P9-CRN-539

ALMANAC OF AMERICA'S WARS

General Editor: John S. Bowman

First published in the United States of America in 1990
by the Mallard Press.
Mallard Press and its accompanying design and logo are
trademarks of BDD Promotional Book Company, Inc.

ISBN 0-792-45268-2

Printed in Hong Kong

Contents

Introduction

For a nation that has prided itself both on its essentially peaceful nature and on its success in avoiding 'foreign entanglements' America has fought a quite remarkable number of wars.

By the time the North American colonists were ready to declare their independence of Great Britain they had already been involved in four major wars with the French and two minor wars with the Dutch and Spanish, and a long guerrilla struggle with the Indians was still in progress. Between 1776 and the time the United States – itself born of war – celebrated its Bicentennial, the nation had contrived to fight eight more wars against foreign enemies, a Civil War that dwarfed all but a handful of international wars, 114 more years of war against the Indians and a host of smaller actions in places as far-flung as Nicaragua, China, Mexico and the Philippines. Even in the relatively peaceful decade since 1976 the United States has committed its regular forces to some form of significant military action on an average of once every 24 months.

If, in the face of this record, Americans nevertheless still have

some warrant for claiming to be a basically peaceful people, it may consist in the fact that for most of the wars on which she embarked America was singularly unprepared. For much of her history it was standard practice for the United States to maintain absurdly small (and often ill-funded, ill-trained and ill-equipped) peacetime military forces.

This traditional 'unfitness for war,' proudly proclaimed a certain Congressman Fisher in 1821, 'is the best feature of our government.' Perhaps, but it certainly did little to shorten the wars America regularly had to fight, and to what extent it may have invited some of those wars is at least moot. In essence, of course, this habitual unpreparedness was founded on an illusion, a popular willingness always to believe – despite the burden of historical evidence – that the war just fought would be the last. 'The war to end all wars' may have been a formulation peculiar to 1918, but it expressed a venerable American idea.

Of a piece with the traditional preference for believing that war would have no place in America's future was a certain reluctance to acknowledge that it had played an important role in America's past. Most standard American history textbooks paid (and to some extent still pay) scant attention to the details of the nations' wars. Military history was treated as a special subject, apart from the mainstream of historical study, the province of a limited number of military professionals and buffs. By the same token, on the rare occasion when a work of military history did manage to find a popular audience – as in the case of Alfred Thayer Mahan's *The Influence of Sea Power Upon History* – it was often treated as a sort of revelation, and the importance of its message was exaggerated beyond the intention of its author.

It was during World War II that the way Americans traditionally thought about war first began to undergo significant change. Not every illusion was dispelled, of course. Such time-honored propensities as believing implicitly in the justice of the national cause and expecting nothing less than total victory were, if anything, reinforced by the war's peculiar morality-play scenario. But in some other important respects World War II fostered a greater realism in American attitudes. Obviously the initial disaster at Pearl Harbor administered a painful lesson about the high cost of military unpreparedness. Other dramatic lessons followed. And in a broader sense, simply because so many Americans either served in the war or, thanks to mass communication, were able to follow it in elaborate detail as it evolved, a whole generation in effect received a crash course in, if not classical military history, at leas military history in-the-making.

By the early 1950s American publishers were for the first time beginning to find a mass market for books on military history. That market persisted even during the Vietnam era and the upsurge of anti-war sentiment in the late 1960s and early 1970s, and it now seems firmly established. The result is that today more Americans know more about their martial heritage than at any time past.

Although the new amateurs of American military history have been increasingly well supplied with reference material in recent years, it has not always been true that the scope of their interests has broadened correspondingly. The editors of military and history book clubs, for example, are well aware that very many of their military-minded subscribers can be assigned to special-interest categories, and that new selections by the club always have to be made with these categories in mind. Thus any good new book about the Civil War, World War II or Vietnam is likely to be well subscribed (though probably not by the same people), whereas equally good books about the Revolution, World War I or the Korean War will probably not do nearly as well. And just as there are 'favorite' wars, there are often favorite aspects of wars – air, land or sea, for example – and even favorite campaigns within wars.

There is, of course, nothing wrong with specialization, provided it does not become so extreme that it blinds us to larger implications. It is certainly interesting to know about the battle tactics of the great Civil War generals, but it is even more instructive to know how – and especially *why* – their tactics differed from those used by the commanders who had to fight in the Mexican War or World War I or even Vietnam. Without that second kind of knowledge, the first is in danger of never rising above antiquarianism.

This chronicle of America's wars is designed to be a useful – even indispensable – corrective for those of us amateur military historians who have constantly to fight the temptation to learn more and more about less and less. Its temporal sweep is majestic, nearly half a millennium long, and its richly illustrated narrative is a model of clarity and concision. Its pages convey an almost overwhelming sense of how nearly incessant warfare has been in our national past – indeed, of how often military operations of bewilderingly different sorts have occurred simultaneously. More important, the book shows vividly how both this warfare, and the various American societies that produced it, evolved over time, constantly readjusting the balance between technical capabilities and political intentions, yet sometimes revealing surprising continuities. In short, this is a good deal more than just a 'look-it-up book,' for it will generously repay thoughtful reading.

Ian MacSiker

EVENTS OF 1521

Settling Portuguese shipowner João Alvares Fagundes establishes a small fishing colony on Cape Breton Island in Nova Scotia. After encountering hostility from both the local Indians and French fishermen, the colony fades away in the next few years. This marks the beginning of hostilities between the various European peoples who will try to colonize North America.

20 FEBRUARY 1521

Settling Spaniard Juan Ponce de Leon, previously the conqueror of Puerto Rico, sets sail from that island with a company of 200 men. Landing in Florida, probably at Charlotte Harbor, Ponce de Leon is wounded in an attack by the natives. The Spanish group leaves for Cuba where Ponce de Leon dies. This aborted attempt to establish a settlement on the mainland of North America will not discourage the Spanish for long.

EVENTS OF 1526

Slavery Black laborers at a Spanish enclave on Carolina's Pedee River revolt against their white masters. This is probably the first slave challenge to European domination on the North American continent. The Pedee dissidents are subdued, but several blacks manage to escape westward to seek refuge with the Indians. Although the conspiracy is quashed, basic tensions have not been eased, and Spain abandons the colony after only six months of operations.

10 SEPTEMBER 1565

Huguenot Policy French colonist Jean Ribault, who has previously established a French Huguenot colony at Parris Island, North Carolina, sets sail from French Fort Caroline near the St. John's River in Florida. Ribault hopes to destroy the newly created Spanish settlement at St. Augustine, Florida, but the Huguenot fleet is wrecked in a storm.

20 SEPTEMBER 1565

Spanish Policy Spaniard Pedro Menendez de Aviles leads a land force to the Huguenot settlement Fort Caroline. Menendez captures the fort, and most of the Huguenot defenders are killed. The fort is renamed San Mateo, and it becomes a Spanish stronghold.

EVENTS OF 1566

Spanish Policy Menendez, the founder of Spanish St. Augustine and now the victor over the French Huguenots, sends a small party under Captain Juan Pardo to 'discover and conquer the interior country from there to Mexico.' Pardo's men build a series of blockhouses as far inland as the slopes of the Blue Ridge Mountains, but within two years most of the Spanish will have been killed by Indians.

12 APRIL 1568

Huguenot Policy Aided by Indians, a small French force captures two Spanish ports at the mouth of the St. John's River in Florida. The victory is followed by a massacre of the Spanish prisoners.

Sir Francis Drake, the great English explorer-cum-adventurer who repeated (1577-80) Magellan's feat of sailing around the world.

A 1598 engraving by the French geographer Théodore DeBry showing American Indians torturing captured Spanish explorers. Such fanciful 'hate literature' tended to justify European brutalities in America.

APRIL 1578

Spanish Policy Acting Spanish Governor Pedro Menendez Marques (nephew of the earlier Menendez) burns the large Indian village at Copocay in Florida and takes many Indian prisoners. This method of subjugating the Indians is indicative of what will follow in the future.

17 JULY 1580

Colonial Conflict Governor Menendez Marques defeats a French naval force led by Gliberto Gil, who dies in the battle. This signals the end of French influence in the coastal Florida area.

25 MARCH 1584

Settling Englishman Sir Walter Raleigh, who has the confidence of Queen Elizabeth I, sends Humphrey Gilbert to explore and settle in North America. After a survey of Spanish defenses in the Caribbean area, Gilbert's expedition lands on Roanoke Island in July. Raleigh names this newly discovered land Virginia in honor of the Queen.

27 JULY 1585

Settling Sir Walter Raleigh sends a colonizing expedition to land again at Roanoke. Beleaguered by Indians and the Spanish, this settlement lasts for a year and then is abandoned when Francis Drake, after a privateering voyage to the Caribbean, offers the settlers passage home. Several weeks later, Richard Grenville arrives at the abandoned colony with supplies. He leaves 15 men at Roanoke.

JUNE-JULY 1586

English Policy Sir Francis Drake attacks and levels the Spanish fort and other buildings at St. Augustine, Florida, but the Spanish remain in control of the area.

22 JULY 1587

Settling John White leads an expedition to the English Roanoke colony. He finds no trace of the 15 settlers left by Richard Grenville. White leaves off another group of settlers and returns to England for supplies.

17 AUGUST 1590

Settling Delayed by the Spanish Armada's attack on England, John White returns to Roanoke to find that all of the settlers have disappeared without a trace.

10 OCTOBER 1599

Spanish Policy A Spanish military force sets out from St. Augustine. This force is meant to punish the Guale Indians, who have previously made attacks that have led to the abandonment of most of the Spanish missions north of St. Augustine. The Spanish soldiers destroy Indian villages and crops. Faced by the ferocity of the assault, the Indians seek peace.

AUGUST 1606

Exploration The Plymouth Company in England sends out its first expedition to explore the Virginia area, to which it has received colonial rights (at least as far as England is concerned). The voyage ends in disaster when the Spanish capture it in the Caribbean. Spain has previously resisted French attempts to settle.

OCTOBER 1606

Exploration A second expedition is sent to North America by the Plymouth Company. Thomas Hanham and Martin Pring complete a detailed investigation of the Atlantic coast. They return to England, full of enthusiasm over what they have seen in America.

24 MAY 1607

Settling The London Company's colonizing group lands at Jamestown, Virginia. The 105 Englishmen will be reduced by starvation and disease to 38 survivors in the next seven months. When Captain John Smith, a former soldier of fortune, becomes council president of Jamestown, he will require that even the gentlemen of the colony do manual labor so that the budding colony can survive.

15 JUNE 1607

Settling The Jamestown colonists erect forts as a defense against potential assaults by either the local Indians or the Spanish to the south.

10 DECEMBER 1607

Indians Captain John Smith leaves Jamestown in an attempt to obtain food from the Indians for the starving colonists. Smith is captured by Indian Chief Powhatan and the two men who are with Smith are killed. Surprisingly, Smith is saved from almost certain death through the intervention of an Indian girl, Pocahontas, the daughter of Powhatan.

OTHER EVENTS OF 1607

Internal Conflict In perhaps the first rebellious incident in the English colonies, a plot against the governing council of Jamestown is revealed. George Kendall, the leader of the cabal, is executed.

2 JANUARY 1608

Internal Conflict Following his release from captivity by the Indians, Captain John Smith is now imprisoned by his adversaries on the Jamestown council. Fortunately, Captain Christopher Newport arrives almost simultaneously from England with further supplies and 110 new colonists. Newport saves Smith from possible execution by his fellow colonists.

JULY 1609

French Policy French explorer Samuel Champlain travels up the Richelieu River on to a large, hitherto unknown lake which will bear his name in the future. In the area of Ticonderoga, Champlain's party attacks a group of Iroquois Indians, who are routed by the French firearms. This small encounter will be of lasting significance, since the Iroquois will maintain a deep enmity toward the French.

5 OCTOBER 1609

Settling In Jamestown, Captain John Smith is injured in a gunpowder explosion and is ousted from his leadership of the Virginia colony. Smith returns to England.

EVENTS OF 1611

Spanish Policy Spanish monarch King Philip III maintains surveillance of the English colony in Virginia. When three Spaniards sail into the James River for that purpose, they are captured and imprisoned for five years. Yet the Spanish are able to keep contact with their fellows, and they urge the destruction of the Jamestown settlement.

APRIL 1613

Indians Pocahontas, daughter of Indian Chief Powhatan, is captured by Sir Samuel Argall and held as a hostage by the Jamestown colonists to gain the release of settlers held captive by the Indians. Puritan clergyman Alexander Whitaker converts the Indian princess to Christianity. On 14 April 1614 English planter John Rolfe will marry Pocahontas, now Rebecca, and eight years of truce will follow between the English settlers and the Indians.

JULY 1613

Colonial Conflict Sir Thomas Dale of Virginia sends Sir Samuel Argall to attack the French Colonial posts in Maine. Argall's group of Englishmen burns the French settlement at Port Royal, and expels the Jesuits from Mount Desert Island. On his return from these successes Argall also anchors at the newly created Dutch fort on Manhattan Island, New York, and forces the Dutch to raise the English flag. These English raids mark the widening imperial designs of England in the New World.

16 SEPTEMBER 1620

Settling The *Mayflower* sets sail for America with 101 colonists aboard. Most of the colonists are not actually Pilgrims; the group includes Miles Standish, the military leader, 14 indentured servants and several craftsmen.

21 DECEMBER 1620

Settling Following an initial exploratory reconnaissance the *Mayflower* anchors off Plymouth, Massachusetts, concluding a 63-day voyage. The colonists begin to disembark.

22 MARCH 1621

Indians The Pilgrims of Plymouth and the Wampanoag Indians led by Chief Massassoit reach a treaty agreement. The Pilgrims and Indians form a defensive alliance and conclude a peace pact, one of the first documented treaties between Europeans and American Indians.

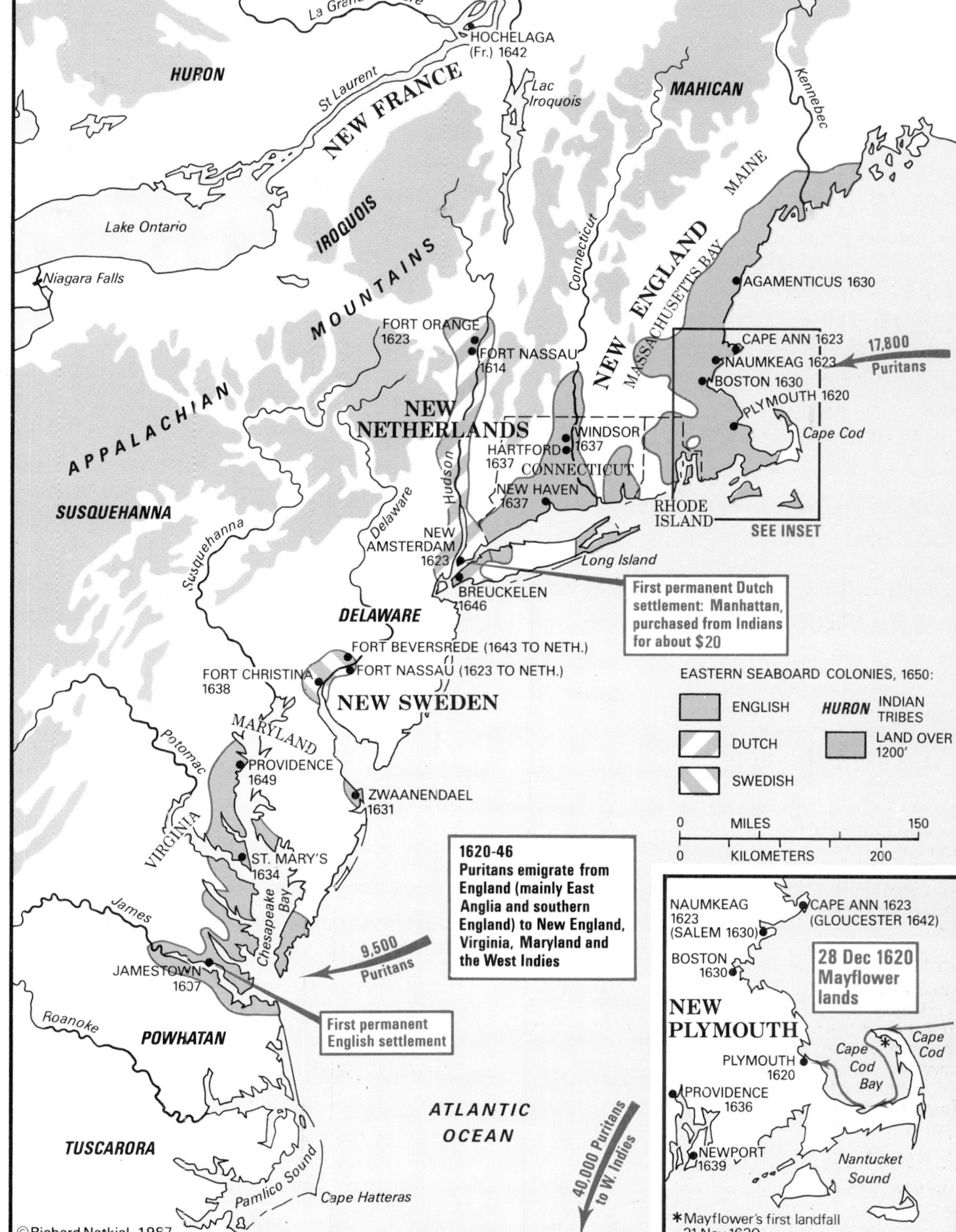

Right: Settlement in North America up to 1650.

Below: A famous but quite impossible painting of *Mayflower*. The set sails while the ship is at anchor only begin the problems with this reconstruction.

22 MARCH 1622

Indian Warfare In Virginia the Opechancanough Indians attack and massacre some 350 English colonists in one day. Despite laws decreeing death for anyone furnishing weapons to the Indians, the warriors have been able to obtain arms and ammunition. The English will emerge victorious, but at a terrible cost in lives.

30 DECEMBER 1622

English Policy The Council for New England appoints Robert Gorges as the first lieutenant-general of the New England territory. In addition, Gorges receives a 300-square-mile land grant along Boston Bay.

MARCH 1623

Settling Miles Standish saves English settlers at Weymouth, Mass., from an Indian attack.

JUNE 1628

Internal Conflict The Plymouth Pilgrims send Miles Standish to eradicate the Merrymount settlement at Quincy, Massachusetts. Thomas Morton, the leader of the settlement, is reviled by the Pilgrims for his dissolute life style. Following his capture, he is sent back to England.

EVENTS OF 1630

Population There are now some 3000 English colonists in Virginia and some 300 in the Plymouth colony.

English Colonists slaughtering Pequot Indians near present-day Mystic, Connecticut, 1637. The Pequots were nearly exterminated in the two-year war, the first big clash between the English and Indians.

6 DECEMBER 1632

Indian Warfare By this date, the Dutch-settled patroonship of Swaanendael, located on the west bank of Delaware Bay, has been eradicated by hostile Indians.

22 APRIL 1635

Colonial Conflict A naval skirmish occurs in the waters off Virginia between the ships of Virginia trader William Claiborne and Lord Baltimore. The incident results from the boundary dispute between Maryland and Virginia. Another such confrontation occurs in May.

AUGUST 1635

Colonial Conflict In New Amsterdam (the Dutch colony in present-day New York City, Long Island and parts of New Jersey) colonists forcibly remove a group of Virginians from the abandoned Dutch Fort Nassau on the Delaware River. The Dutch then set up a military garrison, ensuring their trading rights in the New Jersey area.

20 JULY 1636

Pequot War: Approach New England trader John Oldham is killed by the Pequot Indians, who reside in the area of southern Connecticut and Rhode Island. His murder leads to a series of punitive actions against the Pequots.

24 AUGUST 1636

Pequot War Massachusetts Governor John Endecott organizes a military force to pursue the Pequot Indian War.

26 MAY 1637

Pequot War The first large-scale battle between English colonists and American Indians takes place near present-day Mystic, Connecticut, when Captains John Mason and John Underhill lead colonial forces in attack on Pequot Indians who have been harassing settlers. Pequot forts are burned, and approximately 500 Indian men, women and children die in the fires. The English forces are aided by Mohegan Indians who are under the leadership of Chief Uncas.

5 JUNE 1637

Pequot War Captain John Mason leads a New England force against another sizeable Pequot camp, this one near Stonington, Connecticut, and destroys it completely.

28 JULY 1637

Pequot War Pequot Indians who managed to escape from the previous slaughter at Mystic and Stonington are now massacred by a united force of Connecticut, Massachusetts Bay Colony and Plymouth colonists near Fairfield, Connecticut. The Pequot tribe has been virtually eradicated. For nearly 40 years the English settlers in New England will enjoy a substantial measure of peace from Indian warfare. The same will not, however, be true for the Dutch settlers of New Amsterdam and Long Island.

13 MARCH 1638

English Policy The Ancient and Honorable Artillery Company is chartered in Boston, Massachusetts, one of the first official military units founded in the English colonies.

4 APRIL 1638

English Policy The English Crown rules against Virginia and William Claiborne in the Maryland-Virginia boundary dispute. Claiborne is denied his claim to Kent Island. He later recaptures that island when political conditions deteriorate in England.

21 JANUARY 1642

Dutch Policy Director of the New Netherland colony Willem Kieft calls a meeting of the Twelve (leading family representatives) in New Amsterdam to organize a military response to the increasing raids of the Hudson River Valley Indians upon Dutch settlements. These Indians feel that they are being increasingly hemmed in by the powerful Iroquois tribes to the north and the growing European colonization to the south.

MARCH 1642

Indian Warfare Following an unsuccessful Dutch military campaign against the Hudson River Valley Indians, Jonas Bronck, a settler on the Bronx River, makes a truce with the Indians that will last for one year.

11 DECEMBER 1642

Dutch Policy In response to previous English colonial incursions into the New York and Long Island areas New Netherland Director Willem Kieft creates a new administrative position in the Dutch colony, that of English Secretary.

FEBRUARY 1643

Indian Warfare New Netherland leader Willem Kieft makes an attack on Hudson River Valley Indians at Pavonia. Kieft's forces murder some 80 Indians in their sleep. Following this brutality the Indian tribes rise in fury, and soon Long Island, Westchester and Manhattan are laid waste. With the exception of distant Fort Orange (Albany) and Rensselaerswyck, safety is found only in the immediate vicinity of Fort Amsterdam on Manhattan Island. The Dutch colony is under full siege by the Indian forces.

19 MAY 1643

Colonial Affairs The New England Confederation is formed, uniting New Haven, Massachusetts Bay, Plymouth, and Connecticut for their common defense. John Winthrop of Massachusetts Bay becomes the first president.

25-26 DECEMBER 1643

Indian Warfare Hudson River Valley Indians fleeing from attacks by the Mohawk Indians to the north are massacred by the Dutch when they seek safety in the Dutch settlements. The Indians soon retaliate with a series of raids against Dutch colonists.

29 SEPTEMBER 1643

Indian Warfare Connecticut colonist John Underhill leads a force to the aid of the beleaguered Dutch colonists in their campaign against the Hudson River Valley Indians.

18 MARCH 1644

Indian Warfare In Virginia the Opechancanough Indians rise against the white settlers. The Indian assault seriously endangers the survival of the English colony. Governor William Berkeley plays a heroic role during the conflict. After two years of warfare the Indians are defeated and are forced to cede all the land between the James and York rivers. Peace between the Indians and settlers will last until 1675.

9 AUGUST 1645

Indian Warfare Peace is finally declared between the Dutch of New Amsterdam and the Hudson River Valley Indians. Facilitated by the Mohawk Indians, this pact ends four years of hostilities. On 28 July 1646 Willem Kieft is removed from his position as director of the New Netherland colony, largely because of his ill-judged Indian policy that led to the destruction of numerous Dutch settlements.

EVENTS OF 1646

Colonial Navy The first American warship is commissioned by the united colonies of New Haven and Hartford for patrolling Long Island Sound against possible incursions by the Dutch.

11 MAY 1647

Dutch Policy Peter Stuyvesant arrives in New Amsterdam to assume the position of leader of the Dutch colony of New Netherland, replacing Willem Kieft.

27 APRIL 1648

Settling Peter Stuyvesant orders the construction of Dutch Fort Beversrede at the site of present-day Philadelphia. Meanwhile, Johan Bjornsson Prinz, governor of the New Sweden colony (organized in 1633), builds a series of Swedish forts, concluding with Fort New Krisholm near the mouth of the Schuykill River. There is a growing competition between the Dutch and Swedes for control of lands south of New York.

MAY 1648

Colonial Conflict Swedish forces from Fort Krisholm burn the Dutch Fort Beversrede.

NOVEMBER 1648

Colonial Conflict The Dutch Fort Beversrede is again burned by Swedish troops. Nevertheless, the Dutch hang on to the site until their erection in 1651 of Fort Casimir to control the routes into the colony of New Sweden.

30 JANUARY 1649

International King Charles I of England is executed following his defeat in the English Civil War. Having ended the monarchy, at least temporarily, Oliver Cromwell instigates the creation of the Common-

Peter Stuyvesant (1592-1672) became director-general of the New Netherland colony in 1745. He proved to be a generally effective but unpopular leader.

wealth, with himself as the Lord Protector. Responding to these events, the colony of Virginia declares its continued loyalty to the English royal house of Stuart and offers safe haven to fleeing royalists.

23-29 SEPTEMBER 1650

Colonial Affairs The Treaty of Hartford between New Netherland and the New England Confederacy delineates geographic boundaries between the Dutch and English settlements in southern New England and on Long Island. This treaty is respected by both sides until the 1664 conquest of New Netherland by the English.

OCTOBER 1650

English Policy Responding to the Virginia colony's declaration of allegiance to the Stuart royal line, the English Parliament declares a naval blockade on Virginia.

19 JULY 1651

Colonial Conflict Dutch colonists from New Netherland erect and occupy Fort Casimir on the Delaware River, thereby controlling the routes into the territory of New Sweden.

5 NOVEMBER 1651

Colonial Conflict In the continuing hostilities between Swedish and Dutch colonists in the areas of New Jersey and Maryland, Johan Classen Rising, governor of the New Sweden colony, manages to defeat a Dutch force and capture Fort Casimir on the Delaware River.

12 MARCH 1652

British Policy Virginia Governor Sir William Berkeley (who was important in the 1644 Indian Warfare and will play a role in Bacon's Rebellion in 1676) and his council submit to representatives of Parliament who arrive on two armed vessels. An election follows, and Richard Bennett, one of the parliamentary commissioners, is chosen as the new governor by the burgesses. For the next eight years Virginia enjoys a period of virtual self-rule.

JULY 1652

International War breaks out between the English and the Dutch in Europe.

2 JUNE 1653

Colonial Affairs The Massachusetts Bay Colony refuses to support the New England Confederation vote for war against the Dutch colonists in New Netherland. The New Englanders fear that the Dutch are conspiring with the Nyantic Indians against English settlers in the Connecticut colony.

5 JULY 1653

Colonial Conflict The Dutch garrison of Fort Good Hope at Hartford, Connecticut, is annexed by the Connecticut colony. Although this action takes place during the Anglo-Dutch War (1652-1654), the English and Dutch colonial outposts in America do not formally go to war with each other.

MAY 1654

Colonial Conflict New Netherland Governor Peter Stuyvesant calls a session of his representative assembly to consider the escalation of hostilities with the colonies of the New England Confederation.

20 JUNE 1654

Colonial Conflict New England colonists learn that a peace treaty has been signed between the English and the Dutch just as a colonial military force is ready to leave Boston and march against the Dutch in New Amsterdam.

25 MARCH 1655

Colonial Affairs A civil war in Maryland between royalist Catholics and Puritan parliamentarians concludes with the victory of the Puritan faction led by Maryland Governor William Fuller. Former royalist William Stone is imprisoned, and the Puritans execute four of his men.

26 SEPTEMBER 1655

Colonial Conflict Peter Stuyvesant recaptures the former Dutch Fort Casimir from the Swedes. This action effectively ends all royal Swedish influence on the American continent. The city of New Amsterdam, which has carried on a 15-year campaign against the New Sweden colony – as well as fighting the Hudson River Valley Indians and encountering English settlers in lower Connecticut and Long Island – now receives a large land grant of territory in the Delaware River area from the Dutch West India Company.

EVENTS OF 1657

Slavery Near Hartford, Connecticut, a group of black slaves and local Indians combine in an abortive attempt to displace English rule.

3 SEPTEMBER 1658

International Oliver Cromwell, the Lord Protector of the Commonwealth of England, dies. His son and successor, Richard, proves incapable of effective leadership. On 29 May 1660 Charles II, son of the beheaded Charles I, will enter London after being recalled unconditionally to the throne. Charles executes 13 of the men who signed a death warrant for his father. Many other Puritan regicides escape; among them are Edmund Whalley and Charles Goffe who – it is believed – flee to America and find safety in the small colonial settlement of Hadley, Massachusetts. Goffe will resurface in a dramatic fashion on 1 September 1675.

Stuyvesant surveys the four-ship English fleet that came to besiege New Amsterdam in 1664 in the name of Charles II's brother, the duke of York.

7 JUNE 1663

Indian Warfare Relations between the Hudson River Valley Indians and the Dutch colonists of New Netherland disintegrate to the point that the Indians attack the village of Wiltwyck, near present-day Kingston, New York. This prompts the Dutch to conduct three retaliatory raids against Indian strongholds.

12 MARCH 1664

English Policy The Duke of York, brother of King Charles II, obtains a royal grant that gives him authority over all lands between the Connecticut and Delaware rivers in America. This enormous land grant includes all the current Dutch holdings in North America, as well as substantial areas of Indian land. On 2 April 1664 James, Duke of York, sends English forces under the command of Colonel Richard Nicolls to capture New Netherland.

16 MAY 1664

Indian Warfare The Hudson River Valley Indians surrender the Esopus Valley (present-day New Kingston) to the Dutch.

29 AUGUST 1664

Colonial Conflict An English fleet of four ships, led by Colonel Richard Nicolls, arrives in the harbor of New Amsterdam.

7 SEPTEMBER 1664

Colonial Conflict Following a bloodless naval blockade, New Netherland Governor Peter Stuyvesant surrenders his colony to the English forces under Colonel Richard Nicolls. Stuyvesant is forced to submit against his will, as he lacks the support of many

Stuyvesant's surrender to the English, 8 September 1664. If the burghers had supported Stuyvesant, he might well have repelled the 3-400 attackers.

of his colonists in opposing the English. Nicolls changes the name of New Amsterdam to New York in honor of the English Duke of York, who has authorized this takeover

The head of Indian leader King Philip, killed in the war named for him, was exhibited in Plymouth for the next 20 years as a warning to other Indians.

20 SEPTEMBER 1664

Colonial Conflict Colonel George Cartwright, one of the commissioners sent by the Duke of York, accepts the surrender of the Dutch colonists at Fort Orange (Albany) on the Hudson River. Dutch power, which had opened the Hudson River to European colonization, challenged the English in Connecticut and supplanted the Swedes in Delaware, has been broken by the English forces. Following this annexation of Fort Orange the English become allies of the Iroquois Indians.

5 JANUARY 1665

Colonial Affairs New Haven is annexed by Connecticut.

23 FEBRUARY 1665

English Policy While the Second Anglo-Dutch War rages in Europe, Richard Nicolls, deputy of the Duke of York in America, orders the annexation of all property belonging to the Dutch West India Company in what was formerly New Netherland.

21 JULY 1667

International: End of the Dutch Colonies The Peace of Breda, which formally ends the second Anglo-Dutch War, officially establishes British sovereignty over what had been New Netherland and is now New York.

OTHER EVENTS OF 1667

Dutch Raid on Virginia Holland brings the Second Anglo-Dutch War to Virginia by sending a fleet up the James River. A 20-ship merchant convoy, fully loaded and ready to put out to sea, is destroyed, and a British frigate on escort duty is captured.

8 JULY 1670

International The Treaty of Madrid is signed by England and Spain. Both nations agree to respect the other's rights in the American territories which they occupy.

10 APRIL 1671

Indian Warfare Following a series of hostilities against Massachusetts colonists the Plymouth leaders require Wampanoag Chief, King Philip, or Metacomet (who is a son of Massassoit), to surrender his arms. Philip surrenders only a part of his arsenal of weaponry.

10 APRIL 1671

Indian Warfare Following a series of hostilities against Massachusetts colonists the Plymouth leaders require Wampanoag Chief, King Philip, or Metacomet (who is a son of Massassoit), to surrender his arms. Philip surrenders only a part of his arsenal of weaponry.

Indian forces under King Philip attacked Brookfield, Massachusetts, in August 1675, making effective use of fire arrows against the colonists' log cabins.

OTHER EVENTS OF 1671

Indian Warfare Carolina colonists vanquish the Coosa Indians. A number of Indian prisoners are then enslaved, initiating an experiment with Indian slavery.

8 AUGUST 1673

Dutch Capture of New York Dutch forces demand the surrender of New York, while anchored off Sandy Hook with 23 ships and 1600 men. The Dutch capture and hold possession of New York until 9 February 1674, when the English regain control under the terms of the Treaty of Westminster.

OTHER EVENTS OF 1673

Dutch Raid on Virginia The Dutch, at war with England for the third time in 20 years, attack Virginia from the sea. Virginians are unable to mount an effective defense because farmers, suspecting that rebellion by slaves and indentured servants is imminent, are unwilling to leave their homes undefended.

19 FEBRUARY 1674

International The Third Anglo-Dutch War is ended by the Treaty of Westminster, with the English as the victors. Under this pact the areas reconquered by the Dutch are now returned to England.

8 JUNE 1675

Indians Plymouth colonists try and execute three Wampanoag Indians who are implicated in the murder of an Indian who has accused Wampanoag Chief, King Philip, of conspiracy against the English settlers in the New England area.

20-25 JUNE 1675

King Philip's War King Philip, whose Indian name is Metacomet, leads an Indian attack against Swansea to retaliate for the execution of three Indians on 8 June. The conflict known as King Philip's War has begun.

28 JUNE 1675

King Philip's War Colonial soldiers from Boston and Plymouth unite to form a joint military force against King Philip; they attack the principal Wampanoag fort at Mount Hope, Rhode Island, with little success.

14 JULY 1675

King Philip's War The Nipmuck Indians unite with the Wampanoag Indians to attack the English settlement of Mendon, Massachusetts, thus beginning a series of Indian attacks on the frontier English settlements.

2-4 AUGUST 1675

King Philip's War Combined Wampanoag-Nipmuck Indian warriors, led by King Philip, attack the settlement of Brookfield, Massachusetts.

19 AUGUST 1675

King Philip's War King Philip leads his warriors in an assault upon the settlement of Lancaster, Massachusetts.

1 SEPTEMBER 1675

King Philip's War The Wampanoag and Nipmuck Indians attack the Connecticut River Valley settlements of Deerfield and Hadley, Massachusetts. It is rumored that an unknown gray-bearded white stranger played an important role in turning the Indians back at Hadley. It is believed that this man, the 'Angel of Hadley,' was Charles Goffe, one of the regicides who condemned English King Charles I to death in 1649.

According to legend, the defense of Hadley in 1675 was led by gray-bearded Charles Goffe, one of the men who had signed Charles I's death warrant.

2 SEPTEMBER 1675

King Philip's War Led by King Philip, the Wampanoag and Nipmuck Indians attack the Connecticut River Valley settlement of Northfield, Massachusetts. If King Philip is to have a real opportunity to drive the English into the sea he must first terrify and demoralize the settlements along the Connecticut river, which are less strongly established than either Boston or Plymouth.

9 SEPTEMBER 1675

King Philip's War The New England Confederation officially declares war on King Philip. Each of the colonies is required to provide a quota of men for a combined military force.

12 SEPTEMBER 1675

King Philip's War Indians attack Falmouth, Maine. Further south, they also attack Deerfield, Massachusetts, where they are repulsed.

18 SEPTEMBER 1675

King Philip's War The Indian forces win a major victory at Bloody Brook, two miles south of Deerfield. They massacre 64 of Deerfield's finest fighting men, who are carrying food supplies to Hadley. Following this disaster Deerfield is abandoned, and the survivors move south. In 1682 the tenacious settlers will rebuild Deerfield with stronger fortifications.

27 SEPTEMBER 1675

Bacon's Rebellion: Approach In Virginia a company of militiamen is unable to eliminate the bands of warring Susquehannock Indians who are massacring numbers of Virginia settlers in a series of raids. Governor William Berkeley had saved the Virginia colony from possible annihilation by Indians in 1644, but he is either too timid to engage them again in 1675 or perhaps he too greatly values the profits from trading furs with the Indians.

5 OCTOBER 1675

King Philip's War King Philip's warriors attack Springfield, Massachusetts.

16 OCTOBER 1675

King Philip's War The forces of King Philip attack Hatfield, Massachusetts, which is directly south of the abandoned Deerfield settlement.

30 OCTOBER 1675

King Philip's War The peaceful Indians of Natick and Waban, Massachusetts, are taken away under guard to Deer Island in Boston Harbor, where they are interned.

19 NOVEMBER 1675

King Philip's War Josiah Winslow leads a colonial force in an attack upon the Narragansett Indian stronghold near present-day Kingston, Rhode Island. Most of the Indian warriors escape, but over 300 Indian women and children are killed. It is apparent that the New England forces now fully understand the dangers posed by King Philip's War and will employ almost any means to defeat the tribes.

10 FEBRUARY 1676

King Philip's War The hard winter of 1675-1676 has brought the Indian forces under King Philip to starvation. In search of food they again attack the settlement of Lancaster, Massachusetts.

12 MARCH 1676

King Philip's War Indians attack Plymouth, Massachusetts.

10 MAY 1676

Bacon's Rebellion Nathaniel Bacon, a twenty-eight-year-old English planter who had arrived in Virginia in 1674, leads an unauthorized campaign against the Occaneechee Indians in Virginia. On conclusion of his campaign Bacon writes that, 'wee have left all nations of Indians where wee have bin ingaged in a civill warre amongst themselves, so that wee hope to manadge this advantage to their utter Ruine and destruction.'

18 MAY 1676

King Philip's War Captain William Turner of Boston leads 180 men from Hatfield, Massachusetts, to make a crippling assault on Indian forces camped five miles north of Deerfield. Captain Turner's men achieve a complete surprise and kill many of the Indians in their wigwams, but the English are also attacked on their return to Hatfield. The site of the battle will be named Turner's Falls in memory of the English leader.

26 MAY 1676

Bacon's Rebellion Virginia Governor William Berkeley declares Nathaniel Bacon to be a traitor for fighting the Indians without a proper commission to do so. Bacon is arrested when he arrives in Jamestown to assume his elected seat in the House of Burgesses.

5 JUNE 1676

Bacon's Rebellion Nathaniel Bacon is pardoned after he confesses to having mutinied against the Governor's authority.

12 JUNE 1676

King Philip's War Captain John Talcott leads a combined group of Connecticut River Valley colonists and Mohegan Indians in a decisive battle against King Philip's warriors at Hadley, Massachusetts. Following this defeat and another at Marlboro, Massachusetts, the Indians begin to surrender.

23 JUNE 1676

Bacon's Rebellion Nathaniel Bacon has assembled a group of 500 men. Supported by this force, he requires Governor William Berkeley to sign a commission for Bacon to lead men against the Indians who are terrifying colonists. The Virginia House of Burgesses subsequently passes a series of reforms known as the June Laws.

3 AUGUST 1676

Bacon's Rebellion Bacon requires that some 70 prominent Virginians swear to fight against English troops who, it is known, will soon arrive to support William Berkeley until the English Crown can learn of the reasons that Bacon and others had for fighting against the Indians. The men who swear to this will be remembered by Berkeley in the future.

12 AUGUST 1676

King Philip's War: End King Philip is surprised, shot and killed by an Indian named Alderman in the service of the English. Philip's wife and child are sold into West Indian slavery. The Indian chief's dismembered body is hung in quarters upon four trees, and his head is carried through the streets of Plymouth. Perhaps not a brilliant conspirator, Philip nevertheless had the distinction of leading one of the largest Indian groups against the colonists.

13 SEPTEMBER 1676

Bacon's Rebellion In Virginia, Nathaniel Bacon returns from his campaign against the Indians and drives Governor Berkeley and his followers out of Jamestown. However, Berkeleyan troops have captured a small fleet that was loyal to Bacon, and now the governor has the upper hand militarily in tidewater Virginia.

SEPTEMBER 1676

Colonial Affairs In Maryland a brief rebellion is led by William Davyes and John Pate against the proprietary government. The rebellion is occasioned by objections to prevalent abuses of power and nepotism and reflects the rampant anti-Catholicism within the colony. This uprising fails, and the leaders are both hanged.

26 OCTOBER 1676

Bacon's Rebellion Nathaniel Bacon dies unexpectedly, probably of the 'Bloody Flux.' Bacon is buried in secrecy so that royal officials cannot use his corpse for public display, as Charles II had done to the body of Oliver Cromwell and as the Massachusetts colonists have so recently done to King Philip.

OTHER EVENTS OF 1676

Indian Warfare The Apache Indians in New Mexico rise against the Spanish (who had settled a capital in Santa Fe as early as 1610), but they are quickly put down.

27 APRIL 1677

Bacon's Rebellion: End In Virginia, English Colonel Jeffreys, sent by the English Crown, officially assumes control of the government, replacing Governor Sir William Berkeley. The governor has already executed 23 of the prominent members of the rebel leadership, leading Charles II to characterize Berkeley as a 'bloody old fool who has hanged more men . . . than I have done for the murder of my father.'

AUGUST 1677

Indians Sir Edmund Andros constructs a fort at Pemaquid, Maine, as a stronghold for use against Indian attacks.

3 DECEMBER 1677-1699

Culpeper's Rebellion In Carolina an antiproprietary party headed by John Culpeper sets up a revolutionary government in protest against the arbitrary acts

Demanding a commission to fight against Indians, rebel Nathaniel Bacon and his men confront Virginia Governor William Berkeley in Jamestown in 1675.

Standing under the soon-to-be-famous 'Treaty Elm,' Pennsylvania leader William Penn in 1683 signs a treaty of peace with local Indians.

of the governor, Thomas Miller. Miller escapes to England, where he appeals to the Privy Council for assistance. Culpeper will eventually be tried for treason in England and acquitted. The rebellion is inconclusive, since the abuses of proprietary government are not corrected.

12 APRIL 1678

Indians In Maine, Sir Edmund Andros makes peace with the Indians, thus formally ending King Philip's War. The costs of the war have been high for both the colonists and Indians in terms of lives and property lost. The power of the New England Indian tribes is broken, and from this time onward only the Maine Indian tribes maintain any independence.

EVENTS OF 1680-1692

Indian Warfare The Pueblo Indians of New Mexico revolt against Spanish rule, attacking Santa Fe and killing some 400 settlers and missionaries. Pueblo medicine man Popé tries to wipe out all traces of the Spanish, but attacks by the Apaches weaken the Pueblos. When Popé dies in 1692 the Spanish have reasserted their control in New Mexico.

23 JUNE 1683

Indians Pennsylvania leader William Penn and the Indians negotiate a peace treaty at Shackamaxon under the 'Treaty Elm.'

30 JULY 1684

Indians New York Governor Thomas Dongan negotiates an extension of the peace treaty with the Iroquois Indians in Albany.

6 FEBRUARY 1685

International Upon the death of Charles II the Duke of York becomes James II, King of England.

17 AUGUST 1686

Colonial Conflict The South Carolina settlement of Stuart Town, or Port Royal, is destroyed by a Spanish force from Florida.

24 MARCH 1688

English Policy Sir Edmund Andros issues an order placing the militia of the New England colonies under his direct control.

18 DECEMBER 1688

International King James II (formerly the Duke of York) flees to France, abandoning his throne, upon hearing that influential Englishmen have invited William of Orange to invade England. This forced deposition of James II is known as the Glorious Revolution and will be followed by the removal of James' representatives in North America.

18 APRIL 1689

Colonial Affairs An armed uprising in Boston forces Sir Edmund Andros to surrender, following on the heels of the Glorious Revolution in England. A manifesto lists grievances of the colonists and justifies the rebellion. Andros is returned to England to stand trial for misconduct.

31 MAY 1689

Colonial Affairs Jacob Leslier, a trader formerly employed by the Dutch West India Company, captures the English garrison at New York. Leslier leads an army of farmers from Long Island and Westchester, seeking to establish a popular representative government.

1 AUGUST 1689

Colonial Affairs A Protestant revolution in Maryland is ended through a peace treaty. Rebellion had begun when rumors convinced many that the colony was about to be taken over by the Catholics. On 21 August the Protestant Association will ask the English Crown to assume control of the Maryland colony. This will occur in 1691.

3 AUGUST 1689

Colonial Conflict In Maine a combined French and Indian force captures the English fort at Pemaquid, first erected in 1677.

16 OCTOBER 1689

King William's War: Approach French Count Frontenac arrives at Quebec City to assume his position as Governor of New France. A seventy-year-old veteran soldier, the Count brings the sternness and willpower that are necessary to save the French colony from attacks by the Iroquois Indians that are demoralizing the French colonists. Indeed, French King Louis XIV has charged Frontenac with the responsibility for capturing New York from the English. Knowing that this is totally unrealistic – the population of French Canada is greatly outnumbered by the more populous English colonies – Frontenac sends out French and Indian war parties to raid and terrify the English settlements.

9 FEBRUARY 1690

King William's War: New England The settlement of Schenectady, New York, is burned by a combined group of French soldiers and their Indian allies, sent by Count Frontenac. The attack is followed by others on English settlements in Maine, New Hampshire and Massachusetts.

FEBRUARY 1690

Colonial Affairs Following the destruction of Schenectady panic breaks out in Albany, New York. In exchange for the assurance of southern troops Albany officials agree to recognize the rebel administration of Jacob Leslier in Manhattan. From Long Island Sound to the northern frontier Leslier now controls the New York province.

1 MAY 1690

King William's War: Strategy Delegates from Connecticut, Massachusetts, Plymouth and New York meet at Albany. They vote to make a two-pronged attack upon French Canada. One military force will proceed by way of Lake George, Lake Champlain and the Richelieu River to attack Montreal. The other force will be a naval fleet that will attack Quebec City from the St. Lawrence River.

11 MAY 1690

King William's War: Nova Scotia Massachusetts soldiers led by Sir William Phips, the first native-born American to receive an English knighthood, capture the French town of Port Royal in Nova Scotia. The Catholic chapel there is violated after the surrender, in direct contradiction of the terms of the surrender.

20 MAY 1690

King William's War: New England A combined French and Indian force destroys the English settlement at Casco, Maine, as part of French leader Frontenac's plan to terrify the population of the northern colonies of New England.

9 AUGUST 1690

King William's War: Canadian Campaign Sir William Phips, the conqueror of Port Royal, sails from Nantasket, Massachusetts, in charge of a Puritan armada that intends to capture Quebec City and humble the French in America. This is the largest military operation in New England to date: 32 vessels and 2200 men leave for Canada.

AUGUST 1690

King William's War: Canadian Campaign A combined colonial force led by Fitz-John Winthrop reaches Wood Creek at the head of Lake Champlain. Faced with a lack of canoes and an outbreak of smallpox, the English are forced to return to Albany, sending only a small raiding party forward. Frontenac, however, knows only of the English land movement; unaware of Phips' Puritan armada, the French governor remains at Montreal until 10 October, when he learns of the sailing of the Puritan fleet.

6 OCTOBER 1690

Internal Conflict In the Carolina colony popular leader Seth Sothell captures the government of Charleston and forces Governor James Colleton into exile.

16 OCTOBER 1690

King William's War: Attack on Quebec The fleet commanded by Sir William Phips sails into the St. Lawrence Basin in front of Quebec City. The Puritan fleet has taken two months to reach its destination, and Governor Frontenac has managed to reach Quebec just in time to lead the defense. When Phips sends a demand for immediate surrender Frontenac reminds him of his breach of faith at Port Royal and declares that he will answer Phips only through the mouths of his cannons. Phips lands 1200 men north of the city and readies them for an assault. Bringing his fleet into cannon range, Phips exchanges fire with the guns of Quebec. The English guns cannot reach the heights, while the French score repeated hits upon the English ships. Faced with this and with larger numbers of French and Canadians safe inside the city, Phips withdraws his men and journeys back to Boston.

OTHER EVENTS OF 1690

Colonial Affairs A committee of the General Court of Massachusetts recommends that the Court determine exactly where the colonial frontier is and maintain garrisons of 40 soldiers in each frontier town.

Louis de Buade, Comte de Frontenac (1620-98), was French Canada's governor during King William's war.

A seventeenth-century New England family barricades doors and windows against a threatened attack by a band of hostile Indians.

29 MARCH 1691

English Policy Newly-appointed New England Governor Henry Sloughter arrives in New York. Jacob Leslier surrenders to him on the following day.

10-27 APRIL 1691

Internal Conflict In New York, Jacob Leslier and nine of his compatriots are tried for treason. Leslier and seven others receive the death sentence, although six of the compatriots are eventually pardoned.

18 MARCH 1692

English Policy Pennsylvania is declared a royal colony. The Crown takes over Pennsylvania because the pacifist Quakers refused to involve themselves in the war against France and because William Penn had enjoyed friendly relations with the former King James II.

OTHER EVENTS OF 1692

Colonial Affairs Connecticut sends a troop of soldiers to protect the Massachusetts frontier towns along the Connecticut River, a move toward reducing colonial animosities.

15 AUGUST 1694

Indians Colonial representatives from Connecticut, Massachusetts, New Jersey and New York sign a peace treaty with the Iroquois Indians in Albany to prevent any further alliance between the Iroquois and the French.

15 AUGUST 1696

King William's War: New England A French force led by Le Moyne d'Iberville captures the English fort of Pemaquid in Maine.

15 MARCH 1697

King William's War: New England French and Indian forces conduct a raid against the English settlement of Haverhill, Massachusetts.

30 SEPTEMBER 1697

King William's War: End The Treaty of Ryswick ends King William's War, restoring all colonial possessions as they were before the war began.

EVENTS OF 1700

Population The total population of the American colonies is estimated at 275,000 persons. The largest city is Boston, with around 7000 inhabitants.

23 MAY 1701

Colonial Affairs Captain William Kidd is hanged in London following his trial for piracy. Kidd was a wealthy New York landowner who had previously served as a privateer for the British crown. His execution signals the English determination to crack down on piracy.

4 MAY 1702

Queen Anne's War The European War of the Spanish Succession, known in America as Queen Anne's War, begins when England declares war on France.

10 SEPTEMBER 1702

Queen Anne's War: Florida The Carolina assembly (Carolina will be separated into North and South Carolina on 9 May 1712) authorizes an expedition to seize Spanish St. Augustine in Florida. A mixed force of 500 colonists and Indians burn and pillage the town in December, but the fortress remains impervious to their attacks.

10 AUGUST 1703

Queen Anne's War: New England In the course of Queen Anne's War the Abenaki Indians of Northern New England attack a number of English settlements in Maine.

28-29 FEBRUARY 1704

Queen Anne's War: New England Abenaki Indians and French Canadian soldiers attack and destroy the frontier settlement of Deerfield, Massachusetts. The invaders have used snowshoes to come south from New France (Canada). The massacre of 50 Deerfield colonists and the abduction of 100 others marks the low point of Queen Anne's War for the English colonists in North America. The trials, tribulations and eventual return of some of the captives will be commemorated in a number of books, including *Boy Captive of Old Deerfield*.

1-28 JULY 1704

Queen Anne's War: Nova Scotia Colonel Benjamin Church leads a force of New England colonists in a successful attack on various French settlements in Nova Scotia.

OTHER EVENTS OF 1704

Queen Anne's War: Frontier A combined force of Carolina colonists and friendly Indians led by Governor James Moore attacks and levels 13 of 14 Spanish missions in the Appalachian Indian territory.

24 AUGUST 1706

Queen Anne's War: Carolina French soldiers and Spanish colonists from St. Augustine, Florida, and Havana, Cuba, combine forces to attack Charleston, Carolina. The Carolina settlers are able to fight off the attack.

21 SEPTEMBER 1707

Queen Anne's War: New England Abenaki Indians attack the English settlement at Winter Harbor, Maine.

29 AUGUST 1708

Queen Anne's War: New England A force of French Canadians and their Indian allies attack the English settlement at Haverhill, Massachusetts, where they massacre virtually all of the settlers.

16 OCTOBER 1710

Queen Anne's War: Nova Scotia A combined British and colonial military force besieges the French stronghold at Port Royal, Nova Scotia. The attack is successful, and the English rename the settlement Annapolis, in honor of Queen Anne.

JUNE 1711

Queen Anne's War: Strategy Colonel Francis Nicholson calls a meeting of New England governors at New London, Connecticut, to cooperate on strategy to combat the French in Candada.

30 JUNE 1711

Queen Anne's War: Quebec Expedition Carrying colonial soldiers, a fleet of British warships sails from Nantasket Roads, Massachusetts, to capture Quebec City. Far more ill-fated than Sir Williams Phips' expedition in 1690, the fleet hits reefs in the Seven Islands on 22 August. Nearly ten ships and 1000 men are lost. The campaign is aborted.

22 SEPTEMBER 1711

Tuscarora Indian War The Tuscarora Indian War begins with the massacre of settlers on the Chowan and Roanoke rivers in Carolina. The settlement of New Bern is abandoned. White encroachment, including the enslaving of Indian children, led to the war.

28 JANUARY 1712

Tuscarora Indian War In the Tuscarora Indian War, the militia of Carolina, aided by Indian allies, attacks the Tuscarora Indians on the Neuse River. Three hundred of the Tuscarora are killed in this assault.

6-7 APRIL 1712

Slavery A black insurrection takes place in New York City, and the colonial militia is called out to quell the

Farmers on Virginia's thinly-settled frontier had to fight off almost incessant Indian raids.

rebellion. In the aftermath of the incident 21 blacks are executed.

OTHER EVENTS OF 1712

Tuscarora Indian War Tuscarora Indians attack a settlement of 650 Palatine Germans at New Bern, North Carolina (Carolina has been separated into North and South Carolina on 9 May 1712). The Indians nearly destroy the settlement, and German colonists are scattered over southeastern North Carolina in the aftermath.

23 MARCH 1713

Tuscarora Indian War South Carolinian forces capture the Tuscarora stronghold of Fort Nohucke, thus ending the hostile activities of the Tuscarora Indians, who will move northward and join the Iroquois Indians, becoming the sixth member of the Six Nations.

11 APRIL 1713

International The Treaty of Utrecht ends Queen Anne's War. England gains Nova Scotia, Hudson Bay and Newfoundland, while the French keep Cape Breton Island and the islands in the St. Lawrence River.

15 APRIL 1715

Indian Warfare Thousand of Yamassee, Creek, Choctaw and Catawba Indians attack exposed settlements in South Carolina. Frontier families race to Charleston for protection. In desperation the colony even arms black slaves.

JANUARY 1716

Indian Warfare South Carolina settlers, aided by Cherokee Indians, defeat the Yamassee Indians northwest of Port Royal, South Carolina. The conflict resulted from the increasing incursion of South Carolina settlers into Yamassee territory, with the granting of large land tracts for the purpose of cattle farming. The colonial victory over the Yamassee Indians leads to subsequent gains against the Creek Indians.

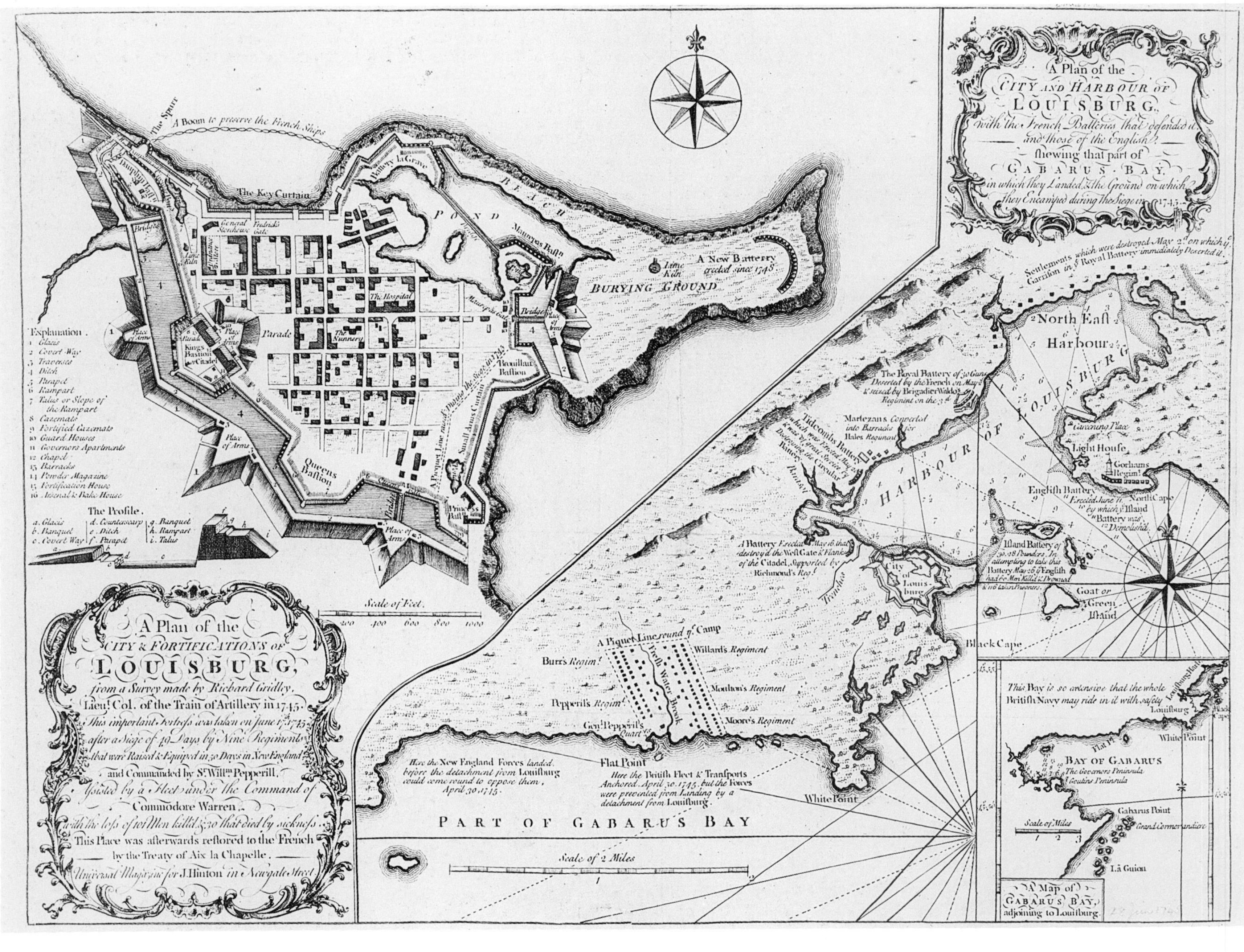

A 1745 map of the great French fort at Louisbourg on Cape Breton Island, guardian of the St. Lawrence estuary. Built in 1720, Fort Louisbourg was captured by the British in 1745 and again in 1758.

27 SEPTEMBER 1718

Colonial Affairs A Carolina coastal expedition captures pirate Steve Bonnet and his crew. Bonnet is tried and hanged on 10 December 1718. During 1718 Edward Teach, better known as Blackbeard, dies in an attack by Virginia colonists.

NOVEMBER 1718

Settling The French city of New Orleans is founded as part of an ambitious program of French expansion along the Mississippi River. The French also erect forts at Kaskaskia (1720), on the mouth of the Illinois River (1726), as well as on the Missouri River (1723).

OTHER EVENTS OF 1718

Indian Warfare The Tuscarora Indians negotiate peace with the North Carolina colonists.

NOVEMBER 1719

Colonial Conflict The settlers of South Carolina, hearing that a Spanish invasion of South Carolina is imminent, hold an unauthorized legislative session to deal with the perceived crisis. Proprietary Governor Robert Johnson is ejected, and James Moore is appointed interim governor.

OTHER EVENTS OF 1719

Colonial Affairs In Pensacola, Florida, the Spanish settlers surrender to French forces led by Louisiana Governor de Bienville.

MAY 1720

Slavery A large group of slaves intent upon capturing Charleston, South Carolina, kills several whites before being subdued. The leaders of this revolt are either hanged or burned.

OTHER EVENTS OF 1720

King George's War: Approach The French construct the fortress of Louisbourg on Cape Breton Island to regulate the traffic in and out of the mouth of the St. Lawrence River. They also build Fort Niagara to protect the lower Great Lakes and to serve as a bulwark against attacks by the Iroquois Indians.

Spanish Policy A Spanish military expedition is almost wiped out by a Pawnee Indian attack. Following this action the Spanish retain Santa Fe and Taos, New Mexico, as their northernmost outposts.

During the War of Jenkins' Ear (1739-42) Georgia's Governor Edward Olgethorpe briefly invaded Florida.

EVENTS OF 1722

Indians In Albany, New York, the Iroquois Six Nations conclude a treaty with Virginia Governor Spotswood. The Indians agree not to cross the Potomac River or the Blue Ridge Mountains.

EVENTS OF 1724

Lovewell's War In Northern New England, Lovewell's War, otherwise known as Dummer's War, climaxes in a bloody massacre of Maine settlers by French Jesuit missionary Father Rale and his Abenaki Indian allies. The New England colonies have erected a chain of northern forts, including Fort

Dummer at present-day Brattleboro, Vermont, the first permanent settlement in that state.

20 FEBRUARY 1725

Lovewell's War In Wakefield, New Hampshire, Captain John Lovewell's men take 10 Indian scalps, the first recorded instance of scalping done by colonists. In Boston the scalps bring a bounty of 100 pounds apiece.

OTHER EVENTS OF 1725

King George's War: Approach New England colonists erect Fort Oswego on Lake Ontario to meet the challenge of the recently-built French Fort Niagara.

FEBRUARY 1727

Anglo-Spanish War Tension is high and hostilities follow between the English and Spanish settlers in North America when the year-long Anglo-Spanish War breaks out.

9 MARCH 1728

Anglo-Spanish War South Carolina militiamen, retaliating against Spanish-protected Indian raiding parties, intrude into Spanish territory to attack the Indian village of Nombre de Dios, directly under the guns of the Spanish fortress at St. Augustine, Florida. The failure of the Spanish to attack the British diminishes the Spanish prestige with the Indians.

EVENTS OF 1729

Slavery A band of escaped black slaves from plantations along the James River in Virginia are tracked into the mountains, where it is discovered that the blacks are readying the land for planting. After a pitched battle with Virginians the slaves are brought home.

Indian Warfare Following a period of expansion, the French settlements in the Mississippi River Valley are attacked by Chickasaw, Natchez and Yazoo Indians. These attacks force the eventual confinement of French settlement to the region of present-day Louisiana.

EVENTS OF 1731

King George's War: Approach The French in Canada erect a fort at Crown Point on Lake Champlain to guard the southern approach to Canada via the Hudson, Lake George, Lake Champlain and the Richelieu River.

EVENTS OF 1734

Slavery The mistaken belief that England has ordered the emancipation of Christian blacks from slavery leads to an insurrection in Burlington County, New Jersey. Several hundred slaves hatch a plot that calls for the murder of all white males and the raping of white women. The details of the rebellion are inadvertently revealed by a drunken slave. Thirty arrests follow, and in the vindictive aftermath one slave is hanged and the others are punished by flogging or ear cropping.

1734-1752

Internal Conflict Small farmers in western North Carolina withhold their rent as protest against the tidewater government and discriminatory legislation enacted by it. Similar east-west colonial conflicts will occur in South Carolina, as well as in Pennsylvania and New Jersey.

1730-1740

Technology This period sees the development of the long or Pennsylvania rifle, later known as the Kentucky rifle.

EVENTS OF 1735

Settling French colonists from Canada settle French territory in the Illinois area of the Mississippi River Valley. To the east, James Oglethorpe, governor of the recently-created Georgia colony, establishes Fort Ofkuskee on the Talapoosa River.

MARCH 1738

Spanish Policy Florida Governor Don Manuel de Montiano proclaims that, in accordance with a declaration made by King Philip V of Spain, all slave runaways from English colonial areas will be freed, armed to fight the British and resettled in a special enclave three miles north of St. Augustine, known as Fort Moosa.

SPRING 1739

Slavery Twenty-three runaway slaves from St. Helen's, South Carolina, make their way through Georgia and into Florida, where they receive a warm welcome from the Spanish.

9 SEPTEMBER 1739

Slavery A black insurrection takes place in South Carolina. A group of blacks sets out on a journey intending to reach St. Augustine, Florida. Surprised by a white attack, the black uprising is quashed at the cost of 44 black and 30 white lives. This is the most serious of the three black uprisings that occur in South Carolina during 1739; the others take place in Stone's Creek and in St. John's Parish in Berkeley County.

19 OCTOBER 1739

International As a result of their struggle for commercial supremacy, England declares war on Spain in the so-called War of Jenkins' Ear. This war will merge with the War of Austrian Succession, known in the colonies as King George's War.

JANUARY 1740

War of Jenkins' Ear Georgia Governor James Oglethorpe invades Spanish Florida. His forces are protected on the west from any possible French attack by friendly Indians. Oglethorpe captures Spanish Forts San Francisco de Pupo and Picolata on the San Juan River.

MAY-JULY 1740

War of Jenkins' Ear The Georgian and Indian forces led by Governor Oglethorpe lay siege to Spanish St. Augustine. Oglethorpe withdraws his force when it is threatened from the rear.

28 FEBRUARY 1741

Slavery Panic develops in New York City after a burglary and a series of fires. Rumors spread that the blacks and poor whites are plotting to seize power. Although little evidence is provided for this theory, 101 blacks are convicted, four whites and 18 blacks are hanged, 13 blacks are burned alive and 70 others are banished.

7 JULY 1742

War of Jenkins' Ear The Battle of Bloody Swamp, a Spanish counterattack for earlier English movement into Florida, is fought on St. Simon's Island, Georgia. The Spanish are severely defeated.

EVENTS OF 1743

War of Jenkins' Ear In punishment for Spanish raids on Georgia settlements in 1742, Georgia Governor James Oglethorpe leads a retaliatory foray against the Spanish settlements around St. Augustine.

15 MARCH 1744

King George's War After signing a pact with Spain, France joins the Spanish war against England. Known in America as King George's War, this conflict will last until 1748.

OTHER EVENTS OF 1744

King George's War The French unsuccessfully attack the British garrison at Port Royal, Nova Scotia.

A scene of the British capture of Louisbourg in 1745 during King George's War.

16 JUNE 1745

King George's War: Capture of Louisbourg A New England military force led by William Pepperell, combined with a fleet commanded by Sir Peter Warren, captures the French fortress of Louisbourg on Cape Breton Island. The siege has taken six weeks. Louisbourg is a tremendous fortress in New World terms, and its fall to a colonial force impresses European leaders.

28-29 NOVEMBER 1745

King George's War: New England A French and Indian force marches overland from Crown Point on Lake Champlain to Saratoga, New York, where it surprises and kills some 30 inhabitants. The French and Indians also assault the fort at Albany.

20 AUGUST 1746

King George's War: Destruction of Fort Massachusetts One of the most serious reverses for the English Colonists during King George's War occurs in East Hoosuck (now Adams), Massachusetts, with the surrender and subsequent destruction of Fort Massachusetts.

18 OCTOBER 1748

King George's War: End The Treaty of Aix-la-Chapelle ends King George's War, restoring the colonies as they were before the hostilities began. The Louisbourg fortress and Cape Breton Island are returned to France. The New England colonists are incensed by this, and the English Crown agrees to bear the costs of the colonial expedition of 1745.

EVENTS OF 1749

French and Indian War: Approach Alarmed by the English incursions into the Ohio River Valley, the French send Celeron de Bienville from Lake Erie to reclaim the Ohio River Valley. During his southward expedition de Bienville places lead plates at the mouth of each major river, documenting the French claims to the area.

EVENTS OF 1750

Population England's North American possessions are by now home to more than 1.1 million colonists. The figure is far from being stable, as it is being constantly swelled by waves of immigrants.

JULY 1752

French and Indian War: Approach Alarmed by the new English presence in the Ohio River Valley, the French seize the English trading post of Pickawillany.

APRIL 1753

French and Indian War: Approach Governor of Canada Marquis Duquesne de Menneville mandates the erection of Fort Presque Isle at present-day Erie, Pennsylvania, of Fort Le Boeuf at the portage to French Creek and of Fort Venango at the fork of French Creek and the Allegheny River.

31 OCTOBER 1753

French and Indian War: Approach Concerned over the French fortifications in the Ohio territory, Virginia Lieutenant Governor Robert Dinwiddie sends 21-year-old George Washington to ascertain the French goals in that area.

JANUARY 1754

French and Indian War: Approach George Washington returns to Virginia and reports that the French are determined to claim the Ohio territory and that they will resist removal with military force.

17 APRIL 1754

French and Indian War: Approach The French capture the forks of the Ohio River, thus setting the stage for conflict with the English colonies of Pennsylvania and Virginia.

28 MAY 1754

French and Indian War In the opening engagement of the French and Indian War (in Europe it will be known as the Seven Years War), George Washington leads 150 Virginians to victory over a French exploratory group. Washington erects Fort Necessity at the Great Meadows. On 3 July 1754 Washington will be forced to surrender the fort to a numerically superior French force led by Coulon de Villiers.

20 FEBRUARY 1755

French and Indian War: Command British General Edward Braddock, in command of two regiments of British troops, arrives in Virginia to take charge as commander-in-chief of all the British forces in the Americas.

14 APRIL 1755

French and Indian War: Fort Duquesne Campaign Leading 1400 British soldiers, General Braddock sets out for French Fort Duquesne, at the site of present-day Pittsburgh, to challenge the French in the Ohio Valley. Lieutenant Colonel George Washington and 450 colonial soldiers accompany Braddock on what will prove a disastrous mission.

19 JUNE 1755

French and Indian War: Nova Scotia Commanded by Colonels Robert Monckton and James Winslow, two thousand New England colonists and some British soldiers capture the French Fort Beausejour in Nova Scotia.

9 JULY 1755

French and Indian War: Defeat of Braddock Braddock and Washington's men are caught in a surprise ambush by 900 French and Indians at a spot only eight miles short of Fort Duquesne. Using wilderness fighting tactics, the French and Indians thoroughly defeat the British force. When the Battle of the Wilderness is over 977 British soldiers have been killed or wounded, including General Braddock, who dies later. George Washington leads the survivors back to Fort Cumberland.

5 SEPTEMBER 1755

French and Indian War: Expulsion of the Acadians The British governor of Nova Scotia, Colonel Charles Lawrence, orders that all those Acadians (originally French colonists who came under English rule in 1713) who refuse to swear allegiance to the English crown be expelled from the colony. On 8 October 1755 some 6000 Acadians are forced from their homes. They are eventually distributed among 12 of the 13 English colonies – Georgia refuses to accept any of the Acadians. The exiled Acadians encounter hardship and penury, in part due to religious discrimination and also because they do not always make genuine efforts to become assimilated into the English colonies. The Acadians find their most sympathetic reception in the colonies of Massachusetts, Connecticut and Pennsylvania.

A discouraged George Washington leads his troops home after having been driven out of Fort Necessity by a superior French force in July 1754.

8 SEPTEMBER 1755

French and Indian War: Battle of Lake George Leading a force of 3500 colonists and 400 Indians, Sir William Johnson has rapidly erected Fort William Henry on Lake George to meet an expected French attack from Canada. In the ensuing Battle of Lake George Johnson defeats 1400 French and Indians led by Baron Dieskau. Johnson has stopped one of the most significant French campaigns.

DECEMBER 1755

French and Indian War: Strategy George Washington convinces colonial assemblies to construct a series of forts from the Potomac River, across the headwaters of the James River and the Roanoke River, to Fort Prince George in South Carolina.

11 MAY 1756

French and Indian War: French Command Louis Joseph, Marquis de Montcalm, arrives in Canada to command the French forces there. His predecessor, Baron Dieskau, had been captured by the British in the Battle of Lake George. Montcalm will prove to be one of France's greatest soldiers in the New World.

14 AUGUST 1756

French and Indian War: Destruction of Fort Oswego Montcalm successfully leads French troops against the English Fort Oswego on Lake Ontario and destroys it.

31 AUGUST 1756

French and Indian War: New York English General Webb is forced to give up the Mohawk Valley to the numerically superior French forces. The settlers in this area relocate to Schenectady and Albany, New York.

Cape Range, nine miles above Quebec, was the point from which British general Wolfe began his final operation against the city in September 1759.

9 AUGUST 1757

French and Indian War: Destruction of Fort William Henry French and Indian forces under Montcalm capture and burn the English Fort William Henry on Lake George, New York. Following the honorable surrender of the garrison, the Indians massacre between 50 and 150 of the English, who are under the protection of the French flag. The scene will be recreated in James Fenimore Cooper's famous novel *The Last of the Mohicans*.

MAY 1758

Indian Warfare The Cherokee Indians begin a series of raids on settlements located in the frontier region of Virginia. The raids continue for one year, and they are countered with retaliatory raids by the settlers.

8 JULY 1758

French and Indian War: Defense of Fort Ticonderoga British General James Abercromby brings some 12,000 men to attack the French Fort Ticonderoga on Lake Champlain. Montcalm is defending the fort with only 3000 French troops. Inexplicably, Abercromby orders a frontal assault, rather than trying to starve the French garrison. The French troops shoot down nearly 2000 British soldiers before the order to retreat is given. This victory is one of the last that the French will enjoy in the French and Indian War.

26 JULY 1758

French and Indian War: Fall of Louisbourg A force of 9000 British soldiers and 500 colonists, led by Generals Jeffrey Amherst and James Wolfe, besiege and capture Louisbourg, the French fortress on Cape Breton Island. The way is now open for an attack on Quebec itself, the heart of New France.

27 AUGUST 1758

French and Indian War: Capture of Fort Frontenac British forces led by Colonel John Bradstreet capture the French Fort Frontenac at the site of present-day Kingston, Ontario.

18 SEPTEMBER 1758

French and Indian War: British Command After his resounding defeat by Montcalm at Fort Ticonderoga, British commander James Abercromby is replaced by General Jeffrey Amherst.

25 NOVEMBER 1758

French and Indian War: Destruction of Fort Duquesne The French blow up Fort Duquesne when a superior British force approaches on a newly-constructed road from the southeast. The losses of Louisbourg and Duquesne shrink the territory of New France and pressage the eventual British victory in North America.

27 JUNE 1759

French and Indian War: Quebec Campaign British General James Wolfe, leading 9000 British soldiers aboard a fleet commanded by Admiral Charles Saunders, arrives in the St. Lawrence River, opposite Quebec City. It has been 67 years since Sir William Phips besieged Quebec.

26 JULY 1759

French and Indian War: Capture of Fort Ticonderoga British General Jeffrey Amherst leads a numerically superior British force against French Fort Ticonderoga. The French blow up parts of the fort and withdraw, first to Crown Point, and then all the way up Lake Champlain to the Richelieu River.

27 JULY 1759

French and Indian War: Quebec Campaign French leader Marquis de Montcalm sends a small fleet of fire ships, trying to burn the British fleet anchored before Quebec. The British sailors manage to tow the fireships aside, but the flames make a splendid show.

13 SEPTEMBER 1759

French and Indian War: Battle of the Plains of Abraham Following a night of scaling the heights of Anse-de-Foulon, a mile and a half from Quebec, Wolfe's British soldiers are arrayed the next morning on the Plains of Abraham, directly south of the city. Montcalm makes an uncharacteristically hasty decision to attack. The Battle of the Plains of Abraham is fought in classic European style: the French advance rapidly forward in disciplined formations, while the British await them in an equally disciplined battle line. When Wolfe gives the order to fire the British pour devastatingly synchronized volleys into the oncoming French. After fifteen minutes the French retreat. Both Wolfe and Montcalm are mortally wounded.

Brigadier General James Wolfe (1727-59) died on the Plains of Abraham at the moment of victory.

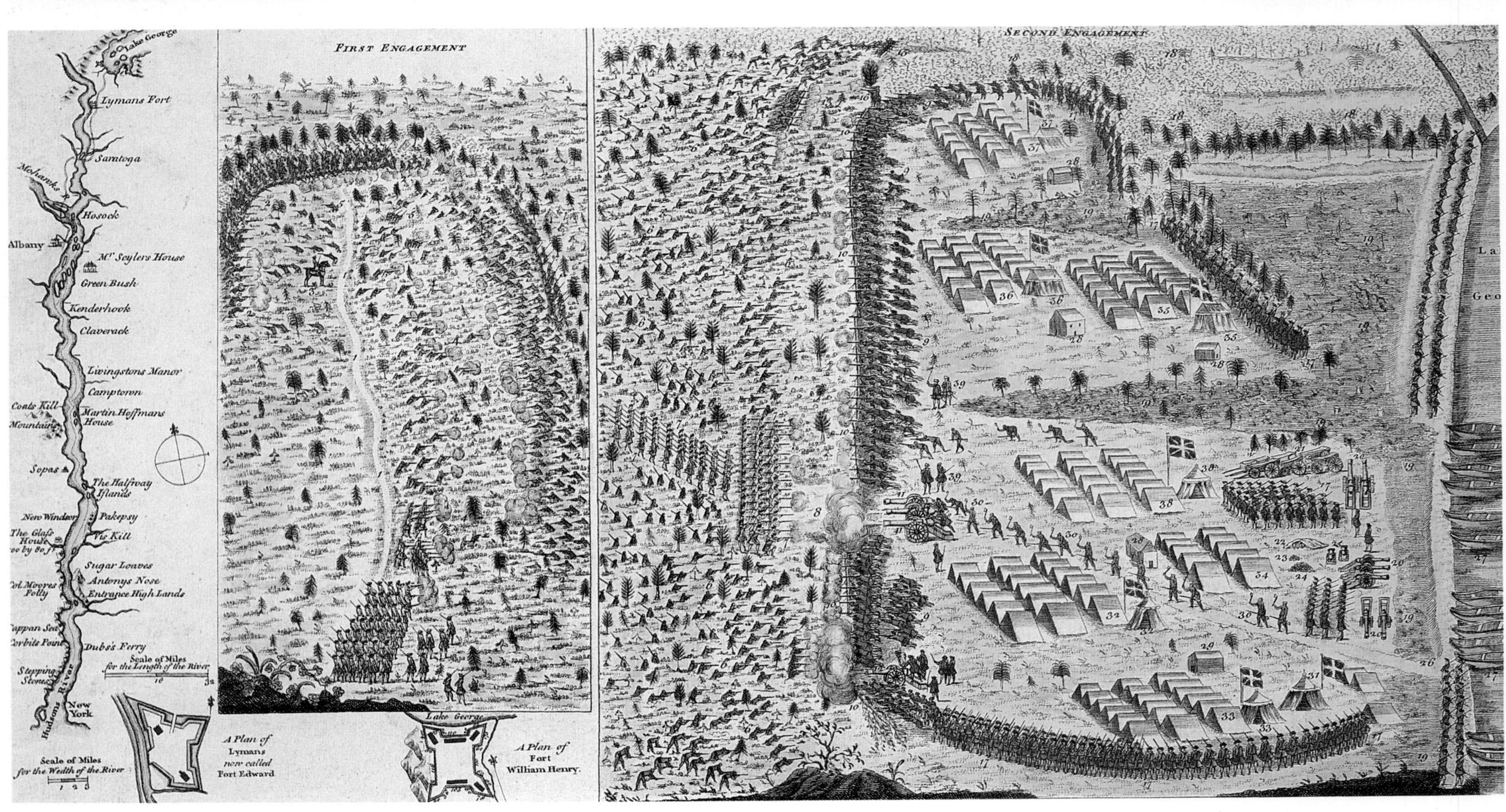
Lake George
Lymans Fort
Saratoga
Mohanks R.
Hosock
Albany
Mr. Seylers House
Green Bush
Kenderhook
Claverack
Livingstons Manor
Camptown
Conts Kill Mountains
Martin Hoffmans House
Sopas
The Halfway Islands
New Windsor
Pakepsy
The Glass House
Vis Kill
Sugar Loaves
Antonys Nose
Entrance High Lands
Col. Moores Folly
Tappan Sea
Corbits Point
Dubs's Ferry
Scale of Miles for the Length of the River
Stepping Stones
Hudsons River
New York
Scale of Miles for the Wedth of the River
FIRST ENGAGEMENT
A Plan of Lymans now called Fort Edward
Lake George
A Plan of Fort William Henry
SECOND ENGAGEMENT

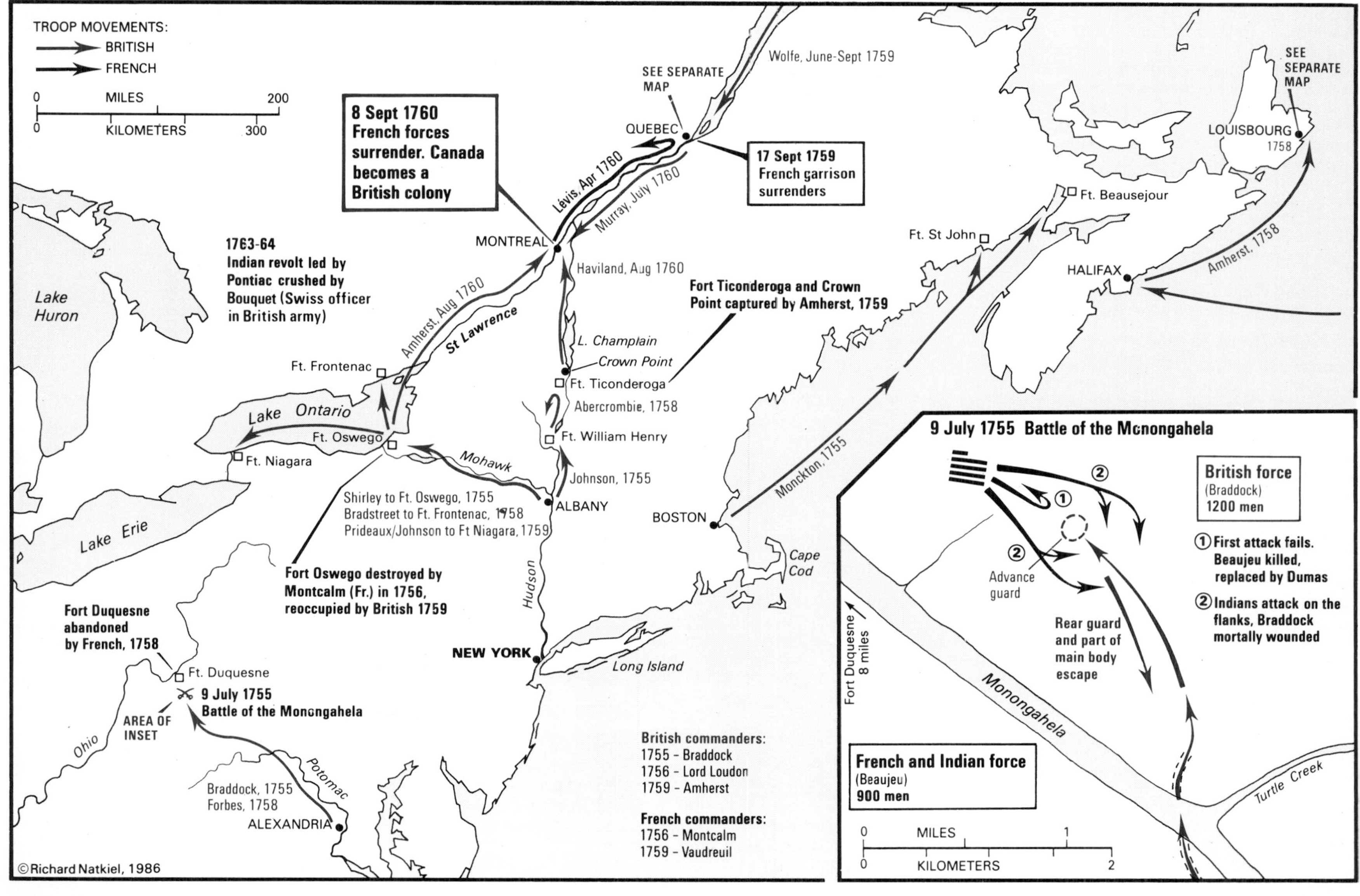

A general map of the French and Indian War, with an inset of Braddock's defeat near Fort Duquesne.

18 SEPTEMBER 1759

French and Indian War: Fall of Quebec The loss at the Plains of Abraham, the death of Montcalm and the lack of food supplies impels the city of Quebec to surrender to the British forces. Although the French and Indian War will continue into 1760, the surrender here spells the end for French Canada.

OCTOBER 1759

Indian Warfare The Cherokee Indian War begins in the southern colonies. These hostilities, particularly in South Carolina, will last into 1761.

1 SEPTEMBER 1760

French and Indian War: Capture of Chambly British forces led by William Haviland march north from Crown Point to seize the French post of Chambly, which is inside Canada.

8 SEPTEMBER 1760

French and Indian War: Fall of Montreal General Jeffrey Amherst has brought a large British force to converge on Montreal, the last major French holding in Canada. French Governor Marquis de Vaudreuil surrenders New France officially to the British.

9 SEPTEMBER 1761

Pontiac's Rebellion: Approach In a conference with the Indians at Detroit the English refuse to acquiesce to the Indian demand that they be supplied with ammunition and lower-priced trade goods. This policy of the British is to lead to further conflict with the Indians, conflict that will culminate in the rebellion led by Pontiac, chief of the Ottawa Indians.

OTHER EVENTS OF 1761

Indian Warfare English Colonel Grant ends the series of devastating raids by the Indians on the western frontier settlements of the southern colonies by forcing the Cherokee Indians to seek peace.

3 NOVEMBER 1762

International In the secret treaty of Fontainbleau, French monarch Louis XV deeds to Spain all French territory west of the Mississippi River, as well as the Isle of Orleans in Louisiana, to compensate Spain for her losses at the hands of the British in the Seven Years War. This maintenance of western lands as Bourbon property will eventually play a role in the acquisition of territory by the United States in the Louisiana Purchase of 1803.

Left top: The French and Indian War began with a sharp British defeat when General Edward Braddock led his troops into a French ambush in July 1755.

Left: A contemporary sketch map of the Battle of Lake George, fought in September 1755.

10 FEBRUARY 1763

French and Indian War: Treaty of Paris The Treaty of Paris officially ends the Seven Years War, known in America as the French and Indian War. Under the terms of this treaty the French surrender Nova Scotia, Cape Breton Island, the St. Lawrence River islands and all of Canada to Britain.

7 MAY 1763

Pontiac's Rebellion A secret plan of Pontiac, chief of the Ottawa Indians, to seize Detroit from the English with a surprise attack, is betrayed. This leads Pontiac to elect the path of all-out warfare, with a devastating effect for the British frontier garrisons west of Niagara – the Indians destroy nearly all of them by mid-June. This active hostility of the Indians is partly the result of the British refusal to agree to the demand of the Indians for lower-priced trade goods and for ammunition.

16 MAY 1763

Pontiac's Rebellion The western British garrison of Fort Sandusky Ohio, is destroyed by rebellious Indian forces.

25 MAY 1763

Pontiac's Rebellion A second British post, Fort Saint Joseph, near present-day Niles, Michigan, is destroyed by Pontiac's Indian forces.

27 MAY 1763

Pontiac's Rebellion The British Fort Miami, near present-day Fort Wayne, Indiana, is destroyed by Indian forces.

1 JUNE 1763

Pontiac's Rebellion The British western garrison of Fort Ouiatenon, near present-day Lafayette, Indiana, is destroyed by the rebel forces of Chief Pontiac.

4 JUNE 1763

Pontiac's Rebellion A deadly game of lacrosse is played by two large teams of Indians outside Fort Michilimackinack, near Mackinaw City, Michigan. When the English garrison gathers to watch the game, the Indians seize concealed weapons and attack, slaughtering all the occupants and burning the fort to the ground.

16 JUNE 1763

Pontiac's Rebellion The British western garrison of Fort Venango, located at the junction of French Creek and the Allegheny River in northwest Pennsylvania, is destroyed by the forces of Chief Pontiac.

18 JUNE 1763

Pontiac's Rebellion The western British post of Fort Le Boeuf in northwest Pennsylvania is destroyed by Pontiac's Indian forces.

20 JUNE 1763

Pontiac's Rebellion The western British garrison of Fort Duquesne is destroyed by Pontiac's forces.

13 JULY 1763

Pontiac's Rebellion General Jeffrey Amherst suggests to Colonel Henry Bouquet that Pontiac's rebellion can be countered by spreading smallpox among the Indians by means of infected blankets. Bouquet points out that this strategem might also prove dangerous to English soldiers.

29 JULY 1763

Pontiac's Rebellion British troops arrive to reinforce the besieged British garrison at Detroit, under the command of Major Henry Gladwin. Detroit is able to resist Pontiac's forces for five months.

31 JULY 1763

Pontiac's Rebellion At the Battle of Bloody Ridge, English forces led by Major Henry Gladwin out of Detroit are turned away by the Indian forces led by Pontiac.

2-6 AUGUST 1763

Pontiac's Rebellion At Bushy Run, near present-day Pittsburgh, Pennsylvania, Colonel Henry Bouquet attacks and defeats Indians who have been besieging Fort Pitt. On 10 August, Bouquet is able to relieve the garrison at Fort Pitt.

NOVEMBER 1763

Pontiac's Rebellion Chief Pontiac ends his unsuccessful five-month siege of the British garrison at Detroit. It is virtually unprecedented for an Indian force to sustain a siege of any duration.

13 DECEMBER 1763

Internal Conflict A mob of settlers from Donegal and Paxton, Pennsylvania, attack the non-belligerent

Indians of Lancaster County. The Pennsylvania assembly mandates the arrest of the 'Paxton Boys' and their trial. The frontiersmen ignore the order and begin a march east. Benjamin Franklin defuses the crisis by convincing the Paxton Boys to drop any idea of doing battle in favor of posting a formal protest. By taking this action they are to receive greater proportional representation for the western settlements in Pennsylvania, thus resulting in greater governmental attention to their needs.

12 APRIL 1764

Pontiac's Rebellion English Colonel John Bradstreet signs peace treaties with a number of Indian tribes at Presque Isle, the site of present-day Erie, Pennsylvania. Chief Pontiac will continue his resistance to the English for another two years.

17 NOVEMBER 1764

Pontiac's Rebellion The Indian War of Chief Pontiac ends when the Indians – but not Pontiac himself – surrender to British forces on the Muskimgham River in the Ohio territory.

22 MARCH 1765

Revolution: Approach The English Parliament passes the Stamp Act, setting its first direct tax on the American colonies. The intent of this act, together with the 1764 Sugar Act, is to raise adequate funds to support at least one-third of the total cost of maintaining a military organization in the colonies: about 300,000 pounds a year needs to be raised. The passage of the Stamp Act meets with almost universal opposition in the colonies. The central objection is to the principle of direct taxation of the colonies by Parliament, with its implication that this tax is the harbinger of more taxes in the future.

22 MARCH 1765

Revolution: Approach The Quartering Act goes into effect in the American colonies. This English law requires the colonies to provide quarters (housing) for English troops stationed in the colonies. The act is to be effective for two years following its institution. It serves to broaden the colonial discontent already provoked by the Sugar Act of 1764.

29 MAY 1765

Revolution: Approach Patrick Henry presents seven Virginia Resolutions to the Virginia House of Burgesses in a speech that ends, 'If this be treason, make the most of it.' The resolutions assert that only Virginia has the legal authority to tax its residents – if not a treasonous idea, surely a revolutionary one. After debate, the House of Burgesses deletes the more radical clauses and passes a version that reaffirms the right of the Virginia colony to self government and its opposition to taxation without representation.

1 NOVEMBER 1765

Revolution: Approach The Stamp Act goes into effect in the colonies. Business is virtually suspended as almost all colonists refuse to use the stamps. (Even the colonial courts close rather than use the stamps.) Business will later be resumed, but without the use of the stamps, in flagrant violation of the parliamentary legislation. In New York City, a mob burns an effigy of 'Liberty,' harasses British soldiers, burns the royal governor in effigy and plunders houses before it is suppressed by law-abiding colonists.

18 MARCH 1766

British Policy King George III signs a bill that repeals the Stamp Act, effective 1 May. However, on the same day that the King signs the bill, Parliament passes the Declaratory Act, which asserts that the British government has complete power to legislate any laws governing the American colonists 'in all cases whatsoever.' The fact that Parliament has found it necessary to outline its generally underexercised powers shows that the American reaction to the Stamp Act has had an important effect.

24 JULY 1766

Indian Warfare Chief Pontiac signs a peace treaty with Sir William Johnson at Oswego, New York. Pontiac is to keep his word, and he will maintain allegiance to the English until his death in 1769.

Irate American colonists burn stamped paper in a protest against the British Stamp Act of 1765, the first direct tax ever levied upon America.

Samuel Adams (1722-1803) of Boston was one of the fieriest of the American patriot leaders. He was the leading force behind the Boston Tea Party of 1773.

10 AUGUST 1766

Revolution: Approach The tension between British troops and New York City colonists who have refused to comply with the Quartering Act results in a violent incident. Some British soldiers destroy a liberty pole, an assembly point erected by the Sons of Liberty, resulting in a skirmish between armed citizens and British soldiers wielding bayonets. Isaac Sears, the leader of the Sons of Liberty, is wounded.

29 JUNE 1767

British Policy The English Parliament passes the Townshend Acts, a new series of internal taxes on the American colonies, including import duties on glass, lead, paints and tea. The projected income from these duties is to help pay for the defense of the colonies, as well as for the governmental and judicial administration of the colonies. To enforce the duties, the colonial supreme court justices are empowered to issue writs of assistance. England is now aware that the American colonies may resist external taxation.

28 OCTOBER 1767

Revolution: Approach In response to the impending imposition of the Townshend Acts, a Boston town meeting decides to resort to a nonimportation movement to force the British to retract the new measures. The colonists compose a list of British luxury item trade goods that are not to be purchased after the end of 1767. On 29 December 1767 a New York City open meeting will choose a committee to design a similar policy.

20 NOVEMBER 1767

British Policy The Townshend Revenue Acts go into effect in the American colonies.

11 FEBRUARY 1768

Revolution: Approach With the approval of the Massachusetts Assembly, Samuel Adams composes a circular letter which explains to other colonial assemblies the steps taken by the Massachusetts general court to oppose the Townshend Acts. The circular essay opposes taxation without representation and concludes with a call for united colonial action against the British governmental policy.

FEBRUARY 1768

Revolution: Approach The British customs commissioners, hindered at every turn by the tactics of Boston agitators, formally request the British government to supply protective military forces. When they receive no reply they repeat their request.

APRIL 1768

Revolution: Approach The legislative assemblies of Connecticut, New Hampshire and New Jersey support the Massachusetts circular letter. Virginia has issued its own circular letter urging support of the Massachusetts position.

17 MAY 1768

British Policy Armed with 50 guns, the British frigate *Romney* arrives in Boston harbor in response to the call of the customs commissioners for protection from Boston's agitators.

1 OCTOBER 1768

British Policy Two regiments of British infantry from Halifax, Nova Scotia, land in Boston, where they are permanently billeted in order to maintain order and enforce the customs laws.

5 NOVEMBER 1768

Indians The Iroquois Indians sign a treaty at Fort Stanwix (now Rome, New York) with the British Commissioner, Sir William Johnson. Under its terms the Iroquois surrender their rights to a vast tract of land, including much of western New York State, and the area between the Ohio and Tennessee Rivers. White settlers will now be free to emigrate into this territory, but other Indians, such as the Shawnees and Cherokees, will not recognize this treaty. There will be an increasing number of confrontations between the whites and Indians, culminating in Lord Dunmore's War in 1774.

OTHER EVENTS OF 1768

Internal Conflict In western North Carolina, frontiersmen begin to resist the authority from the colonial government in the tidewater region; eventually this will develop into a conflict known as the War of the Regulation (1768-1771).

JANUARY-FEBRUARY 1769

British Policy The English Parliament urges the bringing to trial of any inciters to rebellion in the American colonies.

OTHER EVENTS OF 1769

Revolution: Approach Throughout the year merchants in such cities as Philadelphia, Baltimore and Providence join with various colonial assemblies, such as those of New Jersey, North Carolina, Virginia and Maryland, in agreeing to refuse to import many goods from Britain until the Townshend Acts are repealed.

The most serious case of pre-Revolutionary violence was the 'Boston Massacre' of March 1770.

Indian Warfare Chief Pontiac is murdered in Cahokia, Illinois by a Kaskasia Indian, who, according to some accounts, is in the pay of an English trader.

19 JANUARY 1770

Revolution: Approach In an attempt to stop British soldiers from posting broadsides in New York City, the Sons of Liberty, led by Alexander McDougall, engage in a skirmish with British soldiers on Golden Hill. Armed with swords and clubs, the colonists confront 30-40 British soldiers armed with bayonets. No fatalities result, but several participants in the skirmish are seriously wounded.

8 FEBRUARY 1770

Revolution: Approach Alexander McDougall, leader of the New York Sons of Liberty, is arrested for his authorship of a broadside criticizing the New York assembly. Titled, 'To the Betrayed Inhabitants of the City and Colony of New York,' the broadside was issued in December 1769. Refusing to post bond, McDougall remains in prison until 29 April 1770, when he pleads not guilty to the charges and is released on bail. The case never reaches the courts, as the colony's witness dies in the interim.

In 1772 a party of colonists burned the grounded British revenue schooner *Gaspée*, inflated in this old print to look the size of a battleship.

5 MARCH 1770

Boston Massacre A Boston mob teases and confronts British soldiers stationed in the town. There is some confusion as to how the conflict begins, but the soldiers fire their rifles at the crowd, killing three colonists, mortally wounding two and injuring six. This dangerous situation is defused when Massachusetts Governor Thomas Hutchinson agrees to the demands of Samuel Adams that British soldiers be withdrawn from the town to islands in Boston Harbor. British Captain Thomas Preston and eight of his men are arrested for murder by the civil authorities on 9 March 1770. The case comes to trial in October 1770.

12 APRIL 1770

British Policy The British Crown approves the partial repeal of the Townshend Acts, eliminating duties on all imports to the colonies except for tea. At the same time, the Quartering Act is allowed to lapse without renewal. Although tensions are still high in the colonies, reconciliation between England and the colonies is clearly still possible.

OCTOBER-DECEMBER 1770

Colonial Affairs The case of the British soldiers involved in the Boston Massacre comes to trial. Ably defended by colonial lawyers John Adams and Josiah Quincy – both of whom are firm patriots – Captain Thomas Preston and six of his men are acquitted by the civil jury. Two other soldiers are found guilty of manslaughter, are punished with branding and then are released.

15 JANUARY 1771

Internal Conflict The North Carolina assembly passes the 'Bloody Act,' which makes rioters guilty of treason. The enactment of this legislation is triggered by the violent agitation of the Regulators, led by Herman Husbands. Active since 1768 in representing the western frontier settlers, the Regulators protest inequitable representation of the Piedmont region in the North Carolina Assembly, as well as levelling charges of extortion and oppression against the eastern part of the colony.

16 MAY 1771

Internal Conflict North Carolina Governor William Tyron leads 1200 militiamen into the western part of the colony to confront the rebellious Regulators at Alamance Creek, near Hillsboro. Many of the Regulators lack firearms, and Tyron's force overcomes them. A leader of the Regulators, James Few, is executed on the battlefield on 17 May, and 12 others are judged guilty of treason on 17 June. Of these, six are executed. The other six defendants and some 6500 North Carolina settlers in the Piedmont are required to swear an oath of allegiance to North Carolina's government. The rebellion is indicative of the profound regional factionalism of the area.

AUGUST 1771

Internal Conflict A Pennsylvania proprietary force is unable to dislodge Connecticut settlers from the Wyoming Valley region in Pennsylvania.

9 JUNE 1772

Revolution: Approach The British customs schooner *Gaspee* runs aground in Narragansett Bay, off Rhode Island, while pursuing a colonial vessel suspected of smuggling. Led by merchant John Brown, eight boatloads of colonists from Providence, Rhode Island, attack the *Gaspee*, capture it, set wounded Lieutenant William Duddington and his crew ashore and then burn the British ship.

28 OCTOBER 1772

Revolution: Approach Over the opposition of Boston merchant John Hancock and other influential patriots, Samuel Adams is able to issue a call for a Boston town meeting to take place in November in order to consider the imminent threats to self-government in the colonies.

27 APRIL- 7 MAY 1773

British Policy The British Parliament passes legislation that revokes all export duties on English tea going to the American colonies. Nevertheless, in order to save the East India Company from possible bankruptcy, the three-penny per pound import tax on tea remains in effect.

SEPTEMBER 1773

Indian Warfare Daniel Boone is leading a party of settlers from northwestern North Carolina into Kentucky via the Cumberland Gap. A small group, led by his sixteen-year-old son James, camps separately to tend the stock; a band of Shawnees attacks and kills all except two of the group – James is shot in the hips so he cannot run and then is slowly tortured to death.

27 NOVEMBER 1773

Revolution: Approach The first of three ships bearing tea, the *Dartmouth*, arrives in Boston.

16 DECEMBER 1773

The Boston Tea Party Some 8000 Bostonians gather in the Old South Church to hear Samuel Adams, chairman of the meeting, receive the news that Massachusetts Governor Thomas Hutchinson will not allow the ships carrying tea to leave Boston Harbor until the duty on the tea is paid. During the night of 16-17 December, a group of activists disguised as Mohawk Indians board the tea ships and empty all 342 casks of tea into the water. The action will be remembered as 'The Boston Tea Party.'

APRIL 1774

Indian Warfare Taking revenge for the murder of James Boone and his group, a party of settlers led by Daniel Greathouse invite some Indians to enjoy a drink of rum at a place called Baker's Bottom (on the southeastern bank of the Ohio River, above present-day Steubenville) and then proceed to get them drunk and massacre them. Since the victims include the brother and sister of Logan, an Indian chief who regarded himself as a friend of the whites, the Shawnees agree to assist Logan in taking revenge on the many settlers now moving into these lands as a result of the Treaty of Fort Stanwix (1768). The result will be the relatively brief conflict known as Lord Dunmore's (or Shawnee) War.

The American Revolution began with the Battles of Lexington and Concord in April 1775. Here British troops, under colonial attack, return to Boston.

13 MAY 1774

British Policy British General Thomas Gage arrives in Boston to replace Thomas Hutchinson as governor of Massachusetts. Gage has sweeping powers as commander-in-chief of all British forces in the colonies. Four regiments of British soldiers accompany Gage.

10 JUNE 1774

Lord Dunmore's War Dunmore, the governor of the colony of Virginia, calls out the militia of the counties to the west and orders them to erect a line of defenses along the Ohio River. In the ensuing weeks there will be only one major confrontation between the militia and Indians, but Lord Dunmore will proceed to Pittsburgh and then make his way down the Ohio River in September.

1 SEPTEMBER 1774

Revolution: Approach Governor Thomas Gage seizes the Massachusetts colony's arsenal of weaponry at Charlestown.

SEPTEMBER 1774

Revolution: Approach Following his seizure of the arsenal at Charlestown and the colonists' response to this action, Governor Gage fortifies Boston Neck, the strip that connects Boston with the mainland.

Patrick Henry (1736-90), shown here delivering his famous 'give me liberty or give me death' speech, was a Virginian counterpart of Samuel Adams.

10 OCTOBER 1774

Lord Dunmore's War About 1100 backwoodsmen, led by Andrew Lewis, have camped at Point Pleasant, a promontory formed by the right bank of the Kanawha River and the Ohio River. Led by Cornstalk, a Shawnee chief, some 500 Indians attack the camp and engage in a fierce battle that leaves 75 settlers dead (including Lewis's brother) and 140 wounded. Indian losses are unknown (they have removed their casualties) but are believed to be at least as high. Lord Dunmore will arrive nearby a few days later and impose a treaty on Cornstalk and his Shawnees that leaves them powerless against future settlers.

30 NOVEMBER 1774

Revolution: Approach Encouraged by Benjamin Franklin, radical propagandist Thomas Paine emigrates to America and settles in Philadelphia.

14 DECEMBER 1774

Revolution: Approach Warned by rider Paul Revere of a British plan to station soldiers at Portsmouth, New Hampshire, a group of Massachusetts militiamen, led by Major John Sullivan, successfully attacks the arsenal of Fort William and Mary in Portsmouth and captures arms and ammunition. No lives are lost in this encounter, which, but for the lack of a declaration of war, could be called the first battle of the American revolution.

9 FEBRUARY 1775

British Policy Parliament declares the colony of Massachusetts to be in a state of rebellion.

26 FEBRUARY 1775

Revolution: Approach British soldiers land at Salem, Massachusetts, hoping to capture another colonial arsenal, but the British are repulsed with no casualties on either side.

23 MARCH 1775

Revolution: Approach At the second meeting of the Virginia convention in Richmond, Patrick Henry opposes the arbitrary rule of Great Britain with his famous speech that closes, 'Give me liberty or give me death.'

30 MARCH 1775

British Policy King George III endorses the New England Restraining Act, which forbids the New England colonies from trading with any nation other than England after 1 July and also bans them from fishing in the North Atlantic after 20 July. On 13 April the provisions of the Restraining Act will be applied to Maryland, New Jersey, Pennsylvania, South Carolina and Virginia when Parliament hears that these colonies have ratified the Continental Association.

MARCH 1775

Revolution: Approach General Gage warns Captain William De La Place, commander of Ticonderoga, New York, to guard against a possible surprise attack.

1 APRIL 1775

Settlement Daniel Boone founds Boonesborough in present-day Madison County, on the south side of the Kentucky River.

14 APRIL 1775

Revolution: Approach General Gage receives a letter from Lord Dartmouth instructing him to implement the Coercive and other acts and to strike preemptively to prevent further buildup of colonial military resources.

19 APRIL 1775

Revolution: Battles of Lexington and Concord The 'shot heard round the world' is discharged in Concord, Massachusetts, beginning the Revolutionary War in America. Gage has sent Lieutenant Colonel Francis Smith with 700 British soldiers to destroy a significant cache of colonial arms located in Concord. The Boston Committee of Safety sends Paul Revere and William Dawes to warn of the British move. Revere warns rebel leaders John Hancock and Samuel Adams in Lexington and then rides on toward Concord with Dawes and Dr. Samuel Prescott. The three riders encounter a British patrol, which captures Revere, who is later released. Prescott alone reaches Concord, and the colonial part-time soldiers, who are known as Minutemen, are roused to meet the oncoming British soldiers, who have marched under cover of night. In Lexington, an early morning skirmish occurs when some 70 armed minutemen refuse to lay down their arms. Eight Americans are killed and eight others are wounded in the fight. Colonel Smith pushes on to Concord, where his men destroy some colonial arms and supplies. A sharp fight at Concord Bridge demonstrates the colonial will to fight. On the return march to Boston, Smith's men are beset by an increasingly large number of Americans, who fire from behind trees, stone walls and bushes. When the British reach Boston they have lost 273 men. Colonial soldiers soon begin a siege of Boston that lasts for nearly a year. News of the fighting reaches Philadelphia on 24 April, Virginia on 30 April, North Carolina on 7 May and South Carolina on 8 May. There will still be some attempts to reconcile the colonies and England, but the Revolution has begun in earnest and the fate of England's North American empire is gravely at risk.

23 APRIL 1775

Revolution: Massachusetts The Massachusetts Provincial Congress orders the mobilization of 13,600 colonial soldiers, appoints Artemas Ward as commander and requests aid from the other colonies.

10 MAY 1775

Revolution: Capture of Fort Ticonderoga In an early morning attack some 80 Americans led by Colonel Ethan Allen and Colonel Benedict Arnold capture Fort Ticonderoga, New York, from some 40 British soldiers.

11 MAY 1775

Revolution: Naval After news of the fighting at Lexington and Concord reaches Machias, Maine, some 30 Americans on a local vessel exchange fire with, board and capture the British schooner *Margaretta*. This is the first naval engagement of the Revolution.

12 MAY 1775

Revolution: New York Following the capture of Fort Ticonderoga, Seth Warren leads Americans to seize the British fort at Crown Point on Lake Champlain.

16 MAY 1775

Revolution: Canada Benedict Arnold destroys the British fort of St. John's in southern Canada and then withdraws southward.

22 MAY 1775

Revolution: British Command British generals John Burgoyne, Sir Henry Clinton and Sir William Howe arrive in Boston to reinforce and assist General Gage.

12 JUNE 1775

Revolution: British Policy Gage offers pardon to all rebels who will take an oath of allegiance to the Crown.

15 JUNE 1775

Revolution: American Command George Washington, a Virginia planter and a veteran of the French and Indian War, is selected as supreme commander of the new Continental Army. He declines to accept payment for his services, but after eight years of warfare he will submit records of his expenses totalling £24,700.

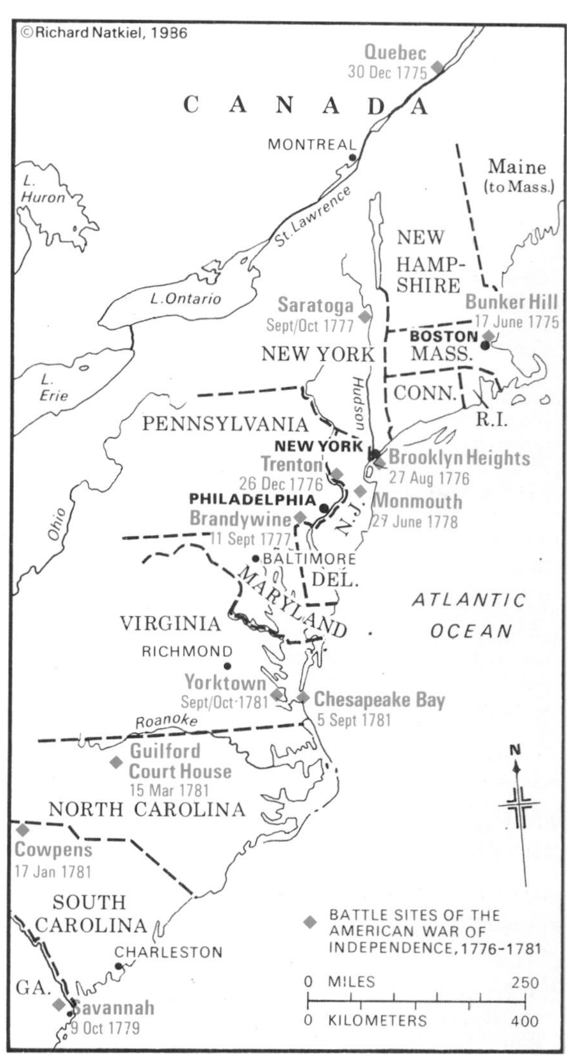

Above: A general map of the American Revolution.

Below: A contemporary painting showing the siege of Boston and the Battle of Bunker Hill.

17 JUNE 1775

Revolution: Battle of Bunker Hill This battle (actually fought on adjacent Breed's Hill) takes place in present-day Charlestown, Massachusetts, directly north of Boston. During the night of 16 June American forces have marched onto the peninsula on which Breed's Hill stands and have dug earthworks; when dawn comes, they are in position. Once cannons are emplaced the Americans can directly menace the city of Boston and all of its inhabitants. After a conference in Boston the British generals decide that the American earthworks must be taken before the enemy can set up their artillery. General William Howe will lead the assault. British soldiers are ferried out to the peninsula, where they group into battle formation at the foot of Breed's Hill. The American defenders are instructed not to fire until they can see the 'whites of their eyes.' The defense is fierce. Howe's experienced British soldiers are carrying equipment that weighs up to 40 pounds per man, and the weather is hot. As the British come nearly to the top of the hill their ranks are blasted with a tremendous American volley of gunfire, followed quickly by a second volley. Dozens of British soldiers are killed immediately, and Howe orders his men to fall back. A second march up the hill yields similar results, although by now the Americans are running out of gunpowder. Howe's third try captures Breed's Hill and sends the Americans running, but at a heavy price: over 1000 British casualties. Howe is deeply sobered by the experience, and in the future he will tend to err on the side of overcaution.

17 JUNE 1775

Revolution: American Command Congress appoints four major generals for the Continental Army – Charles Lee, Israel Putnam, Philip Schuyler and Artemas Ward.

3 JULY 1775

Revolution: American Command George Washington assumes command of the American troops at Cambridge, Massachusetts.

AUGUST 1775

Revolution: Canada Colonel Benedict Arnold leads 1100 patriots, taken from the army at Cambridge, to begin a journey to an ultimate goal of British-held Quebec City in Canada. Utter secrecy is imposed for this mission.

18 SEPTEMBER 1775

Revolution: Canada American General Richard Montgomery, an Irish-born soldier who served in the British army during the French and Indian War, invests British Fort St. John's on the Richelieu River in Canada.

25 SEPTEMBER 1775

Revolution: Canada Colonel Ethan Allen, head of the Green Mountain Boys, is captured while attacking Montreal. He is taken to England and held prisoner until the end of the war.

10 OCTOBER 1775

Revolution: British Command General William Howe replaces Thomas Gage as commander of the British forces in North America. Gage, through having been longer in the colonies, has developed a healthy respect for the American fighting ability.

13 OCTOBER 1775

Revolution: Naval Congress authorizes the commission of a 'swift sailing vessel to carry 10 carriage guns and an appropriate no. of swivels,' thus creating the first American naval ship. Throughout the Revolution, American privateers will harass the British at sea.

18 OCTOBER 1775

Revolution: Naval A British fleet under Captain West attacks Falmouth, Maine, burning 139 houses, 278 stores.

7 NOVEMBER 1775

Revolution: The South Virginia Governor Dunmore institutes official martial law in the colonies and begins to organize a Loyalist army. Dunmore will lose the support of the Virginian planters when he promises freedom to all blacks who leave their masters and join a regiment.

10 NOVEMBER 1775

Revolution: Canada Benedict Arnold and some 5-600 men (he had left Cambridge with 1100) reach Point Levis on the eastern bank of the St. Lawrence River, opposite Quebec City. By 14 November he brings his force to the Plains of Abraham, where Wolfe and Montcalm fought in 1759. Arnold's men have endured an extremely dangerous and strenuous journey in a little over two months, from Cambridge to Maine, up the Kennebec River and then the Chaudiere River.

10 NOVEMBER 1775

Revolution: Military The Marine Corps is organized by authority of the First Continental Congress as a component of the navy. The Marine Corps will be separately organized on 11 July 1789.

13 NOVEMBER 1775

Revolution: Canada The city of Montreal opens its gates to General Montgomery and his American force. The inhabitants had previously made clear to British General Guy Carleton that they would not fight the Americans.

29 NOVEMBER 1775

Revolution: Naval The American cruiser *Lee* captures the British brig *Nancy*, which is laden with guns and ammunition destined for Quebec City. *Nancy* is later renamed *Congress* and will be instrumental in forcing the evacuation of Boston in March 1776.

2 DECEMBER 1775

Revolution: Canada Benedict Arnold and Richard Montgomery join forces at a point 20 miles above Quebec City. Montgomery assumes overall command, and on 5 December he invests Quebec.

11 DECEMBER 1775

Revolution: The South Virginia Governor Dunmore, commanding British and Loyalist troops, is defeated at Great Bridge, near Norfolk, Virginia, by a force of 900 Virginians and North Carolinians.

31 DECEMBER 1775

Revolution: Canada Slightly under 1000 American soldiers, commanded by Montgomery and Arnold, make a desperate assault on Quebec City, one of the strongest fortified cities in the world. Sir Guy Carleton commands the defense, leading some 1500 regular British troops. Montgomery is killed in the first stage of the assault, and his troops are repulsed. Arnold is seriously wounded, about 100 Americans

Above: George Washington when he was 40 (1772). This engraving is based on the Charles Peal portrait.

Below: Lord William Howe, British C-in-C in North America in 1776, had been with Wolfe at Quebec.

are killed and wounded and 300 others are made prisoners.

1 JANUARY 1776

Revolution: The South Virginia Governor Lord Dunmore orders the shelling of the garrison at Norfolk, Virginia, and sends a party ashore to set fire to the town. Its destruction is completed by the Americans to prevent if from becoming a shelter for the British.

24 JANUARY 1776

Revolution: Siege of Boston American Colonel Henry Knox arrives in Cambridge with 43 cannons and 16 mortars that were originally captured by Ethan Allen and Benedict Arnold in May 1775 at Fort Ticonderoga. Knox has successfully undertaken the enormously difficult task of transporting the heavy siege guns across upstate New York and Massachusetts in the dead of winter, using sleds. The guns will be vital in forcing the British out of Boston.

27 FEBRUARY 1776

Revolution: The South A force of North Carolina patriots resoundingly defeats a detachment of Scottish-descent Loyalists at Moore's Creek Bridge, near Wilmington, North Carolina. The Americans take some 900 prisoners and eliminate the possibility of a major Loyalist uprising in the South.

1 MARCH 1776

Revolution: Diplomacy French Foreign Minister Vergennes suggests to Spain that Spain join with France in secret measures of aid to the American colonies.

4-5 MARCH 1776

Revolution: Siege of Boston Led by General John Thomas, American forces occupy Dorchester Heights, overlooking Boston and the harbor from the south. Now the patriots can place the artillery brought by Colonel Knox from Ticonderoga to menace the British presence in Boston.

7-17 MARCH 1776

Revolution: Evacuation of Boston Led by General William Howe, the British evacuate Boston. Much has to be sacrificed. The British cram troops, loyal inhabitants (who have no wish to be left behind), stores and horses into a fleet of 78 troopships. The British leave for Halifax, Nova Scotia. Washington's move to Dorchester Heights has forced the evacuation of Boston. Although there will be future hostilities in the New England land area, the center of British-American combat now shifts south to the New York City area and the middle colonies of New Jersey, Pennsylvania and Maryland.

19 MARCH 1776

Revolution: Naval The Continental Congress authorizes privateering raids on British shipping.

13 APRIL 1776

Revolution: American Strategy Following the evacuation of Boston by the British forces Washington leads the main part of the Continental Army south to New York City, correctly anticipating that British General William Howe will strike there next.

1 MAY-5 JULY 1776

Revolution: Canada After a fruitless three-month siege of Quebec City, American Brigadier General Benedict Arnold leads his forces southward to prepare for the defense of the Lake Champlain region. During this period Sir Guy Carleton, British commander in Canada, prepares to invade New England by way of the same route that Richard Montgomery used in 1775 to reach Quebec City – the Richelieu River, Lake Champlain and the Hudson River.

3 MAY 1776

Revolution: British Southern Campaign British reinforcements commanded by General Charles Cornwallis join General Henry Clinton's forces aboard a British fleet positioned off the Carolinas.

6 MAY 1776

Revolution: Canada A British fleet reaches Quebec City, carrying ten companies of regulars and marines, the advance guard of larger forces soon to follow. American General John Thomas retreats to Montreal, followed by British Generals Carleton and Burgoyne with several thousand British soldiers.

9-16 MAY 1776

Revolution: Naval Commodore of the American Navy, Esek Hopkins, successfully leads an attack on the British naval station in the Bahamas. The Americans occupy Nassau and capture a large military arsenal.

4 JUNE 1776

Revolution: British Southern Campaign American General Charles Lee arrives in Charleston, South Carolina, having travelled from New York to command the American defense in the south.

7 JUNE 1776

Revolution: Political Virginia delegate to the Continental Congress Richard Henry Lee presents a formal resolution calling for independence from Great Britain. A final decision on this resolution is postponed until 1 July.

Revolution: Canada During the American retreat from British-held Canada, General John Sullivan attempts an unsuccessful attack against the British at Three Rivers. Sullivan subsequently retreats to Fort Ticonderoga.

27 JUNE 1776

Revolution: Conspiracy American traitor Thomas Hickey is hanged in New York for conspiring to deliver George Washington to the British.

28 JUNE 1776

Revolution: Defense of Fort Moultrie American forces under General Charles Lee successfully defend Fort Moultrie, a fort made of palmetto logs located on Sullivan's Island in the outer harbor of Charleston, South Carolina. British ships commanded by Sir Peter Parker cannonade the fort for several hours. The British cannon balls sink into the spongy palmetto logs; after the fight some 7000 cannon balls are recovered in and around the fort. All of the British ships are damaged by American gunfire. Aboard the flagship, alone, there are 64 dead and 161 wounded. By comparison, Colonel William Moultrie loses a dozen killed and perhaps 25 wounded. The result of the British loss is that the American southern front will not be reopened until 1778.

JUNE 1776

Revolution: British New York Campaign A large British war fleet, commanded by Admiral Lord Richard Howe, transports a 30,000-man British and Hessian army, led by General William Howe (brother to the Admiral), into New York harbor, thus initiating a new area of conflict.

2 JULY 1776

Revolution: British New York Campaign At New York, British General Howe lands some 10,000 soldiers on Staten Island, unopposed. Through July and early August British reinforcements keep arriving on Staten Island until Howe finally commands some 32,000 troops, of whom 9000 are Hessian mercenaries who have been sold into the service of King George III by their ruler, the Lord of Hesse-Canal in Germany.

4 JULY 1776

Revolution: Declaration of Independence Congress formally endorses the Declaration of Independence (the voting took place on 2 July, even as Howe landed his men on Staten Island). Copies of the document are sent to all of the colonies. Previously, the Revolution has been an armed insurrection; it now continues that aspect but also surpasses it by legitimizing armed rebellion at times, 'When in the course of human events. . .' The final copy will not actually be signed until 2 August 1776.

20-21 JULY 1776

Indian Warfare In North Carolina a force of Cherokee Indians attacks the western settlement of Eaton's Station. In retaliation, the North Carolina militia destroys a neighboring Cherokee village.

12 AUGUST 1776

Revolution: American Policy In an attempt to entice desertions from the British army, the Continental Congress enacts legislation granting free land as bounty to British deserters.

American hero/traitor Benedict Arnold.

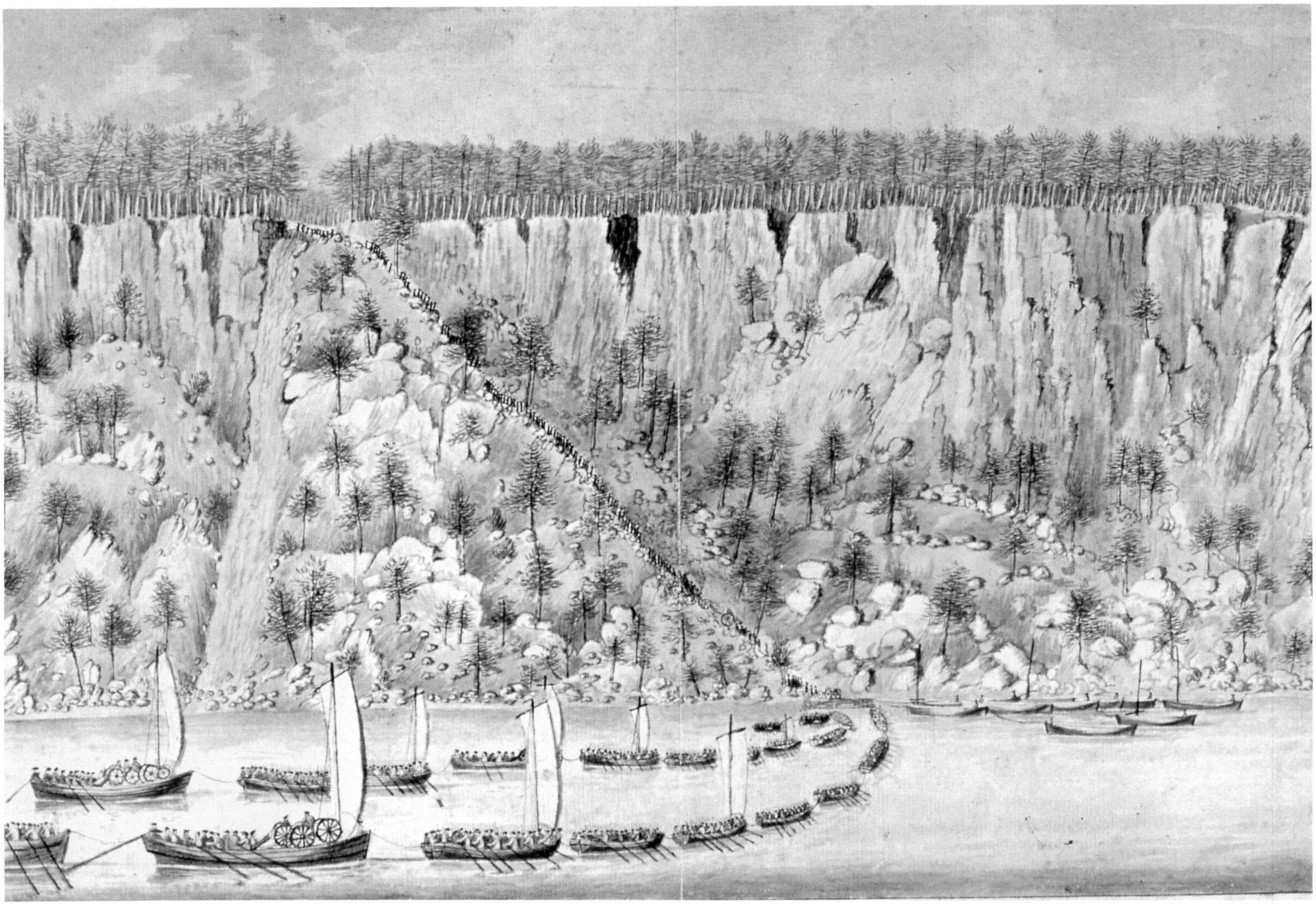

27 AUGUST 1776

Revolution: Battle of Long Island General Howe sends his British and German soldiers forward in the Battle of Long Island. Using Loyalist-provided information, Howe personally leads 10,000 men through virtually undefended Jamaica Pass and hits the unprepared American left wing. Howe's forces inflict some 2000 casualties and capture 1000 Americans. British casualties number only about 300. Howe's classic, perfectly executed battle places Washington in an untenable position. The American leader has perhaps 9000 men faced by an overwhelmingly larger British force, and the Americans have their back to the East River, blocking possible retreat. Howe does not immediately attack the disoriented American force, perhaps because he remembers how well Americans fought from defensive positions at Breed's Hill in June 1775. The British general's decision to wait, while understandable, will cost Britain the best chance it ever has for destroying the heart of the Continental Army.

29-30 AUGUST 1776

Revolution: Evacuation of Brooklyn Heights Under cover of darkness Washington employs a regiment of fishermen from Marblehead, Massachusetts, to evacuate some 9000 American soldiers from Brooklyn Heights across the East River to Manhattan. While he has suffered a costly defeat on Long Island, Washington's skillful retreat saves his army to fight on.

11 SEPTEMBER 1776

Revolution: Diplomacy Colonial representatives John Adams, Benjamin Franklin and Edward Rutledge meet with Admiral Lord Richard Howe in a peace conference on Staten Island. Howe suggests that American grievances will be removed by the British government if the patriots will only lay down their arms. The representatives tell Howe that they will settle for nothing less than independence, and the conference adjourns.

12 SEPTEMBER 1776

Revolution: Evacuation of Manhattan Rather than be trapped in lower Manhattan by the British, who command the surrounding waterways through Richard Howe's fleet, Washington decides to evacuate New York City.

26 SEPTEMBER 1776

Revolution: Diplomacy The Continental Congress appoints Silas Deane, Benjamin Franklin and Thomas Jefferson as diplomatic commissioners, empowered to negotiate treaties (of alliance, it is hoped) with European nations. Deane and Franklin travel to France, and Congress authorizes them to procure financial and military aid for the American cause. In December Jefferson will be replaced by Arthur Lee.

11 OCTOBER 1776

Revolution: Naval General Benedict Arnold's small flotilla of fighting vessels is utterly destroyed in Valcour Bay, Lake Champlain, by British General Carleton's 87-gun fleet. Nevertheless, Arnold's improvised fleet has served an important purpose. Carleton had to spend the late summer and early fall of 1776 building his own superior fleet, and British forces were unable to advance down Lake Champlain until the American ships were eliminated. Now the approaching winter prevents Carleton from making the ambitious movement southward that he originally intended. A British invasion from Canada will have to wait for another eight months.

23 OCTOBER 1776

Revolution: Evacuation of Manhattan At New York City, withdrawing before the advancing forces of General Howe, Washington evacuates his main force from Manhattan Island. While leaving a sizeable garrison at Fort Washington, he marches to White Plains.

28 OCTOBER 1776

Revolution: Battle of White Plains At White Plains, New York, Washington's army fights the British and Hessian forces commanded by Howe and Hessian General Von Knyphausen to a standstill. Each side will claim a victory, although Washington will maintain his position until 30 October.

16 NOVEMBER 1776

Revolution: Capture of Fort Washington Some 13,000 British and Hessians, led by Generals Matthews, Cornwallis, Percy and Von Knyphausen surround and attack Fort Washington at the upper end of Manhattan Island. After some severe fighting American Colonel Magaw surrenders the fort. The British capture 2818 Americans, while losing 458 men in the assault on the fort.

Left top: Lord Howe orders his troops to evacuate Boston, March 1776.

Left: By scaling the New Jersey palisades British troops outflanked Fort Lee in November 1776. This painting is by a British eyewitness, Thomas Davies.

19 NOVEMBER 1776

Revolution: Retreat to New Jersey British General Charles Cornwallis leads 12 British regiments across the Hudson River by way of Yonkers. Cornwallis marches rapidly southward along the west bank of the river. The troops that are available to Washington in New Jersey, disspirited and dwindling in numbers, cannot stand against the British move. Retreating in confusion to Newark, New Jersey, they abandon Fort Lee on the Hudson, across from Fort Washington, without a struggle. The British and Hessians under the leadership of Howe, Cornwallis, Knyphausen and others have now defeated the patriots on Long Island, taken possession of New York City, captured Forts Washington and Lee, and chased Washington into New Jersey. At this point, when the American cause is desperate, Howe fails to pursue the war to what might well be its close. He orders Cornwallis to drive Washington beyond Brunswick (present-day New Brunswick), so that a part of the British army may gain winter quarters in eastern New Jersey. He also sends General Henry Clinton with 6000 men to seize and hold Newport, Rhode Island, as a base for possible campaigns against New England.

21 NOVEMBER 1776

Revolution: Retreat to New Jersey After deciding to abandon the New York area, Washington moves his forces westward to Newark, New Jersey.

29 NOVEMBER 1776

Revolution: New Jersey Advanced British detachments under General Cornwallis move against Newark, New Jersey, and Washington flees to Brunswick with the enemy in close pursuit.

6 DECEMBER 1776

Revolution: Rhode Island General Clinton's force successfully takes and occupies the naval base at Newport, Rhode Island.

11 DECEMBER 1776

Revolution: Retreat Across the Delaware Washington leads some 3000 men – virtually all that remains of an army that numbered around 20,000 before the battle of Long Island in August – across the Delaware River, near Trenton, New Jersey, into Pennsylvania. By gathering all the boats for many miles on both sides of Trenton, Washington makes further advance by Cornwallis difficult. Arriving at the Delaware River, Cornwallis decides to go into winter quarters. With Howe's approval, he sets up posts on the east bank, principally at Bordentown and Trenton.

12 DECEMBER 1776

Revolution: Political Fearing a British attack on Philadelphia, the Continental Congress flees to Baltimore, where it will meet for the next three months. This is the low point of American morale that Thomas Paine epitomizes in *The Crisis* on 19 December 1776. Paine's words are read to the patriot troops. 'These are the times that try men's souls. The summer soldier and the sunshine patriot will, in this crisis, shrink from the service of their country; but he that stands it *now*, deserves the love and thanks of man and woman.'

13 DECEMBER 1776

Revolution: Continental Army American General Charles Lee is captured by a British patrol at Basking Ridge, New Jersey. General John Sullivan assumes control of Lee's men and manages to join Washington's forces in Pennsylvania. By 20 December Washington has over 6000 men available for duty, enough to take the initiative. Indeed, he must do so, for on 31 December 1776 the enlistment period will expire for many of his soldiers.

25-26 DECEMBER 1776

Revolution: Battle of Trenton Washington leads 2400 men back across the Delaware River to make an effective surprise attack on the British-Hessian garrison at Trenton, New Jersey, commanded by Hessian Colonel Johann Rall. Attacking at daybreak and using field artillery to clear the streets, Washington achieves a complete victory in less than one hour. Some 20 Hessians are killed and 909 are made prisoners, while the American loss is two killed, two frozen to death and five wounded. The victory will become a major morale booster.

31 DECEMBER 1776

Frontier Virginia is petitioned by George Rogers Clark to annex the Kentucky settlements, now in danger of Indian attack. This move will also circumvent the plans of Daniel Boone to organize Kentucky as a separate state.

OTHER EVENTS OF 1776

Spanish Policy In Arizona the Spanish establish their second presidio, or fort, at Tucson, an Indian settlement.

2 JANUARY 1777

Revolution: New Jersey British General Cornwallis enters Trenton with 6000 British regulars that he has assembled since learning of Rall's defeat at the Battle of Trenton. As Cornwallis advances Washington withdraws and soon has his back to the Delaware River. Once again, as at Long Island, the Americans are left with no feasible retreat avenue. Again Washington and his generals improvise. Leaving their campfires burning, the Americans quietly file off in the darkness to the south and east, then march around the British by a side road and arrive at Princeton in the morning.

3 JANUARY 1777

Revolution: Battle of Princeton George Washington achieves a second important victory by inflicting heavy losses on the British rear guard at Princeton, New Jersey, and driving the British army toward Brunswick.

6 JANUARY 1777

Revolution: New Jersey Washington establishes winter quarters for his exhausted soldiery in the hills surrounding Morristown, New Jersey.

12 MARCH 1777

Revolution: Political Since Washington has effectively cleared all but the most eastern part of New Jersey of British forces, the Continental Congress returns to Philadelphia from Baltimore.

26 APRIL 1777

Revolution: Connecticut British forces destroy an American storage depot in Danbury, Connecticut.

27 APRIL 1777

Revolution: Battle of Ridgefield A fierce battle is fought in Ridgefield, Connecticut, between 800 Americans under Generals Wooster, Arnold and Silliman and 2000 British led by General Tryon. The Americans are defeated, with a loss of 100 men killed, wounded or missing. The British lose 170 men killed, wounded or missing.

6 MAY 1777

Revolution: British Command British General 'Gentleman Johnny' Burgoyne, a playwright of some talent as well as military man, arrives at Quebec City. Burgoyne presents to General Guy Carleton a letter from British Lord Germain that specifically appoints Burgoyne leader of the British northern front.

14 JUNE 1777

Revolution: Naval Congress designates veteran seaman John Paul Jones, a Scotsman who had once served in the British merchant marine, captain of the 18-gun sloop *Ranger*. Jones is to raid the coastal towns of England, in defiance of the powerful British navy.

British General 'Gentleman Johnny' Burgoyne led the 1777 offensive from Canada that, had it succeeded, would have cut off and surrounded New England.

A scene from the Battle of Bennington, August 1777, the first serious defeat suffered by Burgoyne in his advance on Albany.

15 JUNE 1777

Revolution: Invasion of New England General John Burgoyne leaves Fort St. John's on the Richelieu River in Canada with 6700 rank-and-file infantry, both British and Hessian, 600 artillerymen, 250 dismounted Hessian dragoons (who will have a difficult time in the terrain ahead due to their heavy equipment), about 650 Canadians and Loyalists and 400 Indians. This formidable army is poised to move directly south, via Lake Champlain and Lake George and the Hudson River, to reach Albany, New York, where Burgoyne intends to rendezvous with General Howe's army and that of Colonel Barry St. Leger, who is to reach Albany via Lake Ontario and the Mohawk River Valley. If all goes as planned the thirteen rebellious colonies will be split in two by these three British armies. It is anticipated that once this is accomplished a conquest of the New England area will be a mop-up operation. The strategy was proposed by Burgoyne during the winter of 1776-1777 and approved by the British War Office, headed by Lord Germain. Unfortunately, Germain has failed adequately to impress upon Howe that his presence will be essential on the Hudson River and eventually at Albany.

23 JUNE 1777

Revolution: Invasion of New England As the second prong of the three-fold British move on Albany, Colonel Barry St. Leger departs from Montreal and heads to Fort Oswego on the eastern shore of Lake Ontario.

27 JUNE 1777

Revolution: Invasion of New England Burgoyne's army leaves Crown Point, just above Fort Ticonderoga.

30 JUNE 1777

Revolution: New Jersey The British forces of General Howe leave eastern New Jersey for New York City. Washington, whose forces are tracking the British movements, is still uncertain as to whether Howe will try to move up the Hudson or will sail to capture Philadelphia.

1 JULY 1777

Revolution: Siege of Fort Ticonderoga General Burgoyne's army begins operations against Fort Ticonderoga. The fortress is defended by American General Arthur St. Clair, who commands 2300 Continentals and 900 militiamen. The Americans fail to post a defense on Mount Defiance, which overlooks the promontory that Ticonderoga is located on. Burgoyne's artillerymen commence the difficult task of bringing cannons to the peak, putting themselves in a position to bombard the fort, much as Washington had done to the British forces at Boston in March 1776.

5-6 JULY 1777

Revolution: Fall of Fort Ticonderoga Finding that Burgoyne's enterprising artillerymen, led by Major General William Phillips, have placed guns on Mount Defiance, American commander Arthur St. Clair evacuates Fort Ticonderoga, crossing to the eastern side of Lake Champlain while sending some artillery and supplies by water to Skenesboro (present-day Whitehall). At daybreak the British begin a vigorous pursuit. On 7 July the pursuers fight a fierce battle with St. Clair's rear guard at Hubbardton, Vermont. The British and Hessians, led by General Simon Fraser and the Baron von Riedesel, encounter some of the best Continental infantry, and though the British win the field, the pursuit is halted. The rest of St. Clair's men escape and rejoin the American army at Ford Edward, New York. The fall of Ticonderoga is a large psychological loss to the Americans, and King George is reported to have exulted that, 'I have beaten them! I have beaten the Americans,' on hearing the news. Actually, by missing the opportunity to capture or thoroughly defeat St. Clair's force, Burgoyne has left a nucleus around which further American resistance can gather.

20 JULY 1777

Indian Warfare By the Treaty of Long Island the Overhill Cherokee Indians cede all of their land in western North Carolina east of the Blue Ridge Mountains and the Nolichucky River.

23 JULY 1777

Revolution: Philadelphia Campaign General William Howe initiates his campaign to capture the American capital city of Philadelphia by setting sail for Chesapeake Bay from New York with 15,000 men. Howe leaves General Henry Clinton in command at New York. While Burgoyne has envisaged three British armies (of which Howe's is by far the largest) converging on Albany, Howe's ambitious campaign now removes the southern front from the picture. With their southern front unengaged, American forces will soon outnumber Burgoyne's army.

25 JULY 1777

Revolution: Philadelphia Campaign Americans sight Howe's fleet off the Capes of Delaware. Washington moves nearer Philadelphia, and, at this point, the British fleet sails out to sea again. Washington has to guess Howe's next move and try to match the British speed at sea.

26 JULY 1777

Revolution: Invasion of New England Colonel Barry St. Leger, a veteran British soldier, leaves Fort Oswego on Lake Ontario with 900 regular British soldiers, Tories and Canadian scouts and 1000 allied Indians. St. Leger is now intent on reaching Albany.

27 JULY 1777

Revolution: Invasion of New England Settler Jane McCrea, engaged to marry an officer in Burgoyne's army, is murdered by Burgoyne's Indian allies. The news of this and of other atrocities prompts reluctant Americans to enlist for military service in increasing numbers.

28 JULY 1777

Revolution: Foreign Assistance A French nobleman, 20-year-old Marie Joseph Gilbert du Motier, Marquis de Lafayette, arrives in Philadelphia to volunteer his services to the American cause. Congress will commission the inexperienced Marquis as a major general in the Continental Army. Lafayette is but the most celebrated of a number of Europeans who will enlist to fight with the American forces. Count Pulaski, Baron de Kalb and Baron Von Steuben are among the others.

Burgoyne's camp on the west bank of the Hudson on 20 September 1777, the day after his Pyrrhic victory at the Battle of Freeman's Farm.

29 JULY 1777

Revolution: Invasion of New England Hearing of the impending arrival of British General Burgoyne, Philip Schuyler, commander of the northern American forces, abandons Fort Edwards and withdraws down the Hudson River. As Schuyler's men retreat, they fell trees across the wilderness roads to impede the progress of Burgoyne's army.

30 JULY 1777

Revolution: Invasion of New England Burgoyne has made a significant tactical error in sending his army through the woods at the foot of Lake Champlain. The retreating Americans roll stones into creeks to slow the British movement. Their effort is successful; in 20 days Burgoyne's forces advance only 20 miles, reaching Fort Edward on 29 July.

4 AUGUST 1777

Revolution: American Command General Horatio Gates replaces General Philip Schuyler as the commander of the Continental Army of the North. Schuyler will be accused of negligence and later exonerated by a court martial. Actually, Schuyler's delaying tactics have provided his successor with enough time to gather American military forces to resist Burgoyne.

3-6 AUGUST 1777

Revolution: Relief of Fort Stanwix British and Indian forces led by Colonel Barry St. Leger besiege Fort Stanwix, located at present-day Rome, New York, in the Mohawk River Valley, commanded by Colonel Peter Gansevoort.

6 AUGUST 1777

Revolution: Invasion of New England At Oriskany, New York, a body of American militia marching to the rescue of Fort Stanwix, is ambushed by a party of British and Indians. The militia are defeated and 400 of their number, including their leader, General Herkimer, are killed.

16 AUGUST 1777

Revolution: Battle of Bennington Burgoyne has sent two large sections of Hessian soldiers toward Bennington, Vermont, to obtain supplies and horses. The Hessians are met by some 1600 Massachusetts and New Hampshire militiamen under General Stark. In the first engagement the Americans defeat 600 Hessians under Colonel Baum, and in the second they put to rout 500 Germans under Colonel Breyman. The losses are 280 Germans killed or wounded and 654 made prisoners; 100 Americans killed or wounded. These losses are men that Burgoyne, far from his base of supply in Canada, cannot replace.

22 AUGUST 1777

Revolution: Relief of Fort Stanwix British Colonel Barry St. Leger ends his siege of Fort Stanwix when American reinforcements led by Benedict Arnold approach the area. St. Leger withdraws his force, leaving Burgoyne devoid of a western flank attack on Albany.

25 AUGUST 1777

Revolution: Philadelphia Campaign In his campaign to capture Philadelphia, General Howe disembarks 15,000 men at the head of Chesapeake Bay. It is one of the great 'ifs' of the Revolution: if Howe instead had marched up the Hudson all might have been well with Burgoyne's campaign.

8 SEPTEMBER 1777

Revolution: Invasion of New England General Horatio Gates, who now leads at least 7000 troops, takes up position at Bemis Heights, New York.

9-11 SEPTEMBER 1777

Revolution: Battle of Brandywine In Howe's Philadelphia campaign a battle occurs at Chadd's Ford, Pennsylvania, where Washington's army has blocked the path of the British to Philadelphia. Howe sends General Cornwallis around the Americans to turn their right flank. When it becomes clear to Washington that Howe has again outmaneuvered him, the Americans retreat. The Americans suffer 1000 men killed, wounded or missing; the British lose 93 killed and 509 men wounded.

13-14 SEPTEMBER 1777

Revolution: Invasion of New England General Burgoyne, now aware that Howe is not coming up the Hudson to support him, moves his army, which now consists of 5500 regulars and 800 Tories and Indians, across the Hudson River to its west bank. By making this crossing Burgoyne commits his army to victory or to defeat.

19 SEPTEMBER 1777

Revolution: Battle of Freeman's Farm Near Saratoga, New York, Burgoyne meets the American forces under General Gates. American Colonel Daniel Morgan leads his group of Virginia riflemen to demoralize one British column. General Benedict Arnold attacks the British center column, commanded by Burgoyne and George Hamilton. The fight lasts four hours and breaks off at dark. The Americans retire regularly from the field without being pursued. The British retain the battlefield, but at the cost of 600 men killed or wounded, while the American loss totals 321 men. The British 62nd Regiment, which had left Canada with 500 men, comes out of the battle with less than 60 men still able to fight.

20 SEPTEMBER 1777

Revolution: Paoli Massacre A detachment of 1500 American soldiers under General Anthony Wayne are surprised at midnight by a British division under Lord Grey. Three hundred Americans are killed while crying for quarter. This becomes known as the massacre at Paoli, Pennsylvania.

24 SEPTEMBER 1777

Revolution: Invasion of New England American forces conduct a raid on Fort Ticonderoga, thereby menacing Burgoyne's already tenuous ties with Canada.

25-26 SEPTEMBER 1777

Revolution: Philadelphia Campaign General Howe's army begins to enter Philadelphia, the capital city of the rebellious colonies. Howe might think that the Americans will soon cease to resist, but the American will to fight is not dependent on holding its major cities.

30 SEPTEMBER 1777

Revolution: Political The Continental Congress moves from Lancaster to York, Pennsylvania.

4-5 OCTOBER 1777

Revolution: Battle of Germantown Washington counterattacks in the Battle of Germantown, Pennsylvania. Having suffered losses at Brandywine and Paoli, the American leader is determined to gain a victory in order to bolster the sagging patriot morale. The Continentals surprise the British advance guard at dawn and drive it back. At this point, the Americans come to the Chew house, made of stone. Rather than leave a fortress in their rear, the Americans try to capture the house. Meanwhile, the main body of the British and Hessians has been warned and has hastily formed. The Continentals drive them back at one point and threaten to break through the British lines, but some patriots mistakenly fire on their fellows in a heavy fog, and the continuing conflict at the Chew house leads some of the patriots to believe they may be surrounded. The British take advantage of the confusion and win possession of the field. The Americans suffer some 700 casualties, the British 534. Although technically a loss for Washington, the battle restores a measure of American morale.

A nineteenth-century lithograph purporting to show the fighting around the Chew house at the Battle of Germantown, 4-5 October 1777, Washington's final attempt to drive Howe from Philadelphia. But here the uniforms are anachronistic and there is no fog.

6 OCTOBER 1777

Revolution: Invasion of New England British forces commanded by Sir Henry Clinton and Colonel Campbell simultaneously capture American Forts Clinton and Montgomery on the Hudson River. Two hundred and fifty Americans are killed or wounded, and the British suffer 200 casualties. This British move is meant to pressure the forces that are surrounding Burgoyne, but the action is essentially both too little and too late.

7 OCTOBER 1777

Revolution: Second Battle of Bemis Heights Another important battle is fought between Burgoyne and Gates. Burgoyne sends out a 1500-man force to explore the American positions. The American response is swift; the column is driven back with heavy losses. Benedict Arnold again leads a strike against the center of the British army, and this time he succeeds in gaining complete mastery of the field (although Arnold himself is severely wounded). The British army sustains another 600 casualties and, having been beaten twice consecutively by the Americans, begins to lose heart.

12 OCTOBER 1777

Revolution: Invasion of New England Even though he has learned that General Clinton is moving up the Hudson, Burgoyne decides to flee northward. It is too late: his army is completely surrounded by Gates's forces, which now are much larger than Burgoyne's depleted British and Hessians.

17 OCTOBER 1777

Revolution: Victory at Saratoga General Burgoyne's combined British-Hessian army surrenders at Saratoga, New York. A total of over 5700 men lay down their arms. The shock will be felt in London, Paris and Madrid. The so-called Saratoga Convention provides for the British and Hessians to be permitted to sail to England with the stipulation that none of them will serve in America again during the war. Unfortunately, both the British and the Americans will renege on the agreement. Burgoyne's men are marched to Boston and eventually sent off to Virginia, where they are treated as prisoners of war. Burgoyne himself is allowed to return to England.

2 NOVEMBER 1777

Revolution: Naval Captain John Paul Jones sets sail across the Atlantic on the sloop *Ranger*. He plans to harry English port towns and shipping traffic.

16-20 NOVEMBER 1777

Revolution: Delaware River British forces capture Fort Mifflin and Fort Mercer, thus establishing their power over the Delaware River region.

John Turnbull's painting of Burgoyne's surrender at Saratoga, 17 October 1777. This first great colonial victory prompted France to enter the war.

17 DECEMBER 1777

Revolution: Valley Forge Led by George Washington, the Continental Army enters winter quarters at Valley Forge, Pennsylvania. The winter of 1777-1778 is a harsh one, and the Americans are low on all types of supplies. It is largely through the perseverance and will of Washington, Lafayette and other American leaders that the Continental Army stays intact through the winter.

17 DECEMBER 1777

Revolution: Diplomacy France officially recognizes the independence of the American colonies. The move is prompted by the American victory at Saratoga, and also by the indecisive but still impressive performance of the Continental soldiers at the Battle of Germantown, Pennsylvania.

23 DECEMBER 1777

Revolution: Conway Cabal A purported plot of army officers and a few members of the Continental Congress to replace George Washington with General Horatio Gates is revealed. Public opinion supports Washington, and Major Thomas Conway is forced to resign.

DECEMBER 1777

Revolution: Technology David Bushnell, inventor of a one-man submarine in 1775, lays a minefield of gunpowder kegs to harass British naval operations.

OTHER EVENTS OF 1777

Revolution: Naval It is estimated that over 400 British transports and merchant vessels have been captured by American ships during 1777. While unable directly to challenge the British Navy, the American seamen are waging a 'guerrilla' at sea.

6 FEBRUARY 1778

Revolution: Diplomacy In Paris, French and American agents negotiate and sign two treaties, one of alliance and one of amity and commerce. According to the terms of these treaties the Americans are given leave to conquer Canada (which had belonged to France until 1763) and Bermuda, while France is permitted to conquer the British colonial possessions in the West Indies. Congress ratifies the pacts on 4 May, and in July French Ambassador Alexander Gerard arrives in America to present his credentials. The French are surely more interested in doing damage to Britain than in helping the Americans, but the effect is an alliance that makes Britain now fight a two-front war.

17 FEBRUARY 1778

Revolution: Diplomacy Responding to the Franco-American treaties, British Prime Minister Lord North presents a plan for conciliation with the colonies to the British Parliament.

23 FEBRUARY 1778

Revolution: Valley Forge Prussian Friedrich Wilhelm, Baron von Steuben, arrives at Valley Forge, Pennsylvania, to offer his services to the Continental Army. Von Steuben will be of considerable assistance in training and drilling Washington's soldiers.

16 MARCH 1778

Revolution: Diplomacy The British Parliament creates a Peace Commission which is to be granted wide powers to enter into negotiations with the American revolutionaries.

18 MARCH 1778

Revolution: New Jersey At Quintin's Bridge, some five miles southeast of Salem, New Jersey, Colonel Mawhood's British regulars and Tory allies decoy and massacre a small force of American militia poised to defend against British parties sent from Philadelphia.

14 APRIL-8 MAY 1778

Revolution: Naval American privateer *Ranger*, commanded by Captain John Paul Jones, enters the Irish Sea, takes two prizes and captures a British sloop of war, which is taken to Brest, France. Similar raids by American privateer ships have taken 733 British prizes by 1778.

23 APRIL 1778

Revolution: Naval After capturing two British vessels Captain John Paul Jones completes a raid on the fort at Whitehaven, England, and burns a ship in the harbor there. This is largely a symbolic gesture to show American defiance of the overwhelmingly more powerful British Royal Navy.

24 APRIL 1778

Revolution: Naval In a naval battle off the coast of northern Ireland, Captain John Paul Jones accepts the surrender of the British sloop *Drake*, which he then takes with him to Brest, France.

8 MAY 1778

Revolution: Leadership General Henry Clinton is named to replace General William Howe as commander-in-chief of all the British forces in the American colonies. Clinton, aware of the recent French alliance with the Americans, rightly fears that French sea power may trap him in Philadelphia. Rather than try to defend both Philadelphia and New York City against a possible French attack, Clinton formulates a plan to withdraw British forces from Philadelphia and to march them overland to New York. Sir William Howe's historical legacy will be that of a fine tactical leader who won numerous battles (Bunker Hill, Long Island, Fort Washington, Brandywine) but who lacked the necessary determination to pin Washington down, kill or capture the hard core of the Continental Army and win the war. Yet, Howe's successors, Clinton and later Cornwallis, will experience similar frustrations in trying to fight a war 3000 miles from their homeland against an enemy that does not fight battles by the formal rules of eighteenth century warfare.

General Sir Henry Clinton became the British C-in-C in America in May 1778 after the resignation of Lord Howe.

War leaders at the Continental Army winter quarters at Valley Forge. L to r: Washington, de Kalb, von Steuben, Pulaski, Kosciusko, Lafayette, Mulhenberg.

15 MAY 1778

Revolution: Frontier Beginning a campaign to secure colonial authority over the western frontier territories, George Rogers Clark, with the aid of 150 Virginian volunteers, captures Cahokia on the Mississippi River.

30 MAY 1778

Revolution: Frontier The settlement of Cobleskill, New York, is burned by some 300 Iroquois Indians. The attack initiates a campaign of terror by Loyalists and Indians against American frontier settlements, particularly in the New York-Pennsylvania area.

6 JUNE 1778

Revolution: Diplomacy The British Peace Commission arrives in Philadelphia with offers that will be rejected by the Continental Congress, which, encouraged by its new alliance with France, insists upon unconditional independence from Great Britain.

18 JUNE 1778

Revolution: Evacuation of Philadelphia British General Henry Clinton leads the British army out of Philadelphia in order to march to New York City. Clinton is one of the three British generals who came to American in 1775 to assist Gage; Howe has been removed and Burgoyne was captured at Saratoga.

19 JUNE 1778

Revolution: Pennsylvania-New Jersey Breaking his winter camp at Valley Forge, Pennsylvania, Washington dispatches General Charles Lee to intercept the British forces under Clinton. Just as in December 1776, Washington has endured a trying time (the losses at Brandywine, Germantown and the terrible winter) but now has recovered to the point of pursuing the retreating British army.

26 JUNE 1778

Revolution: New Jersey General Clinton and his British army, laden with a large baggage train and suffering in intense summer heat, reach Monmouth Courthouse, New Jersey. Exhausted, the British stay there during the next day. On 27 June, Washington orders Major General Charles Lee, who commands the advance guard of the American forces, to attack the British rear guard the following day.

28 JUNE 1778

Revolution: Battle of Monmouth A major engagement is fought in scorching 100-degree temperatures near Monmouth Courthouse, New Jersey. Cornwallis, commanding the British rear guard, successfully fends off an assault by Charles Lee's troops. Lee has little faith in his men and issues a few contradictory instructions, and the Americans begin a slow retreat. Cornwallis, now joined by Henry Clinton, pursues the Americans and seems to have gained a victory, when, suddenly, the American forces halt, about face and fiercely resist the British. Washington has arrived on the field, sent Lee off in disgrace and required his men to stand fast. Cornwallis and Clinton make several determined efforts to break the American resistance, but to no avail. The heat and the approaching darkness prevent conclusive action by either army, and the battle breaks off. Clinton's army and baggage train reach New York safely, while Washington holds the field of battle and New Jersey is cleared of British forces. The British are now ensconced in New York City, precisely where they were almost two years before, while Washington's Continental soldiers have the satisfaction of knowing that they can match the British troops in battle. The action at Monmouth in fact proves to be the last major engagement to take place in the northern colonies during the revolution.

30 JUNE 1778

Revolution: Pennsylvania Four hundred Loyalists led by Colonel John Butler and 600 Indians enter the head of the Wyoming Valley in Pennsylvania. On 1 July they take possession of a fort and demand the surrender of the valley. In response, American Colonel Zebulon Butler marches with 350 militia to give battle, which occurs eight miles above Wilkes-Barre. After half an hour's fighting the militiamen begin a disorderly retreat; many of them are killed in hand-to-hand combat, and others are shot while trying to cross a stream. Loyalist leader John Butler reports the taking of 227 scalps and only five prisoners. American Colonel Zebulon Butler and 140 Americans escape the battle. By contrast, the Loyalists and Indians report only a dozen casualties.

2 JULY 1778

Revolution: Political Congress returns to Philadelphia, exactly two years after approving the Declaration of Independence.

4 JULY 1778

Revolution: Frontier George Rogers Clark captures the British garrison at Kaskaskia, at the junction of the Mississippi and Kaskaskia rivers. The French inhabitants swear allegiance to the new American republic. The settlements of Cahokia and Vincennes will follow Kaskaskia's example and raise the American flag.

8 JULY 1778

Revolution: Continental Army George Washington establishes headquarters for the Continental Army at West Point, New York.

9 JULY 1778

Revolution: Articles of Confederation The Articles of Confederation are signed by Continental Congressional delegates from Massachusetts, Rhode Island, Connecticut, New York, Pennsylvania, Virginia and South Carolina. The delegates of the other colonies endorse the document over the course of the next 11 months.

9 JULY 1778

Revolution: Naval A British naval force raids and burns Fairfield, Connecticut. Norwalk, Connecticut is to meet the same fate.

10 JULY 1778

Revolution: Naval French Admiral Charles Henri, Count d'Estaing arrives off New York with a fleet of one 90-gun, one 80-gun and six 74-gun ships. D'Estaing had sailed from Toulon, France, on 13 April and, had he arrived a week earlier, would have caught British Admiral Richard Howe in the process of bringing supplies and Loyalists from Delaware Bay as part of the British evacuation of the Philadelphia area. Now Howe commands a British fleet in New York harbor that is smaller and less heavily gunned than that of the French. A naval battle is avoided, however, because the large French warships cannot pass over the sandbar at the mouth of New York harbor. Chagrined, d'Estaing sails away and concentrates his naval force on the British base at Newport, Rhode Island.

20 JULY 1778

Revolution: Frontier George Rogers Clark captures the British garrison at Fort Vincennes on the Wabash River in present-day Indiana.

29 JULY 1778

Revolution: Naval The French fleet of Count d'Estaing arrives off Newport, Rhode Island. Com-

The Battle of Monmouth, 28 June 1778, was nearly lost by American General Charles Lee. Washington's arrival saved the day. Lee was later courtmartialed.

American militia leader George Rogers Clark, hero of several campaigns on the western frontier.

manding 12 ships of the line and 4 frigates, d'Estaing surrounds and cuts off the retreat of the British vessels that have protected Newport.

8 AUGUST 1778

Revolution: Naval American land forces led by General John Sullivan combine with Count d'Estaing's war fleet to begin a siege of Newport. At this point British Admiral Richard Howe arrives off Newport with a newly reinforced fleet. D'Estaing reembarks his men and sails out to meet Howe.

11 AUGUST 1778

Revolution: Naval A fierce storm scatters the ships of both Howe and d'Estaing before the opposing fleets can begin battle. Following the storm and the subsequent regrouping of the ships the British fleet will return to New York, while d'Estaing will make his way to Boston harbor for a refitting of his ships.

26 AUGUST 1778

Revolution: Diplomacy The British Peace Commission is snubbed. Some of its members try to bribe members of the Continental Congress and are exposed for this action.

29 AUGUST 1778

Revolution: Rhode Island The American forces under Generals Sullivan, Lafayette and Nathaniel Greene occupy Quaker Hill and Turkey Hill near Newport. The British drive them from their positions with some difficulty and at the cost of roughly 250 casualties to each side. Immediately following this action a British fleet carrying reinforcements arrives to back up the garrison, and the siege ends. So far, the French alliance has raised high hopes in the American ranks, but d'Estaing's actions have been disappointing.

7-17 SEPTEMBER 1778

Indian Warfare Shawnee Indians attack and lay siege to Boonesborough, Kentucky, but Daniel Boone manages to repulse the assault.

28 SEPTEMBER 1778

Revolution: Tappan Massacre At Tappan, New York, a massacre occurs when a regiment of American cavalry under Colonel Baylor is surprised by British led by General Gray (who also commanded the British at the Paoli massacre in 1777) while the Americans are asleep. No quarter is given. Out of 104 American privates, 67 are killed, wounded or taken prisoner.

15 OCTOBER 1778

Revolution: Egg Harbor Massacre British Captain Ferguson, with 300 British regulars and a company of Loyalists, in a surprise movement against Little Egg Harbor, New Jersey, makes an attack on an American force led by Polish Count Pulaski. Disregarding cries for quarter, the British massacre some 50 Americans before falling back.

11 NOVEMBER 1778

Revolution: New York Indians and Loyalists (roughly 750 in number) surprise the American garrison and settlers in the area of Cherry Valley, New York, about 13 miles northeast of Cooperstown. Thirty-two inhabitants and 11 Continental soldiers are killed, and all of the houses and barns in the settlements are burned.

27 NOVEMBER 1778

Revolution: Diplomacy Disappointed in their efforts, the members of the British Peace Commission set sail on their return trip to England.

14 DECEMBER 1778

Revolution: Diplomacy The Continental Congress appoints Benjamin Franklin the American diplomatic representative to France. Franklin will cultivate good relations with French Foreign Minister Vergennes.

17 DECEMBER 1778

Revolution: Frontier British soldiers under Colonel Henry Hamilton (who is called Hamilton the Hair Buyer because he pays money for American scalps) retake the western outpost of Vincennes.

29 DECEMBER 1778

Revolution: Southern Campaign British forces led by Major General Prevost capture Savannah, Georgia, after defeating an American force led by General Robert Howe. British commander-in-chief Clinton is content to hold Washington in a stand-off position in and around New York while Clinton sends British forces to defeat and demoralize the American resistance in the southern colonies.

6 JANUARY 1779

Revolution: Southern Campaign Pushing northward from Savannah, British forces led by General Prevost capture Fort Sunbury, Georgia, and attack Augusta, Georgia.

10 JANUARY 1779

Revolution: Naval The French present a dilapidated former merchant ship, the *Duc de Doras*, to American naval Captain John Paul Jones. Jones refits the vessel, mounts 42 guns, and renames the ship *Bonhomme Richard* (the French name for Poor Richard of *Poor Richard's Almanac*), in honor of Benjamin Franklin, the American ambassador to France.

29 January 1779

Revolution: Southern Campaign Augusta, Georgia, is captured by a British force led by Colonel Archibald Campbell.

3 FEBRUARY 1779

Revolution: Southern Campaign American forces led by General William Moultrie, the hero of the defense of Sullivan's Island at Charleston in 1776, successfully defend Port Royal, South Carolina, against a British attack.

7 FEBRUARY 1779

Revolution: Frontier George Rogers Clark leaves Kaskaskia with 170 men. Having learned that British Colonel Hamilton has retaken Vincennes, 240 miles to the east, Clark determines that he must recapture Vincennes to retain credibility with the French inhabitants of the western frontier settlements. Melting snow has swelled river streams, and the lowlands between Kaskaskia and Vincennes are flooded for miles. On 21 February, having been without food for two days, Clark and his men are ferried across the Wabash River.

Benjamin Franklin was brilliantly successful as the American representative in France from 1776 to 1785.

14 FEBRUARY 1779

Revolution: Battle of Kettle Creek American Colonels Andrew Pickens and Dooley lead a surprise assault on 700 Tories led by Colonel Boyd at Kettle Creek, South Carolina. Boyd's force had gathered in western North Carolina and is en route to Augusta, Georgia, held by the British. At Kettle Creek the Tories fight for an hour but then are scattered, and only 300 of them eventually reach Augusta. The result of the battle is that the Loyalist spirit in the Carolinas is broken, and no other large bodies of Tories are organized in that area during the Revolution.

15 FEBRUARY 1779

Revolution: Diplomacy A report of a Congressional committee sets forth goals to be achieved in a possible peace settlement–independence, certain minimum boundaries, complete British evacuation of United States territory, rights to fisheries and free navigation of the Mississippi River. On 14 August Congress will agree on the instructions to guide the peace negotiation, and on 27 September John Adams will be named to negotiate a peace treaty with Great Britain.

25 FEBRUARY 1779

Revolution: Frontier Leading 150 men, Lieutenant Colonel George Rogers Clark forces the surrender of British Colonel Henry Hamilton at Vincennes after manipulating the desertion of Indians who form half of Hamilton's force. Hamilton and 27 of his men are

George Rogers Clark bursts in on a British soiree at Fort Kaskaskia (in present-day Illinois) on 4 July 1778. Within the next six weeks he had claimed most of the surrounding area for Virginia.

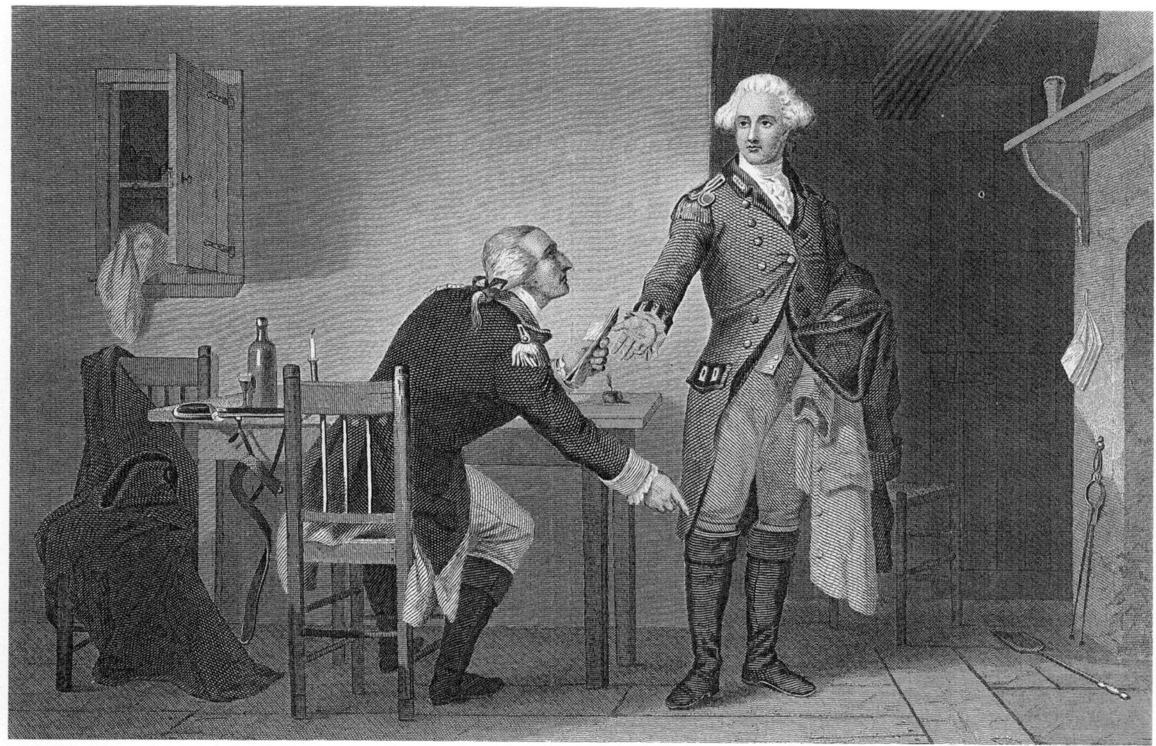

Above: Traitor Benedict Arnold (l) gives British Major John Andre the plans of West Point.

sent to Virginia as prisoners. With this triumph at Vincennes, Clark makes American conquest of the northwest area complete.

1 MARCH 1779

Revolution: Southern Campaign In an unsuccessful attempt to recapture Augusta, Georgia, American General John Ashe loses over 350 of his men in a battle with the British at Briar Creek.

29 APRIL 1779

Revolution: Southern Campaign British General Prevost crosses the Savannah River with 2400 men and a body of Indians to advance against General William Moultrie, who retreats to Charleston, South Carolina.

1-30 APRIL 1779

Indian Warfare American Colonel Evan Shelby destroys a group of Chickamagua Indian settlements in Tennessee in retaliation for raids by those Indians. Following this action by Shelby's North Carolina and Virginia militia all raiding in the area ceases.

10 MAY 1779

Revolution: Southern Campaign British forces capture and burn Portsmouth and Norfolk, Virginia.

11 MAY 1779

Revolution: Southern Campaign An attack on Charleston, South Carolina, is repulsed by the Polish Count Casimir Pulaski, one of the most devoted foreign soldiers to assist the American cause during the Revolution.

23 MAY 1779

Revolution: Arnold's Treachery By this date Benedict Arnold, the hero of Saratoga, the leader of the march on Quebec and the impromptu admiral who delayed the British at Lake Champlain in 1776, has begun to send information regarding American troop movements to British commander Henry Clinton. Arnold's treachery will stun his fellow officers when they later learn of it. It will be suggested that Arnold felt he had received inadequate recognition and honors for his war service.

1 JUNE 1779

Revolution: New York British commander Henry Clinton leads 6000 men up the Hudson River to capture the unfinished American forts at Stony Point and Verplank Point, but he fails to reach his goal of West Point.

19 JUNE 1779

Revolution: The South At Stono Ferry, South Carolina, American troops led by General Benjamin Lincoln unsuccessfully attack the rear of British troops under General Prevost while they are withdrawing from the Charleston area to Savannah, Georgia.

21 JUNE 1779

International Spain, unenthusiastic about American independence but anxious for her own colonial possessions, especially Florida and Louisiana, declares war on England after the British refuse to surrender the fortress of Gibraltar as the price for Spanish neutrality. Britain now has three enemies.

2 JULY 1779

Revolution: Tarleton Raids At Poundridge, New York, British Lieutenant Colonel Banastre Tarleton leads 360 mounted British, Hessian and Tory raiders to burn the home of Major Ebenezer Lockwood, an active American leader. Also burned are the Presbyterian church and other buildings. Tarleton will become known as the most ruthless and deadly of the British commanders.

10 JULY 1779

Revolution: Naval The entire Massachusetts colonial navy (distinct from the United States Navy) is destroyed in the aftermath of a mismanaged project to capture a Loyalist base at Castine, in the district of Maine. After failing to capture a fort, the American ships allow themselves to become bottled up in the Penobscot River by a British naval squadron. The Yankees are forced to burn every ship not captured by the British. All survivors – mariners and militia alike – have to straggle back to the Boston area on foot. Subsequent recriminations actually include a court martial for cowardice for famed patriot Paul Revere (chief of the American artillery), but he is cleared.

Below: American General Anthony Wayne's successful night bayonet attack on the British-held fort at Stony Point on the Hudson, 15 July 1779. All but one of the soldiers in the British garrison were killed or captured in this exemplary American action.

The engagement between John Paul Jones' *Bonhomme Richard* and HBM *Serapis*, September 1779. *Serapis'* advantage in broadside weight was 330 lb to 249 lb.

16 JULY 1779

Revolution: Capture of Stony Point American General 'Mad' Anthony Wayne leads an American force against the British-held fortress of Stony Point, New York, at midnight. Stony Point is garrisoned by 600 men under Colonel Johnson. Wayne's 1200-man force consists of two regiments and two companies of light infantry from North Carolina. It is only when they are a mile and a half from the fort that the American troops are told that they will capture Stony Point. Wayne achieves a complete surprise, but the British garrison surrenders only after a severe hand-to-hand contest, including the use of bayonets by both sides. The fortress is taken at the cost of 98 Americans killed or wounded. The British lose 63 men killed, and 543 are taken prisoner.

22 JULY 1779

Indian Warfare American militia pursue Indians led by Joseph Brant on the eastern bank of the Delaware River, north of present-day Port Jervis. The militia is drawn into an ambush, where they are fired upon from ten in the morning until late in the afternoon. Only 30 of 150 militiamen escape.

JULY 1779

Revolution: Arnold's Treachery Benedict Arnold and Henry Clinton break off their developing relations when Clinton refuses to pay £10,000 to Arnold and to indemnify him against any losses he might suffer after defecting to the British.

14 AUGUST 1779

Revolution: Diplomacy Congress approves a peace plan that contains the stipulations of independence, of defined minimum boundaries, of complete British evacuation of the American territories and of free navigation on the Mississippi River.

19 AUGUST 1779

Revolution: New Jersey American Major General Henry Lee attacks and takes possession of Paulus Hook, present-day Jersey City, New Jersey, the last British stronghold in that state.

29 AUGUST 1779

Indian Warfare At Newtown (present-day Elmira), New York, American General John Sullivan's army of 4000 men fights a brief engagement with 6-800 Tories and Indians led by Major John Butler and Joseph Brant. Following the battle Butler and Brant fall back to the relative safety of British Fort Niagara. Sullivan, who has been sent by Washington specifically to destroy the fighting capacity of the Iroquois Six Nations, will destroy an estimated 40 villages, 1500 fruit trees and corn fields yielding approximately 160,000 bushels.

1-15 SEPTEMBER 1779

Indian Warfare Following the victory at Newtown, Sullivan presses northwest on his mission to destroy Seneca and Cayuga Indian villages. Sullivan's campaign will indeed break the power of the Iroquois, who have generally held sway in upstate New York for at least as long as the period of known English settlement in North America.

8 SEPTEMBER 1779

Revolution: Siege of Savannah French Admiral d'Estaing drops anchor off Tybee Bar, where the Savannah River empties into the Atlantic. Having spent the past year in the French West Indies, d'Estaing now joins with the land forces of General Benjamin Lincoln in an effort to recapture Savannah from British General Prevost. On 16 September, d'Estaing summons Prevost to surrender. The formal siege begins on 23 September, and from 5-8 October a heavy cannon bombardment is maintained by the French and Americans.

23 SEPTEMBER 1779

Revolution: Naval Commanding the *Bonhomme Richard* and a squadron of one American and two French ships, John Paul Jones engages the British 44-gun frigate *Serapis* in battle off the east coast of England. Knowing that the British artillery is superior, Jones brings his ship to close quarters and puts grappling irons aboard his foe, locking the two ships together. American riflemen in the rigging shoot down many British sailors, but the British continue to fire their cannons into the American ship, which soon becomes a battered and sinking hulk. When British Captain Richard Pearson calls on Jones to yield, the Scotsman-turned-American patriot retorts that, 'I have not yet begun to fight!' Pearson eventually surrenders after American sharpshooters have cleared his decks of any crew to maneuver the *Serapis*. Jones then transfers his men to the *Serapis* while the *Bonhomme Richard* burns and sinks. The victory is largely symbolic; American ships cannot defeat the much stronger British navy. But the American will to win cannot be mistaken, and Jones will be lionized by the French court.

27 SEPTEMBER 1779

Revolution: Diplomacy Congress names John Adams to negotiate with England.

SEPTEMBER 1779

Spanish Policy Spanish Governor Galvez of Louisiana captures the British gulf ports of Manhac, Baton Rouge and Natchez.

9 OCTOBER 1779

Revolution: Siege of Savannah D'Estaing and Sullivan make a frontal assault upon the British defenses at Savannah, Georgia. The effort results in disaster. One brigade of the French army gets lost in Yamacraw Swamp, and the French and Americans are successfully repulsed by Prevost's soldiers. Polish Count Casimir Pulaski is mortally wounded in the

The youthful French Marquis de Lafayette (at 19 he commanded a division) was one of many Europeans who volunteered to serve in the Continental Army.

fighting, d'Estaing is twice wounded (not seriously) and the Franco-American allies suffer roughly 800 casualties, about 650 of them French. The siege is given up, and on 20 October d'Estaing's soldiers re-embark and sail away.

11 OCTOBER 1779

Revolution: British Invasion of the South British General Henry Clinton evacuates the naval base at Newport, Rhode Island, in order to concentrate his efforts on the southern campaign.

17 OCTOBER 1779

Revolution: Morristown Washington leads the Continental Army into winter quarters at Morristown, New Jersey, where his men will suffer through a winter that is worse than the one they endured at Valley Forge in 1777-1778. Low morale, low supplies, desertions and attempts at mutiny will plague the American forces.

26 DECEMBER 1779

Revolution: British Invasion of the South British General Henry Clinton embarks 8700 men on transport ships in New York harbor. The soldiers are headed for Charleston, South Carolina, where Clinton has decided the British will strike next. Ten warships and 90 transports leave New York. The British invasion force encounters foul weather, and off Cape Hatteras it is mauled by a terrific storm. One transport ship is actually blown across the Atlantic, to be wrecked on the coast of Cornwall, and virtually all of the horses brought on the expedition are lost.

26 JANUARY 1780

Revolution: Arnold's Court Martial An American court martial finds Benedict Arnold guilty of two charges of misusing his powers when he was commander of Philadelphia, following the British evacuation of that city. On 6 April Washington will, to his own distaste (for he has great respect for Arnold), officially reprimand the war hero. Arnold's treachery is, of course, still unknown to the Americans.

28 JANUARY 1780

Indian Warfare: Fort Nasborough (in 1782 renamed Nashville) is established on the Cumberland River in North Carolina's trans-Appalachian territory to help secure the region from Indian attacks.

1 FEBRUARY 1780

Revolution: British Invasion of the South After having made necessary repairs at the harbor in Savannah, Georgia, Clinton's fleet arrives off Charleston, South Carolina.

14 MARCH 1780

Spanish Policy Galvez, the Spanish governor of New Orleans, captures the British port of Mobile, Alabama.

8 APRIL 1780

Revolution: British Invasion of the South British naval forces initiate the attack on Charleston by sailing past the guns of Fort Moultrie with the loss of 27 men, in sharp contrast to the large losses they suffered in 1776 when they tried to subdue the fort. The British enter Charleston harbor. Meanwhile, Washington has sent Maryland and Delaware Continental troops (some of his very best) to the aid of the garrison at Charleston, which is led by General Benjamin Lincoln.

APRIL 1780

Revolution: Lafayette The Marquis de Lafayette returns to America to a loud welcome in Boston. Lafayette has earnestly pushed French leaders, including Foreign Minister Vergennes, to send another French fleet to America, and also a French army. When Lafayette sees Washington's army he is even more convinced that the American cause has become desperate. Lafayette writes that the American army is reduced to a 'very small number . . . almost perishing for want,' after the terrible winter of 1779-1780.

6 MAY 1780

Revolution: Siege of Charleston At Charleston, Fort Moultrie falls to the British.

8 MAY 1780

Revolution: Siege of Charleston There is an attempt to arrange a surrender at Charleston. The negotiations fail to produce a resolution, in part because Clinton requires a complete, unconditional surrender of the American forces. When the talks break off Clinton's artillery begins to shell the city. The Americans cannot properly match the British cannonade, and the surrender of the city becomes a matter of time.

12 MAY 1780

Revolution: Fall of Charleston Benjamin Lincoln formally surrenders Charleston, South Carolina, to Clinton. The loss of the 5400-man garrison, four ships and considerable arms and weapons constitutes by far the greatest single American loss of the Revolutionary War. The battle which led to the surrender was, significantly, one of the few classic textbook-style engagements fought during the Revolution. Clinton will soon depart for New York, leaving General Charles Cornwallis as commander of all the British forces in the south.

25 MAY 1780

Revolution: Continental Army Washington faces a mutiny of two Connecticut regiments, which demand full rations and immediate payment of salary that is five months in arrears. Pennsylvania troops put down the mutiny near Morristown, New Jersey, and two leaders of the protest are courtmartialed, convicted and hanged.

29 MAY 1780

Revolution: Tarleton Raids British Colonel Banastre Tarleton attacks and massacres a Virginia regiment at Waxhaw, North Carolina. Tarleton is becoming known as 'Bloody Tarleton.'

13 JUNE 1780

Revolution: American Command Congress commissions General Horatio Gates, the victor at Saratoga, as leader of the southern American army. Gates will lead the troops that were sent south by Washington in April.

22 JUNE 1780

Revolution: The South The reinforcements dispatched by Washington arrive in North Carolina after an arduous march through states that sometimes have denied them food rations and supplies. Their temporary leader (soon to be replaced by Gates) is the Baron de Kalb, the son of a Bavarian peasant, who has proved to be dedicated and proficient in serving the American cause. Unfortunately, de Kalb will not survive this campaign.

A contemporary map of British operations against Charleston, 11 February-12 May 1780.

23 JUNE 1780

Revolution: New Jersey At the Battle of Springfield, New Jersey, American forces led by General Nathaniel Greene defeat the British.

11 JULY 1780

Revolution: Rochambeau Led by Jean Baptiste de Vimeur, Count de Rochambeau, 5000 first-rate French soldiers disembark at Newport, Rhode Island. These are the forces for which Lafayette had lobbied in Paris – and which he had also wished to command. Rochambeau is a thorough and competent soldier, and, unlike the Count d'Estaing, Rochambeau has been instructed by his superiors to defer to Washington's wishes and even to be commanded by the American leader. Unfortunately, Rochambeau and the fleet which brought him to America, is soon blockaded in Newport by a British fleet.

25 JULY 1780

Revolution: American Command American General Horatio Gates assumes command of the American southern army at Coxe's Mill, North Carolina.

5 AUGUST 1780

Revolution: American Command Benedict Arnold takes command of a crucial American fortress, West Point, New York.

16 AUGUST 1780

Revolution: Battle of Camden General Gates' southern army is resoundingly defeated at Camden, South Carolina, by British General Cornwallis' better rested, better fed and better led soldiers. Nearly 900 Americans are killed and 1000 taken prisoner. The Baron de Kalb, who has continued serving under Gates, is wounded 12 times before finally collapsing (he dies three days later). Gates rides away from the

debacle at Camden so swiftly that he reaches Hillsborough, North Carolina, 180 miles to the north, in two days time. Behind him, there is no formal American army to oppose Cornwallis. Coming on the heels of the loss of Charleston, this defeat at Camden appears to spell the end of all American hopes for winning in the southern colonies.

18 AUGUST 1780

Revolution: British Invasion of the South At Fishing Creek, South Carolina, American forces led by General Thomas Sumter are defeated by Colonel Banastre 'Bloody' Tarleton. This opens the way for a British invasion of North Carolina.

8 SEPTEMBER 1780

Revolution: British Invasion of the South British forces under Cornwallis begin to invade North Carolina.

21 SEPTEMBER 1780

Revolution: Arnold's Treachery Benedict Arnold and British Major Andre meet on the west bank of the Hudson River, near Haverstraw, New York. Arnold delivers plans of West Point and informs Andre of the weak points of the fortress. While returning to the British lines Andre – in violation of Clinton's specific orders – doffs his British uniform in favor of civilian clothes.

23 SEPTEMBER 1780

Revolution: Arnold's Treachery Major Andre is captured by three New York militiamen before he reaches the British lines. The Americans discover that Andre has plans for West Point in his clothing. Not suspecting Arnold of any wrong-doing, the militiamen send word of Andre's capture to Arnold. On 25 September Arnold, seeing that the game is up, flees to the *Vulture*, a British warship on the Hudson River. Arnold will receive some money and a command in Virginia from Clinton, but the British never fully trust Arnold, and his military prowess on the British side is never as dramatic or powerful as it was when he fought on the American side.

2 OCTOBER 1780

Revolution: Execution of Andre After his conviction as a British spy, Major John Andre is hanged for his role in negotiating with Benedict Arnold. Since Andre was apprehended in civilian clothes, the Americans deny him the rights of a prisoner of war.

7 OCTOBER 1780

Revolution: Battle of King's Mountain At King's Mountain, South Carolina, a Loyalist army of 1100 men led by British Major Patrick Ferguson is resoundingly defeated by a roughly equal force of American frontiersmen led by Colonels Issac Selby and William Campbell. Ferguson had made the error of threatening these 'mountain men.' This sudden extinction of his left flank persuades British General Cornwallis to halt his movement into North Carolina.

14 OCTOBER 1780

Revolution: American Command Having learned of the defeat of Gates at Camden, the Continental Congress permits Washington to chose a successor to Gates. Washington's man is General Nathaniel Greene, an ex-Quaker from Rhode Island who has served with Washington since 1776. On 4 December 1780, Greene takes command of the remnants of the Southern army at Charlotte, North Carolina.

4 NOVEMBER 1780

Revolution: War Effort Congress requests the states to fulfill wartime quotas of flour, pork and hay in support of the common military effort.

19 DECEMBER 1780

Revolution: Arnold Benedict Arnold, now a British commander, sails from Sandy Hook, New Jersey, with approximately 1600 men and orders to create a diversion that will assist Cornwallis in the south.

DECEMBER 1780

Revolution: American Tactics Nathaniel Greene makes a highly unorthodox military move. Already outnumbered by British General Cornwallis, Greene splits his small force into two columns. The first, under his own command, stays close to the coastal region of the Carolinas, while riflemen leader Daniel Morgan takes another column and heads northwest. Cornwallis responds by dispatching Colonel Tarleton to eliminate Morgan, while he, Cornwallis, again begins to invade North Carolina.

Top left: Baron de Kalb is fatally wounded at the disastrous Battle of Camden, SC, in August 1780.

Left: The Battle of Cowpens, SC, January 1781, the first big American victory in the South, was a tactical masterpiece of General Daniel Morgan.

OTHER EVENTS OF 1780

Spanish Policy Spain, through Esteban Miro, governor of Louisiana, enlists Indians to attempt to halt Anglo-American westward expansion.

3 JANUARY 1781

Revolution: Continental Army Mutinous Pennsylvania troops make camp near Princeton, New Jersey, and elect representatives to bargain with state officials. Negotiations resolve the crisis, although over half of the mutineers will leave the army.

5-6 JANUARY 1781

Revolution: Arnold Benedict Arnold's British force marches into Richmond, Virginia, and burns the public records building and stores without losing a man.

17 JANUARY 1781

Revolution: Battle of Cowpens An encounter at Cowpens, South Carolina, is a total victory for American General Daniel Morgan. Having been pursued by British Colonel Tarleton, Morgan stops at the Broad River and deploys his 1100-man force in a defensive posture. Morgan places his untrustworthy militia in front and asks them to fire two rounds before retreating to the rear. Behind the militia are a core of highly disciplined Continental soldiers, and behind them – disguised by a low hilltop – is an American cavalry group. Tarleton leads his equal force (also 1100 men) in a headlong attack upon the Americans. Morgan's plan works better than he could have imagined. The militia inflict some casualties before retreating in an orderly fashion, the Continentals stand fast and at the crucial moment the American cavalry sweeps around and traps the British. Tarleton himself escapes capture by a hair-breath, but 100 British are killed, 229 are wounded and 600 others become prisoners. The Americans lose about 70 men. This one-day elimination of a British army is unique in the Revolution, and Morgan will receive due credit for his victory.

20 JANUARY 1781

Revolution: Continental Army A mutiny of New Jersey troops is quelled by American General Robert Howe, who hangs two of the leaders.

JANUARY 1781

Spanish Policy Spanish forces led by Don Eugenio Pourre capture the British Fort St. Joseph in the Illinois territory, near present-day Niles, Michigan. The Spanish later will claim this region on the basis of Pourre's victory.

14 FEBRUARY 1781

Revolution: The South General Nathaniel Greene, who has since recombined forces with Daniel Morgan, transports his army across the Dan River, near the North Carolina-Virginia border. Cornwallis, who has pursued Greene since learning of Tarleton's defeat at Cowpens, arrives just minutes after the last American has been ferried across. Greene has all the boats, and Cornwallis is stranded. Realizing that his position is weak, Cornwallis falls back to Hillsborough, North Carolina.

15 MARCH 1781

Revolution: Battle of Guilford Courthouse A battle at Guilford Courthouse, North Carolina, is fought between Greene and Cornwallis. The British make several frontal charges against American defenders. The accurate American shooting depletes the British ranks, and at one point it seems that the British line will break. Desperate, Cornwallis makes the decision to have his artillery fire into the fighting groups. The cannon-fire kills both British and Americans, but ultimately, Greene pulls his army away, leaving Cornwallis the master of the field of battle at the cost of 532 men killed, wounded or missing, the bloodiest battle since Bunker Hill. Greene has technically lost a battle, but he has damaged the core of Cornwallis' army. When news of the British 'victory' is reported in London, Opposition Leader Charles Fox will comment that one more such victory would ruin the British army.

17 MARCH 1781

Revolution: The South Cornwallis moves his footsore and battle-weary men to Wilmington, North Carolina.

25 APRIL 1781

Revolution: The South Cornwallis begins a campaign to conquer Virginia. Moving without directly consulting his superior officer, Henry Clinton, Cornwallis leaves Wilmington to join Generals Phillips and Benedict Arnold at Petersburg, Virginia. Although Cornwallis can claim that Virginia needs to be subdued, the painful truth is that Greene has outmaneuvered him and reduced Cornwallis' once-stronger army to the point where the British general has lost his ability to fight Greene in the Carolinas.

C-in-C of the American forces in the South in 1781 was the skillful General Nathaniel Greene.

9 MAY 1781

Spanish Policy Spanish forces complete their capture of all West Florida with the British surrender of Pensacola.

APRIL-JUNE 1781

Indian Warfare The Mohawk Valley in up-state New York is ravaged by Indians operating with the help of the British.

21 MAY 1781

Revolution In Wethersfield, Connecticut, George Washington and French General Rochambeau hold a conference to discuss Franco-American strategy. Rochambeau reluctantly agrees to Washington's plan for a joint attack on Clinton's base in New York. Although he is doubtful that such an attack can succeed, Rochambeau is under orders to play a subordinate role to Washington.

4 JUNE 1781

Revolution: Tarleton Raids British Colonel Banastre Tarleton nearly succeeds in capturing Virginia Governor Thomas Jefferson in an action at Charlottesville, Virginia.

10 JUNE 1781

Revolution: The South General Anthony Wayne and the Marquis de Lafayette join forces in Virginia, bringing their combined force to nearly 5000 men.

11 JUNE 1781

Revolution: Diplomacy Congress decides to supplement John Adams as sole peace negotiator with the addition of a commission composed of Benjamin Franklin, Henry Laurens and Thomas Jefferson.

JUNE 1781

Revolution: New York Washington moves his army from New Windsor to Peekskill, New York, and begins small operations against King's Bridge, New York.

20 JULY 1781

Internal Conflict Rebellious slaves in Williamsburg, Virginia, set fire to several buildings, as well as to the capitol.

1 AUGUST 1781

Revolution: The South Cornwallis arrives at the small coastal town of Yorktown, Virginia, where he hopes to be in close contact with Clinton through the services of the British Navy. The British are confident that they will retain command of the sea. The only time it has even been challenged was in 1778-1779, by French Admiral d'Estaing, whose mission to America ended in failure.

14 AUGUST 1781

Revolution: Yorktown Campaign Washington and Rochambeau learn that French Admiral Francois Joseph Paul, Count de Grasse, has sailed from the West Indies with at least 20 ships of the line to help the American cause. There are two 'buts' – de Grasse will go to Chesapeake Bay, rather than New York, and he can only stay on the American coast until 15 October. By 16 August Washington and Rochambeau have made a crucial decision to march their

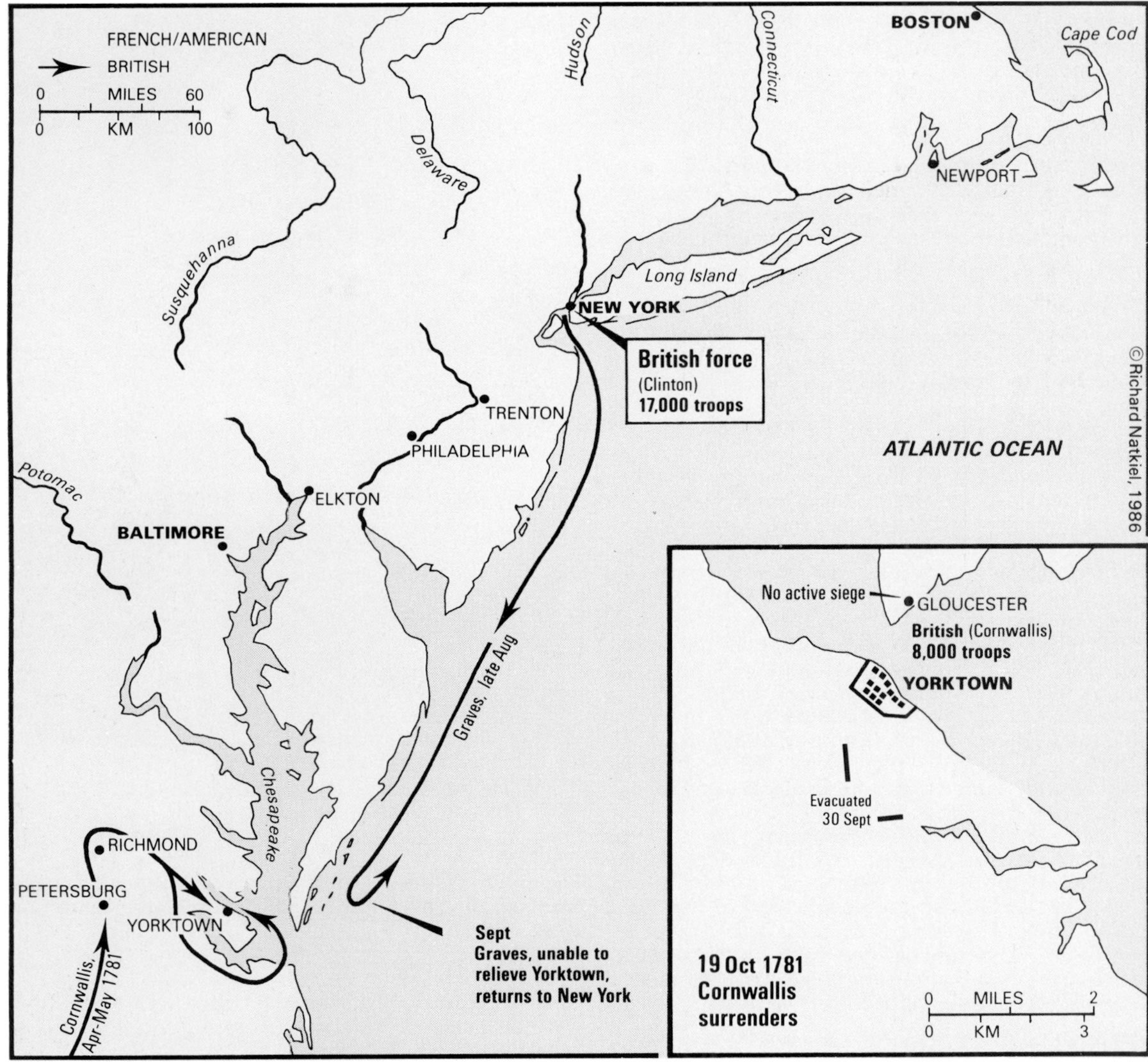

A general map of the Yorktown campaign, with an inset of the siege of Yorktown itself.

combined armies south to Virginia and trap Cornwallis with the assistance of de Grasse. In order to do this Washington gives up his own cherished desire to recapture New York, which he lost in 1776.

22-25 AUGUST 1781

Revolution: Yorktown Campaign The Franco-American forces cross the Hudson River at King's Ferry. By making feints they confuse Clinton into believing that the attack will indeed come at New York.

30 AUGUST 1781

Revolution: Yorktown Campaign The French war fleet of the Count de Grasse sails into Chesapeake Bay. De Grasse brings 28 ships of the line, including his own flagship, the 110-gun *Ville De Paris*, the largest ship in the world, and 3000 French land troops from the West Indies. De Grasse has taken a large gamble in bringing such a force north from the West Indies; if the enterprise ends in failure he will surely be disgraced and the French-American cause in North America will suffer a tremendous loss.

31 AUGUST 1781

Revolution: Yorktown Campaign Count de Grasse lands French troops at Yorktown to join with the Marquis de Lafayette in blocking off any possible retreat by Cornwallis. For his part, the British general probably does not yet realize the great size of the forces that are being arrayed against him.

1 SEPTEMBER 1781

Revolution: Yorktown Campaign The combined Franco-American forces led by Washington and Rochambeau reach Philadelphia. Only at this point does Clinton realize that these forces are heading south to snare Cornwallis.

5-8 SEPTEMBER 1781

Revolution: Battle of the Chesapeake The single most decisive battle of the Revolutionary War is fought outside of Chesapeake Bay, though few, if any, Americans participate in the naval Battle of the Chesapeake. British Admiral Thomas Graves has arrived off the Chesapeake with 19 ships of the line to come to the relief of Cornwallis. De Grasse slips the cables of his ships and heads out of the Bay to meet the British. The French battle line is ragged as it comes out into the Atlantic, and if Graves pounces, he can probably maul the French lead ships. Graves, however, adheres to the standard British mode of operations and waits to engage the French in an orderly line of battle. When the fleets at last close, the French gunners damage several of the British ships badly, and one, the *Terrible*, is later sunk. Both fleets drift southeast for two days, almost always within sight of each other, but without doing any further battle. De Grasse then turns and makes his way back to the Chesapeake. When he arrives there he discovers that French Admiral de Barras, who has commanded the French ships anchored at Newport, Rhode Island, has brought eight more ships into the Chesapeake. (De Barras has also brought heavy siege guns that will be needed for the capture of Yorktown.) Thus when British Admiral Graves returns to the Chesapeake he finds a total of 36 French ships of the line anchored in a good defensive position. Unable to fight such a force, Graves returns to New York to repair his ships and to consider what to do next. The result of the Battle of the Chesapeake is enormous: de Grasse and de Barras have sealed off any possible relief or retreat for Cornwallis, and the siege guns have arrived.

6 SEPTEMBER 1781

Revolution: Arnold Benedict Arnold loots and burns the port of New London, Connecticut.

8 SEPTEMBER 1781

Revolution: The South General Nathaniel Greene leads 2000 American soldiers to victory over British Colonel Stuart in the battle of Eutaw Springs, South Carolina.

14-24 SEPTEMBER 1781

Revolution: Siege of Yorktown With the assistance of French transport vessels, the combined armies of Washington and Rochambeau arrive to surround Cornwallis at Yorktown, Virginia.

6 OCTOBER 1781

Revolution: Siege of Yorktown The Franco-American forces establish the first parallel of their siege of Cornwallis at Yorktown.

14 OCTOBER 1781

Revolution: Siege of Yorktown One American force and one French force attack and capture two British redoubts at Yorktown.

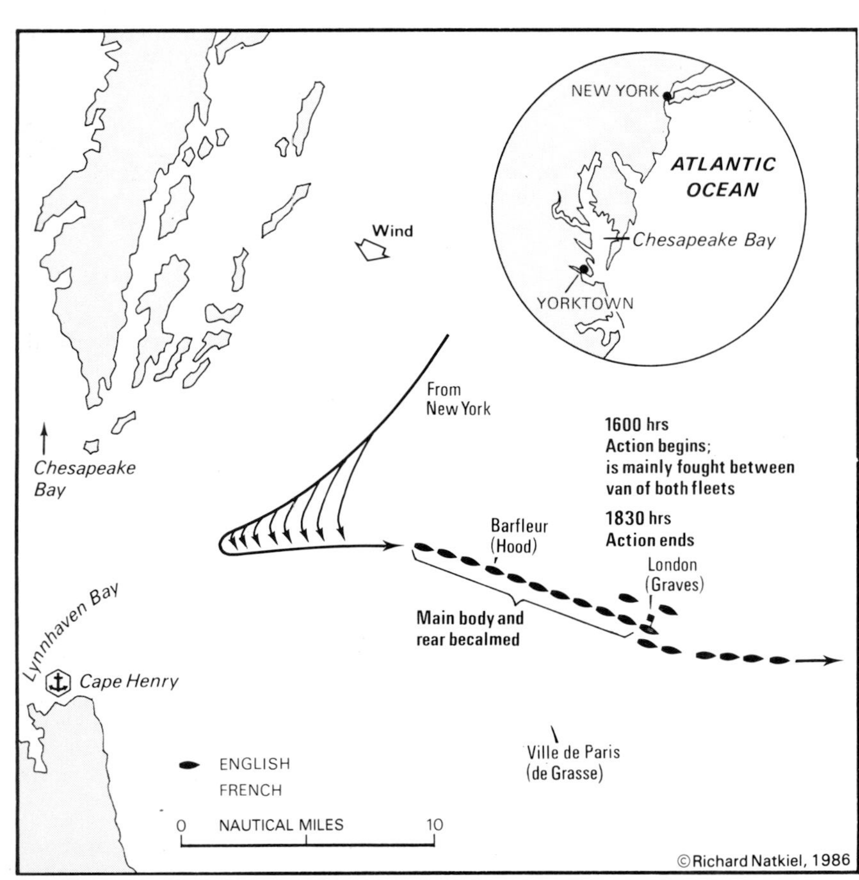

A map of the movements of the British and French fleets at the decisive Battle of the Chesapeake.

The signing of the Treaty of Paris.

16 OCTOBER 1781

Revolution: Siege of Yorktown Cornwallis sends 350 of his men on a sortie against the advanced American redoubts. The British inflict some casualties and spike some cannon, but the losses are readily replaced.

17 OCTOBER 1781

Revolution: Siege of Yorktown Exactly four years to the day after Burgoyne's surrender at Saratoga, Cornwallis asks for a parley to discuss terms of surrendering Yorktown.

19 OCTOBER 1781

Revolution: The Fall of Yorktown Cornwallis' army surrenders to the Franco-American armies led by Washington. As the British march in surrender past the Americans their bands play 'The World Turned Upside Down.'

24 OCTOBER 1781

Revolution: Naval The British fleet of Thomas Graves arrives off Chesapeake Bay carrying 7000 soldiers as a last-ditch effort to save Cornwallis. On learning of the surrender, Clinton's force returns to New York. The last major battle of the Revolution is over.

5 JANUARY 1782

Revolution: The South British forces withdraw from Wilmington, North Carolina.

7 MARCH 1782

Indian Warfare American soldiers massacre 96 peaceful Christian Delaware Indians at Gnadenhutten, Ohio, in retaliation for terrorist raids carried out by other Indians. On 4 June Indians and Loyalists will kill Colonel William Crawford who commanded the soldiers at this massacre.

22 MARCH 1782

Revolution: Diplomacy In England, Lord Rockingham replaces Lord North as prime minister. Rockingham will seek immediate and direct negotiations with the Americans.

4 APRIL 1782

Revolution: British Command Sir Guy Carleton is commissioned as the chief commander of British forces in America, replacing Henry Clinton.

12 APRIL 1782

Revolution: Diplomacy Peace talks begin between British and American representatives in Paris.

11 JUNE 1782

Revolution: The South British forces evacuate Savannah, Georgia.

19 AUGUST 1782

Revolution: Frontier Combined Indian and Loyalist forces, continuing to conduct raids on frontier settlements, attack and defeat a group of American frontiersmen at Blue Licks, near present-day Lexington, Kentucky.

25 AUGUST 1782

Indian Warfare Mohawk chief Joseph Brant leads raids on Pennsylvania territory frontier settlements, burning the village of Hannastown, Pennsylvania.

27 AUGUST 1782

Revolution: The South In the last eastern seaboard engagement of the Revolution, a skirmish occurs between Americans and British troops by South Carolina's Combahee River.

10 NOVEMBER 1782

Revolution: Frontier The last battle of the Revolution is fought by George Rogers Clark against the Shawnee Indian village of Chillicothe in the Ohio territory. Clark's riflemen retaliate against Loyalists and Indians for the defeat at Blue Licks, Kentucky.

30 NOVEMBER 1782

Revolution: Diplomacy American and British representatives sign a preliminary peace treaty in Paris. The French will object to this independent negotiation but will be pacified once again by the ever-persuasive Benjamin Franklin.

14 DECEMBER 1782

Revolution: The South British forces evacuate Charleston, South Carolina.

24 DECEMBER 1782

Revolution: End French troops embark on the voyage home from Boston.

20 JANUARY 1783

Revolution: Diplomacy Preliminary articles of peace are signed between England and France and England and Spain.

Protesting high taxes and inefficient government, a mob led by Daniel Shays in 1786 forces the state supreme court in Springfield, Mass, to close.

4 FEBRUARY 1783

Revolution: End Great Britain officially declares an end to the hostilities in America.

11 APRIL 1783

Revolution: End Congress formally proclaims an end to hostilities in America and to the Revolutionary War against Great Britain.

15 APRIL 1783

Revolution: Peace Treaty Congress ratifies the preliminary peace treaty negotiated in Paris.

26 APRIL 1783

Revolution: End Bound for Canada, some 7000 Loyalists set sail from New York bringing to a total some 100,000 Loyalists who have left for Europe or Canada since the years immediately before the Revolution.

13 JUNE 1783

Revolution: End The main part of Washington's Continental Army disbands.

3 SEPTEMBER 1783

Revolution: Treaty of Paris The Treaty of Paris is signed by Great Britain and the United States in Paris. On the same day, England signs a peace pact with France and Spain at Versailles. By the terms of this treaty Britain cedes Florida to Spain.

25 NOVEMBER 1783

British Policy The last of the British troops leave Manhattan as George Washington and Governor George Clinton enter the city. By 4 December all British soldiers on Staten Island are boarding ships bound for England.

23 DECEMBER 1783

Resignation of Washington After a triumphant journey to Annapolis, Maryland, where the Congress is meeting, George Washington comes before the Congress to resign officially his commission as commander in chief of the Continental Army.

14 JANUARY 1784

Treaty of Paris Congress ratifies the Treaty of Paris, formally ending the Revolutionary War and initiating peace with Great Britain.

8 APRIL 1784

British Policy British Lord Sydney notifies Canadian Governor-General Haldimand that British troops will not withdraw from garrisons on the Great Lakes until the United States complies with the conditions of the Treaty of Paris, specifically those dealing with the treatment of Loyalists and the repayment of debts.

26 JUNE 1784

Transportation Spain officially closes the lower Mississippi River to American navigation.

22 OCTOBER 1784

Indian Affairs In the Second Treaty of Fort Stanwix the Six Nations of the Iroquois Indians give up all claims to the territory west of the Niagara River.

21 JANUARY 1785

Indian Affairs In a treaty negotiated at Fort McIntosh the Chippewa, Delaware, Ottawa and Wyandot Indians cede nearly all land in the present-day state of Ohio to white settlers.

20 JULY 1785

International Congress authorizes John Jay to negotiate with Spain's minister to the United States for free navigation on the Mississippi River. Jay's mission meets with defeat.

10 OCTOBER 1785

International Spain orders Georgia to give up its claim to Bourbon County, a political unit Georgia has established in the area of present-day Alabama and Mississippi, territory also claimed by Spain.

30 NOVEMBER 1785

International United States minister to Great Britain John Adams formally demands that the British relinquish their military posts along the Great Lakes and in Ohio – notably the forts at Detroit, Michilimackinac, Niagara and Oswego.

22 FEBRUARY 1786

International In London, John Adams meets with the ambassador of Tripoli, Africa, to negotiate a settlement to end piracy on American shipping in the Mediterranean Sea and off the coasts of Portugal and Spain. These negotiations fail to resolve the matter.

31 AUGUST 1786

Shays' Rebellion In Northampton, Massachusetts, an armed mob prevents the session of the town court. Similar incidents will soon occur in Worcester, Concord and Great Barrington. On 22-25 August representatives from some 50 Massachusetts towns had protested against the inefficacy of the state government, high legal expenses and taxation.

20 SEPTEMBER 1786

Internal Conflict An armed mob marches on the New Hampshire assembly in an attempt to force the enactment of a paper-money issue.

A federal inspector is tarred and feathered by a mob protesting excise taxes on liquor and stills in 1794, another proof of the new government's weakness.

26 SEPTEMBER 1786

Shays' Rebellion: After Massachusetts Governor James Bowdoin sends 600 militiamen led by General William Shepherd to protect the state's supreme court session in Springfield, an armed band of insurgents led by Daniel Shays, a former Revolutionary War captain and now a bankrupt farmer, confronts the state's forces and causes the court to adjourn.

20 OCTOBER 1786

Shays' Rebellion Fearful of the proximity of Daniel Shays' rebel army to a federal armory in Springfield, Massachusetts, Congress authorizes Secretary of War Henry Knox to raise a 1340-man army from Connecticut and Massachusetts, purportedly for Indian service.

30 NOVEMBER 1786

Internal Conflict An insurrection in eastern Massachusetts is quelled with the capture of rebel leader Job Shattuck.

26 DECEMBER 1786

Shays' Rebellion Daniel Shays assembles a new rebel force of 1200 men near Worcester and marches to Springfield to unite with forces led by Luke Day. Together, these forces outnumber the state militiamen led by General Shepherd, who are guarding the federal arsenal. Massachusetts Governor Bowdoin immediately calls for the short-term mobilization of 4400 men to deal with the insurrection.

18-19 JANUARY 1787

Shays' Rebellion The newly activated Massachusetts militia force of 4400 men led by Revolutionary War veteran Benjamin Lincoln assembles to combat the insurgents who are led by Daniel Shays in Springfield, Massachusetts.

26 JANUARY 1787

Shays' Rebellion Daniel Shays leads his rebel force of 1200 men in an unsuccessful attack on the federal arsenal at Springfield, Massachusetts.

27 JANUARY 1787

Shays' Rebellion General Benjamin Lincoln arrives in Springfield and moves on to chase the rebels northward.

4 FEBRUARY 1787

Shays' Rebellion General Lincoln makes a surprise attack on Shays' insurgents at Petersham, Massachusetts. One hundred and fifty rebels are captured, and Shays flees to Vermont. He is eventually pardoned and he will move to the town of Spartacus, New York. The rebellion is squelched, but its influences will extend to the entire nation, since the individual states now see that federal authority and armaments are needed to deal with possible rebellions.

17 SEPTEMBER 1787

National: The Constitution Thirty-nine delegates to the constitutional convention vote to endorse the final form of the Constitution, prepared by Gouverneur Morris.

21 JUNE 1788

National: The Constitution With the vote of New Hampshire for ratification of the Constitution, the Federal Constitution is formally adopted by the United States.

30 APRIL 1789

National In New York, George Washington is inaugurated as the first president of the United States. His inaugural address urges the 'preservation of the sacred fire of liberty.'

29 SEPTEMBER 1789

National Congress establishes the 1000-man United States Army composed of one regiment of infantry and one battalion of four artillery companies.

18 OCTOBER 1790

Indian Warfare In the first of a number of United States expeditions against the western Indians the forces of General Josiah Harmar are defeated in a battle with Ohio Indians near Fort Wayne. With these hostilities, the five-year-long Indian war begins in the Northwest Territory.

12 JUNE 1791

Slavery Inspired by a slave rebellion on the West Indian island of Haiti, a group of slaves revolts in the Spanish colony of Louisiana.

4 NOVEMBER 1791

Indian Warfare Near the site of Fort Wayne a force of Ohio Indians defeats an expeditionary force led by Arthur St. Clair, governor of the Northwest Territory.

18 JULY 1792

Naval John Paul Jones, the naval hero of the Revolutionary War, dies in Paris.

JULY 1794

Internal Conflict In the Monongahela Valley of western Pennsylvania, the Whiskey Rebellion breaks out among backwoods farmers who oppose the collection of a federal excise tax on liquor and stills. The rebels resort to violent actions such as burning the tax collectors' homes and tarring and feathering revenue officers.

7 AUGUST 1794

Whiskey Rebellion President Washington issues a proclamation directing the insurgents to return to their homes, at the same time calling out a combined Virginia, Maryland, New Jersey and Pennsylvania militia force of 12,900 to put down the insurrection.

20 AUGUST 1794

Indian Warfare: Battle of Fallen Timbers At the Battle of Fallen Timbers in northwest Ohio, alongside the Maumee River, General Anthony Wayne thoroughly defeats a 2000-man Indian force, effectively ending Indian hostilities in the region. One hundred and seven Americans are killed or wounded in the battle.

24 SEPTEMBER 1794

Whiskey Rebellion During the course of the Whiskey Rebellion, President Washington issues a second proclamation ordering the suppression of the insurrection by the militia led by Henry Lee. Faced with the sizable militia force, the insurgents return home quietly, thus ending the rebellion in mid-November. Two hundred rebels are arrested, 25 are tried for treason and two are convicted but later pardoned.

5 SEPTEMBER 1795

International The United States signs a treaty of peace and amity with the Dey of Algiers, agreeing to pay tribute to the Barbary pirates who have preyed upon American commercial shipping in the Mediterranean Sea and off the coasts of Spain and Portugal. The Americans agree to pay $1 million to ransom 115 seamen, and then to make annual tribute payments.

15 NOVEMBER 1796

French Naval War: Approach Relations between France and the United States, which have deteriorated slowly during the seven years since the start of the French Revolution, now take a sharp turn for the worse when French minister Adat announces the suspension of diplomatic relations between the two nations.

4 MARCH 1797

National John Adams is inaugurated as president of the United States, with Thomas Jefferson as the vice-president.

1 JUNE 1797

French Naval War: Approach American Secretary of State Thomas Pickering reports that some 300 American vessels have been captured by the French on the high seas.

28 AUGUST 1797

International The United States signs a treaty with Tunis, Africa, in order to end the costly attacks of the Barbary pirates on American commercial shipping. America agrees to an even higher tribute than that promised in the treaty with Tripoli. This pact will not be ratified until 10 January 1800.

18 OCTOBER 1797

French Naval War: Approach In Paris, American peace commissioners Elbridge Gerry, John Marshall and Charles C. Pinckney are approached by three French agents who suggest an American loan to France and a $240,000 bribe as preconditions for serious negotiations. The Americans refuse the offer, and the so-called XYZ affair (named after the three agents) promotes further ill-will between America and France that will culminate in an undeclared naval war between the two countries.

General Anthony Wayne's victory at the 1794 Battle of Fallen Timbers broke Indian power in northern Ohio.

Incidents between US ships and French commerce raiders multiplied as the century drew to a close. Here the American merchantman *Planter* beats off an attack by a French privateer in July 1799.

21 OCTOBER 1797

Naval The United States ship *Constitution* is launched in Boston. This 44-gun, 1576-ton frigate will serve gloriously in the War of 1812.

28 MAY 1798

French Naval War: Approach Congress authorizes President Adams to order American naval commanders to seize any French armed ships interfering with American commercial shipping.

7 JULY 1798

French Naval War: Approach Congress abrogates the previous American treaties of 1778 with France. America is on the brink of war with her oldest ally, the homeland of Lafayette and Rochambeau.

20 NOVEMBER 1798

French Naval War The American schooner *Retaliation*, commanded by Lieutenant William Bainbridge, is seized by the French off Guadeloupe in the Caribbean.

9 FEBRUARY 1799

French Naval War In the undeclared naval war with France, American Captain Thomas Truxton, commanding the 36-gun frigate USS *Constellation*, captures the 40-gun French frigate *L'Insurgente* off the island of Nevis.

7 JULY 1799

French Naval War The 12-gun French schooner *La Croyable* is captured by the 20-gun sloop-of-war USS *Delaware* off Egg Harbor, New Jersey.

9-10 NOVEMBER 1799

International The French Directoire government is abolished by a coup d'etat that establishes Napoleon Bonaparte, conqueror of Italy and Egypt, as first consul, the virtual ruler of France.

JANUARY-OCTOBER 1800

French Naval War The naval war will swing steadily in the United States' favor as cruising US warships gradually sweep the western Atlantic of French privateers. The 12-gun schooner USS *Enterprise* alone will capture 18 privateers during this period.

1 FEBRUARY 1800

French Naval War In the naval war the 36-gun American frigate *Constellation* engages in an indecisive battle with the 52-gun French *La Vengeance*.

8 MARCH 1800

International Napoleon Bonaparte receives the American peace commissioners William Vans Murray, Oliver Ellsworth and William R. Davie with courtesy. Formal peace talks are to begin in April.

30 AUGUST 1800

Slavery In Virginia, a planned slave rebellion led by a slave named Gabriel Prosser is revealed. Prosser and 37 others are seized and tried on 30 April 1804. Prosser is hanged.

30 SEPTEMBER 1800

International The Treaty of Morfontaine (more commonly known as the Convention of 1800) is signed by the French consulate and the American peace commissioners, thus ending the undeclared naval war between France and the United States. On the very next day Napoleon forces Spain to cede the Louisiana area to France in the secret Treaty of San Ildefonso. The land transfer does not become known in the United States until May 1801.

17 FEBRUARY 1801

National Thomas Jefferson becomes the third president of the United States.

14 MAY 1801

Tripolitan War Increasing his demands for tribute, Pasha Yusuf Karamanli of Tripoli declares war on the United States. President Thomas Jefferson (who was inaugurated on 4 March 1801 as the third president of the United States) will send American naval warships into the Mediterranean Sea. The Tripolitan War will last into 1805.

1 AUGUST 1801

Tripolitan War In the war with Tripoli the 16-gun brig USS *Enterprise* seizes the corsair *Tripoli*.

6 FEBRUARY 1802

Tripolitan War In recognition of the 14 May 1801 declaration of war on the United States by the Pasha of Tripoli,Congress passes legislation authorizing the arming of merchant ships in order to defend American interests. By doing so Congress in effect admits that a state of war exists between the two nations.

2 MAY 1803

International In Paris, American envoys James Monroe and Robert Livingston sign the Louisiana Purchase agreement with Napoleonic France. The Treaty gives the young United States some 828,000 square miles of land between the Mississippi River and the Rocky Mountains for approximately $15,000,000.

23 MAY 1803

Tripolitan War American naval commander Edward Preble is appointed commander of the Mediterranean Squadron, which has been assigned the task of waging the Tripolitan War.

31 OCTOBER 1803

Tripolitan War The 38-gun American frigate *Philadelphia* is captured by the Tripolitans in Tripoli harbor, where the vessel has run aground on a reef. The Tripolitans will convert the vessel to their own uses.

16 FEBRUARY 1804

Tripolitan War: Burning of the *Philadelphia* American naval lieutenant Stephen Decatur wins a stunning surprise victory by sailing his ketch *Intrepid* into Tripoli harbor and burning the previously-captured *Philadelphia*.

Tripolitan gunboats close in on the grounded and helpless 38-gun frigate USS *Philadelphia* in one of the notable incidents of the Tripolitan War.

29 APRIL 1804

Tripolitan War In the Tripolitan War, American Commodore Edward Preble captures two enemy vessels.

AUGUST-SEPTEMBER 1804

Tripolitan War American Commodore Edward Preble bombards the city of Tripoli in a series of five unrelenting attacks.

4 MARCH 1805

National Thomas Jefferson is inaugurated for his second term as president of the United States.

26-29 APRIL 1805

Tripolitan War: Eaton Expedition A small American land invasion force captures the port city of Derna in Tripoli. William Eaton, the energetic United States consul in Tunis, has led a rabble army from Egypt, supplemented by fewer than 10 American marines, to a victory that signals a turning point in the Tripolitan War.

4 JUNE 1805

Tripolitan War: End A peace treaty ends the Tripolitan War after the Americans have installed the Pasha's brother on the throne. In order to get back his throne, Pasha Yusuf grants the American Navy the right to sail the Mediterranean Sea unmolested, while the United States agrees to pay $60,000 as ransom for the crew of the *Philadelphia*. This is to be a one-time payment, and Tripoli surrenders any right to demand further tribute from the United States. Congress will ratify the treaty on 12 April 1806.

22 JUNE 1807

War of 1812: Approach The British 52-gun HMS *Leopard* stops the American 39-gun USS *Chesapeake* just outside the three mile limit off Norfolk, Virginia. The British commander insists that four men on the *Chesapeake* are British deserters, and he demands their surrender. When American Commodore James Barron refuses, the British open fire, killing three men and wounding 18. The *Chesapeake* strikes and the British forcibly remove the four alleged deserters. Only one of the four men is later proven to be a British deserter; he is hanged. This inflamatory incident brings the United States and Britain to the brink of war.

2 JULY 1807

War of 1812: Approach In response to the *Leopard-Chesapeake* incident of 22 June, President Jefferson issues a proclamation calling for all British warships to vacate the territorial waters of the United States.

17 OCTOBER 1807

British Policy The British announce that they intend to enforce even more vigorously their policy of impressing American seamen. Britain is locked in a life-or-death struggle with Napoleonic France, and British leaders want every possible available sailor to serve in the British Royal Navy.

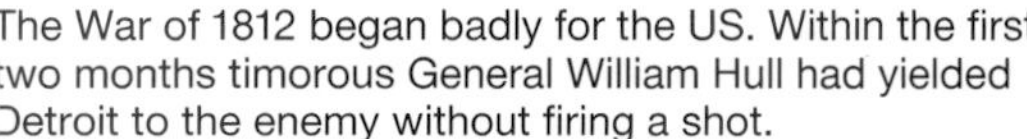

The War of 1812 began badly for the US. Within the first two months timorous General William Hull had yielded Detroit to the enemy without firing a shot.

OCTOBER 1808

International In an attempt to settle the *Chesapeake-Leopard* controversy Great Britain sends special envoy George Rose to the United States to discuss reparation payments. The British persist in demanding the withdrawal of President Jefferson's 2 July 1807 order that all British ships leave American territorial waters; this controversy is not settled until 12 November 1811.

4 MARCH 1809

National James Madison is inaugurated as the fourth president of the United States. Thomas Jefferson, a peace-loving man who presided over the Tripolitan War and the *Chesapeake-Leopard* controversy, now retires to private life in Monticello, his home near Charlottesville, Virginia.

In 1811 General William Henry Harrison defeated a large Indian force at Tippecanoe Creek. British aid to the Indians fed US pro-war sentiment.

2 JULY 1809

Indian Warfare Shawnee Indian chief Tecumseh and his brother, The Prophet, begin a campaign to establish a defensive confederacy of Indian tribes to resist the westward progress of American settlers, who in the past seven years have acquired over 30 million acres of Indian lands north of the Ohio River. The British government of Canada reportedly backs the efforts of Tecumseh.

26 SEPTEMBER 1810

International Americans living in the western portion of Spanish West Florida, the possession of which has been in dispute since the Louisiana Purchase of 1803, rise up in rebellion against their Spanish rulers. They seize the fort at Baton Rouge and declare the region between New Orleans and the Pearl River to be the Republic of West Florida, seeking annexation by the United States. This pattern will be repeated in Texas in the 1830s-1840s.

27 OCTOBER 1810

International President Madison announces the annexation and military occupation of the western region of Spanish West Florida. The area between the Mississippi River and the Perdido River will become the state of Louisiana in 1812.

1 MAY 1811

War of 1812: Approach Off Sandy Hook, New York, the 38-gun British frigate *Guerrière* stops the American brig *Spitfire* and seizes a native-born American seaman. This impressment arouses an outcry in the United States.

31 JULY 1811

Indian Warfare Fearful of the Indian confederacy being formed by Shawnee chief Tecumseh and his brother, The Prophet, the frontier settlers of Vincennes in the Indiana Territory call for the destruction of the main Indian village on the Tippecanoe River.

26 SEPTEMBER 1811

Indian Warfare In the Indiana Territory, Governor William Henry Harrison leads a 1000-man military force out of Vincennes, headed for the Indian capital at the junction of the Tippecanoe and Wabash rivers.

The goal of the expedition is to eradicate the settlement and to thwart the confederacy plans of Tecumseh, who has travelled to the Southwest to seek allies among the Creek Indian tribes. The expeditionary force will erect Fort Harrison 65 miles north of Vincennes in late October.

5 NOVEMBER 1811

War of 1812: Approach President Madison calls for increased preparations for the national defense in light of the continued British and French harassment of American commercial shipping.

7 NOVEMBER 1811

IndianWarfare: Battle of Tippecanoe In the Indiana Territory, Indians led by The Prophet make a surprise attack on Governor Harrison's 1000-man force. In the hard-fought Battle of Tippecanoe, Harrison's men repulse the Indians, despite heavy losses. After razing the Indian village, Harrison's troops withdraw southward to Fort Harrison. Despite the indecisive aftermath of the battle, the settlers acclaim Tippecanoe as a great victory. When Harrison becomes a presidential candidate in the future, a campaign slogan will be 'Tippecanoe and Tyler too,' Tyler being the vice-presidential candidate.

12 NOVEMBER 1811

International Secretary of State James Monroe accepts the offer of the British to settle the *Chesapeake* incident of 22 June 1807.

APRIL 1812

Indian Warfare In the northwest region the peace created by the Battle of Tippecanoe ends as the Indians begin another series of raids on the frontier settlements.

10 APRIL 1812

War of 1812: Approach Congress empowers President Madison to call up 100,000 militia from the states and territories for six months service.

1 JUNE 1812

War of 1812: Approach Motivated by the apparently unyielding position of Great Britain on neutral shipping – specifically the impressment of seamen, interference with trade and the blockade of American ports – as well as by British encouragement of Indian hostilities, President Madison sends a message to Congress asking for a declaration of war against Great Britain.

4 JUNE 1812

War of 1812: Approach The House of Representatives, in a vote of 79 to 49, supports President Madison.

16 JUNE 1812

British Policy In London, British Prime Minister Castlereagh proclaims the suspension of the British orders in council affecting neutral shipping, to be effective 23 June. This move, motivated by worsening economic conditions in England, might mollify some American resentment against Britain if it could reach the United States quickly. However, even the fastest crossing of the Atlantic will be too late.

19 JUNE 1812

War of 1812 President Madison officially proclaims the United States to be in a state of war against Great Britain. This is the first official declaration of war in United States history. The war with France had gone undeclared, and the United States did not formally declare war on Tripoli.

17 JULY 1812

War of 1812: Great Lakes Theater British forces capture the American port of Michilimackinac (Michigan) without firing a shot. Meanwhile, American General Hull has led 2200 soldiers across the Detroit River into British Canada.

8 AUGUST 1812

War of 1812: Great Lakes Theater American General William Hull withdraws his 2200-man force from Canada, retreating to Detroit.

15 AUGUST 1812

War of 1812: Great Lakes Theater At the site of present-day Chicago, Indians massacre the American garrison as it evacuates Fort Dearborn. The fort is burned the following day.

16 AUGUST 1812

War of 1812: Surrender of Detroit American General William Hull surrenders Detroit to British General Isaac Brock without a shot fired. This capitulation gives the British power over the Lake Erie-Lake Michigan area. General Hull, who surrenders because he fears a possible Indian massacre of civilian settlers, is later court martialed and found guilty of cowardice and neglect of duty, but his death sentence will be commuted because of his fine Revolutionary War record.

19 AUGUST 1812

War of 1812: Naval Off Nova Scotia, Captain Isaac Hull leads the 44-gun frigate USS *Constitution* to victory over the British 38-gun frigate *Guerrière* in a half-hour naval battle.

17 SEPTEMBER 1812

War of 1812: US Command William Henry Harrison, the hero of the Battle of Tippecanoe, is commissioned brigadier general and given command of the American northwest army.

13 OCTOBER 1812

War of 1812: Battle of Queenston Heights American General Stephen Van Rensselaer leads 600 men across the Niagara River to capture Queenston Heights, Ontario. British General Isaac Brock is killed in the action, but the Americans are defeated by a 1000-man British force when the New York state militia refuses to come to Rensselaer's aid on the grounds that their commission does not require them to leave the boundaries of the state.

17 OCTOBER 1812

War of 1812: Naval Six hundred miles off the Virginia coast American Captain Jacob Jones' 18-gun sloop of war *Wasp* defeats the British 18-gun brig *Frolic*, with only 10 US casualties, compared to 90 suffered by the British.

25 OCTOBER 1812

War of 1812: Naval Off the Canary Islands the 44-gun frigate *USS United States*, commanded by Commodore Stephen Decatur, captures the 38-gun British frigate *Macedonian* after a two-hour fight.

19 NOVEMBER 1812

War of 1812: New York At Plattsburg, New York, American General Henry Dearborn leads his force against Montreal. However, Dearborn's militia forces refuse to cross the Canadian border, and he is forced to turn back.

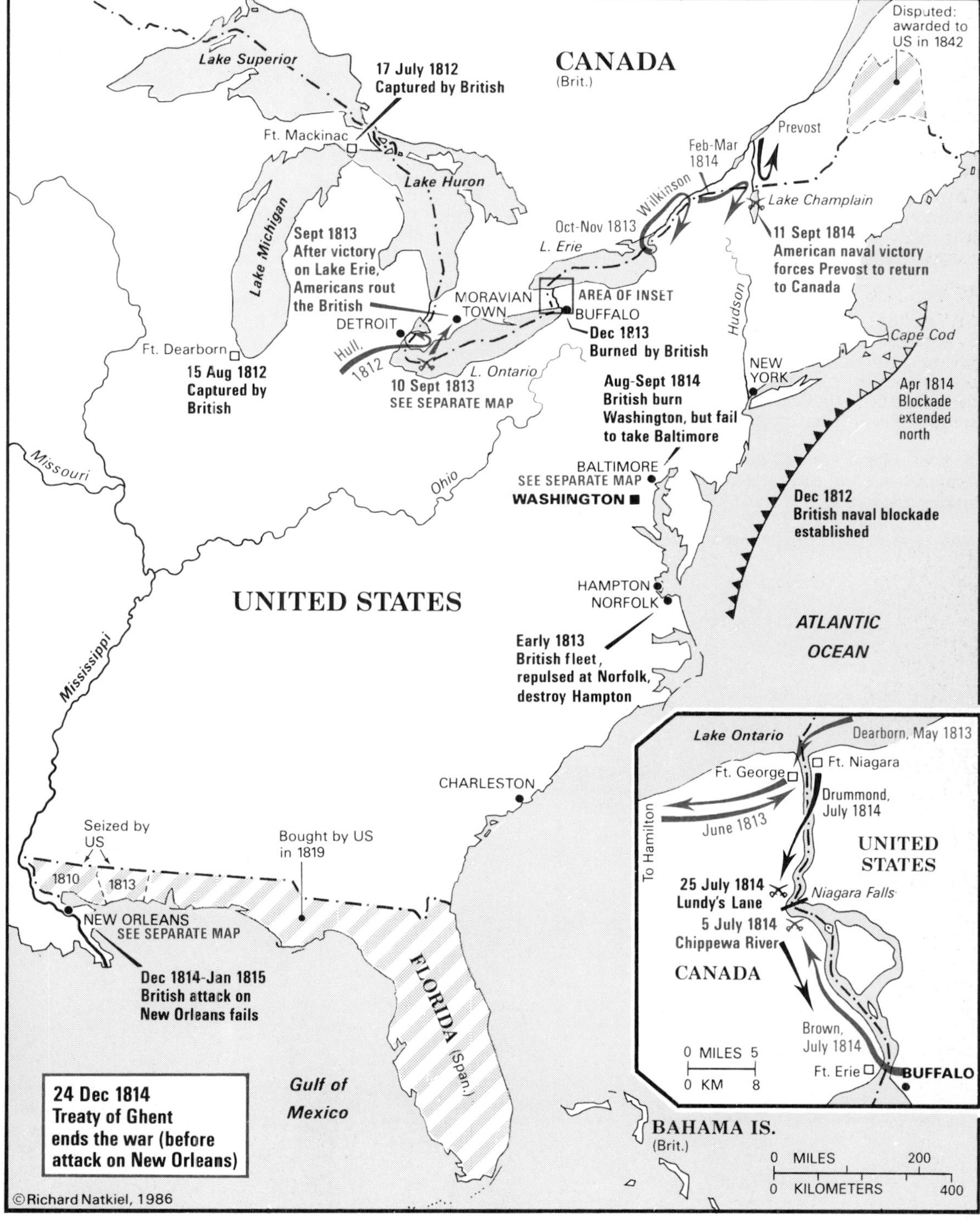

Right: A general map of the War of 1812.

Below: Isaac Brock, the British general to whom Hull surrendered Detroit.

26 DECEMBER 1812

War of 1812: Blockade The British Admiralty officially declares a naval blockade of Chesapeake and Delaware Bays. By 1813 the blockade will have done serious harm to US trade and will have largely confined US warships to their ports.

29 DECEMBER 1812

War of 1812: Naval In a naval engagement off the Brazilian coast American Captain William Bainbridge's 44-gun frigate USS *Constitution* destroys the British 38-gun frigate *Java*. The sight of British cannonballs bouncing off the sides of the *Constitution* gains for her the name of 'Old Ironsides.'

22 JANUARY 1813

War of 1812: Battle of Raisin River American militiamen led by General James Winchester are decisively defeated by a combined British-Indian force in the Battle of Raisin River, at Frenchtown, at the western end of Lake Erie. Some 500 Americans are taken prisoner.

4 MARCH 1813

National James Madison is inaugurated for his second term as president of the United States.

27 MARCH 1813

War of 1812: Lake Erie American Captain Oliver Hazard Perry arrives in Presque Isle (Michigan), where he will supervise the construction of a flotilla initially consisting of two brigs, a schooner, and three gunboats, in order to challenge the British command of Lake Erie.

15 APRIL 1813

War of 1812: The South American forces led by General James Wilkinson capture the Spanish fort at Mobile (Alabama) being used by the British. The Americans will occupy the Mobile region of West Florida between the Pearl and Perdido Rivers.

27 APRIL 1813

War of 1812: Burning of York A combined American military and naval force captures the 600-man British garrison at York, near present-day Toronto. The Americans set fire to the government buildings in what is at this time the capital of upper Canada. This incendiary destruction will serve as motivation for the British to burn Washington DC in 1814.

1-9 MAY 1813

War of 1812: Frontier Shawnee chief Tecumseh and the British lay siege to Fort Meigs, opposite the town of present-day Maumee, Ohio. The fort is successfully defended by General William Henry Harrison.

27 MAY 1813

War of 1812: Capture of Fort George American General Winfield Scott's 4000-man force captures the 1600-man British garrison of Fort George, near the eastern mouth of the Niagara River as it empties into Lake Ontario. The British withdraw from Lake Erie, thereby permitting Captain Oliver Hazard Perry to remove five naval vessels from the Black Rock shipyard and to take them to Presque Isle to reinforce the flotilla that is under construction.

28-29 MAY 1813

War of 1812: Battle of Sackett's Harbor At Sackett's Harbor, near the mouth of Lake Ontario, American General Jacob Brown turns back a British force led by Sir George Prevost, the governor-general of Canada.

1 JUNE 1813

War of 1812: Naval The 38-gun American frigate *Chesapeake*, commanded by Captain James Lawrence, is captured by the British 38-gun frigate *Shannon*, commanded by Captain Philip Broke, following a pitched naval battle that takes place 30 miles off Boston Harbor. The mortally wounded Lawrence exhorts his crew with the words, 'Don't give up the ship,' which will become the rallying cry of the American Navy. This is the most important victory won by the British Navy during the war.

6 JUNE 1813

War of 1812: Battle of Stoney Creek Near Hamilton, Ontario, at Stoney Creek, the retreating British General John Vincent leads 700 men in an attack on the 2000-man American pursuing force. The British capture two American generals, William H. Winder and John Chandler, and force the Americans to fall back to Lake George.

Captain James Lawrence of the frigate USS *Chesapeake* is killed during the duel with HBM *Shannon*. The loss of the *Chesapeake* put an end to a string of American victories in single-ship actions in 1812-13.

On 10 September 1813 US Commodore Oliver Hazard Perry defeated a British naval force on Lake Erie in a long, bloody, strategically vital battle.

2 AUGUST 1813

War of 1812: Frontier In Ohio the British attack on Fort Stephenson at present-day Fremont, Ohio, is turned back by a successful defense led by Major George Croghan.

4 AUGUST 1813

War of 1812: Lake Erie On Lake Erie, Captain Oliver Hazard Perry floats the heavier ships of his newly-constructed American flotilla into deep waters off the island of Put-in-Bay while the British blockading squadron is on another part of the lake.

30 AUGUST 1813

Creek War Mississippi Valley Creek Indians led by William Weatherford, also known as Chief Red Eagle, attack Fort Mims, near Mobile (Alabama). Families in the vicinity have taken refuge in the unprotected stockade. All but 36 of the 553 inhabitants are massacred. This massacre opens the Creek War. Andrew Jackson, major general of the Tennessee militia, calls up a 2000-man volunteer force.

10 SEPTEMBER 1813

War of 1812: Battle of Lake Erie American Captain Oliver Hazard Perry leads his makeshift nine-vessel flotilla to victory over the smaller but heavier British squadron commanded by Captain Robert H. Barclay. Following this victory, which gains control of Lake Erie, Perry sends the message to General William Henry Harrison that, 'We have met the enemy and they are ours; two ships, two brigs, one sloop, one schooner.'

18 SEPTEMBER 1813

War of 1812: Evacuation of Detroit With the loss of naval supremacy on Lake Erie, British General Henry A. Proctor is forced to evacuate Detroit, over the protests of Tecumseh. The American forces of General Harrison follow in hot pursuit.

5 OCTOBER 1813

War of 1812: Battle of the Thames At the Thames River, near present-day Chatham, Ohio, American General Harrison defeats the retreating forces of British and Indians. Tecumseh is killed in the battle, leading to the collapse of the Indian confederacy.

9 NOVEMBER 1813

Creek War Major General Andrew Jackson destroys the Creek Indian village of Talladega in present-day Alabama, killing more than 500 Indian warriors.

11 NOVEMBER 1813

War of 1812: Battle of Chrysler's Farm American General James Wilkison's force is soundly defeated by British forces led by Colonel J. W. Morrison at Chrysler's Farm, some 90 miles southwest of Montreal. On 13 November Wilkison will enter winter quarters at French Mills on the Salmon River.

29-30 DECEMBER 1813

War of 1812: Burning of Buffalo A 1500-man British force led by General Gordon Drummond burns Buffalo, New York, and the nearby strategically important Black Rock Naval Yard, destroying both ships and stores.

30 DECEMBER 1813

War of 1812: Peace Negotiations Bearing a truce flag, the British schooner *Bramble* arrives off Annapolis, Maryland, carrying peace dispatches from England.

22 JANUARY 1814

Creek War in the Creek Indian War, Tennessee militia forces are repulsed at Emuckfaw. The militia will also be defeated at Enotachopco Creek on 24 January and at Calibee Creek on 27 January.

27 JANUARY 1814

National Congress passes legislation authorizing a United States Army of 62,773 men. At this time the effective strength of the regular army stands at about 11,000 men.

27 MARCH 1814

Creek War: Battle of Horseshoe Bend In the Creek Indian War, Tennessee militia forces led by Andrew Jackson and his subordinate General John Coffee achieve a decisive victory over the Creeks and their Cherokee allies at the Battle of Horseshoe Bend, on the Tallapoosa River in present-day Alabama. This battle effectively ends the Creek War.

6 APRIL 1814

International In France, Napoleon Bonaparte is overthrown, thus freeing Great Britain to concentrate her energies upon the American war. Some 14,000 British veterans of the Napoleonic campaigns will be sent to fight in America.

3 JULY 1814

War of 1812: Capture of Fort Erie American General Jacob Brown captures Fort Erie.

5 JULY 1814

War of 1812: Battle of Chippewa American General Winfield Scott defeats a British force at Chippewa, 16 miles north of Fort Erie.

25 JULY 1814

War of 1812: Battle of Lundy's Lane In the most violent battle of the war, American General Jacob Brown's 2600 men engage 3000 British soldiers in an indecisive five-hour conflict at the village of Lundy's Lane, near Niagara Falls. Following the battle the Americans withdraw to Fort Erie.

2 AUGUST 1814

War of 1812: Siege of Fort Erie British forces begin a siege of Fort Erie, the refuge of 2000 American troops.

8 AUGUST 1814

War of 1812: Peace Negotiations In the Flemish town of Ghent peace discussions begin. The American peace commissioners are John Quincy Adams, J. A. Bayard, Henry Clay, Albert Gallatin and Johnathan Russell. The British are represented by Lord Gambier, Henry Goulburn and William Adams. Each side will alter its demands, depending on the most recent news from the field of battle.

19 AUGUST 1814

War of 1812: Washington Campaign Four thousand British troops land at Benedict, Maryland. Their commander is General Robert Ross, a veteran of the Napoleonic Wars. The goal of his force is to seize and destroy the gunboats in the Patuxent River and to conduct raids on Washington and Alexandria.

24 AUGUST 1814

War of 1812: Washington Campaign At the Battle of Bladensburg, Maryland, British General Robert Ross routs some 7000 hastily assembled American troops, thus opening the way for Ross to enter the American capital city of Washington.

24-25 AUGUST 1814

War of 1812: Burning of Washington General Ross' British force marches into Washington unopposed, as United States Army and government officials flee to Virginia. In retaliation for the earlier American burning of York, Ontario, the British set fire to the Capitol, the White House, most government buildings and a number of private houses. A storm forces the British to withdraw and board their ships on the Patuxent River.

11 SEPTEMBER 1814

War of 1812: Battle of Lake Champlain American naval commander Captain Thomas McDonough, commanding an 86-gun squadron of four vessels and 10 gunboats, soundly defeats a larger British squadron on Lake Champlain, thereby spoiling British General Sir George Prevost's plans to invade New York and New England via a joint land and water operation moving south down the lake.

A Currier & Ives print of the death of the Shawnee chief Tecumseh at the Battle of the Thames in 1813.

12-14 SEPTEMBER 1814

War of 1812: Bombardment of Fort McHenry The city of Baltimore effectively defends itself against a land and sea attack by British forces. British General Robert Ross is mortally wounded and the British fleet unsuccessfully bombards Fort McHenry from beyond a line of sunken ship hulks. The British withdraw, and on 14 October their army will sail for Jamaica. The bombardment inspires Francis Scott Key to write 'The Star Spangled Banner.'

5 NOVEMBER 1814

War of 1812: Evacuation of Fort Erie American forces evacuate Fort Erie and subsequently destroy the fort, finally abandoning their plans to invade Canada.

13 DECEMBER 1814

War of 1812: New Orleans Campaign A 50-ship British fleet from Jamaica enters Lake Borne, 40 miles to the east of New Orleans. The 7500 British troops aboard are commanded by Sir Edward Pakenham. As the British disembark American General Andrew Jackson proclaims martial law in New Orleans and rushes his main force from Baton Rouge to New Orleans.

23-24 DECEMBER 1814

War of 1812: New Orleans Campaign Andrew Jackson stalls the British advance on New Orleans by making a night attack with 5000 men, supported by bombardment from the 14-gun schooner *Carolina*. This action provides Jackson with time to complete defensive breastworks and fortifications in a dry canal bed outside of the city.

24 DECEMBER 1814

War of 1812: Treaty of Ghent American and British peace commissioners sign the Treaty of Ghent, ending the War of 1812 (at least on paper). The pact provides for the release of prisoners, the restoration of conquered territory and for an arbitration panel to resolve United States-Canadian boundary disputes. Other issues, such as impressment of sailors, blockades, indemnities and military control of the Great Lakes, are left unresolved or are postponed. Meanwhile, the battles will continue for a short while. Just as the beginning of the War of 1812 might have been averted if news could be communicated across the Atlantic immediately, so now will unnecessary battles be fought and lives lost to no avail.

8 JANUARY 1815

War of 1812: Battle of New Orleans The assault on New Orleans is a disaster for Sir Edward Pakenham and his British soldiers. The British make a frontal attack on Jackson's slightly smaller number of Tennessee and Kentucky sharpshooters, who are protected by barricades and earthworks. It is surprising that British military leaders still make the mistake of frontal assault upon entrenched American positions. In half an hour 2036 British soldiers are killed or wounded, and Pakenham is killed. The American casualties number approximately twenty men killed or wounded, less than one percent of the British losses. This spectacular, yet also unnecessary, battle restores a measure of pride to the Americans in their military ability.

11 FEBRUARY 1815

War of 1812: Treaty of Ghent The news of the signing of the Treaty of Ghent finally reaches the United States.

17 FEBRUARY 1815

War of 1812: Treaty of Ghent The Senate unanimously ratifies the Treaty of Ghent, and President Madison officially declares that the War of 1812 is over.

Captain Stephen Decatur, the foremost US naval hero of the first two decades of the nineteenth century.

Fifth US President James Monroe elucidates his 1823 'Monroe Doctrine' to listening cabinet members.

20 FEBRUARY 1815

War of 1812: Naval In what is in some ways her most brilliant action the famous frigate USS *Constitution*, now commanded by Captain Charles Stewart, captures two British warships, the 32-gun *Cyane* and the 20-gun *Levant*, in a single battle. None of the combatants was aware that the war had already ended.

3 MARCH 1815

International Congress passes legislation authorizing hostilities against the Dey of Algiers, who has reinstated the plunder of American shipping during the War of 1812.

10 MAY 1815

International In New York, Captain Stephen Decatur takes command of a 10-ship fleet setting sail for Algiers. His mission is to end the raids of the Barbary pirates on American commercial shipping in the Mediterranean.

17 JUNE 1815

International Commodore Decatur captures the Algerian frigate *Mashouda*. The Algerian Admiral Hammida is killed by cannon shot. Two days later Decatur will capture the 22-gun brig *Estido*, then tow both ships into Algiers harbor and threaten to bombard the city.

30 JUNE 1815

International The forceful actions of American Commodore Decatur lead the Dey of Algiers to sign a treaty agreeing to cease hostilities against American shipping in the Mediterranean, to free all American prisoners without ransom and to end all demands for tribute payments from America. On 26 July Tunis will sign a comparable treaty and on 5 August so will Tripoli.

27 JULY 1816

Indian Warfare In Spanish-held East Florida a United States military expedition destroys Fort Apalachicola at the request of the state of Georgia. The fort had been a refuge for runaway slaves and hostile Indians, both of which were sheltered by the Seminole Indians.

4 MARCH 1817

National James Monroe is inaugurated as the fifth president of the United States.

20 NOVEMBER 1817

First Seminole War The Seminole Indian War begins when settlers attack Florida Indians, and the Indians retaliate by raiding isolated Georgia homesteads. Americans feel that Spain has incited the Seminoles.

16 DECEMBER 1817

First Seminole War In Flordia, General Andrew Jackson, the hero of the Battle of New Orleans, takes command of an expeditionary force to pacify the hostile Seminole Indians. Secretary of War John C. Calhoun instructs Jackson to do whatever is necessary to end the conflict.

6 JANUARY 1818

First Seminole War: Florida Intrusion General Jackson sends a letter through Tennessee congressman John Rhea to President Monroe, suggesting that he can capture Spanish Florida for the United States in a 60-day military campaign. President Monroe's failure to respond to the letter will be taken by Jackson as a sign of tacit approval of the plan.

24 MAY 1818

First Seminole War: Florida Intrusion General Jackson seizes the Spanish post of Pensacola, Florida, ending the First Seminole War in Florida.

12 JANAURY 1819

First Seminole War: Florida Intrusion Congress fails to endorse a report sponsored by Henry Clay, condemning Andrew Jackson's conduct of the First Seminole War.

3 MARCH 1820

Civil War: Approach The Missouri Compromise becomes official with the proposed admission of Maine into the Union as a free state and of Missouri as a slave state, with the exclusion of slavery from the Louisiana Purchase area north of 36° 30′.

22 MARCH 1820

National Stephen Decatur, hero of the Tripolitan War, is shot and killed in a duel with James Barron.

26 SEPTEMBER 1820

National Legendary Indian fighter Daniel Boone dies in Missouri at the age of 85.

1 JULY 1821

Florida Recently-appointed Governor Andrew Jackson officially receives the Florida territory from the Spanish.

30 MAY 1822

Slavery Free black Denmark Vesey and 34 other blacks are hanged in Charleston, South Carolina, for leading a massive slave uprising. In the aftermath of this rebellion strict slave controls will be instituted in the South.

2 DECEMBER 1823

International: Monroe Doctrine In his annual message to Congress President Monroe presents what comes to be called the Monroe Doctrine, proclaiming that the Americas will no longer be open to European colonization. Barely noticed at the time, this doctrine will become of increasing importance after mid-century.

22 MAY 1824

Commerce Congress adopts the high Tariff Act of 1824, promoted by Henry Clay to protect American industry. Tariffs will be a subject of increasing friction between northern and southern states.

1 DECEMBER 1824

National In the presidential election none of the candidates gains a majority: Andrew Jackson receives 99 electoral votes, John Quincy Adams 84, William H. Crawford 41 and Henry Clay 37. Hence the election is thrown into the House of Representatives.

9 FEBRUARY 1825

National The presidential election is decided in the House when Henry Clay throws his votes to Adams.

British General Edward Packenham's death at the Battle of New Orleans, 8 January 1815.

When Adams appoints Clay as Secretary of State, the Jackson faction will take up the cry of 'bargain and corruption' that will help take Jackson into the White House in four years. The Adams-Clay faction will become known as the National Republicans (or Whigs) in the 1830s; the pro-Jackson faction keeps the Democratic-Republican name and will become the Democratic party after 1828.

12 JANUARY 1828

International Mexico and the US sign a treaty setting their common boundary line along the Sabine River.

3 DECEMBER 1828

National After a virulent name-calling campaign Andrew Jackson is chosen president, with 178 electoral votes to 83 for John Quincy Adams. Southerner John C. Calhoun will be Jackson's vice-president but will resign over sectional policy differences.

8 AUGUST 1829

Transportation In Pennsylvania the first steam-powered locomotive in America is run on the Delaware and Hudson Canal Company's tracks. The British-made engine runs at ten miles per hour. The first American engine will run in South Carolina next year, leading to the inauguration of scheduled passenger service on 25 December 1830. The locomotive is destined to have a major impact on the conduct of war.

25 AUGUST 1829

Texas The Mexican government rejects President Jackson's offer to purchase Texas, where thousands of American settlers now live. The US will persist in negotiations on the matter.

12-27 JANUARY 1830

National North-South sectional tensions over issues of slavery and states' rights are escalating year by year. Robert Y. Hayne of South Carolina debates with Daniel Webster of Massachusetts, the nominal subject being the sale of lands in the West but the real subject that of states' rights versus federal power. Hayne supports Southern ideas of state sovereignty and the right of states to nullify federal laws (mainly anti-slavery ones) with which they disagree. Webster responds with what some will call the greatest American oration ever recorded, centering his remarks on the nature of the Union, emphasizing that states derive their power from the Constitution and that the national government reigns over the people. In ringing tones Webster climaxes, 'Liberty and Union, now and forever, one and inseparable!' In April President Jackson will challenge Southerners at a dinner with the toast, 'Our Federal Union – it must be preserved!' Southern pro-slavery Vice-President John C. Calhoun will respond with the toast, 'The Union – next to our liberty, the most dear.'

1 JANUARY 1831

National In Boston radical abolitionist William Lloyd Garrison begins publishing his newspaper *The Liberator*, which will do much to fan the flames of sectionalism in the coming years.

21 AUGUST 1831

Slavery Nat Turner, a pious but radical slave preacher, leads an uprising of slaves in Virginia. About 70 whites are killed before soldiers put down the rebellion. Turner will be executed, along with 12 of his followers. About 100 blacks have been killed in the search for Turner.

6 APRIL-2 AUGUST 1832

Black Hawk War A small-scale war begins when Indian Chief Black Hawk, who has tried to cross with his Sauk and Fox Indians into their old lands in Illinois, is ordered back into Iowa. After his emissaries are shot in cold blood, Black Hawk retires along the Rock River, devastating settlements in the area. Illinois militia forces slaughter most of the warriors on 2 August. Black Hawk himself is captured by the Winnebago Indians, who hand him over to the whites. (Paradoxically, the chief is sent back to his tribe after being honored in Washington.) The Sauk and Fox are delegated lands west of the Mississippi River. Among those who fight in the war are Abraham Lincoln and Jefferson Davis.

5 DECEMBER 1832

National Andrew Jackson, winning an overwhelming victory for the Democrats, is re-elected president with 219 electoral votes to opponent Henry Clay's 49.

12 FEBRUARY 1833

Civil War: Approach In November, South Carolina adopted an ordinance of nullification and threatened to secede over the high Tariff Acts of 1828 and 1832. Today Henry Clay staves off the threat with a Compromise Tariff that placates the South. The bill will soon pass the Senate and House.

An old engraving of the capture of Black Hawk on 2 August 1832. Among the soldiers who fought in Black Hawk's War were Lincoln and Jefferson Davis.

Left: Sauk and Fox Chief Black Hawk
Above: Statesman, lawyer and orator, Daniel Webster.

6 DECEMBER 1833

Civil War: Approach As part of growing, though still minority, abolitionist sentiment, the American Anti-Slavery Society is organized in Philadelphia. Next October a pro-slavery mob will burn many black homes in the city; such mob action will become common in ensuing years.

28 OCTOBER 1834

Indian Affairs The US government demands that the Seminole Indians leave Florida, as demanded by a treaty signed in 1832.

30 JUNE 1835

Mexico President Santa Anna is turning toward a centralist position and expects to rule over all Mexicans, including Texans. This worsens relations between American settlers and the Mexican government, and escalating clashes will result.

6 JULY 1835

Civil War: Approach A mob in Charleston, South Carolina, burns abolitionist literature that a local post office has impounded. Southern states are beginning to pass prohibitory laws against abolitionist tracts; people who distribute them are threatened with death. The matter is abroil in the North as well: in October, a Boston pro-slavery mob will parade abolitionist William Lloyd Garrison through the streets with a rope around his neck.

NOVEMBER 1835

Second Seminole War Under their leader, Osceola, Seminole Indians in Florida resist their scheduled removal to the West, thereby setting off the Second Seminole War. In the first years of this long (until 1843) and frustrating conflict, fought in the dismal swamps of Florida that are familiar to the Indians and unbearable to the whites, the Indians will devastate much of northeast Florida.

28 DECEMBER 1835

Second Seminole War In a major action of the war General Wiley Thompson and his troops are massacred by Seminoles at Fort King, Florida. Also today, Major Dade and 100 of his men are killed at Fort Brooke, Florida.

23 FEBRUARY 1836

Fall of the Alamo Mexican President Santa Anna leads 3000 men in a siege on the Alamo. There, 187 Americans (who have planned to secede rather than give in to Mexican anti-slavery laws) hold off the assault until 6 March, when the Mexicans overwhelm the fort and kill all the defenders – including frontiersman/politician Davy Crockett. The heroic defense of the Alamo, however, inspires the North American settlers to develop their own plan for governing the territory. In March Texas settlers will draw up a declaration of independence, name Sam Houston as commander of their army and adopt a constitution that legalizes slavery.

21 APRIL 1836

Battle of San Jacinto Under General Sam Houston, Texas settlers defeat Santa Anna's pursuing Mexican

The heroes of the Battle of Resaca de la Palma were the US 2nd Dragoons, whose charges, led by bearded Captain May, overran the Mexican batteries.

army at San Jacinto. The Texans will now ratify their new constitution, elect Houston as president and send an envoy to Washington to demand annexation to the US or recognition as an independent republic. Not wishing to goad Mexico further, and with anti-slavery forces not wanting another slave state, Congress will take the latter course in July; annexation will remain a controversial issue for nearly a decade.

7 DECEMBER 1836

National Martin Van Buren, Jackson's second vice-president and protegé, is elected president, with 170 electoral votes to William Henry Harrison's 73.

19 DECEMBER 1837

Civil War: Approach After acrimonious debate and talk of secession by Southern delegates, the House renews and strengthens a 'gag rule' that forbids discussion of abolitionist petitions.

2 DECEMBER 1840

National The first national campaign carried on largely by hoopla and public relations rather than real issues ends in a Whig victory. The Whigs chanted 'Tippecanoe and Tyler Too' for their candidates – Battle of Tippecanoe hero William Henry Harrison and running mate John Tyler. The Whigs take 234 electoral votes to Van Buren's 60. However, Harrison will die in one month, leaving the presidency, in a time of mounting crisis, to the ineffective Southern sympathizer Tyler.

14 AUGUST 1843

Second Seminole War The war peters out after years of massacres by both sides. US forces have captured and shipped west about 3000 Indians (including leader Osceola) and killed 100. However, about 300 Seminoles are still at large in Florida.

4 DECEMBER 1844

National Former Congressman and Tennessee governor James K. Polk defeats Henry Clay for the presidency. Polk is virtually unknown on the national scene, but his aggressive and expansionist views on annexing Texas, acquiring Oregon from the British (represented by the slogan 'Fifty-four Forty or Fight') and securing California from the Mexicans have struck a receptive chord among Americans.

4 JULY 1845

Mexican War: Approach In convention, the former independent Lone Star Republic of Texas votes itself into the Union as a slave state. Mexico has severed diplomatic relations with the US on learning of annexation sentiment. At the end of the year Polk will offer to pay Mexico for Texas and to buy New Mexico and California as well; the result will be a military takeover of Mexico by a faction against selling the territories. Texas will officially be admitted to the Union on 29 December.

12 JANUARY 1846

Mexican War: Approach Having received word of Mexico's refusal to sell territories, President Polk turns immediately to war. He orders General Zachary Taylor to provoke the Mexicans by moving into territory on the Rio Grande that is claimed by both the US and Mexico. Taylor's 'Army of Observation' has nearly 3500 troops, about half the US Army. He will move to the left bank of the river on 28 March and begin building fortifications.

24 APRIL 1846

Mexican War Despite the evident desire of new Mexican President Mariano Paredes to find some face-saving way of avoiding armed conflict, President Polk persists in provoking war. It comes when a small Mexican cavalry unit inflicts a few casualties on US troops blockading a Mexican town. On 26 April General Taylor reports to Washington that 'hostilities may now be considered as commenced.'

MAY 1846

Mexican War: Battle of Resaca de la Palma Mexican forces attack Fort Texas, constructed by Taylor's men. En route to relieve the fort Taylor defeats a group of enemy at Palo Alto on 8 May and then follows the numerically superior Mexicans to attack again at the Battle of Resaca de la Palma on 9 May. In the latter battle the mounted US Second Dragoons turn the tide by a gallant charge on Mexican cannons. Casualties in the fighting are estimated at 39 American dead and 83 wounded, and 262 Mexicans dead, with 355 wounded and 150 captured. The battle makes Taylor a popular hero.

13 MAY 1846

Mexican War Congress approves a declaration of war on Mexico and authorizes recruitment of 50,000 troops and a budget of $10 million. The debate leading to the declaration shows that the war is yet another divisive issue between North and South: Southerners tend to support the war because they hope it will lead to more slave territory, while Northerners oppose the war for the same reason. In addition, many Americans object to the war as a blatant land grab. Among those opposed will be Henry David Thoreau, who, after spending time in jail for refusing to pay a war tax, will write *Civil Disobedience*; studied by later leaders such as Ghandi and Martin Luther King, that brief essay will be one of the most important results of the Mexican War.

6 JUNE 1846

International A dispute has long simmered between the US and Britain over the border between the Oregon Territory and Canada. President Polk, anxious to gain support for the war with Mexico, submits to the Senate a British treaty that extends the international boundary along latitude 40° to Puget Sound and then to the ocean through the Juan de Fuca Strait. The Senate will ratify the treaty on 15 June.

14 JUNE 1846

Mexican War: California Encouraged by the war, North American settlers proclaim the Republic of California. On 7 July, Commodore John Sloat will land at Monterey and claim California for the US.

8 AUGUST 1846

Wilmot Proviso As a rider to an appropriations bill, the House attaches an amendment by Representative David Wilmot forbidding slavery in any territories acquired from Mexico. The Senate will reject the Proviso in February 1847.

13 AUGUST 1846

Mexican War: California US forces take Los Angeles; Commodore David Stockton will then declare that the US has annexed California.

15 AUGUST 1846

Mexican War: Nevada and New Mexico Colonel Stephen Watts Kearny and the First Dragoons seize Las Vegas without Mexican opposition; Kearny announces the annexation of New Mexico by the US. On 18 August he will occupy Santa Fe and set up a temporary government there.

20-24 SEPTEMBER 1846

Mexican War: Capture of Monterey General Taylor takes Monterey, Mexico, in four days of fierce fighting.

22 SEPTEMBER 1846

Mexican War: California A group of Mexican Californians revolt against the US and take control of the territory south of San Luis Obispo.

6 DECEMBER 1846

Mexican War: Battle of San Pascual Mexican Californians inflict a humiliating defeat on Colonel Kearny and his Dragoons at San Pascual. Nonetheless, Kearny will occupy San Diego on 12 December.

3 JANUARY 1847

Mexican War: Command General Winfield Scott, hero of the War of 1812, takes command of the Gulf expedition in Mexico.

General Winfield Scott and his victorious troops parade before the cathedral in Mexico City on 14 September 1847, climaxing a brilliant campaign.

10 JANUARY 1847

Mexican War: California Kearny, now a general, takes Los Angeles after two skirmishes near the San Gabriel River. This ends hostilities in California. On 13 January the remaining Mexican forces in the area sign the Treaty of Cahuenga.

22-23 FEBRUARY 1847

Mexican War: Battle of Buena Vista Refusing Mexican General Santa Anna's demand for American surrender, General Taylor, with 4800 men, soundly defeat 15,000 enemy at Buena Vista after a hard fought, see-saw battle. The Americans now have control over northern Mexico, and the Mexicans retreat toward the capital at Mexico City.

29 MARCH 1847

Mexican War: Battle of Vera Cruz After two weeks of attacks from land and sea General Scott defeats Santa Anna's Mexicans at Vera Cruz, the most powerful fortress in the Western Hemisphere.

APRIL-MAY 1847

Mexican War: Mexico City Campaign Moving inland from Vera Cruz towards Mexico City, Scott inflicts a further defeat on Santa Anna at Cerro Gordo on 18 April, then takes Jalapa on the 19th and Puebla on 15 May.

20 AUGUST 1847

Mexican War: Battle of Churubusco In spirited fighting General Scott wins Churubusco, near Mexico City. Scott's military leadership in this campaign has been brilliant.

SEPTEMBER 1847

Mexican War: Fall of Mexico City General Scott takes Molino del Rey after a day-long battle on 8 September. After defeating superior forces in a fortified castle in the Battle of Chapultepec on the 13th Scott marches into Mexico City on the 14th, climaxing the whirlwind campaign he began in May at Vera Cruz. The Mexicans immediately agree to negotiate.

2 FEBRUARY 1848

Mexican War: Treaty of Guadalupe Hidalgo The US signs the treaty ending the war with Mexico, receiving over 500,000 square miles that include what will become the states of California, Nevada, Utah, most of New Mexico and Arizona, and parts of Wyoming and Colorado. Texas is also conceded to the US, with the boundary at the Rio Grande. The US agrees to pay Mexico $15 million and an additional $3.25 million in claims around the Rio Grande. The Mexican War makes the United States a transcontinental republic.

7 NOVEMBER 1848

National General Zachary Taylor, a Whig and hero of the Mexican War, is elected president over the Democrats' Lewis Cass of Michigan. Anti-slavery Free Soil Party candidate Martin Van Buren contributed to Taylor's victory by taking a quarter of a million Democratic votes.

29 JANUARY 1850

Compromise of 1850 Henry Clay offers to the Senate a series of resolutions that will eventually become the Compromise of 1850, another in a string of enactments that manage to stave off secession for a time. The resolutions involve admitting California (which is now roaring with a gold rush) as a free state on the grounds that this is the people's own wish; thus the bill approves the principle of 'popular sovereignty' over the matter of slavery in each state. Another element of the bill, placed there to appease slaveowners, is a strict fugitive slave law. With the support of staunch antislavery Representative Daniel Webster, the Compromise will pass Congress in September.

9 JULY 1850

National President Taylor dies of cholera, and Vice-President Millard Fillmore assumes the office.

MARCH 1852

Civil War: Approach Harriet Beecher Stowe's *Uncle Tom's Cabin* is published. Within a year it will sell over a million copies, and its critical portrait of slave life arouses both sides of the slavery question.

2 NOVEMBER 1852

National Pro-slavery Democrat Franklin Pierce defeats Whig General Winfield Scott for the presidency with 254 electoral votes to Scott's 42.

26 MAY 1854

Civil War: Approach After much debate Senator Stephen A. Douglas's Kansas-Nebraska Act passes Congress. It creates two new territories that will be allowed to make their own decision as to slavery. The effect of the Act will be to arouse violent protest from both sides of the issue and to provoke much violence in Kansas over the next years. In February the new Republican Party began forming among anti-slavery opponents of the proposed Kansas-Nebraska bill.

21 MAY 1856

Civil War: Approach Kansas is now virtually in a state of civil war, with separate pro- and anti-slavery governments in violent competition. Today, pro-slavery men attack opposing settlers in Lawrence and kill one man. In retaliation, a band led by fiery abolitionist John Brown will massacre five pro-slavers at Pottawotamie Creek. The territory has become known as 'Bleeding Kansas.'

4 NOVEMBER 1856

National Democrat James Buchanan wins the presidency over Republican John Frémont after a campaign fought openly along the lines of South versus North, pro-slavery versus anti-slavery. Buchanan wins 14 slave states and four free, while Frémont wins 11 free states. The Whig Party, whose candidate, Millard Fillmore, wins only one state, is falling apart as sectionalism rises. For his part, Buchanan will support the idea of popular sovereignty and condemn violence, but he will offer no program or philosophy to stem the tide of violence and sectionalism.

6 MARCH 1857

Civil War: Approach The conservative Supreme Court does its part to bring war closer with the *Dred Scott* decision, ruling that a black slave, even though he once lived in a free state, remains a slave. The most inflammatory aspect of the decision states that slaves are not citizens but are property, and thus the owners' property rights are protected by the Constitution. The decision inflames abolitionists.

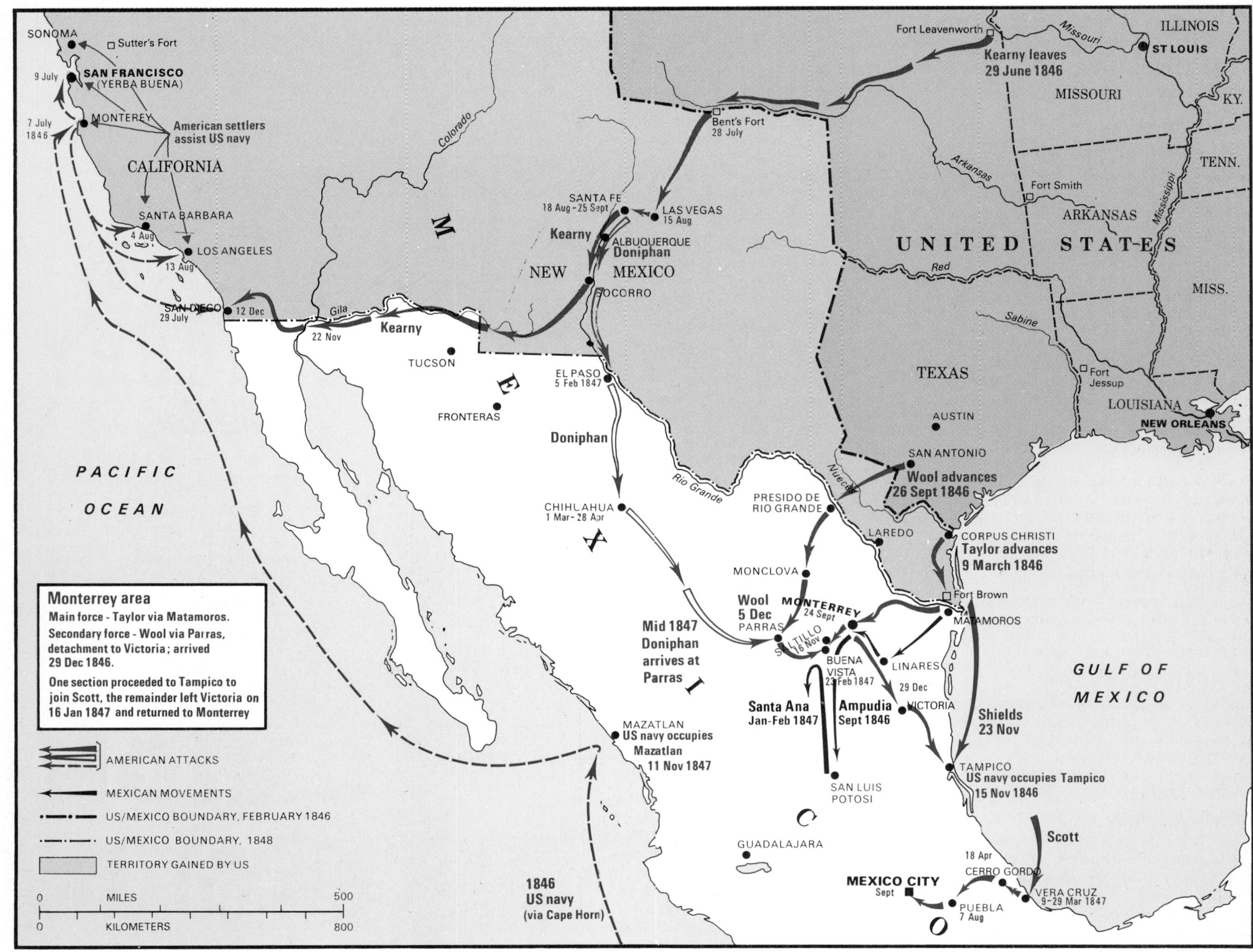

A general map of the Mexican War showing the major campaigns in Mexico itself, as well as those in California and New Mexico.

Inside the captured US arsenal at Harper's Ferry John Brown and his raiders prepare for attack by federal troops, 18 October 1859.

AUGUST-OCTOBER 1858

National: Lincoln-Douglas Debates Republican Senate candidate Abraham Lincoln and incumbent Democratic Senator Stephen A. Douglas meet in a series of seven debates across Illinois. Lincoln is little known outside the state, and Douglas is a national figure. Lincoln takes a strong stand against slavery on moral, social and political grounds, while Douglas defends not slavery as such but the right of Americans to vote their preference (he was the author of the Kansas-Nebraska Act, which confirmed the idea of popular sovereignty). Douglas will be re-elected to his seat, but Lincoln emerges on the national stage as an articulate spokesman for the anti-slavery position.

4 OCTOBER 1859

Regional Kansans vote by a wide margin to ratify an anti-slavery constitution; this further alarms the slaveholding states.

16-18 OCTOBER 1859

Civil War: Approach: John Brown's Raid Crazed abolitionist John Brown leads an armed group of five blacks and 16 whites (including his three sons) in seizing a Federal arsenal at Harper's Ferry, Virginia. He is trying to capture arms for a vague plan to touch off a slave insurrection. Brown and four survivors are captured by US Marines under Colonel Robert E. Lee. Within six weeks Brown will be tried for conspiracy and treason, convicted and hanged. As Brown hoped, his actions have an incendiary effect both on abolitionists and on the South (the latter's greatest fear is of a slave insurrection). Brown's raid and his death light the fuse that eventually touches off the Civil War.

2 FEBRUARY 1860

Civil War: Approach Jefferson Davis, now a Senator from Mississippi, presents resolutions to the Senate to protect slavery and slaveholders in the territories. The resolutions are mainly addressed to the Democratic members in hopes of persuading the coming Democratic convention to reject Stephen Douglas and his concept of popular sovereignty.

27 FEBRUARY 1860

Civil War: Approach Abraham Lincoln speaks to the Young Men's Central Republican Union and describes the power of the Constitution in controlling slavery in the territories.

23 APRIL-3 MAY 1860

Civil War: Approach The Democratic party holds its convention in Charleston, South Carolina. When a pro-slavery platform is rejected, delegates from eight Southern states walk out. The remaining delegates are unable to agree on a candidate, and the convention adjourns.

6-18 MAY 1860

Civil War: Approach In Chicago the Republican party nominates, on its third ballot, Abraham Lincoln as its presidential candidate. To gain the nomination Lincoln has had to present himself as moderate on the question of slavery. The party's platform declares that it is for prohibiting slavery in the territories but against interfering with it in the states.

18-23 JUNE 1860

Civil War: Approach The Democratic party reconvenes, this time in Baltimore, and after another walkout by the anti-Douglas Southerners, he is nominated for the presidency.

28 JUNE 1860

Civil War: Approach Convening in Baltimore, disaffected Southern Democrats nominate their own candidate for president – the current vice-president John C. Breckinridge of Kentucky. The platform, naturally, calls for preservation of slavery.

JULY-OCTOBER 1860

Civil War: Approach As extremists of both sides fan the flames of discontent, the sole issues in the presidential campaign are slavery and sectionalism. Of the candidates, only Stephen Douglas travels widely, trying to broaden his appeal, but it soon becomes clear that his party is split and his hopes are slim. Southern spokesmen grimly prophesy secession if Lincoln is elected.

6 NOVEMBER 1860

National Abraham Lincoln is elected president with a clear majority of electoral college votes but only a plurality in the popular vote. Some Southern leaders now begin speaking of secession as inevitable.

20 DECEMBER 1860

Secession As Congress desperately tries to find a compromise that will cool sectional tensions, a state convention in South Carolina takes the epochal step of seceding from the Union.

26 DECEMBER 1860

Civil War: Approach In a move whose ominousness is clear to all, Major Robert Anderson, commanding Federal garrisons in the harbor of Charleston, South Carolina, moves his forces from Fort Moultrie to the more defensible Fort Sumter in the middle of the harbor.

27 DECEMBER 1860

Civil War: Approach South Carolina state troops seize both Fort Moultrie and Castle Pinckney.

31 DECEMBER 1860

Civil War: Approach Incumbent President Buchanan refuses a request from South Carolina to remove Federal troops from Charleston, declaring that Fort Sumter will be defended "against all hostile attacks." He authorizes a relief ship to the fort.

3 JANUARY 1861

Civil War: Approach The state of Georgia takes over Federal Fort Pulaski.

5 JANUARY 1861

Civil War: Approach The state of Alabama seizes Federal Forts Morgan and Gaines. In New York the ship *Star of the West* sails toward Charleston Harbor with troops and supplies.

6-7 JANUARY 1861

Civil War: Approach The state of Florida takes over a Federal arsenal and Fort Marion, meeting virtually no opposition.

8 JANUARY 1861

Washington President Buchanan urges adoption of the Crittenden Compromise, a Senate bill which would use the Missouri Compromise line to divide proposed slave and non-slave territories. This compromise satisfies no one and will quickly die.

9 JANUARY 1861

Civil War: Approach A state convention in Mississippi votes to secede from the Union. In Charleston harbor the ship *Star of the West*, sent to reinforce Fort Sumter, is fired on by one of the Southern batteries that have appeared in the harbor. The ship turns back.

10 JANUARY 1861

Secession Florida secedes from the Union.

11 JANUARY 1861

Secession Alabama secedes from the Union.

12 JANUARY 1861

Washington Mississippi representatives walk out of the House.
Military Having seized two Federal forts and a naval yard, Florida troops demand the surrender of Fort Pickens.

14 JANUARY 1861

Military Fort Taylor at Key West, Florida, is garrisoned by US troops; it will remain an important Federal base throughout the war.

19 JANUARY 1861

Secession Georgia secedes from the Union.

21 JANUARY 1861

Washington Five Southern Senators, including Jefferson Davis, leave the Senate after emotional farewell speeches.

26 JANUARY 1861

Secession Louisiana secedes from the Union.

29 JANUARY 1861

Washington Congress closes a long and bitter chapter of sectional rivalry by admitting Kansas as a slave-free state.

1 FEBRUARY 1861

Washington William H. Seward, Secretary of State-designate, receives a letter from Lincoln saying "I am inflexible" in reference to extending slavery in the territories.

4 FEBRUARY 1861

Secession While a Peace Convention begins meetings in Washington in a futile attempt to save the Union, a convention of seceding states – presently

A 20 December 1860 poster announces the secession of South Carolina from the Union.

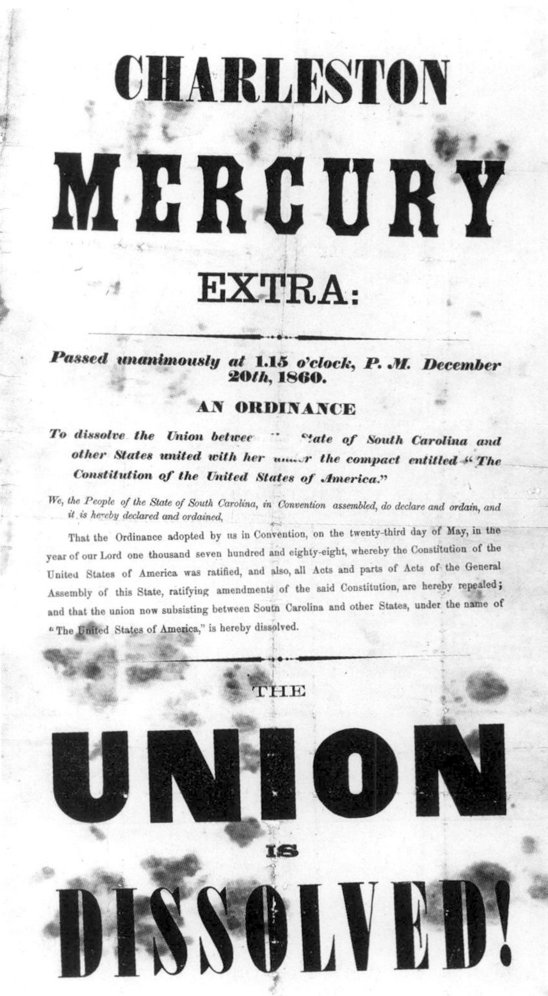

CHARLESTON

MERCURY

EXTRA:

Passed unanimously at 1.15 o'clock, P. M. December 20th, 1860.

AN ORDINANCE

To dissolve the Union betwee[illegible] [illegible]tate of South Carolina and other States united with her [illegible] the compact entitled "The Constitution of the United States of America."

We, the People of the State of South Carolina, in Convention assembled, do declare and ordain, and it is hereby declared and ordained,

That the Ordinance adopted by us in Convention, on the twenty-third day of May, in the year of our Lord one thousand seven hundred and eighty-eight, whereby the Constitution of the United States of America was ratified, and also, all Acts and parts of Acts of the General Assembly of this State, ratifying amendments of the said Constitution, are hereby repealed; and that the union now subsisting between Soutn Carolina and other States, under the name of "The United States of America," is hereby dissolved.

THE

UNION

IS

DISSOLVED!

Onetime US secretary of war Jefferson Davis was elected president of the Confederacy in 1861. He was never as effective a war leader as Lincoln.

Alabama, Florida, Georgia, Louisiana, Mississippi and South Carolina – meet at a convention in Montgomery, Alabama, to form the provisional government of the Confederate States of America.

8 FEBRUARY 1861

Secession The Montgomery convention, called the Confederate Provisional Congress, provisionally adopts a Confederate Constitution. Though it otherwise closely follows the United States Constitution, the document strongly protects slavery.

9 FEBRUARY 1861

Secession The Confederate Provisional Congress unanimously elects Jefferson Davis, a former US Congressman, Secretary of War and Senator, as provisional president of the Confederate States of America. Davis's vice-president is Alexander Stephens, a brilliant but feisty former Congressman who will become a major obstruction to his president. The Congress also decrees that US laws not inconsistent with the new Confederate Constitution are to remain in force.

12 FEBRUARY 1861

Secession Lincoln travels to his inauguration in Washington. He speaks before various groups along the way, calling for allegiance to the Union but trying to avoid hitting sensitive nerves. Meanwhile, Confederate President-elect Jefferson Davis is making his way from his Mississippi plantation to the Confederate Congress, likewise speaking to crowds along the way. Davis observes that a possible outcome of secession is war.

18 FEBRUARY 1861

The Confederacy In Montgomery, Alabama, Jefferson Davis is inaugurated provisional president of the Confederate States of America. "Dixie," the unofficial anthem of the South, is played at the ceremonies.

19 FEBRUARY 1861

Secession A Confederate Cabinet takes shape in Montgomery, Alabama. Secretaries of State, War and the Treasury (Toombs, Walker and Memminger) are joined by Attorney General Judah Bejamin, Secretary of the Navy Stephen Mallory and Postmaster General John Reagan. Meanwhile, in New York, Lincoln, on his way to Washington, is hailed by a crowd of 500,000 as he passes through the city.

22 FEBRUARY 1861

National President-elect Lincoln receives an assassination threat in Baltimore and leaves by a secret train for Washington.

23 FEBRUARY 1861

Secession As the President-elect arrives in Washington, Texas secedes from the Union.

27 FEBRUARY 1861

Secession New Confederate President Jefferson Davis appoints three ambassadors to approach officials in Washington with offers of peaceful negotiation of differences based on Southern independence. Davis also receives word from Governor Pickens in Charleston, South Carolina, who insists on the need to take over Fort Sumter.

28 FEBRUARY 1861

Secession North Carolina votes, by the slimmest of margins, not to hold a convention to consider secession.

3 MARCH 1861

Military Aged General Winfield Scott, head of the Federal Army, indicates in a letter to Secretary of State Seward that relief of Fort Sumter is not practical.

4 MARCH 1861

National Abraham Lincoln is inaugurated 16th president of the United States, with Hannibal Hamlin as his vice-president. In spite of his personal anti-slavery convictions, Lincoln in his inaugural address is generally conciliatory, stating, 'I have no purpose . . . to interfere with the institution of slavery.' Nonetheless, he warns, 'No state, on its own mere action, can get out of the Union,' thus defining the conflict as concerning secession, not slavery. After placing the responsibility for war on Southern actions – 'in *your* hands, my dissatisfied fellow countrymen, and not in *mine*, is the momentous issue of civil war' – Lincoln concludes on a hopeful peroration: "The mystic chords of memory will yet swell the chorus of the Union, when again touched, as they surely will be, by the better angels of our nature." Unfortunately, these words do little to pacify the secessionist states.

5 MARCH 1861

Military President Lincoln and General Scott confer about the urgent situation at Fort Sumter, which cannot be maintained without provisions and reinforcements.

11 MARCH 1861

The Confederacy The Confederate Congress adopts a Constitution based on the US Constitution but stressing states' rights and protecting the institution of slavery.

13 MARCH 1861

Washington Wishing to avoid any semblance of recognizing the Confederacy, Lincoln tells Secretary of State Seward to refuse meetings with the peace ambassadors sent by Jefferson Davis.

18 MARCH 1861

Secession A convention in slave-holding Arkansas narrowly defeats a secession resolution but agrees to a popular vote on the question.

29 MARCH 1861

Washington After conferring exhaustively with government and military officials, Lincoln finally announces his plans for Fort Sumter: There will be no evacuation, but rather ships will be sent to supply and support the troops already there.

1 APRIL 1861

Washington President Lincoln receives a peremptory letter from Secretary of State Seward suggesting various devious foreign policy maneuvers, that Fort Sumter ought to be abandoned and that Seward might assume responsibility for dealing with the Confederacy. Seeing the letter correctly as a power play by Seward, Lincoln tactfully but firmly reminds his secretary who is president.

5 APRIL 1861

Washington The Navy orders ships to sail for Fort Sumter with provisions.

6 APRIL 1861

Washington The US State Department advises South Carolina Governor Pickens that it is going to provision rather than reinforce Fort Sumter, on condition that there be no resistance to the landing of the supplies.

7 APRIL 1861

Secession General P.G.T. Beauregard, commander of Southern forces in Charleston Harbor, sends word to Fort Sumter's commander, Major Robert A. Anderson, that no further communication between the Fort and Charleston will be permitted.

11 APRIL 1861

The Confederacy Anticipating the arrival of the supply ships for Fort Sumter, messengers from General Beauregard go by boat to the fort to demand the immediate surrender of the garrison, which is now encircled by Confederate batteries. Major Anderson refuses, but the Confederate government decides to give him a day to reconsider so as to 'avoid the effusion of blood.'

12 APRIL 1861

Civil War: Battle of Fort Sumter The war begins with an orderly and gentlemanly process. In the early morning hours Confederate messengers return to Fort Sumter to ask Major Anderson for a time of probable evacuation. Anderson estimates noon of 15 April as the time when he would have to evacuate if he receives no further supplies or orders from Washington. The Confederacy, knowing that supplies are probably on the way, refuses to wait and notifies Anderson that hostilities will begin in one hour. The messengers leave, and Anderson gives orders to his men. At 4:30 AM, in Fort Johnson on James Island, Captain G.S. James pulls the lanyard on a cannon. As fire erupts from all the Confederate batteries around the harbor, Federal return fire is only token. The barrage continues throughout the

Beneath the still-unfinished dome of the Capitol Abraham Lincoln is inaugurated 16th president of the United States on 4 March 1861.

G-in-C of the Union army at the outbreak of the Civil War was veteran soldier Winfield Scott.

day and night. During the day the Federal supply vessels are observed out at sea, but they do not try to reach Fort Sumter.

13 APRIL 1861

Civil War: Battle of Fort Sumter As the Confederate barrage continues, Major Anderson, running out of ammunition and food and with no casualties, decides that he and his men have done their duty. He surrenders to a Confederate delegation at 2:30 PM.

14 APRIL 1861

Civil War: Battle of Fort Sumter The Confederates have agreed that Major Anderson's garrison may fire 100 guns before evacuating Fort Sumter. During this salute some sparks accidentally ignite a cannon cartridge as it is being loaded, killing Private Daniel Hough, who becomes the first death of the war. The Federals march out and sail off to a heroes' welcome in New York; with equal ceremony, the Confederacy marches in. Fort Sumter will remain in the South's hands to the end of the war, despite massive Federal shelling, a potent symbol to both sides.

15 APRIL 1861

Civil War President Lincoln, declaring not war, but rather a state of 'insurrection,' calls for 75,000 volunteers for three months' service.

17 APRIL 1861

Secession In the wake of Sumter, Virginia secedes from the Union, and Missouri and Tennessee decline to send volunteers. The border slave states of Kentucky and North Carolina will also refuse to send volunteers; holding the border states in the Union will require all Lincoln's political skill, but he will keep them loyal.

19 APRIL 1861

Civil War The President orders a blockade of all ports in the Confederacy. Gradually reducing Southern supply imports, the blockade will be an increasingly significant element of Northern strategy.

20 APRIL 1861

The Confederacy After agonized consideration, Colonel Robert E. Lee resigns his US Army commission and assumes a commission for the Confederacy, declaring that he could not raise his hand against his native state of Virginia.

21 APRIL 1861

Secession Anti-secessionists meet in western Virginia, resolving to support the Union despite the stand taken by the remainder of the state.

27 APRIL 1861

Washington In a bold and controversial action, Lincoln suspends the writ of habeas corpus in an area stretching from Philadelphia to Washington, and then leaves General Scott in charge of handling any protest arising out of his action. Lincoln does this in part to subdue the rioting that has been plaguing Baltimore and disrupting troop transport.
The Confederacy Richmond, Virginia, is offered by the Virginia Convention as a capital for the Confederacy, to replace Montgomery, Alabama.

29 APRIL 1861

Secession The State legislature of slaveholding Maryland repudiates secession by a wide margin.

30 APRIL 1861

The West Federal troops evacuate Indian Territory forts, leaving the Five Civilized Nations – Cherokees, Chicksaws, Choctaws, Creeks and Seminoles – virtually under Confederate jurisdiction and control.

1 MAY 1861

Civil War: Eastern Theater Confederate troops under Colonel Thomas J. Jackson are sent to Harper's Ferry, Virginia, by General Robert E. Lee.
Civil War: Naval Federals seize two Confederate ships in Atlantic waters and the United States Navy blockades the mouth of the James River.

3 MAY 1861

Civil War: Washington Lincoln sends out a call for 42,000 Army volunteers and 18,000 seamen. He also forms the Department of the Ohio, to be commanded by George B. McClellan. General Winfield Scott, General-in-Chief of the Federal Army, suggests that, with the aid of a powerful blockade, it would be possible to envelop the states along the length of the Mississippi River and thereby choke off the insurrection. This 'Anaconda Plan,' as it comes to be known, will not be implemented, though at long length the North will stumble on to the same strategy.
International The Confederacy has sent commissioners to London to meet with the British Foreign Minister in an attempt to gain recognition for the Confederacy. The United States complains to the British Ministry about this meeting.

6 MAY 1861

Secession Arkansas secedes from the Union.
Civil War: The Confederacy Jefferson Davis approves a bill from the Confederate Congress declaring a state of war with the United States.

7 MAY 1861

Border States Pro- and anti-secessionists clash in Nashville, Tennessee, resulting in injuries and one fatality.

10 MAY 1861

Civil War: The Confederacy President Davis orders the purchase of warships and munitions for the Confederacy. Naval Secretary Mallory suggests ironclads as logical additions to the small Confederate Navy, hoping this will enable them to challenge the much stronger Union fleet.
Civil War: The West Missouri state militia clash with Federal troops in St. Louis, Missouri; the Federals subdue the rioters, but 29 people are reportedly killed or fatally injured. Rioting and fatalities will continue into the next day.

13 MAY 1861

International England proclaims neutrality in the conflict, dashing Southern hopes for a foreign ally; France and Spain will soon make similar declarations.

18 MAY 1861

Civil War: Eastern Theater In its first offensive against the South the Union engages rebel batteries at Sewall's Point, Virginia.

20 MAY 1861

Secession A North Carolina convention votes for secession.
The Confederacy The Confederate Congress votes to relocate their capital to Richmond, Virginia.

24 MAY 1861

Civil War: Eastern Theater Federal troops occupy Alexandria, Virginia, in a move to protect Washington; Virginia troops mount little resistance. The first Union combat fatality of the war occurs during this move: 24-year-old Elmer Ellsworth dies in an attempt to remove a Confederate flag from a hotel roof. The man who shot Ellsworth, hotel keeper James Jackson, is then shot by a Union soldier. Both North and South thereby gain martyrs.
Slavery In an action provoking questions as to the disposition of slaves by the North, General Benjamin F. Butler holds three slaves at Fort Monroe. The issue is quickly interpreted as one of whether slaves are to be regarded as contraband of war; this will become an increasingly complex controversy.

27 MAY 1861

Washington In a case testing the legality of Lincoln's suspension of the writ of habeas corpus, Chief Justice Roger B. Taney – who is something of a pro-slaver – decrees the arrest of John Merryman illegal; Merryman has been imprisoned for recruiting Confederate soldiers. It is Lincoln's view that in time of rebellion such virtually dictatorial presidential decrees are required in order to preserve public safety.

29 MAY 1861

Washington Secretary of War Simon Cameron receives Dorothea Dix, accepting her offer of help in setting up hospitals for the Union wounded.

31 MAY 1861

Civil War: The West Union troops, which have evacuated forts in Indian Territory, reach Fort Leavenworth, Kansas, on the Chisholm Trail.
Civil War: The Confederacy General P.G.T. Beauregard is given command of the Confederate Army of the Potomac in northern Virginia.

1 JUNE 1861

Civil War: Eastern Theater Northern Virginia sees fighting at Arlington Mills and Fairfax County Courthouse. Confederate Captain John Q. Marr is killed in the skirmishing, becoming one of the early Southern fatalities.
International British territorial waters and ports are proclaimed off-limits to belligerents carrying spoils of war.

3 JUNE 1861

Civil War: Eastern Theater Union forces surprise Confederates at Phillippi in Western Virginia and

South Carolina batteries bombard US Fort Sumter in Charleston Harbor, 12-13 April 1861.

In May 1861 Lincoln called for 60,000 army and navy volunteers to fight for the Union. Before the war ended about three times that many would be killed.

easily send the Rebels running. This victory will encourage loyalists to form a pro-Union government of West Virginia, permanently dividing the state.

8 JUNE 1861

Secession By popular vote, Tennessee secedes from the Union, the 11th and final state to do so.

10 JUNE 1861

Civil War: Eastern Theater At Bethel Church, Virginia, Federal troops are defeated by aggressive Confederates. Union losses are 18 dead and 53 wounded; Southern losses one dead, seven wounded.

12 JUNE 1861

Civil War: Trans-Mississippi Factional agitation has torn Missouri for weeks; pro-Southern Governor Claiborne calls for 50,000 volunteers to repel what he perceives as a Federal takeover of the state.

14 JUNE 1861

Civil War: Eastern Theater Harper's Ferry, Virginia, is abandoned by Rebels hoping to avoid being cut off by McClellan and Patterson.

17 JUNE 1861

Civil War: Trans-Mississippi Union troops establish themselves at the Missouri state capital of Jefferson City.

1 JULY 1861

Civil War: Washington In order to fill the need for Union troops, the War Department decrees that both Kentucky and Tennessee are to be canvassed for

A general map of Civil War battles and campaigns.

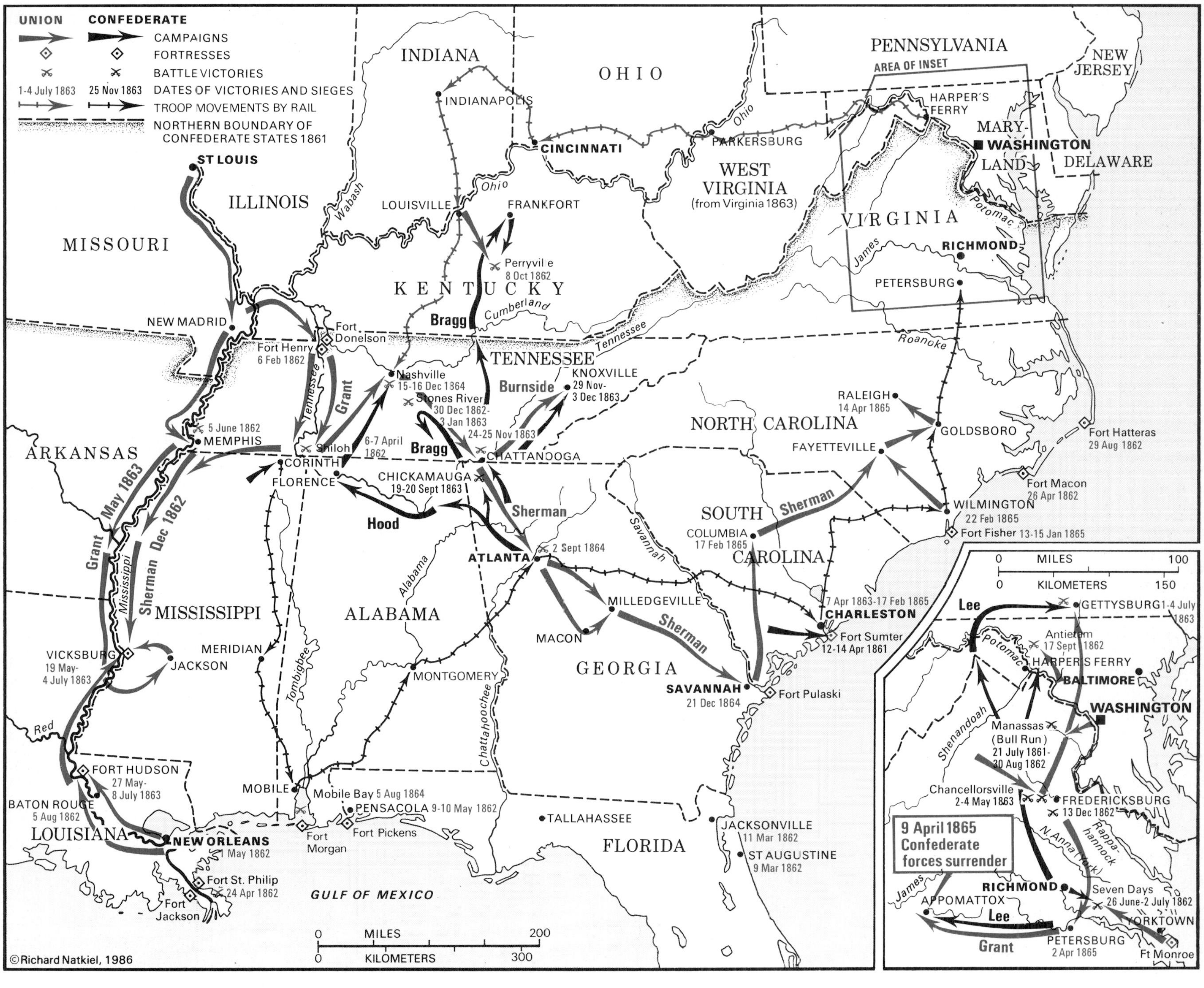

The first Battle of Bull Run, 21 July 1861, was a disaster for the Union and a chilling proof of the superiority of Southern generalship.

volunteers. This is depite the fact that Tennessee has seceded and Kentucky has voted to remain neutral.

2 JULY 1861

Civil War: Eastern Theater Federal troops under General Robert Patterson head for the Shenandoah Valley, where they intend to curtail the movement of Confederates toward Manassas, Virginia. Next day the Southern commander, General Joseph E. Johnston, will pull back.

4 JULY 1861

Civil War: Washington On Independence Day President Lincoln calls a special session of the Twenty-Seventh Congress. He tells them that the North has done everything in its power to maintain peace. Blaming the South for the Fort Sumter affair, the president emphasizes that the questions facing the nation have to do with the United States' maintaining 'its territorial integrity, against its own domestic foes.' He makes a request for an additional 400,000 men for the Union army.

5 JULY 1861

Civil War: Trans-Mississippi Federal forces attack pro-secessionist Missouri troops under the command of Governor Claiborne Jackson. Outnumbering the Federals three to one, the Missouri troops drive back General Franz Sigel and his Union forces. Though Sigel's losses are much lower, the South hails the engagement as a victory.

10 JULY 1861

Civil War: Eastern Theater In western Virginia, General McClellan sends troops under General William S. Rosecrans to intercept Confederates at Rich Mountain, and under General T.A. Morris to do the same at Laurel Hill, Virginia.

11 JULY 1861

Civil War: Eastern Theater Rosecrans defeats the rebels at Rich Mountain, Virginia, and Confederates at Laurel Mountain withdraw upon the attack of General Morris.

13 JULY 1861

Civil War: Eastern Theater At Carrickford, Virginia, Union troops crush Confederate forces, securing McClellan's control of the entire area of West Virginia. In addition to providing a vital communications link, this victory gives Union troops a base of operations from which to launch raids into Virginia proper and protects the new pro-Union government of West Virginia. As well, the campaign gives George B. McClellan a leading position among Union generals.

14 JULY 1861

Civil War: Eastern Theater After the victories in West Virginia the North is anxious to press further into Virginia. To that end General McDowell advances on Fairfax Courthouse, Virginia, with 40,000 Union troops.

17 JULY 1861

Civil War: Eastern Theater General Beauregard, stationed near Manassas, Virginia, with about 22,000 men, requests aid in repulsing the Federal advance. Confederate President Davis orders General Joseph E. Johnston to Manassas with reinforcements.

18 JULY 1861

Civil War: Eastern Theater Blackburn's Ford, Virginia, proves to be a preview of the upcoming battle at Manassas. McDowell's inexperienced Union soldiers are camped at nearby Centreville; he sends a small party forward to examine the area around Blackburn's Ford. The men meet Confederates under the command of James Longstreet, and a brisk skirmish ensues before Longstreet pushes the Federals back.

20 JULY 1861

Civil War: Eastern Theater Both Union and Confederate forces prepare for battle around Manassas, Virginia. McDowell is situated with some 30,600 men near Sudley Ford on Bull Run, a creek running by Manassas. He misses a good opportunity to attack today before Confederate reinforcements arrive to give them a strength of over 30,000, under Beauregard. The creek will make the battle known as First Bull Run to Northerners, while Southerners call it First Manassas (the North tends to name battles by the nearest river, the South by the nearest town).

21 JULY 1861

Civil War: First Battle of Bull Run Not knowing that Johnston and Jackson have reinforced the Rebels (for the first time in history, this strategic reinforcement is done by railroad), McDowell hopes to surprise an outnumbered enemy by striking them on the left flank of their position at Stone Bridge. But the Confederates detect the Union advance, and General N.G. Evans meets McDowell's troops as the latter approach from Sudley Ford. Evans holds the Southern position until around noon. The Confederates then fall back to Henry House Hill, where Evans, Jackson and others make a strong stand (the valiant resistance of Jackson's men will earn the unit and their commander the historic nickname 'Stonewall'). McDowell's forces, smelling victory, advance on Henry House Hill around 2 o'clock; but despite several Union attempts to charge their position, the Rebels, with help from Jeb Stuart's cavalry, hold fast and finally drive the Federals back. Then panic strikes the retreating Union forces when a shell destroys a wagon. The main road of retreat is blocked, and the Federals scatter in terror. During the night the demoralized Northern soldiers have begun to straggle into the streets of Washington. It is a stunning triumph for the South. Their losses are 387 dead, 1582 wounded and 12 missing; Union losses are 418 dead, 1011 wounded and 1216 missing. Lincoln, learning of the rout, closets himself with his Cabinet. In the first great battle of the war Southern generalship and fighting ability have proven their superiority, and hopes decline for a quick end to the bloodshed.

25 JULY 1861

Civil War: Washington The Crittenden Resolution passes the Senate; it states that the war is to be fought to preserve the Union and uphold the Constitution, not to alter the slavery status quo.

27 JULY 1861

Civil War: Washington President Lincoln hands over command of the Federal Division of the Potomac to General George B. McClellan, hero of the West Virginia campaign. McClellan replaces General McDowell, who was routed at Bull Run.

30 JULY 1861

Civil War: Slavery War Secretary Cameron is pressed by General Benjamin Butler at Fort Monroe, Virginia, to make a firm policy in the sensitive matter of former slaves now in Federal hands. Butler has in his area about 900 former slaves and is unclear as to their status as still-legal property.

Trans-Mississippi After months of unrest, pro-Union forces gain the upper hand in Missouri, the State Convention voting to appoint a new Unionist governor and state officers. Next day, Hamilton Gamble becomes governor, and Missouri is tentatively in the Union fold.

31 JULY 1861

Civil War: Washington President Lincoln names a hard-drinking, failed Union officer from the Mexican War as General of Volunteers. His name: Ulysses S. Grant.

1 AUGUST 1861

Civil War: The Confederacy Confederate President Davis urges General Johnston to pursue the Federals after his victory at Bull Run and sends General Robert E. Lee to command the defeated Southern forces in West Virginia.

2 AUGUST 1861

Civil War: Washington To aid in financing the war, the US Congress passes the first income tax law. Governmental calls for volunteers increase steadily and the stated length of service has changed from three months to two years.

6 AUGUST 1861

Civil War: Washington Congress empowers President Lincoln to pass measures concerning Army and Navy actions. Lincoln decides that slaves used by the South against the North will be freed. He also establishes a Union military camp near Lexington as a show of force in neutral Kentucky.

8 AUGUST 1861

Civil War: Slavery Responding to General Butler's queries about fugitive slaves, Secretary of War Cameron advises him that fugitives from the Union states should be returned, those from Confederate states not returned.

10 AUGUST 1861

Civil War: Battle of Wilson's Creek General Nathaniel Lyon is killed at Wilson's Creek, Missouri, where he had led 5400 men to meet 11,600 Rebel troops under the command of General Benjamin McCulloch. The Confederates are joined in the encounter by pro-Southern Missouri militia. While Union troops are defeated, they put up a valiant fight, falling back only after Lyon's death. Southern losses are 421 killed and 1300 wounded; Federal losses are 263 killed and 721 wounded. The battle is the second important encounter between the sides and, following Bull Run, another heartening victory for the Confederacy. It also leaves Missouri an area of contention for the next four years.

16 AUGUST 1861

Civil War: The North Several northern newspapers are brought to court for alleged pro-Southern leanings, among them the Brooklyn *Eagle*, New York *Journal of Commerce* and New York *Daily News*.

19 AUGUST 1861

Civil War: The Confederacy In an action which does little to settle the discord in Missouri, the Confederate Congress allies with pro-Southern elements in the state, essentially providing for the establishment of a Confederate state government.

24 AUGUST 1861

Civil War: The Confederacy As part of its continuing efforts to gain European recognition, the Confederacy appoints three new commissioners to Europe: John Slidell to France, James Mason to Britain and Pierre Rost to Spain.

27 AUGUST 1861

Civil War: Eastern Theater A Union expeditionary force of 900 men and eight vessels under Commodore Silas Stringham and General Benjamin Butler lands troops under fire at Cape Hatteras, North Carolina. The Federals take Forts Clark and Hatteras this day and the next, with few casualties to either side. This victory gives the North a strategic point on Hatteras Inlet from which to operate against Confederate blockade-running ships.

At first an unlikely candidate, Ulysses S. Grant eventually proved to be the war-winning general for whom Lincoln sought so long.

Robert Edward Lee, the greatest of the Southern commanders, was neither a convinced rebel nor a pro-slaver, but simply a loyal Virginian.

30 AUGUST 1861

Civil War: Trans-Mississippi Without authorization, maverick Union General John C. Frémont declares martial law throughout Missouri. To make matters still stickier, he confiscates all property of Confederates and declares the state's slaves to be free. Seeing these actions as likely to alienate Union sentiment in Missouri and the other slaveholding border states, President Lincoln will declare Frémont's decrees 'dictatorial.'

3 SEPTEMBER 1861

Civil War: Western Theater Anticipating a Northern military takeover in neutral Kentucky, Southern General Leonidas Polk orders troops into the state to hold Confederate positions.

6 SEPTEMBER 1861

Civil War: Western Theater General Ulysses S. Grant moves his forces into Paducah, Kentucky, in order to prevent Polk's rebels from seizing the city. Grant's action, though it leads to no fighting, proves to be strategically important, as it secures for the North an area that will become central to next year's western river campaign.

11 SEPTEMBER 1861

Civil War: The Battle of Cheat Mountain In his first campaign of the war, General Robert E. Lee mounts a surprise attack on the forces of Federal General John Reynolds at Cheat Mountain and Elkwater, in western Virginia. However, the Rebel advance bogs down in rain and rough terrain, and the Federals hold their ground, with 21 casualties to the South's 100. This Union victory secures the area of West Virginia for the North, and gives a misleadingly inauspicious beginning to the Civil War career of Robert E. Lee.

12 SEPTEMBER 1861

Civil War: Washington After much consulting on the matter, President Lincoln sends a messenger to Missouri with instructions to urge moderation and modification of General Frémont's proclamation of 30 August.

13 SEPTEMBER 1861

Civil War: Naval In the first significant naval action of the war Union Lieutenant J.H. Russel makes a daring raid on a Southern navy yard in Pensacola, Florida, burning a Confederate privateer.

19 SEPTEMBER 1861

Civil War: Western Theater In Kentucky the Confederates are making a strong defense along a line including the area around Cumberland Gap, Bowling Green and Columbus. Pro-Union Kentucky troops are driven out of the vicinity of Barboursville by General Felix Zollicoffer's rebel forces.

20 SEPTEMBER 1861

Civil War: Trans-Mississippi In Lexington, Missouri, Federal general Mulligan has been under seige by Confederate forces for the past week while Mulligan urgently requests reinforcements from General John Frémont, who is in command of the area. Today the 3600 Federals in Lexington finally surrender after an enemy assault. Frémont's failure to aid Mulligan further weakens his already shaky position.

23 SEPTEMBER 1861

Civil War: Trans-Mississippi After a local newspaper editor criticizes his inaction to relieve the seige in Lexington, Missouri, General Frémont closes the newspaper and arrests the editor.

27 SEPTEMBER 1861

Civil War: Washington Amidst mounting pressures for the Federal armies to take decisive action, President Lincoln and General McClellan confer over plans for an offensive in Virginia.

John C. Frémont typified the incompetence of Union commanders in the early years of the war.

1 OCTOBER 1861

Civil War: The Confederacy Meeting in Centreville, Virginia, Confederate President Jefferson Davis and his generals Johnston, Beauregard and Smith meet to discuss the current military situation. After assessing Southern strength they decide that an offensive on the North at this time would be foolhardy; they will wait until spring and monitor developments in the North. For the duration of the war Southern leaders will debate the wisdom of an offensive versus a defensive strategy.

3 OCTOBER 1861

Civil War: The Confederacy The governor of Louisiana, Thomas O. Moore, bans the shipment of cotton to Europe in order to place pressure on European nations. Threatening to deprive Europe of cotton unless they recognize and trade with the Confederacy is a critical element of Southern strategy, but it will prove to be ineffective.

4 OCTOBER 1861

Civil War: Naval Ship designer John Ericsson of New York submits a contract, approved by the Cabinet, to build ironclad warships according to his own innovative designs. The first of those ships will be the *Monitor*.

Civil War: The Confederacy The Confederate government signs treaties with the Cherokee, Shawnee and Seneca tribes. This will enable the Rebels to utilize willing Indians in their campaigns.

7 OCTOBER 1861

Civil War: Trans-Mississippi In Missouri, General Frémont has gathered troops and set out on a mission to intercept Confederate General Sterling Price, who captured Lexington in September. This belated campaign does little to redeem Frémont in the view of Washington. Meanwhile, Secretary of War Cameron is on his way to the area to assess Frémont's leadership, which has lately been a favorite topic of concern in Washington.

12 OCTOBER 1861

Civil War: Trans-Mississippi Missouri continues in uproar, partly as a result of Frémont's political and military gambits. Fighting goes on for two days near Clintonville and Pomme de Terre, and Southern raiders under partisan fighter Jeff Thompson push into the Ironton area.

Civil War: Naval At the mouth of the Mississippi River the Confederate iron-armored *Manassas* confronts the USS *Richmond* and the USS *Vincennes*. Despite running aground, both Federal ships manage to pull back. The Federal blockade resumes after a short time, but the clash puts the Union at a psychological disadvantage.

Civil War: International John Slidell, Confederate commissioner to France, and James Mason, Commissioner to Britain, successfully slip past the Union blockade of Charleston, South Carolina, on the *Theodora*. They are en route to Europe via Cuba to help their government buy armaments and to work for recognition of the Confederacy.

16 OCTOBER 1861

Civil War: Trans-Mississippi Lexington, Missouri, is retaken by Union forces after being captured in September, but most of the Rebels have evacuated the town.

21 OCTOBER 1861

Civil War: Battle of Ball's Bluff Union General Charles Stone, assisted by Colonel Edward Baker, pushes toward Leesburg, Virginia, on orders from Washington to make a 'slight demonstration.' The Federals run squarely into a Confederate ambush at Ball's Bluff. With retreat imminent, Colonel Baker is killed. His men attempt to withdraw in steep and hilly terrain along the river bank but fall into confusion and then into panic. Men are drowned and shot as boats swamp and as the Union troops try to escape up the steep cliffs. It is yet another sad debacle for the Union resulting from inept leadership. The North loses 48 killed, 158 wounded and 714 captured or missing. Total Southern losses are 149.

23 OCTOBER 1861

Civil War: Western Theater Skirmishing breaks out in Kentucky near West Liberty and at Hodgenville. This line of Confederate troops in supposedly neutral Kentucky is a matter of concern to the Union and to its new commander in the area, General William Tecumseh Sherman.

24 OCTOBER 1861

Civil War: Washington After much delicate political maneuvering, President Lincoln is at last ready to sack General John C. Frémont in Missouri. Frémont is famous and popular as an explorer, known worldwide as 'The Pathfinder,' and he is a favorite of the intensely anti-slave Radical Republicans; but Frémont has manifestly made a mess of things in Missouri, militarily and politically. Lincoln sends orders to turn over command of the Western troops to General David Hunter, unless Frémont is 'in the immediate presence of the enemy, in expectation of a battle.' Meanwhile, Frémont, suspecting what is going on, is endeavoring to put himself in exactly that position by dislodging Sterling Price's Confederates from Missouri. Unfortunately, Frémont does not presently know where the enemy is.

25 OCTOBER 1861

Civil War: Naval At Greenpoint, Long Island, the keel is laid for the first Union ironclad ship, the *Monitor*.

31 OCTOBER 1861

Civil War: Washington General Winfield Scott, heroic old veteran of the War of 1812 and the Mexican War, requests to be relieved as General-in-Chief of the Union Army, and the president grants the request on 1 November. Scott is indeed tired and creaky, but his military mind, as seen in the 'Ana-

The death of Union Colonel Edward Baker at the Battle of Ball's Bluff, Virginia, in October 1861, another humiliating defeat for the North.

conda Plan,' seems as keen as ever. The more compelling reason for his resignation is a power play by popular and ambitious young General George B. McClellan, who is appointed to Scott's position at the head of the Union war effort. McClellan, who glories in the nickname 'The Little Napoleon,' will immediately set to the task of building his Army of the Potomac with an energy and efficiency that he will never demonstrate on the battlefield.

1 NOVEMBER 1861

Civil War: Trans-Mississippi In Missouri, General Frémont has located his enemy and communicates with Rebel general Price, agreeing to exchange prisoners. This decision is made without Lincoln's authorization, and the President later abrogates it.

6 NOVEMBER 1861

Civil War: The Confederacy The South holds elections, confirming Jefferson Davis as president for six years; Davis is again joined to his querulous vice-president, Alexander Stephens.

7 NOVEMBER 1861

Civil War: Battle of Belmont General Ulysses S. Grant ships a force of 3500 men on the Mississippi to Belmont, Missouri, opposite Confederate defenses under General Polk. While Grant attacks Confederate positions in the area, Polk crosses the river with a force of 10,000 and nearly cuts Grant off from his transports. Grant, who had gotten incorrect reports about Polk's strength, gets his men back on the river, but the action is inconclusive and untypical of the later Grant. Federal losses are 607, and Southern losses 642.

Civil War: Naval The Federal Port Royal expedition, having left Hampton Roads, Virginia, in late October with 17 wooden cruisers and 12,000 men, sails into Port Royal Sound on the South Carolina coast. After a bombardment the Federals take possession of Forts Beauregard and Walker, which gives the North a base for its blockade fleet. Union casualties in the engagement are 31. Confederate casualties are 66.

8 NOVEMBER 1861

Civil War: Western Theater Pro-Union Kentucky mountain men rise up against General Felix Zollicoffer's Rebel troops in the state, forcing the general to request reinforcements.

Civil War: International A dangerous international incident is touched off when the US ship *San Jacinto* stops the British *Trent*, sailing from Cuba to England, and arrests two Confederate commissioners on their way to Europe – John Slidell and James Mason. This '*Trent* Affair' causes an international dispute of such magnitude as to threaten war between Britain and the United States. The Union violation of British neutrality also gives the South potent propaganda.

13 NOVEMBER 1861

Civil War: Washington In a foretaste of their ensuing relations, President Lincoln calls on his new Commander-in-Chief, General McClellan, at the General's home. Informed that the president is waiting, McClellan simply goes to bed. It is the day after a torchlight parade in Washington celebrating McClellan's elevation.

15 NOVEMBER 1861

Civil War: International The ramifications of the *Trent* affair begin to unfold as the *San Jacinto* arrives at Fort Monroe, Virginia, and Confederate commissioners Slidell and Mason are dispatched to prison in Boston. Federal Captain Wilkes, at first hailed as a hero for waylaying the British ship, will receive a distinctly cooler welcome in Washington as president and cabinet realize that they have a major international embarrassment on their hands.

18 NOVEMBER 1861

Civil War: Secession A North Carolina delegation repudiates the state's 20 May order of secession and appoints a new pro-Union governor. Conversely, in Kentucky Confederate soldiers adopt a secession ordinance and set up a Rebel government; now both Kentucky and Missouri have two contending governments – though Unionist sentiment is stronger in both states, both are also slaveholding.

Civil War: The Confederacy The Provisional government of the Confederate States of America convenes in its fifth session at the new capital of Richmond.

21 NOVEMBER 1861

Civil War: The Confederacy Jefferson Davis reorganizes his cabinet, naming Judah Benjamin as secretary of war and Thomas Bragg as attorney general.

25 NOVEMBER 1861

Civil War: Naval The Confederate Naval Department prepares to convert the captured former USS *Merrimack*, now the CSS *Virginia*, to a fully ironclad vessel.

General Winfield Scott meets with Lincoln and his cabinet for a last time before Scott's resignation as General-in-Chief in October 1861.

30 NOVEMBER 1861

Civil War: International The *Trent* affair heats up. In a letter to Great Britain's Minister to the United States, the British Foreign Secretary, Lord John Russell, communicates Britain's displeasure at the seizure of Confederate diplomats Slidell and Mason. He further requests that the Union apologize for seizing a British ship and release the two men to British jurisdiction. The British Navy is placed on alert but told to avoid hostilities. The British Minister, Lord Lyons, is instructed to leave Washington in a week if there is no satisfactory response from the US government. In the streets of London demonstrators carry signs reading 'Outrage on the British Flag.'

1 DECEMBER 1861

Civil War: Naval The US gunboat *Penguin* seizes the Confederate blockade runner *Albion*, capturing armaments, foodstuffs, tin, copper and military equipment valued near $100,000.

3 DECEMBER 1861

Civil War: Washington President Lincoln makes his State of the Union address to the Thirty-Seventh Congress, saying 'the Union must be preserved, and hence all indispensable means must be employed.'

5 DECEMBER 1861

Civil War: Washington The Secretary of War reports that the Union regular army has 20,334 men and that volunteers total 640,637. The Naval Secretary tallies 22,000 sailors and marines.

9 DECEMBER 1861

Civil War: Washington As a result of criticism and debate over the string of Union military debacles, the US Senate calls for the establishment of the Joint Committee on the Conduct of the War to oversee the president's decisions. This committee is the special provenance of the Radical Republicans, who are critical of Lincoln's conciliation of the South and his assumption of almost dictatorial powers.

10 DECEMBER 1861

Civil War: The Confederacy The Confederate Congress formally admits Kentucky as the 13th Confederate state, but rising Union sentiment in Kentucky will soon drive most Rebel forces out.

11 DECEMBER 1861

Civil War: The Confederacy Charleston, South Carolina, is ravaged by a fire which destroys half the city. This damage to one of its prime cities does much psychological harm to the whole Confederacy.

17 DECEMBER 1861

Civil War: Eastern Theater Though the war has entered its usual winter slowdown, the inevitable minor military actions take place around the country. At Chisholm Island, South Carolina, there is skirmishing, and Rockville in that state sees confrontations between the sides. The Union garrison at Hilton Head poses such a threat to Confederates at Rockville that Southerners leave the vicinity. Near Harper's Ferry, Virginia, General 'Stonewall' Jackson carries out maneuvers along the Potomac River with his Rebel troops.

18 DECEMBER 1861

Civil War: Washington President Lincoln and his Cabinet meet to discuss the *Trent* affair; meanwhile the British Minister in Washington receives orders from London concerning Britains's demands for Slidell and Mason's immediate release. General McClellan and the president confer about upcoming military strategy.

20 DECEMBER 1861

Civil War: International The British Navy sends two ships to Canada in order to have forces in readiness if the *Trent* affair should necessitate formal military action against the United States.

26 DECEMBER 1861

Civil War: Washington After many meetings the cabinet acknowledges the seizure of Confederate diplomats from a British ship on the high seas was illegal, and the United States agrees to surrender James Mason and John Slidell into the keeping of Great Britain. Secretary of State Seward orders the men released from their confinement at Fort Warren in Massachusetts.

Civil War: Trans-Mississippi St. Louis, Missouri, is

placed under martial law by the Union commander in the area, General Henry Halleck. The order is unpopular at best. Rebel irregular Jeff Thompson continues his raiding in the state.

1 JANUARY 1862

Civil War: International James Mason and John Slidell, the two Confederate commissioners seized on the *Trent* and now released by the Union government, board a British schooner en route to England to continue their interrupted efforts to gain recognition and support for the Confederacy. With their departure the *Trent* affair is effectively closed.

6 JANUARY 1862

Civil War: Washington There is growing sentiment in official circles against General McClellan, who appears reluctant to commit troops to any concerted action. Accordingly, a group of senators approach President Lincoln with the suggestion that McClellan be replaced. Instead, the president tries to get some action from General Don Carlos Buell in Kentucky; the president recommends that Buell's forces advance in order to provide support for 'our friends in East Tennessee.'

9 JANUARY 1862

Washington It is a matter of intense concern to the president that neither General Buell in Kentucky nor General Halleck in Missouri have responded to the administration's urging that the Western troops advance. Lincoln discusses the issue with General McClellan, who is recuperating from illness. The Congress, meanwhile, is absorbed in discussion of the slavery problem, considering petitions which would curtail or terminate slavery with or without reimbursing slaveowners. There are questions about what to do with massive numbers of freed slaves. Some suggest that they be colonized elsewhere in the world.

10 JANUARY 1862

Civil War: Eastern Theater Federal troops evacuate Romney, Virginia, as Stonewall Jackson's Rebels push into the area. The town will be a winter camp for the Confederates.

11 JANUARY 1862

Civil War: Washington President Lincoln accepts the resignation of Simon Cameron as war secretary, replacing him on 13 January with Edwin M. Stanton. While Cameron and his department have been under considerable criticism for fraud and general incompetence, there has been no evidence that Cameron himself is corrupt. Stanton, a lawyer and former attorney general, is allied with the Radical Republicans and is a champion of General McClellan. He will prove both a capable secretary and a regular critic of the president.

Union General Henry Halleck succeeded Frémont as the major commander in the Western Theater.

18 JANUARY 1862

Civil War: Western Theater Climaxing weeks of maneuvering between Union and Confederate forces in Kentucky, Federals under General George H. Thomas close in on Felix Zollicoffer's Confederates at Mill Spring and Somerset on the Cumberland River. Southern General Crittenden's troops should be partically protected by Zollicoffer's men but are not because of the latter's careless positioning of his troops.

19 JANUARY 1862

Civil War: Battle of Logan Cross Roads (Also known as Mill Springs) Aided by Zollicoffer's poor placement, General Thomas's Federals drive the Confederates across the Cumberland River. Zollicoffer is shot and killed when he begins giving orders to a Union officer under the impression that the Northerner is one of his own men. After fierce fighting the Rebels withdraw under Crittenden with losses of 125 killed, 309 wounded and 99 missing. Union losses are 39 killed, 207 wounded and 15 captured. The result of the battle is a gap in the Confederate line of defense in the Tennessee-Kentucky area, as well as considerable losses of weapons and materiel for the South.

27 JANUARY 1862

Civil War: Washington After months of delay and frustration President Lincoln issues *General War Order Number One*: 'that the 22nd of February 1862 be the day for a general movement of the Land and Naval forces of the United States against the insurgent forces.' General-in-Chief McClellan will ignore the order.

30 JANUARY 1862

Civil War: Naval In a ceremony at Greenpoint, Long Island, the strange-looking turreted ironclad ship *Monitor* is launched. John Ericsson, the Swedish-born designer of this ship and similar ironclads to follow, states that such vessels are critical to the Northern war effort and 'will admonish the leaders of the Southern Rebellion that the batteries on the banks of their rivers will no longer present barriers to the entrance of the Union forces.'

1 FEBRUARY 1862

Civil War: Western Theater Cairo, Illinois, sees preparations for an expedition under General Grant that aims to seize Fort Henry, a Confederate garrison on the Tennessee River.

3 FEBRUARY 1862

Civil War: Washington President Lincoln communicates with General McClellan, who continues to ignore the president's wishes for the disposition of the Army of the Potomac. Lincoln favors a direct overland movement into Virginia; his general-in-chief wants to land troops on the coast and then march inland to the Confederate capital at Richmond.

5 FEBRUARY 1862

Civil War: Western Theater Having shipped his 15,000 men and four gunboats up the Tennessee River from Cairo, Illinois, to attempt the first strategic penetration of the Confederacy, General Grant is ready to open his attack on Fort Henry. After having sent most of his garrison overland to Fort Donelson, Southern General Lloyd Tilighman has 100 artillerymen to resist the attack.

6 FEBRUARY 1862

Civil War: Fall of Fort Henry At around 11 in the morning Federal gunboats begin shelling Fort Henry, which responds with its artillery, but after a short time Southern General Tilighman surrenders 80 surviving artillerymen and 16 hospital patients to Grant, who has not had to commit his ground troops. The North counts 11 dead and 31 wounded.

7 FEBRUARY 1862

Civil War: Western Theater Grant's forces now prepare to strike Fort Donelson on the Cumberland River near Dover, Tennessee. Confederate troops are ordered into the area as the Kentucky defenses further deteriorate.

8 FEBRUARY 1862

Civil War: Eastern Theater Federal General Ambrose Burnside, opening an expedition along the North Carolina coast with an armada of 65 vessels, mounts an attack with 7500 men on Roanoke Island in Pamlico Sound. Confederate Colonel Shaw, in command, makes an attempt to hold the Southern position, but his resistance is futile. Shaw surrenders 2500 men after losses of 143 killed, wounded and missing; Federal casualties are 14 in the naval force and 264 in the infantry. The Confederates relinquish 30 guns in this defeat and lose an important position on the Atlantic coast. Burnside prepares to push on with his expedition.

Feisty but effective Edwin Stanton became Lincoln's secretary of war in January 1862.

11 FEBRUARY 1862

Civil War: Western Theater General Grant begins to march his troops toward Fort Donelson while General McClernands' forces pull out of Fort Henry in support. Federal gunboats advance up the Cumberland.

13 FEBRUARY 1862

Civil War: Siege of Fort Donelson Having the previous day positioned the 40,000 troops now under his command around Fort Donelson and the town of Dover, Tennessee, and having readied gunboats, Grant besieges the enemy garrison. Donelson has been reinforced by the troops of Confederate General John Floyd, who is now in command. In the evening the Federals camp on the field amidst plunging temperatures and a roaring blizzard.

14 FEBRUARY 1862

Civil War: Siege of Fort Donelson Four Union ironclads and several wooden gunboats arrive and shell Fort Donelson, but the fort's batteries drive the ships away. The day ends with the Federals surrounding the fort on the land side.

15 FEBRUARY 1862

Civil War: Siege of Fort Donelson Fighting continues on the Cumberland River as Confederates under General Gideon Pillow break through Federal lines to provide an avenue of escape toward Nashville, Tennessee. However, Floyd bungles the attempt to exploit his gains, ordering his troops back into the fort, and Grant partially closes the escape route. Outnumbered two to one, Floyd passes command to Pillow, who passes it to Simon Buckner – who happens to be an old West Point friend of Grant's. Floyd and Pillow then escape across the river with some 3000 men while one of their subordinates, Nathan Bedford Forrest, leads a body of cavalry out through the backwaters.

16 FEBRUARY 1862

Civil War: Fall of Fort Donelson General Buckner asks for terms from his friend Grant, who somewhat rakishly replies with a message that will become immortal in military annals: 'No terms except unconditional and immediate surrender can be accepted. I propose to move immediately upon your works. I am sir, very respectfully, Your obt. svt. U S Grant.' Buckner is highly put out with this reply, but he has no choice but to surrender. Estimates of casualties are uncertain; best guesses are that during the siege the North has lost 500 killed, 2108 wounded and 224 missing. The South's total losses are placed at 2000 killed or wounded and 14,623 missing – mostly captured. This is the first decisive Union victory of the war. Kentucky and much of Tennessee are lost to the

South, and the Cumberland and Tennessee Rivers are under Union control. The stage is set for a vertical splitting of the Confederacy by a drive down the Mississippi River. As important, news of the victory makes Grant a Major General and a famous man; his initials become the basis of new nickname: Unconditional Surrender Grant.

18 FEBRUARY 1862

Civil War: The Confederacy The two houses of the First Congress of the Confederate States of America meets, succeeding the Provisional Congress.

21 FEBRUARY 1862

Civil War: The North Convicted slave trader Nathaniel Gordon is hanged in New York, the first person on whom the Union has ever imposed this punishment.

Civil War: Trans-Mississippi A Confederate victory results when the forces of General H. H. Sibley attack Union troops near Fort Craig, at Valverde, New Mexico Territory. After a two-hour engagement the Federals under Colonel E. R. S. Canby lose 68 dead, with 160 wounded and 35 missing out of a total of 3810 men. The Southerners, numbering 2600, suffer 31 deaths, 154 wounded and one missing. Colonel 'Kit' Carson commands part of the Union forces in the battle. The victorious Confederates move toward Santa Fe after seizing six Union cannons.

22 FEBRUARY 1862

Civil War: The Confederacy After his election to the presidency of the Confederacy (up to now he has been provisional president), Jefferson Davis is inaugurated at the new capital of Richmond, Virginia.

24 FEBRUARY 1862

Civil War: Western Theater General Buell's Federals take over Nashville, Tennessee.

27 FEBRUARY 1862

Civil War: Naval The Union ironclad ship *Monitor* sails from New York harbor under sealed orders.

1 MARCH 1862

Civil War: The Confederacy Richmond, Virginia, witnesses the arrest of John Minor Botts for treason against the Confederacy. A former Virginian congressman and avowed neutral, Botts is seized along with 30 others. The Confederate capital is now under martial law.

3 MARCH 1862

Civil War: Western Theater General Henry Halleck, commanding the Federal Department of the Missouri since the ouster of General Frémont, relieves General Ulysses Grant of command. Halleck accuses his general of tardy appearance during the Fort Donelson takeover. Grant's forces are at this point moving up the Tennessee River, with massive Confederate forces in the vicinity.

4 MARCH 1862

Civil War: Washington The Senate confirms antislavery Southern Democrat Andrew Johnson as military governor of Tennessee, which is increasingly Union-controlled.

Civil War: The Confederacy President Davis calls General Robert E. Lee from command in South Carolina to become a military advisor in Richmond.

7 MARCH 1862

Civil War: Battle of Pea Ridge (Also called Elkhorn Tavern) Federal forces under General Samuel Curtis at Pea Ridge, Arkansas, are surprised by General Van Dorn's Confederate troops in an attack from the latter's northern position. About 14,000 Confederates, including some Indian troops, make valiant attempts to rout the Union soldiers, but the North holds the line.

8 MARCH 1862

Civil War: Washington The president and General-in-Chief McClellan discuss plans for the latter's giant Army of the Potomac, which has been built to conquer Virginia. Lincoln agrees, somewhat reluctantly, to McClellan's intention to move his forces by water to the peninsula southeast of Richmond. The president, to McClellan's chagrin, insists that some of the Union forces be left in the Washington defenses.

Civil War: The Battle of Pea Ridge The conclusion of the battle at Pea Ridge, Arkansas – the most significant of the war's battles in the trans-Mississippi theater – sees the deaths of Confederate Generals McCulloch and McIntosh. Federals under General Curtis drive Van Dorn's forces in confusion from the field, and the Confederates retreat to the Arkansas River, with orders to reinforce Confederate positions along the Mississippi River. In the two-day battle the Union has suffered 1384 casualties among 11,250 engaged, and the South 800 casualties among 14,000 engaged.

Civil War: Naval Off the coast of Virginia at Hampton Roads the new Rebel ironclad *Virginia* (formerly – and often in subsequent histories – the USS *Merrimack*) approaches a squadron of Federal vessels, which prove helpless in battle with the heavily armored Confederate ship. In the ensuing encounter two Union vessels are put out of commission and a third is heavily damaged. Flag Officer Franklin Buchanan of the *Virginia* is slightly wounded.

9 MARCH 1862

Civil War: First Battle of the Ironclads As the Southern ironclad *Virginia* (formerly *Merrimack*) steams out to finish off the Federal flotilla remaining in Hampton Roads, Virginia, the Confederates see a strange object slip around the bow of the grounded USS *Minnesota* and head directly for them. Some Southern sailors take the object for a boiler on a raft, but it is the turreted Union ironclad *Monitor*, which opens fire at about nine in the morning, beginning the first duel of ironclad ships in history. The fighting continues inconclusively for two hours before damage forces both commanders to pull back (Lieutenant Lorimer Worden in the *Monitor*, Lieutenant Catesby ap Roger Jones now commanding the *Virginia*). Several times in the next few days the *Virginia* will challenge the *Monitor*, but the experimental Union ship will be under orders not to risk an engagement; she has served her purpose to save the Union fleet in the area. As governments around the world are quick to realize, a new era in naval warfare has begun.

Union batteries fire on Fort Donelson, Tennessee, in February 1862, the first step in Grant's long campaign to break Rebel power on the Mississippi.

The Battle of Pea Ridge, Arkansas, fought on 7-8 March 1862, the largest trans-Mississippi battle of the war and an important Union victory.

A new era in naval warfare began with the duel of the ironclads USS *Monitor* (r) and CSS *Virginia* (ex-*Merrimack*) off Hampton Roads in March 1862. *Monitor* was armed with two 11-inch Dahlgren guns; *Virginia* with three 8-inch, two 7-inch and two 6-inch cannons. *Monitor*'s design was produced by Swedish engineer John Ericsson.

11 MARCH 1862

Civil War: Washington Frustrated by the slowness of his General-in-Chief McClellan and wishing him to concentrate on the upcoming invasion of Virginia, President Lincoln relieves McClellan as head of the Union armies but leaves him in command of the Army of the Potomac.

14 MARCH 1862

Civil War: Eastern Theater The 14,000-man Confederate garrison at New Berne, North Carolina, is driven away by General Burnside's 11,000 Federals. This position will be maintained by the North for the rest of the war, proving to be a useful point of departure for inland expeditions. In this action of Burnside's North Carolina Expedition the Federals lose 471 casualties to the South's 578.

15 MARCH 1862

Civil War: Western Theater General Grant resumes command of field forces in Tennessee after General Halleck absolves Grant of charges of misconduct at Fort Donelson. To the public, meanwhile, Grant is the hero of that campaign.

17 MARCH 1862

Civil War: Eastern Theater: Peninsular Campaign After many delays, General George B. McClellan and the 12 divisions of his Army of the Potomac move out of Washington and head for Fort Monroe, at the tip of the peninsula between the James and York Rivers in Virginia. The intention of this campaign is to capture the Confederate capital at Richmond and thereby end the war.

18 MARCH 1862

Civil War: The Confederacy Jefferson Davis names his friend Judah Benjamin as secretary of state. Benjamin has been War Secretary but has been much criticized in that position.

23 MARCH 1862

Civil War: Battle of Kernstown About 9000 Union troops clash with 4200 Confederates under 'Stonewall' Jackson at Kernstown, Virginia. Skirmishing of the previous day had led the Southerners to assume a smaller enemy force, but, although outnumbered, Jackson's troops perform admirably. They finally retreat after suffering 80 killed, 375 wounded and 263 missing, compared to Union losses of 118 killed, 450 injured and 22 missing. This battle is preliminary to Jackson's historic Shenandoah Valley Campaign. Despite the Union victory, President Lincoln makes one of his greatest strategic blunders: now fearing an offensive on the Federal capital, the president orders that General McDowell's 40,000 troops stay in Washington instead of joining McClellan on the Peninsula, thereby weakening the vital Peninsular Campaign. In addition, the assault at Kernstown suggests the possibility of a threat on Harper's Ferry, and General Banks's troops are ordered to return to that vicinity rather than reinforce McClellan. Jackson's loss at Kernstown thereby proves to be as useful to the South as a victory. Lincoln's fears for Washington have perhaps prolonged the war by years.

24 MARCH 1862

Civil War: Slavery The emancipation issue continues to be fraught with emotion. In Cincinnati, Ohio, fiery abolitionist Wendell Phillips speaks and is greeted with a barrage of eggs and rocks. Lincoln, commenting on proposals for compensated emancipation, notes in a letter to prominent newspaperman Horace Greeley that 'we should urge it persuasively, and not menacingly, upon the South.' Lincoln is still hoping – probably not very realistically – for some sort of peaceful settlement.

28 MARCH 1862

Civil War: Trans-Mississippi New Mexico Territory sees a battle at La Glorietta Pass; Union troops under Colonel John Slough clash with Confederates under Colonel W. R. Scurry, the Federals finally falling back. Confederate supply wagons at nearby Johnson's Ranch are attacked by Major John Chivington's men, driving the Southerners back to Santa Fe and effectively stopping a Confederate invasion of the territory. Of 1100 Confederates, 36 are killed and 60 wounded. Union troops totalling 1324 lose 31 killed and over 50 wounded.

29 MARCH 1862

Civil War: Western Theater General Albert Sidney Johnston pulls his Confederate forces together at Corinth, Mississippi, to oppose Grant's presence in the area. Second in command to Johnston is General Beauregard.

3 APRIL 1862

Civil War: Washington The US Senate abolishes slavery in the District of Columbia. President Lincoln is gravely concerned about the defense of the nation's capital and continues to wrangle with General McClellan about the number of troops detailed to guard Washington. McClellan, meanwhile, has 112,000 men on the Peninsula in Virginia, more than enough for his campaign. But McClellan has been receiving immensely exaggerated intelligence reports of enemy strength at Yorktown, which the Federals are preparing to beseige. In fact, the Confederate line of defense consists of 17,000 men under General Joseph E. Johnston, and these troops are spread thin along an eight-mile front. If McClellan only knew, Yorktown – and, indeed, Richmond – are ripe for the picking. But McClellan is not a man who will be remembered for taking risks.

6 APRIL 1862

Civil War: Battle of Shiloh Several days of preparations by A. S. Johnston's Confederate forces in Corinth, Mississippi, have gone unnoticed by Grant, and in the early morning these Rebels fall crushingly on the Northern forces at Pittsburgh Landing, Tennessee. (Grant, meanwhile, is at Savannah, Tennessee.) In short order the surprised Yankees are pushed back through their camps to the Landing; only a heroic stand by General Prentiss' division in an area dubbed the 'Hornets' Nest' prevents the Northerners from being driven into the Tennessee River. Grant arrives around eight in the morning and begins to organize his forces in front of the river bank. Then, at 2:30 in the afternoon, the Southern assault falters when General Johnston is killed. An ailing General Beauregard takes command, but he is not able to press his advantage. In the afternoon Federal batteries and gunboats shell the Confederate positions, keeping up the barrage through a wet and miserable night. Meanwhile, copious Federal reinforcements begin to arrive.

7 APRIL 1862

Civil War: Battle of Shiloh Having spent the night shelling the Southern positions, collecting reinforcements and reorganizing his troops, Grant mounts a strong counterattack in the early morning. For hours, ailing Confederate General Beauregard, in command after the death of A. S. Johnston, keeps up fierce resistance while waiting for the arrival of 20,000 reinforcements under Van Dorn. The heaviest fighting is around a crossroads at Shiloh Church. Finally, learning that Van Dorn cannot make it in time, Beauregard orders a retreat to Corinth, Mississippi. After being surprised at the outset, Grant has organized a stunning recovery for his Federal forces, but the cost of victory is appalling: Union losses are 1754 killed, 8408 wounded and 2885 missing, a total of 13,047 casualties out of 62,682 engaged. Confederate losses are 1723 killed, 8012 wounded and 959 missing, a total of 10,694 casualties out of 40,335 engaged. Now the Union has split the Rebel forces along the Mississippi River and further weakened Confederate power in Tennessee. Grant's initial mistake will cause him problems for a while, but Lincoln will keep him in command with the eloquent observation: "I can't spare this man. He fights." Beauregard's career will never entirely recover from his defeat at Shiloh.

10 APRIL 1862

Civil War: Eastern Theater In the harbor of Savannah, Georgia, Union General Quincy Adams Gillmore assaults Fort Pulaski. The Confederates have about 40 guns, but Federal long-range cannons cause severe damage to the masonry fort during the night. On the 11th, 360 Confederates surrender, giving the Union command of the coastal approaches to Savannah. Only one soldier has been killed on each side.

11 APRIL 1862

Civil War: Western Theater In Tennessee several hundred Confederates are captured when the town of Huntsville is occupied by Federals. The Union begins to marshal its forces for a push toward Beauregard's forces in Corinth, Mississippi. In command of the Federals is General Henry Halleck, who has taken over from Grant – his being surprised at Shiloh has again temporarily put Grant in disfavor.

12 APRIL 1862

Civil War: Great Locomotive Chase In a minor but later legendary episode James Andrews, a spy for the Union, has led a group of 21 men through Confederate lines to Kenesaw, Georgia, in order to seize a train on the Western and Atlantic Railroad. Taking the locomotive *General*, Andrews and his raiders head northward, pursued by Confederates in the locomotive *Texas*. The raiders are finally caught by the Southerners. Andrews and seven others will be executed as spys.

Civil War: Peninsular Campaign Confederate General Joseph Johnston sends troops to support besieged Yorktown, Virginia. The situation on the Peninsula seems ill-omened for the vastly outnumbered Confederates.

Union General Ambrose Burnside could, as Lincoln said, 'snatch defeat from the jaws of victory.'

In April 1862 Grant won a shoestring victory at Shiloh on the Tennessee River. It was the bloodiest battle to date, but worse was to come.

16 APRIL 1862

Civil War: The Confederacy President Jefferson Davis gives his approval to a military draft of Southerners between the ages of 18 and 35. This action, while manifestly necessary, offends Southern traditions of states' rights and rugged individualism, and many voices are raised against conscription – one of many such internal tensions that will hamper the Confederate war effort.

23 APRIL 1862

Civil War: Naval After several days of preparatory bombardment Flag Officer David Farragut orders the Federal fleet on the Mississippi River to move past Rebel Forts Jackson and St. Philip and sail toward New Orleans. The Union ships will slip past the Southern defenses the next day with a loss of only one ship (the South loses 8 ships).

25 APRIL 1862

Civil War: Naval Farragut's forces seize the city of New Orleans, Louisiana, after the withdrawal of the Confederate garrison. There is little civilian resistance to the Union takeover; the city will formally surrender on 29 April. Northern control of the Mississippi is now nearing completion.

27 APRIL 1862

Civil War: Western Theater As a result of the fall of New Orleans to the North, four Rebel forts – Livingston, Quitman, Pike and Wood – surrender to the North. The following day both Forts Jackson and St. Philip surrender, removing any Confederate resistance to Northern action on the Mississippi as far up as New Orleans. Federal General Ben Butler becomes military governor of the area.

2 MAY 1862

Civil War: Peninsular Campaign Having held the vastly superior Union Army of the Potomac at bay for a month, largely by bluffing (aided by Union commander McClellan's susceptibility to inflated reports of enemy strength), General Joseph Johnston pulls his forces out of Yorktown, Virginia, to strongly entrenched positions near Richmond. McClellan's men enter Yorktown, but the Union general has amply demonstrated the timidity which will hamstring his campaigns – and thereby the Federal war effort.
Civil War: Western Theater Federal forces under General Halleck are lumbering slowly toward Beauregard's army at Corinth, Mississippi, to which the Confederates retreated after the battle of Shiloh.

5 MAY 1862

Civil War: Peninsular Campaign In the wake of the Confederate evacuation of Yorktown, Virginia, there is serious fighting between advancing Federals and retreating Confederates at Williamsburg. In all, 1703 Southerners are lost during the encounter, which claims 456 Union troops, with 373 listed as missing.

8 MAY 1862

Civil War: Jackson's Valley Campaign In the first victory of a campaign that will become an historic model of a diversionary operation, Stonewall Jackson attacks Federal forces at McDowell, Virginia, in the Shenandoah Valley. Jackson has made his way to McDowell by a roundabout and secret combination of forced marches – 92 miles in four days – and entraining. At McDowell his 10,000 Confederates turn back an attack by 6000 Federals under General Schenck. Jackson then prepares to push his men north up the Valley to continue his diversion, which is tying up many of the troops McClellan desperately wants for the Federal Peninsular Campaign.

9 MAY 1862

Civil War: Peninsular Campaign Frustrated with his general's slow advance toward Richmond, President Lincoln meets in Virginia with General McClellan.
Civil War: Western Theater General David Hunter, commander of the Federal Department of the South, frees slaves in South Carolina, Florida and Georgia. This order, not approved by officials in Washington, is later repudiated by Lincoln.

11 MAY 1862

Civil War: Naval The Confederate ironclad *Virginia* (formerly *Merrimack*), which fought to a draw with the USS *Monitor* in history's first battle of ironclads, is deliberately destroyed by the Confederate navy, which must abandon the ship's base at Norfolk in the face of the Union advance into Virginia.

14 MAY 1862

Civil War: Peninsular Campaign As McClellan's Federal army pulls into White House, 20 miles from Richmond, Virginia, panic breaks out in the Confederate capital, many civilians fleeing the city. However, the ill-fated Peninsular Campaign is near the end of its advance. McClellan, whose forces are in fact overwhelmingly superior, is still convinced that he is outnumbered.

16 MAY 1862

Civil War: Western Theater General Ben Butler, a politically-appointed officer beloved of the Radical Republicans but otherwise inept in both political and military arenas, ignites a bitter controversy in New Orleans with what becomes infamous as his 'Woman Order.' It states that any woman in the city who insults the Union or Federal soldiers shall be treated as a prostitute. The city erupts with outrage. While Lincoln will not wish to take the political risk of rescinding Butler's order, he will ease Butler out of his post as military governor in December.

20 MAY 1862

Civil War: Peninsular Campaign The Federal Army of the Potomac under General McClellan is now in sight of the steeples of the enemy capital of Richmond, Virginia, eight miles away. Meanwhile, to prevent Union General Banks from moving his troops to support McClellan, Stonewall Jackson and Richard Ewell take their 16,000 Confederates into the Luray Valley area of the Shenandoah to block Banks' path east.

23 MAY 1862

Civil War: Jackson's Valley Campaign In Virginia's Shenandoah Valley, Southern Generals Stonewall Jackson and Richard Ewell overwhelm 1000 Federals at Front Royal. This places pressure on Banks in nearby Strasburg.

24 MAY 1862

Civil War: Washington Jackson's Valley Campaign is having its intended effect: instead of sending General McDowell's 20,000 men to reinforce McClellan near Richmond, Lincoln sends McDowell into the Shenandoah to cooperate with Generals Frémont and Banks against Jackson's forces.

CSA General Joseph E. Johnston fought throughout the war, often skillfully but usually unluckily.

25 MAY 1862

Civil War: Jackson's Valley Campaign So fast does Stonewall Jackson's command move that they have been dubbed the 'foot cavalry.' Having marched them all night, Jackson sends his men to attack the Federal command of Banks, who is now at Winchester, Virginia. In a morning assault Jackson and Ewell send the Yankees running, but the Rebels are too exhausted to pursue. The engagements at Front Royal and Winchester claim 400 Confederate casualties; Federal losses are around 3000.

29 MAY 1862

Civil War: Western Theater Before the approach of General Halleck's Federal forces General Beauregard pulls his troops in good order out of Corinth, Mississippi. The slow-moving Halleck thereby loses his chance to strike the main enemy force in the area. The Federals will occupy the city the next day, finding most materiel of value destroyed.

31 MAY-1 JUNE 1862

Civil War: Battle of Fair Oaks McClellan's Federal Army of the Potomac is largely spread out along the Chickahominy River west of Richmond. However, the Union IV Corps under Keyes is isolated south of the river at Fair Oaks. On 31 May a large Confederate force under J. E. Johnston falls on that isolated corps. Johnston's attack is somewhat disorganized, and the timely arrival of Union reinforcements results in an inconclusive battle. A Confederate attack on 1 June,

Victor at New Orleans in 1862 and Mobile Bay in 1864, David Farragut was the war's best admiral.

At the Battle of Fair Oaks CSA General J.E. Johnston failed to destroy McClellan's army on the Virginia Peninsula. Lee was then sent to replace Johnston.

led by James Longstreet, is not able to crack Union defenses. Both sides in the battle of Fair Oaks have approximately 41,800 troops engaged; Federal losses are 5031, Southern losses 6134. General Johnston is severely wounded during the first day's fighting, but this proves a fortuitous boon for the South, for Johnston's replacement is General Robert E. Lee. He gives his new command a name that will resound in history – the Army of Northern Virginia.

6 JUNE 1862

Civil War: Naval As crowds gather onshore before dawn, Federal and Confederate naval forces clash near Memphis, Tennessee. In two hours the Southern fleet is reduced to one vessel, which escapes, leaving Memphis open to Union occupation and the Mississippi River closer to complete Northern control.

8 JUNE 1862

Civil War: Jackson's Valley Campaign The previous evening Stonewall Jackson and Richard Ewell have found themselves squarely between two enemy columns under Frémont and Shields. Today, at the battle of Cross Keys, Virginia, Jackson manages to avoid their pincer movement. In the fighting, Ewell's division of 6500 bests Frémont's force of 10,500.

9 JUNE 1862

Civil War: Jackson's Valley Campaign Fighting continues in the area of Cross Keys, Virginia, but the main battle today, between Jackson's troops and those of Frémont and Shields, takes place at Port Republic. After some faltering efforts in the first hours of battle the Confederates mount a strong stand and push the Northerners back. The battle here at Port Republic and the engagement at Cross Keys are the end of Jackson's remarkable Shenandoah Valley Campaign. During one month Jackson and his men have marched more than 250 miles, fought four pitched battles and endless skirmishes, captured enormous quantities of materiel and over 400 prisoners and thrown the entire Federal war effort into confusion. His job completed in the Shenandoah, Jackson now prepares to march to the aid of Robert E. Lee.

12 JUNE 1862

Civil War: Peninsular Campaign In one of the legendary operations of the war Confederate General James Ewell Brown 'Jeb' Stuart, commander of cavalry for Lee's Army of Northern Virginia, takes his troopers on a reconnaissance of the Federal position on the Peninsula. Riding completely around McClellan's Army of the Potomac, Stuart goes beyond scouting to raid the Federal communications and, as important, humiliates the enemy. This four-day operation will go down in history as Stuart's First Ride Around McClellan; typically, the flamboyant Stuart will be the first to sing its praises. It is the first of many times that Stuart will demonstrate brilliantly the use of cavalry for strategic raids.

17 JUNE 1862

Civil War: Washington President Lincoln oversees the reorganization of commands in the East. Resentful at being placed under General John Pope, General John Frémont resigns from the new Army of Virginia, to be replaced by Franz Sigel (completing a triumvirate of ineptitude). The maverick Frémont will spend the remainder of the war awaiting orders.

25 JUNE 1862

Civil War: Seven Days Battles In the first major engagements of his Civil War career, and the first with his new command the Army of Northern Virginia, Robert E. Lee attempts to drive McClellan's Army of the Potomac away from Richmond. McClellan, having moved most of his army south of the Chickahominy River, is ready to make his long-delayed move directly on the Confederate capital. Today in the battle of Oak Grove, the Federals move forward with little difficulty, driving back Lee's outnumbered forces.

26 JUNE 1862

Civil War: Seven days Battles At Mechanicsville, Lee seizes the initiative, holding the Federals south of the Chickahominy while striking the Federal V Corps, which is isolated north of the river. However, the Confederate commanders are unable to coordinate their movements – especially Jackson, just back from his Valley campaign and now apparently exhausted and uncharacteristically slow. Federal casualties at Mechanicsville are 361 out of 15,631 engaged. Southern losses are around 1484 out of 16,356 engaged.

27 JUNE 1862

Civil War: Seven Days Battles Having failed to dislodge the Army of the Potomac the previous day, Lee attacks again, this time on a new Federal defensive position at Gaines Mill. After a day of heavy fighting, with Jackson again proving undependable, the exposed Federal V Corps is driven back somewhat, while Magruder, with his 25,000 men, successfully ties up the main body of 60,000 Northerners. Federal losses in the battles of Gaines Mill are 6837 out of 34,214 engaged. Southern casualties are 8751 out of 57,018 engaged. Despite his army's success in fighting off Lee's offensive, McClellan in the evening makes the foolish decision to abandon his attempt to take Richmond; he retreats to the James River.

28 JUNE 1862

Civil War: Seven Days Battles Today McClellan's Army of the Potomac and Lee's Army of Northern Virginia tangle at Garnett's and Golding's farms, west of Richmond. This minor action actually has begun the previous day as part of Magruder's holding action on the Federals south of the Chickahominy. Inconclusive fighting continues through today.

Civil War: Naval Admiral David Farragut takes his fleet past the shore batteries of Vicksburg, the last remaining Confederate stronghold on the Mississippi River. This action, while it does not weaken Southern control of Vicksburg, does prove that the batteries can be run.

29 JUNE 1862

Civil War: Seven Days Battles The opposing sides clash at the battle of Savage Station, McClellan's Army of the Potomac now withdrawing from Richmond behind a screening force, and Lee trying unsuccessfully to break through Union lines. Once again Confederate efforts are hampered by the sluggish movement of Jackson and his men.

30 JUNE 1862

Civil War: Seven Days Battles The sixth day of battle in Virginia is a heavy engagement at White Oak Swamp. Yet again Southern movements are confused and Jackson indecisive, and the Federals hold their lines with 2853 casualties. Confederate losses are 3615.

1 JULY 1862

Civil War: Seven Days Battles Lee unwisely decides to attack strong Union positions on the high ground of Malvern Hill. The Rebel assault is torn apart by a storm of Union artillery. Says Southern General D. H. Hill, 'It was not war – it was murder.' In this last engagement of the Seven Day's Battles, Lee suffers 5355 casualties to the Federals' 3214. Lee and his generals, especially Jackson, have been ineffective throughout the week. Presumably they have learned many lessons from the Seven Days, for they will never again fumble like this. Lee pulls back to the defenses of Richmond. McClellan's withdrawal to Harrison's Landing on the James River is due more to his own failings than to Lee's offensive. After 16,000 Union and 20,000 Southern casualties, the Union's Peninsular Campaign, which might have taken Richmond and ended the war, has collapsed.

Dashing James Ewell Brown 'Jeb' Stuart was by far the South's most successful cavalry commander.

4 JULY 1862

Civil War: Western Theater In Kentucky, Confederate raider John Hunt Morgan begins a series of operations which later earn him recognition from the Confederate Congress for his 'varied, heroic, and invaluable services in Tennessee and Kentucky.'

11 JULY 1862

Civil War: Washington Still searching for an effective supreme commander, Lincoln names General Henry W. Halleck as general-in-chief of the Union armies. This returns command of the Army of West Tennessee to U. S. Grant.

13 JULY 1862

Civil War: Western Theater At Murfreesboro, Tennessee, Federal forces are defeated by General Nathan Bedford Forrest's small command. The North loses large amounts of military supplies in this defeat.

17 JULY 1862

Civil War: Western Theater Confederate raider John Hunt Morgan and his men continue depredations in Kentucky, making a surprise attack at Cynthiana. After several hours of fighting the Federals are overcome and Southern troops occupy the town. Three days later, however, Morgan's raiders are dispersed by Union cavalry near Owensville.

A favored ruse of the commerce raider CSS *Alabama* was to set fire to prize vessels in order to decoy other potential prizes into coming to their rescue.

22 JULY 1862

Civil War: Washington Resigned to the necessity of war, aware of growing abolitionist sentiment in the North and responding to his own deeply-felt convictions, President Lincoln submits to his surprised cabinet the first draft of the Emancipation Proclamation, which orders the freeing of slaves within the Confederacy only. Although the cabinet's response is favorable, Lincoln is persuaded to keep the proclamation quiet until Union fortunes improve in the war.

29 JULY 1862

Civil War: International Northern diplomats in England fail to prevent the Confederate seagoing raider *Alabama* from sailing out of Liverpool. Under the command of Captain Raphael Semmes, the *Alabama* will inflict much damage to Federal shipping in the Atlantic. This will result in claims brought by Washington against the British government, claims which will be settled only after the war.

Civil War: The North A Cincinnati paper coins the term "Copperhead" to denote Southern sympathizers, most of them Democrats, in the North.

9 AUGUST 1862

Civil War: Second Bull Run Campaign Stonewall Jackson's Confederates are positioned near Culpepper, Virginia, and intend to strike Union General John Pope's Army of Virginia. Federal General Banks attacks Jackson first, but in the ensuing battle of Cedar Mountain the Yankees are pushed back upon the arrival of Southern reinforcements under A. P. Hill. By now Jackson knows that McClellan's Army of the Potomac is ready to move into the region to reinforce Pope. At Cedar Mountain, the beginning of the Second Bull Run Campaign (known to the South as Second Manassas), Union losses are 314 dead, 1445 wounded and 622 missing. Southern casualties are 1341.

16 AUGUST 1862

Civil War: Second Bull Run Campaign Following orders to join his command to that of General Pope, McClellan moves the Army of the Potomac out of Harrison's Landing and proceeds northward.

18 AUGUST 1862

Indian Warfare A Sioux uprising flares in Minnesota, led by Chief Little Crow. It will be suppressed by Colonel Henry Sibley in September.

19 AUGUST 1862

Civil War: The North Horace Greeley, powerful abolitionist editor of the *New York Tribune*, criticizes Lincoln's seeming lack of concern for the plight of black people in an editorial called 'The Prayer of Twenty Millions.' Despite having already drafted the Emancipation Proclamation, Lincoln replies to the editorial on 22 August, 'My paramount object . . . is to save the Union, and it is not either to save or to destroy slavery.'

22 AUGUST 1862

Civil War: Second Bull Run Campaign In a daring raid Confederate cavalry under Fitzhugh Lee (R. E. Lee's nephew) overruns Union General Pope's headquarters near Catlett's Station, Virginia (Pope is away at the time). Captured orders confirm that McClellan is on the way to reinforce Pope, which would make for a Federal army of 130,000. Lee, deciding to strike before the combination can be effected, will send Jackson and Stuart on a wide envelopment to operate on Union supply lines.

Second only to Lee in the pantheon of great CSA generals was Thomas Jonathan 'Stonewall' Jackson.

26 AUGUST 1862

Civil War: Second Bull Run Campaign The campaign heats up as Confederates under Stonewall Jackson move in on Union General John Pope's Army of Virginia. The Southerners seize Manassas Junction, destroying a Federal supply depot there (after eating and drinking as much of it as possible) and take over the railroad line. As Jackson divides his troops and encircles Pope's position, it dawns on the latter that he is in trouble, and in the evening Pope begins to withdraw.

27 AUGUST 1862

Civil War: Second Bull Run Campaign Kettle Run, Virginia, is one of several areas of heavy skirmishing. The Confederates have interrupted communications between Washington and the Federal Army of Virginia. Moreover, Jackson's maneuvers have thoroughly mystified General Pope, who is now pulling back northward from positions along the Rappahannock River.

28 AUGUST 1862

Civil War: Second Bull Run Campaign Jackson has managed to convince Pope that his forces are in retreat, and Pope is trying to find him. In fact, Jackson has entrenched in an ideal defensive position behind a railroad ditch at the foot of Sudley Mountain, near Groveton, Virginia. Jackson's problem is to hold Pope until the arrival of Lee with Longstreet's corps. Accordingly, Jackson engages the Federals and thereby discloses his position. A fierce skirmish ensues at Groveton. Pope orders a concentration in the area with the intention of destroying Jackson. (Meanwhile, Pope foolishly ignores reports of Longstreet's approach.)

29 AUGUST 1862

Civil War: The Second Battle of Bull Run General Pope mounts a series of uncoordinated attacks on Jackson, trying to cut off the latter's supposed retreat. But Jackson has no intention of withdrawing; in a strong position, with 20,000 men against Pope's 62,000 Federals, the Confederates fight determinedly to hold Pope until the arrival of Longstreet and Lee. Longstreet arrives in mid-morning, but puts off his attack until next day.

30 AUGUST 1862

Civil War: Second Battle of Bull Run Ignoring reports of Longstreet's forces on his left flank, Pope orders a general assault on Jackson's position across the railroad. Lee waits until Pope has committed his forces, then sends Longstreet to turn the enemy left flank. A Union retreat follows, though a fierce Federal stand at Henry House Hill allows a reasonably orderly pullback. In their first great battle, Lee and Jackson have outmaneuvered, outfought and generally humiliated the hapless General Pope. Lee has not destroyed the enemy army, but the combined operations of the Peninsular Campaign, Jack-

The burning of the Mumma farm at the Battle of Antietam. This day, 17 September 1862, bloodiest of the war, produced a total of 4808 killed.

son's Valley Campaign and Second Bull Run have eliminated the immediate threat to Virginia. Casualiies in the Second Bull Run are, for the Union, 1724 killed, 8372 wounded and 5958 missing, a total of 16,054 – 21 percent of the 75,696 engaged. Southern losses are 1481 killed, 7627 wounded and 89 missing, a total of 9197 – 19 percent of the 48,527 engaged.

1 SEPTEMBER 1862

Civil War: Second Bull Run Campaign The final action of the Second Bull Run campaign breaks out when Lee tries to envelop the Federal retreat. Jackson's corps strikes Federals under Stevens and Kearny near Chantilly, Virginia. After a day-long engagement the Federals withdraw. Stevens and Kearny are among the dead in the battle of Chantilly. Meanwhile, Pope is pulling the bulk of his forces back to Washington.

2 SEPTEMBER 1862

Civil War: Washington In the wake of Pope's humiliation at Second Bull Run, President Lincoln orders General McClellan to subsume the Union Army of Virginia into his Army of the Potomac. Few politicians are enthusiastic about McClellan's command after the aborted Peninsular Campaign, but he seems the only man available, and he remains popular with his troops.

4 SEPTEMBER 1862

Civil War: Antietam Campaign Having bested the Federals at Second Bull Run, Robert E. Lee makes the fateful decision to invade Maryland and begins to move the Army of Northern Virginia into the state. Within a few days Washington and cities in Maryland will fall into panic.

8 SEPTEMBER 1862

Civil War: Antietam Campaign Hoping to calm fears of civilians in Maryland and perhaps enlist Confederate supporters there, Lee makes a public speech saying, 'We know no enemies among you, and will protect all, of every opinion. It is for you to decide your destiny freely, and without constraint.' The support that Lee hoped for in the state, however, will not materialize – the first of his several miscalculations in the invasion.

9 SEPTEMBER 1862

Civil War: Antietam Campaign Pursuant to his invasion of the North, Lee issues Special Order No. 191, directing Jackson's corps southward to seize Harper's Ferry while Longstreet moves toward Hagerstown, Maryland. Meanwhile, McClellan is now moving cautiously west toward Lee with the Army of the Potomac.

13 SEPTEMBER 1862

Civil War: Antietam Campaign A Union soldier finds a paper wrapped around two cigars in a field; the paper proves to be a copy of Lee's Special Order No. 191, which is soon in the hands of General McClellan. Now McClellan has complete information on the divided enemy forces and the opportunity to smash Lee one corps at a time. Before the day is out Lee is informed that McClellan has the order and plans accordingly. Meanwhile, Jackson has arrived at Harper's Ferry. The most sanguinary battle of the war to date is fast approaching.

14 SEPTEMBER 1862

Civil War: Antietam Campaign The battle of Crampton's Gap, the first of several engagements making up the Antietam Campaign, breaks out around noon. As Confederates under McLaws prepare to attack Harper's Ferry, Virginia, Union troops under Franklin strike them from the rear. After a day of fighting the Confederates pull back, but Jackson still takes Harper's Ferry the next day. In a separate battle at South Mountain, General Pleasonton attacks Rebels defending Turner's Gap and drives them away.

15 SEPTEMBER 1862

Civil War: Antietam Campaign Stonewall Jackson captures Harper's Ferry and nearly 11,000 Federals. At Sharpsburg, on Antietam Creek, Lee has made the audacious decision to stand and fight McClellan with only 19,000 Confederate troops available (40,000 are at Harper's Ferry) to the Union's 75,000. Lee's gamble is based on his low – and accurate – opinion of McClellan's generalship. With his slowness to strike, the Union commander has fumbled away the once-in-a-lifetime opportunity that capturing Lee's order gave him.

17 SEPTEMBER 1862

Civil War: Battle of Antietam (or Sharpsburg) In position behind the creek, his back to the Potomac and with only about a third of his army present, Lee awaits McClellan's attack. It begins at dawn, Federals under Hooker falling onto the Confederate left. The fighting is bloody in the extreme, but the assaults are piecemeal and ineffective. As the fighting on the left wanes in exhaustion, scattered Union attacks strike the middle of the Rebel line. After more severe fighting, particularly in a sunken road dubbed 'Bloody Lane,' the Southern line holds on by a thread. Finally, in midafternoon, Federal General Burnside fights his men across a small bridge over the creek (having failed to notice the creek is shallow enough to wade) and makes headway against Lee's right. Then, as the Confederate line is on the verge of collapse, A. P. Hill's men arrive after a forced march from Harper's Ferry and pour a withering fire into the advancing Yankees, saving the day for the South. The opposing forces have fought to a draw at the battle of Antietam; McClellan's generalship once again proves inadequate. Nonetheless, the Union Army of the Potomac has at least not been humiliated this time. In the bloodiest single day the war will see the North has lost 2108 killed, 9549 wounded and 753 missing, a total of 12,410 casualties among 75,316 effectives. The South's losses are 2700 killed, 9024 wounded and 2000 missing – 13,724 casualties out of 51,844 engaged.

18 SEPTEMBER 1862

Civil War: Antietam Campaign Having defiantly stayed in position at Antietam Creek through the day, Lee in the evening begins to withdraw – undefeated but with his invasion of Maryland stymied. McClellan makes no attempt to pursue. Confederates will pull out of Harper's Ferry the next day.

Civil War: Western Theater Southern forces under General Sterling Price attack Federals under General W. S. Rosecrans at Iuka, Mississippi. After several hours the Northerners have overwhelmed Price's men, who retreat toward the south.

22 SEPTEMBER 1862

Civil War: Emancipation Proclamation Deciding that Antietam is more or less the victory he has been waiting for, President Lincoln releases the Emancipation Proclamation. Though the document only frees slaves in the Confederacy, and thus actually frees none at all, it is still an epochal event. Transforming the war from an action against secession to a crusade against slavery, the Proclamation effectively forestalls European recognition of the Confederacy and somewhat placates Northern abolitionists. A political as well as moral masterstroke, the Emancipation Proclamation is the beginning of the end of human slavery in America.

2 OCTOBER 1862

Civil War: Western Theater A battle breaks out in Mississippi as Confederates under Van Dorn and Price drive Federals under Rosecrans into a defensive position near Corinth.

4 OCTOBER 1862

Civil War: Western Theater The second day of battle at Corinth, Mississippi, sees Rosecrans' Federals hit hard by Van Dorn's forces. Nevertheless, after heavy fighting the Southerners are forced to withdraw before nightfall. The Confederate offensive thus fails in its attempt to secure the railroad and, more important, to drive Rosecrans into Ohio.

8 OCTOBER 1862

Civil War: Western Theater A Confederate invasion of Kentucky, which began in late August under General Braxton Bragg, climaxes in the battle of Perryville. Northern troops are poorly handled by General Don Carlos Buell, but Buell nonetheless is able to drive Bragg back and finally out of the state. Union losses in the battle are 4211 out of 36,940 effectives. Southern losses are 3396 out of an estimated 16,000 engaged.

9 OCTOBER 1862

Civil War: Eastern Theater At Chambersburg, Pennsylvania, Confederate cavalry General 'Jeb' Stuart begins several days of raiding which carries him as far as Cashtown, Pennsylvania. In the process Stuart will take his 1800 troopers around McClellan's army for the second time, with Federal cavalry helpless to stop him or his depredations on Union communications.

18 OCTOBER 1862

Civil War: Western Theater Confederate raider John Hunt Morgan, with 1500 men, routs Federal cavalry outside Lexington, Kentucky, and enters the city.

22 OCTOBER 1862

Civil War: Western Theater Confederate General Bragg gets his army safely out of Kentucky after his invasion attempt. For allowing that escape, Federal General Don Carlos Buell will be cashiered from command in Kentucky and Tennessee. His replacement will be General W. S. Rosecrans, who also heads the Department of the Cumberland.

28 OCTOBER 1862

Civil War: Eastern Theater After much exasperated prodding from the President, General McClellan is moving his Army of the Potomac toward Lee's forces at Warrenton, Virginia.

4 NOVEMBER

Civil War: Western Theater Having gathered forces in preparation for a campaign against Vicksburg, the last Confederate stronghold on the Mississippi River, General U. S. Grant occupies La Grange and Grand Junction in the area.

5 NOVEMBER 1862

Civil War: Washington In one of the more significant command changes of the war President Lincoln removes General George B. McClellan from his command of the Army of the Potomac. McClellan has built the army admirably, but he has been unconscionably slow to move, insubordinate in his relations with the president and ineffective on the battlefield. Yet Lincoln makes an unfortunate choice for McClellan's replacement: General Ambrose E. Burnside, who will prove one of the most blundering leaders of the war.

8 NOVEMBER 1862

Civil War: Washington Dealing with another troublesome general, Lincoln relieves Ben Butler as head of the Department of the Gulf, replacing him with General Nathaniel Banks.

14 NOVEMBER 1862

Civil War: Eastern Theater The newly-appointed chief of the Army of the Potomac, General Burnside, reorganizes his command, appointing Generals Sumner, Hooker and Franklin as corps commanders. On the next day he will put his army on the road to Fredericksburg, Virginia, where Lee's forces await.

18 NOVEMBER 1862

Civil War: Fredericksburg Campaign General Burnside and the army of the Potomac arrive in Falmouth, Virginia, on the banks of the Rappahannock River across from the Confederate position at Fredericksburg.

24 NOVEMBER 1862

Civil War: The Confederacy President Davis appoints General Joseph E. Johnston as commander of the Army in the West.

28 NOVEMBER 1862

Civil War: Trans-Mississippi Federal forces under General James Blunt stage an attack on Confederate positions at Cane Hill, Arkansas. The 8000 Southern troops there are under General John Marmaduke. Blunt's 5000 men pursue Marmaduke into the Boston Mountains after beating them back, but the chase is called off due to the strategic danger it creates.

Right: Lincoln speaks with McClellan in the field.

ABRAHAM LINCOLN AND HIS Emancipation Proclamation

Whereas On the Twenty-second day of September, in the year of our Lord one thousand eight hundred and sixty-two, a Proclamation was issued by the President of the United States, containing among other things the following, to-wit:

"That on the first day of January, in the year of our Lord one thousand eight hundred and sixty-three, all persons held as slaves within any State, or designated part of a State, the people whereof shall then be in rebellion against the United States, shall be then, thenceforward and forever free, and the executive government of the United States, including the military and naval authority thereof, will recognize and maintain the freedom of such persons, and will do no act or acts to repress such persons, or any of them, in any efforts they may make for their actual freedom.

"That the executive will, on the first day of January aforesaid, by proclamation, designate the States and parts of States, if any, in which the people thereof respectively shall then be in rebellion against the United States, and the fact that any State, or the people thereof, shall on that day be in good faith represented in the Congress of the United States by members chosen thereto at elections wherein a majority of the qualified voters of such State shall have participated, shall, in the absence of strong countervailing testimony, be deemed conclusive evidence that such State and the people thereof are not then in rebellion against the United States."

Now, therefore, I, ABRAHAM LINCOLN, President of the United States, by virtue of the power in me vested as Commander-in-Chief of the Army and Navy of the United States in time of actual armed rebellion against the authority and government of the United States, and as a fit and necessary war measure for suppressing said rebellion, do, on this first day of January, in the year of our Lord one thousand eight hundred and sixty-three, and in accordance with my purpose so to do, publicly proclaim for the full period of one hundred days from the day the first above mentioned order, and designate as the States and parts of States wherein the people thereof respectively are this day in rebellion against the United States, the following, to-wit:

ARKANSAS, TEXAS, LOUISIANA (except the parishes of St. Bernard, Plaquemines, Jefferson, St. John, St. Charles, St. James, Ascension, Assumption, Terre Bonne, Lafourche, St. Mary, St. Martin, and Orleans, including the city of New Orleans), MISSISSIPPI, ALABAMA, FLORIDA, GEORGIA, SOUTH CAROLINA, NORTH CAROLINA and VIRGINIA (except the forty-eight counties designated as West Virginia, and also the counties of Berkley, Accomac, Northampton, Elizabeth City, York, Princess Ann and Norfolk, including the cities of Norfolk and Portsmouth), and which excepted parts are, for the present, left precisely as if this Proclamation were not issued.

And by virtue of the power and for the purpose aforesaid, I do order and declare that all persons held as slaves within said designated States and parts of States are and henceforward shall be free; and that the executive government of the United States, including the military and naval authorities thereof, will recognize and maintain the freedom of said persons

And I hereby enjoin upon the people so declared to be free, to abstain from all violence, unless in necessary self-defence, and I recommend to them that in all cases, when allowed, they labor faithfully for reasonable wages.

And I further declare and make known that such persons of suitable condition, will be received into the armed service of the United States to garrison forts, positions, stations and other places, and to man vessels of all sorts in said service.

And upon this act, sincerely believed to be an act of justice, warranted by the Constitution, upon military necessity, I invoke the considerate judgment of mankind, and the gracious favor of Almighty God.

In testimony whereof, I have hereunto set my name, and caused the seal of the United States to be affixed.

L.S. Done at the City of Washington, this first day of January, in the year of our Lord one thousand eight hundred and sixty-three, and of the Independence of the United States the eighty-Seventh.

By the President: ABRAHAM LINCOLN.

WILLIAM H. SEWARD, Secretary of State.

NOTE.—The rest of the slaves were afterwards freed by Legislation and Constitutional Amendments.

Below: Lincoln's Emancipation Proclamation of 1 January 1863 in fact freed no slaves, since it applied only to slaves in seceded states.

7 DECEMBER 1862

Civil War: Western Theater Hartville, Tennessee, is the scene of another raid by John Hunt Morgan and his men. The Federal garrison under Colonel A. B. Moore suffers losses of 2096, 1800 of them taken prisoner.

Civil War: Trans-Mississippi In Arkansas the battle of Prairie Grove takes place as Confederate General Thomas Hindman surprises Northern troops under Generals James Blunt and Francis Herron. The 10,000 Federals are unable to repel 10,000 Rebels. Losses are 1251 for the Union, 1317 for the South.

Civil War: Fredericksburg Campaign The Federal Army of the Potomac under General Burnside is still gearing up for the assault on Lee at Fredericksburg, Virginia. The slowness of Burnside's preparations has given Lee all the time he could wish to arrange his defenses.

13 DECEMBER 1862

Civil War: Battle of Fredericksburg Approximately 78,500 men of the Confederate Army of Northern Virginia are in strong defenses on the heights above Fredericksburg, and the 122,000 of the Federal Army of the Potomac are ready to attack. Before noon the corps of General William Franklin advances with flags flying on Stonewall Jackson's corps at the right of the Southern line. Jackson waits until the enemy is in good range, then unleashes a storm of fire that drives the Federals back with heavy losses. Soon after, General Sumner advances on positions north of the city after a preliminary – and ineffective – bombardment. Sumner's peacemeal attacks hit the virtually invulnerable Confederate positions on Marye's Heights. Lee finds that his opponent is preceding precisely as the Confederates have hoped: he is throwing virtually random frontal assaults on Southern defenses that are as strong as positions can be. The result is one of the most appalling slaughters of the war: at the end of the day 12,700 Northerners lie dead or wounded on the slopes. Confederate losses are less than half the North's, approximately 5300. As one Union soldier observes, 'It can hardly be in human nature for men to show more valor, or generals to manifest less judgment, than were perceptible on our side that day.' Another says more succinctly, 'They may as well have tried to take Hell.'

15 DECEMBER 1862

Civil War: Fredericksburg Campaign Following the debacle of Fredericksburg the stricken Army of the Potomac withdraws toward Falmouth, Virginia. Lee does not pursue.

Civil War: Western Theater In Tennessee, General Grant's forces, preparing for their campaign against Vicksburg, are harassed by enemy raids on their communications by General Nathan Bedford Forrest, who is a master of the art.

26 DECEMBER 1862

Indian Affairs Following a Sioux Indian uprising in Minnesota which claimed the lives of over 450 white settlers, 38 Sioux are hanged at Mankato, Minnesota. President Lincoln has commuted the sentences of over 300 other Indians who had likewise been sentenced by the court to die.

27 DECEMBER 1862

Civil War: Western Theater Federal forces under General W. T. Sherman push toward Vicksburg, Mississippi, as part of Grant's operations against the city. Sherman's assault on the land defenses of the city on 29 December will fail, and Grant will turn to other ideas about how to take the city.

30 DECEMBER 1862

Civil War: Naval In stormy waters off Cape Hatteras the pioneering Union ironclad USS *Monitor* goes to the bottom with 16 men and officers; another 47 are rescued. The Union now has a growing fleet of turreted ironclads on the model of the *Monitor*, while the South is building its less sophisticated, but still effective, ironclads on the model of the *Virginia* (or *Merrimack*).

31 DECEMBER 1862-2 JANUARY 1863

Civil War: Battle of Stones River Murfreesboro, Tennessee, sees a major battle between the two main armies of the region – the Federal Army of the Cumberland under W. S. Rosecrans and the Confederate Army of Tennessee under Braxton Bragg. Having tangled once before at the battle of Perryville, Kentucky, the two commanders have now faced off just west of Stones River. Both have planned to attack in the morning by striking the enemy right; if pursued, the plans would turn both armies like a revolving door. Instead, the Southern attack erupts first. There follows a confused and bitter day of fighting that leaves the Union army battered and on the defensive. On 1 January there is only minor skirmishing as the exhausted armies recoup. Then, on the 2nd, a major assault by Confederate General Breckenridge – ordered by Bragg over the objections of Breckinridge – is turned back with heavy losses. But by the end of the day the Confederates have won a tactical victory, the result more of fierce and fearless fighting by the Southerners than of effective leadership by Bragg. Both sides have taken heavy losses in the battle of Stones River, the Federals losing 12,906 out of 41,400 engaged, the South 11,739 out of 34,739 engaged. Despite his relative success, Bragg will pull away from Murfreesboro on the 3rd and head for East Tennessee.

1 JANUARY 1863

Civil War: Washington Lincoln's Emancipation Proclamation takes effect.

11 JANUARY 1863

Civil War: Trans-Mississippi Fort Hindman, Arkansas, is seized by coordinated Federal land and naval attacks under General John A. McClernand and Admiral David Dixon Porter. During the battle the Union suffers 1061 casualties out of 28,944 engaged. Virtually the entire Southern garrison of 5000 is captured.

The Confederate raider *Florida* destroys the clipper ship *Jacob Bell* in February 1863.

20 JANUARY 1863

Civil War: Eastern Theater After his bloody failure to take Fredericksburg by assault Union General Burnside decides to try an envelopment of Lee's position in the town. The Army of the Potomac pulls out for Fredericksburg today, but immediately runs into torrential rains which turn the route into a morass. After two days of what comes to be called the 'Mud March' the attempt is abandoned, and the demoralized army turns back. Having crowned a debacle with a fiasco, Burnside takes the traditional route of blaming his subordinates, but he still finds himself cashiered by Lincoln on 25 January.

22 JANUARY 1863

Civil War: Western Theater General Grant is given overall responsibility for operations in the vicinity of Arkansas, his primary task still being to conquer Vicksburg, Mississippi. He begins a series of experimental approaches to the Confederate stronghold, ordering a canal dug through marshy areas across from the city.

26 JANUARY 1863

Civil War: Eastern Theater General Joseph Hooker, 48, called 'Fighting Joe' by the press, succeeds Burnside in command of the Federal Army of the Potomac (122,000 infantry, 12,000 cavalrymen and a battery of 400 cannons). Hooker is an experienced but somewhat dissolute commander who has schemed actively to get the command. He confidently proclaims 'May God have mercy on General Lee, for I will have none!' Hearing the news, Lee does not seem anxious about his soul or his army. On the departure of General McClellan, Lee had observed with gentle irony, "I am sorry to see him go, for we always understood each other so well. I fear they may continue to make these changes until they find someone whom I don't understand.' Hooker, Lee suspects, will be no challenge to his understanding of Union generals.

31 JANUARY 1863

Civil War: Naval In Charleston Harbor, South Carolina, there is a spectacular battle between Southern gunboats and the Northern blockading fleet. The Confederate ironclads *Chicora* and *Palmetto State* severely damage the Federal *Mercedita* and *Keystone State*, but the harbor remains under the control of the Federal blockade.

3 FEBRUARY 1863

Civil War: Western Theater At Yazoo Pass in Arkansas, Grant's soldiers break through a levee, providing a passage for troops along the Yazoo River north of Vicksburg. It is another of Grant's experiments with ways to reach the city, but nothing will come of it.

5 FEBRUARY 1863

Civil War: Eastern Theater Showing unexpected planning abilities, General Hooker reorganizes the Army of the Potomac and tones up its equipment and morale in preparation for operations against Lee's Army of Northern Virginia, which is still at Fredericksburg and dealing with much Union cavalry reconnaissance in the area.

Union General Joseph 'Fighting Joe' Hooker had a reputation for courage and aggressiveness, but he was no match for Lee at Chancellorsville in 1863.

7 FEBRUARY 1863

Civil War: Naval Though the Union blockade of the Confederacy will be increasingly effective in cutting off supplies to the South, blockade-running has developed into a fine art in the Rebel navy, dozens of sleek, fast, black-painted ships pursuing the trade. Today three blockade-runners break through the Federal cordon at Charleston, South Carolina.

12 FEBRUARY 1863

Civil War: Western Theater The war has wound down for the winter, but a typical day's skirmishing claims lives around the country. In a minor action at Bolivar, Tennessee, four Union men are dead and five injured in a Confederate attack. At Sandy Ridge, North Carolina, Federal troops skirmish with the enemy.

Civil War: Naval Captain Ellet's *Queen of the West* fires on and manages to destroy a number of Confederate wagons carrying supplies and ammunition along the Red River. Off the West Indies, the Southern blockade runner *Florida* seizes and destroys the Yankee clipper *Jacob Bell*, with its $2 million of Chinese tea and other goods. The Union ironclad *Indianola* runs the Rebel batteries at Vicksburg; on 14 February it will connect with a ship carrying survivors of the *Queen of the West*, which has been run aground when a boiler threatens to explode.

15 FEBRUARY 1863

Civil War: Western Theater At Cainsville, Tennessee, Federals hold off an attack by John Hunt Morgan's raiders. Two Union men are killed, 12 wounded; Confederate losses include 20 dead and a large number wounded and captured.

16 FEBRUARY 1863

Civil War: Washington The Senate passes a conscription act with the support of the president. This new draft law is intended to fill the ranks of the Union Army, which is not adequately served by voluntary enlistment. It is estimated that by the end of 1862 100,000 soldiers have deserted the army.

17 FEBRUARY 1863

Civil War: Naval The ironclad gunboat USS *Indianola* is now in position at the junction of the Red River and the Mississippi, intending to waylay Southern vessels headed upriver to Vicksburg.

24 FEBRUARY 1863

Civil War: Naval In a blow to its river operations on the Mississippi the Federal Navy loses the *Indianola* to an attack from Confederate rams.

25 FEBRUARY 1863

Civil War: The Confederacy Inflation plagues the South; in Charleston, South Carolina, a half-pound loaf of bread costs $25 and flour is selling for $65 a barrel (in Confederate money).

3 MARCH 1863

Civil War: Washington Congress passes the new Enrollment Act, often called the Conscription Act, which calls for the three-year enlistment of all able-bodied white males between 20 and 45 years of age. (Substitutes or payment of $300 can be used for exemption.) The Act is well-received by the military, who are pleased at the prospect of fresh troops. The public response will be embodied in the Draft Riots of July. The Financial Bill passed by Congress at this time is intended to aid the Federal economy, in part by the issuing of treasury notes. In addition, Congress authorizes suspension of the writ of habeas corpus throughout the entire Union; 36 Democratic Representatives protest this action.

5 MARCH 1863

Civil War: Western Theater The Confederate garrison at Vicksburg, Mississippi, steps up preparations and fortifications against Grant's coming assault on the city. Union forces are constructing a mile-long canal to bypass the shore batteries at Vicksburg. (The canal, like several other experiments, will eventually be abandoned.)

8 MARCH 1863

Civil War: Eastern Theater General E. H. Stoughton, commander of the Federal garrison at Fairfax Court House, Virginia, is awakened by a slap on his behind and finds himself the prisoner of Confederate raider John Singleton Mosby, who seizes a number of other prisoners, horses and equipment in a daring night raid of the style for which he will become famous.

11 MARCH 1863

Civil War: Western Theater In an effective counter to Northern operations against Vicksburg, Mississippi, Confederates construct a defensive outpost called Fort Pemberton. Union forces attempting to move past the fort on the Yalobusha River find that their gunboats are unable to withstand the new batteries. After six days of exchanging fire Grant's troops are obliged to give up yet another experiment of the Vicksburg campaign.

14 MARCH 1863

Civil War: Naval Port Hudson, Louisiana, where Confederate troops are stationed north of Baton Rouge, is subjected to bombardment from Union gunboats under Admiral David Farragut. This attempt by Federals to move past Port Hudson to Vicksburg costs the Navy the USS *Mississippi*, which runs aground and is eventually burned. The USS *Hartford* and the *Albatross* make it past Port Hudson, but two other vessels in the flotilla sustain considerable damage and are forced to turn back. During this action 65 Federals are listed as killed or missing.

17 MARCH 1863

Civil War: Eastern Theater General Hooker sends an Army of the Potomac cavalry corps under General William Wood Averell to attack General Fitz Lee at Culpeper, Virginia. Taking 2100 men and six artillery pieces, Averell engages 800 Southern horsemen at the battle of Kelly's Ford. After a full day of fighting the Federals pull back with 78 casualties, to 133 for the South.

20 MARCH 1863

Civil War: Western Theater In Mississippi, General Grant makes another abortive attempt to reach Vicksburg by water, this time via Steele Bayou, with 11 ships supported by General William Tecumseh Sherman's infantry.

22 MARCH 1863

Civil War: Western Theater In Kentucky there are several encounters between North and South; Confederate raider John Hunt Morgan and his cavalry harass Federal positions, and Rebels under John Pegram operate against Union forces. These operations will continue through the month.

24 MARCH 1863

Civil War: Western Theater Northern troops try to reach Vicksburg by way of Black Bayou; the attempt will be turned back tomorrow. General Grant thereupon will decide to end his experiments at reaching Vicksburg by roundabout water routes and will now concentrate on a more elaborate strategy.

26 MARCH 1863

Civil War: Washington In a letter which reveals some of Lincoln's thinking concerning the former slave population the president writes to Tennessee Governor Andrew Johnson: 'The colored population is the great *available*, and yet unavailed of, force for restoring the Union. The bare sight of fifty thousand armed and drilled black soldiers on the banks of the Mississippi, would end the rebellion at once.' However, Northern resistance to the idea of black soldiers will limit the number of actively engaged black regiments throughout the war.

Civil War: The North Following the Emancipation Proclamation loyal slaveholding states begin to consider voluntary emancipation. Today West Virginia citizens approve a referendum mandating gradual emancipation.

29 MARCH 1863

Civil War: Vicksburg Campaign Beginning the final phase of his series of operations against the vital Confederate stronghold of Vicksburg – the key to Union control of the Mississippi River – Grant directs General McClernand to open a road from Millikens Bend to New Carthage, just south of Vicksburg on the opposite (west) bank. McClernand will complete the road on 6 April, opening the way for Grant's whole Army of the Tennessee. This move is to be supported by a flotilla under Admiral Porter, who is ordered to take his ships past the formidable Vicksburg batteries.

31 MARCH 1863

Civil War: Eastern Theater Drainesville, Virginia, sees Union cavalry clash with Southern partisan rangers under the redoubtable John Singleton Mosby. In a victory typical of him Mosby thrashes the Federals, who sustain 60 casualties.

2 APRIL 1863

Civil War: The Confederacy A bread riot breaks out in the Confederate capital of Richmond, Virginia. A mob initially demands bread from a bakery wagon and soon begins attacking nearby shops. President Davis, backed up by militia, appears personally to break up the mob.

5 APRIL 1863

Civil War: International The British detain several Confederate vessels in Liverpool harbor, which puts the South on notice that they can expect less sympathy from Palmerston's government.

7 APRIL 1863

Civil War: Naval In Charleston Harbor, South Carolina, nine Union ironclad vessels bombard Fort Sumter. Confederate fire from Forts Sumter and Moultrie drive the attack away with extensive damage to the Union ships and 15 casualties. This action demonstrates that Charleston cannot be taken by naval operations alone.

10 APRIL 1863

Civil War: The Confederacy President Jefferson Davis advises the South to concentrate on food crops rather than tobacco. His past promises that the overseas demand for cotton will bring recognition and wealth from Europe have proven empty – the Southern economy is now nearly at the breaking point. A newspaper estimates that in the first two years of war the weekly cost of feeding a family has increased from $6.65 to $68.25.

Civil War: Western Theater Near Franklin, Tennessee, Federals under General Granger attack enemy forces under General Van Dorn. The Rebels are defeated in a brief battle which claims 100 Northerners dead and wounded and 300 Southern casualties.

11 APRIL 1863

Civil War: Washington Having recently met with General Hooker in Virginia, President Lincoln now meets with his cabinet and with General-in-Chief Henry Halleck to discuss war strategy with emphasis on General Grant's Vicksburg campaign.

Civil War: Western Theater In Louisiana, Federal General Nathaniel Banks takes 17,000 men on an ex-

Union ironclads bombard Fort Sumter in April 1863. The US Navy attacked the fort repeatedly throughout the war, but it remained in Rebel hands to the end.

pedition toward the Red River; this is intended to help operations on the Mississippi, but the expedition will come to little.

13 APRIL 1863

Civil War: Eastern Theater Intending a Jeb Stuart-style raid on Lee's communications, General Hooker sends 10,000 cavalry under General George Stoneman on a raid across the Rappahannock River. Lee, informed of this raid will simply ignore the Federal cavalrymen, who will later limp home with heavy losses.

15 APRIL 1863

Civil War: Eastern Theater General Hooker reports that his refurbished Army of the Potomac has nearly 130,000 men, in contrast with the approximately 60,000 of General Lee's Army of Northern Virginia, still in the Fredericksburg area (Longstreet's command being absent on a foraging mission). The Union commander has developed a promising plan: leaving a force to hold Lee in position, Hooker will march the bulk of his army around in a wide strategic envelopment, coming in behind Lee from the west.

16 APRIL 1863

Civil War: Vicksburg Campaign In the first big gamble of his final operations on Vicksburg, Mississippi, Grant sends Admiral David Dixon Porter and 12 vessels on a dramatic nighttime run past the formidable Vicksburg batteries. Though every Union ship is hit during a furious bombardment, only one sinks.

17 APRIL 1863

Civil War: Vicksburg Campaign In yet another element of his complex Vicksburg strategy Grant orders Colonel Benjamin Grierson and 1700 cavalry on a raid south from La Grange, Tennessee. The raid is intended to divert the Confederates in Mississippi from Grant's real threat – moving ships and men south of Vicksburg preparatory to an assault from the land.

22 APRIL 1863

Civil War: Vicksburg Campaign Grant sends 18 more vessels past the Confederate batteries of Vicksburg, with less success than on the 16th – one transport and six barges are sunk.

24 APRIL 1863

Civil War: The Confederacy In a much-deplored move the Confederate Congress places an eight percent tax on all agricultural products grown in the previous year and a ten percent tax on profits made from the purchase or sale of most food, clothing and iron. A graduated income tax is also instituted.

25 APRIL 1863

Civil War: Eastern Theater Federals clash with the enemy in Greenland Gap, Virginia; the North loses 15 dead and 60 prisoners, the Confederates estimate close to 100 killed and a large number of prisoners lost.

26 APRIL 1863

Civil War: Western Theater With the armies of Union General Rosecrans and Confederate General Bragg inactive in middle Tennessee, Rebel raiders Nathan Bedford Forrest and John Hunt Morgan have been harassing Federal communications. To try and stop these depredations, Union Colonel Abel Streight sets out with mule-mounted troops to track the enemy raiders. Instead, Streight will soon find Forrest pursuing him.

Civil War: Trans-Mississippi A Union garrison at Cape Girardeau, Missouri, is attacked by enemy under General John Marmaduke, but the Federals repel the assault, losing 12 casualties to the South's nearly 250.

27 APRIL 1863

Civil War: Eastern Theater Leaving 30,000 under General Sedgwick to hold the Confederates in place at Fredericksburg, Hooker moves 70,000 men along the Rappahannock River on the wide envelopment that he proclaims will finish Lee off once and for all. The Federals will cross the river the following days.

30 APRIL 1863

Civil War: The Confederacy Increasingly concerned with Grant's threat to Vicksburg, President Davis advises General Joseph E. Johnston of the situation in the city; Johnston will soon be sent to aid Vicksburg commander John C. Pemberton.

Civil War: Chancellorsville Campaign General Hooker, encamped near a clearing in the Virginia Wilderness called Chancellorsville, confidently reports that, 'the operations of the last three days have determined that our enemy must ingloriously fly, or come out from behind their defenses.'

Civil War: Vicksburg Campaign Grant moves his Army of the Tennessee across the Mississippi River to the east bank – the Vicksburg side – while Sherman mounts an attack at Haines' Bluff to cover the move. Confederate commander Pemberton is duly confused, taking Sherman's feint for the main attack. Now at last, after so many months of frustrating operations, Grant is ready to take on the Confederate city directly. First, however, he will march east to deal with other Confederate forces in the area.

The Battle of Chancellorsville, 2-3 May 1863, was both Lee's masterpiece and the South's costliest victory: 1665 killed, including Jackson.

Twelve ships of Admiral David Porter's Mississippi flotilla run past the guns of the strong Vicksburg batteries on 17 April 1863. One ship was sunk.

1 MAY 1863

Civil War: Chancellorsville Campaign Pushing through the Virginia Wilderness toward Fredericksburg in Hooker's intended envelopment, Federal advance units are surprised to find themselves opposed by Rebel units two miles from the Chancellorsville clearing. Lee, keeping track of Hooker's movements by way of Stuart's cavalry, has divined his enemy's strategy and is countering it with a bold one of his own: the Confederate commander has divided his outnumbered forces, leaving 10,000 to bluff Sedgwick at Fredericksburg and marching over 50,000 to confront Hooker. The latter, buffaloed at the first brush with an enemy force that is not part of his plan, abandons the advance and orders his army to pull back and dig in. Having cowed the enemy and learned that the Federal right flank is vulnerable, Lee and Stonewall Jackson have a late-night conference to plan a surprise for General Hooker.

Civil War: Vicksburg Campaign After crossing the Mississippi the previous day, Union troops advance on the enemy at Port Gibson, which is evacuated by the Confederates after an all-day fight.

2 MAY 1863

Civil War: Battle of Chancellorsville Another great battle breaks out between Hooker's Union Army of the Potomac and Lee's Army of Northern Virginia. Holding the Federals in place with feinting attacks during the day, Lee sends Stonewall Jackson and 26,000 men on a 16-mile march across the Federal front, a move which the demoralized Hooker fails to detect. At 6 o'clock Jackson's men pounce onto the undefended Yankee right and send the Northerners running in terror. The collapsed flank streams back toward Chancellorsville, and only the coming of darkness and scattered Union resistance halt the Southern advance before it destroys the Army of the Potomac. However, after this brilliant success the South suffers a serious loss: during a night reconnaissance Stonewall Jackson is accidentally wounded by his own men.

Civil War: Vicksburg Campaign Colonel Grierson and his cavalrymen arrive in Baton Rouge, Louisiana, ending their diversionary raid. In 16 days they have ridden through 600 miles of hostile territory, wrecked some 60 miles of railroad, destroyed massive amounts of supplies, captured 500 enemy and suffered only 27 casualties. In the process they have tied up enemy forces in the area and thoroughly confused the Confederate commanders. Elsewhere today, Grant's men push further into Mississippi.

3 MAY 1863

Civil War: Battle of Chancellorsville The second day of battle begins as Jeb Stuart, commanding the troops of the wounded Jackson, strikes the Federals at dawn, driving them back in confusion; finally Hooker's headquarters at the Chancellorsville mansion comes under heavy fire, and Hooker himself is dazed by a shell. Meanwhile, Union commander Sedgwick storms the Confederate positions at Fredericksburg and marches to aid Hooker, threatening to catch Lee in a vise. But the Confederate commander, hearing of Sedgwick's approach, leaves a small part of his army to contain Hooker and marches with the rest to deal with Sedgwick.

Civil War: Vicksburg Campaign The Confederate garrison at Grand Gulf, Mississippi, is evacuated before Grant's advance. Meanwhile, in Alabama, Union General Streight, whose riders had been sent out to run down Nathan Bedford Forrest, is himself captured after days of pursuit. Bluffing Streight by marching his smaller forces in a circle, Forrest gains the surrender of 1466 Yankees to his force of 500.

4 MAY 1863

Civil War: Battle of Chancellorsville Today Lee completes his masterpiece. Having held the bulk of the Union army in place to the east, Lee surrounds the forces of General Sedgwick on three sides and drives him back across the Rappahannock. In one of history's most brilliant tactical victories, Lee has soundly beaten an enemy over twice his size. Union losses in the battle have been 1575 killed and 9594 wounded, a total of 11,116 out of 97,382 effectives. Southern casualties are estimated at 12,821 killed, wounded and missing out of 60,892 effectives (Lee thus has much more severe percentage losses). Years later the Federal commander will say of his failure of nerve at Chancellorsville, 'To tell the truth, I just lost confidence in Joe Hooker.'

6 MAY 1863

Civil War: Eastern Theater After his humiliating defeat at Chancellorsville, General Hooker begins his withdrawal across the Rappahannock. Had Hooker waited one more day to run, he would have given Lee a chance to make a planned and probably disastrous assault on the Federal positions. As Stonewall Jackson lies wounded, Lee puts General A. P. Hill in charge of Jackson's corps.

7 MAY 1863

Civil War: The Confederacy Jubilant over the victory at Chancellorsville, Southern leaders turn to the problem of Vicksburg. President Davis writes the city's commander, General Pemberton, 'To hold both Vicksburg and Port Hudson is necessary to our connection with Trans-Mississippi. You may expect whatever it is in my power to do for your aid.'

10 MAY 1863

Civil War: The Confederacy After the enigmatic final words 'Let us cross over the river and rest under the shade of the trees,' General Stonewall Jackson dies in Virginia at age 39. He has been Lee's right arm, and the Confederacy will never recover from his loss.

12 MAY 1863

Civil War: Vicksburg Campaign General Grant has made the historic decision to break away from his supply line and march his army across enemy territory to take Jackson, the capital of Mississippi, before returning to assault Vicksburg. (This is in defiance of orders from Washington to march south and aid Banks' Red River campaign at Port Hudson.) Today Grant starts his army of 44,000 northeast across the state. Immediately one of his corps gets into a sharp skirmish at Raymond, both sides suffering some 500 casualties before the Southerners pull back toward Jackson, where General Johnston is preparing to resist Grant's advance.

14 MAY 1863

Civil War: Vicksburg Campaign Despite a downpour, Grant's men pitch into Johnston's forces outside Jackson. After some stiff fighting the outnumbered Confederates are forced out of the city, and the Federals occupy the capital in late afternoon. To the south, Federal General Banks moves his forces toward Port Hudson, after Vicksburg the second most critical Confederate position on the Mississippi River.

15 MAY 1863

Civil War: Vicksburg Campaign Vicksburg commander Pemberton moves out of the city to operate against Grant's supply line, not suspecting that Grant has no supply line.

16 MAY 1863

Civil War: Vicksburg Campaign General Pemberton finally locates the advance forces of General Grant, which are now moving west toward Vicksburg, and tries to stop them. The result is the battle of Champion's Hill, the most severe engagement of the campaign. The forces engaged are not radically unequal: Grant has 29,000 men of McPherson's and McClernand's corps (Sherman's corps is still moving out of Jackson), and Confederate General Pemberton some 22,000. McClernand makes contact with the Rebel left flank about 9:30 AM, but he waits over four hours to make what should have been the initial attack. This gives Pemberton time to shift troops to meet McPherson's assault on his right. The fighting surges back and forth indecisively for some time, Champion's Hill changing hands repeatedly, before the Confederates are forced to pull back toward Vicksburg with Grant in pursuit. Union casualties in the battle are 410 killed, 1844 wounded and 187 missing, a total of 2441. Southern losses are 381 killed, around 1800 wounded and 1670 missing, a total of 3851.

17 MAY 1863

Civil War: Vicksburg Campaign Grant catches up with Pemberton's rear guard before the Big Black River, and Sherman's corps pitches into the enemy center. Many Rebels are forced into the river to swim or sink. The remaining defenders notice that Yankees are heading for the only bridge, and something of a footrace ensues. The Confederates reach the bridge first, while their artillery remains behind to slow the Northerners. Pemberton's men escape by a hairsbreadth, burning the bridge behind them but leaving behind 1700 prisoners. Meanwhile, to the south, Union General Banks pushes to a point directly across the Mississippi from the Rebel stronghold of Port Hudson.

18 MAY 1863

Civil War: Vicksburg Campaign As Grant moves his men across reconstructed bridges over the Big Black River, General Pemberton pulls his Confederates into Vicksburg to prepare for a siege.

19 MAY 1863

Civil War: Vicksburg Campaign Having arrived in force at Vicksburg, Mississippi, Grant impatiently orders a general assault of the city's fortifications. The Federals are repulsed with 1000 casualties.

22 MAY 1863

Civil War: Vicksburg Campaign Grant mounts a second frontal assault on the defenses of Vicksburg, and it proves a bloody failure. The 13,000 Confeder-

General John Pemberton, who commanded the Vicksburg garrison, had been a pre-war friend of Grant.

The Vicksburg campaign caused worldwide interest. Here a Dublin newspaper reports on the fighting in June under banner headlines.

IMPORTANT FROM AMERICA!!

Awful Slaughter at Vicksburg,

And Elsewhere,

The Bloody Conflict between the North & South

CONTINUED!

We regret to say that this unnatural war seems still to rush upon the unhappy Yanky with fearful impetuosity, so as to stun the entire population and saturate the States of America with blood, by sacrificing the lives of hundreds of thousands of honest men, at the whim or caprice of a few noxious individuals. Federal accounts state that the siege still continues, —and, that the incredible number of 3,600 bombs were thrown into the city of Vicksburg in an hour! The streets are ploughed up with shot and shell, and that the inhabitants dwell in caves which they have excavated in the sides of the Bluff!

In the force under Banks and Sheridan there was a battalion of Negroes, who are said to have fought well. They suffered terribly, for out of a regiment of 900, 600 were killed or wounded in an hour!

The Prize Court at Key West has laid down the law of confiscation so as to insure the condemnation of every British Ship a Federal vessel may seize,—'Any vessel bound to Nassau, with the intention of sailing from thence to a blockaded port, is liable to condemnation." As the prize court constitutes inself sole judge of the intention, and as Matamoras has been, de facto blockaded, all British vessels bound for that port will, of course, be at once condemned. The Key west correspondent of the New-York Herald has good reason to say that " nowhere else is prise law rigidly enforced, vessels being condemned at the rate of two each week."

Although 49,688 emigrants had arrived in New York from Ireland since the first of January, 1863, and though the negroes are said to be the " best hope of restoring the Union," the enrollment is being enforced.

Queenstown, Saturday,—The following is the latest " correspondence " from Vicksberg. One regiment only, the 22nd Iowa Volunteers, commanded by Colonel William M. Stone, by almost superhuman efforts, and after immense loss, planted its colours on the rebel rampart. There it remained all day long, the colonel hourly demanding aid, until at nightfall, after having been exposed all day to a destructive fire, the lieutenant-colonel and 15 men only remained and they were taken in great triumph to Vicksburg. Every man who entered the fort in the morning was killed or wounded except these sixteen. Colonel Stone was struck in the arm whilst on the bastion, loudly calling for reinforcements. It was a stupid blunder, or worse, to storm the works at all. It needs not a military eye to discover that it is impossible to lead men over an abrupt embankment twenty feet high, with ditches from ten to twelve feet deep. It was doubtless, necessary that the experiment should be tried. It has proven a costly one. Twenty-five hundred killed and wounded is a fearful loss.

The northerns are evidently constructing a new line of works between the outer line opposed to us and the city. While the charge was being made on the 22nd some of our sharpshooters, posted in the trees overlooking the fortifications, could plainly see contrabands and white men digging for dear life.

OUR LOSSES.

I regret to learn that Colonel Abbot, of the 30th Iowa, was killed on the 22nd instant. He was a brave officer, and his loss is universally regretted. In the battle of Champion's Hill, on the 16th, instant, the tenth Iowa lost, killed, wounded, and missing, one hundred and sixty-one men. Among the killed were three commissioned officers and 7 wounded. In the recent charge on the fortifications the twenty-second Iowa, lost two hundred and fifty men; General Stevenson's Brigade, two hundred and sixty; General Ransom's Brigade, three hundred and fifty-eight; General Carr's division, five hundred; General Blair's division, five hundred and fifty; Gereyal Steele's division, heavily, estimated six hundred; General Osterhans' division two hundred, estimated; and General Smith's three hundred and fifty, estimated. This is rather under than over the estimate.

CANNONADING.

To-day there has been vigorous cannonading at intervals from batteries on the right and left of the railroad. A misdirected shot fell in our own ranks killing three soldiers of the thirty-second Ohio, and seriously wounding as many more.

Over one hundred women and children have been killed by our bombardment.

New-York, June 14—General Banks fliocially reports that the conduct of the Negro troops has been most praiseworthy, and there is no longer any doubt that the Government will find in the Negroes effective supporters.

General Banks' loss from the 23rd to the 30th. ult., was 1,000 men, including many of his ablest officers.

General Sherman has died of his wounds.

General Neal Dow is also dangerously wounded.

ANOTHER BATTLE.

Three brigades of Federal Cavalry, and 2,000 infantry crossed the Rappahannock on Tuesday at Beverley Ford, and had a severe engagement with General Stuart's cavalry, lasting all day, when the Confederates received heavy infantry reinforcements, and the Federals recrossed the river bringing away their dead and wounded. Sharp firing was kept up from the confederate rifle pits during the crossing, and 40 of the Federals were killed or wounded. A portion of Federal land and naval farces at Yorktown, made an incursion into King William Country. Virginia, via the Mattapony River. On the 4th inst. a Foundry at Ayltes, with all its machinery, several mills, and large quantities of grain, were destroyed, and many horses, mules, and cattle were captured. The expedition returned to Yorktown the following day.

The agricultural resources of the Yazoo country are described as being most abundant

John F. Nugent and Co., Steam-Machine Printers, 35, New-Row West, Dublin. N.B.—No connection with any other person of the name.

ate defenders turn back 35,000 Federals and inflict 3200 casualties. Southern casualties are around 500. Grant is forced to concede that the city's defenses – a line nine miles long over broken ground, with nine forts as strong points – are immune to direct attack. (In his memoirs, Grant admits the assault was a mistake.) The Yankees resign themselves to the tedious but inexorable tactic of the siege.

25 MAY 1863

Civil War: Naval Pursuing its raiding on the high seas, the CSS *Alabama*, under Captain Raphael Semmes, seizes two Federal vessels off the coast of Bahia, Brazil.

27 MAY 1863

Civil War: Western Theater The Federal siege of Port Hudson, Louisiana, begins as forces under General Nathaniel Banks assault the works of the city. Confederate forces there are some 4500 under General Franklin Gardner. The Union attack is made by 13,000 men, but is disorganized and easily repulsed by the defenders.

Civil War:Vicksburg Campaign In an attempt to seize Fort Hill, the northernmost strongpoint of the Vicksburg defensive line Admiral David Dixon Porter shells it from the river. Confederate batteries manage to sink Porter's gunboat, which goes down with 40 Federal casualties. Once again, the city's defenses have proven their mettle.

30 MAY 1863

Civil War: The Confederacy General Robert E. Lee and President Jefferson Davis meet to discuss the desperate situation at Vicksburg, Mississippi. They agree that General Johnston's failure to attack Grant from the rear as he marched toward Vicksburg has perhaps cost the Confederacy that vital city.

3 JUNE 1863

Civil War: Eastern Theater Following his extraordinary victories at Fredericksburg and Chancellorsville, General Robert E. Lee has made the fateful decision to march into Pennsylvania on a second invasion of Northern territory. To that end he has reorganized the Army of Northern Virginia into three corps under Generals James Longstreet, Richard Ewell (succeeding Stonewall Jackson) and A. P. Hill, plus the cavalry corps of J. E. B. Stuart. Lee's army is now at the peak of its strength, with some 89,000 men, and at the peak of its confidence as well. Today Lee's army pulls out of its field of triumph at Fredericksburg, Virginia, and heads north, leaving Hill's corps behind temporarily to occupy Hooker's Army of the Potomac.

5 JUNE 1863

Civil War: Eastern Theater General Hooker suspects that Lee is on the move and sends General Sedgwick with a reconnaissance in force to probe the Confederate positions at Fredericksburg. The result is the battle of Franklin's Crossing (or Deep Run), in which the Federals, with some difficulty, drive the enemy out of rifle pits below the town. Sedgwick reports that Lee's main force is still present; Hooker, still suspicious, orders a cavalry reconnaissance.

Within days of his being appointed commander of the Army of the Potomac US General George Meade (center) had to fight the war's greatest battle.

7 JUNE 1863

Civil War: Western Theater There is action at Milliken's Bend in Louisiana, as Rebels under General McCulloch push the Yankees back to the Mississippi; but the Federal commander, General George Thomas, makes a stand with the help of two Union gunboats. Finally, the Confederates pull back. They have suffered 185 casualties to the North's 652.

8 JUNE 1863

Civil War: Eastern Theater General Lee attends a review of General Jeb Stuart's cavalry, which is produced in Stuart's customary extravagant style (he is nicknamed 'The Cavalier') and which – in a portent of mistakes to come – somewhat tires his men and horses with enemy at hand.

Civil War: Vicksburg Campaign In Mississippi, General Grant orders a 24-hour bombardment of Vicksburg that sends residents running to shelter in houses and caves.

9 JUNE 1863

Civil War: Battle of Brandy Station At 4 AM the first and greatest pure cavalry battle of the war breaks out at Brandy Station, Virginia, when Alfred Pleasonton's Federal horsemen strike Stuart's cavalry along the Rappahannock River. The Southerners are scattered all down the line before Stuart organizes enough resistance to send the Yankees back across the river. Though the Federals have retreated, Stuart and his men note the ominous new aggressiveness of the Union cavalry, which has so far been outclassed by the Rebel riders. Approximate Union losses in the battle of Brandy Station are 930, Southern losses around 485. Meanwhile, Lee has concentrated his infantry around Culpeper, from which he will begin to move out tomorrow.

13 JUNE 1863

Civil War: Eastern Theater As Lee moves the bulk of his army toward Pennsylvania, he sends General Ewell's corps to deal with General Milroy's Federal garrison at Winchester. To support Ewell, today Southern units drive away a Union garrison and occupy Berryville, Virginia.

14 JUNE 1863

Civil War: Eastern Theater Confederates surround and drive away the Federal garrison at Martinsburg, West Virginia. This isolates Milroy's Federal garrison at Winchester, which Confederate General Ewell is preparing to attack.

Civil War: Western Theater Continuing his operations at Port Hudson, Louisiana, Federal General Banks sends 6000 troops against the fort; the 3750 Confederates hold off the attack.

15 JUNE 1863

Civil War: Washington To help deal with the threat of Lee's invasion President Lincoln asks for 100,000 militia to be called out in Pennsylvania, Maryland, Ohio and West Virginia.

Civil War: Eastern Theater General Ewell mounts his attack on Milroy's Federal garrison at Winchester, Virginia. By the end of the fighting the Federals have suffered a debacle – 4443 casualties, 3358 of them captured, and enormous quantities of arms, supplies and horses lost. Southern casualties are around 269. Meanwhile, Chambersburg, Pennsylvania, sees raiding by Jeb Stuart's Southern cavalry.

16 JUNE 1863

Civil War: Eastern Theater Now certain of Lee's intentions, General Hooker and the Army of the Potomac are shadowing the Southern advance; today Hooker's army is at Fairfax Court House in Virginia as Lee's army crosses the Potomac.

18 JUNE 1863

Civil War: Vicksburg Campaign General Grant has read a letter to the press written by General McClernand, in which Grant's subordinate takes most of the credit for the campaign. Grant dismisses McClernand today, replacing him with General Ord.

22 JUNE 1863

Civil War: Eastern Theater As Pleasonton's Union cavalrymen try to penetrate Jeb Stuart's counterreconnaissance screen for Lee's advancing army, a running series of cavalry skirmishes flare up through the week. Today the fighting is near Aldie, Virginia. These skirmishes have the effect of keeping Lee unaware that Hooker is shadowing him.

Jefferson Davis with his cabinet. Davis was much criticized for making unpopular appointments and for interfering with his generals' strategy.

23 JUNE 1863

Civil War: Western Theater Under the command of General William Rosecrans, the Federal Army of the Cumberland begins operations to dislodge General Braxton Bragg and the Confederate Army of Tennessee from their long-held position in middle Tennessee. Part of the purpose of the campaign is to keep Bragg from going to the aid of besieged Vicksburg, and Rosecrans will be successful in that task.

24 JUNE 1863

Civil War: Eastern Theater Sharpsburg, Maryland, sees skirmishing between units of Hooker's army and troops under Longstreet and Hill. The latter are moving to join forces with Ewell, who has arrived in Maryland as part of Lee's advance toward Pennsylvania. Meanwhile, making a major strategic blunder, General Lee has authorized Jeb Stuart to take his cavalry on a raid, which begins today, around Hooker's army. Since the Federal forces are more spread out than Stuart realizes, this raid will take far more time than expected, with the result that Lee's infantry will be moving into enemy territory virtually without intelligence information – in effect, marching blind.

25 JUNE 1863

Civil War: Vicksburg Campaign In his siege of Vicksburg, General Grant tries the old expedient of a mine; a tunnel dug under the enemy defenses is filled with powder and blown up. Anticipating the attempt, General Pemberton has erected a backup defense. In any case, the explosion does not open a breach big enough for the Federals to use. Within the city the population is harassed by mortar fire, and food is a rare commodity. The horses have been eaten, and rats are becoming an endangered species.

27 JUNE 1863

Civil War: Washington General Hooker has sent a message to President Lincoln requesting authorization for the evacuation of Harpers Ferry, which Hooker feels is useful to his operation against Lee. With the approval of the president General-in-Chief Halleck countermands the order, hoping that Hooker will resign in protest. In this way officials hope to finesse Hooker out of command after his failure at Chancellorsville.

Civil War: Eastern Theater Lee's Army of Northern Virginia moves into Chambersburg, Pennsylvania, after having forced the surrender of York. Near Fairfax Court House, Virginia, the raiding cavalry of Jeb Stuart captures a number of Union riders.

Civil War: Western Theater Several days of skirmishing between the forces of Generals Rosecrans and Bragg climaxes in fights at Guy's Gap and Shelbyville. These engagements have maneuvered Bragg to fall back to Tullahoma, Tennessee, and prevent his marching to the aid of Vicksburg. Northern casualties in the fighting have been 560; Southern losses 1634.

28 JUNE 1863

Civil War: Washington As was hoped, General Joseph E. Hooker resigns from command of the Federal Army of the Potomac when he learns that Halleck has countermanded Hooker's order about Harper's Ferry. Lincoln and Halleck have his replacement ready: General George G. Meade, who has been commanding the V Corps. Meade takes over the Union's main army virtually on the eve of battle, making the fifth change of command in ten months. It is a terrifying prospect, and Meade is reluctant in the extreme. Hearing the news, Lee reaches into his rich fund of knowledge about enemy generals and prophesies accurately, 'General Meade will make no blunder on my front.'

Civil War: Eastern Theater After learning that the Federal army has crossed north of the Potomac River, Lee makes a change in his original plan to concentrate at Harrisburg, Pennsylvania. The new strategy requires that his army concentrate at Gettysburg and Cashtown – both towns with useful road crossings. General Meade, meanwhile, will make the same decision for the same reason.

29 JUNE 1863

Civil War: Gettysburg Campaign At Winchester, Maryland, there is a fierce cavalry skirmish between Stuart's men and Union riders; Stuart's troopers send the Yankees running. Meanwhile, General Meade moves the Army of the Potomac toward Gettysburg, converging accidentally with Lee's army.

30 JUNE 1863

Civil War: Gettysburg Campaign Unknown to anyone, the two great armies of the East are on the eve of the greatest battle to be seen on the American continent. In Hanover, Pennsylvania, Stuart continues his raiding. A fierce Union counterattack by Judson Kilpatrick's cavalry nearly captures Stuart and results in over 100 casualties on both sides. To the west, General Meade sends the corps of General John Reynolds to occupy the little town of Gettysburg, which is about to explode onto the pages of American history.

Civil War: Western Theater Fighting continues in middle Tennessee as General Bragg pulls his Confederates back from Tullahoma across the Tennessee River. His campaign to contain Bragg carried out, Rosecrans settles his army in Chattahoochee.

1 JULY 1863

Civil War: Battle of Gettysburg The battle breaks out when Federal cavalry General John Buford sees a line of Confederates marching toward him into Gettysburg. Union troopers spread out in a thin line to the west of town and begin peppering away with their new repeating carbines. The fighting heats up quickly as infantry divisions are thrown into the fray by both sides; the Confederates move up faster, with the result that the Federals are slowly pushed back with heavy losses. By the end of the day Lee's forces have driven the Army of the Potomac from the town and captured some 4000; killed in the fighting is General John Reynolds, commander of the I Corps and one of the finest officers in the Union. In late afternoon Union General Winfield Scott Hancock begins to organize a defensive position at Cemetery Hill, south of town. As dusk approaches Southern General Richard S. Ewell arrives with orders from Lee to attack Cemetery Hill 'if possible.' After taking a look, Ewell decides an attack is not possible; if he had made the attack, he would likely have swept over the Federals and possibly changed the course of American history. Meade is moving his divisions up fast; Cemetery Ridge will be his strongpoint.

2 JULY 1863

Civil War: Battle of Gettysburg During the night, General Meade follows Hancock's advice in arranging his lines, curving defenses around Culp's Hill above Cemetery Hill and pushing them south down Cemetery Ridge – without, as it turns out, extending them far enough into the small hills called the Round Tops – until the Union line looks like a great fishhook. It is on the Round Tops that Lee orders his main attack to strike in the morning, under the direction of General James Longstreet. Ewell and Hill are to make attacks further north to hold the Federals in place, while Longstreet rolls up the Union line from the south. However, in this second day's fighting nothing goes as Lee planned. After various delays by Longstreet, action does not begin until 4 in the afternoon; by then Federal General Daniel Sickles has inexplicably moved his corps down from the heights, making a vulnerable salient. As a furious Meade tries to pull Sickles back, firing erupts, and Rebel General John B Hood begins pushing his men toward the Round Tops. Federal General G. K. Warren arrives on Little Round Top to find Hood approaching and no defenses there at all. Warren begins frantically to pull troops in, and only a desperate bayonet charge by Colonel Joshua Chamberlain's 20th Maine division prevents Hood from taking Little Round Top. Thereafter the fighting works its way north along the Union line. First, Sickles' salient is smashed by Confederate General McLaws' men, but Meade is able to marshal enough reinforcements to reform the position on the ridge. Then a Southern charge in the center nearly splits Hancock's line before it is repulsed. Finally, Ewell makes a weak attempt on Culp's Hill. It has been a day of almosts for the Confederate Army of Northern Virginia, but the Army of the Potomac has held the line.

3 JULY 1863

Civil War: Battle of Gettysburg The third day of battle begins with another abortive attack on Culp's Hill by Ewell and with a bungled Federal counterattack. Then the battlefield sinks back to silence as the haze breaks up and the morning turns clear and oppressively sultry. In midmorning the Federals watch Southern cannons moving into position opposite them until there is a line of 150 guns. At 12:30 all 150 cannons erupt at once, and Federal generals realize that Lee is preparing some sort of assault. After an hour and a half of cannonade from both sides, the worst bombardment ever seen on American soil and perhaps on any soil to that time, the guns fall silent. At about three in the afternoon 15,000 Confederates emerge from the woods marching straight toward Gibbon's II Corps. It is Lee's last big gamble, a grand charge in the old Napoleonic style. For some reason history will call it 'Pickett's Charge,' though Longstreet is – over his protest – in command. The Federals hold fire for long minutes until the enemy is in range, and then a storm of fire strikes the Southerners. The Confederate right flank brushes past some concealed Vermont regiments, who open up a blistering musket fire. Both Rebel flanks begin to falter, then the left gives way, but the center pushes forward until a spearhead is over the low stone wall of the Northern line. This is the high tide of the Confederacy. Suddenly Federal reinforcements arrive, a leaderless band of Yankees which swarms around the enemy. The Confederate spearhead seems to dissolve, becoming a rabble of terrified men pouring back down the slope to their own lines. Robert E. Lee and the Army of Northern Virginia have been defeated; never again will they have the strength to mount such an offensive. The casualties have been by far the most horrible of the war. Of 88,289 Federals engaged, 3155 are killed, 14,529 wounded and 5365 missing, a total of 23,049. For the South, of 75,000 engaged, 3903 are killed, 18,735 wounded and 5425 missing, a total of 28,063. Lee has lost over a third of his army.

Civil War: Surrender of Vicksburg Lee's defeat is not the only disaster for the South today. After his long campaign on and siege of Vicksburg, Mississippi, General Ulysses S. Grant sees white flags appear on the ramparts of the beleagured city. Soon General Pemberton, the Confederate commander, appears and the two discuss terms. Grant first demands the same kind of unconditional surrender he asked of Fort Donelson; Pemberton curtly declines. At length Grant agrees to parole surrendered Confederates until exchanged, instead of imprisoning them. Pemberton hastens to agree. Grant will later receive criticism for giving up his captives.

4 JULY 1863

Civil War: Eastern Theater Robert E. Lee and his defeated Army of Northern Virginia begin a miserable retreat in driving rain, the wounded bouncing behind in springless wagons. The rain does, however, have the effect of preventing Federal pursuit.

Civil War: Surrender of Vicksburg At three o'clock in the afternoon of this Independence Day 30,000 ragged and hungry Confederates file out of Vicksburg to stack their arms. At Gettysburg the South has just lost a great battle; here in Vicksburg the Confederacy has probably lost the war. With the fall of

A contemporary engraving of Pickett's (actually Longstreet's) famous charge on 3 July 1863 at the decisive Battle of Gettysburg.

Hand-to-hand fighting on Cemetery Ridge on the last day of the Battle of Gettysburg. The division led by CSA General Pickett lost 3393 of its 4500 men.

Port Hudson imminent, the North will soon control the Mississippi River, and the Confederacy will be split in two.

7 JULY 1863

Civil War: Eastern Theater Lee's army entrenches at Hagerstown, Maryland, ready to cross the storm-swollen Potomac as soon as the waters fall.

8 JULY 1863

Civil War: Western Theater Isolated by the fall of Vicksburg, Confederates in Port Hudson, Louisiana, surrender to General Banks after six weeks of siege, leaving the whole of the Mississippi River under Federal control (the formal surrender is next day). Lincoln will write, 'The Father of Waters runs unvexed to the sea.' Elsewhere, Confederate raider John Hunt Morgan and 2500 cavalrymen begin a sweep through Indiana and toward Ohio.

10 JULY 1863

Civil War: Eastern Theater General Meade begins to move units of the Army of the Potomac toward Lee, who is still entrenched before the swollen Potomac.

12 JULY 1863

Civil War: Eastern Theater Meade's advance makes contact with Lee's army but engages only in light reconnaissance. Lee, building fires to give the illusion of a settled camp, begins to move his troops over the lowering Potomac. Meade contemplates a full-scale attack next day but is dissuaded by his staff.

13 JULY 1863

Civil War: Draft Riots Following the first drawing of names for the draft in New York, resentment over the Federal Enrollment Act boils over into a four-day riot that begins when a mob of over 50,000 people swarm into the city's draft office, setting it afire. The mob is virulently anti-black: over the next few days an evacuated black orphanage and the offices of Horace Greeley's abolitionist *Tribune* are torched by rioters, and blacks are beaten and killed at random. But the rioters also loot businesses, beat to death a Union colonel and assault the home of the mayor. At length, Federal troops put down the mob, leaving over 1000 dead and wounded in one of the darkest homefront episodes of the war and the worst race riot in American history. Less serious draft riots break out in Boston and other towns in the East and Ohio.

Civil War: Eastern Theater Lee and the Army of Northern Virginia complete their evacuation over the Potomac and head for the Shenandoah.

14 JULY 1863

Civil War: Eastern Theater Finally pressing toward an attack, Meade moves into Lee's positions on the Potomac and discovers them to be abandoned. This day Lincoln writes in an unsent letter to Meade, 'Your golden opportunity [to destroy Lee] is gone, and I am distressed immeasurably because of it.'

18 JULY 1863

Civil War: Western Theater Federal forces in Charleston Harbor, South Carolina, having mounted an unsuccessful assault on Battery Wagner on 11 July, try another attack after an extensive naval bombardment. This one also fails, with 1515 Federal casualties to the defenders' 174. Leading the Union assault is the 54th Massachusetts Colored Infantry,

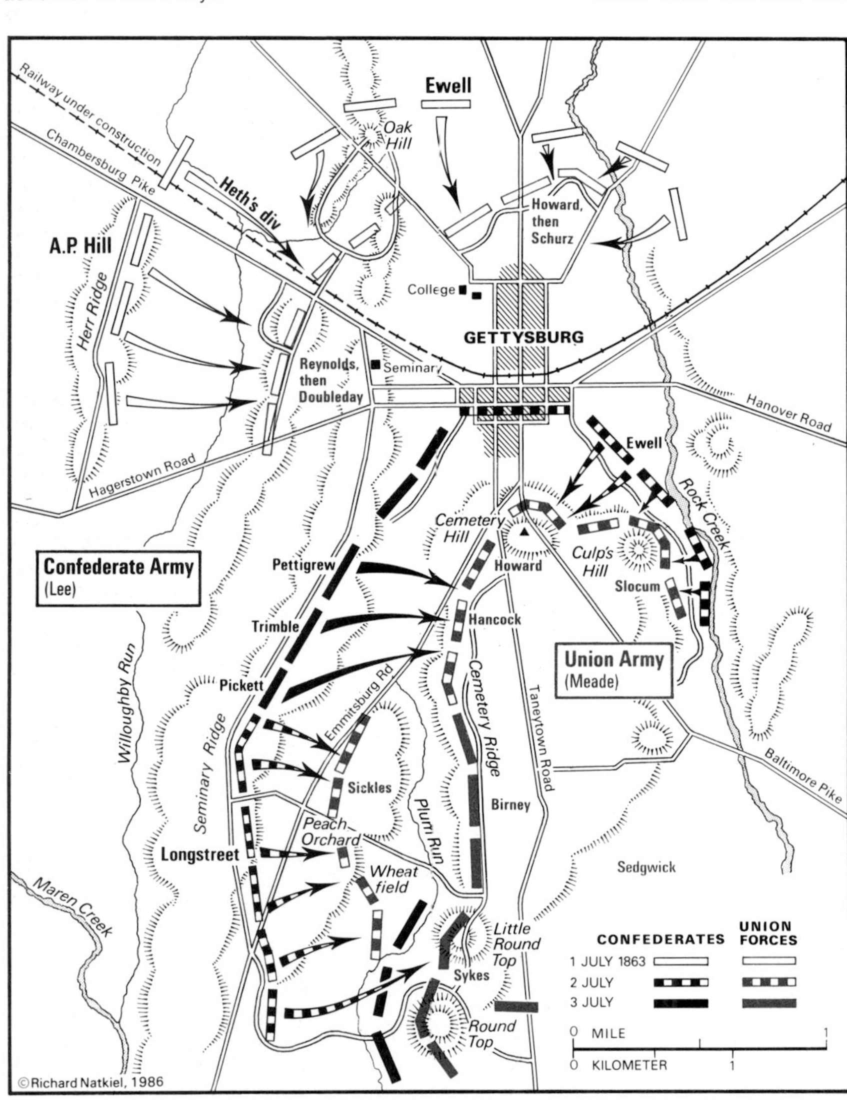

A general map of the Battle of Gettysburg showing the action on all three days.

An engraving from *Leslie's* showing the draft riot in New York City in July 1863. It degenerated into the worst race riot in US history.

Some of the dead at Gettysburg. During the entire campaign the South suffered some 30,000 casualties, which could now no longer be replaced.

who lose 272 of 650; their white commander, Colonel R. G. Shaw, is killed. The Federals will settle into a siege of the battery.

19 JULY 1863

Civil War: Western Theater After being harried by Federals throughout their raid, John Hunt Morgan and his men are overwhelmed by Union forces in Ohio. Some 800 Confederates are captured, but, hotly pursued, Morgan and 300 men escape toward Pennsylvania.

20 JULY 1863

Civil War: Eastern Theater General Meade has moved his army across the Potomac in pursuit of Lee. Today he sends parties to take over the passes of the Blue Ridge Mountains in hopes of intercepting Lee's column. Meade's pursuit will not succeed in cornering Lee.

26 JULY 1863

Civil War: Western Theater Confederate raider John Hunt Morgan and the last of his men are brought to bay at New Lisbon, Ohio, after an exhausting but strategically pointless expedition (hoped-for Copperhead support has failed to materialize in Ohio). Morgan and his officers will soon be dispatched to Ohio State Penitentiary.

28 JULY 1863

Civil War: Eastern Theater Meade and the Army of the Potomac are now in a part of Virginia dominated by daring Confederate raider John S. Mosby, who begins a series of hit-and-run harassing maneuvers around the Yankees.

8 AUGUST 1863

Civil War: The Confederacy Robert E. Lee, dejected and in ill health, writes President Davis offering his resignation as commander of the Army of Northern Virginia. Davis will refuse the request, knowing that if the Confederacy has any hopes left, they are in Lee's hands.

16 AUGUST 1863

Civil War: Western Theater The Federal Army of the Cumberland under General William S. Rosecrans pulls out eastward from Tullahoma, Tennessee, toward Chattanooga, where Braxton Bragg's Army of Tennessee is concentrating. At the same time, Union General Ambrose Burnside moves down from Kentucky toward eastern Tennessee. Rosecrans plans to envelop Bragg between himself and Burnside; anticipating this strategy, Bragg requests reinforcements and reorganizes his command. South of Chattanooga, Union Generals Thomas and McCook are brought up to threaten Bragg's only railway link. The stage and the principal actors are now preparing for the bloody engagements of the Chickamauga and Chattanooga Campaigns in Tennessee and Georgia.

17 AUGUST 1863

Civil War: Eastern Theater Beginning months of intermittent and futile bombardment, Union land and naval batteries shell Confederate-held Fort Sumter in Charleston Harbor, South Carolina. The fort, scene of the first battle of the war, is a potent symbol for both sides.

20 AUGUST 1863

Indian Wars In Arizona Territory, Colonel 'Kit' Carson begins a campaign against the Navaho Indians, who have been raiding settlers for years. In the first months of 1864 Carson will defeat his erstwhile friends, the Navaho, and send them on the infamous 'Long March' to Bosque Redondo, during which hundreds of Indians will die of starvation.

21 AUGUST 1863

Civil War: Chickamauga Campaign Rosecrans' army reaches the Tennessee River outside Chattanooga and prepares for the coming offensive.
Civil War: Trans-Mississippi Around 450 irregular Confederate raiders under William Clarke Quantrill stage a dawn terrorist raid on Lawrence, Kansas, leaving 150 civilians dead, 30 wounded and much of the town a smoking ruin. For some time the town of Lawrence has been strongly Unionist and abolitionist, thus earning Quantrill's enmity. This strategically pointless raid demonstrates not only the raiders' barbarity, but also a certain Southern loss of faith in conventional military operations. Guerilla-style raiding by men such as Mosby and Forrest will become increasingly part of the Southern war effort, though Quantrill will remain a renegade to most Confederates.

29 AUGUST 1863

Civil War: Naval In Charleston Harbor, South Carolina, the experimental Confederate submarine *H. L. Hunley* sinks, drowning five crewmen. The little vessel is soon raised.

1 SEPTEMBER 1863

Civil War: Chickamauga Campaign Moving toward Chattanooga, Rosecrans' army begins a four-day crossing of the Tennessee River largely unopposed by Bragg; the latter meanwhile receives reinforcements.

2 SEPTEMBER 1863

Civil War: Western Theater Without opposition, Federal General Burnside's forces occupy Knoxville, Tennessee, to remain there as a potential resource for Rosecran's operations around Chattanooga (but Burnside will prove of little use to Rosecrans or anyone else in coming months).

4 SEPTEMBER 1863

Civil War: Western Theater General Ulysses S. Grant, in a perhaps drunken mishap, is fallen on by his horse in New Orleans; he will be partly lame for weeks.

5 SEPTEMBER 1863

Civil War: Chickamauga Campaign Rosecrans, now convinced that Bragg is fleeing him, moves his forces toward Georgia, taking the risky step of separating his army into three groups in order to go quickly through three widely spaced gaps in the mountains.
Civil War: International Despite Federal protests, British shipbuilders have been constructing vessels for the Confederacy, the most notorious of them being the raider CSS *Alabama*. Finally responding to Washington's protests, the British government today seizes in Liverpool's Laird Shipyards two new ironclads fitted with ramming spars that have been ordered by the Confederacy. This seizure of the so-called 'Laird Rams' halts the growth of the Confederate Navy and ends the last major diplomatic crisis between Washington and Britain during the war.

6 SEPTEMBER 1863

Civil War: Chickamauga Campaign As Federal troops close around the city General Bragg evacuates Chattanooga. Elsewhere, in Charleston, South Carolina, Confederate commander P. G. T. Beauregard decides it is too costly to resist upcoming Federal assaults on Battery Wagner and Battery Gregg. He evacuates these forts, and the Union will move into them next day. Fort Sumter, though, will hold out until the end of the war.

8 SEPTEMBER 1863

Civil War: Chickamauga Campaign Bragg's 65,000-man Confederate Army of Tennessee marches out of Chattanooga and withdraws toward Lafayette, Georgia.

9 SEPTEMBER 1863

Civil War: Chicamauga Campaign Rosecrans' Federal Army of the Cumberland is now spread out in three groups across 40 miles of mountains. Generals Crittenden, Thomas and McCook pursue what their commander, Rosecrans, believes to be a fleeing enemy, but in fact, the Union army is racing into a trap. Bragg's army is gathering at Lafayette, Georgia, preparing to defeat in detail the widely-separated Federal forces. In Virginia, Longstreet's divisions leave Lee's army by train to reinforce Bragg.

10 SEPTEMBER 1863

Civil War: Chickamauga Campaign Having created a brilliant trap, Bragg and his staff now proceed to spring it too soon and ineptly. Bragg orders an attack at McLemore's Cove, but it fails to be mounted. During the day both Crittenden and Thomas discover strong parties of Confederates in their paths, and both are able to fall back and regroup. Another attack ordered by Bragg tomorrow will also fail to materialize.

12 SEPTEMBER 1863

Civil War: Chickamauga Campaign By this time Rosecrans has realized the perilous position of his divided forces, and he issues urgent orders to move toward the center. Bragg has ordered General Polk to attack next day at Chickamauga Creek; this attack, too, will not be mounted.

17 SEPTEMBER 1863

Civil War: Chickamauga Campaign Union divisions move toward concentration around Lee and Gordon's Mill on Chickamauga Creek. Bragg, now on the east bank of the creek, begins to make battle plans: he proposes to turn the Union left flank and get behind Rosecrans, cutting off the roads to Chattanooga. The stage is now set for the bloodiest battle of the war in the Western Theater. The name of its site, the creek called Chickamauga, comes from an ancient Cherokee word meaning 'River of Death.'

18 SEPTEMBER 1863

Civil War: Chickamauga Campaign Bragg has planned a major attack today but cannot get his forces to the west bank of the creek in time. Cavalry skirmishes break out, and the first of Longstreet's forces arrive from Virginia. All day and night Rosecrans arranges his troops, anticipating Bragg's strategy to get behind him. Because of the dense woods in much of the area, neither commander can determine the strength and position of his enemy or, often, of his own forces.

19 SEPTEMBER 1863

Civil War: Battle of Chickamauga Dawn finds the rival armies facing one another along a six-mile front, the Federals on the west bank of the creek, Southerners on the east. The fighting breaks out when Union General George H. Thomas sends men to reconnoiter near Chickamauga Creek on the Federal left. These troops run into the dismounted cavalry of Nathan Bedford Forrest, who returns fire and calls for infantry help. Soon hostilities erupt along most of the battle line. Throughout the ensuing day of confused but fierce fighting Bragg pursues his plan to get behind the enemy left wing. Rosecrans responds by moving division after division to his left, extending his battle line north. By the end of the day losses are enormous on both sides, but neither has gained any significant advantage. During the afternoon Longstreet has arrived with the bulk of his troops. He finds Bragg during the night and is told the next day's plan – Polk will attack at dawn in the north, and the attack will be joined successively down the line, to climax with an all-out assault by Longstreet on the Union right. Meanwhile, Rosecrans decides to remain on the defensive and sets his men to building breastworks.

20 SEPTEMBER 1863

Civil War: Battle of Chickamauga At dawn Bragg, unable in the dense forest and morning fog to see his own troops, waits impatiently for Polk to attack. After over an hour of inactivity the Southern com-

CSA General John Hood is wounded at the Battle of Chickamauga in September 1863. He had already lost the use of his left arm from a wound, and now he loses his right leg, yet he continues in service.

mander finds that Polk has been casually breakfasting in a farmhouse. Bragg swears 'in a manner that would have powerfully assisted a mule team in getting up a mountain,' and about 9:30 AM orders an attack against Thomas on the Union left. Once again the Confederates struggle to flank the Federals, but Thomas's men hold their breastworks, and the fighting sways back and forth indecisively. Then, about eleven o'clock, there occurs a strange and fateful error. An aide who has been riding behind the Union position reports to Rosecrans that there is a gap in the line between Wood's and Reynolds' division on the right flank. Intending to seal that gap, Rosecrans sends an order to Wood to move left, to 'close up on and support' Reynolds. But the aide has made a disastrous mistake: there is no gap in the Union line. Between Wood and Reynolds is Brannans's division, nearly invisible in the woods: thus the actual positions are Reynolds-Brannan-Wood. Wood, confused by Rosecrans' order, orders his division to pull out and march behind Brannan toward Reynolds. As they begin to move out of line, Longstreet charges in a solid column directly into this gap. The Union line immediately falls apart, the right wing in disorderly rout and Thomas's men pushed left toward Snodgrass Hill. Thousands of Federals are killed or captured, and most of the rest are running. Along with McCook and Crittenden, a demoralized Rosecrans flees to Chattanooga, assuming his whole army is being destroyed. But Rosecrans is wrong: on the Federal left Thomas has maintained control of his troops and takes a strong position on Snodgrass Hill. For the rest of the day, Thomas's men desperately turn back wave after wave of attacks as nearly the whole Confederate army swarms up the precipitous slopes. At three o'clock in the afternoon Thomas is reinforced by General Granger with the Reserve Corps, and together they hold the position until nightfall and then withdraw in good order to Chattanooga. His heroic defense has saved the Union forces from utter rout, and General George Henry Thomas will be known forevermore as 'The Rock of Chickamauga.' The losses on both sides have been staggering. In two days of fighting the Union has suffered 1657 killed, 9756 wounded and 4757 missing, totaling 16,170 casualties out of 58,222 effectives. The Confederates have suffered 2312 dead, 14,674 wounded and 1468 missing, totaling 18,454 out of 66,326 effectives. Both sides have thus lost about 28 percent of their strength.

21 SEPTEMBER 1863

Civil War: Chattanooga Campaign As the beaten Union army gathers in Chattanooga, Bragg is urged by Longstreet to pursue the retreating enemy, and Forrest rages at his commander, 'You are a coward and a damned scoundrel. You may as well not issue any more orders to me, for I will not obey them.' But Bragg, who apparently cannot absorb the fact that he has won, does not give orders to pursue until four in the afternoon – too late to reach the city.

22 SEPTEMBER 1863

Civil War: Chattanooga Campaign Bragg orders an attack on Union positions in Chattanooga, but the Confederates reach the area to find the enemy 'ready to receive and entertain us.' Realizing the Federals have now dug in, Bragg cancels the attack. By failing to pursue the Federal retreat before it can organize, Bragg has let another opportunity slip through his fingers. Now his forces occupy the heights of Missionary Ridge and Lookout Mountain to begin a siege of Chattanooga.

23 SEPTEMBER 1863

Civil War: Washington Lincoln sends General Hooker with two corps from the Army of the Potomac (which is still stalking Lee in Virginia) to support Rosecrans. These 20,000 Federals will arrive in Alabama over the next weeks with large amounts of supplies.

30 SEPTEMBER 1863

Civil War: Chattanooga Campaign Bragg orders cavalry under Wheeler to raid the Federals' supply line into Chattanooga. The raids will continue into October, reducing Rosecrans to one muddy mountain road on which to bring in a trickle of supplies. Bragg is confident he can starve the Yankees out of Chattanooga.

5 OCTOBER 1863

Civil War: Naval In an attempt to loosen the Federal blockade of Charleston Harbor the Confederate semi-submersible vessel *David* hits a Federal ironclad with a spar torpedo. The Union ship is damaged but not sunk, and the *David* is likewise. This is the first successful Southern submarine attack of the war, but in general, the experimental submarines of the war cause more fatalities to crews than to enemies.

9 OCTOBER 1863

Civil War: Eastern Theater Lee, wishing to capitalize on Meade's loss of two corps to Chattanooga, moves the Army of Northern Virginia from the Rapidan River to the west and north, trying to flank Meade's Army of the Potomac and drive them from Virginia. Over the next month Lee forces Meade to retreat some 40 miles for a time, but achieves little real strategic gain.

10 OCTOBER 1863

Civil War: Chattanooga Campaign Confederate President Davis arrives on the scene near Chattanooga to survey the siege and to attempt mediation in the growing feud between the fractious Bragg and his generals, who dislike their commander and have served him badly.

14 OCTOBER 1863

Civil War: Eastern Theater Lee attempts to cut off Meade's withdrawal with an attack near Bristoe Station. There ensues a day of inconclusive but costly maneuvering which gains no clear results; though Meade is forced back near the Potomac, his column is not broken. Lee loses 1900 to Meade's 548.

16 OCTOBER 1863

Civil War: Washington The government announces sweeping changes in the organization of the army. The Departments of Ohio, Cumberland and Tennessee are combined into the Military Division of the Mississippi, the whole to be commanded by General Ulysses S. Grant. The new commander, still limping from his horse accident, is ordered to Chattanooga to try to extract the besieged and starving Union forces there. En route, Grant will relieve the demoralized Rosecrans from command of the Army of the Cumberland and replace him with 'Rock of Chickamauga' George H. Thomas.

20 OCTOBER 1863

Civil War: Eastern Theater The Army of Northern Virginia gathers on its old line across the Rappahannock. This 'Bristoe Campaign' has accomplished little so far except to add to the war's casualty statistics: between 10 and 21 October the South has lost 1381, the Union 2292.

24 OCTOBER 1863

Civil War: Chattanooga Campaign Having arrived in Chattanooga the previous day, Grant begins deal-

Below left: A ship's boy on a US Navy frigate.

Below: Grant at Cold Harbor in 1864.

ing with the siege with his customary decisiveness. He issues orders for opening a river supply route to Bridgeport, Alabama, which will come to be called the 'Cracker Line.'

27 OCTOBER 1863

Civil War: Chattanooga Campaign With little interference from Bragg, the Federals place a pontoon bridge over the Tennessee River at Brown's Ford, over which Hooker's corps march to reinforce Chattanooga.

30 OCTOBER 1863

Civil War: Chattanooga Campaign A Federal steamship arrives in Chattanooga with 40,000 rations and tons of feed. The 'Cracker Line' is now open, and Union soldiers and animals are back on full rations.

4 NOVEMBER 1863

Civil War: Chattanooga Campaign In a move that weakens his forces around Chattanooga, Bragg sends Longstreet's men, including Wheeler's cavalry, to reinforce Confederate forces around Knoxville, which is still occupied by Burnside's Union army. Although this poses a threat to Knoxville, Grant decides not to weaken his own army by reinforcing Burnside but rather to attack Bragg as soon as possible. First, however, Grant must await the arrival of reinforcements under his old partner, General Sherman.

7 NOVEMBER 1863

Civil War: Eastern Theater Meade sends troops across the Rapahannock to strike Lee. By dusk an advance by two brigades succeeds in overunning the Confederate positions. Two Southern divisions lose 2023 in dead and captured, a figure that shocks the Rebels, who are not accustomed to such treatment from the Army of the Potomac. Lee withdraws to the Rapidan, and the contending armies have thus returned to the positions they held in Virginia at the beginning of the 'Bristoe campaign.'

9 NOVEMBER 1863

Civil War: Washington Pursuing one of his favorite pastimes, President Lincoln attends the theater; he enjoys a play called *The Marble Heart*, starring John Wilkes Booth.

15 NOVEMBER 1863

Civil War: Chattanooga Campaign Federal General W. T. Sherman arrives at Bridgeport, Alabama, with 17,000 men. Sherman goes on to Chattanooga to confer with Grant on the impending offensive.

16 NOVEMBER 1863

Civil War: Knoxville Campaign At Campbell's Station near Knoxville, Longstreet's Confederates try and fail to cut off Burnside's retreat into the city. However, Longstreet lacks the means to mount a proper siege.

19 NOVEMBER 1863

Civil War: Gettysburg Address A crowd of 15,000 people gather in Pennsylvania for the dedication of a military cemetery on the Gettysburg battlefield. Edward Everett, the main speaker, gives a florid two-hour discourse on the battle. After Everett concludes, Lincoln rises and in his high voice gives what he calls his 'little speech,' which has been carefully written over the last few days. When he has finished, the reception is polite but unenthusiastic; the President considers the address a 'flat failure.' No one seems to foresee that these ten sentences will come to be considered one of the most moving and exquisite utterences in the language.

23 NOVEMBER 1863

Civil War: Battle of Chattanooga Having carefully formed plans for his offensive, Grant is now ready to try to break the Army of the Cumberland out of Bragg's siege of Chattanooga. At dawn Union batteries open up on Missionary Ridge. Soon thereafter Southern troops on the ridge are entertained by the appearance below of 20,000 Union troops clad in their best uniforms and marching in ranks to the music of military bands. Suddenly the parade wheels and charges furiously toward the slopes; in short order the Federals overrun Orchard Knob, which will become Grant's command post the following day. By the end of the fighting the Union has established a salient in the Confederate positions.

24 NOVEMBER 1863

Civil War: Battle of Chattanooga After midnight some of Sherman's troops move across the Tennessee River on pontoon boats. By afternoon all his men are across the river on a new pontoon bridge and move to attack the north end of Missionary Ridge. Meanwhile, Hooker mounts an assault on Lookout Mountain. A dense fog enshrouds the slopes and thus Hooker's engagement there, during which he overruns the weak Confederate positions. This action will become known as 'The Battle Above the Clouds.' On the left wing, Sherman has by late afternoon encountered only enemy outposts as he seizes what he thinks is the northern end of Missionary Ridge; he is surprised to discover that he has only occupied an outlying hill. Nevertheless, by the end of the day Union efforts have been everywhere successful.

25 NOVEMBER 1863

Civil War: Battle of Chattanooga: Missionary Ridge Dawn reveals to the Union army the Stars and Stripes flying at the summit of Lookout Mountain, which elicits cheers all over Chattanooga. Grant orders his wings to advance, Sherman in the north and Hooker in the south, and holds his main attack on the center until the flanks have gained ground. However, both these attacks soon bog down. Fearing that his main attack on the center is being fatally delayed, Grant signals Thomas's men to begin the assault on the heavily entrenched enemy center at the top of Missionary Ridge. Certain that there will be fierce resistance, Grant orders the troops to stop halfway up the ridge and reorganize. In his memoirs, Grant recalls the result: 'In an incredibly short time Generals Sheridan and Wood were driving the enemy before them toward Missionary Ridge . . . Our men drove the troops in front of the lower line of rifle pits so rapidly, and followed them so closely, that Rebel and Union troops went over the first line of works almost at the same time.' Rather than stopping to reorganize as ordered, the Federals continue their charge up the ridge without pause; to do otherwise would leave them open to a murderous fire from the crest when the fleeing Southerners get out of the way. Grant turns and asks Thomas, 'Who ordered those men up the hill?' Thomas replies that they must have ordered themselves. Grant replies, 'Someone will suffer for it, if it turns out badly.' But this assault, one of the most spectacular of its kind in history – an advance up a heavily-occupied slope into the mouths of the enemy guns – turns out triumphantly for the Union. Shouting 'Chickamauga!' as they charge, the Federals overrun line after line of defenses. Finally the Confederates turn in panic-stricken rout; thousands are captured, and Bragg himself barely escapes. Meanwhile, Hooker is rolling up enemy positions to the south. Sherman is still meeting resistance in the north, but his opponents will retreat in the night toward where the defeated Confederate Army of Tennessee is gathering in Ringgold, Georgia. Casualties in the Battle of Chattanooga are comparatively low for such a major engagement: Union forces lose 5824 from all causes out of 56,359 effectives; the South loses 6667 out of 64,165 effectives. Though Bragg's army has not been vitally damaged, the result of his year's campaigning has been another debilitating defeat for the Confederacy.

26 NOVEMBER 1863

Civil War: Eastern Theater Skirmishing breaks out around the Rapidan River in Virginia as, after much prodding from Lincoln, Mead's Army of the Potomac begins an offensive against Lee's greatly outnumbered Army of Northern Virginia. Meade hopes to turn the Confederate right flank and force them back to Richmond. This Federal offensive will falter over the next few days, however; in early December Meade will withdraw across the Rapidan and settle his army into winter quarters. Elsewhere, Confederate raider John Hunt Morgan and some of his officers escape from Ohio State Penitentiary and head South. The future career of Morgan, however, will lack its earlier success.

Lincoln delivering the Gettysburg Address. Few who heard the speech realized that they had been listening to a masterpiece of oratory.

29 NOVEMBER 1863

Civil War: Knoxville Campaign After long preparation Longstreet launches his final attack on Federal positions at Fort Sanders, seeking to dislodge Burnside's forces from nearby Knoxville. The advance, made in bitter cold, is slowed by Union wire entanglements and then bogs down in a ditch for lack of scaling ladders to mount the parapet. It ends a half-hearted and bungled assault, the South's last chance to shake the Union occupation of Knoxville.

30 NOVEMBER 1863

Civil War: The Confederacy President Davis accepts the resignation of General Braxton Bragg as commander of the Army of Tennessee; Bragg has allowed his important victory at Chickamauga to end in an inexcusable rout at Chattanooga.

3 DECEMBER 1863

Civil War: Knoxville Campaign In the face of advancing Union reinforcements Longstreet abandons his siege of Knoxville and moves his troops toward winter quarters in Tennessee. Thus ends the Knoxville Campaign, a Federal victory largely by default. Federal commander Burnside, by failing now to pursue Longstreet, obliges Grant to keep a large force in the state until spring. This failure will interrupt, but alas not end, Burnside's career.

8 DECEMBER 1863

Civil War: Washington At the end of his annual message to Congress, President Lincoln makes his first major statement of proposed Reconstruction policy: most Confederates taking an oath of allegiance to the Union will receive a full pardon with all property except slaves restored. The President's plan receives widespread approval in the North.

9 DECEMBER 1863

Civil War: Western Theater At his own request, General Burnside is relieved as Federal commander at Knoxville and is succeeded by General J. G. Foster. Burnside has been much criticized for failing to support Union operations around Chattanooga and for not pursuing Longstreet. It will be said of Burnside that it is to his discredit that he is a poor commander and to his credit that he knows it.

16 DECEMBER 1863

Civil War: The Confederacy President Davis names General J. E. Johnston, recently opposing Grant in Mississippi, as successor to Bragg as commander of the Department of Tennessee.

William Tecumseh Sherman, the most effective Union commander after Grant, is surrounded by a galaxy of other Northern generals in this old engraving.

31 DECEMBER 1863

Civil War: The Confederacy The Richmond (Virginia) *Examiner* observes, 'Today closes the gloomiest year of our struggle.' Few in the South would disagree. The superior manpower and material resources of the North have begun to tell, and the Union is soon to prepare a unified strategy for the final conquest of the Confederacy.

4 JANUARY 1864

Civil War: The Confederacy President Davis authorizes General Lee to commandeer food supplies in Virginia. Southern troops and animals in winter quarters are seriously underfed, but the civilian population of the Confederacy has also suffered considerable deprivation. Such orders contribute to a decline in the autocratic Davis's popularity.

3 FEBRUARY 1864

Civil War: Meridian Campaign After the fall of Vicksburg, Lincoln has turned his attention to enemy territory in the trans-Mississippi. In order to drive Rebels out of Louisiana and Arkansas, a campaign is planned on the Red River, but this cannot be implemented until the waters rise in March. General W. T. Sherman, ordered to commence preparations for the Red River operation, decides to destroy the two primary railroads of central Mississippi. Beginning his Meridian Campaign, Sherman leaves Vicksburg today with 25,000 men. In conjunction with this infantry move General W. Sooy Smith and 7000 cavalry are to leave Memphis, Tennessee, and drive enemy cavalry from northern Mississippi, then sweep down the rail line toward Meridian to join Sherman.

9 FEBRUARY 1864

Civil War: Western Theater In the largest and most dramatic escape of the war Union prisoners dig their way out of Libby Prison in Richmond, Virginia. While conditions in the prison camps of both sides are poor and growing worse, those in Libby Prison are to be exceeded in infamy only by Andersonville. Nearly half the 109 Union officers who today escape Libby Prison will be recaptured.

14 FEBRUARY 1864

Civil War: Meridian Campaign With little opposition Sherman's infantry marches into Meridian, Mississippi. In a preview of his style in Georgia, Sherman does considerably more damage than his proposed plan of dismantling railroad lines: he orders a rampage that over the next days will level depots, storehouses, hospitals, offices, hotels and the like. Meanwhile, he awaits the arrival of Sooy Smith's cavalry.

The motto of CSA cavalry leader Nathan Bedford Forrest was 'get there fustest with the mostest.'

17 FEBRUARY 1864

Civil War: The Confederacy The privilege of the writ of habeas corpus is suspended by the Confederate Congress, though this applies only to arrests made by highest authority. The Congress also extends the limits of conscription to white men between 17 and 50. Among those condemning conscription is Vice-President Alexander Stephens; the growing hostility between Davis and Stevens is a serious handicap to the Confederate government.

Civil War: Naval The tiny cigar-shaped Confederate semi-submersible *H L Hunley* strikes the USS *Housatonic* with a spar torpedo in Charleston harbor, South Carolina. Both ships go down, the Rebel ship losing its crew. Although this attack will worry the Union blockading fleet, effective submarine warfare is still many years in the future. In its testing and its single action the *Hunley* has drowned 33 sailors.

20 FEBRUARY 1864

Civil War: Meridian Campaign Giving up his wait for the arrival of Sooy Smith (whose cavalry is bogged down in eastern Mississippi), Sherman begins a slow withdrawal from Meridian back to Vicksburg. His casualties have been light, and he has devastated the town. After he leaves, the Confederates return and begin repairing the railroad.

Civil War: Battle of Olustee In January, President Lincoln wrote to Major General Gillmore urging him to bring Florida under Union control and form a state government. After a series of forays from Jacksonville, the Federals have concentrated some 5500 troops near Olustee, Florida. The Confederates in the area number 5200. In the morning a Union cavalry brigade opens battle at Olustee with a successful advance against enemy outposts; then two Federal infantry regiments break and flee. Other brigades replace those that have run, holding their ground with heavy losses until the Confederates have nearly exhausted their ammunition. After dark Union troops withdraw. Losses are high, particularly to Union black soldiers; a total of 1861 casualties are counted by the Union, to the South's 934.

22 FEBRUARY 1864

Civil War: Meridian Campaign Having been sent into retreat on 21 February by a brush with cavalry under Nathan Bedford Forrest, General Sooy Smith's Union cavalry tries to make a stand near Okolona, Mississippi. But Forrest dislodges the Yankees, who mount a series of delaying actions as they retreat. In late afternoon some Federals mount a charge against Forrest which checks his advance, but then the Union troops withdraw in disorder to Memphis, ending the Meridian Campaign on a note of defeat.

24 FEBRUARY 1864

Civil War: Washington Congress approves the revival of the old rank of lieutenant general, thus paving the way for U. S. Grant to become General-in-Chief of the Union army. Among other measures voted concerning enlistment and the draft, Lincoln approves a plan to free slaves who enlist after paying their masters $300 compensation.

25 FEBRUARY 1864

Civil War: Western Theater In what will be called the 'Federal Demonstration on Dalton,' General George H. Thomas and his army probe Confederate positions under Johnston near Dalton, Georgia. The Rebels drive Thomas back, showing that they are present in force. The North suffers 345 casualties in the engagement, and the South 167.

28 FEBRUARY 1864

Civil War: Eastern Theater President Lincoln and War Secretary Stanton have authorized a raid that will attempt to seize the Confederate capital of Richmond by a surprise attack, free Union prisoners and distribute amnesty proclamations. The man who has proposed this harebrained scheme is dare-devil cavalry General Judson Kilpatrick, who today takes 3500 mounted raiders across the Rapidan. With Kilpatrick is one-legged Colonel Ulric Dahlgren, son of Union Admiral Dahlgren.

29 FEBRUARY 1864

Civil War: Kilpatrick-Dahlgren Raid The raid takes shape as the two leaders separate at Spotsylvania, Kilpatrick moving with the main body toward Richmond and Dahlgren heading for Goochland. During the night the Confederate War Department learns of the raid and orders emergency measures.

1 MARCH 1864

Civil War: Kilpatrick-Dahlgren Raid The Union cavalry leaders close in on Richmond in two columns as Confederate militia gather to resist in the lightly-defended city. Approaching the outskirts, Kilpatrick runs into these militia and takes them for a major enemy force. After light skirmishing the Union general withdraws across the Chickahominy River, leaving Dahlgren to his fate. By nightfall Dahlgren and his 500-man detachment have advanced to within three miles of the capital but then decide to retreat in light of increasing enemy resistance.

2 MARCH 1864

Civil War: Washington The Senate confirms Grant's nomination as lieutenant general. In addition to being the highest ranking officer, Grant will become General-in-Chief of the United States Army.

Civil War: Kilpatrick-Dahlgren Raid As the Union raid grinds to its miserable conclusion Kilpatrick is harassed as he retreats, and Dahlgren's men are pulling away from Richmond in two groups; in the evening one contingent will rejoin Kilpatrick. All day Confederate cavalry pursue Dahlgren and his other detachment, who are moving north. Late in the day the Rebels circle ahead, join others at Mantapike Hill and set up an ambush. Around 11 in the evening Dahlgren and his men ride into the trap. In short order Dahlgren is killed and 92 of his troopers are captured. Then something is found that is to make Dahlgren's name notorious. Two documents taken from the Union colonel's body call not only for the release of prisoners in Richmond but also the burning of the city and the summary execution of President Davis and his cabinet. These documents will be sent to Robert E. Lee, who will forward copies to Union General Meade with a demand for explanation. A subsequent Federal investigation into the matter will never find the source of the orders, but the affair does great damage to the honor of the Union.

10 MARCH 1864

Civil War: Red River Campaign Beginning the Red River Campaign, Union forces leave Vicksburg and head down the Mississippi River toward the Red River, which runs through northwestern Louisiana. The infantry is accompanied by 13 ironclads and seven gunboats. The goal of the operation is to establish Union control of Louisiana and eastern Texas; it is to be coordinated by General Nathaniel Banks.

14 MARCH 1864

Civil War: Red River Campaign Moving up the Red River, Union forces easily overwhelm the partly-completed Rebel Fort de Russy, near Simsport, Louisiana. Meanwhile, the Federal fleet bursts through a dam nine miles below and proceeds up the river.

16 MARCH 1864

Civil War: Red River Campaign Nine Union gunboats have arrived in Alexandria, Louisiana. Federal troops occupy the town and await the arrival of further land forces.

17 MARCH 1864

Civil War: Western Theater Generals Grant and Sherman confer in Nashville, Tennessee, planning operations against General Johnston and his Confederate army in Dalton, Georgia. Formally receiving command of the Union armies on this date, Grant announces, 'Headquarters will be in the field, and . . . with the Army of the Potomac.' Grant, in other words, is going to take over Meade's army for the final showdown with Lee.

24 MARCH 1864

Civil War: Red River Campaign Union General Nathaniel Banks arrives in Alexandria, Louisiana, to take command of the Union forces assembling there. He discovers two major problems: first, he is ordered to return Sherman's 10,000 troops, which are needed for the Atlanta campaign; second, the Red River is so low as to make it barely passable for his flotilla. Nonetheless, Banks orders an advance to Shreveport.

4 APRIL 1864

Mexican situation Concerned about the French puppet regime developing in Mexico and its threat to Texas, the House of Representatives passes a resolution saying the US will not tolerate a monarchy in Mexico.

5 APRIL 1864

Civil War: Red River Campaign Confederates fall back from the Federal advance and group around Mansfield, Louisiana, placing themselves between Banks and his goal of Shreveport. By this time the Federal land forces are marching on a single narrow road, encumbered by a wagon train that stretches for 12 miles through enemy-held wilderness. The Union flotilla, meanwhile, continues to make poor headway up the low waters of the Red River.

Dour James Longstreet became Lee's most trusted lieutenant after the death of Stonewall Jackson.

Scorched earth was not solely a Northern policy. Here, the ruins of Manassas Railroad Junction in the wake of a Southern retreat.

7 APRIL 1864

Civil War: The Confederacy The government orders General Longstreet and his corps to leave Georgia and rejoin Lee. This is in anticipation of Grant's operations against the Confederate Army of Northern Virginia.

8 APRIL 1864

Civil War: Washington By a vote of 38 to 6 the Senate passes the Thirteenth Amendment to the Constitution, abolishing slavery in the United States and all areas under its jurisdiction. The vote shows that by now the North clearly perceives the importance and moral significance of the gesture. Final adoption of the amendment will come in 1865.

Civil War: Red River Campaign Confederate General Taylor moves his army from Mansfield, Louisiana, to Sabine Crossroads to meet the advance of Banks toward Shreveport. Taylor orders a general assault, which drives the Federals back with 2235 casualties out of 12,000 engaged. Southern losses are 1000 out of 8800 engaged.

9 APRIL 1864

Civil War: Red River Campaign Taylor tries to follow up his previous day's victory by attacking Union positions at Pleasant Hill. After some gains early in the fighting the Rebels are repulsed by a counterattack. The battle ends with Taylor's forces withdrawing in some confusion. While the engagement is technically a Northern victory, it has in fact halted the progress of the Red River Campaign, which has been plagued by problems and mistakes from the beginning. The end of Federal efforts on the river marks the last important operation by either side in Louisiana. Now Banks will have to face the problem of withdrawing his flotilla on the lowering waters of the river.

12 APRIL 1864

Civil War: Western Theater Nathan Bedford Forrest, on a raiding expedition against Federal operations in Tennessee and Kentucky, surrounds Fort Pillow on the Mississippi in Tennessee. The fort is held by about 557 Union troops, nearly half of them black. Forrest places his men in sheltered positions and then mounts a swift attack, and the fort is soon overrun. There are only 100 Confederate casualties, but what sends shockwaves through the country are the Union casualties and the apparent reasons for them. Southern accounts will claim that the Federal losses – 231 killed and 100 wounded, with 168 whites and only 58 blacks captured – occur because the Yankees refuse to surrender in the face of certain defeat. The Northern report, which history will in some degree vindicate, states that the fort surrendered quickly and that what followed was a massacre of helpless Union troops, especially blacks. Whatever the true extent of Southern atrocities in the engagement, the accusations will inflame the North.

The first great clash between Grant and Lee took place on 5-6 May 1864 when the Rebels attacked the Union army in Virginia's Wilderness area.

17 APRIL 1864

Civil War: Washington Grant orders that no more prisoners be exchanged with the South until such releases are balanced equally, as they have not been and probably cannot be. Though this order increases the drain on the South's dwindling supply of manpower, it also condemns many Union prisoners to slow death from starvation and disease in overcrowded Southern prisons.

20 APRIL 1864

Civil War: Western Theater Confederate forces capture the 2500-man Federal garrison at Plymouth, North Carolina, and occupy the city. This victory raises Confederate spirits considerably, but the city has little strategic significance, and Grant has already concluded that it is not worth defending.

21 APRIL 1864

Civil War: Red River Campaign Continuing his withdrawal from a disastrous campaign, Banks marches his land forces to Cloutiersville, Louisiana. Meanwhile, the Federal rear guard is driven from Natchitoches by Rebel cavalry, who continue pursuit.

26 APRIL 1864

Civil War: Red River Campaign Federal troops and some of the fleet have arrived in Alexandria, Louisiana, but the rest of the flotilla remains stuck above the rapids near the city. Union Colonel Joseph Bailey proposes an extraordinary plan to build a series of dams to raise the river; when the required seven feet of depth is reached, chutes will be opened for the ships to slip through. For their part, the Confederates keep up strong harassment.

27 APRIL 1864

Civil War: Washington The plans are made, the armies poised and Grant has issued orders pursuant to his grand strategy for ending the war. There are to be simultaneous advances on five fronts: Sherman is to march toward Atlanta; Ben Butler will move his army up the Peninsula toward Richmond; Franz Sigel will clear Virginia's Shenandoah Valley; Banks will march on Mobile, Alabama; and Grant and Meade will move on Richmond from the north.

28 APRIL 1864

Civil War: Eastern Theater As they have been doing since late 1863, Federal batteries continue their shelling of Fort Sumter in Charleston harbor, South Carolina, today sending 510 rounds into the unconquerable mass of rubble. The shelling will be intense over the next seven days.

3 MAY 1864

Civil War: Eastern Theater The Army of the Potomac, still nominally under Meade but in fact commanded by Grant, is on the eve of a new campaign. A few days before, Grant has written Halleck (who is now Chief of Staff), 'The Army of the Potomac is in splendid condition and evidently feels like whipping somebody.' Grant plans to march through the dense forest of the Virginia Wilderness, hoping to cut Lee off from Richmond. The Federals will cross the Rapidan River tomorrow, 122,000 strong, to take on Lee's 66,000 hungry and ill-clad men.

4 MAY 1864

Civil War: Washington Over Lincoln's objections the House of Representatives passes the Wade-Davis Reconstruction Bill, which contains stiffly punitive measures directed toward the South. If put into law, this will destroy Lincoln's more moderate reconstruction plans; however, some Radical Republicans oppose the bill as insufficiently severe.

5 MAY 1864

Civil War: Battle of the Wilderness Grant begins to learn what kind of opponent he is facing when Lee

The tone of Grant's Richmond offensive was set in the Wilderness: a total of over 25,000 casualties.

makes a surprise attack on the Federal column in the Wilderness. The armies are soon struggling in a desperate battle. Because of the thick woods, the forces often grapple at almost point-blank range, battle lines becoming confused in the smoke-filled forest. Late in the afternoon Confederate General Hill's advance along the Plank Road is met by Hancock, and a separate battle ensues. But as evening falls nothing significant has been gained by either side. Also today, General Butler and 40,000 men land at Bermuda Hundred, in the peninsula formed by the James and Appomattox Rivers, to move on Richmond as part of Grant's grand strategy.

6 MAY 1864

Civil War: Battle of the Wilderness During the night Grant orders a general attack for five in the morning, but before that can be launched Rebels attack the Union right flank, and firing gradually spreads along the line. Federal General Hancock moves against the weak positions of Hill, enveloping them along the Orange Plank Road. Then, at the critical moment, Longstreet's men make a dramatic appearance, moving down the Orange Plank Road at a trot. Soon the Union advance is checked, and the Federals are thrown back to their original breastworks. About 10 in the morning Longstreet decides to take the offensive against the Federal left flank. He finds an unfinished railroad cut that provides a clear route to the enemy flank and sends troops to the attack, rolling up the Union line northward in confusion. But then disaster strikes the Confederate advance – Longstreet is seriously wounded by the fire of his own men, and after Longstreet is carried from the field the Southern advance falters. Late in the afternoon Confederate General John B. Gordon mounts an assault on the Union right. The surprised Yankees are driven from a large portion of their works before the attack is halted by the arrival of darkness. Elsewhere during the day, Federal cavalry under their new commander Philip Sheridan have skirmished inconclusively with Jeb Stuart's horsemen at Todd's Tavern. Casualties in two days of inconclusive fighting in the Wilderness have been staggering. The North has lost 2246 killed and 12,073 wounded, these and other casualties totaling 17,666 out of 101,895 engaged. Confederate losses are estimated at 7750 out of 61,025 engaged. But the tragedy is not quite over: as darkness falls brushfires break out in the forest, and some 200 Federal wounded die in the flames. Between the James and Appomattox Rivers, meanwhile, Butler's Federal army begins to entrench across the neck of the peninsula. Richmond lies fifteen miles to the north, and there are only some 10,000 Confederate troops in the area.

7 MAY 1864

Civil War: Eastern Theater As the exhausted men of both armies lie in their trenches in rainy weather, Grant decides to try again to flank Lee, sidling around the Rebels toward Richmond. But Lee has anticipated the move and orders his forces to hurry to the road crossing at Spotsylvania.

Civil War: Western Theater Since November of 1873 the great armies of the West have been stationary. Now Sherman is in command in Chattanooga with over 100,000 men of three Federal armies under Thomas, McPherson and Schofield. His opponent, commanding the Confederate Army of Tennessee, is General J. E. Johnston with 62,000 men. Today Sherman begins his advance deep into the Confederacy toward the vital supply and communications center of Atlanta; striking on Johnston's left flank, Federals drive the enemy from Tunnel Hill near Dalton.

8 MAY 1864

Civil War: Spotsylvania Campaign After a forced march Grant's advance divisions arrive to find the Rebels blocking their path at Spotsylvania. After the Confederates throw back weak Federal assaults both armies begin moving up in strength and begin entrenching. In the afternoon General Sheridan convinces Grant to let him make a cavalry raid toward Richmond that will disrupt supply lines and tie up Jeb Stuart's cavalry. Thus begins Sheridan's Richmond Raid, which will set out tomorrow.

9 MAY 1864

Civil War: Atlanta Campaign In Georgia five assaults by Sherman's Federals are repulsed from the crest of Dug Gap by Johnston's Confederates. Union cavalry are also driven from Poplar Place with heavy losses. However, these engagements will convince Johnston that he must abandon Dalton.

Civil War: Red River Campaign The innovative Union plan to raise the river with dams and then open them for passage proves its worth when a gunboat slips through a gap torn in a dam above Alexandria, Louisiana. During the next few days the rest of the Union flotilla will likewise be saved, ending the Red River Campaign with less loss than might have been expected.

10 MAY 1864

Civil War: Spotsylvania Campaign Lee's army has erected breastworks and entrenchments all along the line, with a vulnerable horseshoe-shaped salient bulging from one section. During the day Grant throws three Union corps against the Confederate left and left-center. These attacks are repulsed with heavy Northern losses. Meanwhile, Sheridan's cavalry is at Beaver Dam Station, where they have destroyed quantities of Lee's supplies. Sheridan moves on toward Richmond as Stuart's Confederate cavalry ride to intercept them. Elsewhere, on the peninsula below Richmond, Federal General Ben Butler has not been able to advance toward the Confederate capital.

11 MAY 1864

Civil War: Spotsylvania Campaign Grant orders a frontal assault on the Confederate horseshoe salient for tomorrow. During the day he writes to Chief of Staff Halleck, 'I . . . propose to fight it out on this line if it takes all summer.'

Civil War: Battle of Yellow Tavern Jeb Stuart and his Rebel cavalry reach Yellow Tavern in the morning and position themselves to block Sheridan's way to Richmond. Sheridan's men arrive before noon and mount a few probing attacks before a full-scale assault in the late afternoon. It is during this action that General Jeb Stuart, at age 31 one of the most colorful and effective of Southern leaders, is mortally wounded; he will die in Richmond tomorrow. Showing that they have finally become a match for the Southern horsemen, the Federals drive the enemy cavalry from the field. But the engagement gives the Confederates time to strengthen Richmond, and Sheridan, realizing that it will be unwise to move on the Confederate capital, begins to ride south to link up with Butler. With the deaths of Jackson and now of Stuart, Lee has lost the two partners he can least afford to lose.

12 MAY 1864

Civil War: Battle of Spotsylvania At 4 in the morning of what is to become one of the bloodiest days of the war, 20,000 Federals fall on to the Confederate horseshoe salient. The Federals quickly capture over 2000 enemy and 20 cannon. The remaining defenders fall back to a second line of breastworks on the neck of the salient and begin to pour a murderous fire into the advancing Northerners. By 10 o'clock the Federals have been driven back to a stand on the north side of the salient. There follows a truly terrible day of fighting in driving rain, with the contending forces only a few yards apart across the breastworks. The Army of Northern Virginia manages to hold the line, and during the night Lee orders his forces back to new breastworks across the neck of the salient. In the fighting for this small piece of territory the Union has suffered 6800 casualties to the South's 5000, and a corner of the salient has earned the name 'Bloody Angle.'

Civil War: Atlanta Campaign During the night General Johnston moves his Confederate Army of Tennessee out of Dalton, Georgia, establishing new defenses around Resaca to resist Sherman's advance. The two generals have established the pattern of the campaign: as if in a formal dance, Sherman will move his superior forces to one flank or the other of his enemy, and Johnston will retreat.

A view of the terrain near Spotsylvania, where Lee and Grant again clashed just two days after the Battle of the Wilderness had ended.

14 MAY 1864

Civil War: Eastern Theater Another element in Grant's overall strategy takes shape as General Franz Sigel moves south toward the Shenandoah Valley, one of the primary sources of Southern food supplies.

Civil War: Atlanta Campaign There is heavy fighting as Sherman's men try unsuccessfully to crack Johnston's defenses around Resaca, Georgia. By the end of the day the lines have not significantly changed.

15 MAY 1864

Civil War: Eastern Theater As Sigel moves his 6500 Federals south down the Shenandoah he runs into enemy cavalry, who delay his advance until the arrival of reinforcements at New Market. Before noon the Northerners have been pushed back about a half mile. A series of costly but effective Southern assaults follows, and finally Sigel orders a general retreat. In the fighting the Federals have lost 831 and the Confederates 820, out of 5000 Rebel troops engaged.

Civil War: Atlanta Campaign There is a second day of sharp but inconclusive fighting around Resaca, Georgia. Sherman is unable to break through Confederate defenses. But when Johnston learns that Federals have crossed the Oostenaula River and are moving on his rear, he orders another withdrawal.

16 MAY 1864

Civil War: Eastern Theater In the early morning ten brigades of Confederates under General Beauregard attack Butler's lines on the right at Drewry's Bluff. The Federals repulse five charges before they are overwhelmed and 400 are captured. But the fighting on the Federal left is inconclusive, the center holds and Butler's innovative use of wire entanglements proves effective in stopping enemy advances. Nonetheless, Butler at length gives up and orders a retreat. By next morning the Federals will be back at Bermuda Hundred, there to be, in Grant's phrase, 'bottled up' by the enemy. Thus, in two days, Butler's and Sigel's elements of Grant's master plan have foundered, as has the Red River Campaign. Grant himself, meanwhile, has so far been stymied by Lee. Only Sherman in Georgia is making progress.

A symbolic post-war engraving of Sherman's March to the Sea summarizes the devastation wrought in this application of the doctrine of 'total war.'

18 MAY 1864

Civil War: Spotsylvania Campaign In early morning a new Federal attack is mounted on the breastworks at the neck of the former salient. After brief fighting Grant abandons the attempt and once more begins sidling his army to the left, trying to get around Lee's right flank. In the Spotsylvania Campaign, now drawing to a close, Federal casualties have been 17,500 out of 110,000 engaged. Since the beginning of his campaigns against Lee, Grant has lost over 33,000 of his army.

Civil War: Atlanta Campaign Johnston again entrenches his army, this time near Cassville, Georgia, with Sherman in hot pursuit. Deciding to strike at the Federals, Johnston orders John B. Hood to mount an assault. Hood, dashing as a field commander but blundering as a tactician, fumbles the attempt. Finding Union forces creeping around both his flanks, Johnston is again forced to move.

20 MAY 1864

Civil War: Eastern Theater Grant sends Hancock's corps toward Hanover Junction in Virginia, but once again Lee second-guesses his enemy and orders his men to march to Hanover Junction and entrench. The armies are again racing to the east and south toward Richmond.

22 MAY 1864

Civil War: Atlanta Campaign Sherman again flanks Johnston's army, going around the Confederate left at Altoona, Georgia, and heading toward Dallas.

At the cavalry Battle of Trevilian Station in June 1864 US General George A. Custer (on black horse r) displayed the rashness that would be his undoing.

23 MAY 1864

Civil War: Battle of North Anna River Lee has entrenched his Army of Northern Virginia in a wedge, with the point on the North Anna River near Hanover Junction. Arriving and joining battle, the Federal Army of the Potomac splits in two during fierce but indecisive fighting; Lee thus has a rare opportunity to deal Grant a serious blow. But on this day Lee is ill, delirious with fever, and cannot organize an offensive.

24 MAY 1864

Civil War: Battle of North Anna River Now split into three parts, Federals attack both sides of the Confederate wedge while another force moves on the point. Lee is still feverish and not able to direct his army, but the Rebel line holds. Meanwhile, Sheridan arrives back at the Army of the Potomac after his cavalry raid around Lee's army, during which he has destroyed vital supplies and killed the great Confederate cavalry commander Jeb Stuart.

Civil War: Western Theater Realizing that Sherman is moving around him, Johnston orders his forces out of Altoona to Dallas, Georgia.

25 MAY 1864

Civil War: Battle of North Anna River The battle concludes with Grant spending another day vainly trying to find a vulnerable point in Lee's lines.

Civil War: Western Theater: Atlanta Campaign Sherman attacks Hood's position at New Hope Church, but his men are turned back by concentrated fire from 16 cannon and 5000 Rebel muskets.

26 MAY 1864

Civil War: Eastern Theater Failing to find a weakness in Lee's position, Grant and Meade late at night move the Army of the Potomac northward back across the North Anna and for the fourth time begin sidling toward Lee's right. For their part, the Con-

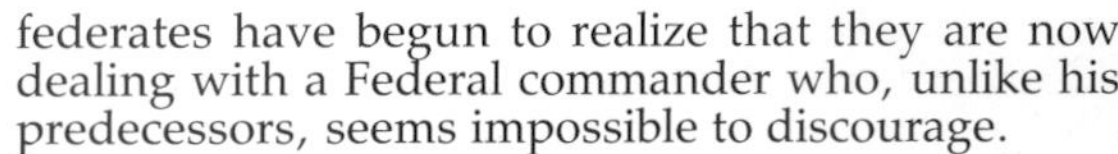

federates have begun to realize that they are now dealing with a Federal commander who, unlike his predecessors, seems impossible to discourage.

27 MAY 1864

Civil War: Atlanta Campaign Heavy fighting is seen around the New Hope-Dallas area as the opposing forces jockey for position. Sherman suffers 1400 casualties in unsuccessful attempts to turn Johnston's right. By the end of the month both sides will have lost around 9000 men in the campaign.

31 MAY 1864

Civil War: The North A group of Radical Republicans hostile to Lincoln meets in Cleveland, Ohio, to nominate General John C. Frémont for president.

1 JUNE 1864

Civil War: Battle of Cold Harbor Before dawn Lee moves against Federals holding the important road junction of Cold Harbor in Virginia. After two attacks are repulsed Lee calls for reinforcements and turns back three Federal assaults late in the day. As the Confederates dig in, Grant orders an attack tomorrow morning.

Civil War: Atlanta Campaign Sherman issues orders to protect his supply line, which is growing steadily longer and more vulnerable. The main threat to that line is the raiding of Nathan Bedford Forrest, of whom Sherman writes with his customary ferocity, 'That devil Forrest . . . must be hunted down and killed if it costs ten thousand lives and bankrupts the Federal treasury.' To this end Sherman sends General Samuel D. Sturgis with 3200 cavalry and 4800 infantry to hunt down Forrest. General Sturgis leaves Memphis today. Meanwhile, Rebel raider John Morgan is harassing Sherman's supply lines in Kentucky.

2 JUNE 1864

Civil War: Battle of Cold Harbor Grant's planned assault is put off for a day due to slow troop movements and rain. Union soldiers understand all too well what a charge on to Lee's strong entrenchments will entail: a Union observer sees men sewing name tags on to their coats so their bodies can be identified after the battle is over.

Civil War: Eastern Theater In the Shenandoah Valley, General Sigel has been replaced by General David Hunter, who is ordered by Grant to do what Sigel failed to do and sweep the area. Hunter is headed south for Staunton with 16,000 men; his opponent is W. E. Jones with 8500 men.

3 JUNE 1864

Civil War: Battle of Cold Harbor Grant has determined to strike a decisive blow at Lee's army, hammering enemy lines in a direct assault like the ones that initially overran Bloody Angle at Spotsylvania and secured the heights of Chattanooga. The attack begins at 4:30 in the morning, thousands of soldiers of the Army of the Potomac marching straight toward the Army of Northern Virginia. As they march, an observer will recall, 'there rang out suddenly on the summer air such a crash of artillery and musketry as is seldom heard in war.' Though Union men fall in waves like mown wheat, for a short time, the Confederate breastworks are reached. But then a countercharge hurls the Federals back. Within the space of a half hour 7000 Northerners have died or been wounded. Incredibly, after the failure of the initial assault, Grant orders two more. The last order is essentially ignored. Grant will admit in his memoirs, 'No advantage whatever was gained from the heavy loss we sustained.' But the horror continues after the battle. The wounded are abandoned between the lines, and not until 7 June will Union stretcher parties be sent out, by which time all but two men of the thousands of wounded have slowly died in full sight of both lines. In a month of incessant campaigning Federal losses have been 50,000, 41 percent of their original strength. A Northern writer notes that the Army of the Potomac 'has literally marched in blood and agony from the Rapidan to the James.' Lee has lost 32,000 men, 46 percent of his strength. As Grant well knows, his own losses can be replaced, but Lee's cannot.

4 JUNE 1864

Civil War: Atlanta Campaign Realizing that Sherman is flanking him again, Johnston moves the Army of Tennessee out of the New Hope-Dallas area toward lines already prepared in the mountains before Marietta, Georgia.

5 JUNE 1864

Civil War: Eastern Theater Confederate General Jones makes a stand against Hunter's advance toward Staunton, Virginia, but in a day of fighting the Federals rout the Confederates. Hunter loses 780 men to the South's 1600. General Jones is killed among the Southern casualties. Tomorrow Hunter will enter Staunton unopposed.

7 JUNE 1864

Civil War: Eastern Theater As the opposing armies lie in their entrenchments at Cold Harbor, Grant finally gives up his hopes of striking Lee a decisive blow and marching on Richmond. Instead, he decides to turn his army south toward Petersburg, which is in effect the back door to Richmond. As a diversion for his coming move Grant sends Sheridan's cavalry west to join Hunter in the Shenandoah. This will be known as Sheridan's Trevilian Raid.

8 JUNE 1864

Civil War: The North By a comfortable majority Abraham Lincoln is nominated for president by the National Union convention in Baltimore. Democratic former Senator Andrew Johnson of Tennessee, who has been staunchly Unionist, is nominated for vice-president over the incumbent Hannibal Hamlin. It is felt that a Southern Democrat who supports the war will strengthen the ticket. The party platform calls for reunification, pursuing the war to its end, no compromise with the South and passage of the Thirteenth Amendment ending slavery.

10 JUNE 1864

Civil War: Battle of Brice's Cross Roads A Union force under General Sturgis, sent by Sherman to hunt down Nathan Bedford Forrest, meet their foe at Brice's Cross Roads in Mississippi. The Confederate raider has learned of the Yankee approach and his pickets are waiting at the crossroads. While his pickets halt the enemy, Forrest moves up his artillery and main force. When the Federals arrive in strength, tired from a forced march in fierce heat, they find themselves under heavy attack. With his instinctive genius for tactics (he is self-taught in warfare), Forrest pressures both Union flanks, which begin to give way late in the afternoon. Finally the Federals panic and run. Sturgis has been defeated by a force less than half as large as his own and has lost 223 killed, 394 wounded and 1623 captured, in addition to 16 guns and his entire 250-wagon supply train. The Confederate commander reports losing 492 of 3500 engaged. It is 'that devil' Forrest's finest moment, and he will chase Sturgis clear back to Memphis. Elsewhere, John Hunt Morgan and his new outfit are raiding in Lexington, Kentucky.

11 JUNE 1864

Civil War: Battle of Trevilian Station Lee has dispatched cavalry under Wade Hampton, Stuart's successor, to stop Sheridan's advance into Virginia (which is a diversion from Grant's planned movement on Petersburg). Hampton finds Sheridan near Trevilian Station and pitches his troopers into the Yankees, only to discover more Federals at his rear; these prove to be George Armstrong Custer's men, striking between the divisions of Hampton and Fitz Lee. Hampton turns to attack Custer, squeezing him between two columns. It takes much of the day for Federal reinforcements to extricate the over-impetuous Custer from his predicament. The first day of fighting ends with the Union holding Trevilian Station and the Rebel columns separated.

Two scenes from the Battle of Cold Harbor, 1-3 June 1864, in which Grant failed to dislodge Lee from entrenched positions. In this first month of his Richmond campaign Grant had lost some 60,000 men, the equal of Lee's total strength.

12 JUNE 1864

Civil War: Petersburg Campaign After several days of careful and secretive preparations the Army of the Potomac pulls quietly out of position at Cold Harbor and steals toward the James River. Grant seems for once to have outsmarted Lee, who does not discover the move for several days, thus leaving Grant's goal, Petersburg, weakly defended.

Civil War: Battle of Trevilian Station After the previous day's success for Sheridan, the battle ends with a failed Federal attack on Hampton's entrenchments. Federal losses have been 1007 out of 8000 engaged; Southern casualties are comparable. Sheridan thereupon decides not to join Hunter in the Valley as planned, but rather to rejoin Grant.

Civil War: Western Theater His luck running out, Confederate raider John Hunt Morgan is defeated by Federals in Cynthiana, Kentucky, losing nearly half his party of 1300 men. Morgan and the remainder flee toward Abingdon, Virginia, where they arrive on 20 June.

15 JUNE 1864

Civil War: Petersburg Campaign Still not suspecting Grant's move, Lee refuses an urgent request for reinforcements from General Beauregard, who is commanding in Petersburg. At that moment the 5400 Confederates defending Petersburg are under assault by W. F. 'Baldy' Smith's corps of 16,000. But though his attacks on the city slowly gain ground, Smith makes one of the great blunders of the war in deciding not to try and take the city in the evening. Had he done so, the war would likely have been shortened by months. During the night Confederate General Beauregard begins to take men from Bermuda Hundred to reinforce Petersburg.

16 JUNE 1864

Civil War: Petersburg Campaign Beauregard, having pulled in most of his Bermuda Hundred line, now has 14,000 men to defend Petersburg as the Army of the Potomac gathers near the city. During the day Grant and Meade direct renewed assaults, which by late evening have captured several positions.

17 JUNE 1864

Civil War: Petersburg Campaign Another series of Federal attacks on Petersburg make slow and costly headway, and late in the day Beauregard actually retakes some positions. During the night the Rebels pull back into tighter and tougher positions. Lee, at last perceiving the Federal threat, sends reinforcements.

18 JUNE 1864

Civil War: Petersburg Campaign During the day a series of badly-coordinated Federal assaults are launched against Petersburg. These attacks are repulsed; a larger push in mid-afternoon makes progress but is terribly costly. As the fighting ends with darkness Grant gives up the idea of direct assault. In four days of attempts the North has lost 1688 killed, 8513 wounded and 1185 captured or missing, a total of 11,386 casualties out of 63,797 engaged. Now that Southern reinforcements have arrived along with Lee himself, the city is now effectively impregnable to attack. The only course hereafter is a siege, and Grant begins making preparations to that end.

Civil War: Eastern Theater In Virginia's Shenandoah Valley, Hunter's attempt to clear the area of enemy is stymied when Confederate General Jubal Early drives him back.

19 JUNE 1864

Civil War: Naval As crowds of observers watch from nearby cliffs and from ships the CSS *Alabama* under Captain Raphael Semmes sallies out of the coast of Cherbourg, France, to challenge the USS *Kearsarge*. A fierce battle ensues, the ships circling closer and closer and blazing away with their cannons. At length the superior marksmanship of the Union sailors wins the day. While the men watch from the *Kearsarge*, the Rebel ship slides under the waves, and a British yacht picks up a number of sailors, including Captain Semmes. Thus ends the high-seas career of the legendary Confederate commerce raider *Alabama*, which has taken 65 Union merchant ships during the war.

25 JUNE 1864

Civil War: Siege of Petersburg As Grant slowly extends his siege lines around the city, meeting determined resistance, an engineer submits a plan to dig an enormous mine under the enemy breastworks. The idea is promoted by General Ambrose Burnside, who is anxious to recoup his reputation after the disaster of Fredericksburg.

27 JUNE 1864

Civil War: Battle of Kennesaw Mountain In his Atlanta campaign, impatient with the undramatic flanking maneuvers he has been using so success-

In June 1864 USS *Kearsarge* finally caught and sank the elusive Confederate raider *Alabama*. Shown here is one of *Kearsarge*'s two massive 11in Rodman guns.

fully against Johnston's Confederates, Sherman decides on a frontal assault on enemy positions at Kennesaw Mountain, near Marietta, Georgia. But in three major advances uphill into a hail of shot and shell the Federals capture not one breastwork. As one Southern soldier will recall, 'I will ever think that the reason they did not capture our works was the impossibility of their living men to pass over the bodies of their dead.' Federal casualties in the defeat are 1999 killed and wounded and 52 missing, over 2000 lost out of 16,229 attackers. Confederates number some 270 killed and wounded and 172 missing out of 17,333 engaged. On 2 July Sherman will return to his flanking game and maneuver Johnston away from Marietta.

30 JUNE 1864

Civil War: Eastern Theater Confederate General Jubal Early and 10,000 men pull out of Staunton, Virginia, and head north toward the Federal capital of Washington, DC.

4 JULY 1864

Civil War: Washington Lincoln pocket-vetoes the Radical Republicans' Wade-Davis Bill, with its punitive plans for reconstruction. In the storm of protest that follows Lincoln will stand firmly by his more lenient policies.

5 JULY 1864

Civil War: Early's Washington Raid Avoiding Federal pursuit, Early begins crossing the Potomac into Maryland as panic breaks out in Washington. Grant and Chief of Staff Halleck begin to organize resistance, and the Maryland militia is called out.

8 JULY 1864

Civil War: Atlanta Campaign Against the wishes of President Davis, General Johnston responds to new Union flanking movements by ordering the Army of Tennessee back to breastworks near Atlanta.

9 JULY 1864

Civil War: Early's Washington Raid Near Frederick Maryland, Early routs a motley force of 6000 Federal troops and militia; most of the 2000 Union casualties are the missing. Early presses on toward Washington, stopping to demand a $200,000 levy in Frederick.

11 JULY 1864

Civil War: Early's Washington Raid By noon Early's army arrives on the outskirts of Washington at Silver Springs. Skirmishing flares at Fort Stevens. Visiting there with his wife, President Lincoln exposes himself to fire as he looks over the parapets. Then Early, learning of reinforcements moving into the capital, decides to give up the idea of assaulting Washington.

12 JULY 1864

Civil War: Early's Washington Raid Before withdrawing and concluding their raid Early's men skirmish on the outskirts of Washington. Once again Lincoln stands on a parapet to watch the firing at Fort Stevens, prompting an officer to shout, 'Get down, you fool!'

14 JULY 1864

Civil War: Battle of Tupelo In the Western Theater Union General A. J. Smith, sent by Sherman in another attempt to stop Nathan Bedford Forrest's depredations, finds himself under attack by Forrest and S. D. Lee at Tupelo, Mississippi. But Smith has dug in firmly and his men turn back a series of Rebel frontal assaults during the day and a flanking attempt in the evening.

15 JULY 1864

Civil War: Battle of Tupelo A further Confederate attempt on Smith's entrenchments is repulsed with little loss to either side, but Smith begins to retreat in the afternoon. The Rebels pursue, and in the skirmishing Forrest is slightly wounded. While Forrest has not trounced the Federals with his usual dash and has lost a good many men, neither has Smith much interfered with Forrest's operations. Federal casualties in the two days have been 674 out of 14,000 engaged, and Southern losses are 1326 out of around 11,600 engaged.

17 JULY 1864

Civil War: Atlanta Campaign A telegram arrives from President Davis relieving the cautious J. E. Johnston from command of the Confederate Army of Tennessee. His replacement is General John B. Hood, who can be counted on to take the offensive. As it happens, nothing could suit Sherman's purposes better.

19 JULY 1864

Civil War: Atlanta Campaign Sherman is closing in on Atlanta. McPherson is on one wing, moving through Decatur to the east. Thomas is on the other wing to the north. And Schofield is advancing in the center.

20 JULY 1864

Civil War: Atlanta Campaign Today Sherman's men are introduced to Hood's style. Federal General Thomas's army is resting in the afternoon astride Peach Tree Creek when Hood's men attack in force. The fighting is desperate and often hand-to-hand before Thomas moves up cannon to create a devastating enfilade fire. After two hours of determined assault, the Confederates fall back with losses of 4796 out of 20,000. Federal casualties are about 1779 out of about the same number engaged.

22 JULY 1864

Civil War: Battle of Atlanta Around noon McPherson and Sherman are conferring when firing is heard from the left; McPherson rides off to investigate. After a 15-mile march Confederate General Hardee has made an attack, which Hood intends will flank McPherson and get in the rear of the Federals. McPherson arrives to find his men mounting a successful counterattack, but on his return he is shot dead off his horse by Confederate skirmishers. New charges by the Rebels then gain some ground, but by three in the afternoon these attacks are floundering. Realizing this, Hood orders another attack closer to the Federal center. This makes some headway before being repulsed by a counterattack. Meanwhile, Wheeler's cavalry is moving unsuccessfully against the enemy in Decatur. As evening falls Hood's forces have failed for the second time to strike a decisive blow, and his men sink back into the strong defenses of Atlanta. Federal losses for the day are 430 killed, 1559 wounded and 1733 missing, for 3722 casualties out of over 30,000 engaged. Southern losses are estimated at 8000 out of 36,934 engaged. Now Sherman will settle into a siege of Atlanta; he orders operations to cut off the city's supply lines.

28 JULY 1864

Civil War: Atlanta Campaign At Ezra Church, Hood tries again to strike a decisive blow against Sherman. This third Confederate sortie from Atlanta is repulsed with losses up to 5000, though Hood briefly halts Federal destruction of one of his last remaining railroads.

30 JULY 1864

Civil War: Petersburg Mine Assault After weeks of preparation a gigantic powder-filled mine sponsored by General Ambrose Burnside is ready to be detonated under the defenses of Petersburg. The previous day word came from Meade that the black troops specially trained to lead the assault are not to be used, since if it fails the Union will be accused of sacrificing its black soldiers on an experimental operation. Burnside is chagrined by the news, and his ensuing orders are perfunctory. In late afternoon the mine is detonated: one of the largest man-made explosions seen on earth to this time sends flames, earth, cannon and bodies a hundred feet into the air amidst a mushroom-shaped cloud. When all has settled there is an enormous crater stretching into the Confederate works. Into this hole Federal soldiers are sent almost randomly. After the Confederates collect themselves they find the enemy virtually at their feet. They turn a withering fire into the crater, and the Yankee attackers become primarily engaged in hiding. Finally, in desperation, Burnside orders in the black troops originally trained to lead the assault. These men advance resolutely, only to be cut to pieces. The whole inglorious affair ends with surviving Union soldiers rushing devil-take-the-hindmost back to their own lines. The North has suffered 3748 casualties out of 20,708 engaged; the Confederates about 1500 out of 11,466. Following what Grant will dub this 'stupendous failure,' the incapable Burnside will be cashiered for the third and final time (and will go on to a successful career in politics).

1 AUGUST 1864

Civil War: Sheridan's Valley Campaign Grant gives General Philip H. Sheridan a force of 48,000 cavalry and infantry and the mission of clearing the enemy, especially the forces of Jubal Early, out of Virginia's Shenandoah Valley.

5 AUGUST 1864

Civil War: Battle of Mobile Bay At 6 in the morning Admiral David Farragut's Federal fleet begins to run past three enemy forts into the important Confederate port of Mobile Bay. Defending at sea are the powerful ironclad ram *Tennessee* and three gunboats. Soon a Federal ironclad is sunk by a floating mine (called, in those days, a torpedo). It is after this that the 63-year-old Farragut, standing high in the rigging of his flagship, *Hartford*, bellows, 'Damn the torpedos, full speed ahead!' (or something to that effect). The Union fleet does just that, led into the bay by the *Hartford* with little further damage. After being rammed and shelled the CSS *Tennessee* is finally disabled and the bay is secured. Besides removing a valuable port from the Confederacy, the battle gives the Union army a staging area for planned operations against Mobile. Federal bombardment from the water will conquer the forts in the bay by the end of the month, but the city will continue to hold out.

12 AUGUST 1864

Civil War: Sheridan's Valley Campaign Sheridan stalks Jubal Early's Confederates in the Shenandoah. It will be some weeks before the antagonists do more than scouting and skirmishing.

21 AUGUST 1864

Civil War: Siege of Petersburg In one of several attempts to dislodge Federals from the much-needed Weldon Railroad, A. P. Hill attacks Union forces south of Petersburg. The attack fails, with heavy Southern losses. Another attack on 25 August will be harder on the Union, but the railroad will remain broken.

27 AUGUST 1864

Civil War: Atlanta Campaign General W. T. Sherman has slowly extended his lines around Atlanta, choking off the city's supplies, and has noted that Hood has weakened his forces by sending cavalry off to raid Federal supply lines. Now the time has come to begin the final act of the campaign. Sherman sends two corps on a wide circuit of the city. Hood thinks the Yankees are retreating, but in fact they are moving to break Hood's last rail lines into the city, which they will accomplish over the next days.

29 AUGUST 1864

Civil War: The North The Democratic National Convention meets in Chicago. On the 31st the Democrats will make their choice for a presidential candidate: General George B. McClellan, whom Lincoln had cashiered as head of the Army of the Potomac. The Democratic platform calls for an end to hostilities, but McClellan will repudiate the anti-war plank.

1 SEPTEMBER 1864

Civil War: Atlanta Campaign His last rail line being cut the previous day, General Hood orders his Army of Tennessee out of Atlanta, Georgia. The Confederate rearguard blows up remaining supplies as they leave, sending smoke and fire through the city. Tomorrow, as Union troops begin to move in, Sherman will wire Lincoln, 'Atlanta is ours, and fairly won.' Both men know that the fall of Atlanta adds vitally to Lincoln's chances of reelection, which have hitherto looked slim.

4 SEPTEMBER 1864

Civil War: Western Theater Union troops surround the celebrated Rebel raider John Hunt Morgan while he and his remaining men are bivouacked at Greeneville, Tennessee. One hundred Confederates are killed and captured. Among the dead is Morgan, one of the most dashing – though never the luckiest – of Southern irregulars.

5 SEPTEMBER 1864

Reconstruction Following the reconstruction procedure Lincoln has outlined for the readmission of states to the Union, those citizens of Louisiana who have taken a loyalty oath go to the polls and ratify a new state constitution abolishing slavery.

11 SEPTEMBER 1864

Civil War: Western Theater General Sherman has issued an order for the evacuation of all civilians from Atlanta. The order will never be enforced in full, but in the next days 446 families will be driven out, an event unprecedented in the war. Sherman resists protests from the citizens and from General Hood, replying, 'You might as well appeal against the thunder-storm.' His aim is to so devastate the city that it can be of no use to the Confederacy, and he will pursue that goal relentlessly.

Union monitors and frigates batter the Confederate ironclad *Tennessee* into submission at the Battle of Mobile Bay on 5 August 1864.

16 SEPTEMBER 1864

Civil War: Sheridan's Valley Campaign Having skirmished with Early around the Shenandoah for over a month, Sheridan confers with Grant at Charles Town, West Virginia. Now that Early has weakened his forces by sending a division to reinforce Lee, the Union generals decide that the time for decisive action has come.

17 SEPTEMBER 1864

Civil War: The North John C. Frémont, who was nominated for president by a Radical Republican splinter group, withdraws from the race and throws his support to Lincoln.

19 SEPTEMBER 1864

Civil War: Sheridan's Valley Campaign Sheridan attacks Early at Winchester, Virginia. In the morning bottlenecks develop as the Union troops try to cross a river to engage the enemy; later, however, Sheridan organizes a large number of his troops to attack the enemy breastworks. By the end of the day Early is in full retreat. Union losses are 653 killed, 3719 wounded and 618 missing. Early leaves 3000 wounded in Winchester as the rest flee, and Sheridan bags another 2000 prisoners during the day. News of the victory will further enhance Republican election prospects in the North.

Civil War: Trans-Mississippi General Sterling Price leads 12,000 cavalrymen into Missouri in a last attempt to recover the state for the Confederacy. He will raid through October but will never threaten Union control.

After Sherman captured Atlanta in September 1864 he destroyed installations of military value in the city including the railroad depot, shown here.

22 SEPTEMBER 1864

Civil War: Sheridan's Valley Campaign In Virginia, Sheridan catches up with Early again at Fishers Hill. Though the Confederates have taken a strong defensive position, Sheridan drives them to a headlong retreat up the Valley. In this one-sided battle the Federals lose only 528, while the Confederates lose 1235 men and 12 guns. It will be almost a month before Early is ready to fight again. Meanwhile, Sheridan is ordered to destroy as much of the Valley's food-producing capacity as he can lay his hands on: '. . . we want the Shenandoah Valley to remain a barren waste,' writes Grant. The fertile area is no longer to be the breadbasket of the Confederacy.

29 SEPTEMBER 1864

Civil War: Siege of Petersburg As part of his continuing operations to chip away at the Confederate defenses Grant orders an attack on Forts Harrison and Gilmer, part of the Petersburg-Richmond lines. Federals capture Harrison, but the move against Gilmer fails; Rebel attempt to retake Harrison will be repulsed with heavy losses tomorrow.

1 OCTOBER 1864

Civil War: Western Theater General John B. Hood begins a futile campaign to drive Sherman out of Georgia, moving his army around Atlanta to strike Sherman's railroad line at Salt Springs. In support of Hood's army General Nathan Bedford Forrest and his cavalry have been operating in Sherman's rear. Today they skirmish with Federals at Athens and Huntsville, Alabama.

5 OCTOBER 1864

Civil War: Western Theater Still pursuing Hood's goal of somehow crippling Sherman in Georgia, Confederates strike a Union position at Allatoona, Georgia, trying to destroy a railroad bridge. The commander there receives a message – 'General Sherman says hold fast. We are coming.' – which is later embellished into the saying (and revival hymn) 'Hold the fort; I am coming.' In fact, the promised reinforcements do not come, but the Federals hold the fort anyway.

7 OCTOBER 1864

Civil War: Sheridan's Valley Campaign Sheridan writes Grant that in the Shenandoah so far his men have burned 2000 barns filled with wheat and other foodstuffs, destroyed in excess of 70 flour mills, driven off 4000 head of livestock and killed over 3000 sheep to feed his army.

9 OCTOBER 1864

Civil War: Sheridan's Valley Campaign Furious at Early's harassment, Sheridan has ordered cavalry commander Torbert to 'whip the enemy or be whipped yourself.' At Tom's Brook in Virginia today Torbert does as ordered. A spirited two-hour cavalry battle ends with the Confederates fleeing up the Valley with losses of 300 prisoners and 57 casualties.

13 OCTOBER 1864

Civil War: Sheridan's Valley Campaign Taking advantage of Sheridan's withdrawal to Cedar Creek, Jubal Early moves his forces back to their old lines at Fishers Hill and begins to probe Federal positions. Further north, J. S. Mosby and his partisan rangers derail a passenger train near Kearneyville, rob a Federal paymaster and burn the train. It is another day's work in what has come to be called 'Mosby's Confederacy.'

15 OCTOBER 1864

Civil War: Trans-Mississippi As part of General Price's raid in Missouri, Confederate cavalry capture Glasgow, forcing the surrender of the 400-man Federal garrison. Others occupy the town of Sedalia after the Yankees flee.

17 OCTOBER 1864

Civil War: Western Theater General Hood moves his army toward Gadsden, Alabama, breaking off, for the most part, his attacks on Sherman's supply lines. The Confederate general now hopes that by heading north, and eventually into Tennessee, he will force Sherman to follow him, thus maneuvering the Yankees out of Georgia. Sherman, by far the sharper strategist, will not fall for the bait.

Civil War: Trans-Mississippi Federal resistance to the Price raid in Missouri stiffens: the Confederates ride toward Lexington with enemy closing in from three directions.

19 OCTOBER 1864

Civil War: St. Albans Raid A small group of Confederate raiders crosses the Canadian border and descends upon the small Vermont town of St. Albans. The men rob three banks, but citizen resistance prevents them from burning the town. Eleven of the raiders escape over the border, to be arrested and later released by Canadian authorities.

Civil War: Battle of Cedar Creek Out of the early morning fog Jubal Early mounts a savage attack on Sheridan's positions. Completely surprised, the Federal left flank falls back in disarray, forming ragged lines to the rear. Sheridan has spent last night in Winchester after a conference in Washington. He wakes up to sounds of firing in the distance; then, approaching on horseback, he runs into streams of Federal stragglers retreating from Cedar Creek. What follows will make Sheridan a legend. Galloping up and down waving his hat, Sheridan begins to rally his men with commands and vigorous curses, turning them around and organizing a counterattack against the Confederates, whose advance has slowed as they sample the Yankee camp's food and liquor. By late afternoon Sheridan has arranged his forces and leads them screaming to the charge. Early's men are forced back through the camps they earlier captured and finally into headlong retreat. Although Union casualties at Cedar Creek are higher (5665 for the North compared to an estimated 2910 for the South), Sheridan has effectively ended the power of Jubal Early in the Shenandoah. Now the Federals can continue their destruction with little real resistance.

22 OCTOBER 1864

Civil War: Trans-Mississippi Trying to defeat the three Federal forces closing in on him before they can unite, General Price orders Shelby's troops to attack the enemy in front while Marmaduke holds the Yankees at the rear. Shelby successfully forces the Federals to fall back to Brush Creek.

23 OCTOBER 1864

Civil War: Battle of Westport In the Trans-Mississippi Theater, following up their success of yesterday, Shelby's cavalry again strikes Federals near Westport, Missouri, but this time Shelby is repulsed. Meanwhile, Pleasonton's Union cavalry break through Marmaduke's rearguard defense, driving the Rebels from the field; Pleasonton then closes in on Shelby and forces a retreat. The battle, the biggest engagement of the war west of the Mississippi, involves some 20,000 Union troops and over 8000 Confederates. Casualties are about 1500 on each side. This effectively marks the end of Price's raid in Missouri and the last serious threat to Union control of the state. Price will retreat under close pursuit and arrive in Arkansas in early December, having lost heavily in men and supplies.

1 NOVEMBER 1864

Civil War: Western Theater Federal General Alfred J. Smith, who has been in Missouri to help check Price's raid, moves his men to Nashville to reinforce General George Thomas against an expected attack by Hood.

8 NOVEMBER 1864

Civil War: The North With 55 percent of the popular vote and a comfortable majority of electoral votes, Abraham Lincoln is reelected to the presidency, with Tennessee war-governor Andrew Johnson as his vice-president. Significantly, the strongest support for Lincoln has come from soldiers on active duty.

16 NOVEMBER 1864

Civil War: March to the Sea Having devastated Atlanta, General W. T. Sherman and his army leave the city, heading east for Savannah, Georgia. The intention is for the 62,000 men to forage in the Georgia countryside. Sherman has said that they should take any livestock they need from the inhabitants and, if they meet resistance, should 'enforce a devastation more or less relentless.' These orders, inevitably, will be enforced loosely and liberally. To oppose Sherman the Confederates have only about 13,000 men in Georgia; Hood and the Confederate Army of Tennessee are in northern Alabama. Sherman's goals are to split the Confederacy horizontally and show the world that a Union army can march at will through the heart of the South, and in the process humiliate and demoralize the enemy. All those goals will be amply realized.

Personally humane, Sherman was implacable when it came to applying his scorched earth military policy.

The Savannah waterfront in 1865. Sherman took this vital Georgia port city, virtually unopposed, on 21 December 1864.

21 NOVEMBER 1864

Civil War: Western Theater General John B. Hood moves the 38,000 men of his Confederate Army of Tennessee out of Florence, Alabama, northward for an invasion of Tennessee.

26 NOVEMBER 1864

Civil War: Western Theater Hood's army arrives outside Columbia, Tennessee, to find Federals well-entrenched along the Duck River. Hood will decide to try to cut off the Yankees from the north.

29 NOVEMBER 1864

Civil War: Western Theater Having been driven off to Franklin by Forrest's cavalry, Schofield's cavalry commander sends word that Hood is trying to trap the Federals. Meanwhile, Confederate infantry begin to cross over the Duck River to the north. In mid-afternoon Schofield – who had expected an attack from the south – starts his army to Franklin, getting them past Hood during the night.

Indian Wars: Approach Colorado militia under Indian-hating Colonel John M. Chivington descend upon a Southern Cheyenne and Arapaho village at Sand Creek, Colorado Territory. Numerous atrocities are committed by the soldiers, who kill 105 Indian women and children and 28 men. Among the Indians escaping is Chief Black Kettle. Chivington's losses are nine killed and 38 wounded, many of these caused by wild firing from the whites. The incident, which will be condemned by the Federal government, comes to be called the 'Chivington Massacre' and will have devastating repercussions on future Indian/white relations in the West.

30 NOVEMBER 1864

Civil War: Franklin and Nashville Campaign In the Western Theater, having escaped the trap Hood planned for him, General Schofield arrives in Franklin with 32,000 men and deploys them south and west of the town. In mid-afternoon Hood arrives with his Army of Tennessee and launches a full-scale assault over two miles of open field against entrenched Federals. Bloody hand-to-hand fighting develops as the Southerners several times reach enemy lines, only to be repulsed with heavy losses. In the evening Hood finally calls off his attacks, and during the night Schofield withdraws toward Nashville. Casualties are 2326 out of 27,939 engaged for the North, 6252 out of 26,897 engaged for the South.

Civil War: March to the Sea In Georgia, Sherman and his men are cutting a burning and ravaged swath 50 miles wide across the landscape, moving about ten miles a day and impeded little by local enemy forces. Today there is a skirmish at Louisville.

2 DECEMBER 1864

Civil War: Franklin and Nashville Campaign Hood has arrived at the outskirts of Nashville, Tennessee, hard on the heels of Schofield's Federals. Strong

Union lines, prepared by Thomas during the last month, ring the Tennessee capital. Hood begins to fortify his own positions.

7 DECEMBER 1864

Civil War: Franklin and Nashville Campaign In Murfreesboro, Tennessee, Union General Milroy is ordered to make a reconnaissance in force against Nathan Bedford Forrest's Rebels, sent there by Hood two days earlier. Milroy inflicts one of Forrest's few defeats, forcing the Southerners from the field and capturing over 200 men and 14 guns.

10 DECEMBER 1864

Civil War: March to the Sea The end now in sight for their historic and devastating march across Georgia, General Sherman and his 60,000 men arrive south of Savannah. Defending the city are 18,000 well-entrenched Confederates. Sherman decides against an assault and besieges the city. To provide a route for supplies from the Federal navy, Sherman must capture nearby Fort McAllister; this is accomplished on 13 December.

15 DECEMBER 1864

Civil War: Franklin and Nashville Campaign General George Thomas, after much delay caused by lack of horses and icy weather – and after goading and threats of cashiering from Grant – mounts an attack on Hood's Confederates around Nashville. Using one contingent to hit the enemy right with a diversion, Thomas throws the bulk of his army at the Confederate left. During the fighting the Southerners gradually contract their lines as the Union assault pushes them from their original positions. Thomas believes Hood will withdraw during the night. The South would have been better off had Hood done so.

16 DECEMBER 1864

Civil War: Franklin and Nashville Campaign Basically repeating the same tactics as yesterday, Thomas strikes Hood's forces a decisive blow and sends them running in retreat. The right flank fights off the Federals with a desperate rearguard action, while the remaining Rebels flee south toward Franklin. Casualties are 387 killed, 2562 wounded and 112 missing out of 50,000 Federals engaged. There are around 1500 casualties out of 23,000 engaged for the South. Thomas reports capturing 4462 enemy soldiers. The hard-fighting but rather obtuse General John B. Hood has finally battered his Army of Tennessee nearly to pieces against the Union juggernaut.

20 DECEMBER 1864

Civil War: March to the Sea As Sherman's men move to encircle Savannah and cut off the Confederates' escape route General Hardee pulls his men out of the city northward toward South Carolina, where he hopes to link up with troops in that state.

21 DECEMBER 1864

Civil War: March to the Sea Concluding their historic march to the sea, Sherman and his Federal troops occupy Savannah, Georgia. Tomorrow Sherman will telegraph Lincoln, 'I beg to present you, as a Christmas gift, the city of Savannah.' It has been a brilliant campaign and an ominous one. Sherman's determination to visit the sufferings of war on enemy civilians will set a precedent for the future, which will call this strategy Total War. Sherman's own self-justification will run, 'War is barbarism. You cannot refine it.' Later that will become the more succinct and accurate, 'War is hell.'

CSA General John Bell Hood vainly tried to divert Sherman by attacking his supply lines in Tennessee.

On the day that Sherman entered Savannah, garrison troops under CSA General William Hardee destroyed the city's navy yard by setting it ablaze.

24 DECEMBER 1864

Civil War: Eastern Theater A 60-vessel Union fleet begins shelling Fort Fisher at Wilmington, North Carolina, which is the last major port available to Rebel blockade runners. Infantry under General Ben Butler prepare to assault tomorrow.

25 DECEMBER 1864

Civil War: Eastern Theater Butler's men land north of Fort Fisher and struggle to within 75 yards of the garrison before fire from the 500 Confederate defenders checks the advance. Hearing that Southern reinforcements are approaching, Butler withdraws his men. This blundering attack, one of Butler's several inept performances, will finally give Lincoln the excuse he has long sought to cashier the general, who is a favorite of the Radical Republicans. Ben Butler will officially be relieved on 7 January.

9 JANUARY 1865

Civil War: Western Theater The remains of John B. Hood's Confederate Army of Tennessee arrive in Tupelo, Mississippi, at the end of their long retreat from disaster at Nashville. President Davis plans to transfer troops from Hood's army to reinforce Hardee's men opposing Sherman, who is now turning his sights to the Carolinas.

13 JANUARY 1865

Civil War: Eastern Theater Another Union attempt on Fort Fisher in the port of Wilmington, North Carolina, begins, this time under the command of General A. H. Terry. Today a Federal fleet of 59 ships shell the fort, which now has some 2000 defenders and 47 guns, with 6000 other Confederate troops in the area under Braxton Bragg. Nonetheless, in midafternoon Federals establish a beachhead north of the fort and dig in to resist counterattacks; these preparations will go on through tomorrow.

15 JANUARY 1865

Civil War: Eastern Theater In the morning the Union fleet opens up on Fort Fisher again, now at point-blank range. In midafternoon Terry, with detachments of his 8000 men, launches a two-pronged attack against the fort, one from the ocean side and the other from the northwest, while another detachment remains entrenched to stop Confederate reinforcements (though Bragg never commits his troops). At 10:00 in the evening the fort capitulates. Southern casualties are about 500, with another 1900 captured. Union losses are 1341. The fall of Fort Fisher closes 'the last gateway between the Confederate States and the outside world.'

19 JANUARY 1865

Civil War: The Confederacy After much prodding from Davis, General Robert E. Lee agrees to accept the position of general-in-chief of Confederate armies. Hitherto President Davis has run the war effort, to its considerable detriment. By now the South's military condition is virtually hopeless.

Civil War: Carolinas Campaign General Sherman issues orders that will move his army into South Carolina on a campaign similar to the March to the Sea. Heavy rains will delay the march until early February. Ultimately, Sherman plans to cut a swath clear to Petersburg, where he will join Grant to smash Lee (in the end this will not be necessary). Resisting Sherman are entirely inadequate Confederate forces under General W. J. Hardee.

31 JANUARY 1865

Civil War: Washington By a vote of 119 to 56 the House of Representatives passes the proposed Thirteenth Amendment to the Constitution which prohibits slavery. The amendment will now go to the states, where it must be ratified by three-quarters. Tomorrow, Lincoln's home state of Illinois will become the first to ratify. By 8 December 1865 26 more states will have ratified, and it will become law.

1 FEBRUARY 1865

Civil War: Carolinas Campaign Divided into two wings, Sherman's army begins its march through South Carolina. Confederate General Hardee commands some 12,500 troops to resist Sherman's 60,000. Aside from their ordered work of destruction, groups of Federals will also ravage much private property on their own. Sherman has written of the state that is the object of his campaign, 'I almost tremble at her fate.'

3 FEBRUARY 1865

Civil War: The North President Lincoln and Secretary of State Seward meet with three Confederate commissioners – including Vice-President Stephens – on a ship off Hampton Roads, Virginia, to discuss possibilities for peace. The talks are cordial, but the effort fails when Lincoln insists on Southern recognition of Federal authority and observes that the Thirteenth Amendment is likely to pass (as of today, six states have ratified).

11 FEBRUARY 1865

Civil War: Carolinas Campaign Sherman's army reaches the Augusta and Charleston Railroad, placing itself between Rebel forces around Augusta and Hardee's forces in Charleston, and thus separating Hardee from potential reinforcements. Hardee expects an attack on Charleston, not suspecting Sherman is heading for Columbia.

16 FEBRUARY 1865

Civil War: Carolinas Campaign Sherman's army arrives just south of Columbia, South Carolina. General Beauregard, commanding there, notifies Lee that nothing can be done to save the state capital and pulls out of the city. To the east, General Hardee makes preparations to evacuate his troops from Charleston.

17 FEBRUARY 1865

Civil War: Carolinas Campaign Sherman's Federals occupy Columbia, the capital of South Carolina. During the night fires break out in a number of homes, and the wind-fanned flames reduce two-thirds of the city to ashes. Responsibility for the fire will never be ascertained.

18 FEBRUARY 1865

Civil War: The Confederacy In a letter that plainly shows both the desperation of the Confederacy and abandonment of its very foundation, General Lee endorses the idea of arming freed slaves for the Confederate armies. A few regiments of Rebel black troops will be organized but will never see service.

The ruins of Columbia, SC. An accidental fire had destroyed much of the city when Sherman entered it, and more was deliberately destroyed thereafter.

19 FEBRUARY 1865

Civil War: Carolinas Campaign Having completed his destruction of most of Columbia, South Carolina, Sherman pulls his men out and heads north for Goldsborough.

21 FEBRUARY 1865

Civil War: Carolinas Campaign After much pressure from Union forces on land and sea General Braxton Bragg orders the evacuation of Southern forces from Wilmington, North Carolina, the last major Confederate port. Union troops will occupy the city tomorrow.

2 MARCH 1865

Civil War: Sheridan's Valley Campaign At Waynesborough, in Virginia's Shenandoah Valley, a detachment of Sheridan's army led by General George Armstrong Custer attacks and scatters the last remnant of Jubal Early's Confederates. Although Early and his staff escape to Richmond, more than 1000 Rebels are taken prisoner. This action marks the end of the last campaign in the Shenandoah Valley.

4 MARCH 1865

Civil War: Washington Abraham Lincoln is inaugurated for his second term as president. In the unforgettable conclusion of his address Lincoln looks forward to the future: 'With malice toward none; with charity toward all; with firmness in the right . . . let us strive on to finish the work we are in; to bind up the nation's wounds . . . to do all which may achieve and cherish a just, and a lasting peace, among ourselves, and with all nations.' From a balcony just behind the president these words are heard by actor John Wilkes Booth.

21 MARCH 1865

Civil War: Carolinas Campaign After three days of fighting Sherman maneuvers his old Georgia opponent Joseph Johnston away from Bentonville, North Carolina. Johnston has made a valiant try to check Sherman's advance, one that will also prove to be the last such effort. Having fought his way through the Carolinas, Sherman will march on to Goldsborough.

23 MARCH 1865

Civil War: Carolinas Campaign Sherman's army reaches Goldsborough, North Carolina, after marching the 425 miles from Savannah in 50 days, despite steady enemy resistance. Though history will remember it less, Sherman's Carolinas Campaign has been still more brilliant than the March to the Sea – and nearly as destructive.

25 MARCH 1865

Civil War: Siege of Petersburg In a last desperate attempt to take the offensive and cut the Federal supply line to City Point – which might force Grant to contract his siege lines – Robert E. Lee orders a full-scale assault on Fort Steedman and nearby Federal lines. The offensive makes progress for a time, but Northern troops counterattack and drive the Rebels back into the city. During the action the North suffers close to 1150 casualties, while the South loses nearly 4000, many of them in capture.

27 MARCH 1865

Civil War: Washington At City Point, Virginia, Lincoln begins a two-day conference with Generals Grant and Sherman and Admiral David Porter. During the talks Lincoln apparently proposes that as soon as Southerners lay down their arms, they be granted full citizenship rights; in pursuing this idea later Sherman will find himself the center of controversy.

29 MARCH 1865

Civil War: Appomattox Campaign Beginning the final major campaign of the Civil War, Grant sends Sheridan's cavalry and infantry units to envelop the Confederate right flank to the southwest of Petersburg. If successful, this will cut Lee's last railroad line and threaten his escape route to the west. Lee sends Generals Pickett and Fitz Lee to block Sheridan, and the sides clash inconclusively in the area. Heavy rains will impede Federal efforts over the next days, though skirmishing continues.

1 APRIL 1865

Civil War: Battle of Five Forks As the loss of Five Forks would threaten the Confederate line of retreat, Lee orders General Pickett to hold that position 'at all costs.' But Sheridan's forces overwhelm Pickett during the day, isolating his command from the main Confederate force in Petersburg; over half of Pickett's 10,000 men are captured.

2 APRIL 1865

Civil War: The Confederacy President Davis receives a message from General Lee informing him that after the defeat at Five Forks, Confederate defenses in Petersburg are no longer tenable and the city must be evacuated – which means that the Confederate government in Richmond must evacuate as well. In the night Davis and several members of his cabinet board a special train bound for Danville, Virginia. Behind them Confederate forces blow up factories, warehouses and arsenals, creating fires that gut much of the city.

Civil War: Fall of Petersburg Grant mounts a full-scale assault on the defenses of Petersburg, breaking through at several points. During the night Lee makes a run for it, leading his forces out of the city toward Amelia Court House. Of the 18,579 Confederates engaged, there are 3361 casualties. Among the Southern dead is A. P. Hill, one of Lee's greatest generals.

Civil War: Raid on Selma After breaking through strong defensive positions held by 5000 Rebels under Nathan Bedford Forrest, Union troops occupy Selma, Alabama. The Federals bag some 2700 prisoners and nearly capture Forrest himself.

3 APRIL 1865

Civil War: Fall of Richmond In the morning Union General Godfrey Weitzel formally accepts the surrender of Richmond, Virginia, until yesterday the capital of the Confederacy. To the south Union troops take over Petersburg.

4 APRIL 1865

Civil War: The North Cheered by throngs of Union soldiers and black slaves, President Lincoln walks the streets of Richmond and for a few minutes sits at the desk in the house of Jefferson Davis.

Civil War: The Confederacy From Danville, Virginia, Jefferson Davis issues a proclamation saying the struggle is entering a 'new phase,' and the Confederacy must not give up hope.

Civil War: Appomattox Campaign Lee's forces clash with pursuing Federals at Tabernacle Church and Amelia Court House. Hoped-for supplies are cut off to the latter place, and Lee's already-disintegrating army faces starvation. Meanwhile, Sheridan's cavalry arrives at Jetersville on the Danville Railroad. Lee is now trapped between Meade's troops from the east and Sheridan's from the south and west.

6 APRIL 1865

Civil War: Appomattox Campaign As Lee's army approaches Farmville it accidentally diverges into two segments, each heading in a different direction. Sheridan's men fall on Ewell's wing at Saylor's Creek and capture 8000, one-third of Lee's remaining strength. The remainder of the once-triumphant Army of Northern Virginia limps on to the west.

7 APRIL 1865

Civil War: Appomattox Campaign Grant sends General Lee a message asking for surrender, and Lee inquires as to terms; the two will trade messages for a day. Meanwhile, there is fighting at Farmville, which delays the Confederate retreat, while Sheridan's cavalry circles around the south to place itself directly in the path of the Southern army.

9 APRIL 1865

Civil War: Lee's Surrender The last remnants of the Army of Northern Virginia find Sheridan blocking their path at Appomattox Court House, Virginia. Lee

Fires set by Rebels fleeing Richmond on 2-3 April 1865 got out of hand and gutted much of the city.

sends cavalry around the Federal right flank, and his infantry and artillery break through the center of Sheridan's line. For a few moments there is open country in front of the Rebels. Then, from over a hill, appear Union infantry, line after line of blue, and Sheridan sounds his bugle for the charge. Before anyone moves a horseman appears galloping from behind Southern lines. He carries a white flag. In early afternoon Grant and Lee meet at the McLean House in Appomattox and come to surrender terms. The Confederates will lay down their arms (keeping sidearms and horses) and go home. Lee emerges silently from the house to be saluted by the men he fought so long and so well. He rides back to tell his army, 'Go to your homes and resume your occupations. Obey the laws and become as good citizens as you were soldiers.' Though hostilities will continue here and there through the month, it is only mopping up. With the surrender of the South's greatest general and its greatest remaining army the Civil War is essentially over.

10 APRIL 1865

Civil War: Washington A brass band leads crowds to the White House as news of Lee's surrender sweeps the city. Lincoln asks the band to play 'Dixie,' remarking that it has always been a favorite of his and that it now belongs to the Union.

Civil War: Eastern Theater General Robert E. Lee gives his last address to the Army of Northern Virginia, saying, 'with an increasing admiration of your constancy and devotion to your country, and a grateful remembrance of your kind and generous consideration of myself, I bid you an affectionate farewell.'

11 APRIL 1865

Reconstruction: Washington Addressing crowds around the White House, President Lincoln urges reconstruction in the spirit of generous conciliation and proposes that the 'most intelligent' freed slaves be given the vote. It is Lincoln's last public appearance.

14 APRIL 1865

Civil War: Assassination of Lincoln President Lincoln goes to a play at Ford's Theater. There actor and fanatical Southern patriot John Wilkes Booth mortally wounds the president before making an escape. Lincoln dies next morning, and Andrew Johnson takes the oath of office as president.

18 APRIL 1865

Civil War: Western Theater Confederate General J. E. Johnston surrenders the last major Confederate army to Sherman in North Carolina. Sherman agrees to terms following Lincoln's liberal pronouncements in their last meeting; these terms will unleash a storm of criticism, nearly wrecking Sherman's career, and will be rescinded. Minor Confederate resistance will continue in the South for several weeks as the war winds to a halt.

26 APRIL 1865

Civil War: Assassination of Lincoln Assassin John Wilkes Booth is cornered and shot to death near Bowling Green, Virginia.

10 MAY 1865

Civil War: Aftermath Jefferson Davis is captured in Georgia and jailed. Davis will be pardoned in 1868 when President Johnson grants amnesty to all former Confederates.

29 MAY 1865

Reconstruction President Johnson begins to put his own plans for the South into effect. An essential difference between his plan and the one Congress will subsequently adopt is the lack of protection for blacks. Johnson sees the South as part of a federation, whereas Congress will pursue a more punitive policy. Soon the battle lines are drawn between Johnson's 'restoration' policy and Congress's 'reconstruction.'

10 JULY 1865

Transportation The Union Pacific Company lays its first rail at Omaha, Nebraska, beginning the transcontinental railway that will bring settlers and buffalo hunters pouring West – and in the process inflame and ultimately help dispossess the Indians.

26 JULY 1865

Indian Wars: Approach In revenge for the Chivington massacre of late 1864 a band of over 1000 Cheyenne, Sioux and other tribes attack a small military station at the North Platte River, on the Oregon-California road.

14 OCTOBER 1865

Indian Wars: Approach Having failed to subdue the Indians involved in the July North Platte raid by military means, the government decides to negotiate. Federal commissioners and leaders of the Southern Plains tribes conclude a council and sign treaties at the mouth of the Little Arkansas River in western Kansas. Tribal leaders present include Black Kettle (a peace advocate who escaped the Chivington massacre) for the Southern Cheyenne, Ten Bears for the Comanches and Satanta for the Kiowas. The objective of the government is to create a railroad corridor between the Platte and Arkansas Rivers. By these Little Arkansas Treaties the tribes cede much territory to the US; however, the Senate will refuse to ratify the pacts, and federal officials will not make any serious effort to protect the tribal territorial rights guaranteed by the treaties.

Lincoln, attending the play *Our American Cousin* at Ford's Theater in Washington, is fatally shot by John Wilkes Booth at 10:15 PM, 14 April 1865.

4 DECEMBER 1865

Reconstruction The Thirty-Ninth Congress convenes. By now all Confederate states except Mississippi have formally accepted requirements for readmission to the Union and representation in Congress. But many of the Southern delegates who show up are former high-ranking Confederates, including Vice-President Stephens. The House refuses to seat the Southern delegates and proceeds to discuss punishment for the South. Congress will soon set up a Joint Committee on Reconstruction.

9 APRIL 1866

Reconstruction Congress enacts the Civil Rights Bill in response to the repressive new Black Codes promulgated in the South. The bill grants full citizenship to all born on US soil (Indians excepted) and mandates that all citizens are to have equal protection of civil laws. President Johnson vetoes the bill but is overridden. Johnson and the Congress are now involved in an intense power struggle.

JUNE 1866

Indian Wars: Approach A delegation of Brule and Oglala Sioux, led by Chief Red Cloud, meets with US officials at Fort Laramie. The whites demand that the Northern Plains tribes consent to the improvement and fortification of the Bozeman Trail, which runs from Fort Laramie to mines in Montana Territory and across prime Sioux buffalo-hunting territory. At the same time, Colonel Henry B. Carrington arrives at Fort Laramie with 700 soldiers under orders to establish a chain of forts along the Trail. Declaring, 'White Chief goes with soldiers to steal the road before Indians say Yes or No,' Red Cloud demands that the forts be closed. In the next weeks, Carrington's men will begin erecting forts.

Indian Wars: Approach With the end of the Civil War and new overland trails and railroads west, the consciousness of the nation begins stretching toward the Pacific and to the lands now in the possession of native American peoples. The strongest Plains Indian tribes are the expert horsemen Sioux-Cheyennes in the north, the fierce Apaches in Arizona and New Mexico and the horseback-fighting Comanches, Kiowas, Arapahoes and Southern Cheyennes in Texas and Indian Territory (later Oklahoma). Together, these total between 2 and 300,000 Indians of nearly a hundred tribes spread over a million square miles. In July, Congress authorizes four new cavalry regiments, the 7th, 8th, 9th and 10th; the 9th and 10th cavalry are black outfits with white officers. Commanding the 7th Cavalry is young Colonel George Armstrong Custer. Over the next 25 years Army strength in this vast area of the middle US will number only around 5000 troops, most of them cavalry.

16 JULY 1866

First Sioux War The war begins as Red Cloud's Oglalas drive off horses belonging to Colonel Carrington's troopers. For the rest of the summer Red Cloud's Sioux and their allies engage in hit-and-run warfare along the Bozeman Trail and its new forts.

DECEMBER 1866

Paiute War: Approach General George Crook arrives at Fort Boise to take command of operations against the Paiutes in Oregon and Idaho. Crook is to become the greatest Indian fighter of his time. Tough as a warrior himself, Crook is an avid student of Indian culture; his great innovation will be using Indian allies to track and fight hostiles.

21 DECEMBER 1866

First Sioux War: Fetterman Massacre A Subordinate of Colonel Carrington, Captain William J. Fetterman, is ambushed with 80 soldiers near Fort Phil Kearny on the Bozeman Trail. The whites leave the fort to help a wood-cutting party, which is under attack by Indian decoys. Almost 2000 Sioux, Cheyenne and Arapaho warriors fall on Fetterman and his men and wipe out the detachment. This is the worst defeat the

Sioux Chief Red Cloud led Indian resistance to government plans to improve and fortify the Bozeman Trail. He fought troops and settlers for two years (1866-68) and forced the government to back down.

The signing of the Fort Laramie Treaty ending the First Sioux War, April 1868. Spotted Tail stands. Fourth from the right in back is General Sherman.

US Army has yet suffered in Indian fighting. Leading the Indians is a young war chief of Red Cloud's named Crazy Horse.

MARCH 1867

Indian Wars: Washington In response to the Fetterman Massacre, Congress passes a bill calling for 'establishing peace with certain Indian tribes now at war with the United States.' A Peace Commission is formed and a plan developed to confine all Great Plains Indians to two reservations in areas that it is presumed will never be inhabitable by whites. On the first day of this month Nebraska is admitted as the thirty-seventh state.

11 MARCH 1867

Reconstruction Giving in to Congress, which is now more or less running the country, President Johnson issues directives pursuant to the First Reconstruction Act, passed over his veto. Some 20,000 troops will occupy the South, protecting black voting rights and keeping the peace in five military districts.

APRIL 1867

Indian Wars General William Tecumseh Sherman, now in command of military operations in the West, has devised a plan to drive all the Plains tribes away from a broad belt of territory on both sides of the transcontinental railroad and the Kansas Pacific. General Winfield Scott Hancock leads a large cavalry and infantry force across western Kansas in pursuit of the ultimately fruitless plan. At Pawnee Fork his troops burn a Cheyenne village as the Indians flee. In retaliation, through the summer Indians stop almost all white travel across western Kansas and briefly halt work on the Kansas Pacific Railroad line.

1 AUGUST 1867

First Sioux War: Hayfield Fight Red Cloud's forces continue their war against the US Army forts along the Bozeman Trail. Over 500 Cheyennes, led by Dull Knife and Two Moon, attack about 30 soldiers and civilians in a hayfield near Fort C. F. Smith. The defenders turn back the attack.

2 AUGUST 1867

First Sioux War: Wagon Box Fight Some 800 Sioux warriors under Red Cloud force a group of woodcutters near Fort Phil Kearny back to a line of wagon boxes, which are used as cover. The defenders inflict 200 Indian casualties, against their own five, but do not substantially damage Red Cloud's power.

21 OCTOBER 1867

First Sioux War: Medicine Lodge Treaties The government has decided to come to terms with Red Cloud's confederation: the leaders of the Southern Plains tribes conclude a series of treaties with members of the Peace Commission established by Congress. The signings take place on Medicine Lodge Creek in southwestern Kansas. US representatives include General Alfred H. Terry. Indian leaders include Satank and Satanta for the Kiowas, Ten Bears and Little Horn for the Comanches and Black Kettle and Tall Bear for the Southern Cheyennes and Arapahoes. The Medicine Lodge Treaties assign a 3,000,000-acre reservation in western Indian Territory to the Kiowas and Comanches. A week later the Southern Cheyenne and Arapaho tribes receive an area between the Cimarron and Arkansas Rivers. This is the beginning of the government's two-decade campaign to confine the Great Plains tribes on reservations.

25 NOVEMBER 1867

Washington Congress's power play over the Executive comes to a head when the impeachment of President Johnson is formally proposed by the Judiciary Committee of the House. This proposal will fail, as will a second, but a third proposal will lead to full Congressional impeachment proceedings early next year.

16 MARCH 1868

Washington The threat to Executive power is averted when the final vote on impeachment of President Johnson fails in Congress by one vote.

29 APRIL 1868

First Sioux War: Fort Laramie Treaties The war ends on Red Cloud's terms in a meeting with US commissioners at Fort Laramie. The US agrees to cease improvements on the Bozeman Trail and to abandon its forts; the Powder River region is designated 'unceded Indian territory,' and all of later South Dakota is set aside as the Great Sioux Reservation. The Sioux are also promised the use of their old hunting grounds east of the Bighorn Mountains in southern Montana Territory. It is the end of Red Cloud's fighting days. He will prove the only Indian leader to have won a major campaign against white encroachment, and he will remain a powerful dealer with whites through many years of gradual chipping away at his gains.

Colonel George A. Custer's 7th Cavalry storms into a sleeping Cheyenne village on the Washita River on the morning of 27 November 1868.

1 JULY 1868

Paiute War At Camp Harney, Oregon, the Paiutes sue for peace from General George Crook after his determined campaign of the last two years.

25 JULY 1868

Washington Congress creates the Territory of Wyoming, most of it detached from the huge Dakota Territory. Through the southern reaches of the new territory passes the transcontinental railroad; cities such as Cheyenne and Laramie sprout in its wake.

28 JULY 1868

Washington The Fourteenth Amendment to the Constitution is passed by Congress. It guarantees full citizenship to blacks and all others either born in the US or naturalized – with the notable exception of native Americans, who are denied citizenship.

17 SEPTEMBER 1868

Cheyenne War: Battle of Beecher's Island General Philip H. Sheridan, now commanding the Division of the Missouri, has ordered a campaign to track down and kill any Indians sighted along the path of the Kansas Pacific Railroad. Today Colonel George A. Forsyth and 50 scouts are surrounded by numbers of Sioux and Cheyenne warriors in eastern Colorado Territory. Forsyth's men set up sand-pit breastworks on an island and are besieged for eight days before a relief column arrives. During the battle Roman Nose, a fierce Northern Cheyenne leader, is killed.

27 NOVEMBER 1868

Cheyenne War: Massacre at the Washita River As part of Sheridan's campaign the 7th Cavalry, led by Colonel George A. Custer, strikes a large Cheyenne camp on the upper Washita River in Indian Territory. In heavy snow Custer attacks from four directions at dawn. The troopers catch the sleeping Indians completely by surprise – especially since they are a largely peaceful contingent under the peacemaker Black Kettle. Among the 103 Indians slaughtered – 92 of them women, children and old men – is Black Kettle. Nineteen white troopers are killed and mutilated when they are led down a trail into a trap (Custer has ridden from the field without trying to find the detachment). Custer's men also destroy 800 Indian ponies, burn every lodge and gather a train of women and children as prisoners.

2 FEBRUARY 1869

Technology James Oliver patents the chilled iron plow, made of iron with a cutting edge of tempered steel; it will help make homesteading possible on the hard prairie. Later legendary as 'the plow that broke the plains,' the blade will do its part in breaking the Indians as well.

4 MARCH 1869

Indian Affairs Civil War hero Ulysses S. Grant is inaugurated 18th president of the United States. Grant appoints William T. Sherman as general of the army, and Philip Sheridan is named to command of military forces west of the Mississippi River. Grant also chooses the first native American commissioner of Indian affairs: Ely Parker, an Iroquois who served on Grant's staff in the war. Parker will appoint many Quakers to posts as Indian agents on the theory that Quakers are more honest and peaceful; sometimes this will prove to be the case. Before the inauguration Grant proclaimed, 'All Indians disposed to peace will find the new policy a peace policy'; those Indians otherwise disposed will receive 'a sharp and severe war policy.' For his part, Sheridan has observed, 'The only good Indian is a dead Indian,' and his superior Sherman more or less concurs. In theory, however, the goal of Federal Indian operations is to 'civilize' the natives by turning them into small farmers and decent Christians. Meanwhile, they must exist on the government dole in reservations, thus becoming the prey of corrupt Indian agents.

15 MARCH 1869

Cheyenne War Custer parlays with hostile Cheyennes at Staked Plain in the Texas Panhandle. During the talks he treacherously siezes four chiefs, whom he threatens to hang. The Cheyennes thereupon release two white women hostages and agree to return to the reservation. An elite warrior group called the Dog Soldiers, however, remains on the warpath.

10 APRIL 1869

Indian Affairs Congress creates the Board of Indian Commissioners. Intended to supervise all federal spending for tribes, the Board will become another link in the government's manipulation of the Indians.

10 MAY 1869

Transportation At Promontory Point in Utah Territory the nation's first transcontinental railroad is completed when the Central Pacific and Union Pacific join tracks with a golden spike. Regular train service begins in five days, with average traveling time eight to ten days coast to coast.

11 JULY 1869

Cheyenne War: Battle of Summit Springs Eight companies of the US 5th Cavalry attack the summer encampment of Tall Bull and his Cheyenne Dog Soldiers at Summit Springs, in northeast Colorado Territory. Tall Bull and 52 Indians are killed, finally ending Indian power in Kansas and the surrounding country. 'Buffalo Bill' Cody has played a key role in scouting the hostiles in the area (and later incorporates the battle into his Wild West Show).

15 FEBRUARY 1870

Transportation Construction of a second transcontinental railroad, the Northern Pacific, begins in Minnesota. Financing problems will delay its completion until 1883.

3 MARCH 1871

Indian Affairs Reversing previous policy, Congress passes the Indian Appropriation Act. It declares that henceforth no Indian tribe or nation will be treated or recognized as a sovereign power with which the government must contract by treaty. Instead, Indian tribes shall be subject to all national laws and to administrative decrees, particularly those of the Commissioner of Indian Affairs. In short, having previously been treated as nations with whom treaties must be negotiated, Indian tribes and nations are now essentially wards of the State and utterly in its power. All treaties negotiated before 1871 and based on tribal sovereignty, however, are to remain in force.

30 APRIL 1871

Apache War: Massacre at Camp Grant An Apache War begins in New Mexico and Arizona Territories when a group of whites, Mexicans and rival Indians burst into a camp of sleeping Apaches and butcher some 100 men, women and children. This outrage will ignite the area, and Apache depredations will continue intermittently over the next 15 years. General George Crook is called in to head the Department of Arizona and oversee operations against the hostile Apaches.

MAY 1871

Indian Wars At Salt Creek Prairie in Texas, Kiowas under Chief Satanta ambush a wagon train and massacre the settlers. Later Satanta will boast of his raid to General Sherman at Fort Sill, where the Indians are on the dole. After a tumultuous conference, with guns and arrows aimed, Satanta and two other chiefs are arrested; but Satanta will be released and return to the warpath some years later.

SUMMER 1871

Red River Wars General Ranald S. Mackenzie, one of the Cavalry's most active Indian fighters, begins a series of whirlwind campaigns against the Indians in and around Texas. His major opponent is half-breed Comanche chief Quanah Parker, who will finally surrender in 1875.

1 MARCH 1872

Washington Pressed by growing agitation for conservation of the country's natural resources, Congress creates Yellowstone National Park, the country's first such park, 2,142,720 acres in extent.

AUTUMN 1872

Apache War After two weeks of negotiations with General O. O. Howard, Chiricahua Apache chief Cochise gets his way: he and his people are granted a reservation at Apache Pass in Arizona. Cochise will end his days peacefully, after years of bloody raiding, but many Chiricahuas will return to the warpath.

5 NOVEMBER 1872

National Despite the scandals ringing his administration, Grant wins reelection to the presidency by a landslide over former newspaperman Horace Greeley.

29 NOVEMBER 1872

Modoc War For several months Modoc Indians have been living away from their assigned Klamath Reservation in Oregon. Today Captain James Jackson and 38 soldiers of the 1st Cavalry attempt to move the Modocs and their leader, called Captain Jack, back to the reservation. Shooting breaks out, and the Modocs will take refuge in virtually impregnable lava beds south of Tule Lake in northern California. In the course of their flight south the Modocs kill at least a dozen settlers.

16 JANUARY 1873

Modoc War: Battle of the Stronghold Colonel Frank Wheaten tries to dislodge the Modocs from the Indians' stronghold in the lava beds. The Modocs keep the soldiers pinned down with accurate rifle fire, then retreat in darkness to a new stronghold. The government will next try negotiations.

Satanta, or White Bear, here wearing an officer's coat and a peace medal, was the warlike leader of the Kiowas in the Red River Wars.

27 MARCH 1873

Apache War: Battle of Turret Peak General George Crook began his campaign against the Apaches in November 1872 using Indian scouts to find hostiles, who were then doggedly harried in a series of sorties. Today Crook climaxes the first phase of his efforts by whipping Apache holdouts at Turret Peak. In the next weeks some 6000 Apaches will enroll on the local reservations.

11 APRIL 1873

Modoc War A peace council with the Modoc Indians, who have been holed up unassailably in lava beds in northern California, turns into a massacre. Modoc leader Captain Jack fatally shoots General E. R. S. Canby, and another Indian kills Reverend Eleazer Thomas. This episode begins a month-long chase of 50 Modocs by almost 1000 soldiers. It ends when Captain Jack and his dwindling band surrender on 1 June. In October, Captain Jack and three other war leaders will be hanged.

27 JUNE 1874

Red River Wars: Battle of Adobe Walls In the Texas Panhandle 700 Kiowa, Comanche, Cheyenne and Arapaho warriors under Comanche Chief Quanah Parker attack a group of 28 buffalo hunters. With the aid of rapid-fire Sharps rifles the hunters hold the Indians at bay during a full day of fighting. (One of the defenders is 'Bat' Masterson, later a famous sheriff in Dodge City.) The Indians will then turn on settlers all over the area in a campaign of murder, torture and abduction.

20 JULY 1874

Red River Wars Responding to the depredations in and around Texas, Washington authorizes General Sheridan to attack hostiles wherever they may be found. Against stiffening Army resistance the hostiles break into small bands around the Texas Panhandle, the bands led by chiefs including the Cheyenne Medicine Arrows and the Kiowa Satanta.

28 SEPTEMBER 1874

Red River Wars: Battle of Palo Duro Canyon General Mackenzie strikes a village of Kiowas, Comanches and Cheyennes in Palo Duro Canyon. Though most of the braves escape, Mackenzie kills their herd of 1500 ponies, leaving the Indians virtually powerless. Over the next months hundreds of Kiowas and Comanches surrender at Fort Sill, Texas, ending the Red River Wars and Indian/white hostilities on the north Texas plains. To help prevent further violence 72 warrior chiefs are sent to a military prison in St. Augustine, Florida.

AUGUST 1875

Second Sioux War: Approach A military expedition led by Colonel George A. Custer emerges from the Black Hills of western Dakota Territory with extravagant reports of gold in the area. The land is part of the

Colonel George A. Custer (l) during the Civil War, when he held the temporary rank of Major General.

Great Sioux Reservation, which was given to the Indians on the assumption that it was useless to anybody else. But these reports will bring a flood of white miners into the area, and they will quickly come into conflict with the Sioux.

OCTOBER 1875

Second Sioux War: Approach The government attempts to buy some of the Indian lands north of the Platte, but the Sioux refuse to sell. An old story is about to be reenacted.

9 NOVEMBER 1875

Second Sioux War: Approach Indian Inspector E. C. Watkins identifies hundreds of Hunkpapa Sioux under Sitting Bull, and Oglala Sioux under Crazy Horse, as hostiles. On his recommendation it is ordered that the Indians remove to a more restricted reservation before the end of January 1876 or face Federal action. The real reason is that whites want the gold in the Black Hills.

1 FEBRUARY 1876

Second Sioux War: Approach Secretary of the Interior Z. Chandler, noting that the Sioux under Sitting Bull have refused to return to their reservation or report to agency posts, turns the situation over to the War Department. On 10 February, General Alfred H. Terry, commander of the Department of Dakota, receives orders for military action against the Sioux and Cheyenne tribes.

17 MARCH 1876

Second Sioux War: Battle of Powder River The war begins when a subordinate of General George Crook, Colonel Joseph J. Reynolds, attacks a village of Oglalas and Cheyennes in the Powder River Valley. The Indians mount a counterattack that sends Reynolds' men running. Crook will later accuse Reynolds of mismanaging the attack and thus emboldening the Indians. Sitting Bull has put together a powerful alliance of Sioux and Cheyennes.

17 MAY 1876

Second Sioux War General Terry leaves Fort Abraham Lincoln in Dakota Territory with a column that includes Colonel George Custer and the 7th Cavalry. As part of a three-pronged operation planned by General Sheridan, Terry will move west until he reaches the Yellowstone River, then move upstream and locate the Indians. Colonel John Gibbon is moving east from Fort Ellis, Montana Territory, and General George Crook is moving northward from Fort Fetterman in Wyoming Territory. The officers have been told that they can expect to encounter no more than 500 hostiles in any one group.

9 JUNE 1876

Second Sioux War Sioux Chief Crazy Horse attacks General Crook's column on the Tongue River but is easily repulsed. Crook suspects this is an attack for show, to be followed by a more serious one.

17 JUNE 1876

Second Sioux War: Battle of the Rosebud River Braves led by Crazy Horse mount a furious assault on Crook's camp on the Rosebud, trying to force the troopers either to break into vulnerable units or to back into a box canyon where they will be trapped. Crook is nearly swamped before he tries the ruse of using his horses as bait. When the Indians head for the horses, Crook picks them off with men stationed on high ground. Crazy Horse is driven back, but Crook's men are shaken and will contribute nothing to the coming campaign.

21 JUNE 1876

Second Sioux War Aboard a steamer on the Yellowstone River Gibbon, Terry and Custer meet to plan strategy. They are unaware of Crook's near-disaster at the Rosebud or of the true strength of the Sioux-

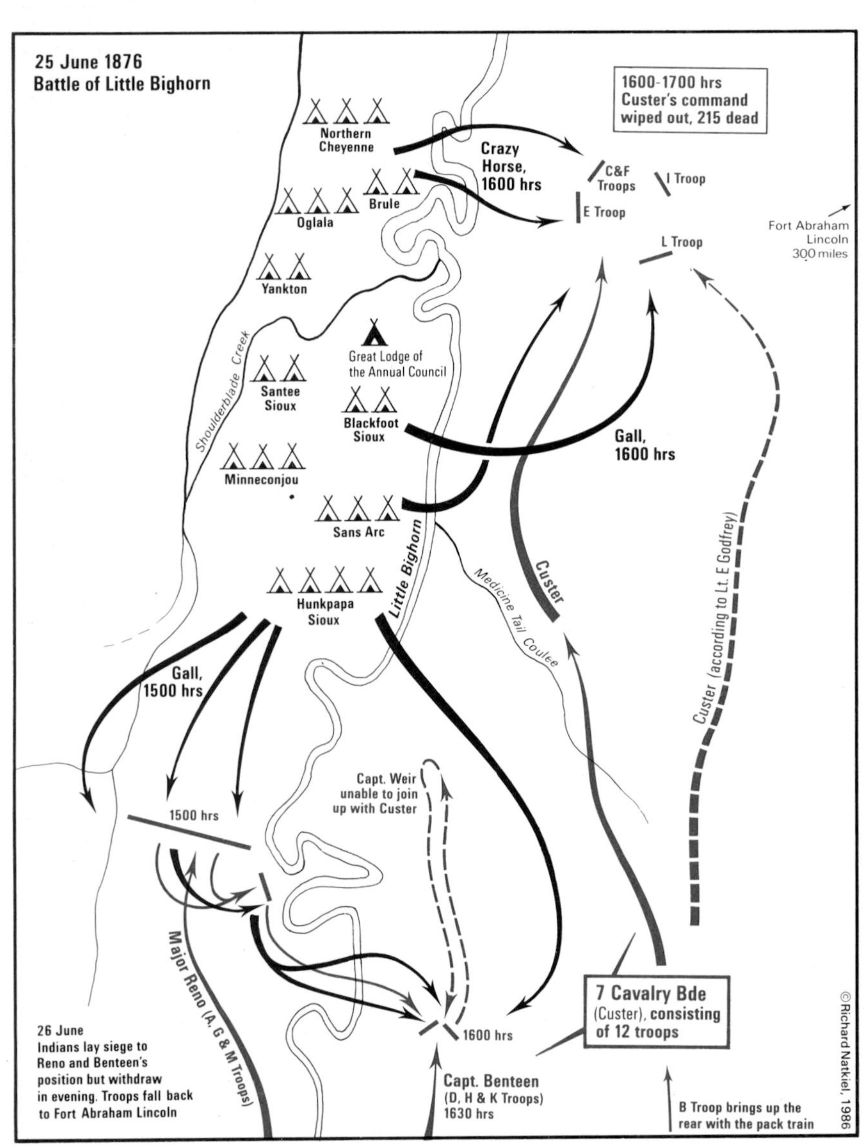

A map reconstructing the movements of Custer and the Indians at the Battle of the Little Bighorn.

Sitting Bull, the great Hunkpapa medicine man who unified the Sioux against the Army in 1876.

Cheyenne alliance. It is decided that Custer and his 7th Cavalry will ride south along Rosebud Creek to the headwaters of the Little Bighorn River and there reverse direction and ride north. Gibbon and Terry are to follow the Yellowstone to the Bighorn River, then ascend to the Little Bighorn. Terry observes, 'Now Custer, don't be greedy, but wait for us.' 'No,' replies Custer ambiguously, 'I will not.'

25 JUNE 1876

Second Sioux War: Battle of the Little Bighorn Colonel George Custer and 600 men of his 7th Cavalry arrive 12 miles southeast of Sitting Bull's village on the Little Bighorn River. The village is far larger than Custer realizes; it includes some 3000 warriors under war chiefs Crazy Horse, Gall and Lame White Man. To attack the village, Custer splits his regiment. Captain Frederick Benteen takes three troops to search in the west. Major Marcus Reno takes another three troops across the Little Bighorn and moves northwest to attack. Custer, with five troops, moves along the bluffs east of the river with the intention of striking the flank side of the village. One company of troopers is detailed to the pack train, further reducing Custer's detachment. On the west side of the Little Bighorn is the largest gathering of Indians ever seen in North America. In six circles are 10 to 15,000 Cheyenne, Sans Arcs, Minneconjou Sioux, Oglala Sioux, Blackfeet and Hunkpapa Sioux in an encampment about three miles long. Reno and his men attempt to strike the south end of the village, but braves emerge to drive the troopers across the river with heavy losses; the remainder of Reno's command scramble up to the heights to establish a defense. Custer, having ridden four miles upstream, and assuming Reno is engaged and Benteen approaching, suddenly finds himself under attack from the south and west by Indians streaming out of the village. No white man survives to tell the tale, but later studies will conclude that Custer's men are driven up on to a low ridge where there is no cover. There, in five clumps, the 213 troopers make their stand as the Indians close in, largely on foot and armed with rifles. Before long all the whites' horses have been killed or stampeded. The end comes very fast: as the men are picked off one by one, Custer's north flank crumples. Crazy Horse himself leads a charge on the clump of men around Custer, who, already mortally wounded, has barricaded himself behind dead horses under his regimental pennant. As the Indians creep forward a dying trooper suddenly rises on one arm, holding the Indians at bay with a revolver; a Sioux tears the gun away and shoots the trooper in the head. Then the only sound is the victory cries of the Indians. It has taken less than an hour for George Custer to preside over one of the worst defeats in American history. Meanwhile, Captain Benteen and his three troops, realizing it is futile to try to join Custer, join Reno on the bluffs near the river to fight off waves of Indian assaults that go on all through the next day. Finally the Indians leave; behind a curtain of smoke from a prairie fire, the surviving troopers see the gigantic village pulling away toward the Bighorn Mountains.

27 JUNE 1876

Second Sioux War: Battle of the Little Bighorn The columns under General Terry and Colonel Gibbon discover the remains of Custer's men, most of the bodies mutilated beyond recognition. Custer has been stripped of his buckskins and has two bullet wounds, but is otherwise untouched. The column also picks up Reno and Benteen. Those killed in the Battle of the Little Bighorn, including Custer and his 212 men, total some 265; total casualties with wounded are some 600, over half the 7th Cavalry. In the next weeks news of the disaster will inflame the country against the Indians, but Benteen's later assessment is more astute: 'There were a great deal too many Indians who were powerful good shots on the other side. We were at their hearths and homes – and they were fighting for all the good God gives anyone to fight for.'

25 NOVEMBER 1876

Second Sioux War: Defeat of Dull Knife Following Custer's defeat the Army steps up its campaign to drive all Indians from the Bighorn and Powder River region. Today Colonel Ranald Mackenzie attacks the Cheyenne village of Dull Knife in the Bighorn Mountains. Over 200 lodges and hundreds of Indian ponies are destroyed and over a thousand Cheyennes flee to the wilderness. Numerous items belonging to dead members of the 7th Cavalry are discovered in the village.

8 JANUARY 1877

Second Sioux War: Battle of Wolf Mountain In bitter cold and driving snow Colonel Nelson A. Miles attacks 500 Sioux and Cheyenne warriors under Crazy Horse. The Indians are driven away by infantry charges and artillery. Sioux resistance is crumbling, and in the next months bands will begin to give up. Sitting Bull and the Hunkpapas flee to Canada during January.

5 MARCH 1877

National Rutherford B. Hayes is inaugurated 19th president of the United States.

6 MAY 1877

Second Sioux War Having received peace offers from General Crook via Chief Spotted Tail, Crazy Horse appears at the head of 1000 Indians at the Red Cloud Agency. Throwing three rifles to the ground, the great fighter gives up the warpath.

17 JUNE 1877

Nez Percé War: Battle of White Bird Canyon The Nez Percé, until recently a peaceful tribe who boasted that they had never killed a white man, have in recent years been increasingly victimized by white settlers' land grabs and depredations. Now corrupt Indian agents have ordered the tribe to leave their lands in Wallowa Valley, Oregon, and remove to a reservation. The Nez Percé chiefs, led by Joseph and his brother Ollokot, go on the warpath during the tribe's march. Today at White Bird Canyon, The Nez Percé cut to pieces a detachment of cavalry from Fort Lapwai and then continue on to the north.

11 JULY 1877

Nez Percé War: Battle of Clearwater Three hundred Nez Percé fight off 600 of General O. O. Howard's regular soldiers. The Indians then turn east, heading for the Canadian border and safety as the Army begins to assemble forces to give chase.

9 AUGUST 1877

Nez Percé War: Battle of Big Hole River Colonel John Gibbon's column of 200 men catches up with the Nez Percé at the Big Hole River and attacks, driving the tribe from their teepees and killing some 90. However, under the leadership of Ollokot, the Nez Percé counterattack, recapture their village and pin down the whites for two days. Gibbon withdraws with 71 casualties as the Indians continue east across Yellowstone National Park – in the process frightening vacationers, among whom is General Sherman. On 13 September the Indians will drive away pursuing cavalry at Canyon Creek in Montana.

2 SEPTEMBER 1877

Apache War After months of suffering from disease and hunger at the San Carlos Reservation around 300 Chiricahua Apaches under Victorio and Geronimo break from the reservation. They will be rounded up in New Mexico in a month, and a year later ordered back to the reservation.

5 SEPTEMBER 1877

Second Sioux War Crazy Horse, brilliant chief of the Oglala Sioux, is bayoneted by a soldier at Fort Robinson in Nebraska; reportedly he has pulled a knife upon learning that he is to be imprisoned. Crazy Horse dies, in around his 35th year, a few hours later. His death marks the end of the Second Sioux War.

"Custer's Last Stand" became a favorite subject of popular art, but since there were no eyewitnesses, most depictions were wildly imaginative.

30 SEPTEMBER 1877

Nez Percé War: Battle of Snake Creek Less than 40 miles from the sanctuary of Canada, Chief Joseph's remaining 100 warriors are attacked by a column of 400 veteran cavalrymen under Colonel Miles. The Indians hold out for four days, but on 5 October, reduced to less than 50 unwounded warriors, Chief Joseph pronounces his immortal words of surrender, which seem to encompass the whole tragedy of the native American peoples: 'Tell General Howard that I know his heart . . . I am tired of fighting. Our chiefs are killed. It is cold, and we have no blankets. The little children are freezing to death. My people – some of them – have run away to the hills, and we have no blankets, no food . . . I want to have time to look for my children and to see how many of them I can find; maybe I shall find them among the dead. Hear me, my chiefs: my heart is sick and sad. From where the sun now stands, I will fight no more forever.' By the time they surrender the Nez Percé have, in 11 weeks, fought 13 engagements with ten Army units and traveled 1600 miles. Despite years of joint effort by Chief Joseph and General Howard, the Nez Percé will never be allowed to return to their homeland. Joseph, much honored by his erstwhile enemies, will survive until 1904, finally dying, reportedly of a broken heart.

8 JUNE 1878

Bannock-Paiute War After the usual episodes of crowding by settlers, 200 Bannock warriors under Buffalo Horn have been raiding in southern Idaho. Today Buffalo Horn is killed in a skirmish with a group of white volunteers. His men ride to Oregon to join with Paiutes under Chief Egan.

23 JUNE 1878

Bannock-Paiute War Captain Reuben F. Bernard, General Howard's cavalry commander, scatters Chief Egan's camp at Silver Creek. Pursued by the troopers, the Indians cross the Strawberry Mountains, pillaging settlements as they go.

8 JULY 1878

Bannock-Paiute War Howard dislodges the Bannock-Paiute hostiles from cliffs at Birch Creek and sends them running. On 12 July they show up at the Umatilla Agency, and a six-hour skirmish with Howard ensues before the hostiles take to the mountains again. However, a band of Umatilla Indians follows and kills Chief Egan. The Utes surrender on 12 August, and in the next weeks Howard hunts down the remaining hostile Bannocks.

SUMMER 1879

Ute War: Approach The last Indians with a reservation in Colorado, the Utes, come under increasing pressure from whites coveting their 12,000,000 acres of land. During this period the Utes are blamed for any regional malady, including a series of forest fires.

General George Crook, whom the Apaches called "Gray Wolf," one of the most unorthodox and successful of the Army's Indian-fighting officers.

4 SEPTEMBER 1879

Apache War Enraged by Army efforts to force his people back to the miserable San Carlos Reservation, Apache chief Victorio and 60 braves attack a cavalry unit near Ojo Caliente, kill eight black soldiers and take off on a bloody rampage around New Mexico and Arizona. Other hostile Apaches will join, and thousands of Army troops will vainly try to stop Victorio over the next year.

29 SEPTEMBER-5 OCTOBER 1879

Ute War: Battle of Milk Creek At Milk Creek in northwestern Colorado Territory fighting breaks out betwen the Ute Indians and 250 soldiers under Major. Thomas Thornburgh. Twelve soldiers, including Thornburgh, are killed and 43 wounded during the week-long battle. In what they believe is a last stand to save their reservation 37 Utes are killed before pulling away on 5 October. Meanwhile, at the White River Agency, the Ute Indian agent, Nathaniel Meeker, is killed along with other whites. Meeker's wife and daughter and several other women are abducted (they will be released on 21 October, and Mrs. Meeker will later write a book describing her ordeal). A call is issued for volunteers and militia to 'wipe out the red devils.' The Utes will remain at large for nearly a year, but negotiations pursued by sympathetic Secretary of the Interior Carl Schurz will finally end hostilities – and lose the Utes their land.

12 FEBRUARY 1880

Indian Affairs President Hayes issues a warning to illegal settlers, ranchers, and trespassers who have been stealing lands in Indian Territory. The warning will have little effect.

Geronimo (r) with three of his Chiricahua Apache warriors. General Crook once described the Apaches as the "tigers of the human race."

AUGUST 1880

Ute War Bowing to pressure from Coloradans and to agreements with the government, the Utes give up their reservation and move to new reservations in Utah and Colorado.

15-16 OCTOBER 1880

Apache War: Battle of Tres Castillos A band of Mexican militiamen under Colonel Joaquin Terrazas runs Victorio and his Apaches to ground in the Tres Castillos mountains of Mexico. In the first day of fighting the Mexicans pin the Apaches down in the hills. After a breakout attempt by the Indians is turned back during the night the Mexicans hear the Apaches singing their death songs. Next day the Indians fight to the last – the Mexicans finally find 62 men and 16 women dead and take 68 prisoners. Among the dead is Victorio.

2 NOVEMBER 1880

National After an acrimonious campaign, Republican James A. Garfield wins the presidency over Civil War general Winfield Scott Hancock. The new vice-president is Chester A. Arthur.

2 JULY 1881

National While waiting for a train President Garfield is shot in the back by an unbalanced office-seeker (who says he hopes Arthur, in becoming president, will return to the unbounded spoils system). Garfield will linger through the summer before dying on 19 September; Arthur will be inaugurated the next day.

19 JULY 1881

The West Sitting Bull and 186 destitute Sioux return from four-year exile in Canada and give themselves up at Fort Buford, Dakota Territory. For some years, Sitting Bull will play the role of legendary Indian among whites, including a stint in Buffalo Bill's Wild West Show. But the old chief never relinquishes his hatred of what whites have done to his people, and he will finally become another victim of that process.

A studio portrait of the Apache leader Geronimo. In fact, his name was Goyathlay, and "Geronimo" was a nickname bestowed on him by the Mexicans.

30 SEPTEMBER 1881

Apache War Simmering unrest between soldiers and Indians around Fort Apache leads to a breakout from the San Carlos Reservation: 74 Apaches including Geronimo, Chato and Nachez head for Mexico, where they will join with other hostiles who have been raiding from bases in the Sierra Madre. As usual, General George Crook will be detailed to chase the renegades. Also as usual, his force will include many Indians, in this case five companies of White Mountain Apaches – 'the wildest I could get,' says Crook.

1 MAY 1883

Apache War After a raid into Arizona and New Mexico by Apaches based in Mexico, General Crook takes a detachment – 193 Apache scouts plus cavalry and pack mules – across the border into the Sierra Madre to chase down the renegades. On 15 May Crook's men find and attack the camp of Chief Chato. Demoralized to find themselves fighting their own people, the hostiles agree to give up and go back to the San Carlos Reservation. Chief Geronimo will show up there, belatedly, in March 1884, and for a while will farm peacefully.

4 JULY 1883

The West The first of Buffalo Bill Cody's Wild West shows is presented as part of a holiday celebration in North Platte, Nebraska. Next summer Cody will take the show on the road; over the years it will do much to create the popular myth of the West.

4 NOVEMBER 1884

National Democrat Grover Cleveland is elected president over James G. Blaine after another heavy mudslinging campaign in the style of the times. Cleveland is a low-tariff man and thus somewhat more sympathetic to farmers and labor than most recent presidents.

17 MAY 1885

Apache War Chafing under the restrictions imposed on them in the San Carlos Reservation, over a hundred Apaches, male and female, including Geronimo and Nachez, again bolt the reservation and head for Mexico as a wave of panic seizes whites. General Philip Sheridan, commanding the area, will soon show up to criticize Crook's past handling of Apache campaigns, especially the use of Indian scouts. Nonetheless, in December Crook will head into Mexico after the hostiles with his accustomed mixture of Apache scouts and white cavalrymen.

2 SEPTEMBER 1885

Labor Strife Following a decade of smoldering resentment against Chinese mine workers, white laborers at Rock Spring in Wyoming territory go on a rampage, killing 28 Chinese and wounding 15 others. Several hundred more Chinese are chased from the town. Federal soldiers will be sent to return and protect the Chinese, and troops will remain in the area for the next 13 years. Cheap Chinese labor, meanwhile, is becoming scarce following an 1882 Congressional law suspending Chinese immigration.

10 JANUARY 1886

Apache War Captain Emmett Crawford, a subordinate of Crook, locates Geronimo's hideout deep in the Mexican mountains. Geronimo immediately makes peace overtures, but during the talks a detachment of Mexican soldiers shows up. These soldiers happen to be Tarahumari Indians and old foes of the Apaches. In a confused melee the Tarahumaris fire on Crawford's Apache scouts, in the process killing Crawford. A shootout follows between American and Mexican forces, while Geronimo and his men watch, doubtless with some amusement. After further deaths on both sides things calm down, and Geronimo agrees to return to the reservation. But the unreliable old chief will dally in returning as public outcry over Crook's policies mounts.

25 MARCH 1886

Apache War In the Mountains of Mexico, General Crook and Geronimo hold a tense conference about the Chiricahua chief's failure to honor his pledge to return to the reservation. Saying that if the Indians refuse, 'I'll keep after you and kill the last one, if it takes fifty years,' Crook extracts an agreement that the hostiles will give up and be allowed to return to Arizona after a two-year detention. Geronimo duly returns, but after a drinking bout once again bolts and rides the range. Crook tells his commander, Sheridan, that Geronimo will return when he sobers up, and in any case Crook must run his business as he wishes or be relieved. On 12 April Sheridan relieves Crook and replaces him with General Nelson A. Miles, who can be expected to follow usual Army procedures. It is the end of George Crook's fighting days; no one before or after will duplicate his success in Indian-fighting. Paradoxically, Crook has at times been the best white friend the Indians had.

4 SEPTEMBER 1886

Apache War The long intermittent war between Apaches and whites comes to an end when Geronimo and his group of renegades give themselves up to General Miles at Skeleton Canyon in Arizona Territory. The old chief and other leaders will be exiled for eight years to Fort Marion, Florida, but Geronimo will survive to ride in a carriage next to Comanche chief Quanah Parker at the inaugural parade of Theodore Roosevelt.

8 FEBRUARY 1887

Indian Affairs Today President Cleveland signs the Dawes Severalty Act, ending the reservation system. It mandates dissolution of tribes as legal entities and authorizes the president to divide the lands of any tribe, giving each Indian head of a family 160 acres, with lesser amounts to single individuals. Instead of being legally transferred directly to the Indians, the plots are to be held in trust by the government for 25 years. After this period full ownership will be conferred on the Indians and US citizenship granted. Reservation lands remaining after the distribution of the allotments are to be declared surplus and will thenceforth be open for settlement by white homesteaders. As a result of this act Indian tribes in the West will eventually lose some 86 million acres of land, 62 percent of their prior possessions.

6 NOVEMBER 1888

National In the presidential election Grover Cleveland receives the larger popular vote, but Republican Benjamin Harrison – a pro-business, high-tariff man – wins the electoral vote and the election.

2 MARCH 1889

Indian Affairs After providing for final Indian claims Congress authorizes transfer of the Unassigned Lands in Indian Territory to the public domain.

NOVEMBER 1890

Messiah War Among Plains Indians there has grown up a mystical movement called the Ghost Dance. A Paiute prophet named Wovoka, blending elements of Christianity and traditional Indian religions, has preached a mystical doctrine of rebirth. Adherents have come to believe that by dancing in magical shirts they can become invulnerable to bullets, make the whites go away and resurrect the buffalo. By 1890 the movement is widespread, and the Oglala Sioux and other tribes, all of them near starvation on the government dole, are becoming emboldened by the new beliefs. Old Chief Sitting Bull, while probably not a believer, has begun to see the Ghost Dance movement as offering some foundation for renewed Indian resistance. As agitation grows on the Pine Ridge and Standing Rock reservations in South Dakota an order goes out to arrest Sitting Bull. When his friend 'Buffalo Bill' Cody shows up to speak for the chief, soldiers and agents are detailed to keep Cody distracted.

Burying the dead at Wounded Knee on 1 January 1891. The Battle (or, rather, massacre) of Wounded Knee was the last major encounter of the Indian Wars.

15 DECEMBER 1890

Messiah War A group of native Indian reservation police surround Sitting Bull's cabin and prepare to arrest him. A crowd of Indian supporters resists, and shots are fired. In an instant Sitting Bull is shot by two Indian policemen, men of his own tribe, and falls dead. On 23 December Chief Big Foot and 350 Minneconjou Sioux, most of them women and children, head for Pine Ridge agency. Big Foot, once but no longer a Ghost Dancer, intends to help pacify the unrest the movement is causing in the agency. The 7th Cavalry – Custer's old outfit, who have been awaiting a chance for revenge on the Sioux since the Last Stand – are dispatched to head off Big Foot.

29 DECEMBER 1890

Messiah War: Massacre at Wounded Knee The previous day the 7th Cavalry caught up with Big Foot's band at Wounded Knee, about 30 miles from Pine Ridge Agency in South Dakota. Today the soldiers establish a ring – including four machine gunners – around the Sioux and begin to disarm the terrified Indians. As that is being done a shot is accidentally set off, and some warriors grab their rifles. It is all the excuse the 7th cavalry needs. They empty their guns into the largely unarmed Indians; within a few moments Big Foot and over 200 others, mostly women and children, are mown down. Losses for the cavalry are 25 dead and 39 wounded.

30 DECEMBER 1890

Messiah War Outraged by the slaughter at Wounded Knee, a group of Sioux ambush the 7th Cavalry near Pine Ridge Agency. The black 9th Cavalry comes to the rescue of the 7th, and hostilities quickly die down – the Indians are too hungry and weak to fight for long.

14 JANUARY 1891

Messiah War General Nelson A. Miles announces that the Sioux are returning to their reservation; all will be back at Pine Ridge Agency on 19 January. The Ghost Dance movement will survive for a time, but its power as the impetus of the last substantial Indian uprising in history is finished. The Great Indian Wars are over; the story of the Indians from now on will be one of victimization, not fighting.

8 NOVEMBER 1892

National Grover Cleveland becomes the first man to serve two separate terms as president when he beats Benjamin Harrison by a small margin of popular votes.

3 NOVEMBER 1896

National William McKinley, a conservative, high-tariff politician, is elected president over the Populist-supported Democrat William Jennings Bryan.

4 MARCH 1897

National William McKinley is inaugurated as president of the United States. A revolution continues in Cuba aimed at seeking independence from Spain. The American public is becoming increasingly restive over continuing Spanish oppression on the island. McKinley, however, wishes to focus on domestic business conditions and economic recovery from the continuing depression of 1893 and therefore will try to avoid conflict with Spain over Cuba.

25 JANUARY 1898

Cuba The United States battleship *Maine* arrives in Havana harbor. President McKinley is concerned about the safety of American citizens following renewed violence in the city of Havana and has sent the *Maine* there as a symbol of that concern.

15 FEBRUARY 1898

Cuba Following a tremendous explosion the battleship *Maine* sinks in Havana harbor. Of the 350 officers and men aboard 252 are dead or missing. Fourteen more will later die from their injuries. Although no one is certain who or what caused the explosion, the American public is quick to place full blame on Spain. 'Remember the *Maine*' becomes a national rallying cry for those desiring war with Spain.

25 FEBRUARY 1898

Approach to War Assistant Secretary of the Navy Theodore Roosevelt orders the United States Asiatic Squadron, under the command of Commodore George Dewey, to proceed from Japan to Hong Kong. In the absence of Navy Secretary John Long, Roosevelt orders Dewey to coal his ships and, in the event of war with Spain, to commence offensive naval operations against the Spanish-held Philippine Islands and the Spanish naval squadron based at Manila Bay.

9 MARCH 1898

Approach to War As a signal of national resolve Congress unanimously passes a $50 million supplemental defense appropriation.

29 MARCH 1898

Approach to War The United States insists that Spanish forces in Cuba end their brutal policy of massive population relocation as part of an attempt to pacify the island and that Spain take immediate steps to bring about independence for Cuba. In response Spain equivocates and stalls for time.

11 APRIL 1898

Approach to War Under mounting public and congressional pressure President McKinley asks Congress to authorize armed intervention in Cuba. McKinley cites the inability of Spain to end the revolutionary insurrection.

19 APRIL 1898

Approach to War Congress passes a joint resolution calling for armed intervention in Cuba by the United States if Spain refuses to withdraw from Cuba immediately and grant that island full independence. President McKinley will sign the resolution the next day, 20 April.

21 APRIL 1898

Approach to War The United States North Atlantic Squadron, under the command of Rear Admiral William Sampson, is ordered to steam from Key West, Florida, and begin a naval blockade of the north coast of Cuba.

863,956 WORLDS CIRCULATED YESTERDAY

The World.

"Circulation Books Open to All."

VOL. XXXVIII. NO. 13,330. NEW YORK, THURSDAY, FEBRUARY 17, 1898.

MAINE EXPLOSION CAUSED BY BOMB OR TORPEDO?

Capt. Sigsbee and Consul-General Lee Are in Doubt---The World Has Sent a Special Tug, With Submarine Divers, to Havana to Find Out---Lee Asks for an Immediate Court of Inquiry---260 Men Dead.

IN A SUPPRESSED DESPATCH TO THE STATE DEPARTMENT, THE CAPTAIN SAYS THE ACCIDENT WAS MADE POSSIBLE BY AN ENEMY.

Dr. E. C. Pendleton, Just Arrived from Havana, Says He Overheard Talk There of a Plot to Blow Up the Ship--Capt. Zalinski, the Dynamite Expert, and Other Experts Report to The World that the Wreck Was Not Accidental---Washington Officials Ready for Vigorous Action if Spanish Responsibility Can Be Shown---Divers to Be Sent Down to Make Careful Examinations.

DRAWN FROM A DESCRIPTION BY EYE-WITNESSES ON THE STEAMER CITY OF WASHINGTON WHO SAW THE EXPLOSION. FOLLOWED BY "A VOLCANO OF FIRE AND SHOWERS OF BOATS, BODIES, IRON AND GUNS" CABLED TO THE WORLD BY ITS OWN CORRESPONDENT IN HAVANA, SYLVESTER SCOVEL.

THE WHOLE STORY OF THE DISASTER TOLD IN A FEW WORDS.

Screaming, provocative and misleading headlines of Joseph Pulitzer's 'yellow press' daily *The World* report the sinking of the *Maine* in February 1898.

23 APRIL 1898

Spanish-American War Spain declares war on the United States.

25 APRIL 1898

Spanish-American War The United States declares war on Spain. Commodore Dewey receives orders to attack the Spanish squadron located at Manila Bay, Philippines. Dewey departs 27 April.

27 APRIL 1898

Spanish-American War: Naval Admiral Sampson's North Atlantic Squadron begins to implement a naval blockade of Cuba, primarily along the north coast. American ships come under fire for the first time in the war as they exchange fire with a Spanish battery at Matanzas, Cuba.

1 MAY 1898

Spanish-American War: The Battle of Manila Bay In Manila Bay the United States Asiatic Squadron under the command of Commodore George Dewey defeats a decrepit Spanish force of seven ships. The American victory by six ships of the squadron is due mainly to superior gun range and firepower. Spanish losses are three ships sunk, with the others severely damaged. The American ships suffer only minor damage, and only nine sailors are wounded. This victory eliminates the only effective Spanish naval presence in the Pacific Ocean.

2 MAY 1898

Spanish-American War: Naval In the Philippines, Commodore Dewey moves his naval squadron to Cavite where it will be protected and out of range of Spanish shore batteries at Manila.

3 MAY 1898

Spanish-American War: Naval A naval landing party from Dewey's ships captures the Spanish arsenal at Cavite. Meanwhile, American warships *Baltimore* and *Raleigh* force the Spanish batteries at Corregidor to surrender, thereby guaranteeing safe passage in and out of the entrance of Manila Bay.

7 MAY 1898

Spanish-American War: National The naval victory at Manila Bay has made an instant national hero of George Dewey. The Navy Department informs him of his promotion to Rear Admiral and that additional navy and army reinforcements will be sent to the Philippines.

11 MAY 1898

Spanish-American War: Naval The first Americans are killed in action in the war when the torpedo boat *Winslow* sustains heavy damage from a Spanish gunboat and shore batteries in the harbor at Cárdenás, Cuba. One officer and three enlisted men are killed and three men are wounded.

12 MAY 1898

Spanish-American War: Leaders Major General Wesley Merritt, the second-ranking officer in the United States Army, is selected to command the American military expedition to the Philippines to relieve Admiral Dewey.

13 MAY 1898

Spanish-American War: Philippines In order 'to retain possession and thus control the Philippine Islands,' Admiral Dewey requests 5000 American troops. Dewey estimates the size of the Spanish garrison at 10,000 men, but Dewey has the assistance of the guns of his naval squadron, along with that of 30,000 Filipino insurgents.

19 MAY 1898

Spanish-American War: Philippines Filipino revolutionary Emilio Aguinaldo arrives at Cavite, Philippines, aboard the American ship *McCulloch* from exile in Hong Kong. Following his arrival Aguinaldo confers with Admiral Dewey and agrees to lead a Filipino uprising against the Spanish garrison at Manila.

19 MAY 1898

Spanish-American War: Naval The Atlantic Flying Squadron under the command of Commodore Winfield Schley leaves Key West, Florida bound for Cienfuegos on the south coast of Cuba. This powerful force is led by the battleships *Texas*, *Massachusetts* and *Iowa* and is searching for a Spanish naval force, under the command of Admiral Pascual Cervera y Topete. The Spanish squadron is reported to have left Spain seeking to relieve the American naval blockade of Cuba. On this same day Admiral Cervera arrives at Santiago de Cuba, on the southeast coast of Cuba. The United States Navy, although engaged in a desperate search for Cervera, remains unaware of his presence there for ten days.

25 MAY 1898

Spanish-American War: Philippines The initial American military contingent leaves San Francisco bound for the Philippines. On board three transports, accompanied by the protected cruiser *Charleston*, are almost 2500 officers and men under the command of Brigadier General Thomas Anderson.

29 MAY 1898

Spanish-American War: Naval The Atlantic Flying Squadron arrives at Santiago de Cuba and blockades Admiral Cervera's inferior Spanish fleet in port. The Spanish force consists of four armored cruisers and three destroyers.

JUNE 1898

Spanish-American War: Naval Elements of Admiral Sampson's North Atlantic Squadron, led by the most powerful ship in the United States Navy, the battleship *Oregon*, arrive at Santiago de Cuba to support the blockade of the Spanish fleet. This brings the American total to four battleships plus other support vessels.

10 JUNE 1898

Spanish-American War: Invasion of Cuba The first American armed forces land in Cuba at Guantánamo Bay, just east of Santiago de Cuba. The First Marine Battalion consists of 24 officers and 623 enlisted men under the command of Lieutenant Colonel Robert Huntington. During the next several days the Marines clear the area of Spanish forces with the aid of Cuban rebels. Six Americans are reported killed in action.

12 JUNE 1898

Spanish-American War: Philippines Following military successes by Filipino rebels who effectively

Filipino rebel leader Emilio Aguinaldo welcomed the US conquest of the Philippines but turned against the US when it did not give the nation independence.

besiege the Spanish garrison in the city of Manila, the revolutionary leader Emilio Aguinaldo proclaims the independence of the Philippines.

14 JUNE 1898

Spanish-American War: Invasion of Cuba After hectic and confused preparations the United States Fifth Army Corps, with supporting volunteer units, leaves Tampa, Florida, bound for Santiago de Cuba. Under the command of Major General William Shafter, this force consists of 819 officers and 16,058 enlisted men aboard 29 transports. Shafter's orders are to 'capture or destroy the garrison there, and cover the Navy as it sends its men in small boats to remove torpedoes, or with the aid of the Navy, capture or destroy the Spanish fleet now reported to be in Santiago harbor.' How General Shafter will carry out this mission is left up to him.

15 JUNE 1898

Spanish-American War: Philippines A second military expedition leaves San Francisco bound for the Philippines. It consists of 3500 troops on three transports under the command of Brigadier General Francis Greene. It will arrive in Manila Bay on 17 July.

21 JUNE 1898

Spanish-American War: Guam The initial American expedition bound for Manila Bay, under orders from the Navy Department, seizes the Spanish island of Guam in the western Pacific Ocean. Only 60 Spanish troops occupy the garrison there, and they surrender without incident.

22 JUNE 1898

Spanish-American War: Invasion of Cuba The Fifth Army Corps begins amphibious landings at Daiquirí, about 20 miles east of Santiago de Cuba. General Shafter rejects the Navy's preference for the Army to move along the coastline and attack the gun emplacements guarding the narrow opening of the harbor at Santiago de Cuba. Instead, Shafter plans to move along a more interior route and directly strike at the city itself and the fortifications guarding it.

23 JUNE 1898

Spanish-American War: Invasion of Cuba Units of the Fifth Army Corps advance seven miles west to Siboney where additional detachments come ashore. A small force of Spanish troops retreats west toward Santiago de Cuba. The landings will be completed by 26 June.

24 JUNE 1898

Spanish-American War: Battle of Las Guásimas In the first major land battle of the war Major General Joseph Wheeler leads an attack on Spanish positions at Las Guásimas. Wheeler's force consists of three regiments of dismounted cavalry and a brigade of infantry amounting to about 1000 men. The cavalry includes the First United States Volunteer Cavalry, more popularly known as the 'Rough Riders'. The Rough Riders are commanded by Colonel Leonard Wood and Lieutenant Colonel Theodore Roosevelt. After a sharp fight the Spanish forces retreat. American losses are 16 killed and 52 wounded. Wheeler, who had been acting without orders, is told to hold his position in order for American forces to concentrate for the main assault on Santiago de Cuba.

25-29 JUNE 1898

Spanish-American War: Philippines A third contingent of almost 5000 troops under the command of Brigadier General Arthur MacArthur leaves San Francisco aboard seven transports bound for Manila Bay. They will arrive between 25 July and 31 July. Together, the three expeditions are known as the Eighth Army Corps and comprise almost 11,000 officers and men.

26 JUNE 1898

Spanish-American War: Puerto Rico Secretary of War Russell Alger issues orders for a military expedition to take Puerto Rico from Spanish control. General of the Army Nelson Miles is to command. A force of 27,000 troops is assigned to this mission.

30 JUNE 1898

Spanish-American War: Cuba Preparations are made to attack a Spanish fort at El Caney, about six miles northeast of the city of Santiago de Cuba, along with Kettle Hill and San Juan Hill on the San Juan Heights rising two miles east of the city. Colonel Wood has been reassigned to take over the Second Brigade of dismounted cavalry, leaving Lieutenant Colonel Theodore Roosevelt in command of the Rough Riders.

1 JULY 1898

Spanish-American War: Battles of El Caney, Kettle Hill and San Juan Hill In the early morning Brigadier General Henry Lawton's division of 5400 Regular Army troops begins an attack on El Caney, which is defended by about 500 Spanish soldiers. By late afternoon the fort is finally taken after heavy resistance. American losses are 81 killed and 360 wounded. Only about 100 Spaniards escape to Santiago de Cuba. Meanwhile, Brigadier General Jacob Kent's infantry division is ordered to attack San Juan Hill, while General Samuel Sumner's dismounted cavalry division is sent against Spanish positions on Kettle Hill, just to the north of San Juan Hill. The attack is scheduled for early morning, but dense jungle and lack of reconnaissance cause considerable delay. Attempting to move into position to attack San Juan Hill, General Kent's infantry division encounters heavy Spanish gunfire causing many casualties. The attack does not begin until early afternoon. When it does begin a timely Gatling-gun covering fire enables the American troops to take the now weakly-defended hill in a matter of minutes. Meanwhile, General Sumner's cavalrymen on foot assault Kettle Hill, with Lieutenant Colonel Roosevelt being among the first to reach the crest, only to find the Spanish forces there had fled. Among the units participating in this action is the 10th Cavalry, consisting of black soldiers but led by white officers. One of these officers is Lieutenant John J. Pershing, whose later well-known nickname 'Black Jack' stems from the color of the men he leads. Once in possession of the San Juan Heights the American troops begin rapidly to dig in, being only a few hundred yards from the next line of Spanish fortifications. Of the 3000 troops actually taking part in this attack 205 are killed and 1180 are wounded due to skirmishing over the next few days. Many soldiers will later die of their wounds due to inadequate means of evacuation and lack of proper medical facilities.

A contemporary lithograph shows a somewhat fanciful version of the storming of San Juan Hill outside Santiago, Cuba, on 1 July 1898.

3 JULY 1898

Spanish-American War: Naval Battle of Santiago Seven American warships lie in a semi-circle off the channel entrance to the harbor at Santiago de Cuba. From east to west they are the converted yacht *Gloucester;* the battleships *Indiana, Oregon, Iowa,* and *Texas;* the armored cruiser *Brooklyn;* and the converted yacht *Vixen*. Given the desperate situation at Santiago de Cuba, Admiral Cervera's naval squadron attempts to run the blockade and flee westward. The Spanish force which emerges consists of only four armored cruisers and two destroyers. Due to the extremely narrow channel entrance to the harbor each Spanish ship is forced to exit the harbor singly, thereby exposing it to the combined firepower of the American fleet. Admiral Cervera's flagship, the *Infanta Maria Teresa*, is the first to emerge and is quickly disabled and forced ashore. Four more Spanish ships are rapidly sunk or run aground. One Spanish ship, the *Cristóbal Colón*, manages to flee 50 miles westward before also being forced ashore. Within a space of a few hours the only effective Spanish naval force in the Caribbean is completely destroyed. No American ships are seriously damaged and only one American sailor is killed in the battle. Admiral Cervera is captured along with more than 1700 Spanish sailors. Spanish casualties are 323 reported killed and 151 wounded.

Colonel Theodore Roosevelt at the head of the First United States Volunteer Cavalry, better known to history as 'The Rough Riders.'

3 JULY 1898

Spanish-American War: Siege of Santiago General Shafter, in command of American land forces, demands the surrender of the Spanish garrison at Santiago de Cuba. Shafter threatens that he shall be forced to shell the city otherwise. The new Spanish commander, General José Toral, refuses.

4 JULY 1898

Spanish-American War: Siege of Santiago Under cover of darkness a Spanish naval crew attempts to block the narrow channel leading to the harbor of Santiago de Cuba by sinking an old cruiser. The ship is struck by heavy fire from the American battleships *Texas* and *Massachusetts*. The Spanish attempt fails when the ship comes to rest east of the channel. Meanwhile, in order to maintain pressure on Spain to end the war, Secretary of War Alger directs General Shafter to take the city 'as speedily as possible.' In response, General Shafter requests reinforcements be sent immediately. General Nelson Miles is assigned to reinforce the Fifth Army Corps rather than proceed directly to Puerto Rico.

7 JULY 1898

National President McKinley signs a joint resolution of Congress providing for the annexation of the Hawaiian Islands by the United States. In the context of the war with Spain and the extension of American military power to the Far East, Hawaii has become a strategic outpost of tremendous importance.

8 JULY 1898

Spanish-American War: Siege of Santiago General Toral, commander of Spanish forces at Santiago de Cuba, offers to relinquish the city in exchange for an uncontested retreat by his forces.

9 JULY 1898

Spanish-American War: Siege of Santiago In response to a rejection of General Toral's proposal by Washington, General Shafter demands an unconditional surrender of the Spanish garrison by 3 PM, 10 July. If refused, a bombardment of the city is to commence one hour later.

10-11 JULY 1898

Spanish-American War: Siege of Santiago American naval warships bombard Santiago de Cuba. Only a few ships take part, and the shelling is ineffective due to General Shafter's concern that naval gunfire concentrate safely away from American positions around the city. At 1 PM on 11 July Shafter orders another ceasefire and passes on to General Toral a proposal from Secretary of War Alger offering to return Spanish prisoners to Spain at the expense of the United States.

11 JULY 1898

Spanish-American War: Siege of Santiago The Commanding General of the Army, Nelson Miles, arrives at Santiago de Cuba with reinforcements. General Shafter remains in command of all military operations on land around the city.

13 JULY 1898

Spanish-American War: Siege of Santiago Generals Miles and Shafter meet with General Toral under a flag of truce to discuss terms of surrender. Miles demands unconditional surrender, but promises to ship the Spanish garrison back to Spain. The truce is extended until noon, 14 July, to allow Toral time to consult his government.

The last major Spanish resistance in Cuba ended on 17 July 1898 with the surrender of Santiago. Here the US colors are hoisted over the city square.

General Arthur MacArthur (front center) was mainly responsible for Aguinaldo's defeat. He was named the military governor of the Philippines in 1900.

17 JULY 1898

Spanish-American War: Fall of Santiago The Spanish army of 8000 men in the besieged city of Santiago de Cuba formally surrenders to American forces led by General Shafter. The surrender also includes all other Spanish forces in eastern Cuba, numbering an additional 12,000 troops.

20 JULY 1898

Spanish-American War: Puerto Rico General James Wilson departs Charleston, South Carolina, with 3600 troops for the invasion of Puerto Rico. Another 2900 soldiers under the command of Brigadier Theodore Schwan will depart from Tampa, Florida, in support on 24 July.

21 JULY 1898

Spanish-American War: Puerto Rico From Guantánamo Bay, Cuba, General Nelson Miles departs for Puerto Rico with 3400 men aboard transports. A naval escort is led by the battleship *Massachusetts*.

25 JULY 1898

Spanish-American War: Puerto Rico General Miles makes an unopposed landing at Guánica, on the south coast of Puerto Rico, after the harbor is secured by sailors from the armed yacht *Gloucester*.

26 JULY 1898

Spanish-American War: Puerto Rico The first military skirmish takes place in Puerto Rico as seven companies of soldiers led by Brigadier General George Garretson encounter Spanish resistance outside the town of Yauco, six miles north of Guánica. The Spanish defenders retreat, and the town is occupied two days later on 28 July.

27 JULY 1898

Spanish-American War In a letter American Ambassador to England John Hay coins a phrase which later becomes a popular way of describing the conflict with Spain when he refers to it as 'the splendid little war.'

28 JULY 1898

Spanish-American War: Puerto Rico General James Wilson arrives from Charleston with his forces and disembarks at Ponce, located east of Guánica. Spanish troops retreat north toward San Juan.

31 JULY 1898

Spanish-American War: Philippines In the Philippines Spanish defenders open fire on American positions held by the Eighth Army Corps south of the city of Manila. Ten Americans are killed and 33 wounded. Additional skirmishing will lead to five more Americans killed and 20 wounded.

31 JULY 1898

Spanish-American War: Puerto Rico General Theodore Schwan arrives at Guánica, Puerto Rico, with about 2900 men.

3-5 AUGUST 1898

Spanish-American War: Puerto Rico Major General John Brooke lands 5000 troops at Arroyo, on the southeast coast of Puerto Rico. Recent reinforcements bring American forces on the island to more than 15,000 soldiers. There are an estimated 8000 Spanish defenders on the island dispersed at strategic but isolated, locations.

5 AUGUST 1898

Spanish-American War: Puerto Rico American military forces begin to move north toward the interior of Puerto Rico in four separate columns. At Guayama a military column under the command of General Brooke encounters Spanish resistance, and five Americans are wounded.

7 AUGUST 1898

Spanish-American War: Disease Tropical disease, including malaria and yellow fever, has brought severe illness and even death to approximately one-fourth of the 16,000 soldiers of the Fifth Army Corps at Santiago de Cuba. Due to the oppressive conditions and fears of an even greater epidemic the US Army orders the entire force evacuated to Montauk Point in eastern Long Island, New York. Troops begin to arrive there 14 August.

7 AUGUST 1898

Spanish-American War: Philippines Brigadier General Arthur MacArthur completes the deployment of the third contingent of the Eighth Army

Corps south of Manila in the Philippines. American forces ashore now number more than 8500.

9 AUGUST 1898

Spanish-American War: Puerto Rico Pushing northeast from Ponce, Puerto Rico, the military column under General Wilson encounters heavy Spanish resistance when troops led by Brigadier General Oswald Ernst meet Spanish forces at Coamo. In a flanking maneuver a small American detachment is able to get behind the defenders. Reported Spanish losses are 40 casualties and 167 captured.

9 AUGUST 1898

Spanish-American War: Philippines American military commanders, noting the hopeless position of the Spanish garrison in Manila, issue a call for surrender. The Spanish reply that, as a matter of national and personal honor, they must offer at least some resistance before surrendering.

10 AUGUST 1898

Spanish-American War: Puerto Rico The American left wing under General Schwan encounters about 1400 Spanish troops at Hormigueros, near the west coast of the island. After sustaining about 50 casualties the Spanish force retreats northeast. American losses are one killed and 16 wounded. American troops pursue the enemy northeast toward the north coast of the island.

12 AUGUST 1898

Spanish-American War: Peace Negotiations President McKinley and the French Ambassador to the United States, Jules Cambon, who is acting on behalf of the Spanish government, affix their signatures to a protocol ending the war. Spain agrees to grant independence to Cuba and cede Puerto Rico to the United States, along with an island in the western Pacific Ocean. The future of the Philippines is to be decided at a peace conference to be held in Paris for the purpose of concluding a formal treaty.

12 AUGUST 1898

Spanish-American War: Puerto Rico American forces prepare to assault Spanish entrenchments in central Puerto Rico on 13 August preliminary to an attack on San Juan. However, General Miles receives word by telegram from Washington that the United States and Spain have signed an agreement halting all military operations. This brings an end to all combat operations in Puerto Rico. American casualties in the campaign are slight. In six engagements only seven Americans are killed and 36 wounded.

13 AUGUST 1898

Spanish-American War: Philippines Warships from Admiral Dewey's naval squadron begin a morning bombardment of a Spanish fort, Fort San Antonio Abad, south of the city of Manila. This fort anchors the right of the Spanish defense perimeter. According to a previous agreement, the fort does not fire on the American naval squadron, and the Americans avoid targeting the city. The Spanish do not want Filipino insurgents to occupy the city and are willing to surrender after a bombardment to preserve their honor. After a desultory shelling of an hour the bombardment comes to an end. Thereafter, the Eighth Army Corps, divided into two brigades, assaults the Spanish defenses south of the city. The Spanish lines are overrun by early afternoon. General Greene, commanding on the American left, suffers one killed and 54 wounded. On the right, the brigade under General Arthur MacArthur attacks two blockhouses and loses five killed and 38 wounded. A white flag is then raised over the city, and the Spanish garrison surrenders. American forces move in and assume control of Manila. The battle actually occurs after Spain and the United States have agreed to a cessation of hostilities, but word does not reach the Philippines until 16 August because Admiral Dewey had earlier severed Spanish cable communications to Hong Kong.

3 OCTOBER 1898

Spanish-American War: Casualties The Fifth Army Corps is formally disbanded at Camp Wikoff, Long Island. The unit has suffered 243 men killed in action and 1445 wounded. An additional 771 men have died from tropical disease.

10 DECEMBER 1898

Spanish-American War: Treaty of Paris A formal treaty of peace is signed in Paris by two commissions representing the United States and Spain. The United States had previously forced Spain to give up Cuba and Puerto Rico in a protocol signed 12 August. During the subsequent negotiations President McKinley decided to demand the annexation of the Philippine Islands, and Spain is forced to accept $20 million as compensation. The United States also retains Guam in the western Pacific. The Senate will confirm the treaty on 6 February 1899.

US Marines slog through jungle in the Philippines near Olongopo in 1900. Rebel resistance did not finally come to an end until 1902.

4 FEBRUARY 1899

Philippines A nighttime firefight breaks out on the outskirts of Manila between American occupying forces and Filipino insurgents. The Filipinos now fully realize that the United States has no intention of granting the Philippines complete independence or even autonomy under a protectorate. The American force is commanded by Major General Ewell Otis and numbers 11,000 men. The Filipino force is led by Emilio Aguinaldo and consists of 20,000 men. The Americans, however, hold excellent defensive positions and, with superior firepower, are able to repel the weak probing movements of the attacking force.

5 FEBRUARY 1899

Philippines Major General Arthur MacArthur, the commander of the northern sector of the American defensive position, receives permission to counterattack and is easily able to drive the poorly-armed Filipinos opposite him well back of their original lines of the preceding day. Meanwhile, Brigadier General Thomas Anderson also receives permission to attack. Approximately 700 Filipino rebels are trapped by a bend in the River Pasig, which divides the two American sectors. Almost all the trapped Filipinos are killed, wounded or captured.

6 FEBRUARY 1899

Philippines American forces continue their push east from Manila and capture a pumping station supplying Manila with water. The rebel forces are driven well beyond the city and disperse into the countryside. American losses are 59 killed and 278 wounded. General Otis estimates Filipino losses at approximately 3000 men. American reinforcements, including regular army units that are veterans of the recent war, will arrive over the next two months.

24 FEBRUARY 1899

Nicaragua American naval ships are sent to the city of Bluefields, located in a rich banana-growing region on the Atlantic coast of Nicaragua, to 'protect lives and property.' A landing party from the USS *Marietta* is sent ashore. The occasion is an uprising in the region against the central government of President José Santos Zelaya. The government soon crushes the insurgency.

31 MARCH 1899

Philippines General MacArthur's forces capture the insurgent capital at Malolos, 20 miles northwest of Manila. Aguinaldo and his followers flee further into the countryside.

27 MAY 1899

Philippines General MacArthur's division arrives at the town of Calumpit, which is separated from them by the Rio Grande de Pampanga River. Opposing MacArthur are some 6000 rebel troops. The American force has no pontoon bridges and is unable to use a broken-down railroad bridge which spans the river because of the enemy force which guards the opposite end. Two volunteers, Privates Edward White and W. B. Tremblay, swim across the 80-yard expanse of water and attach a rope to the opposite bank. They are quickly followed by Colonel Frederick Funston and eight men, who pull themselves across the river in a raft. After several trips Colonel Funston leads 43 men to the rebel position at the end of the bridge and drives them off. For this action White, Tremblay and Funston receive the Congressional Medal of Honor, and Funston is promoted to Brigadier General of Volunteers.

29 MAY 1899

Philippines The rebel government asks General Otis for an armistice of 15 days to discuss ending the war. Otis refuses to grant an armistice, telling a delegation that is sent to Manila that a cessation of hostilities depends entirely upon the surrender of arms by the rebels and the disbanding of their military organization. The Filipino delegation promises to return in three weeks but never does.

JUNE 1899

Philippines General Otis halts offensive operations in the Philippines against rebel forces in order to reorganize his forces. The forced marches and accompanying heat and tropical disease have taken a heavy toll. American casualties stand at 107 officers and 1667 enlisted men. There are approximately 35,000 American troops in the Philippines.

NOVEMBER 1899

Philippines Having decided to resume the offensive, General Otis plans a three-pronged assault on insurgent strongholds north of Manila. One column, led by General Henry Lawton and his cavalry commander, Brigadier General Samuel Young, relentlessly pursue Aguinaldo and his ever-dwindling band of followers for weeks. Aguinaldo himself narrowly escapes capture. No organized body of rebels remains following this action. Generals Otis and MacArthur believe that the insurrection is over. General Otis will depart in May 1900 believing his task is accomplished.

30 DECEMBER 1899

China An English Christian missionary is killed by members of a secret society whose name in Chinese means 'The Righteous and Harmonious Fists', and today an Imperial Edict is issued that is ambivalent in its criticism of the incident – only one of a growing number of attacks on foreigners and Christians by secret societies. At this point awareness of the mounting tension is limited to the international diplomatic community in Peking. For some decades now China has been increasingly exploited by foreigners; indeed it has been invaded and divided up by commercial and governmental representatives of Britain, France, Germany, Italy, Russia and Japan. Mining and railroad projects have forced large concessions from the Chinese, and ports have been appropriated by foreigners for naval stations. Hard-pressed for cash and credit, China has signed away much of its future income, and foreigners are gaining a stranglehold on the Chinese economy. Meanwhile, some 2000 Christian missionaries have gained the right to protect themselves and their families by 'extraterritoriality.' During the 1890s, therefore, several secret societies have grown up, dedicated to getting rid of the foreigners, especially Europeans and Christians. The best known is The Righteous and Harmonious Fists, and because of this name and the fact that members engage in calisthenics, Westerners have taken to calling them 'The Boxers'. The Boxers are a small group, but they can mobilize large numbers of Chinese in northern China who resent the foreign presence and power. Dowager Empress Tzu Hsi and her advisers are willing to exploit the resentment and let the Boxers do what the Imperial Court cannot do: attack the Westerners.

27 JANUARY 1900

Boxer Rebellion Harassment and outright attacks on foreigners and Chinese who cooperate with them or convert to Christianity continues. Foreign diplomats in Peking write formal notes of protest demanding that the Chinese government stop the Boxers and other groups leading the attacks on Westerners and Christians.

31 JANUARY 1900

Philippines The final report of the USA's Philippine Commission favors territorial government for the islands, with home rule in local affairs but with United States assumption of ultimate responsibility for the government. Today's report seems too little and too late for the Filipino's fighting under Emilio Aguinaldo.

17 MAY 1900

Boxer Rebellion Three villages within 100 miles of Peking are burned by Boxers, and 60 Chinese Christians killed. Christians begin to take refuge in Peking, Tientsin and other treaty ports. Most foreign powers still do regard this as a serious situation.

28 MAY 1900

Boxer Rebellion A mob of Chinese led by Boxers attacks and burns the Fengtai Railway Station, junction of the Peking-Tientsin line, 16 miles from Peking, where the diplomatic corps and foreign legations are situated. In light of the fact that some foreign missionaries have already been killed by the Boxers, the diplomatic corps request military assistance from their warships stationed off the coast of China.

Grim-faced Chinese Boxers await their fate after having been captured by forces of the US cavalry near Tientsin in 1900. In fact, many Boxers were executed after the uprising was put down.

31 MAY 1900

Boxer Rebellion In response to the urgent call for military assistance, 337 officers and men from six nations travel by railway from the coastal port of Taku to Peking. Included among this detachment is an American force consisting of 54 Marines and sailors led by Captains John Myers and Newt Hall. American troops are participating in interallied operations for the first time.

9 JUNE 1900

Boxer Rebellion All telegraph and railway communications to and from the Legation Quarter in Peking are severed. The total military force present to defend this area, approximately three-fourths of a mile square, are 20 officers and 389 men, including 155 Americans.

10 JUNE 1900

Boxer Rebellion An international relief expedition of 2078 men under the command of British Admiral Sir Edward Seymour leaves Tientsin by rail for Peking. Included in this force are 112 Americans under the command of Captain Bowman McCall, commanding officer of USS *Newark*.

10-26 JUNE 1900

Boxer Rebellion The relief expedition is subjected to sniping and attacks by Boxers and Chinese troops. The railway is severed both in the direction of Peking and Tientsin. The multinational force begins to fall back toward Tientsin, which is 20 miles away, on foot along the Pei-Ho River. They are forced to fight their way through each village before safely reaching the foreign settlements near Tientsin. Of the 62 killed and 232 wounded in the allied force are four American sailors killed and 28 wounded, including Captain McCall.

13 JUNE 1900

Boxer Rebellion Boxer and regular Chinese troops launch the first of a series of artillery barrages and fanatical assaults against the fortified foreign legation in Peking. These attacks will continue almost ceaselessly for the next 55 days.

21 JUNE 1900

Boxer Rebellion A relief force of 137 Marines led by Major Littleton Waller runs into a mass of Boxers and Chinese troops 12 miles from Tientsin. Although joined by 450 Russian troops, this contingent is forced to retreat with the loss of 3 Marines killed and seven wounded.

21 JUNE 1900

Philippines General Arthur MacArthur, US military governor of the Philippines, issues an amnesty proclamation to those Filipinos who will renounce the insurgent movement and accept US sovereignty. There will be little response.

24 JUNE 1900

Boxer Rebellion Aided by additional allied troops, Major Waller and his Marines link up with the original multinational expeditionary force near Tientsin. The railway line between the coastal port of Taku and Tientsin, which earlier had been cut off, is restored.

13-14 JULY 1900

Boxer Rebellion With approximately 14,000 allied troops now deployed near Tientsin, an attack is made on that heavily fortified city surrounded by walls on all sides. Japanese forces carry the main assault against the south wall, supported by British forces and 900 American Marines. Under heavy fire, including enfilading fire from across the Pei-Ho River, the attack is called off by nightfall. It is resumed when Japanese forces blow up the gate on the south wall and pour through the gap, followed by the remainder of the allied force. American losses are 24 killed and 98 wounded.

4 AUGUST 1900

Boxer Rebellion A newly-organized relief expedition of almost 16,000 men departs Tientsin for Peking. No word has been received from the foreign legation since 4 July, and their fate is unknown. Additional American troops have recently arrived, including the 6th US Cavalry, the 14th US Infantry and the 1st Marine Regiment. The American contingent now numbers over 2000 men.

6 AUGUST 1900

Boxer Rebellion The allied force attacks entrenched Chinese positions at Yangtsun, 20 miles from Tientsin. Spearheading a frontal assault are the US 9th and 14th Infantry and the 1st Marine Regiment. After a four-hour fight the Chinese positions are successfully taken.

12 AUGUST 1900

Boxer Rebellion Allied forces capture the walled city of Tungchow, only 14 miles east of Peking. Final preparations are made for the attack on Peking.

13-14 AUGUST 1900

Boxer Rebellion Russian, Japanese, American and British forces push west and launch an all-out attack against the heavily protected, four-walled Tatar City in Peking. After an all-day battle allied troops reach and rescue the foreign legation nestled in the southwest corner of the Tatar City. Since the siege began 66 members of the legation have been killed and 150 wounded. Two American Marines protecting the legation are listed as killed.

15 AUGUST 1900

Boxer Rebellion Allied forces continue their sweep of the remainder of the Tatar City. The American objective is the sacred Forbidden City, lying in the innermost part of the multi-walled enclosure. Using coordinated infantry assaults and artillery fire, units from the 14th and 9th Infantry are on the verge of the sanctum of the Imperial Court itself when a ceasefire is sounded. The Boxer Rebellion is crushed. The ferocity of this conflict may be measured by the fact that 60 Congressional Medals of Honor will be awarded to both American defenders of the foreign legation and members of the expeditionary relief force.

20 DECEMBER 1900

Philippines Renewed guerrilla attacks on American soldiers and Filipino sympathizers force General MacArthur to declare martial law throughout the islands. Some 79 rebels are tried for murder and hanged.

2 MARCH 1901

National Congress passes the Platt Amendment, which sets forth conditions under which the United States will withdraw its forces and allow Cuba to govern itself under a new constitution. Conditions include a prohibition on Cuba's making any treaty with a foreign power and authorization for the US to intervene to preserve law and order or Cuban independence. It also provides for the establishment of naval stations on the island. One will be established at Guantánamo Bay.

23 MARCH 1901

Philippines American Army General Frederick Funston and a group of officers, pretending to be prisoners of Filipino scouts, are led into the camp of Emilio Aguinaldo, the leader of the insurgents. Aguinaldo is captured.

Marines parade through Peking in the aftermath of the Boxer Rebellion. The US forgave China most of the $25 million indemnity it was suppcsed to pay.

19 APRIL 1901

Philippines Recently-captured rebel leader Emilio Aguinaldo issues a proclamation advising his countrymen to end their rebellion and use peaceful means to work with the United States toward independence. But many insurgents will not heed his words, and resistance will continue on into 1902.

4 JULY 1901

Philippines William Howard Taft is installed as the first governor-general of the Philippines. Taft declares an amnesty for all who take an oath of allegiance to the United States.

7 SEPTEMBER 1901

Boxer Rebellion: End Representatives of 11 foreign nations and China sign what is known as the Peace of Peking, or the Boxer Protocol. It establishes that China is to pay $333 million in indemnities (with the United States to get $25 million) and permits the stationing of foreign troops in Peking.

14 SEPTEMBER 1901

National President William McKinley, who had been shot in Buffalo on 9 September, dies of his wounds. His vice-president, Theodore Roosevelt, takes the oath of office as president. Roosevelt believes that the United States must realize its potential as a great power, that the safety of the nation requires expansion and that a strong naval battle fleet should serve as the foundation for this. Roosevelt also believes that the United States must take responsibility for and protect weaker nations in the Caribbean. He will be known for the adage: 'Speak softly and carry a big stick.'

28 SEPTEMBER 1901

Philippines In the town of Balangiga, on the island of Samar in the southern islands, Company C, 9th US Infantry, is attacked and nearly massacred by a force of guerrillas disguised as workmen. Of the 74 men in the company only four escape uninjured. Of the rest, 48 are killed or missing.

7-10 NOVEMBER 1901

Philippines In retaliation for the massacre at Balangiga, American forces under orders from Brigadier General Jacob (Hell-Roaring Jake) Smith burn 225 houses and kill 39 Filipinos. Smith tells his field commander, Major Littleton Waller: 'I want no prisoners. I wish you to burn and kill; the more you burn and kill the better it will please me.' Smith is later court-martialed for his actions.

18 NOVEMBER 1901

Great Britain-USA The United States and Great Britain sign the Second Hay-Pauncefote Treaty abrogating the Clayton-Bulwar Treaty of 1850. Britain has now accepted the condition – rejected in the First Hay-Pauncefote Treaty – that the US be allowed to fortify and defend any canal it builds across the isthmus of Central America. The US Senate will consent to this treaty on 16 December.

20 MAY 1902

Cuba The United States withdraws its troops from Cuba as the first president, Tomas Estrada Palma, is installed.

4 JULY 1902

Philippines President Roosevelt proclaims an end to hostilities in the islands, with the exception of the non-Christian Moro province in the southern islands. Amnesty is offered to all rebels willing to take an oath of allegiance to the United States. American military strength has been reduced from a peak of 70,000 to 34,000 men. In more than three years of fighting, American losses are listed as 4243 killed and 2818 wounded. Over the next decade the Moros will frequently rise up and be fought by US troops.

2 NOVEMBER 1903

Colombia Three American warships, led by the USS *Nashville*, receive orders from President Roosevelt to keep open the Panama Railroad and to prevent movement along it by hostile forces. In fact, Roosevelt is ordering the US Navy to prevent Colombia from landing troops on its province of Panama to put down an imminent uprising.

3 NOVEMBER 1903

Colombia The expected uprising by Panamanians occurs early in the evening. Sailors from the USS *Nashville* prevent 400 Colombian soldiers from moving along the Panama Railroad to stop the revolution.

6 NOVEMBER 1903

Colombia At 11:35 AM, President Roosevelt is notified by the US Consul in Panama that the independent Republic exits. By 12:51 PM, Secretary of State John Hay instructs the consul to declare *de facto* recognition. This is the quickest recognition ever granted to a new government by the United States.

11 NOVEMBER 1903

Panama-USA The United States and the new Republic of Panama sign the Hay-Bruneau-Villa Treaty – over the protests of Colombia – giving the US permanent rights to a 10-mile strip in return for $10 million and an annual fee of $250,000 after nine years. Panamanian independence is also guaranteed, and the US will be allowed to occupy and control the strip as well as construct a canal there.

JANUARY-FEBRUARY 1904

Dominican Republic Marine detachments are landed a number of times at various points to protect lives and property of US and other foreign nationals during a civil war.

20 MAY 1904

National At a New York dinner a speech written by President Roosevelt is read for him by a close associate, Elihu Root, and is the first statement of what becomes known as the 'Roosevelt Corollary' to the Monroe Doctrine. Roosevelt warns that instability or 'brutal wrongdoing' in some cases 'may finally require intervention by some civilized nation, and in the Western Hemisphere the United States cannot ignore this duty.' This addition to the Monroe Doctrine is designed to prevent intervention by other European states that will not be tolerated by the United States.

JUNE 1904

Dominican Republic Agreements signed aboard the USS *Detroit* end a civil war in the Dominican Republic. Carlos Morales remains as president at least in part due to support of the American Navy, which had sent ships to that country to protect foreign life and property at places where fighting seemed likely.

30 DECEMBER 1904

Dominican Republic In the first application of the Roosevelt Corollary, Secretary of State John Hay instructs the American minister to the Dominican Republic, Thomas Dawson, to ascertain whether the

President Theodore Roosevelt's 1904 'Corollary' to the Monroe Doctrine justified US intervention in the internal affairs of Latin American states.

Warships of the 'Great White Fleet' return to San Francisco after their 1906 round-the-world cruise to display US naval might.

Dominican government would agree to US control of its customs houses and to adjudicate pending claims upon the government by Italy, Belgium and Germany. These countries are threatening to intervene in Dominican affairs by seizing control of the customs houses by force in order to settle their claims. Commander Dillingham of the USS *Detroit* is sent as a special commissioner to help in the negotiations.

1 APRIL 1905

Dominican Republic The United States and the Dominican Republic agree that the US will direct the Dominican Customs Service in order to preserve the financial stability of that country and prevent foreign intervention. The Navy and Marine Corps are directed to put the customs service into order and enforce the collection of revenue.

5 SEPTEMBER 1905

Dominican Republic President Roosevelt instructs the American naval commander, Admiral Bradford, 'to stop any revolution' in the Dominican Republic during the establishment of a customs receivership by the United States in that country.

24 FEBRUARY 1906

Cuba Tomas Estrada Palma defeats José Gomez in the election for president, but Gomez and his followers refuse to accept the results and sponsor an uprising. Among other charges, Gomez labels Estrada Palma a tool of 'Yankee imperialism', and soon Palma is calling for US troops to help put down the uprising.

The Roosevelt Corollary led to a long series of US interventions in Latin America. Here US Marines battle insurgents in the Dominican Republic in 1916.

29 SEPTEMBER 1906

Cuba Under the Platt Amendment, Secretary of War William Howard Taft assumes control of the island of Cuba as provisional governor following the resignation of virtually the entire Cuban government. President Tomas Estrada Palma resigns in order to force the United States to intervene and settle the civil war that has broken out following the disputed election. A force of 2000 US Marines is brought ashore to ensure order from naval warships in Havana harbor.

19 MARCH 1907

Honduras Nicaragua and Honduras are at war. The Honduran army is routed at the Battle of Namasigue. Nicaraguan troops then proceed to take possession of several Honduran ports on the Atlantic coast. In response, US warships land Marines at several points to protect US citizens and property in the area.

12 APRIL 1907

Nicaragua Following a ceasefire signed between Nicaragua and Honduras aboard the USS *Chicago* off the Pacific coast, US Marines are dispatched to ensure order on Tigre Island in the Gulf of Fonseca.

28 JANUARY 1909

Cuba General José Miguel Gomez is inaugurated as president of Cuba. All American troops and officials of the provisional government who have been in place since September 1906 are withdrawn.

4 MARCH 1909

National William Howard Taft is inaugurated as president of the United States. Like Roosevelt, Taft believes the United States must support stable governments and economic progress as the best means of warding off European interference. Although Taft proposes to substitute 'dollars for bullets', Taft and his active secretary of state, Philander C. Knox, will demonstrate a greater willingness to consider the use of force when diplomacy has failed.

11 OCTOBER 1909

Nicaragua Another uprising is declared against the Nicaraguan central government and takes place in the Atlantic coast region around Bluefields. The rebellion is supported by American companies operating in the region, and many American citizens serve as mercenaries for the insurgent forces.

16 NOVEMBER 1909

Nicaragua Two American mercenaries, Lee Roy Cannon and Leonard Croce, who had held the rank of colonel during the recent rebellion, are executed by firing squad for crimes against the state.

1 DECEMBER 1909

Nicaragua-USA American Secretary of State Philander C. Knox breaks diplomatic relations with Nicaragua following the recent execution of two American citizens for armed insurgency.

16 DECEMBER 1909

Nicaragua A conservative revolution, coupled with US pressure, forces President José Santos Zelaya from office.

19 MAY 1910

Nicaragua The civil war continues. Nicaraguan factions seem ready to bring anarchy to Bluefields. Commander Gilmer of the USS *Paducah* declares the area a neutral zone, tells both sides there must be no fighting in the city and lands 100 sailors and Marines to enforce his demands. Two companies of Marines under Major Smedley Butler will relieve this force on 31 May and will remain until 5 September.

1 JANUARY 1911

Nicaragua-USA After a change of government in Nicaragua the United States reestablishes diplomatic relations with that country.

4 AUGUST 1912

Nicaragua Civil war has broken once again in this country, splitting the ruling Conservative Party into rival factions. Liberals opposed to the government also stage uprisings. In response to a request by Nicaraguan Foreign Minister Diego Chamorro, 100 US sailors and Marines are sent ashore from the USS *Annapolis* at Corinto and proceed to Managua to serve as a legation guard. They will be reinforced by 350 Marines from the Canal Zone under the command of Major Smedley Butler.

20 AUGUST 1912

Nicaragua A party of 40 sailors and 100 Marines attempting to reach the port of Corinto by railroad from Managua are stopped by a mob at Leon and forced to return to Managua on foot. An additional 1500 Marines will arrive over the next two months to reinforce the legation guard.

3 OCTOBER 1912

Nicaragua A force of US sailors and Marines takes part in the Battle of Coyotepe and Barranca Hills against revolutionary forces. American losses are seven killed, but the town is captured, and the rebel leader, General Zeledon, is killed by his own troops as he attempts to flee.

3-4 OCTOBER 1912

Nicaragua A force of 900 sailors from the USS *Annapolis* and USS *California* and Marines commanded by Colonel J. H. Pendleton assist Nicaraguan government forces in a battle at Masaya in defense of a railway line. Three US servicemen are killed and five are wounded.

The touchiest of the US interventions were those involving Mexico. When the US occupied Vera Cruz in 1914 the two states nearly went to war.

6 OCTOBER 1912

Nicaragua A US Marine force of 1200 soldiers under Colonel C. C. Long engage rebel forces in street fighting in the city of Leon. The city, the last rebel stronghold, is shortly surrendered to the Americans. The civil war ends in Nicaragua. US Marines will occupy several towns for a short time to restore order and prevent an outbreak of atrocities. The greater part of the American expeditionary force leaves the country soon thereafter, but 100 Marines will remain in Nicaragua as a legation guard. This legation guard will remain for 13 years, during which time no major civil disturbances will take place. Before this year the US Navy had frequently made a show of force to protect American or foreign property or to discourage revolutionary activities, but this is the first time that American forces have gone into battle to help suppress a revolution against a foreign government.

18 FEBRUARY 1913

Mexico President Francisco Madero is overthrown by the ruthless General Victoriano Huerta, friend of the landowners. Four days later Madero is executed 'while attempting to escape' as the US masses troops on the Mexican border. The US refuses to recognize Huerta, who is opposed by a revolutionary movement led by Venustiano Carranza.

4 MARCH 1913

National Woodrow Wilson is inaugurated as president of the United States. He believes that the United States has a distinct moral duty to promote democratic government in countries within its sphere of influence. Feeling personally responsible for spreading moral enlightment, Wilson will become determined 'to teach the South American republics to elect good men.' His forcefully expressed liberalism makes it hard to foresee that his administration will go further than any of its predecessors in intervening in the internal affairs of several Latin American republics.

15 JUNE 1913

Philippines Following a three-day struggle against an overwhelming force of American infantry and artillery, more than 300 Muslim warriors are killed, along with many women and children, having been trapped in a volcano on the island of Jolo. No American soldiers are reported killed. This event marks the end of Muslim resistance to American sovereignty in the southern islands.

1 NOVEMBER 1913

Mexico Less than a week after a US nonintervention promise, President Wilson demands that Mexican dictator Huerta resign.

9-11 APRIL 1914

Mexico President Wilson has refused to recognize Huerta as President of Mexico on the ground that he has not been elected by the people. When sailors from the USS *Dolphin* go ashore for supplies at Tampico they are arrested and marched off to jail. Although they are quickly released by President Huerta, Rear Admiral Henry Mayo demands an apology and a 21-gun salute to the American flag. Huerta refuses the latter, and on 11 April the US breaks off diplomatic relations.

20 APRIL 1914

National President Wilson, having dispatched more naval ships to Mexico, asks a joint session of Congress to approve armed force, if necessary, to make Huerta agree to American terms. Congress votes approval.

21 APRIL 1914

Mexico: Siege of Vera Cruz President Wilson orders Rear Admiral Frank Fletcher to interdict arms and ammunition aboard a German cargo steamer at Vera Cruz bound for Huerta's troops. Fletcher's orders are to 'take the Customs House immediately and prevent delivery of arms and ammunition.' In the first American invasion of Mexico since 1846 a Marine detachment from the US cruiser *Prairie* lands without resistance, seizing a cable station and nearby power plant. Additional Marines and sailors follow from the battleships *Utah* and *Florida*. This force moves on, taking the customs house, post office and railway station. By nightfall about one-half of Vera Cruz is in American hands, and 19 Americans and 200 Mexicans are dead. That evening the USS *San Francisco* and USS *Chester* arrive in port and land still more reinforcements.

22 APRIL 1914

Mexico: Siege of Vera Cruz The battleships *Arkansas, New Hampshire, New Jersey* and *South Carolina* arrive off Vera Cruz. This force is commanded by Rear Admiral Charles Badger, commander-in-chief of the US Fleet. Additional reinforcements include the 1st and 2nd Marine Regiments under the command of Colonel John A. Lejeune. The Marines engage in close combat in the city of Vera Cruz, supported by gunfire from the naval squadron.

24 APRIL 1914

Mexico: Fall of Vera Cruz Armed resistance to the American occupying force in Vera Cruz ends. US forces ashore, mainly Marines, total almost 7500 officers and men.

25 APRIL 1914

Mexico President Wilson is persuaded by the ABC powers – Argentina, Brazil and Chile – to accept mediation in the conflict with Mexico. Negotiations are to begin within a month.

28 APRIL 1914

Mexico A reinforced Army brigade commanded by Brigadier General Frederick Funston arrives in Vera Cruz to replace naval seamen ashore. The naval fleet departs, but 3141 Marines remain to support Army troops.

20 MAY-30 JUNE 1914

Mexico-USA Representatives of the US and Mexico meet at Niagara Falls, New York, with representatives of Argentina, Brazil and Chile to resolve differences. Huerta resigns and is replaced by General Carranza as 'provisional' president. Its goal achieved, the US signs an agreement with Mexico on 24 June.

28 JULY 1914

World War I Ever since the assassination of the Archduke Francis Ferdinand, heir to the Austrian throne, Europe has been in a crisis and moving toward war. The Austro-Hungarian government blames Serbia for the assassination and on this day declares war on Serbia.

1 AUGUST 1914

World War I Russia proceeds with a general mobilization in support of Serbia. In response, Germany declares war on Russia.

3 AUGUST 1914

World War I Germany declares war on France, an ally of Russia.

The inauguration of Woodrow Wilson, January 1913. Although inclined to pacifism, Wilson took such a moralistic stance about free elections that the US interfered constantly in Latin American politics.

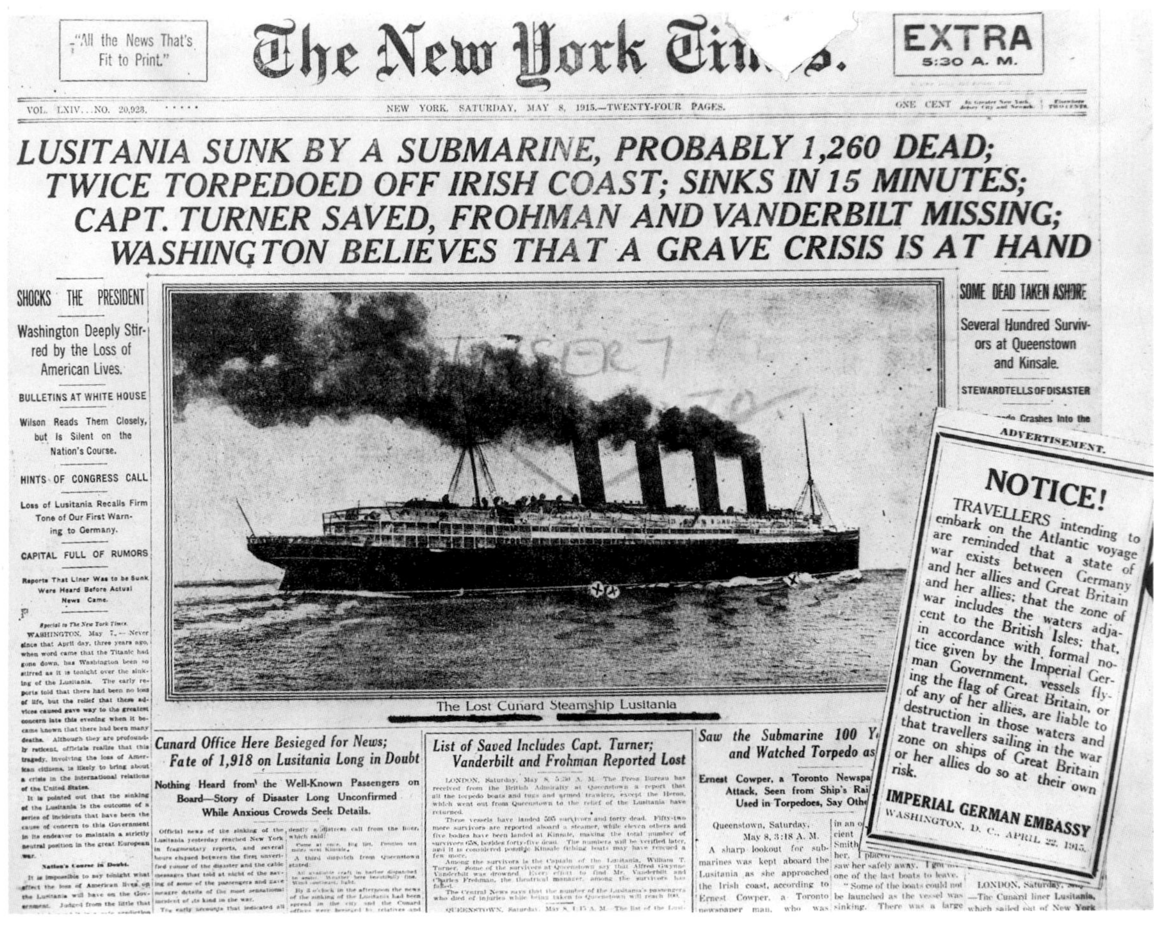

"All the News That's Fit to Print."

The New York Times.

EXTRA 5:30 A. M.

VOL. LXIV...NO. 20,923. NEW YORK, SATURDAY, MAY 8, 1915.—TWENTY-FOUR PAGES. ONE CENT

LUSITANIA SUNK BY A SUBMARINE, PROBABLY 1,260 DEAD; TWICE TORPEDOED OFF IRISH COAST; SINKS IN 15 MINUTES; CAPT. TURNER SAVED, FROHMAN AND VANDERBILT MISSING; WASHINGTON BELIEVES THAT A GRAVE CRISIS IS AT HAND

SHOCKS THE PRESIDENT

Washington Deeply Stirred by the Loss of American Lives.

BULLETINS AT WHITE HOUSE

Wilson Reads Them Closely, but Is Silent on the Nation's Course.

HINTS OF CONGRESS CALL

Loss of Lusitania Recalls Firm Tone of Our First Warning to Germany.

CAPITAL FULL OF RUMORS

Reports That Liner Was to be Sunk Were Heard Before Actual News Came.

SOME DEAD TAKEN ASHORE

Several Hundred Survivors at Queenstown and Kinsale.

STEWARD TELLS OF DISASTER

The Lost Cunard Steamship Lusitania

Cunard Office Here Besieged for News; Fate of 1,918 on Lusitania Long in Doubt

Nothing Heard from the Well-Known Passengers on Board—Story of Disaster Long Unconfirmed While Anxious Crowds Seek Details.

List of Saved Includes Capt. Turner; Vanderbilt and Frohman Reported Lost

Saw the Submarine 100 Y... and Watched Torpedo as...

ADVERTISEMENT.

NOTICE!

TRAVELLERS intending to embark on the Atlantic voyage are reminded that a state of war exists between Germany and her allies and Great Britain and her allies; that the zone of war includes the waters adjacent to the British Isles; that, in accordance with formal notice given by the Imperial German Government, vessels flying the flag of Great Britain, or of any of her allies, are liable to destruction in those waters and that travellers sailing in the war zone on ships of Great Britain or her allies do so at their own risk.

IMPERIAL GERMAN EMBASSY

WASHINGTON, D. C., APRIL 22, 1915.

New York Times headlines of 8 May 1915 report the sinking of the liner *Lusitania* by a German U-boat. Rather than endorse Wilson's violent protests to Germany pacifist Secretary of State Bryan resigned.

4 AUGUST 1914

World War I German troops enter Belgium. Great Britain sends an ultimatum demanding that Germany respect Belgian territory and neutrality. As German troops continue to march Britain declares war on Germany at midnight.

National The United States proclaims neutrality in the war in Europe. The following day the United States will offer to mediate.

19 AUGUST 1914

National In a message to the Senate, President Wilson urges the American people to be 'neutral in fact as well as in name.' But many young Americans will join the British forces, form the Lafayette Escadrille in France or serve as ambulance drivers. Isolationists and pacifists endorse neutrality, as do those who favor Germany.

23 AUGUST 1914

World War I Japan declares war on Germany.

NOVEMBER 1914

World War I Following a two-month race to the sea by Allied and German military forces, both sides stabilize their positions and begin the kind of attrition warfare that will persist until 1918.

23 NOVEMBER 1914

Mexico American occupation forces are withdrawn from Vera Cruz after Venustiano Carranza replaces Huerta as President.

4 FEBRUARY 1915

World War I Germany announces a submarine blockade of the British Isles and declares the entire area a war zone.

10 FEBRUARY 1915

US Approach to War President Wilson warns Germany that the US will hold it 'to a strict accountability' for 'property endangered or lives lost.'

1 MAY 1915

US Approach to War Without warning the American tanker *Gulflight* is sunk by a German submarine. Germany offers reparations and promises not to attack again without warning. On this same day the German Embassy publishes in New York newspapers a warning that anyone sailing into the war zone on a British ship will be doing so at his own risk. And on this day the British liner *Lusitania* sails with many Americans aboard.

7 MAY 1915

US Approach to War The British liner *Lusitania* is sunk without warning off the Irish coast. Of the 1924 passengers aboard 1198 die, including 128 Americans.

9 JUNE 1915

US Approach to War President Wilson sends a note to Germany demanding reparations for the sinking of the *Lusitania* and prevention of 'recurrence of anything so obviously subversive of the principles of warfare.' Wilson also refuses to recognize the 'war zone' that Germany has proclaimed around the British Isles.

National William Jennings Bryan officially resigns as secretary of state following a letter written to President Wilson the previous day. Bryan wants to hold Germany accountable for the sinking, but he also wants to hold Britain similarly accountable for violations of American neutral rights.

28 JULY 1915

Haiti Complete anarchy breaks out in Port-au-Prince following the murder of President Vibrun Guillaume Sam. In response, sailors and Marines are put ashore from the cruiser USS *Washington*. Over the next several weeks additional reinforcements arrive, including five companies from the 2nd Marine Regiment and the 1st Marine Brigade commanded by Colonel Littleton Waller. The Marines take over operation of the customs house, police and public works projects.

10 AUGUST 1915

National General Leonard Wood sets up a training camp in Plattsburg, New York, the first of many such 'Plattsburgs' that will train volunteer civilians. President Wilson will endorse the idea on 4 November.

16 SEPTEMBER 1915

Haiti A treaty is imposed on Haiti by the United States which officially makes Haiti a military protectorate and authorizes American intervention should renewed violence break out. The US Navy is in control of Port-au-Prince and other coastal cities, but much of the interior is still controlled by armed guerrillas. US Marine patrols are attacked several times during the next few months. The United States assumes control of most government, police, and financial services.

24 OCTOBER 1915

Haiti During the evening a Marine patrol of 40 men is ambushed in Northern Haiti by a large force of guerrillas. Finding a good defensive position, the Marines wait until daybreak then counterattack in three separate squads. The Marines discover a guerrilla fort and overrun the position. Eight guerrillas are reported killed and 10 wounded. One American soldier is slightly wounded. The three squad leaders, Captain William Upshur, Lieutenant Edward Ostermann and Gunnery Sergeant Dan Daly will receive the Medal of Honor. This is Daly's second award. The first was for service at Peking during the relief of the foreign legations.

17 NOVEMBER 1915

Haiti The Marine force in Haiti has discovered the last remaining stronghold of rebel resistance, known as Fort Rivière. At daybreak three companies of Marines, led by Major Smedley Butler, open fire and attack the fort. Caught by surprise, many guerrillas attempt to flee over the walls of the fort but are killed by the firepower of the Marines. During the attack Butler leads 27 Marines through a drain pipe in single file gaining access to the interior of the fort. The Marines report 72 rebels killed. Only a few Marines are wounded. Butler and two others will receive Medals of Honor. It is Butler's second award. The fort is blown up, guerrilla resistance ends and the Marines begin a 19-year occupation of Haiti.

1 DECEMBER 1915

US Approach to War After several sensational revelations of German espionage the United States requests that Germany withdraw its military and naval attachés from its Embassy in Washington.

10 JANUARY 1916

Mexico In retaliation for President Wilson's recognition of the Carranza government members of Francisco "Pancho" Villa's revolutionary army take 17 American mining engineers from a train and shoot 16 of them in cold blood.

9 MARCH 1916

Mexico In a pre-dawn raid the Mexican bandit Pancho Villa and a large group of followers attack the town of Columbus, New Mexico, located three miles from the border. Columbus is the headquarters of the US 13th Cavalry. As the Mexicans begin to burn and loot the town the aroused troopers respond with rifle and machinegun fire, driving off Villa's invasion force. Seven American soldiers are killed and five are wounded; civilian losses are eight killed and two wounded. Pursued by two troops of cavalry, the bandits retreat south across the border.

General John J. Pershing (l) confers with General Leonard Wood during the 1916 Mexican campaign.

Rickety Curtiss JN-4 aircraft were used to no great effect in Pershing's 1916 pursuit of Pancho Villa.

15 MARCH 1916

Mexico General John Pershing enters Mexico in two separate columns with a force that will eventually grow to 10,000 officers and men. His mission – officially designated the 'Punitive Expedition' – is to break up Villa's army and capture Villa himself.

18 MARCH 1916

Mexico Pershing establishes headquarters at Colonia Dublán, 50 miles south of the border. Pershing dispatches the 7th and 10th Cavalry south in two flanking columns designed to trap Villa before he can retreat too deep into Mexico.

29 MARCH 1916

Mexico Pershing's expedition has its first encounter with Mexican bandits at Guerrero, 250 miles south of the border. Colonel George Dodd, with 370 officers and men of the 7th Cavalry, attacks some 500 of Villa's men in town just as they are preparing to leave. Heavy fighting breaks out in town, and the Mexicans scatter and flee. Pursued for several hours, 30 Mexicans are confirmed killed, but the estimate is much higher. Four American troopers are wounded.

12 APRIL 1916

Mexico After a ride of 140 miles Major Frank Tompkins reaches the town of Parral with less than 100 troopers of the 13th Cavalry. They are forced back out of town by 500 Mexican government soldiers. Fighting a rearguard action, the squadron is reinforced by the 10th Cavalry by nightfall. American losses are two killed and seven wounded.

18 APRIL 1916

US Approach to War Secretary of State Robert Lansing warns Germany that America may break diplomatic relations unless so-called 'unrestricted' submarine warfare is halted. America's relations with Germany are becoming ever more strained as the public rallies around President Wilson's toughening position.

21 APRIL 1916

Mexico Colonel Dodd and 190 troopers of the 7th Cavalry surprise almost 200 of Villa's men in a canyon at Tomochic, 30 miles southwest of Guerrero. Thirty Mexicans are reported killed in the fighting. The remainder of the Mexican force flees. Ten Americans are killed and three wounded.

5 MAY 1916

Mexico Major Robert Howze and six troops of the 11th Cavalry run into 120 of Villa's men at Ojos Azules. In a one and one-half hour fight 61 Mexicans are reported killed. There are no American casualties.

9 MAY 1916

Mexico Because of the threat of war between the United States and Mexico, General Pershing is ordered to retreat northward and concentrate his force. President Wilson orders the mobilization of National Guard units along the Mexican border.

13 MAY 1916

Dominican Republic There is a renewed civil war in the Dominican Republic. American warships threaten to bombard Santo Domingo if the revolutionary leader, Desiderio Arias, does not immediately evacuate the city with his followers.

15 MAY 1916

Dominican Republic Sailors and Marines from American warships occupy Santo Domingo after rebel forces leave the city. Additional reinforcements will arrive over the next several weeks, beginning an American occupation that will last until 1924.

21 JUNE 1916

Mexico President Carranza has ordered his soldiers to fire on American soldiers on Mexican soil. En route to Ahumada two troops of the 10th Cavalry attempt to force their way through Carrizal past government soldiers. Captain Charles Boyd of Troop C attacks a machine gun, is killed and fighting breaks out. Captain Lewis Morey of Troop K is also seriously wounded. Ten Americans are killed, ten are wounded and 24 are taken prisoner. The Mexican government warns that there will be a repetition of this incident unless American soldiers leave Mexico. The US government refuses to leave until the border is secure.

26 JUNE 1916

Dominican Republic Two columns of Marines advance on the city of Santiago, which is held by a rebel force under the leadership of Desiderio Arias. The 4th Marine Regiment, with more than 800 men, moves southeast from Monte Cristi. A second column of two companies moves south along the railroad from Puerto Plata.

27 JUNE 1916

Dominican Republic Colonel Joseph Pendleton leads the 4th Marine Regiment in an assault against rebel defensive positions approximately 20 miles south of Monte Cristi. Under the cover of artillery fire the rebel lines are captured. One Marine is killed and four wounded.

5 JULY 1916

Dominican Republic American forces capture and occupy Santiago when rebel forces finally decide to surrender.

29 AUGUST 1916

US Approach to War Congress approves increased appropriations for the Army and Navy of almost $580,000,000. The Navy is put on a wartime basis, and the Council of National Defense is created to oversee and coordinate industry and resources for a defense buildup.

29 NOVEMBER 1916

Dominican Republic A formal military occupation is declared by the United States. Captain Harry S. Knapp is appointed military governor. Meanwhile, at San Francisco de Macoris, a provincial capital in the northeast section of the country, the governor, Juan Peréz, stages a revolt. As the gates of the old Spanish fort of Forteleza begin to close Lieutenant E. C. Williams and 12 other Marines rush the fort. Eight of his men are shot down, but Williams and four of his men reach the gate of the fort and force an entry. Additional reinforcements quickly arrive to secure the fort and the city. Williams will receive the Medal of Honor for his actions.

31 JANUARY 1917

US Approach to War Despite President Wilson's warnings Germany declares that it will renew a policy of unrestricted submarine warfare in the North Atlantic Ocean. This decision enflames anti-German sentiment in the US.

3 FEBRUARY 1917

US Approach to War Citing Germany's announcement of unrestricted submarine warfare as reason enough to intervene, Wilson says: 'this government has no alternative consistent with the dignity and honor of the United States.' The same day the American steamer *Housatonic* is sunk without having received warning.

Marine headquarters in Santiago, Dominican Republic. US intervention there lasted from 1916 to 1924.

5 FEBRUARY 1917

Mexico Following several months of quiet in northern Mexico and war looming with Germany, the last American troops of the Punitive Expedition leave Mexico.

25 FEBRUARY 1917

US Approach to War A telegram from the German Foreign Minister Zimmerman to the German ambassador in Mexico has been intercepted and decoded by British agents. In the note Zimmerman, seeing war with the United States as inevitable, instructs his ambassador to offer Mexico Texas, Arizona and New Mexico in return for a declaration of war against the United States. On this day the decoded contents of the message are handed over to the United States. The public release of the message in the US will push war fever to a new high.

26 FEBRUARY 1917

US Approach to War President Wilson asks Congress for authority to arm American merchant ships to protect American lives and shipping. A small group in the Senate, however, blocks passage of the bill. In response Wilson will order the arming of merchant ships on his own authority on March 9.

18 MARCH 1917

US Approach to War Three American ships, the *City of Memphis*, the *Illinois* and the *Vigilancia*, are sunk by German submarines with heavy loss of life.

2 APRIL 1917

US Approach to War The policy of neutrality destroyed by Germany's policy of unrestricted submarine warfare, President Wilson declares that 'the world must be made safe for democracy' and asks Congress for a declaration of war against Germany.

6 APRIL 1917

World War I: US Declaration of War Congress votes a declaration of war against Germany, with only six senators and 50 representatives opposed.

18 MAY 1917

World War I: Preparations Having declared war, the United States has taken steps to prepare for combat. On May 4 six destroyers arrived in Queenstown, Ireland, to aid in convoying ships to England. On May 15 the first officers' training camps opened. This day, Congress passes the Selective Service Act, calling for enrollment of all men between 21 and 30, who will be drafted by lot into the army.

28 JUNE 1917

World War I: France The first American combat troops, the US 1st Division, arrive in France. General John Pershing is the overall commander of the American Expeditionary Force.

4 JULY 1917

World War I: France As General Pershing lays a wreath at the tomb of the Marquis de Lafayette, a member of his staff, Captain Charles Stanton declares: 'Lafayette, we are here.'

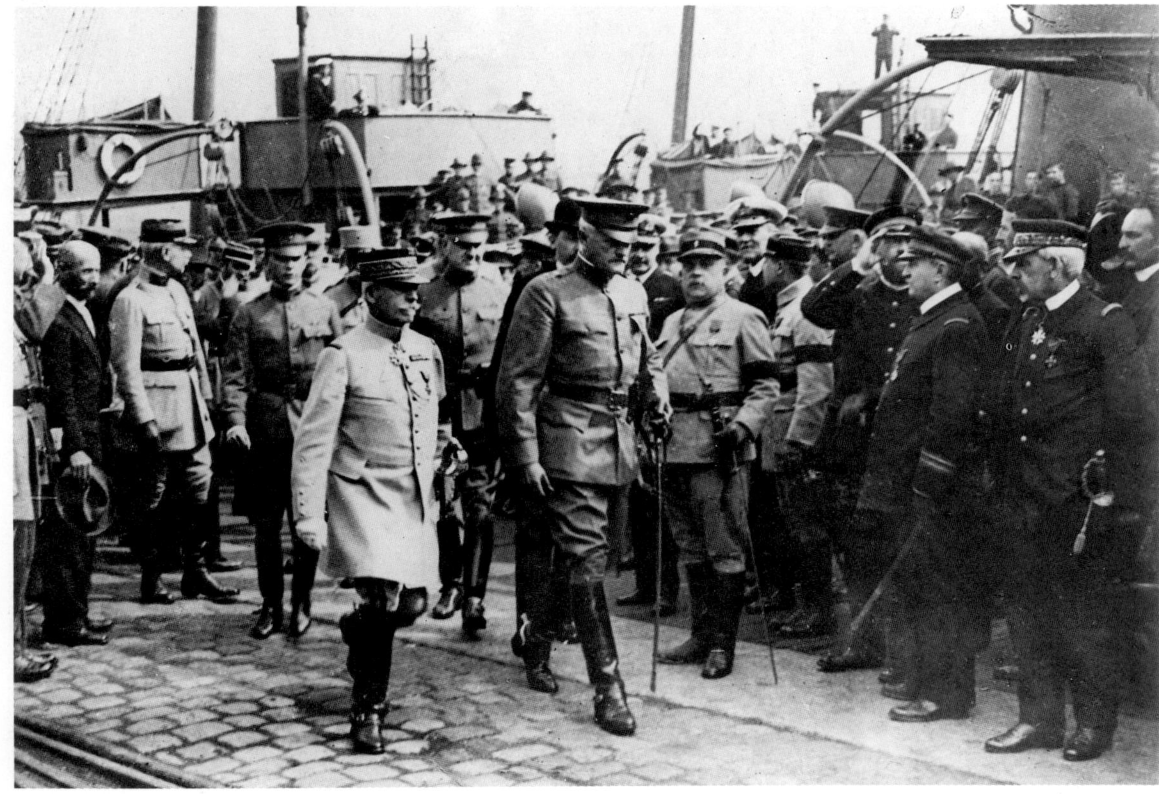

General John Pershing, commander of the American Expeditionary Force lands in France in June 1917. He held this command until 11 November 1918.

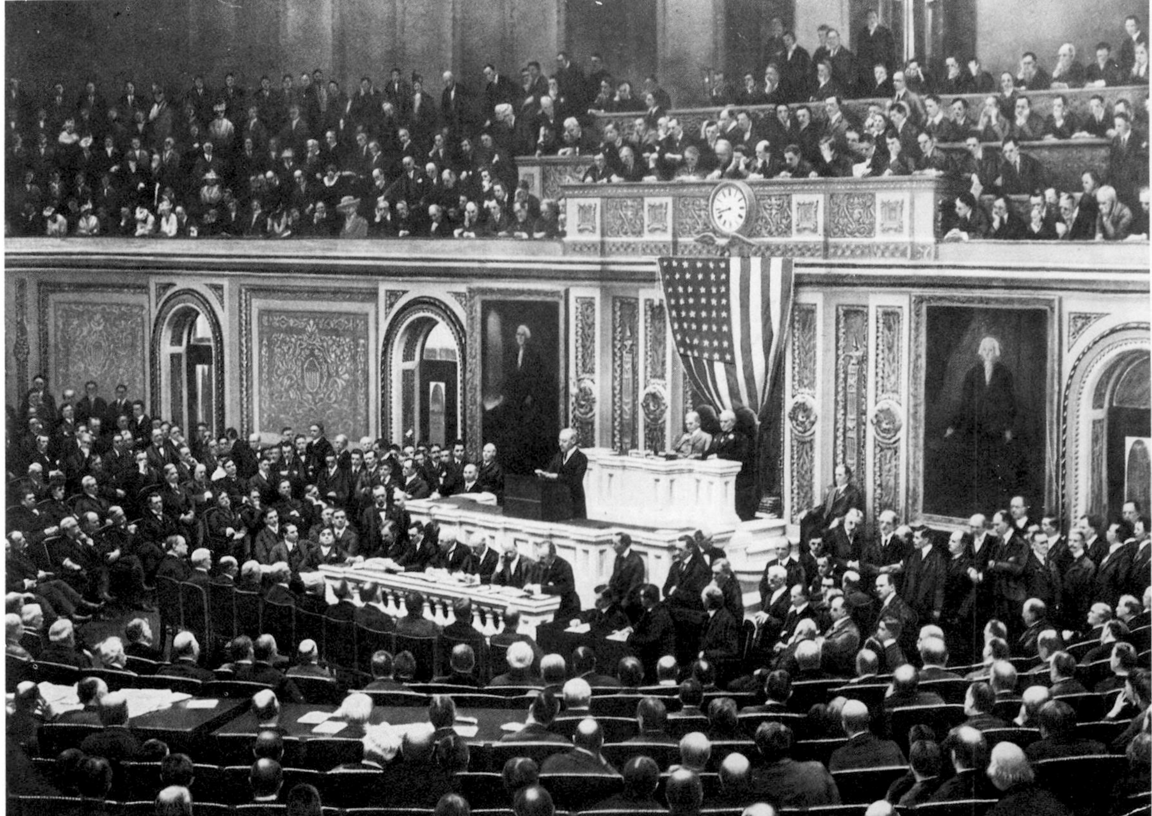

President Wilson asks a special session of Congress for a declaration of war on Germany on 2 April 1917. The resolution passed the Senate, 82-6, on 4 April, and the House, 373-50, on 6 April.

21 OCTOBER 1917

World War I: France Four battalions of the US 1st Division enter the front lines in the Sommerviller sector, east of Nancy. They are under the direct command of French officers.

27 OCTOBER 1917

World War I: First Combat Soldiers of the 1st Division wound and capture their first German soldier, a mail orderly named Leonard Hoffman. Hoffman later dies of his wounds.

3 NOVEMBER 1917

World War I: First Casualties German troopers launch a trench raid against a company of the 1st Division in front of Bathelémont, resulting in the first American ground combat casualties of the war. Eleven Americans are captured, and Corporal James Gresham and Privates Thomas Enright and Merle Hay are killed.

7 NOVEMBER 1917

Russia: Revolution Since the abdication of Czar Nicolas II in March 1917 Russia has been ruled by a liberal parliamentary regime. This government, headed by Alexandr Kerensky, has continued to wage war against Germany and Austria. The continuing war, however, has undermined support for the government, and on this day it is overthrown by the Bolshevik faction of the Russian Social Democratic Party, led by Nicolai Lenin. The Bolsheviks make contact with Germany and indicate their desire to end Russia's participation in the war.

20 NOVEMBER-7 DECEMBER 1917

World War I: Cambrai At the Battle of Cambrai the United States 11th Regiment of Engineers is caught up in the British retreat and takes part in the fighting around the Gouzeaucourt railway yards. Six Americans are killed, 13 are wounded and 11 are taken prisoner.

6 DECEMBER 1917

World War I: Naval In the worst American naval loss of the war the destroyer *Jacob Jones* is struck by a torpedo from a German submarine off the southeast coast of England. The ship sinks in eight minutes, with a more than 50 percent loss: 64 officers and men out of a crew of 110.

8 JANUARY 1918

World War I: Fourteen Points In a speech before Congress, President Wilson sets out his 'Fourteen Points' for world peace. Most of them are specific to borders, national sovereignty, reparations, and war-related issues. The final point asks for 'a general association of nations . . . under specific covenants for the purpose of affording mutual guarantees of political independence and territorial integrity to great and small states alike.' The concept evolves into what will become the League of Nations.

3 MARCH 1918

World War I: Russia The Treaty of Brest-Litovsk officially ends hostilities between Russia and the Central Powers. Germany is rapidly shifting its military forces to the Western Front.

21 MARCH 1918

World War I: German Preparations Freed from the Eastern Front, the German Army determines to make a final assault on the Allies on the Western Front before American reinforcements become overwhelming. With 207 divisions, against the Allies' 173, the Germans launch a major offensive in an attempt to split the British and French forces along the Western Front.

28 MARCH 1918

World War I: German Offensive German attacks along the Western Front have driven back the British Fifth Army more than 30 miles during the past six days. The American Expeditionary Force has only six divisions in France at this time, with only the 1st and 2nd Divisions in the lines. On this day General Pershing offers French generals Ferdinand Foch and Henri Philippe Pétain any American division that can be of service.

3 APRIL 1918

World War I: German Offensive In the Ansauville sector, just southeast of the St. Mihiel salient, the 26th Division relieves the 1st Division. During the past three months at the front the 1st has suffered 549 casualties, mostly through trench raids and gas attacks.

12 APRIL 1918

World War I: German Offensive The 104th Infantry Regiment of the 26th Division repulses a German attack at Seicheprey, near St. Mihiel. The unit is awarded the *Croix de Guerre* by the French – the first American unit to be so decorated.

14 APRIL 1918

World War I: Command General Ferdinand Foch is made supreme commander of Allied forces, including the Americans. With General Pershing he makes a special plea to President Wilson to get more troops over to Europe quickly.

20 APRIL 1918

World War I: German Offensive In the Ansauville sector an estimated 2800 Germans attack two advance companies of the 102nd Infantry of the 26th Division in front of Seicheprey. Both companies are overrun. German troops capture the forward defensive position and move into the town itself. The Germans then withdraw during the night. The 669 reported casualties include 81 Americans killed and 187 captured or missing.

29 APRIL 1918

World War I: Air War American Army Air Corps pilot Lieutenant 'Eddie' Rickenbacker downs his first German plane. Rickenbacker will total 26 'kills' before the end of the war, more than any other American. The Army will eventually award Rickenbacker the Medal of Honor in 1931.

MAY 1918

Russia: Revolution Almost complete anarchy reigns in Russia as the Allies turn against the Bolsheviks. They feel betrayed by the Bolshevik withdrawal from the war and point out that they gave quantities of arms and other supplies to the Czar's government, which they do not want used by the Bolsheviks. The Allies detest the Bolshevik regime, which has claimed its goal as the overthrow of all established 'bourgeois' states. Before the summer is over the Allies will land thousands of troops on Russian soil.

27-30 MAY 1918

World War I: German Offensive In their third great offensive of 1918 the German Army sweeps across the Aisne River, pushing back French forces more than 20 miles in three days.

28 MAY 1918

World War I: Cantigny In their first independent action of the war units of the US 1st Division attack the German-held town of Cantigny in northern France. The village, which commands the surrounding hills, is captured by American troops supported by French tanks.

29-30 MAY 1918

World War I: Cantigny The 1st Division continues to fight off German counterattacks at Cantigny. Over the past few days the Division reports 1067 casualties, including 200 men killed.

31 MAY 1918

World War I: Château-Thierry The German offensive pushes French forces across the Marne River. Following a 110-mile, 22-hour journey, two companies of the Seventh Machine Gun Battalion, 3rd Division, take up defensive positions south of the Marne guarding the bridges at Château-Thierry.

1 JUNE 1918

World War I: Château-Thierry The guns of the Seventh Machine Gun Battalion assist French forces in defending two bridges across the Marne at Château-Thierry. The American troops lose five killed and 32 wounded. German forces seize key hill positions to the west, capture Vaux and are astride the road leading to Paris. The US 2nd Division begins to deploy west of Château-Thierry, with the 9th Infantry moving into position south of the Paris Road at Le Thiolet and facing Vaux. The 6th Marine Regiment establishes a line through Clerembaut's Woods north of the Paris Road stretching almost to Belleau Wood.

2 JUNE 1918

World War I: Belleau Wood The line of the 2nd Division is extended northward by the 23rd Infantry, 5th Marines and 2nd Engineers. As retreating French troops pass through the lines of the 2nd Division, a German attack on the left flank of the division northwest of Champillon is met and broken by the Marines.

4 JUNE 1918

World War I: Belleau Wood Command of the front before the 2nd Division formally passes from French to American control. The Marine brigade moving into position to attack suffers more than 200 casualties from artillery fire alone.

The greatest American ace of World War I would be Captain Eddie Rickenbacker (26 victories), shown here with his Hat-in-the-Ring-Squadron Spad 13.

6 JUNE 1918

World War I: Belleau Wood On the extreme left of the 2nd Division the 1st Battalion of the 5th Marines, along with French forces launch an attack on key hill positions. This objective is taken in the first assault, bringing the American left in front of Belleau Wood along its west border. Late in the afternoon the 3rd Battalion of the Sixth Marines attacks the southern face of the woods, while the 3rd Battalion of the Fifth Marines moves against the western edge of the woods. The Marines to the west are forced to cross 400 yards of open wheat fields and never reach the woods themselves; they suffer tremendous casualties. The Marines on the southern flank, with better cover, are able to gain the woods. Here the scene is one of close-in fighting and assaults against German machine gun positions. Gunnery Sergeant Charles Hoffmann will be awarded the Medal of Honor for destroying five machine gun nests. Marine forces also move into the village of Bouresches, southeast of Belleau Wood. The Marine brigade participating in these actions loses 1087 casualties. This is the most suffered by the Marines on a single day during the entire war.

7 JUNE 1918

World War I: Belleau Wood Marine units are unable to penetrate further into Belleau Wood. The terrain is dominated by well-placed German machine guns. The Marines withdraw to the southern edge of the woods to allow artillery to fire on German positions.

11 JUNE 1918

World War I: Belleau Wood The attack by US Marines in Belleau Wood is renewed. The attack advances beyond the center of the woods but is forced to halt there.

18 JUNE 1918

World War I: Belleau Wood The 7th Infantry of the 3rd Division replaces the Marines in Belleau Wood. Attacks by the 7th will be repulsed by the Germans on June 18 and 21.

23 JUNE 1918

World War I: Belleau Wood Marine units return to Belleau Wood.

25 JUNE 1918

World War I: Belleau Wood The Marines finally clear Belleau Wood of German troops and capture 500 prisoners. The Marine brigade has suffered 5200 casualties, including more than 750 killed. The rest of the 2nd Division suffers 3200 casualties.

Marines of the 4th Brigade in hand-to-hand combat in Belleau Wood. American success in this battle (1 June-6 July 1918) helped Pershing to keep the command of the AEF from passing to the French.

German troops running through barbed wire near the Aisne River. Some 270,000 US troops took part in Foch's Aisne-Marne Offensive of July-August 1918.

26 JUNE 1918

World War I: Belleau Wood Major Maurice Shearer, commander of the Third Battalion of the 5th Marine Regiment, reports: 'Woods now US Marine Corps entirely.'

JULY 1918

World War I: US Deployment A total of 306,350 American soldiers will arrive in French and English ports during this month alone – more than any other single month of the war.

1 JULY 1918

World War I: Vaux The 9th and 23rd Infantry of the 2nd Division attack the village of Vaux, recently captured by the Germans. This successful attack ends the activities of the 2nd Division along the Paris Road. The Division has suffered 9777 casualties of whom 1811 are listed as killed.

4 JULY 1918

World War I: US Deployment There is a public announcement that there are now 1 million American soldiers in France. The American I Army Corps is formed, consisting of the 3rd and 2nd Divisions, plus the 26th, 28th, 4th, 32nd and 42nd Divisions. These units are responsible for the front between Belleau Wood and the Marne. In other action the Australian Corps, with the support of four companies of the US 33rd Division, makes a successful attack on the Vaire Woods and Hamel on the Somme River, east of Amiens. There are 134 American casualties.

15 JULY 1918

World War I: German Offensive Following a devastating artillery barrage German forces cross the Marne east of Château-Thierry. Positioned between French forces south of the river is the US 3rd Division and, to their east, four companies of the newly-arrived 28th Division. These four companies are quickly overrun and almost all are killed or captured by the German wave. Other supporting companies of the 28th are forced to fight their way south to a new defensive position. As French resistance begins to break down the 109th Infantry forms the main line of resistance on a wooded ridge south of the river. Meanwhile, the 3rd Division puts up a stubborn resistance to the German attack. Although American forward positions are taken, isolated pockets of resistance and counterattacks continue. The 38th Infantry on the right of the 3rd Division holds the key position on the riverbank before the Surmelin Valley, through which the main German assault south of Marne would have to develop. The French on the right and the 30th Infantry to the left are forced to give way, exposing the 38th to attack from three sides in an ever-deepening salient. Yet this regiment is able to hold the main line of resistance along the forward slopes of the hills, and it is here that the German attack falters. By mid-afternoon the German advance is stopped everywhere along the front of the 3rd Division. The Allies will counterattack the following day, and German troops will be forced back across the Marne on July 20. The 38th Infantry Regiment will become known as the 'Rock of the Marne.'

17 JULY 1918

Russia: Allied Intervention Under intense pressure from Britain and France, President Wilson agrees to dispatch a contingent of American troops to Murmansk and Archangel in northern Russia in order to guard Allied military supplies that have accumulated there.

18 JULY 1918

World War I: Aisne-Marne Offensive The Allied counterattack to the latest German offensive begins. The French XX Corps, consisting of the French 1st Moroccan Division and flanked by the US 1st Division on its left and the 2nd Division on its right, attacks the western edge of the extended German salient between the Aisne and the Marne rivers. Their objective is the key supply center of Soissons. In a stunning surprise attack the 1st Division advances four miles and captures 1500 prisoners and 30 guns. The 2nd Division also advances well into the German position and takes Vierzy. At the apex of the salient several battalions of the US 4th Division are attached to the left of the French Sixth Army and join in attacking German forces near Belleau Wood. To their right the 26th Division moves into the base of the Marne salient.

19 JULY 1918

World War I: Aisne-Marne Offensive Further advances are made into the Aisne-Marne salient. The 6th Marines of the 2nd Division drive deeper into the German lines, along with the 1st Division and the Moroccan Division. The 2nd Division is relieved during the night by the 56th French. The 2nd has moved six miles in two days, taking 3000 Germans prisoner and capturing 66 guns at a cost of 4000 casualties. Other units make small gains.

20 JULY 1918

World War I: Aisne-Marne Offensive The 1st Division is ordered forward to capture the small town of Berzy-le-Sec. One brigade advances on the town, while the other brigade moves into the Chazelle ravine and on to the heights of Buzancy. The American troops are unable to take Berzy-le-Sec. To the south the 4th and 26th Divisions continue to push across the Marne River. The 4th Division is relieved in the evening. In its first battle the 4th has lost 397 killed and 1869 wounded.

21 JULY 1918

World War I: Aisne-Marne Offensive The First Brigade of the 1st Division takes the heights southwest of Buzancy. The Second Brigade, despite heavy losses and under a steady fire, seize the heights and hold their position on the crest east of Berzy-le-Sec. The Division will be relieved on the following day after having driven into the most sensitive point of the Aisne-Marne salient south of Soissons. In four days of fighting the 1st Division has sustained 7317 casualties. The 3rd Division begins to cross the Marne, east of Château-Thierry, to the right of the 26th Division. As combined American and French forces close in on Château-Thierry the 26th Division crosses the main Château-Thierry-Soissons highway. The 3rd Division begins to expand its bridgehead north of the Marne as French troops capture Château-Thierry.

22 JULY 1918

World War I: Aisne-Marne Offensive The German Army decides to abandon the entire Aisne-Marne salient and retreat 30 miles. The Germans, however, are determined to buy time in order to evacuate their heavy guns and other supplies. The 26th Division takes heavy casualties in capturing the villages of Epieds and Trugny that are centers of German resistance. A fierce counterattack drives the American troops from the two villages, and by the end of the day the 26th is in its original position along its entire front. At the same time, the 3rd Division advances up the slopes on the north bank of the Marne and take Jaulgonne in the center. The 1st Battalion of the 38th Infantry reaches Le Charmel, on the right, but is forced to abandon the town due to lack of support.

The US used horse-mounted cavalry in battle as late as 12 October 1918. The cavalry of other nations, like these crested French dragoons, had already learned the folly of trying to use war horses in a conflict dominated by the machine gun.

23 JULY 1918

World War I: Aisne-Marne Offensive The 3rd and 26th Divisions continue to press the attack against a stubborn German holding-action. Having held the Allied army for the necessary 48 hours in order to cover their retreat, the Germans withdraw from their Epieds defensive line. The 56th Brigade of the 28th Division replaces the 52nd Brigade of the 26th in the line.

24 JULY 1918

World War I: Aisne-Marne Offensive Two brigades from the 26th and 28th Divisions make a rapid advance to the northeast in pursuit of retreating German forces from the Marne salient. To the right the 3rd Division advances on a crest of hills north of the Marne and reach the outskirts of Le Charmel.

25 JULY 1918

World War I: Aisne-Marne Offensive The US 3rd Division captures Le Charmel. The 28th, 42nd and 32nd Divisions parade through Château-Thierry and move into position to support the Allied advance. This night the 42nd takes over the entire American I Corps front, relieving the brigades from the 26th and 28th Divisions, plus the French 167th.

26 JULY 1918

World War I: Aisne-Marne Offensive As the 42nd and 3rd Divisions attempt to renew the advance German resistance stiffens once again. The 42nd is held up at a German strong point centered on La Croix Rouge Farm. The 167th and 168th Infantry attempt to advance on the farm across an open clearing of more than a mile. Although faced with flanking fire from the adjacent woods, the two regiments are able to capture the farm by nightfall at the cost of hundreds of casualties.

27 JULY 1918

World War I: Aisne-Marne Offensive As German forces once again retreat to a line behind the Ourcq River the 42nd and 3rd Divisions are joined by the 28th, which occupies the center.

28 JULY 1918

World War I: Aisne-Marne Offensive The 42nd, 28th and 3rd Divisions attempt to move against German positions on the heights overlooking the Ourcq from the north. The German Army command is determined to hold this line for a few more days to allow a further withdrawal. The general direction of the American attack is to the northeast. Despite heavy German artillery and machine gun fire the 3rd Division is able to capture the town of Roncheres. The 28th Division also crosses the Ourcq but is forced back across by the end of the day, with heavy losses. Meanwhile, the 42nd, with the support of French troops on its left, carries the main burden of the attack. The 42nd crosses the Ourcq at several points but is unable to gain the crests of the strategic hills north of the river and is forced to cling to the lower slopes of the north bank. German forces counterattack, driving a wedge between two regiments of the 42nd. The American troops drive into the town of Sergy late in the afternoon, only to be forced out twice. By the end of the day, despite suffering thousands of casualties, no key German positions on the heights are captured.

29 JULY 1918

World War I: Aisne-Marne Offensive The attack along the Ourcq is renewed. The 28th Division crosses the river but is forced back for the second consecutive day. A second attack is made at midmorning, but a fierce flanking fire forces the American troops back down the slopes. A third assault is launched late in the afternoon with the support of the 3rd Division. An attempt to capture a German stronghold at Grimpettes Woods is unsuccessful, and the 28th and 3rd Divisions are once again forced to withdraw to the river bottom. Meanwhile, two attack battalions of the 4th Division reinforce the American position around Sergy, with one battalion capturing the town. During the evening the 32nd Division replaces the 3rd.

30 JULY 1918

World War I: Aisne-Marne Offensive Three divisions (42nd, 28th and 32nd), along with two battalions from the 4th, move forward in a general assault along the Ourcq River. The Germans halt the attack on the American left. There is heavy fighting around Seringes. The main German line northwest of Sergy is pierced in the center by units of the 42nd and the two battalions from the 4th. However, these troops are forced to retreat to cover their flanks. A German counterattack forces the Americans back through Sergy, but the Americans are able to reorganize and capture the village again. On the right the 28th and 32nd Divisions break through the Hill 188-Grimpettes Woods line by seizing the hill and driving deep into the woods. The 28th continues to press forward in the afternoon, clearing out the entire woods down to Cierges. The 32nd moves in from the east, leaving American units in complete control of the woods. This is the most important piece of ground gained along the Ourcq and represents a definite breach of the main German defensive line. The Germans counterattack once again, but the Americans cling to their position during a nighttime bayonet encounter.

31 JULY 1918

World War I: Aisne-Marne Offensive For the fourth consecutive day the 42nd Division attacks in the hills north of the Ourcq but makes no progress. The 32nd replaces the 28th on the American right and launches a successful assault on Cierges. The 32nd then moves into position to attack two key hills that dominate the entire front above Cierges.

1 AUGUST 1918

World War I: Aisne-Marne Offensive The 32nd Division seizes the strategic hills above Cierges that are the key to the entire German defensive position along the Ourcq. During the night the German forces give up this defensive line and retreat north to the Vesle River.

2 AUGUST 1918

World War I: Aisne-Marne Offensive The 42nd Division is removed from the front lines north of the Ourcq. Over the past eight days the Division has suffered 5500 casualties.

2-3 AUGUST 1918

World War I: Aisne-Marne Offensive The French Sixth Army, including two American Army Corps, pursue the retreating German Army north of the Ourcq. The 32nd Division leads III Corps, and the 4th Division guides I Corps.

3 AUGUST 1918

Russia: Allied Intervention The first Allied troops land at Archangel, the Russian port on the White Sea, following landings at Murmansk to the north during July. Included in the Allied force are three battalions of the 339th Infantry Regiment, plus supporting units, under the command of Lieutenant Colonel George Stewart. A total of almost 5000 American troops will see duty in northern Russia. On the same day, the first British troops land at Vladivostok, on Russia's Far East coast.

4 AUGUST 1918

World War I: Aisne-Marne Offensive The 4th Division captures several villages on the south bank of the Vesle and attempts to move across the river. The 32nd assaults the town of Fismes, moves into the city, and is driven out by a German counterattack. A second attack captures most of the city.

5 AUGUST 1918

World War I: Aisne-Marne Offensive American forces attempt to cross the Vesle. Although the river is only 15 yards wide it is too swift and deep to ford. Only a few patrols are successful. The 32nd Division continues to consolidate its position in the city of Fismes. During the night the 28th Division relieves the 32nd, while the 6th Brigade of the 3rd moves into the sector immediately to the right of the 28th.

6 AUGUST 1918

World War I: Aisne-Marne Offensive The entire 4th Division moves to attack across the Vesle, but only the 1st Battalion of the 58th Infantry manages to get across. The battalion attacks German positions along a railroad embankment several hundred yards from and parallel to the river. The battalion then reforms and moves on to the heights, where it faces flanking fire from villages on two sides. Confined to the lower slopes along the Soissons-Reims highway, the battalion digs in.

7 AUGUST 1918

World War I: Aisne-Marne Offensive The 47th Infantry of the 4th Division attempts to move across the Vesle and reinforce the American advance. Attempts to construct bridges prove futile in the face of concentrated German shell and machine gun fire. About 350 men do succeed in crossing to the left of the 58th Infantry. They pass the railroad embankment and reach the highway. However, flanking fire from the village of Bazoches to the left forces a retreat back to the railroad embankment. By nightfall, the 4th Division can only count less than 1000 men across the river in two isolated groups in exposed forward positions. To the right, attempts by the 28th Division and a brigade from the 3rd to cross the Vesle on both sides of Fismes fails.

8 AUGUST 1918

World War I: Aisne-Marne Offensive The 28th Division establishes a toehold on the north bank of the Vesle and moves into the small village of Fismette.

Marines man a French Hotchkiss machine gun against German air attack. The war demonstrated that the machine gun was a poor antiaircraft weapon.

9 AUGUST 1918

World War I: Aisne-Marne Offensive The 4th Division once again attempts to cross the Vesle. American troops move into Bazoches, battling German forces located there. The Germans withdraw and call in an air attack on American infantry in the village. The Americans are forced to retreat, and German soldiers move back in. The line of the 4th is consolidated along the railroad embankment. Meanwhile, the 131st Regiment of the 33rd Division, in support of British forces to the north, attacks a German stronghold at Gressaire Wood, east of Amiens along the Somme River. This action is part of a general British offensive in the area. After heavy fighting, the regiment successfully takes the position that had threatened the flank of the British advance. During the next ten days the American regiment will continue to participate in the offensive while losing 78 killed and 677 wounded.

10 AUGUST 1918

World War I: US Deployment The first independent American army, the First Army, with General John Pershing in command, is officially formed. The headquarters of the army is moved to Neufchâteau to prepare for the attack on the St. Mihiel salient, southeast of Verdun.

10-13 AUGUST 1918

World War I: Aisne-Marne Offensive With a military stalemate on the Vesle front, the 77th Division relieves the 4th. The division suffers more than 1000 casualties moving into position and organizing its front due to German shellfire. The American III Corps assumes responsibility for the entire front.

15 AUGUST 1918

International The United States and the Bolshevik government of the Soviet Union break diplomatic relations.

16 AUGUST 1918

Russia: Allied Intervention The 27th Infantry Regiment from Manila, lead unit of the American Expeditionary Force to Siberia, lands at Vladivostok. It will be followed by the 31st Infantry on August 22, plus other supporting units. Under the command of Major General William Graves, the American troops in Siberia will number more than 10,000 men. These troops will be spread out in detached companies to guard rail lines, mines, warehouses and other strategic points along the Tran-Siberian Railway.

27 AUGUST 1918

World War I: Aisne-Marne Offensive An attack by the French Tenth Army, north of Soissons, puts pressure on the German defensive line on the Vesle. American troops move into Bazoches but are driven out with losses of 133 men killed or missing. A battalion of the 77th Division attempts to storm a knoll known as Château Diable – a German center of resistance – but is driven back with more than 100 casualties. In the center of the American position the Germans counterattack at Fismette. The Americans

The US 27th Infantry Regiment, part of the anti-Bolshevik Allied forces sent to Russia, parades down a street in Vladivostok on 16 August 1918.

are forced back to the riverbank itself, and under covering fire from two companies they are forced back to Fismes. Out of the two companies only about 30 Americans escape, with the rest being either killed or captured. At the end of the day, German forces still hold the three local strong points of Bazoches, Château Diable and Fismette. During the night the 32nd Division is pulled out of the front lines at the Vesle and is attached to the French Tenth Army northwest of Soissons.

30 AUGUST 1918

World War I: Aisne-Marne Offensive The 32nd Division attacks and captures the town of Juvigny. Further south, the American First Army, with a total of 15 divisions, is given control of the St. Mihiel front.

31 AUGUST 1918

World War I: Aisne-Marne Offensive The 32nd Division pushes east from Juvigny, across a series of ravines on the north bank of the Aisne River. Another 555 German soldiers are captured.

2 SEPTEMBER 1918

World War I: Allied Strategy General Pershing confers with Marshall Foch and General Pétain, who agree to Pershing's insistence that the American First Army remain intact. A plan for the remainder of 1918 is agreed upon. The British are to attack in the direction of Cambrai; the French are to drive across the Aisne on both sides of Reims; and the American Army is to attack between the Argonne Forest and the Meuse River.

3 SEPTEMBER 1918

World War I: Aisne-Marne Offensive The German Army is forced to retreat from the Vesle River by the advance of the French Tenth Army to the west.

4 SEPTEMBER 1918

World War I: Aisne-Marne Offensive American troops move into the former German defensive positions north of the Vesle. They cross the heights and begin to move north and northeast toward the Aisne River over the next two weeks. The 28th and 77th Divisions are withdrawn for the Meuse-Argonne offensive.

12 SEPTEMBER 1918

World War I: St. Mihiel Offensive The German Army has held a 200-square-mile salient of French territory, with an apex anchored at St. Mihiel, since their opening offensive of 1914. General Pershing has gathered more than 550,000 American, plus an additional 110,000 French troops, to reduce the salient and protect the American right flank for the Meuse-Argonne offensive. In a pre-dawn attack the US 1st, 42nd, 5th, 2nd, 89th and 90th Divisions assault the south face of the salient. The French II Corps places pressure on the apex at St. Mihiel, while the 26th and 4th Divisions move against the western face of the German position. On the first day a large advance is made from both the south and west. During the night the 26th and 1st Divisions are ordered to push forward to cut off retreating German troops. In this, however, they will be largely unsuccessful.

13 SEPTEMBER 1918

World War I: St. Mihiel Offensive In the early morning lead units of the 26th Division reach the town of Vigneulles in the center of the salient. They are joined a few hours later by the 1st Division, thereby splitting the St. Mihiel salient in half. German forces move quickly to evacuate the northern half of the salient. American forces continue to advance, eliminating the entire salient by nightfall and completely straightening out the German lines in the area. The American Army captures nearly 16,000 prisoners and 443 guns, at a cost of more than 7000 casualties in the initial phase of the operation and an additional 7000 in mopping up operations.

14 SEPTEMBER 1918

World War I: US Deployment The American Army begins to move north to the Meuse-Argonne front.

21 SEPTEMBER 1918

World War I: US Deployment The American II Corps, consisting of the US 27th and 30th Divisions, is transferred to the British Fourth Army. It is to form the spearpoint for an assault on the German Hindenburg line in front of the Cambrai-St. Quentin tunnel, near the village of Bellicourt in northern France.

26 SEPTEMBER 1918

World War I: Meuse-Argonne Offensive All the Allied armies are flung against the German lines in a simultaneous series of offensives. The American First Army is selected to attack the center hinge of the Hindenburg line north of Verdun between the Meuse River to the east and the Argonne Forest to the west. Three army corps are concentrated for the assault, with 2700 guns, 189 tanks and 821 airplanes. To attack from west to east is the 77th Division, moving into the Argonne Forest, along with the 28th, 35th, 91st, 37th, 79th and 4th, with the 80th and 33rd assigned to guard the flanks along the Meuse. Following a tremendous artillery barrage, the greatest American attack of the war unfolds. Nine American divisions overrun the advance German positions, driving northward along a 24-mile front. There is slower going on the left through the dense Argonne Forest, but a significant advance is made in the center. The 4th Division makes the furthest gains east of the heights of Montfaucon, actually breaking through the second German defense line.

27 SEPTEMBER 1918

World War I: Cambrai-St. Quentin Offensive Preliminary to the main assault on the Hindenburg line along the Cambrai-St. Quentin tunnel, the 106th Infantry of the 27th Division attacks German outposts 1700 yards before the main German position. The regiment, stretched too thin along a 4000 yard front, fails to carry the key German strong points known as the Knoll, Guillemont Farm and Quennemont Farm.

World War I: Meuse-Argonne Offensive On the second day of the Meuse-Argonne offensive German resistance is much stronger. American infantry has outpaced artillery support and faces bitter machine gun defense. It is also extremely difficult to move forward supplies across a battlefield destroyed by four years of fighting. The second German defensive line is broken at a dozen places along the heights of Montfaucon. The 77th Division and the left of the 28th remain tangled in the Argonne Forest.

28 SEPTEMBER 1918

World War I: Cambrai-St. Quentin Offensive The American II Corps, with the 27th Division on the left and the 30th on the right, attempt to move into position to assault the Cambrai-St. Quentin tunnel line. The 30th reaches its jump-off point due to Australian troops having cleared out the outpost system on its front. However, the attempt by the 27th to move into position encounters a determined German resistance that develops into a night battle. By morning the 27th Division is still more than 1000 yards short of its assigned position.

World War I: Meuse-Argonne Offensive The Germans are completely forced out from their second main defensive position. American units seize Aprémont, Épinonville, Nantillois and several other strong points. However, ahead lies the strongest German line of defense, running just north of the Argonne Forest and the heights of the Meuse. This

defensive line is anchored on Cunel, Romagne and Landres Saint-George. The entire position is known as the Kriemhilde Stellung. As American forces move up the valley before an ever-increasing series of heights they are taking fire from three sides: from the heights on the main position ahead, from the cliffs at the outer edge of the Argonne on the left and from the heights of the Meuse on the opposite bank to the right.

29 SEPTEMBER 1918

World War I: Cambrai-St. Quentin Offensive The British Fourth Army, led by two American divisions, attack the German defenses anchored on the Cambrai-St. Quentin tunnel and canal system. Supported by the British IX Corps on their right, which crosses the open canal, the 30th Division attacks the southern half of the almost five-mile-long tunnel. That line is quickly overrun, along with the village of Bellicourt and, beyond that, Nauroy. Meanwhile, the attack battalions of the 27th Division still must contend with a well-defended outpost system. Hand-to-hand fighting erupts at the German strong points at the Knoll, Guillemont Farm and Quennemont Farm. Lead units reach the main German defensive ridge about noon, but thousands of German troops emerge from the tunnel and hidden dugouts, reducing the entire front to complete anarchy. The 3rd Australian Division moves up in support of the Americans, but it will take two more days of fighting to secure the front. In this action the 27th Division suffers 4642 casualties, the 30th 3136.

World War I: Meuse-Argonne Offensive The order is given to attack again. Six Americans divisions in the center encounter strong resistance and face a series of German counterattacks. After some small gains every division is forced to withdraw to cover their flanks or find better cover.

30 SEPTEMBER 1918

World War I: Meuse-Argonne Offensive A halt is called to the Meuse-Argonne offensive. After four days of battle the maximum American advance is only eight miles. Preparations are made for a renewed assault. Three veteran divisions, the 1st, 3rd and 32nd, are brought up, replacing the 35th, 37th and 79th. The 91st is also withdrawn. The American divisional front, from left to right, now consists of the 77th, 28th, 1st, 32nd, 3rd, 80th, 4th and 33rd.

1 OCTOBER 1918

World War I: French Southern Offensive The US 2nd Division relieves the French 61st Division following its attack toward Blanc Mont in Champagne area near Reims. The French have driven the Germans back several miles but have been unable to carry the main German position known as the Essen Trench. Prior to a general assault the 2nd Division will spend the next 24 hours clearing German outposts away from its jump-off line.

2 OCTOBER 1918

World War I: Meuse-Argonne Offensive The First Battalion of the 308th Regiment, 77th Division, is cut off from American lines deep in the Argonne Forest. This unit becomes popularly known as the 'Lost Battalion' and is not relieved until October 7, following a general advance along the entire front. During the next few days the battalion fights off numerous attacks while refusing to surrender. Of the 600 men in the unit only 194 will march out of the forest. Its commander, Major Charles W. Whittlesey, will be awarded the Medal of Honor for his actions, along with two other men from his unit.

3 OCTOBER 1918

World War I: French Southern Offensive The US 2nd Division assaults Blanc Mont. The two brigades of the division pass on either side of Vipers' Wood and converge north of the woods for the main assault up the slopes of the mountain. With the 6th Marines on the left and the 9th Infantry on the right, the manuever is executed perfectly, despite the flanking fire from the woods. The 5th Marine Regiment, on the left of the 6th, attacks a deadly hook in the German trenches known as the Essen Hook. In the afternoon the 5th Marines and 23rd Infantry move from support to lead the continuing attack. The 2nd Division's position on the mountain is strengthened, forcing a triangular salient in the very center of the main German defensive position.

4 OCTOBER 1918

World War I: Meuse-Argonne Offensive The attack is renewed. In the center the 32nd, 3rd and 80th Divisions are repulsed. The 4th Division, to their im-

Left: US troops used French tanks in the Argonne.

Below: A map of the Meuse-Argonne Offensive.

Opposite below: US infantry at St. Mihiel.

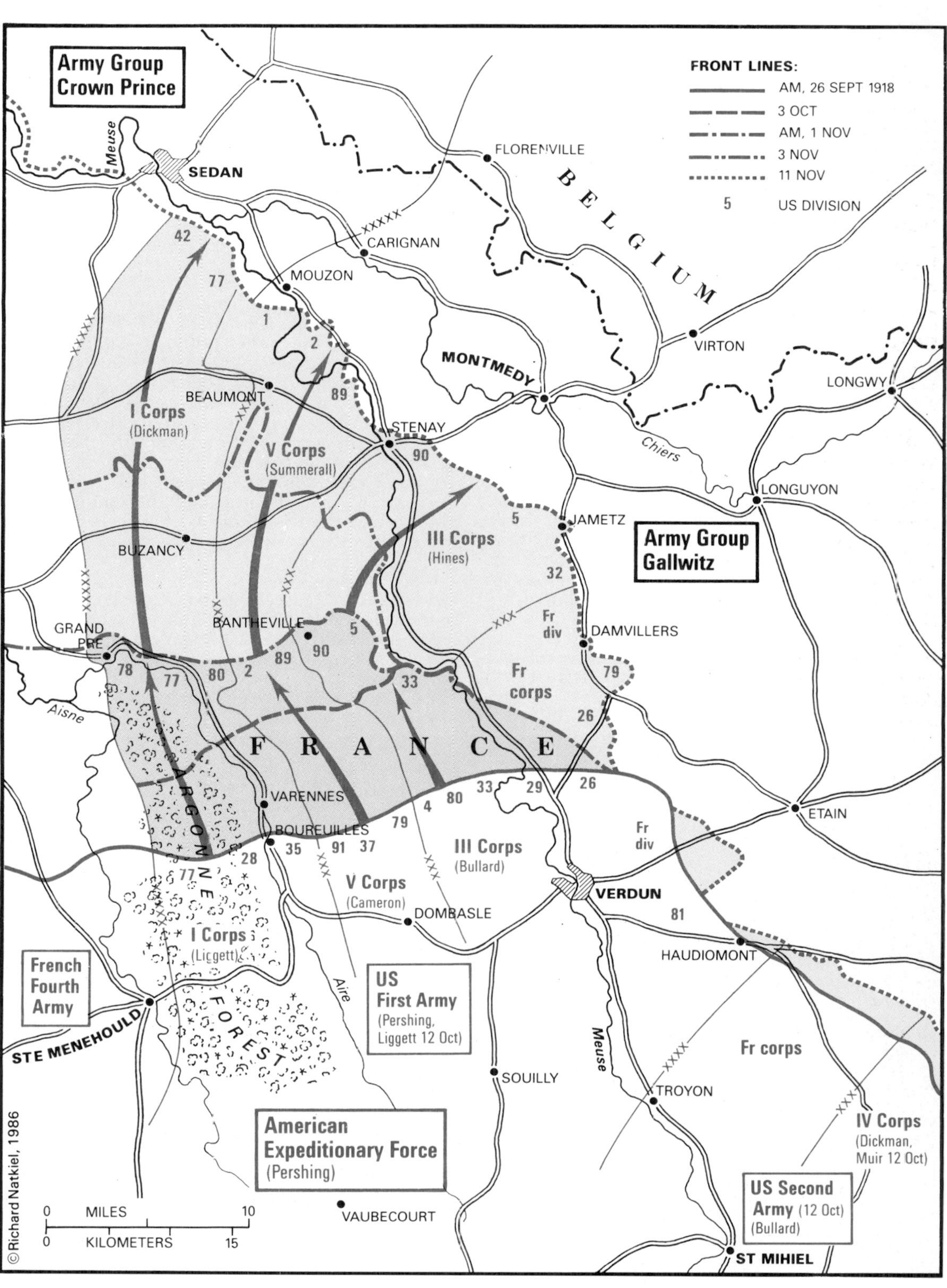

mediate right, makes some gains. On the extreme left the 77th and 28th remain entangled in the Argonne Forest. The 1st Division has the most success, as the 16th Infantry drives the Germans from Fléville and the 18th Infantry takes Exermont.

World War I: French Southern Offensive At Blanc Mont the 2nd Division fights off a German counterattack against its exposed salient. The 23rd Infantry attempts to advance but makes no gain. French forces on the left of the 2nd advance but are unable to drive the Germans off the western slopes. During the evening the 6th Marines secure the American left by linking up with the French to the southwest.

5 OCTOBER 1918

World War I: French Southern Offensive In an early morning attack the 6th Marines storm and capture the actual crest of Blanc Mont capturing its garrison of 209 soldiers. The entire ridge is now held by the 2nd Division. The 6th Marines press on and attack up the road toward Saint-Etienne in the afternoon. This further penetration of the German lines along the entire front allows French divisions on either side to advance.

World War I: Meuse-Argonne Offensive The attack continues, led by the 1st Division. The 32nd moves forward in support of the right flank of the 1st. To the right the 80th and 4th encounter German strong points in the well-fortified woods. The 77th continues to be mired in the Argonne. The heights of Romagne and Cunel remain in German hands.

6 OCTOBER 1918

World War I: French Southern Offensive After a day of sharp exchanges the 2nd Division is relieved by the 71st Brigade of the 36th. The 36th Division encounters heavy German fire masking a retreat to the Aisne River. German forces remain in possession of Saint-Etienne.

7 OCTOBER 1918

World War I: Armistice Negotiations President Wilson receives a request for an armistice from Germany and Austria. Wilson asks for clarifications as the Germans send more notes over the next few weeks. Finally, on October 23, Wilson feels satisfied that the Germans are accepting his terms and agrees to transmit their request to the Allies.

World War I: Meuse-Argonne Offensive The 82nd Division has been brought to the front during the previous evening and placed between the right of the 28th and the left of the 1st. The 82nd and the right of the 28th attack almost due west, storming the steep eastern ridge of the Argonne, while the 77th continues a frontal push northward through the forest. All three units make significant gains.

8 OCTOBER 1918

World War I: Meuse-Argonne Offensive The attack by the American First Army continues on the left against the ridges and cliffs on the eastern edge of the Argonne Forest. Involved are the 82nd Division, supported by the 28th and 77th from the south. These units undermine the German defensive position in the area sufficiently to cause the German Army to begin to withdraw from the forest. On the right of the First Army the American 33rd and 29th Divisions (along with a French Corps) push across the Meuse to eliminate the threat to that flank from the heights of the Meuse.

US infantrymen enter ruined Varennes on the first day (26 September 1918) of the great Meuse-Argonne Offensive, the largest US attack of the war.

World War I: Southern French Offensive The 71st Brigade of the 36th Division attempts to attack across the Saint-Etienne-Orfeuil road. Without adequate tank and artillery support, the movement of the brigade across the open fields in the face of machine gun fire is halted. One regiment manages to reach the outskirts of Saint-Etienne. In this action the 71st Brigade sustains almost 1400 casualties.

World War I: Meuse-Argonne Offensive In the Argonne Forest a small group of American soldiers is ambushed by a numerically superior German force. One soldier, Corporal Alvin York, singlehandedly shoots several German snipers and survives a machine gun barrage, followed by a bayonet assault by five German soldiers. York then forces the surrender of several dozen German troops. Behind enemy lines, and with only seven other American soldiers, York captures additional German positions, taking still more prisoners. Altogether York is credited with killing 25 German soldiers and capturing 132, while 'acting virtually alone.' He is also credited with putting 35 German machine guns out of action while armed with only a rifle and a pistol. For his actions York is promoted to sergeant. Marshall Foch awards York the *Croix de Guerre*, and the United States awards him the Distinguished Service Cross and, five months later, the Medal of Honor.

9 OCTOBER 1918

World War I: Meuse-Argonne Offensive Following successful attacks on both flanks an assault in the center is ordered. The 181st Brigade is brought up for additional firepower. The 1st and 32nd Divisions advance northward over hills and through woods. The 32nd actually reaches Romagne and pushes into the main German defensive position. However, a German counterattack forces a retreat from Romagne to a trench line south of the village. The 3rd and 80th Divisions make small advances in their approach to the Kriemhilde Stellung. An attack by the 4th is broken up by an artillery barrage. On the extreme left the 77th Division is in pursuit of the rapidly retreating Germans as they evacuate the Argonne Forest. The 28th Division is withdrawn.

10 OCTOBER 1918

World War I: Meuse-Argonne Offensive An attack is ordered all along the front of the American First Army. The 1st Division, to the left of the center, drives a wedge into the Romagne Forest between the Argonne and the Romagne heights. Small advances are made by the 3rd, 80th and 4th Divisions. On the left the 77th finally emerges from the Argonne after two weeks of fighting. The left flank of the First Army is finally level with the remainder of the front.

11 OCTOBER 1918

World War I: Meuse-Argonne Offensive The general offensive continues. On the left the 82nd Division fails to gain the north bank of the Aire River. The 32nd is thrown back from the Romagne Heights. The 3rd Division is forced to retreat several times before Cunel. However, on the right the 4th Division paces an advance driving a salient into the woods northeast of Cunel. This represents the first real penetration of the Kriemhilde line.

11-14 OCTOBER 1918

World War I: Meuse-Argonne Offensive The First Army consolidates its position and brings forward reinforcements. The 1st Division is replaced by the 42nd, and the 80th by the 5th. The 3rd Division moves to the right to take over the line held by the 4th. The 4th Division faces east to guard the right flank of the army.

12 OCTOBER 1918

World War I: Meuse-Argonne Offensive The growing size of the First Army forces a reorganization of American forces. The portion of the line east of the Meuse-Argonne battlefield is transferred to the newly-organized Second Army under the command of Lieutenant General Robert Bullard. On 16 October Lieutenant General Hunter Liggett is given command of the First Army. General Pershing becomes overall commander of the American field armies.

14 OCTOBER 1918

World War I: Meuse-Argonne Offensive The fourth major offensive by First Army begins in the Meuse-Argonne. On the left the 77th Division crosses the Aire, west of St. Juvin, capturing the village with the help of units of the 82nd. The 5th Division moves against the heights of Cunel and occupies a German strong point there. The 32nd Division closes in on

US machine gunners set up shop in a shell crater during the Meuse-Argonne fighting. US casualties in this offensive were 122,000, about 10 percent.

American doughboys of the 7th Division cheer the news that hostilities are to end at the eleventh hour, eleventh day, eleventh month of 1918.

Romagne from both flanks and the center, capturing the crest. The center of the German defensive line is now in possession of American troops.

15 OCTOBER 1918

World War I: Meuse-Argonne Offensive The Germans attempt to regain their positions by launching a series of counterattacks against the American 82nd and 42nd Divisions. The 32nd advances past Romagne through the Romagne Woods. Meanwhile, the 29th and 33rd Divisions continue to attack along the heights of the Meuse east of the river.

16-31 OCTOBER 1918

World War I: Meuse-Argonne Offensive Most of the First Army prepares to break the last German resistance along the Kriemhilde line and drive the German Army north toward Sedan. So far, the offensive between the Meuse and the Argonne has advanced 12 miles and captured 18,600 prisoners. The aim of the American Army is the decisive and final defeat of the German forces west of the Meuse and, thereafter, an immediate pursuit across the Meuse. During this period several American divisions push out of the woods north of Romagne and Cunel.

31 OCTOBER 1918

World War I: Meuse-Argonne Offensive Final preparations are made for the assault against Landres Saint Georges, the last German strongpoint on the Kriemhilde line. Beyond that lies one final German defensive line along Barricourt Ridge.
World War I: Flanders Offensive The 91st and 37th US Divisions report to the French Sixth Army in Flanders, at the extreme left of the Allied line in Belgium. In an early-morning attack led by the two American divisions the 37th captures a crest known as Cruyshaute Ridge and digs in. The 91st moves in and around the woods known as the Spitalls Bosschen, collapsing the southern half of the German line in the area. Both divisions will advance to the Scheldt River on the following day.

1 NOVEMBER 1918

World War I: Meuse-Argonne Offensive The offensive is renewed by seven American divisions. On the left the 77th and 78th Divisions are thrown back with heavy losses. On the right, however, the 89th and 90th make large gains. In the center the Marines and infantry of the 2nd Division move directly up the slopes against Landres Saint-Georges. Flanked by the 80th and 89th, the 2nd Division moves through Landreville and Chennery and seizes the heights of Barricourt, the highest ridge between the Argonne Forest and Meuse River. To the right of the 2nd the 89th turns to the northeast and advances through the Barricourt Woods. On the left the 90th Division also pivots to the northeast. In danger of being overrun in the center, German forces begin to withdraw from north of the Argonne Forest.

2 NOVEMBER 1918

World War I: Meuse-Argonne Offensive Due to the general German withdrawal before the American left flank, the 78th, 77th and 80th Divisions make an almost uncontested advance, seizing Buzancy. Other American units also advance.

2-4 NOVEMBER 1918

World War I: Flanders Offensive In the north at Audenarde attempts by the 37th and 91st Divisions to cross the Scheldt River prove unsuccessful. The American divisions are finally withdrawn in preparation for a renewed attack.

3 NOVEMBER 1918

World War I: Meuse-Argonne Offensive The German defensive line is completely destroyed by a series of attacks that prevent the German forces from establishing new defensive position. On the left the 78th, 77th and 80th Divisions continue to drive northward. On the right the 5th and 90th Divisions also advance, move east and gain the bank of the Meuse. In the center the 2nd Division pushes a salient of more than nine miles into the crumbling German defenses. The scene is now one of a general rout. German forces are retreating east to the Meuse as fast as possible and moving out of the entire area south of Sedan.

5 NOVEMBER 1918

World War I: Meuse-Argonne Offensive The entire line of hills east of the Meuse is captured by the 5th Division.

6 NOVEMBER 1918

World War I: Meuse-Argonne Offensive With the German Army line hopelessly broken, the American First Army gains the entire west bank of the Meuse almost as far north as Sedan. On this day the German government appeals for an immediate cessation of hostilities upon virtually any terms the Allies should impose.

7 NOVEMBER 1918

World War I: Meuse-Argonne Offensive After receiving orders to attack the heights south of Sedan the 1st and 42nd Divisions are withdrawn, leaving Sedan to the French Fourth Army. The weight of the American offensive pivots to the east.

9 NOVEMBER 1918

World War I: Armistice Negotiations As Allied armies continue to advance rapidly on the Western Front, Germany accepts Allied terms of peace calling for evacuation of all conquered territory and surrender of arms.

11 NOVEMBER 1918

World War I: Armistice Following an armistice signed in a railroad car in the forest of Compiègne, north of Paris, hostilities officially end at 11 in the morning. The Meuse-Argonne offensive has cost the American Army 26,277 killed and 95,786 wounded. During the course of the war, slightly more than 50,000 American soldiers are killed in action or later die of their wounds, with another 198,000 wounded. There are also 69,540 deaths due to other causes, mostly disease.

11-14 NOVEMBER 1918

Russia: Allied Intervention The Allied intervention forces assume defensive positions south of Archangel. On this day the Soviet 6th Army, led by Leon Trotsky, attacks and continues the assault for four days. An American garrison at Touglas loses 28 killed and 70 wounded in heavy fighting.

1 DECEMBER 1918

Germany American troops cross into Germany and will occupy Coblenz on the Rhine on 11 December.

19 JANUARY 1919

France The Paris Peace Conference begins in the Palace of Versailles. Consideration of the German treaty will take until June.

20 JUNE 1919

Russia: Allied Intervention Company H of the 27th Infantry attempts to free five captured American soldiers at the village of Novitskaya in eastern Siberia. The Americans lose four killed as the Bolsheviks retreat with the prisoners. The prisoners will be freed 28 June by negotiation.

Clemenceau rises to ask the German delegates to sign the Versailles Peace Treaty, 28 June 1919.

25 JUNE 1919

Russia: Allied Intervention At Romanovka in eastern Siberia a platoon from the US 31st Infantry is attacked by a strong Bolshevik force. Out of 72 soldiers the unit loses 19 killed and 25 wounded.

27 JUNE 1919

Russia: Allied Intervention American troops begin to leave north Russia at Archangel. American losses during the mission have been 144 killed in action and another 100 dead from disease or accidents. A little over 300 American soldiers have been wounded.

28 JUNE 1919

France: Versailles Peace Treaty The signing of the Versailles Treaty concludes the peace Conference. Germany is forced to admit its guilt for the war, return Alsace-Lorraine to France, give up its overseas colonies and pay reparations of some $15 billion. President Wilson has persuaded the delegates to accept a League of Nations to help solve differences between nations and to prevent future hostilities. The isolationist US Senate, however, will refuse to ratify the treaty.

31 OCTOBER 1919

Haiti The Haitian 'caco' guerrillas have once again staged a violent uprising which has included an attack on Port-au-Prince on 7 October. The "cacos" are led by a rebel chief known as Charlmagne Peralte. During the night 1200 guerrillas attack the town of Grande Rivière, but US Marine forces have anticipated the attack and ambush the guerrillas. Meanwhile, Sergeant Herman Hanneken, Corporal William Button and 20 loyal natives discover the hideout of the rebel leader. Disguised as natives they are able to penetrate the rebel defenses and kill Charlmagne. For their actions Hanneken and Button receive the Medal of Honor.

1 APRIL 1920

Russia: Allied Intervention The last American troops leave Siberia at Vladivostok. American losses in Siberia have been 35 killed and 52 wounded.

4 MARCH 1921

National Warren G. Harding is inaugurated president. Harding has promised a "return to normalcy" and has campaigned against American participation in the League of Nations.

12 NOVEMBER 1921

International The United States opens the Washington Disarmament Conference. The primary object is the limitation of naval armaments and an agreement on the position of all powers in the Far East and the Pacific Ocean. It is agreed that Britain, the US, Japan, France and Italy will limit the size of their national fleets of capital ships (battleships and aircraft carriers) on a ratio of 5:5:3:1.67:1.67 respectively. The treaty will be signed on 6 February 1922.

13 DECEMBER 1921

International A Four-Power Treaty pledges Britain, the United States, Japan and France to consult in the event of a threat to peace in the Pacific region and to respect each others' possessions there. This treaty replaces the Anglo-Japanese Treaty of 1902. A Nine-Power Treaty recognizes the principle of the 'open door' in China and respect for Chinese sovereignty and territorial integrity.

Japanese troops roll into Manchuria in 1932. The Japanese curtly rejected US and League of Nations protests and in 1933 withdrew from the League.

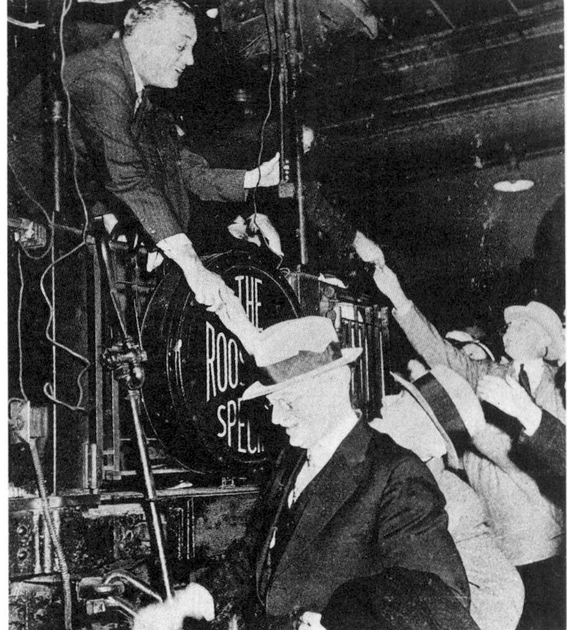

10 JANUARY 1923

Germany The last American troops are withdrawn from Germany.

3 AUGUST 1923

National Calvin Coolidge is sworn in as president following the sudden death of President Harding. Like Harding, Coolidge will be primarily occupied with domestic affairs.

12 JULY 1924

Dominican Republic The US military occupation ends with the establishment of civilian government. The last American troops will leave in September.

6 MAY 1926

Nicaragua US Marines land in Nicaragua to quell a revolt and shore up the government of Aldolpho Diaz. The US military will remain until 1933.

16 MARCH 1927

China A civil war has been raging in China since 1924. As Nationalist forces, led by Chiang Kai-shek, drive northward toward Shanghai the 4th Marine Regiment of more than 1200 men is landed at that port city. They are there to assist other American and foreign forces in guarding lives and property. By early next year there will be almost 5000 American troops in China.

15-16 JULY 1927

Nicaragua Following a period of civil strife there are now some 3000 US Marines in Nicaragua under the command of Major General Frank McCoy. César Augusto Sandino has refused to acquiesce to US government-supervised elections and has begun guerrilla warfare. In northwestern Nicaragua, Sandino and 600 men attack the village of Ocotal, which is held by Captain G. D. Hatfield, with about 20 Marines and 50 members of Nicaragua's National Guard. Two rebel attacks are repulsed. In response five Marine planes attack Sandino's force with bombs and machine gun fire, killing an estimated 50 rebels. One Marine is reported killed and one wounded in the fighting. This is only one of a continuing series of battles between rebel forces and Marine units.

Above left: Franklin Roosevelt campaigning in 1932. He beat Hoover by 413 electoral votes.

Above: Within days of Roosevelt's inauguration in 1933 Adolf Hitler became chancellor of Germany.

27 AUGUST 1928

International The Pact of Paris, also known as the Kellogg-Briand Pact after its two formulators, is signed by the United States and 14 other nations. The Pact, which outlaws war as an instrument of national policy, will eventually be signed by 62 nations.

4 MARCH 1929

National Herbert Hoover is inaugurated as president. Hoover assures the world that the United States has 'no desire for territorial expansion, for economic or other domination of other people.'

21 JANUARY-22 APRIL 1930

International An international naval conference meets in London to continue work begun at the Washington Conference of 1921-22. The United States, Great Britain and Japan agree on ratios, sizes and building schedules for their fleets, but France and Italy reject them. The US Senate will consent to this treaty of 21 July.

18 SEPTEMBER 1931

China Japanese troops in a railway zone in Manchuria attack Chinese troops, whom they accuse of blowing up a piece of the track on the Japanese-owned South Manchuria Railway. The subsequent occupation of all Manchuria launches Japan on a course that will lead to its participation in World War II.

7 JANUARY 1932

International Prompted by Japan's attacks upon Chinese forces in Manchuria, Secretary of State Henry Stimson sends diplomatic notes to Japan and China announcing that the United States will refuse to recognize Japanese sovereignty over any Chinese territory taken by force in violation of the Nine-Power Treaty of 1921 and the Pact of Paris of 1928.

3 JANUARY 1933

Nicaragua The last troops of the 2nd Marine Brigade are withdrawn from Nicaragua after almost seven years of intervention. The Marines have engaged in more than 150 clashes, losing 47 men killed in combat.

30 JANUARY 1933

Germany Adolph Hitler, leader of the National Socialist Party – popularly known as the Nazis – becomes Chancellor of Germany. He receives strong support for his denunciation of the Versailles Treaty and for his promise to make the nation strong and respected again. Hitler and the Nazis will move quickly to consolidate their power and eliminate opposition.

4 MARCH 1933

National Franklin Delano Roosevelt is inaugurated as president. For several years Roosevelt will be preoccupied with domestic relief and recovery from the Great Depression. Roosevelt will adopt a 'good neighbor' policy toward Latin America and will end American military intervention there. Eventually Roosevelt will be forced to deal with the international crisis caused by the increasing aggression of Germany, Japan and Italy.

27 MARCH 1933

Japan Following condemnation by the League of Nations of Japanese military expansion in Manchu-

ria, Japan announces it will withdraw from the League in two years.

14 OCTOBER 1933

International The Geneva disarmament conference breaks up as Germany proclaims withdrawal from the disarmament initiative, as well as from the League of Nations effective 23 October.

15 AUGUST 1934

Haiti The last US Marines leave Haiti, where they have been stationed since 1915.

29 DECEMBER 1934

Japan Japan denounces the Washington Naval Treaty of 1922 and the London Naval Treaty of 1930 and says that it will withdraw from both as of December 1936.

16 MARCH 1935

Germany Hitler denounces the terms of the Treaty of Versailles that mandate German disarmament. Going further, he reinstates conscription and declares that the German Army will be upgraded to 36 divisions.

31 AUGUST 1935

National President Roosevelt signs the Neutrality Act, which forbids shipment of arms and munitions once a state of war exists. The act authorizes the president to prohibit American civilians from traveling on ships of belligerents.

5 OCTOBER 1935

National Italy has begun an invasion of Ethiopia. President Roosevelt proclaims the existence of a state of war between Ethiopia and Italy and declares the provisions of the Neutrality Act to be in effect.

9 DECEMBER 1935

International The Second London Naval Conference convenes in London. When Japan is denied a request to maintain a navy equal to that of Britain and the United States, it will leave the conference.

29 FEBRUARY 1936

National A Second Neutrality Act extends the 1935 Act through 1 May 1937 and adds a prohibition against granting any loans or credits to belligerents.

7 MARCH 1936

Germany German troops reoccupy the Rhineland in violation of the Locarno Treaty of 1925, which designated the area as a demilitarized zone. Britain and France do nothing.

9 MAY 1936

International Italy formally annexes Ethiopia after a cruel and one-sided war.

17 JULY 1936

Spain A civil war begins as Spanish Army units in Morocco proclaim a revolution against the Madrid government, now headed by the leftist-orientated Popular Front. The following day the uprising engulfs mainland military posts. However, in Madrid and Barcelona the government resists. Rebel leaders have behind them most of the army and air force and a large number of North African troops.

7 AUGUST 1936

National Despite heavy involvement by Germany, Italy and the Soviet Union in the Spanish Civil War, the US government issues a proclamation of nonintervention. However, more than 3000 young Americans will flock to Spain to fight with the Popular Front over the next two years. They will form the Lincoln Battalion and fight alongside other International Brigades.

1 MAY 1937

National President Roosevelt signs the third Neutrality Act, extending the earlier acts of 1935 and 1936. The Act not only continues the ban of export of arms to belligerents and prohibits these nations from selling their securities in the United States, but bans American ships from transporting arms into the belligerent zones. It also requires belligerent nations to pay cash for certain non-military goods purchased in the USA and to carry them on their own ships.

8 JULY 1937

China Open warfare begins between Japan and China. Japanese troops move south through the Great Wall, facing only weak opposition from the Chinese. Japanese troops will capture Peking on 28 July. Shanghai will fall on 8 November.

12 DECEMBER 1937

China The US gunboat *Panay* is bombed by Japanese planes on the Yangtze River and sinks. Two are killed, and 43 are wounded. On 13 December Nanking will fall to Japanese forces. On 14 December Japan apologizes for the *Panay* incident, agrees to pay an indemnity and promises to make every possible effort to avoid future incidents.

12 MARCH 1938

Germany Meeting no resistance, the German Army occupies Austria. The next day Austria is proclaimed a province of the German Reich.

The massive 1936 Nazi Party rally in Nuremberg's Zeppelinwiese arena. By this time the rallies had not only become frankly militaristic but had abandoned all pretense that the forces and weapons displayed were for defense, as required by treaty.

30 SEPTEMBER 1938

International At a conference in Munich, British Prime Minister Neville Chamberlain and French Premier Edouard Daladier agree to Adolf Hitler's demands for cession of the Czechoslovakian territory known as the Sudetenland to Germany. Chamberlain returns home to cheering crowds, announcing 'peace in our time.'

21 OCTOBER 1938

China Japanese forces capture Canton. On 25 October Japanese troops will seize Hankow as the Chinese government withdraws to Chungking. The Japanese now control China's major ports, and the Chinese can get supplies only through the Soviet Union or by the Burma Road. In November Japan will announce a 'new order' for East Asia.

12 JANUARY 1939

National President Roosevelt requests an additional appropriation of $5.25 million for defense. He will submit requests for more appropriations on 4 March and 29 April, anticipating that the nation may become engaged in a military conflict.

14-16 MARCH 1939

Germany The German Army moves into the remainder of Czechoslovakia and incorporates it into the Third Reich.

1 APRIL 1939

International Following the unconditional surrender of the Popular Front forces in Spain, the United States recognizes the government of General Francisco Franco.

14 JULY 1939

National President Roosevelt asks Congress for a repeal of the arms embargo. On 18 July, Roosevelt will ask Congress to revise the neutrality laws.

1 SEPTEMBER 1939

Poland Without a declaration of war, Germany invades Poland.

3 SEPTEMBER 1939

World War II War begins as Great Britain, France, Australia and New Zealand declare war on Germany.

German troops invade Czechoslovakia in March 1939, six months after Hitler had promised at Munich that he had 'no further territorial ambitions.'

5 SEPTEMBER 1939

National The United States announces neutrality in the second World War. On 8 September President Roosevelt proclaims a limited national emergency.

4 NOVEMBER 1939

US Approach to War President Roosevelt signs the Neutrality Act of 1939, repealing the embargo on arms. This act allows the sale of arms to belligerents so long as they pay cash and transport them on non-American ships. The act is clearly intended to help Britain and France.

9 APRIL 1940

World War II Germany invades Norway and Denmark. Rapid German advances cause Britain to begin an evacuation of forces on 27 April.

10 MAY 1940

World War II Germany invades Luxembourg, the Netherlands and Belgium. Winston Churchill replaces Neville Chamberlain as Prime Minister.

15 MAY 1940

US Approach to War British Prime Minister Churchill sends the first in a long series of telegrams to President Roosevelt, presenting a 'shopping list' for old destroyers, aircraft and other arms.

5 JUNE 1940

World War II The German Army invades France. Paris will fall 14 June. France will surrender 22 June.

11 JUNE 1940

US Approach to War Congress passes the Naval Supply Act authorizing almost $1.5 million for naval construction.

20 JULY 1940

US Approach to War Congress appropriates $4 billion to construct a two-ocean navy and build 15,000 naval aircraft.

26 JULY 1940

US Approach to War For the second time this month President Roosevelt invokes the Export Control Act of 2 July to restrict American exports to Japan. The list of banned items includes aviation gasoline, iron and steel.

3 SEPTEMBER 1940

US Approach to War The United States agrees to give Britain 50 destroyers in exchange for the right to construct naval and air bases on various British possessions in the Western Hemisphere.

16 SEPTEMBER 1940

US Approach to War President Roosevelt signs the Selective Training and Service Act, requiring men between the ages of 21 and 35 to register for military training.

JANUARY 1941

World War II In the ongoing Battle of the Atlantic a total of 21 Allied ships are sunk by German U-Boats in January. The British are beginning to use their new secret device called radar, but it will take time for problems to be ironed out. English casualties for the month in the aerial Battle of Britain will be 1500 dead and 2000 injured.

2 JANUARY 1941

National President Roosevelt announces a program to produce 200 7500-ton freighters to be known as Liberty Ships.

5 JANUARY 1941

World War II The major British offensive in North Africa against the Italians continues its drive west across the northern coast of Egypt and into Libya. Today Bardia is taken; Tobruk will fall to the Allies on 22 January. The advance will continue successfully into February.

6 JANUARY 1941

Washington In his annual State-of-the-Union address President Roosevelt asks Congress to support lend-lease for the Allies in their fight against the Axis powers. He also defines what he calls the 'four freedoms', which Americans and all democratic peoples are dedicated to preserving: freedom of speech and expression, freedom of worship, freedom from want and freedom from fear. This 'Four Freedoms Speech' will strike a responsive chord in Americans and, during the war, will serve as an Allied motto. Also in the speech, Roosevelt again refers to the US as the 'arsenal of democracy.' On 8 January the president will submit a budget of over $17 billion, some two-thirds of which is for defense.

27 JANUARY-29 MARCH 1941

US Approach to War There are secret staff talks in Washington between British and American representatives. They decide that Allied policy in the event of war with Germany and Japan should be to pursue the defeat of Germany first. These talks mark an important stage in the developing cooperation between the two nations.

1 FEBRUARY 1941

Command The US Navy is reorganized into three fleets: the Atlantic, the Pacific and the Asiatic.

7 FEBRUARY 1941

World War II The British campaign across the northern coast of Africa finishes triumphantly near Benghazi, Libya. Though outnumbered five to one, the Allies have captured 130,000 of the Italian army and much materiel. However, the need for troops in Greece deprives General Sir Archibald Wavell of the forces he needs to drive the Italians from Africa. On 12 February Nazi General Erwin Rommel will arrive in Tripoli to take charge of an Axis counter-drive.

1 MARCH 1941

World War II Bulgaria joins the Axis.

11 MARCH 1941

US Approach to War Despite vigorous opposition from isolationists and America-First agitators, the House passes and Roosevelt signs the Lend-Lease Act. It empowers the president to lend arms and other materiel to any country considered vital to US interests. In practice, the bill means that Britain can continue to order American supplies without necessarily having to pay for them until after the war. Though there are many restrictions on the application of Lend-Lease that will decrease its usefulness, by the end of 1946 nearly $51 billion in aid will have been extended to the Allies.

Victorious German troops parade down the Champs-Elysées on 14 June 1940.

24 MARCH 1941

World War II German General Erwin Rommel begins his campaign to drive the Allies back from their gains on the coast of East Africa. Today Rommel recaptures El Agheila in Libya. Much Allied strength in the area has been sent to Greece. Rommel's forces include four Italian divisions and one German, the latter with a strong tank component. Rommel's lighting drive along the coast to the east will arrive at Tobruk in mid-April, but there it will bog down before Allied resistance.

4 APRIL 1941

US Approach to War Roosevelt agrees to allow British warships to be repaired and refueled in the US.

6 APRIL 1941

World War II German forces invade Yugoslavia and Greece. The Yugoslav Army will capitulate on 17 April, and resistance will end on the Greek mainland by the end of the month.

7 APRIL 1941

US Approach to War US naval and air bases open in Bermuda. The carrier *Ranger* and other ships are to be based there under the euphemistic designation Central Atlantic Neutrality Patrol.

11 APRIL 1941

US Approach to War As German U-Boats have been taking an increasing toll on Allied and neutral merchant ships crossing the Atlantic, President Roosevelt announces that the US will extend its patrols and security zone to the line of 26 degrees west. The Red Sea is declared to be no longer a 'combat zone', and thus US ships may now carry cargos to ports there – including supplies for the British in Egypt. (Germany will ignore the American declaration, and on 21 May a U-boat will sink the American merchant ship *Robin Moor* inside the line.) Also today, Roosevelt creates the Office of Price Administration, which will play an important part in holding back price increases and inflation in the coming wartime economy.

21-27 APRIL 1941

US Approach to War US military officers meet with their British and Dutch counterparts in Singapore and draw up a plan for strategic operations against Japan in case it attacks the US.

25 APRIL 1941

Washington President Roosevelt formally orders US warships to report the movement of German warships west of Iceland. (This is being done unofficially already.)

4 MAY 1941

World War II Rommel halts his initial attack on Tobruk, Libya. The Germans will continue to beseige the city but will not succeed in extending their lines.

9-11 MAY 1941

World War II British ships force a German U-boat to the surface and capture it; on board are code books and an Enigma cipher machine, which will prove invaluable to the Allies throughout the war (Germany will never discover that the machine has been captured).

10-11 MAY 1941

World War II In the heaviest air raid on a British city during the Blitz, German bombers raid London, damaging the houses of Parliament. However, British airmen have turned the tide in the Battle of Britain: this is the last major German attack for three years, and a turning point in the war. 'Never in the field of human conflict,' Churchill will proclaim of the heroic efforts of British flyers, 'was so much owed by so many to so few.' The German Luftwaffe has lost some 2600 planes during the Battle of Britain. English fighting has been much aided by the still-secret device called radar.

20 MAY 1941

World War II The Germans begin a massive airborne attack on the Greek island of Crete. Allied forces there consists mostly of troops recently evacuated from Greece; the German conquest of the island will be completed on 31 May.

27 MAY 1941

US Approach to War President Roosevelt issues a proclamation declaring that a state of unlimited national emergency exists. He has come to this point after seeing Greece and Yugoslavia fall to the Axis; and after the sinking of the *Robin Moor* on 20 May, Roosevelt feels the American people will be sympathetic to the proclamation.

World War II After a long pursuit that began on 23 May, British naval forces sink the giant 'unsinkable' German battleship *Bismarck* 400 miles off the coast of France.

1 JUNE 1941

US Approach to War The Coast Guard begins patrol operations off the southern Greenland coast.

4 JUNE 1941

World War II British forces have smashed insurgent forces in Iraq, and today a new Iraqi Cabinet is formed under British auspices.

After failing to destroy the RAF in the Battle of Britain the Luftwaffe took to 'blitzing' British cities. This is Coventry in November 1940.

5 JUNE 1941

US Approach to War The US Army appropriations bill calls for over $10 billion; it will be passed on 28 June. Tomorrow a new law comes into force allowing the government to take over foreign ships laid up in the US.

8 JUNE 1941

World War II The British and de Gaulle's Free French forces attack Vichy French forces in Syria. The Allies will defeat the Vichy army in six days.

14 JUNE 1941

US Approach to War President Roosevelt, using his emergency powers, freezes the assets of Germany and Italy in the US. Within the week the president will order German and Italian consulates closed in the US.

22 JUNE 1941

World War II Betraying his nonaggression pact with Stalin, Hitler begins a massive invasion of Russia under the code name *Operation Barbarossa.* Despite Germany's evident preparations over the past months and the warnings Stalin has received from many sources, the Soviet army is taken almost completely by surprise and loses very heavily in the first encounters. Hitler has sent to the attack some 140 divisions, three million men, along with 7100 guns,

The German battleship *Bismarck* fires at the British battle cruiser *Hood*, 24 May 1941. *Hood* blew up and sank, losing all but three of her crew of 1416.

The Placentia Bay (Newfoundland) Conference of August 1941 where the Atlantic Charter was signed. L to r: Roosevelt, Churchill, Marshall and Dill.

3300 tanks and 2770 aircraft, under the commanders who conquered France – Field Marshals Bock, Leeb and Rundstedt. So confident is Hitler that this new blitzkrieg will succeed as it did in France that he has not issued winter uniforms to his troops. Opposing the Nazi onslaught, on a front 2000 miles long from the Artic to the Black Sea, are some 2 million men of the Red Army under General Zhukov. Within days, as the Germans make rapid progress pushing east on the whole front, both England and the US will pledge to aid the Soviet Union. Meanwhile, Russia's losses are reaching catastrophic levels.

28 JUNE 1941

US Approach to War An executive order sets up the Office of Scientific Research and Development to coordinate US scientific-technological work related to defense and war – including radar, sonar and early research on the atomic bomb.

2 JULY 1941

Japan An Imperial conference between Emperor Hirohito and government and military officials confirms a plan to seize bases in Indochina even at the risk of war. US authorities know of this decision immediately due to their breaking Japanese diplomatic codes.

4 JULY 1941

National In an Independence Day broadcast Roosevelt says the US 'will never survive as a happy and fertile oasis of liberty surrounded by a cruel desert of dictatorship.'

7 JULY 1941

US Approach to War American forces land on the island of Iceland to garrison it and protect nearby shipping from submarine attack.

11 JULY 1941

Washington The president appoints William Donovan to head a new civilian intelligence agency. This appointment will lead to the creation of the Office for Strategic Services (OSS), which will in turn develop into the CIA.

12 JULY 1941

World War II As German bombs fall on the city for the first time and German forces drive closer, Britain and the Soviet Union sign an agreement in Moscow providing for mutual assistance and forbidding the making of a separate peace. Russia, however reluctantly, is now among the Allies.

21 JULY 1941

Washington Roosevelt asks Congress to extend the military draft period from one year to 30 months. This measure passes the Senate and House in August, but the fact that the bill passes by only one vote in the House shows that anti-war sentiment is still strong.

25 JULY 1941

US Approach to War President Roosevelt announces that all Japanese assets in the US are frozen. This is in retaliation for Japanese seizure of bases in French Indochina on the 24th. The US order will effectively halt all trade between the US and Japan, including the export of goods that Japan needs for its war machine. The order enrages the Japanese, who now have one more reason to consider seriously the possibility of making an attack on the US.

26 JULY 1941

US Approach to War Roosevelt orders that the Philippine Army be incorporated into the US Army, the combined forces in the islands to be under the command of General Douglas MacArthur.

1 AUGUST 1941

US Approach to War President Roosevelt forbids the export of oil and aviation fuel from the US except to the Western Hemisphere and British possessions. This decision is critical for the Japanese, because they have no oil of their own. Now Japan must either change her foreign policy drastically or go to war and try to gain access to the oil of the East Indies.

5 AUGUST 1941

World War II The German drive into Russia continues to make steady progress through mounting but still ineffectual Soviet resistance. Today fighting ceases at the city of Smolensk, on the way to Moscow. The Germans claim to have taken 310,000 prisoners and to have killed many of the 700,000-man Red Army force.

When, in October 1941, bellicose General Hideki Tojo became Japan's premier, hopes that the US and Japan could avoid war receded.

9-12 AUGUST 1941

Diplomacy: The Atlantic Charter Churchill and Roosevelt and their military staffs meet at Placentia Bay in Newfoundland, the discussions covering the situation in Europe and the Far East. They agree to send strong warnings to the Japanese; it is understood that America will probably enter the war if Japan attacks British or Dutch possessions in the East Indies or Malaya. A message is also sent to Stalin proposing a meeting in Moscow to arrange a supply line to the Soviet Union. The Newfoundland conference is best remembered for the agreement later called the Atlantic Charter, which proposes overriding goals of modern civilization; these include renunciation of aggression, the right of peoples to choose their own governments, the support of access to raw materials, guarantees of freedom from want and fear, freedom of the seas and the disarmament of aggressors. By 24 September the Allies and their friends – including the USSR – will endorse the Atlantic Charter. It will become in effect the blueprint for establishing the United Nations.

17 AUGUST 1941

US Approach to War The US presents a formal warning to the Japanese along the lines agreed upon in Newfoundland – though somewhat toned down. On 28 August a note from Japan's moderate Premier Konoye will insist that his country wishes to pursue 'courses of peace and harmony' with the US. On 3 September Roosevelt will turn down a proposed meeting with Konoye.

25 AUGUST 1941

World War II With little opposition British and Soviet forces move into Iran to protect its oil supplies. A new Iranian government will agree to occupation on 9 September.

1 SEPTEMBER 1941

US Approach to War The US Atlantic Fleet forms a Denmark Strait patrol. The US Navy is now allowed to escort convoys in the Atlantic provided at least one American merchant ship is present.

4 SEPTEMBER 1941

US Approach to War In a convoy operation the US destroyer *Greer* is attacked by a German U-boat but is not damaged. In fact, the German commander has mistaken the destroyer for a British ship, but Roosevelt will present the incident to the public as an example of German aggression.

6 SEPTEMBER 1941

Japan Premier Konoye gives in to military pressure, and a conference decides that, in view of declining oil stocks, war preparations should be completed by mid-October. Meanwhile, Konoye continues to make conciliatory proposals to the US, but these are judged insincere.

11 SEPTEMBER 1941

US Approach to War As a result of increasing numbers of attacks on US merchant and military shipping President Roosevelt orders US Navy planes and ships to shoot on sight any Axis ships within the zone delineated on 11 April. On 16 September the Navy will declare responsibility for protecting all shipping as far east as Iceland.

15 SEPTEMBER 1941

World War II By today the German invading army has managed to sever nearly all land connections between Leningrad and the rest of the Soviet Union. Though supplies trickle in, several hundred thousand civilians will starve to death before the German seige is fully lifted in 1944.

27 SEPTEMBER 1941

Production The first batch of 14 Liberty ships is launched from various shipyards. Another 312 are on order.

28 SEPTEMBER-1 OCTOBER 1941

Allied Planning The conference suggested in Newfoundland by Churchill and Roosevelt takes place in Moscow. On 1 October a joint declaration states that the Soviets will continue to receive an increasing amount of help from Britain and America. Meanwhile, after capturing Kiev, the Germans again concentrate on the advance toward Moscow.

9 OCTOBER 1941

US Approach to War Roosevelt asks Congress to allow US merchant ships to be armed and to repeal sections of the Neutrality Act.

16 OCTOBER 1941

Japan Prime Minister Konoye resigns and is replaced by General Hideki Tojo, who also continues as war minister. These changes mark the increasing ascendency of the war party, though the decision to open hostilities has not yet finally been taken.

German troops in Russia slog through early snow in 1941. Harsh winter weather did more to foil the Barbarossa Offensive than any Russian general.

17 OCTOBER 1941

US Approach to War The US destroyer *Kearney* is torpedoed by a German U-Boat off Iceland; although the destroyer does not sink, 11 Americans are killed. In a radio address on 27 October, Roosevelt will say of the incident, 'America has been attacked, the shooting has started.' But he holds back from calling for open war, knowing many Americans are still reluctant to take the final step.

28 OCTOBER 1941

World War II Most of the German attacks toward Moscow are now being halted, partly due to fierce Russian resistance but due even more to the weather. By day the ground is soft and muddy, by night severe frosts weaken the inadequately clad German troops and damage their vehicles. Nazi tank commanders will decide to put off a major drive until the ground freezes.

31 OCTOBER 1941

US Approach to War The US destroyer *Reuben James*, on convoy duty off Iceland, is sunk by a German U-Boat, with the loss of 100 American lives. It is the first American naval vessel to be lost.

3 NOVEMBER 1941

US Approach to War The ambassador to Japan, Joseph Grew, warns that the Japanese may be planning a sudden attack on American positions. On 7 November Secretary of State Cordell Hull will repeat this warning to President Roosevelt.

15 NOVEMBER 1941

World War II The German Moscow offensive is renewed; the main effort is to be made by converging Panzer (tank) forces. Russian reinforcements are pouring in from Siberia; German units are understrength due both to losses in fighting and to casualties from the severe weather. Soviet counterattacks will begin on 17 November and will be so effective that the Germans will contain them with difficulty.

17 NOVEMBER 1941

US Approach to War Japanese officials begin negotiations with the US State Department in Washington. On 20 November they will propose that the US remove restrictions on trade with Japan and refrain from interfering with Japan's activities in China and the Pacific. On 26 November Secretary of State Hull will reject these proposals, and the Japanese will in turn reject his demands that the Japanese pull out of China and Indochina.

18 NOVEMBER 1941

World War II The British begin a new tank offensive into Libya called Operation Crusader. General Rommel, commanding the Afrika Korps, is taken by surprise, but will still mount stiff resistance in the Tobruk area.

26-27 NOVEMBER 1941

US Approach to War Roosevelt and Secretary Hull present a stiff 10-point note of final terms, demanding that Japan leave China and Indochina and recognize Chiang Kai-shek's Chinese Nationalist Government. In return, America promises to negotiate new trade and raw materials agreements. On the 26th all six of Japan's fleet carriers leave their bases to move across the Pacific toward Hawaii. On the 27th US authorities issue a war warning to their overseas commanders.

28 NOVEMBER 1941

World War II Some 22,000 Italian troops in East Africa surrender to the Allies at Gondar, spelling the end of Mussolini's East African Roman Empire. However, the Allies have been unable to break Rommel's hold on the garrison at Tobruk.

29 NOVEMBER 1941

Japan A Japanese government conference decides that America's final terms are unacceptable and that Japan must go to war. Emperor Hirohito gives his ceremonial assent on 1 December.

2 DECEMBER 1941

US Approach to War The code order 'Climb Mount Niitaka' goes out to the Japanese carrier force steaming across the Pacific toward Hawaii. The order indicates that negotiations have broken down and that the carriers are to attack the American naval base at Pearl Harbor. Included in this naval force are all six of Japan's fleet (*ie.* heavy) carriers.

5 DECEMBER 1941

World War II In the face of severe cold, blizzards and Red Army resistance, the German advance on Moscow has stalled 25 miles from the city; Hitler agrees that the offensive must be halted. Tomorrow, with large numbers of troops and tanks pulled apparently from nowhere, Russian Generals Zhukov, Rokossovsky and Kuznetsov will commence a savage counterattack.

6 DECEMBER 1941

US Approach to War President Roosevelt appeals directly to Emperor Hirohito to exercise his influence to prevent war. This is considered an insult by the Japanese; it is bad form to burden the Emperor with such decisions. Late in the day the Japanese begin transmitting a 14-part message to their diplomats. The first 13 parts are intercepted by the American code-breaking service and passed to the president. Although the crucial 14th part is not yet intercepted, Roosevelt correctly interprets the message as meaning war.

7 DECEMBER 1941

World War II: Attack on Pearl Harbor The 14th part of the Japanese signal, stating specifically that relations are being broken off, reaches Washington in the morning and is decoded around 9 o'clock. A little after 10 an order to the Japanese Embassy in Washington to deliver the main message at one o'clock is similarly intercepted. It is quickly realized that this timing coincides roughly with dawn at Pearl Harbor. Various delays ensue in finding new Chief of Staff General George Marshall (who is out riding) and then in transmitting a warning message to Pearl Harbor; this message arrives far too late. At 7:55, Honolulu time, 423 planes from Admiral Nagumo's six-carrier Japanese fleet strike the American Naval base at Pearl Harbor. There is complete tactical and strategic surprise. In two waves of attacks by torpedo bombers, dive bombers, high-level bombers and fighters, the Japanese succeed in crippling all eight of the US battleships in the port, with five of them being sunk (three will later be salvaged and rebuilt). Three cruisers and three destroyers also go to the bottom, and 188 aircraft are destroyed on the ground. The attack is a devastating blow to the US Pacific Fleet. In addition to the losses in ships and planes, 2403 soldiers, sailors and civilians are killed and 1178 wounded. Japanese losses are reported at 29 planes.

A panoramic view of the Japanese attack on Pearl Harbor. The black column of smoke in the center rises from the stricken battleship *Arizona*.

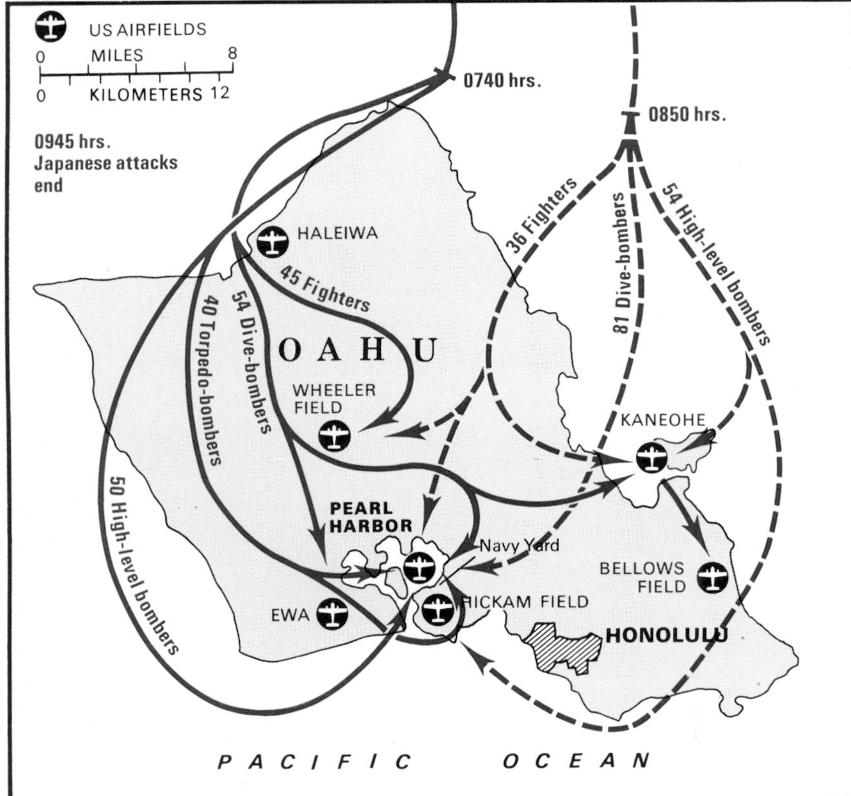

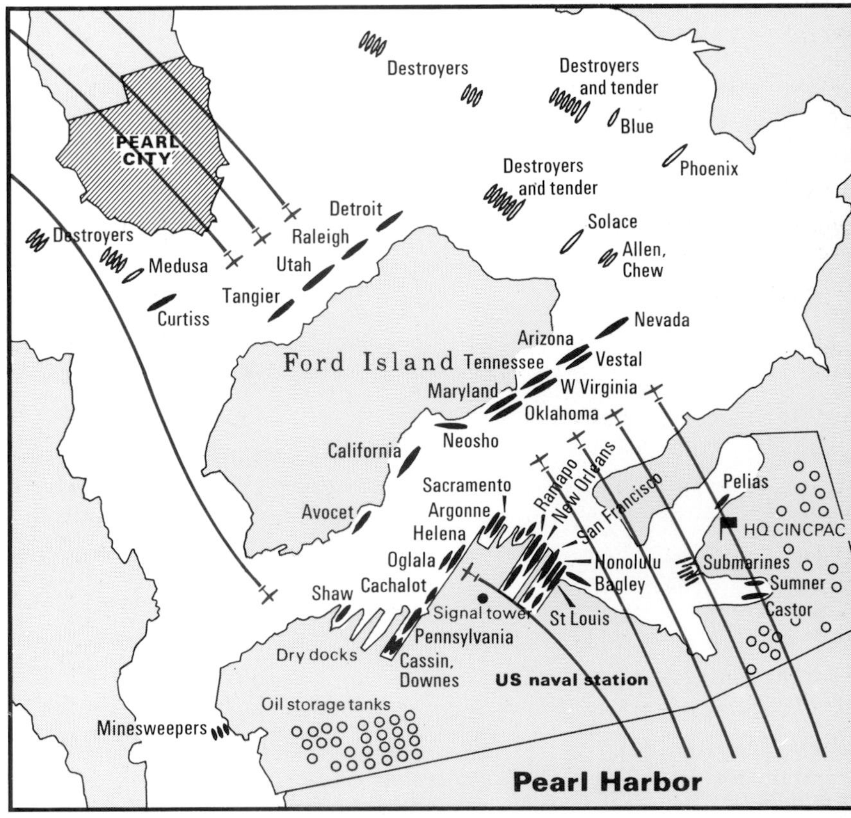

Above and right: Maps of the Japanese attack on Hawaii on 7 December 1941, with a detailed view of the initial assault on Pearl Harbor.

However, some critical elements of the fleet have, by accident, escaped – all three aircraft carriers happen to be away and thus are spared to become a major element in US strategy, and massive oil storage tanks escape unhurt. But these pieces of luck are not due to foresight by the commanders at Pearl Harbor; Admiral H. E. Kimmel, commander of the Pacific Fleet, and General Walter Short, Army commander in Hawaii, will be dismissed for their lack of preparedness. Only in the evening do the Japanese officially declare war on the US. Though Japan has a navy immensely superior in the Pacific, Admiral Yamamoto, who planned the Pearl Harbor attack, knows that Japan cannot fight the US for long before the American production capacity swamps Japanese capacity. Accordingly, Japan must move quickly to secure territory in the Pacific in the hope that America will give into the inevitable and make peace. To that end, today there are Japanese air raids on Guam and Wake islands, a destroyer bombardment of Midway and bombing of Manila and Singapore.

8 DECEMBER 1941

World War II: America Enters As public fury over the attack at Pearl Harbor breaks out across the country President Roosevelt appears before a special joint session of Congress and, declaring 7 December 'a date which will live in infamy,' asks for a declaration of war on Japan. Both houses so vote, with only one dissent. Meanwhile, Australia, New Zealand, the Netherlands, the Free French, Yugoslavia and several South American countries also declare war on Japan. China declares war on the Axis powers.

World War II: Philippines A Japanese offensive begins on the islands with air attacks and a seizure of the small garrison on Batan Island north of Luzon. During the day Japanese bombs destroy some 100 American airplanes on the ground in the Philippines. The US commander in the area is General Douglas MacArthur, whose 130,000 men, most of them of the Philippine Army, are poorly trained and equipped. After the air strike MacArthur has only 17 bombers and 40 fighters in operation – and after Pearl Harbor, the Pacific Fleet will be of little use.

World War II: Malaysia The Japanese land troops at Kota Bharu, bomb Singapore and also make landings in Thailand. British forces in these areas are uniformly weak. Elsewhere in the Pacific there are attacks on Wake Island and Hong Kong, and the Japanese occupy Shanghai.

10 DECEMBER 1941

World War II: Philippines There are Japanese landings and air attacks on Luzon and 2000 Japanese land at Aparri on the north coast.

World War II: Marianas A Japanese force captures the island of Guam, which is defended by only 300 US troops.

World War II: North Africa British forces advance into Libya, finally breaking Rommel's siege at Tobruk.

World War II: South China Sea Japanese aircraft sink HMS *Prince of Wales* and HMS *Repulse*, the only British capital ships in Asian waters.

The US battleships *West Virginia* and *Tennessee* ablaze in Pearl Harbor. All eight battleships in port were put out of commission, two permanently.

11 DECEMBER 1941

World War II: International Germany and Italy declare war on the US; Congress in turn declares war on Germany and Italy. For his part, Hitler has made a fatal mistake in underestimating the power America will wield in the coming conflict.

16-17 DECEMBER 1941

World War II: Malaya British forces withdraw before a second wave of Japanese landings.

17 DECEMBER 1941

World War II: Command Admiral Chester Nimitz replaces Admiral Kimmel in command of the US Pacific Fleet.

18-19 DECEMBER 1941

World War II: Hong Kong Japanese forces land on Hong Kong and repel British counterattacks. The colony will hold out only for another six days.

20 DECEMBER 1941

World War II: National President Roosevelt signs the Draft Act, which calls for all US males between the ages of 18 and 65 to register, and for all men from ages 20 through 44 to be liable for active military duty.

World War II: Command Admiral Ernest J. King is appointed commander in chief, US Fleet. King will become the central architect of victory in the Pacific.

21-23 DECEMBER 1941

World War II: The Pacific As part of wide-ranging seizures of positions on the Pacific Islands and the Indochinese mainland, the Japanese establish a beachhead at Lingayen Gulf on Luzon, Philippines. On the 23rd the American Marines at Wake Island surrender to Japanese forces. On the 25th British Hong Kong capitulates.

22 DECEMBER 1941-7 JANUARY 1942

World War II: Allied Planning Roosevelt, Churchill and their staffs meet in Washington at the Arcadia Conference. The two main conclusions of the conference are to confirm the policy of beating Germany first (in the course of the war operations on the two enemies will turn out to proceed more nearly together) and to establish the Combined Chiefs of Staff as the directing body for the whole Allied military effort. A general strategic program is set up: US buildup in Britain toward a future offensive against Germany, continued bombing of Germany and German-occupied Europe and defensive operations to contain the Japanese in the Pacific.

24 DECEMBER 1941

World War II: Philippines The Japanese land 7000 men at Lamon Bay in Luzon. MacArthur begins a series of delaying actions as he withdraws to the Bataan Peninsula. On the 27th the general will abandon Manila to the enemy.

1 JANUARY 1942

World War II: International Representatives of 26 nations, including the US, sign the Declaration of the United Nations, affirming their cooperation against the Axis. (During the war these 'United Nations' will be called the 'Allies.')

2 JANUARY 1942
World War II: Philippines The Japanese occupy Manila as US and Philippine forces withdraw to the Bataan Peninsula. There General MacArthur will set up headquarters in Corregidor ('The Rock'), a strongly fortified island guarding the entrance to Manila Bay.

3 JANUARY 1942
World War II: Allied Command Chiang Kai-shek is named commander in chief of Allied forces in China.

6 JANUARY 1942
World War II: National In his State-of-the-Union address President Roosevelt calls for production of vast quantities of war materiel to defeat the Axis. The next day he will submit a budget of nearly $59 billion, of which $52 billion is for the war.

9 JANUARY 1942
World War II: Philippines Japanese attacks begin on MacArthur's positions on Bataan.

11 JANUARY 1942
World War II: Dutch East Indies Japanese forces commence an invasion of the Dutch East Indies. By 12 March the Dutch defenders will surrender.

13 JANUARY 1942
World War II: Battle of the Atlantic German U-Boats begin operations off the US East Coast. Finding virtually no American precautions in place, the Germans will sink 150,000 tons of Allied shipping in the first month.

14 JANUARY 1942
World War II: National President Roosevelt orders all aliens in the US to register with the government. The brunt of this proclamation will fall on Japanese-Americans, called *nisei*, most of them living on the West Coast. Secret plans are already underway to move the *nisei* to concentration camps, on the theory that their race alone will lead them to support the Japanese – though there will never be any evidence of such disloyalty.

15-28 JANUARY 1942
International At the Rio de Janeiro Conference in Brazil foreign ministers of 21 American nations resolve to break relations with the Axis (though Chile and Argentina will not do so until late in the war).

20 JANUARY 1942
World War II: Holocaust At what will be called the Wannsee Conference in Berlin, Hitler approves a plan for the 'Final Solution' to the 'Jewish Problem'. The plan calls for the transportation of all European Jews to extermination camps.

21 JANUARY 1942
World War II: North Africa Rommel and the 100 tanks of the Afrika Korps begin a surprise counterattack against the Allies, starting with British positions at El Agheila. This advance will make rapid progress over the next weeks, driving the Allies back eastward along the coast, roughly along the same line that has changed hands twice already, and ending again in Egypt at El Alamein.

By 1941 all European Jews under Nazi domination were forced to wear yellow Star of David badges.

The interior of a railway carrying Japanese-Americans to forced detention in an assembly camp in the aftermath of the Pearl Harbor attack.

29 JANUARY 1942
World War II: Command General Millard F. Harmon becomes chief of staff of the Air Force, succeeding General Carl Spaatz, who will now lead the Air Force Combat Command.

1 FEBRUARY 1942
World War II: Pacific American naval task forces under Admirals Halsey and Fletcher attack Japanese air bases in the Marshall and Gilbert Islands.

8-15 FEBRUARY 1942
World War II: Fall of Singapore Since the first of the month the British have withdrawn from the Malayan mainland to Singapore. On the 8th the Japanese invade the island, and by the 15th, the British (including 15,000 Australian troops among the 138,000-man garrison) are forced to surrender. It is the greatest disaster in British military history.

16 FEBRUARY 1942
World War II: Japan General Tojo outlines Japanese war aims to the Diet. He speaks of a 'new order of coexistence and coprosperity on ethical principles in Greater East Asia.'

19 FEBRUARY 1942
World War II: Command Having shown great talent for logistics, General Dwight D. Eisenhower is appointed chief of the War Plans Division of the US Army General Staff.

24 FEBRUARY 1942
World War II: Pacific An American task force, led by Admiral Halsey from the USS *Enterprise*, mounts a successful attack on Japanese positions at Wake Island, but does not loosen the enemy's hold.

27-29 FEBRUARY 1942
World War II: Battle of the Java Sea An Allied squadron, comprising five cruisers and 11 destroyers of four nationalities, tries to intercept an invasion force bound for Java. In a series of running battles the Allied flotilla is virtually wiped out; the Japanese suffer only slight damage and go on to land on Java on 28 February. Among the US losses are the cruiser *Houston*, the destroyer *Pope* and seaplane tender *Langley*.

MARCH 1942
World War II: Holocaust Large-scale transportation of Jews to the Nazi concentration camps gets fully under way. The five extermination camps – Auschwitz, Chelmno, Treblinka, Sobibor and Belsen – are distinguished from the 'ordinary' concentration camps. In the former the inmates are simply to be killed, largely in gas chambers; in the latter they are expected to be worked to death.

1 MARCH 1942
World War II: Russia The Soviet Army begins a new counteroffensive in the Crimea. The Germans estimate that by now they have lost some 1,500,000 in the Russian campaign.

7 MARCH 1942
World War II: New Guinea The Japanese invasion fleet begins landings on Dutch New Guinea.
World War II: Burma British troops evacuate Rangoon before the Japanese onslaught. As Rangoon is the only significant port in Burma, all supplies for the Allies must now come overland from India.

9 MARCH 1942
World War II: Command Admiral Harold Stark is appointed to command US naval forces in European waters. Admiral Ernest J. King, commander in chief of the US Navy, will take over Stark's work as chief of naval operations.
World War II: East Indies The Dutch commander on Java surrenders 100,000 Allied troops as the Japanese take control of the island.

11 MARCH 1942
World War II: Philippines General Douglas MacArthur leaves Luzon with the later-legendary declaration 'I shall return!' MacArthur is on orders from Washington to go to Australia, where he will assume supreme command of Allied forces in the southwest Pacific; these forces will shortly begin concentrating in Australia. General Jonathan Wainwright is left in Command in the Philippines.
World War II: Burma General Joseph Stilwell is appointed to command the Chinese Fifth and Sixth Armies, which are now concentrating around Mandalay and in the Shan States.

30 MARCH 1942
World War II: Command The Joint Chiefs of Staff divide the Pacific into two commands: Admiral Chester Nimitz is to control the Pacific Ocean Zone and General Douglas MacArthur the Southwest Pacific. This division presages later friction between the two as to how the reconquest should be attempted.

APRIL 1942
World War II: Battle of the Atlantic German U-Boats off the American East Coast continue to prey on Allied shipping. On 1 April a partial convoy system off the East Coast begins. Axis submarines will sink 74 ships during the month, largely in the Atlantic and the Indian Oceans. The Allied convoy system, however, is beginning to be effective in protecting surface ships. American submarine operations will be hampered by defective torpedo design into 1943.
World War II: British Air Operations The RAF pursues extensive bombing of enemy targets, largely saturation bombing at night. This month the range of targets includes industrial areas in Germany and France and several of the Atlantic ports in France and Norway. There are also offensive fighter sweeps over occupied France nearly every day. German industry, however, proves able to weather bomb attacks and increases its output.

The order to abandon ship is given on board USS *Lexington*, fatally damaged in the Battle of the Coral Sea in May 1942.

World War II: Mediterranean Axis air attacks and harbor mining make the situation of the Maltese steadily more desperate.

4-9APRIL 1942

World War II: Indian Ocean A Japanese carrier force attacks a British fleet in the Indian Ocean, sinking 120,000 tons of merchant shipping along with one carrier, two cruisers and four smaller Royal Navy ships.

8 APRIL 1942

World War II: Mediterranean The worst air attacks of the war hit beleaguered Malta, but the defenders hold fast. On 16 April King George VI will award the Maltese the George Cross for collective heroism.

9 APRIL 1942

World War II: Philippines After holding out for three months some 75,000 Philippine and US troops surrender on the Bataan Peninsula of Luzon. In what will be called the Bataan Death March, Allied prisoners will be force-marched by the Japanese to a prison camp 100 miles away; thousands of the prisoners will die of starvation and savage treatment by their captors. Fighting continues in isolated areas of Luzon and the other islands, with some US and Filipino units operating as guerillas. General Wainwright remains on Corregidor.

14 APRIL 1942

World War II: Battle of the Atlantic The destroyer USS *Roper* sinks the German *U.85*. This is the first submarine kill by an American ship.
World War II: The Doolittle Raid on Tokyo Sixteen US B-25 bombers led by General James H. Doolittle take off from the carrier *Hornet* about 650 miles off Japan and raid Tokyo and three other Japanese cities. Those that are not shot down fly on to land in China. To increase their range, the bombers have been practically disarmed, so little material damage is done to the enemy. The effect on the morale of both sides, however, is enormous. As the Allies rejoice, the Japanese begin to bring more fighter forces home to strengthen their defenses and make the unwise decision to extend their perimeter of defense in the Pacific. The direct results of that decision will be the Battles of the Coral Sea and Midway.

29 APRIL 1942

World War II: Burma The Japanese enter Lashio, Burma, cutting off the overland route to China. All supplies for Allied forces must now come in by air. Mandalay will fall to the Japanese on 1 May.

2 MAY 1942

World War II: Battle of the Coral Sea The buildup to a historic battle begins when a Japanese fleet under Admiral Inouye is divided into five groups with the principal task of capturing Port Moresby in southeastern New Guinea. From there the Japanese plan to operate on Allied shipping lanes to Australia and perhaps invade Australia itself. Largely because of American ability to read the Japanese codes, Admiral Nimitz is able to respond, ordering a concentration of Allied task forces to oppose the Japanese.

4 MAY 1942

World War II: Battle of the Coral Sea Aircraft from the carrier *Yorktown*, 100 miles south of Guadalcanal, attack Japanese forces off Tulagi. The *Yorktown* then returns south to join the Allied fleet.

5 MAY 1942

World War II: Battle of the Coral Sea Admiral Takagi's carriers enter the Coral Sea from the west. Admiral Frank J. Fletcher's task force is refuelling in the area, but the Japanese make no contact.
World War II: Philippines Japanese forces land on the island fortress of Corregidor. General Wainwright will surrender with his 15,000 American and Filipino troops on 6 May, and the next day he will broadcast a request for all US forces in the Philippines to surrender. Despite the loss of the Philippines, the American-Filipino resistance has had the good effect of tying up great numbers of Japanese forces for five months when they might have been employed elsewhere.
World War II: Burma In Burma with his Chinese troops, American General Joseph Stilwell learns that the Japanese have entered China via the Burma Road; Stilwell decides that his forces must retire toward India, not China.

7 MAY 1942

World War II: Battle of the Coral Sea Admiral Fletcher sends Task Force 44 to attack the Japanese transports bound for Port Moresby. The Japanese sight these ships and make an assault, unsuccessfully, with land-based aircraft. But the Japanese do manage to sink an American tanker and a destroyer, while Fletcher's planes sink the small aircraft carrier *Shoho*. Late in the day Admiral Takagi loses 21 planes in trying to locate and attack Fletcher's carriers; some Japanese pilots are so confused that they attempt to land on the US carrier *Yorktown*.

8 MAY 1942

World War II: Battle of the Coral Sea Reconnaissance aircraft from the opposing forces sight their enemy virtually simultaneously, and all the carriers dispatch strikes. The *Lexington* is badly hit and abandoned (she is later disposed of by an American destroyer), and the *Yorktown* is seriously damaged. In return, American planes seriously damage the *Shokaku*. By the end of the battle, the Japanese have suffered less injury to their carriers than the Americans, but Takagi has lost 105 carrier aircraft to Fletcher's 81. Tactically, the Battle of the Coral Sea is a draw, but strategically, it is an Allied victory: it ends the Japanese threat to Port Moresby and halts the expansion of enemy territory to the southeast. The engagement has also been the first naval battle in history fought entirely by airplanes – a carrier-to-carrier conflict in which the opposing ships were never in visual contact.

15 MAY 1942

World War II: National President Roosevelt signs the Congressional act establishing the Women's Auxiliary Army Corps (WAAC) – later to become simply the Women's Army Corps (WAC). On 30 July Congress will establish the WAVES, a women's naval reserve. Civilian gasoline rationing of three gallons per week goes into effect in 17 eastern states.
World War II: Burma The first British forces retreating from Burma reach India. The British and the Chinese have suffered terrible casualties in losing Burma to the Japanese, and China now has no overland communications.

25 MAY 1942

World War II: Battle of Midway: Approach Both Japanese and US ships move from ports around the Pacific and begin converging on Midway, a small island in the central Pacific. The Japanese apparently intend to seize Midway Island for use as an air base to threaten Hawaii, but their deeper purpose is to lure the remaining US carriers into battle and to destroy them. They are unaware that *Yorktown*, damaged in the Coral Sea, will be available to fight them.

28 MAY 1942

World War II: Battle of Midway: Approach All Japanese naval forces have set out under the supreme command of Admiral Yamamoto. The plan is complex: Admiral Kakuta is to launch landings on the Aleutians as a diversion to keep American forces away from the elaborate main attack at Midway, which is expected to achieve complete surprise.

SBD dive bombers crowd USS *Enterprise*'s flight deck in this photograph taken shortly before the Battle of Midway.

However, American code-breakers have given Admiral Nimitz, if not complete information, at least enough to organize his resistance. Admiral Raymond A. Spruance's Task Force 16 sails from Oahu with the carriers *Enterprise* and *Hornet* and escorts. Admiral Frank J. Fletcher's Task Force 17, centered on the carrier *Yorktown*, follows soon after.

30-31 MAY 1942

World War II: British Air Operations Over a thousand British bombers rain their cargo on to Cologne, leaving some 45,000 Germans of the city homeless. The British lose 40 planes. Next month there will be similar raids on Essen and Bremen.

2 JUNE 1942

World War II: Battle of Midway: Approach The US carrier groups from Pearl Harbor join other US forces northeast of Midway. The three carriers under Fletcher and Spruance – *Enterprise, Hornet*, and the hastily-repaired *Yorktown* – have about 250 aircraft, approximately the same number carried by the Japanese main force of four fleet carriers and one light carrier.

3 JUNE 1942

World War II: Battle of Midway The gigantic Japanese Midway Invasion Group and their supports – 162 warships altogether – are found by American air reconnaissance and are unsuccessfully attacked by Flying Fortress bombers operating from Midway.

3-21 JUNE 1942

World War II: Aleutians Yamamoto's intended diversion from the Midway battle has some success when the Japanese take Kiska and Attu, two of the Aleutian islands off Alaska.

4 JUNE 1942

World War II: Battle of Midway Today one of the most critical battles in history erupts in full force near the island of Midway. Believing that the American ships are still at Pearl Harbor, 14 Japanese submarines patrol between Midway and Hawaii. The Japanese operations begin according to plan, 108 planes striking Midway. The Americans send up land-based planes to intercept, but the Japanese slaughter the flyers and release their bombs in two attacks. Meanwhile, American Midway-based dive bombers attacking the Japanese carriers are also roughly handled, losing 17 of 52 and scoring no hits. The US carriers begin searching for Admiral Nagumo's ships at dawn, and the first strikes are soon launched. Rearming his reserve planes for the second strike on Midway, Nagumo learns of an American carrier in the area and thus faces a quandary: the aircraft now on decks need fuel and bombs and his first strike force is due back shortly. Nagumo makes the fateful decision to recover all his aircraft first and then send a coordinated strike against the American ships. At about 9:30 in the morning the first American carrier planes come into action, but are badly coordinated – at first only 41 torpedo bombers attack, losing 35 planes and scoring no hits. They have managed, however, to lure almost all the Japanese Zeros down to low level, and the tight cruising formation of the enemy ships has been disrupted, weakening their AA defense. Just before 10:30, when the Japanese have at last organized their strike, American dive-bombers descend in a blistering attack. Within five minutes three Japanese fleet carriers, *Akagi, Kaga* and *Soryu*, their decks packed with aircraft ready to take off, have all been fatally hit. The undamaged *Hiryu* launches its planes against the *Yorktown*, critically damaging it. Late in the afternoon American planes inflict comparably lethal damage on the *Hiryu*. All four stricken Japanese fleet carriers sink or are scuttled within the next 24 hours.

5 JUNE 1942

World War II: National The United States declares war on Bulgaria, Hungary and Rumania.

5-7 JUNE 1942

World War II: Battle of Midway At first Admiral Yamamoto considers closing in to fight a surface battle with the American task forces, but he abandons the idea and retreats on 6 June. With that concession of defeat ends one of the most important battles in history. In addition to the four Japanese carriers, a heavy cruiser and some 275 planes have been lost, along with many expert pilots. Now the Japanese Navy has only two fleet carriers left. The Americans have lost the *Yorktown*, a destroyer and 147 aircraft, but they still have four fleet carriers, by far the most important class of warships at sea. The Battle of Midway has ended both the Japanese threat to Hawaii and their naval superiority in the Pacific. It will embolden the American command to pursue more aggressive Pacific campaigns, despite the 'Germany first' policy.

10-21 JUNE 1942

World War II: North Africa After driving the British from the Gazala Line, Rommel and his Afrika Korps capture the vital coast city of Tobruk, in Libya, with 30,000 prisoners and mountains of stores. Promoted to field marshal by Hitler after this brilliant campaign, Rommel convinces his superiors to let him push on into Egypt.

13-17 JUNE 1942

World War II: Espionage Eight Germans land from submarines off the coasts of Long Island, New York, and Florida, ordered to engage in sabotage and spying. All are quickly apprehended; six will be electrocuted and the other two imprisoned.

18-21 JUNE 1942

World War II: Allied Planning Churchill and Roosevelt and their advisors confer in Washington. There is much discussion of plans for a Second Front, but the British feel that an immediate offensive into France is impractical. The two leaders also discuss the future of atomic research, agreeing that the two counties will work together. Finally, learning of the fall of Tobruk to Rommel on 21 April, Roosevelt orders 300 American tanks and 100 self-propelled guns to be sent to the British in North Africa. These supplies will make a critical difference in the next weeks.

25 JUNE 1942

World War II: Command Major General Dwight D. Eisenhower is appointed commander of US forces in the European theater.

30 JUNE 1942

World War II: National Congress appropriates nearly $43 billion for the armed services.
World War II: North Africa Rommel's advance drives the British back to El Alamein in Egypt, where the Allied commander, Sir Claude Auchinleck, is determined to make a stand. The Germans will pursue their attacks through the month.

4 JULY 1942

World War II: Air War The first US B-17 Flying Fortress pilots join with the Royal Air Force in a raid on Dutch airfields. On the 7th General Carl Spaatz will take over command of US air forces in Europe.
World War II: Eastern Front The Germans complete their conquest of the major port city of Sevastopol in the southern Crimea.

9 JULY 1942

World War II: Arctic Convoys Convoy PQ-17, which left Iceland on 27 June with 36 freighters, a tanker and escort, begins to arrive in Russian ports after a disastrous passage: 24 ships have been lost to German submarine and air attacks. Despite this setback, the Allied convoy system is proving increasingly effective.
World War II: Russia The German offensive in the USSR divides, one group advancing through Rostov into the vital oilfields of the Caucasus and the other moving toward Stalingrad. Both will make progress for a time, but Red Army resistance mounts steadily.

15 JULY 1942

World War II: India and China The first supplies flown 'Over the Hump' into China reach Chiang Kaishek's forces.

19 JULY 1942

World War II: Battle of the Atlantic Due to improved Allied convoy operations the final two German U-Boats sent to prey off the US East Coast are ordered to other areas.

22 JULY 1942

World War II: Allied Planning Roosevelt agrees with the British that a second front in Europe is not possible in 1942 and instructs his negotiators in London to find 'another place for US troops to fight in 1942.' A British plan to invade French North Africa, previously mooted as 'Gymnast,' is adopted in talks over the next few days and is renamed 'Operation Torch.'

5-13 AUGUST 1942

World War II: Battle of the Atlantic Convoy SC-94 is attacked by a U-Boat pack during passage across the Atlantic. This marks the return of U-Boats to large-scale operations on the main North Atlantic routes. SC-94 loses 11 ships, but two of the attacking subs are sunk and four are damaged.

7 AUGUST 1942

World War II: Aleutians The Japanese-held island of Kiska is bombarded by an American naval task force.
World War II: Invasion of Guadalcanal With three carriers under Admiral Frank J. Fletcher in support, an amphibious task force of US Marines lands on Guadalcanal and small adjacent islands of the Solomons. This is the beginning of an agonizing six-month struggle to drive the Japanese from the area and thereby protect and strengthen the supply life-line to Australia. It will be the first time American forces have had to deal with the coordination of sea, air and land forces in amphibious warfare, as well as with the difficult requirements of jungle fighting, which will later have to be pursued all over the Pacific. The landings on Guadalcanal find little opposition at first.

8 AUGUST 1942

World War II: Guadalcanal The remainder of the first American wave lands on Guadalcanal. Troops advancing inland easily overrun the Japanese airstrip, which is renamed Henderson Field. The capture of the small islands of Tulagi and Gavutu is also completed. Because of intense enemy air and submarine activity, Fletcher decides to withdraw his carriers, but the cruisers and transports near Guadalcanal remain.
World War II: Allied Command Roosevelt and Churchill agree that General Dwight D. Eisenhower will lead Operation Torch into French North Africa.

Smoke billows from USS *Yorktown*, hit by aircraft from the Japanese carrier *Hiryu* at the Battle of Midway. *Yorktown* probably would have survived the damage from the air strike, but she was torpedoed the next day by a Japanese submarine and sank 24 hours later.

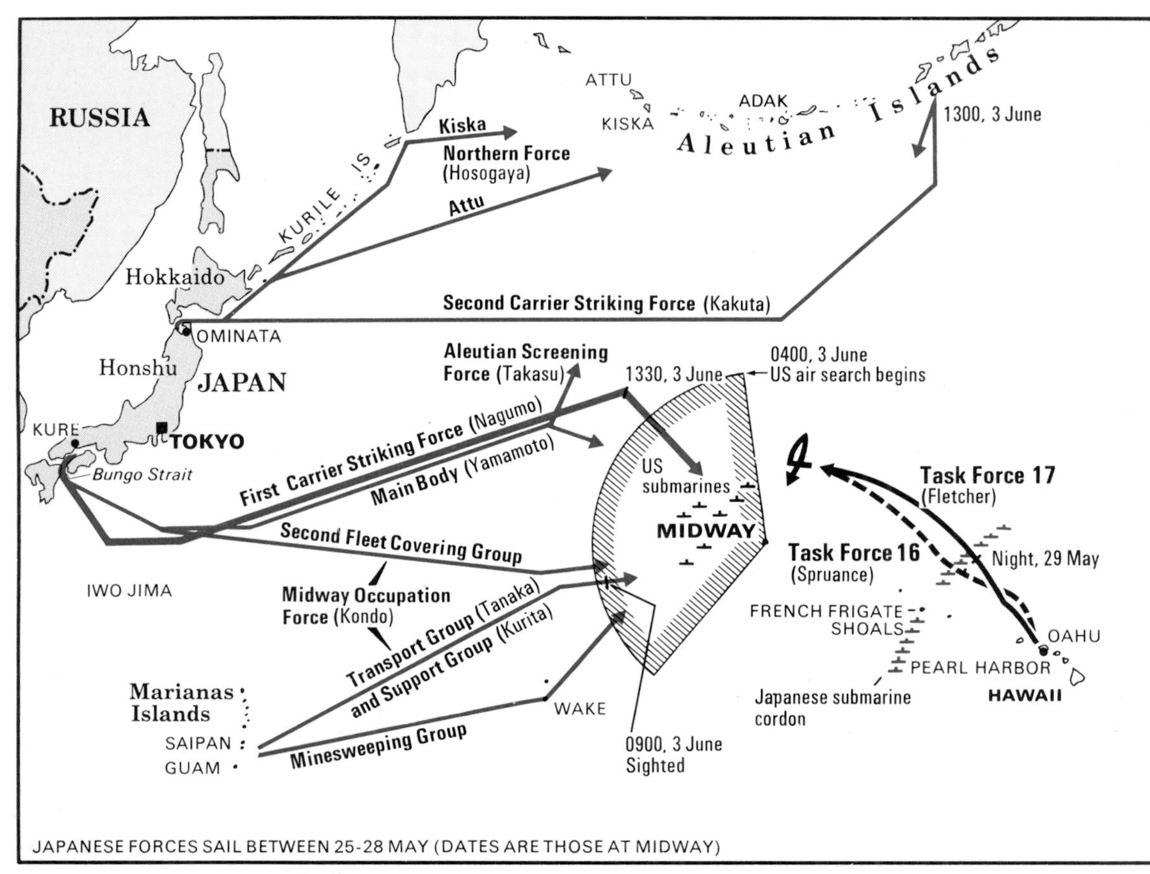

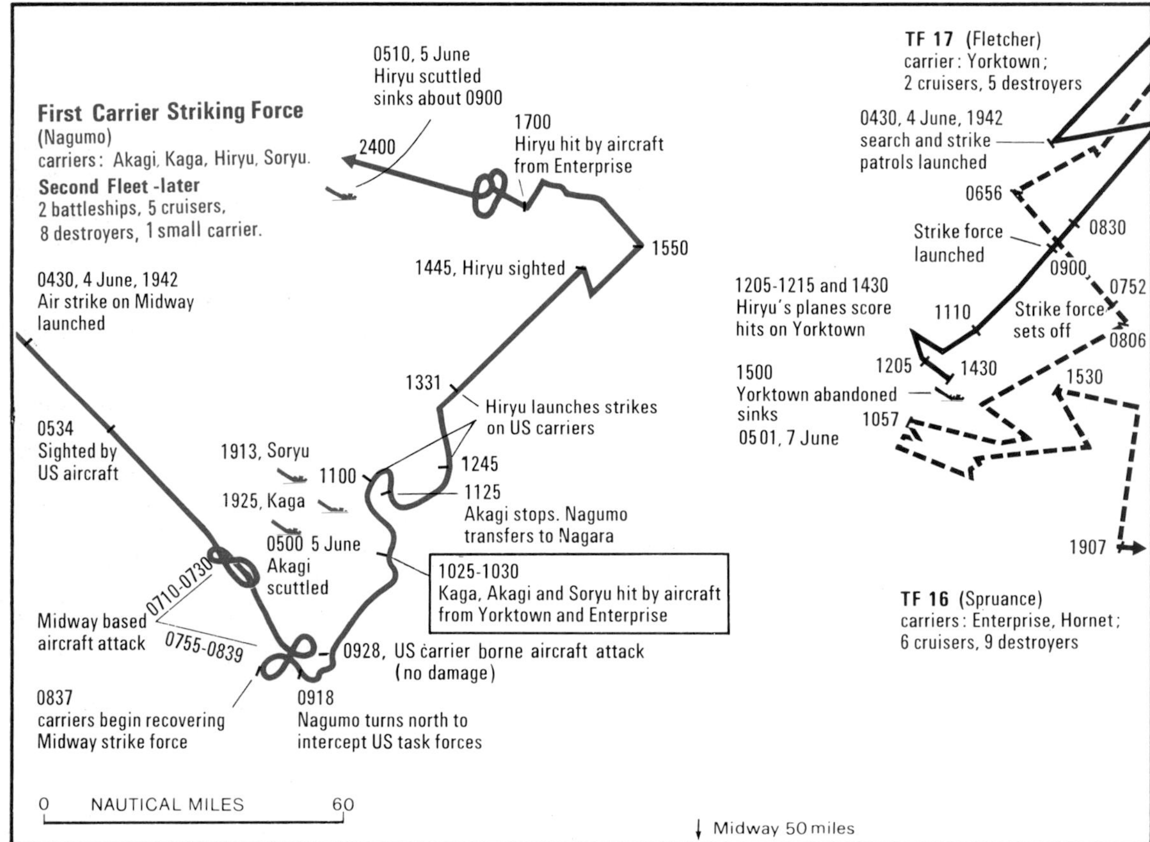

9 AUGUST 1942

World War II: Battle of Savo Island Just after midnight a Japanese cruiser squadron enters Sealark Channel (later renamed Ironbottom Sound) between Savo Island and Guadalcanal. The Allied naval forces are not well prepared for night fighting and are decisively beaten, losing one Australian and three US cruisers and one US destroyer and sinking none of the enemy. The Japanese fail in their aim of attacking the transports unloading off Lunga Point, but the transports are withdrawn in the face of the threat, leaving the Marines short of heavy equipment and supplies.

12-15 AUGUST 1942

World War II: Allied Diplomacy Churchill and American diplomat Averell Harriman confer with Stalin in Moscow, essentially to apologize for the inability of the other Allies to open a European Second Front this year, which would take pressure off the Russians. This tends to confirm Stalin's suspicions that the Allies are content to let Russia bear the brunt of fighting Germany.

17 AUGUST 1942

World War II: Air War Rouen, France, is the target for the first independent American B-17 bombing raid over Europe. Between now and the end of the year the US Eighth Air Force will fly 1547 sorties, losing only 32 aircraft. None of these raids will as yet penetrate Germany.

18 AUGUST 1942

World War II: Guadalcanal The first Japanese reinforcements land at Taivu on Guadalcanal – some 1000 men under Colonel Ichiki. They march toward the American positions believing that there are only some 3000 enemy, but in fact, there are more than 10,000 American Marines and infantry on the island, and Henderson Field is now ready to receive aircraft. The first group of 31 fighters lands on 20 August.

19 AUGUST 1942

World War II: Western Europe Six thousand troops – mostly British and Canadian, with some Free French and American Rangers – make an amphibious commando raid on German installations at Dieppe, France. In practice, the raid proves a disaster, with 3600 Allied casualties and enormous losses of materiel compared to little damage to the enemy, but valuable lessons are learned about amphibious operations.

21 AUGUST 1942

World War II: Guadalcanal Ichiki's forces make a series of wild attacks across the Tenaru River and are wiped out by US troops. Meanwhile, American supplies and reinforcements are pouring into the island.

23 AUGUST 1942

World War II: Battle of the Eastern Solomons Both sides send major warships to cover attempts to ferry supplies to Guadalcanal. Admiral Frank J. Fletcher's Task Force 61 consists of the carriers *Saratoga*, *Enterprise* and *Wasp*. Admiral Nagumo's squadron is typically operating in several separate groups but includes both of Japan's remaining fleet carriers. Today Fletcher dispatches a strike, but the planes fail to locate any targets.

24 AUGUST 1942

World War II: Battle of the Eastern Solomons In the morning American flyers from Fletcher's squadron sink Nagumo's light carrier *Ryujo* and damage the fleet carrier *Shokaku*, but shortly after, Japanese planes damage the *Enterprise*. At the end of the day both carrier groups retire without decisive results.

25 AUGUST 1942

World War II: Solomons American planes damage two Japanese transports and sink a destroyer on the way to Guadalcanal. The Japanese will decide to use fast destroyers to bring in supplies at night.

27 AUGUST 1942

World War II: Solomons The carrier *Saratoga* is damaged in an attack by a Japanese submarine; the ship will be out of action until the end of October, leaving the *Wasp* now the only undamaged US carrier left in the area. In the next few days the Japanese on Guadalcanal will receive major reinforcements on the destroyer flotilla the Marines dub the 'Tokyo Express.'

30 AUGUST-6 SEPTEMBER 1942

World War II: North Africa Rommel launches a major attack at El Alamein designed to clear Egypt of the British. But the defenders, now commanded by General Sir Bernard Montgomery, will use their

Above: Maps of the Battle of Midway.

Left: General Dwight Eisenhower in October 1942.

superior artillery and air force to hammer the Germans back to their starting line.

1 SEPTEMBER 1942

World War II: Stalingrad The Germans are mounting a major assault on Stalingrad; today in fierce fighting they reach the suburbs of the city.

7-8 SEPTEMBER 1942

World War II: Guadalcanal Some 600 Marine Raiders assault the Japanese base at Taivu, doing considerable damage and disrupting Japanese preparations for an attack on the main American position.

10 SEPTEMBER 1942

World War II: Production A commission reports that the US 'will face both a military and civilian collapse' unless something is done immediately about the rubber supply. Tomorrow the US will sign an agreement to purchase Mexico's entire rubber production, but it will be the rapid development of a synthetic rubber industry that will come to the rescue.

12-14 SEPTEMBER 1942

World War II: Guadalcanal For three days the Japanese mount fierce attacks, especially around 'Bloody Ridge.' With the help of reinforcements flown in from the *Wasp* and effective artillery support, American troops turn back these attacks; the Japanese withdraw on the 14th after suffering some 1200 casualties. However, that day the Japanese navy inflicts a major blow when a submarine sinks the carrier USS *Wasp* and a destroyer; the battleship *North Carolina* is also damaged. For the present, the US has no functioning carriers in the area.

16 SEPTEMBER 1942

World War II: New Guinea The Japanese have mounted a number of attacks against Australian troops on New Guinea, but today these are brought to a halt before Ioribaiwa. With the benefit of local air superiority and American reinforcements now arriving at Port Moresby, the Allies can now plan an offensive.

17 SEPTEMBER 1942

World War II: Atomic Research Atomic research in the US is placed under military control, and General Leslie Groves is appointed to direct the program. Groves will prove an able administrator, but he is deeply concerned about security. He is strongly opposed to sharing information with the British.

18 SEPTEMBER 1942

World War II: Guadalcanal As transports bring supplies and the 7th Marine Regiment to reinforce the island, American strength builds to about 23,000 well-supplied men.

23 SEPTEMBER 1942

World War II: New Guinea The Australians begin a counteroffensive against the Japanese as more American reinforcements land at Port Moresby. Australian General Blamey commands the operation under orders from MacArthur. The Japanese will begin to fall back on the 27th.

A B-17E Flying Fortress banks over Sizo Island in 1942. Devastating against industrial targets, the B-17 was not suited for the Pacific island war.

25 SEPTEMBER 1942

World War II: Production The Maritime Commission announces that 488 cargo ships were constructed in the last year.

1 OCTOBER 1942

World War II: New Guinea The campaign heats up: General MacArthur orders an Allied advance on Gona and Buna. Australian forces have already begun to pursue a Japanese retreat along the Kokoda Trail. A US force is to move over the parallel Kapa Kapa Trail to join the Australians in cutting off the Japanese at the Kumusi River. There are also to be landings along the north coast.

2 OCTOBER 1942

World War II: National President Roosevelt is granted power to control wages, salaries and agricultural prices.

4 OCTOBER 1942

World War II: Stalingrad Nazi General Friedrich Paulus begins a fresh series of attacks on Stalingrad, which will become the scene of the fiercest and longest-lasting fighting of the German offensives.

6 OCTOBER 1942

World War II: Production An additional Lend-Lease agreement is signed under which the US will deliver 4.4 million tons of supplies to the Soviet Union.

7 OCTOBER 1942

World War II: Guadalcanal The 1st Marine Division attacks west from the American beachhead along the River Matanikau in an attempt to free Henderson Field from enemy artillery fire. This attack will be halted in three days after the Marines have wiped out a Japanese battalion.

11-12 OCTOBER 1942

World War II: Battle of Cape Esperance As both sides are engaged in mounting supply operations to their forces on Guadalcanal, opposing squadrons of cruisers and destroyers meet off Cape Esperance, and a confused night action ensues, both sides at times firing on their own ships. By the end of the fight the US has lost one destroyer, with three other ships seriously damaged. The Japanese have lost a heavy cruiser and a destroyer, with several other ships damaged.

13-14 OCTOBER 1942

World War II: Guadalcanal Japanese warships bombard Henderson Field, destroying half of the approximately 100 American airplanes.

Marine reinforcements come on shore at Guadalcanal.

Landing craft disgorge troops and equipment onto a North African beach in November 1942 at the start of the Allies' Operation Torch.

18 OCTOBER 1942

World War II: Command Admiral William 'Bull' Halsey replaces Admiral Robert Lee Ghormley in charge of the South Pacific Command Area. Admiral Nimitz has brought in the aggressive Halsey to break the stalemate in the Solomons campaign.

21 OCTOBER 1942

World War II: National Congress passes the largest tax bill in US history to date, calling for some $9 billion in new taxes and including a 'Victory Tax' of 5 percent on all incomes over $624, to be levied until the war ends.

World War II: Guadalcanal Japanese forces, now 20,000 strong, begin a series of attacks against the American positions, but due to inadequate intelligence information and difficult terrain the Japanese effort turns out to be badly planned and coordinated.

21-30 OCTOBER 1942

World War II: Operation Torch On the 23rd General Mark Clark lands in Algiers for secret talks with French leaders, from whom the US and Britain hope to enlist support for Operation Torch, the invasion of Algeria and Morocco under the command of General Dwight D. Eisenhower. Meanwhile, a large fleet of Allied transports is en route to the area with no resistance from Axis forces, who have not yet perceived the threat.

23 OCTOBER-3 NOVEMBER 1942

World War II: Battle of El Alamein General Bernard Montgomery unleashes a carefully-prepared attack against Rommel's Afrika Corps (now commanded in Rommel's absence by General Stumme, who dies of a heart attack during the battle). In one of the most important Allied victories of the war Montgomery will drive the enemy back, and by 10 November the Axis powers will be in full retreat out of Egypt. The tide has now turned in North Africa.

USS *Hornet* under air attack (two 'Kates' and a diving 'Val' are visible) off the Solomons in the Battle of Santa Cruz in October 1942.

25-26 OCTOBER 1942

World War II: The Battle of Santa Cruz The Japanese navy has mounted a major operation to support the offensive on Guadalcanal, which has been making little headway. In the two-day naval Battle of Santa Cruz the US fleet meets the Japanese and suffers an apparent defeat: the carrier *Hornet* is sunk and the *Enterprise* damaged, again reducing the US to no functioning carriers in the area. However, enemy losses in aircraft and crew have been severe, the fleet carrier *Shokaku* and the light carrier *Zuiho* have been damaged and thus the Japanese will have to abandon their immediate offensive efforts. Both sides are now nearly exhausted, but the Japanese have lost the initiative.

2 NOVEMBER 1942

World War II: New Guinea In their advance against the Japanese, Australian forces take Kokoda, whose airstrip will now be available to supply the offensive from the air.

5 NOVEMBER 1942

World War II: Operation Torch General Eisenhower arrives in Gibraltar to set up his headquarters for Operation Torch, the Allied invasion of North Africa, which is intended to drive the Axis off the continent and to relieve German pressure on Russia. Admiral Sir Andrew Cunningham will command the naval forces, and General James Doolittle and Air Marshal Welsh the air forces. General Sir Kenneth Anderson will lead the British First Army, which will be the main ground force.

8 NOVEMBER 1942

World War II: Operation Torch The Allied invasion of French North Africa gets underway as some 107,000 American and British troops land in three groups – the American Western and Central and the British Eastern Task Forces, respectively, at Casablanca, Oran and Algiers. Vichy-French resistance to the invasion is minor, partly because several French commanders are not opposed to an Allied success. Admiral Darlan, Vichy commander in North Africa, falls into Allied hands in Algiers, which has quickly fallen.

10 NOVEMBER 1942

World War II: Operation Torch Oran falls to US troops (Casablanca will fall on the 11th). Vichy Admiral Darlan broadcasts orders to all French forces in North Africa to stop fighting the Allies. As Hitler meets with Axis leaders in Munich to discuss the situation Churchill announces that recent events in Africa mark 'the end of the beginning' of Allied war efforts.

11 NOVEMBER 1942

World War II: Operation Torch French authorities in North Africa sign an armistice with the Allies. Realizing that Vichy leaders are of doubtful loyalty to the Axis, Hitler orders German troops into Vichy France and prepares an attempt to capture the main French fleet at Toulon. In Algeria, British troops move eastward but are impeded by German planes and infantry that have been rushed into Tunisia.

11-13 NOVEMBER 1942

World War II: New Guinea The Australian offensive against the enemy has made steady progress; today the Japanese pull back across the Kumusi River, and their resistance crumbles around Gona and Buna.

12 NOVEMBER 1942

World War II: National The draft age is lowered from 20 to 18. Roosevelt estimates that the US armed forces will contain nearly 10 million men by the end of 1943.

13 NOVEMBER 1942

World War II: Operation Torch The British have now taken Bône and are advancing from Algiers. A formal agreement is signed recognizing Vichy Admiral Darlan as head of the French civil government in North Africa. General Giraud is to command the Free French forces.

World War II: The Naval Battle of Guadalcanal Beginning another offensive, the Japanese send a large convoy of transports with 11,000 men toward the island. To give cover to the operation and bombard Henderson Field, Admiral Abe leads a squadron, which runs into Admiral Callaghan's ships. In a brief but severe fight Callaghan sinks two enemy ships and damages the rest, in the process losing six of his own ships; but the Japanese transport convoy turns back.

14-15 NOVEMBER 1942

World War II: Naval Battle of Guadalcanal Early on the 14th Admiral Tanaka's destroyers and transports come under heavy air attack by planes from Henderson Field and the *Enterprise*. Tanaka continues his advance, however, leading at night to another battle off Savo Island. Admiral Lee has brought up battleships and destroyers to challenge Admiral Kondo's covering force; shortly before midnight these forces collide. The battleship *South Dakota* is hit and forced out of the battle, but later a devastating seven-minute burst of fire from the battleship *Washington* sinks the Japanese battleship *Kirishima*. In three days of fighting, the Japanese have lost two battleships (the other being the *Hiei*), one cruiser, three destroyers and 11 transports (the latter drowning thousands of ground troops in them); three more enemy cruisers and six destroyers have been damaged. Admiral Halsey's victorious fleet has lost two light cruisers and seven destroyers, with eight other vessels damaged. After this battle control of the seas around Guadalcanal passes to the Americans. The Japanese are forced to supply their increasingly sick and hungry troops on Guadalcanal by submarine.

15 NOVEMBER 1942

World War II: Tunisia and Algeria The British capture Tabarka while US paratroops take an airfield near Tebéssa. The German buildup has been rapid; there are now 10,000 enemy troops taking up positions in Tunisia. The Nazis also have over 100 combat planes in well-established bases, while the Allies are forced to use temporary landing grounds farther from the front.

17-20 NOVEMBER 1942

World War II: Malta A British convoy gets from Gibralter to Malta with only one vessel hit. The period of heavy attacks on the island, which began early in 1941, is over.

18 NOVEMBER 1942

World War II: Guadalcanal US ground troops begin expanding their perimeter on the island; the Japanese will not again be strong enough to drive the Americans back into their original perimeter.

19-24 NOVEMBER 1942

World War II: Stalingrad Soviet forces commence a winter offensive along the Don, while some 300,000 German troops in Stalingrad are slowly surrounded and isolated by a gigantic Red Army pincer movement. Despite Hitler's orders to hold out to the death, German troops at Stalingrad will begin surrendering on the 25th; the last units will not give up until early February 1943.

19 NOVEMBER 1942

World War II: New Guinea US troops begin an unsuccessful attack on Buna, which the Japanese have been reinforcing. Bitter but indecisive fighting will continue for weeks.

23 NOVEMBER 1942

World War II: Libya Montgomery halts his advance to reorganize his forces, which have now chased Rommel almost 600 miles in two weeks.

27 NOVEMBER 1942

World War II: France The Germans have planned to make use of the French warships in the harbor of Toulon. Today, on the orders of Admiral Laborde, sailors scuttle the whole fleet – three battleships, seven cruisers, 16 submarines and 46 other craft.

30 NOVEMBER–1 DECEMBER 1942

World War II: Battle of Tassafaronga Off Guadalcanal the regular night run of the Tokyo Express again develops into a major battle between the naval forces of Admiral Tanaka and Admiral Wright. Although radar helps Wright get off the first shells and torpedoes, the American fire is ineffective, fatally damaging only one enemy destroyer. In the Japanese return fire one cruiser is sunk and three are seriously damaged. Nonetheless, Tanaka fails to deliver his supplies to the starving Japanese forces on the island.

DECEMBER 1942

World War II: Battle of the Atlantic During 1942 Allied shipping losses have been 7.8 million tons, of which less than 7 million tons has been replaced by new construction. German U-Boat strength has increased to 212 operational boats, and the underwater fleet has accounted for 80 percent of Allied shipping losses. The year 1943 will see American production begin to reverse the pattern of Allied losses.

1 DECEMBER 1942

World War II: Tunisia There is a strong German counterattack near Tebourba, which the Allies repulse after taking heavy casualties. The German buildup in the area continues. General Carl Spaatz takes over command of the Allied Air Forces in Northwest Africa.

2 DECEMBER 1942

World War II: Atomic Research The first manmade self-sustaining chain reaction is achieved in an atomic pile at Chicago University.
World War II: New Guinea Japanese land reinforcements for the garrison at Buna. General Robert Eichelberger takes over command of American forces in the area, with orders from MacArthur to 'Take Buna or don't come back alive.'

While the Anglo-Americans were going over to the offensive in the Pacific and defeating the Germans in North Africa, the Russians were slowly winning the ultimately decisive battle for possession of the shattered city of Stalingrad.

6 DECEMBER 1942

World War II: Tunisia In one of a series of successful attacks German forces push the Allies back near Medjez el Bab. On the 8th the Nazis will occupy Bizerta, capturing 16 French warships.

7-8 DECEMBER 1942

World War II: Guadalcanal The Japanese continue to have major problems supplying their forces on the island. On these days a seven-destroyer convoy has to turn back after attacks by American PT boats.

14 DECEMBER 1942

World War II: New Guinea Japanese reinforcements land west of Gona and begin to march along the coast toward the Australian flank. US forces take Buna village, but the far tougher obstacle of the Buna Government Station still remains in Japanese hands.

18 DECEMBER 1942

World War II: New Guinea Cape Endiadere, east of Buna, is taken by Allied forces led by the Australians. Fierce fighting continues around Buna.

24 DECEMBER 1942

World War II: French North Africa Admiral Darlan, the Vichy leader who has cooperated with the Allies, is assassinated; General Giraud will take over as French high commissioner for North Africa. General Eisenhower decides to postpone the stalled Allied offensive operations in Tunisia until the rainy season is over.

28 DECEMBER 1942

World War II: Atomic Research Roosevelt confirms the policy of noncooperation with the British that his advisers have recommended. The British are upset by the decision, feeling that it contradicts former agreements. The top-secret American research is now known as the Manhattan Project, under the direction of General Leslie Groves; the team of scientists in Chicago is directed by Enrico Fermi.

31 DECEMBER 1942

World War II: Guadalcanal With a crippled Pacific fleet that is no longer able to supply their forces on Guadalcanal, the Japanese High Command decides to evacuate the island. The orders will be issued on 4 January.

2 JANUARY 1943

World War II: Russia A Soviet offensive drives German forces in the area of the Caucasus into withdrawal. At Stalingrad the trapped Germans are still fighting, but their offensive is doomed.
World War II: New Guinea Finally cracking Japanese resistance after weeks of vicious struggle, General Eichelberger's 1 Corps storm Japanese posts at Buna. Fighting continues around Sanananda.

9 JANUARY 1943

World War II: New Guinea Australian forces are airlifted to Wau to establish a forward base for the next phase of the Allied offensive, to begin when the capture of Buna and Sananand is achieved. In that sector the Americans take Tarakena village but are held up when they try to advance on Sanananda. On the 13th General Robert Eichelberger will take overall command of the fighting troops on the island.

14-24 JANUARY 1943

World War II: Allied Planning President Roosevelt and Prime Minister Churchill meet at Casablanca, Morocco, accompanied by their chiefs of staff and other Allied representatives. The conference starts under a strain, as the British feel the Americans are abandoning the agreed-upon policy of defeating Germany first, while the Americans feel the British are doing too little against the Japanese. But the conference ends with general agreement on such strategies as the invasion of Sicily and Italy, continuous bombing of Germany, maintaining supplies to Russia and the eventual invasion of France. General Eisenhower is given command of the North African Theater. At the closing press conference Roosevelt announces the Allies will demand 'unconditional surrender' of Germany and Japan; some will later argue that this policy unnecessarily prolongs the war.

18 JANUARY 1943

World War II: Tunisia In a German offensive Tiger tanks are used for the first time in this theater at Bou Arada. Neither the British nor the Americans have anything to match this monster vehicle, with its massive armor and powerful 88mm gun.

21 JANUARY 1943

World War II: Air War The Casablanca Directive is issued to British and American strategic bombing forces in Europe, setting out the priorities for continuing Allied attacks. Most of the doctrine is in line with the American practice of daylight precision bombing of industrial targets, as opposed to the usual British style of nighttime saturation bombing. However, US Air Forces as yet have too few resources to carry out these plans, and the RAF bombers have too little accuracy.

22 JANUARY 1943

World War II: North Africa Rommel's retreating German forces pull out of Tripoli, the main port of Libya. Montgomery, the first British general to win a major battle against the Germans, will pull his British Eighth Army into the city on the 23rd and begin using the port a week later in support of Eisenhower's Operation Torch.
World War II: New Guinea The last Japanese are cleared from Papua by Allied forces. The Japanese have lost about 7000 killed in the campaign so far; the Allies about half that number. Enemy resistance at Sanananda and Giruwa is now down to isolated pockets.

23 JANUARY 1943

World War II: Guadalcanal The American offensive is now making rapid gains, but US commanders fail to realize that this is due to Japanese withdrawals toward Cape Esperance.

27 JANUARY 1943

World War II: Air War In the first raid by the USAAF over a German target, 55 US B-17 bombers raid Wilhelmshaven, losing three of their number but claiming to have shot down 22 German planes. American bomber commanders believe that their B-17 Fortress and B-24 Liberator aircraft will make it possible for them to make unescorted daylight missions over Germany to bomb industrial targets with accuracy, thus sparing the civilian population. The fortunate results of this first raid help to confirm, for the moment, this erroneous conclusion.

Above: German General Erwin Rommel.

Above right: British General Bernard Montgomery, who defeated Rommel at El Alamein.

29-30 JANUARY 1943

World War II: Solomons The US Navy's TF 18, covering a supply operation to Guadalcanal, is attacked by Japanese aircraft off Rennel Island, and a heavy cruiser is sunk.

30 JANUARY 1943

World War II: Germany On the 10th anniversary of Hitler's regime Hermann Goering and Joseph Goebbels deliver speeches in Berlin; the RAF celebrates the occasion with its first daylight raid on Berlin, its attacks timed to coincide with the festivities. Meanwhile, Admiral Karl Doenitz is appointed head of the German Navy.

World War II: Tunisia A German Panzer division equipped with Tiger tanks drives back inexperienced French and American troops around Faid.

31 JANUARY-2 FEBRUARY 1943

World War II: Stalingrad Field Marshal Paulus surrenders his German units at Stalingrad; within two days the remaining Germans in the area surrender. With 150,000 Germans and 50,000 Russians dead in the fighting, the surrender at Stalingrad marks the end of Hitler's Russian ambitions and an extraordinary comeback for Marshal Zhukov and his forces, who had been overwhelmed by the early Nazi offensive. From now on the Germans will largely be in retreat before the Red Army, and that retreat will end only in Berlin.

1 FEBRUARY 1943

World War II: Guadalcanal An American force lands near Cape Esperance, but despite this interference the Japanese evacuation begins.

4 FEBRUARY 1943

World War II: Libya and Tunisia The first units of Montgomery's British Eighth Army cross the border of Libya into Tunisia.

9 FEBRUARY 1943

World War II: Guadalcanal After the last Japanese troops slip away on convoys during the night, US forces link up to complete their recapture of Guadalcanal, ending the first great American operation of the war. The Japanese have lost about 10,000 killed, the Americans 1600. It is an important victory both strategically and psychologically, but the fanatical Japanese resistance on the island presages terrible fighting to come in the Pacific.

14-22 FEBRUARY 1943

World War II: North Africa Axis forces in Tunisia mount an offensive that temporarily drives the Americans back at the Kasserine Pass, but on 21-22 February a fierce fight near Thala ends with Rommel's forces exhausted. Although the Germans will make some attacks in the next two weeks, they are ready to evacuate Tunisia. One factor in the Thala battle is the effective British system for controlling air support, which will be adopted in future American campaigns.

19 FEBRUARY 1943

World War II: Solomons American reinforcements are being landed on Guadalcanal in preparation for the next move, invasion of the Russell Islands. By the end of the month some 9000 American troops will occupy these islands without resistance.

MARCH 1943

World War II: Battle of the Atlantic This month will be described as the period when the Germans came closest to defeating the convoy system supplying the British and the Russians from North America. Allied shipping losses for March will total 120 ships, most sunk by U-Boats, many in North Atlantic convoys. The German U-Boat fleet loses 15, only six of these in battles with convoys. Nonetheless, within two months the Allies will have gained the upper hand in the struggle with the U-Boats, helped in large part by growing skill with the captured German Enigma code machine.

World War II: Air War This month RAF Bomber Command will mount ten major attacks on targets in Germany, dropping more than 8000 tons of bombs. American targets will include Vegesack and Wilhelmshaven. On 5-6 March a heavy British raid on Essen will begin what Air Marshal Harris calls the 'Battle of the Ruhr'. By the time it ends on 12 July this 'Battle' will involve 43 major raids on the Nazis' industrial heartland, but, to compensate for the 1000 Allied aircraft lost, there will be no vital damage to German production.

2-4 MARCH 1943

World War II: Battle of the Bismarck Sea Off New Guinea, US and Australian planes destroy a Japanese convoy, sinking eight transports and four destroyers, shooting down 25 Japanese planes and killing at least 3500 enemy. Losses for the allies are five planes. The Japanese regard the battle as a major disaster for their operations in New Guinea.

8 MARCH 1943

World War II: Diplomacy The US ambassador to the USSR, Admiral W. M. Standley, claims that the Russian leaders are not telling their people about all the aid the US is sending. On 11 March the Russian ambassador to the US will thank America for its aid, but this does not quite deal with the US charge, which is substantially true.

18 MARCH 1943

World War II: Tunisia Beginning a new offensive in Tunisia, General George S. Patton's II Corps takes Gafsa and pushes forward toward El Guettar.

20-28 MARCH 1943

World War II: Tunisia The British under Montgomery drive Axis forces into retreat from the Mareth Line. In April the Axis will take defensive positions around Bizerta and Tunis.

1 APRIL 1943

World War II: National Meats, fats and cheese are placed under rationing. On the 8th Roosevelt will freeze prices, wages and salaries in an effort to stem inflation.

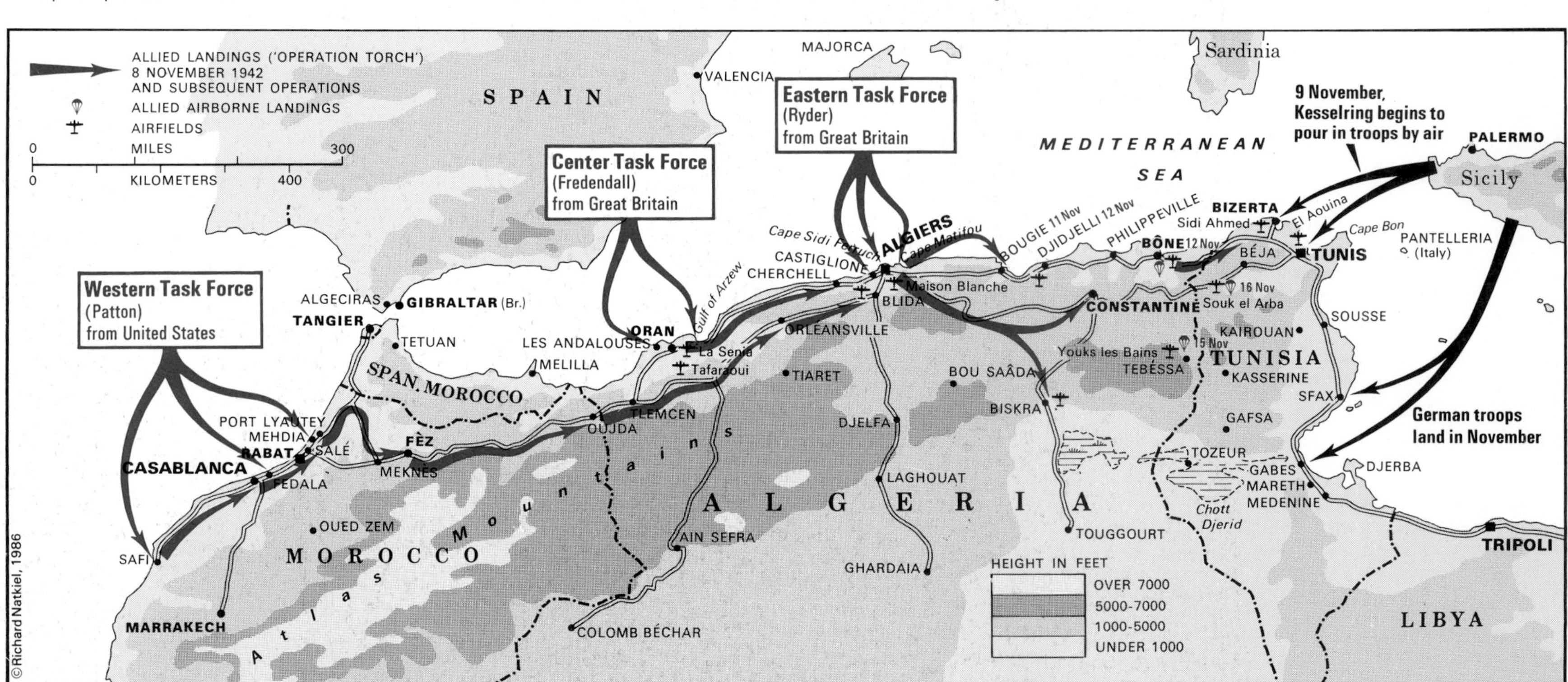

A map of Operation Torch.

The Red Banner is hoisted in Stalingrad following the surrender of the 90,000 German troops remaining in the city on 2 February 1943.

3 APRIL 1943

World War II: Tunisia German resistance has stalled Patton's advance at El Guettar.

7 APRIL 1943

World War II: Solomons In an attempt to set back American offensive preparations, Yamamoto mounts an all-out air offensive called Operation 1. Today there is a Japanese raid against Guadalcanal and Tulagi by 180 planes, in which a US destroyer and two other vessels are sunk.

17 APRIL 1943

World War II: Air War In one of the Eighth Air Force's largest operations yet 115 B-17 bombers are sent to attack Bremen aircraft factories. Sixteen aircraft fail to return.

18 APRIL 1943

World War II: Solomons An aircraft carrying Admiral Yamamoto is shot down by American P-38 Lightning fighters over Bougainville. Yamamoto is killed. The operation was mounted after interception of a coded message announcing a visit by the admiral. Now Japan has lost her leading strategist, and it is a considerable blow to the national morale as well. Admiral Koga will succeed Yamamoto as commander of the Combined Fleet.

19 APRIL-16 MAY 1943

World War II: Holocaust Some 50,000 Jews of the Warsaw Ghetto, having seen nearly half a million of their families and friends removed to concentration camps, rise against the Germans. The Jewish resistance fights valiantly, but after inflicting 10,000 casualties the Nazis blow up the synagogue, send the remaining Jews to extermination camps and raze the Ghetto.

22 APRIL 1943

World War II: Tunisia The Allies begin a series of attacks on last-ditch German positions in the hills. General Omar Bradley's II Corps assaults Hill 609 in 'Mousetrap Valley,' intending to advance to Mateur. The British mount attacks on other positions. Meanwhile, Allied pilots shoot down 30 air transports trying to supply the Axis forces; this had been a regular event in the last weeks.

26 APRIL 1943

World War II: Tunisia This week sees heavy fighting as the Allies strike strong Axis defensive positions. Today the British take Longstop Hill, much aided by their new Churchill heavy tanks. Djebel Bou Aoukaz will fall to the British tomorrow after vicious fighting, but the Germans will retake it.

World War II: South Pacific New plans are agreed to for coming American islands operations, codenamed 'Cartwheel.' Admiral Halsey's South Pacific Area forces are to advance northwest through New Georgia and Bougainville in the Solomons. MacArthur's Southwest Pacific Area is to continue its advance up the eastern coast of New Guinea until he and Halsey can join to isolate the Japanese bases at Rabaul on New Britain and Kavieng on New Ireland.

30 APRIL 1943

World War II: Covert War As part of the coming Allied invasion of Sicily, called Operation Husky, a British submarine releases a corpse with false documents off the Spanish port of Huelva. The body will be identified by the Germans as that of a British major carrying letters to Allied commanders on a plan to invade Greece. This brilliant bit of British disinformation (later subject of the film *The Man Who Never Was*) will contribute much to the German failure to anticipate the invasion of Sicily.

MAY 1943

World War II: Battle of the Atlantic The Allied convoy system turns a vital corner: after sinking 50 Allied ships but in the process losing 41 U-Boats, Nazi Admiral Doenitz decides to pull his subs out of the north Atlantic routes. On the Allied side, the US Tenth Fleet is created under Admiral Ernest King to coordinate US antisubmarine operations.

1 MAY 1943

World War II: Labor John L. Lewis orders a strike of the United Mine Workers to protest the wage freeze. When Roosevelt orders a government takeover of soft-coal mines, Lewis calls off the strike.

5-13 MAY 1943

World War II: Tunisia Allied forces in Tunisia unleash their final campaign to drive the Axis from the continent: on the 5th the British retake Djebel Bou Aoukaz; on the 6th the British break through toward Tunis, and the Americans head for Bizerta, Ferryville and Protville; on the 7th Allied forces burst forward all along the line, taking Tunis and Bizerta. Some 250,000 disorganized enemy troops have surrendered by the 13th. It is the end of Axis efforts to gain an African empire.

11 MAY 1943

World War II: Aleutians Supported by a strong naval task force, the American 7th Division begins to land on Attu in a campaign to recapture it from the Japanese. All units get ashore safely but are held up by enemy and by difficult inland terrain.

11-27 MAY 1943

World War II: Allied Planning Roosevelt and Churchill and their staffs meet in Washington at the Trident Conference. The main topics of discussion are the planned invasions of Europe and the commitment of forces to Europe and the Pacific. Despite considerable differences, the two sides work out compromises on all matters, setting the target day for D-Day as 1 May 1944 and naming General Sir Frederick E. Morgan to head the staff planning the invasion (his position is officially Chief of Staff to the Supreme Allied Commander).

15 MAY 1943

World War II: Aleutians An American assault at Massacre Bay is repulsed, but another in the north of Attu does better – although there are American casualties from badly placed US bombing as well as from the enemy. Tomorrow, attacks at Holtz Bay will drive the Japanese back. US forces on Attu now outnumber the enemy four to one, but bad weather and rough terrain hinder operations.

24-27 MAY 1943

World War II: Aleutians The American drive on Attu has been making steady progress. Fighting is especially fierce on these days, as the Japanese are gradually driven off Fish Hook Ridge. On 27 May work is begun on an airfield at Alexai Point.

27 MAY 1943

World War II: Allied Planning Prime Minister Winston Churchill and American Chief of Staff George C. Marshall leave Washington for North Africa for talks with General Eisenhower on Operation Husky, the coming Sicily campaign.

29 MAY 1943

World War II: Aleutians On Attu the Japanese mount a final fanatical attack on American forces in Chicagof Harbor. This attack will fail by tomorrow, completing the gruelling US capture of the island. The Japanese have lost 2350 killed, including many suicides, and only 28 wounded have been captured. American losses are 600 dead and 1200 wounded.

A German Type VII U-boat. By early 1943 U-boats were sinking ships faster than the Allies could replace them by new construction. Thereafter the balance shifted slowly back in the Allies' favor.

British troops roll into Tunis on 7 May 1943 at the same moment that US troops occupy Bizerta. On 12 May all the Germans in Tunisia surrendered.

10 JUNE 1943

World War II: Air War The Allied Joint Chiefs of Staff issue the Pointblank Directive – formal instructions for priorities and goals of the bomber offensive in the long buildup to D-Day. Once again American doctrine of daylight precision bombing will prevail on paper, but the British and American commands will continue in their usual styles, with little coordination between the two countries. In the end German industrial production will not be overwhelmed by the countless tons of bombs.

11 JUNE 1943

World War II: Operation Husky: Approach After taking heavy bombing, the 11,000-strong Italian garrison on Pantelleria Island surrenders without a fight on the approach of an Allied assault force. This is the beginning of Operation Husky, the invasion of Sicily. On the 14th the Allies will occupy Lampione, thereby completing control of all the islands between Sicily and Tunisia. In the coming week convoys for the invasion will leave the US and Britain.

16 JUNE 1943

World War II: Solomons The Japanese have been mounting major air assaults in the area on US ships that are preparing for operations against New Georgia Island. Today American pilots claim 93 enemy aircraft shot down. On the 21st Marines will land without opposition on southern New Georgia.

28-29 JUNE 1943

World War II: New Guinea Another Allied push is underway. Now Kiriwina and Woodlark Islands are occupied by US troops, who start building an airfield. An Allied landing at Nassau Bay on the 30th will be hotly contested by the Japanese.

30 JUNE 1943

World War II: Solomons There are American landings on several islands in the New Georgia group, particularly Rendova. The landings are all successful, but resistance is heavy on Vangunu.
World War II: New Guinea An American/Australian unit known as McKechnie Force lands at Nassau Bay near Salamaua and is immediately involved in heavy fighting to consolidate and extend a bridgehead in preparation for the main operation.

JULY 1943

World War II: Battle of the Atlantic US hunter-killer escort groups sink a number of U-Boats in the Gibraltar and Azores area, and the British are also successful. Nonetheles, German subs sink 61 ships this month in all theaters.
World War II: Air War Besides the regular bombing of Axis targets in Germany, France and Norway there is stepped-up bombing of Italy in support of the coming invasion. Targets begin with Sicily and later include Naples, Bari and Rome. In China, Chennault's Fourteenth Air Force bombs Hankow, Pailochi, Hainan and Hong Kong.

3 JULY 1943

World War II: New Guinea After heavy fighting in the Mubo area Australians advancing from Wau join up with the Americans from the Nassau Bay landing force in the region of the Bitoi River.
World War II: New Georgia US forces make an unresisted landing on Zanana, but the advance toward Munda tomorrow will be hotly contested by the Japanese.

5-17 JULY 1943

World War II: The Battle of Kursk German and Russian forces totalling 2 million men, 6000 tanks and 5000 planes clash in the Ukraine in the largest tank engagement of the war. By the end of the battle the Germans have failed to make any significant gains, and the strategic advantage in Russia passes to the Red Army.

5-6 JULY 1943

World War II: Solomons During 5 July further US forces land in the north of New Georgia; fighting continues on the Zanana-Munda track. During the night some 3000 Japanese troops land on Vila as the opposing navies battle at sea. The next days will see steady fighting on the islands and progress by the US.

9 JULY 1943

World War II: Operation Husky The Allied landing force for Operation Husky, the invasion of Sicily, is being concentrated around Malta, but bad weather is proving troublesome. Defending the island are some 240,000 demoralized and poorly equipped Italian troops and numbers of expert German troops. The Allies have about 1200 transports, 2000 landing craft, 3700 planes and some 480,000 men (about half of them British) under the command of General Dwight D. Eisenhower. The deputy commander is Field Marshal Sir Harold Alexander, who also heads the 15th Army Group, composed of General George Patton's Seventh Army and Field Marshal Bernard Montgomery's Eighth Army. The Allies have mounted an elaborate and generally successful deception operation pointing to both Greece and Sardinia. Hitler has swallowed the bait and reinforced both. Mussolini correctly expects Sicily but does little about it. The invasion begins the night of 9 July with airborne landings, which are unsuccessful in their objectives but which do cause considerable disruption.

10 JULY 1943

World War II: Operation Husky The main Allied landings for Operation Husky begin. Patton's Seventh Army quickly takes Gela, Licata and Vittoria on the southern coast, while Montgomery's British overwhelm Syracuse on the eastern coast.

11 JULY 1943

World War II: Operation Husky The British continue to advance almost unopposed, taking Palazzolo. The Americans run into trouble, attacked by a Panzer division near Gela, but the Germans are repulsed with the help of naval gunfire. Despite further resistance, largely from German units, the advance will make good progress in the next days.

12-13 JULY 1943

World War II: Solomons An American task force of three cruisers and ten destroyers meet a comparable

Troops swarm ashore at the beginning of Operation Husky, the Anglo-American invasion of Sicily. The main landings took place on 10 July 1943.

Although Mussolini foresaw the invasion of Sicily more clearly than Hitler, he did little to improve the defenses of the island.

Japanese squadron off Kolombangara. Japanese torpedoes sink one destroyer and damage two cruisers, but the Americans virtually blow an enemy cruiser out of the water with radar-directed gunfire. US forces are meanwhile consolidating their positions on Rendova and New Georgia, despite fierce resistance.

13 JULY 1943

World War II: New Guinea Japanese positions at Mubo are overrun, and their force is virtually wiped out.

15 JULY 1943

World War II: Operation Husky General Patton moves west along the coast, while Omar Bradley's II corps bisects Sicily to the north. The Allied offensive continues to take towns almost daily.

17 JULY 1943

World War II: New Guinea Australian and American units move toward Salamaua in a holding action to prepare a later move against Lae and the Markham Valley.

19 JULY 1943

World War II: Italy As Hitler and Mussolini hold a tense conference to the north some 500 US bombers raid selected targets in and around Rome. The Allies have avoided the city so far because of its unique historical, religious and artistic significance, and special care is taken on this raid to avoid historic sites.

20 JULY 1943

World War II: Atomic Research Again switching policies, Roosevelt issues a firm order that the US share atomic research with the British. This will be confirmed in August at a conference in Quebec, which also forbids giving atomic information to any third party.

22 JULY 1943

World War II: Operation Husky Patton's troops enter Palermo, the capital. Axis troops are retreating to the northeast tip of the island as the British move up the southeastern coast.

24 JULY-2 AUGUST 1943

World War II: Air War RAF and USAAF planes make a series of bombing raids on Hamburg, Germany, that result in some 50,000 civilian deaths and 800,000 homeless. Most of the casualties result from fire storms created by incendiary bombs. (A fire storm occurs when fires become so intense that they devour all the oxygen in an area and suck more in, creating hurricane-force winds which both feed the fires and move them along at great speed.)

25 JULY 1943

World War II: Italy At a meeting King Victor Emmanuel forces Mussolini to resign after 21 years as *Il Duce* of Italy. On leaving the meeting, Mussolini is arrested. Marshal Pietro Badoglio is named prime minister. While pretending to support the Axis he will begin looking for ways to extricate Italy from the war.

World War II: Solomons A major American push begins on New Georgia, with little initial success except near Bartley Ridge. In the next days there will be slow progress, aided by heavy air and artillery support. Ground fighting for the Americans in the Pacific will largely be a ghastly process of flushing fight-to-the-death enemy out of holes, with much use of grenades and flame throwers.

28 JULY 1943

World War II: Aleutians Late in the day the Japanese evacuate almost all the remainder of the Kiska Island garrison without being spotted; thus heavy American bombing of the island continues into August.

4-5 AUGUST 1943

World War II: Solomons In their steady push to the northwest up the island chain US forces complete the capture of Munda and its airfield. Fighting will continue on the island, however, as the Americans try to prevent the enemy from escaping to Kolombangara.

8 AUGUST 1943

World War II: Operation Husky The Allied advance is making steady progress. Today, in an amphibious operation supported by one cruiser and three destroyers, the Americans land a small force east of Sant Agata, and the Germans evacuate the town. Elsewhere, Cesaro falls to the Americans, and Bronte and Acireale to the British.

13-24 AUGUST 1943

World War II: Allied Planning Roosevelt, Churchill and Canadian Prime Minister Mackenzie King meet in Quebec with military planners to discuss the invasion of France and campaigns in the Pacific. It is agreed that the supreme commander of the invasion will be an American and that continuing aid will be sent to Chiang Kai-shek in China. Pacific operations will continue under US control. Admiral Lord Louis Mountbatten is selected to lead a new Southeast Asia Command (SEAC).

15 AUGUST 1943

World War II: Aleutians An American/Canadian assault force of 34,000 men supported by three battleships lands on Kiska to find the enemy gone.

16-23 AUGUST 1943

World War II: New Guinea At Wewak the US Fifth Air Force, flying from Australia, destroys or disables 300 Japanese planes and kills 1500 enemy pilots and ground crew. This is a major blow to Japan's Pacific operations.

17 AUGUST 1943

World War II: Operation Husky General Patton's troops enter Messina on the northeast tip of the island a few hours before the British, completing the conquest of Sicily. One disappointment for the Allies is the extent of the evacuations the Germans and Italians have managed – over 100,000 enemy troops with large quantities of materiel have escaped across the narrow Strait of Messina. In the invasion the Germans have lost about 10,000 dead and captured plus many wounded; British and American forces have suffered about 7000 killed and 15,000 wounded. More than 100,000 Italians have been captured. Though the victory has secured a major steppingstone to Italy and brought down Mussolini, the escape of so many enemy makes the coming invasion of the continent an even more daunting prospect.

17-18 AUGUST 1943

World War II: Air War On the 17th American B-17s raid ball-bearing factories at Schweinfurt and Regensburg, but 51 aircraft are lost, one-fifth of the attacking force, calling into question American doctrine of daylight bombing. During the night the German rocket research center at Peenemunde is hit to good effect by nearly 600 RAF bombers.

22-28 AUGUST 1943

World War II: Central Pacific Without opposition, US forces occupy various islands in the Ellice group and begin building airfields.

23 AUGUST 1943

World War II: Russia As the Germans evacuate Kharkov the Red Army pushes strongly near the Mius River. The Russians are now driving the enemy back on a broad front.

25 AUGUST 1943

World War II: Solomons The battle for New Georgia is over; the last Japanese resistance at Bairoko is wiped out. However, many enemy have escaped to Arundel and Kolombangara. Americans will begin operations on Arundel on the 27th.

The flamboyant George Patton, as commander of the US 7th Army in Sicily, began to emerge as one of the most talented of American generals.

26 AUGUST 1943

World War II: Diplomacy The US, Britain, Russia and China give limited recognition to General Charles de Gaulle's French Committee of National Liberation. De Gaulle will coordinate valuable Resistance support for the coming invasion of France.

31 AUGUST-1 SEPTEMBER 1943

World War II: Central Pacific The US light carrier *Independence* and the new fleet carriers *Essex* and *Yorktown* attack Marcus Island with slight losses to either side. The carriers are part of the new Fast Carrier Task Force.

SEPTEMBER 1943

World War II: Pacific US submarines sink 160,000 tons of Japanese shipping, not an unusual total in the increasingly effective American submarine campaign.

1 SEPTEMBER 1943

World War II: Central Pacific US forces land on Baker Island and soon have prepared an airstrip to support a coming campaign in the Gilbert Islands.

3 SEPTEMBER 1943

World War II: Operation Avalanche The invasion of mainland Italy, Operation Avalanche, begins at dawn when units of Montgomery's Eighth Army land to the north of Reggio, finding little resistance. By the end of the day Reggio and four other towns are taken. In the next days the British will begin a slow advance up the toe of Calabria. Meanwhile, an Italian general representing Marshal Badoglio signs a secret armistice with the Allies, agreeing to stop Italian military resistance on 8 September. The agreement is kept secret until that date to forestall a German takeover.

4 SEPTEMBER 1943

World War II: New Guinea Supported by a naval task force, Allied forces land on Huon gulf, east of Lae, with little enemy resistance. Tomorrow an American parachute regiment will land in the Markham Valley in the rear of the town.

World War II: Solomons US forces begin to move out from their beachhead on Arundel; tomorrow they will run into stiff Japanese resistance.

8 SEPTEMBER 1943

World War II: New Guinea The Australians advance with some difficulty on Lae from the east. The Japanese begin to withdraw from Salamaua as the Australians push forward in that sector. US destroyers shell Lae.

9 SEPTEMBER 1943

World War II: Operation Avalanche US General Mark Clark's Fifth Army lands at Salerno, south of Naples, meeting stiff resistance from the Germans. A British division siezes the port of Taranto without opposition. On the left flank US Rangers and British Commandos operate on the mountain passes, pre-

Above: US troops of General Mark Clark's 5th Army land at Salerno on 9 September 1948. Fierce German counterattacks kept the beachhead's fate in doubt until the 16th, when the enemy pulled back.

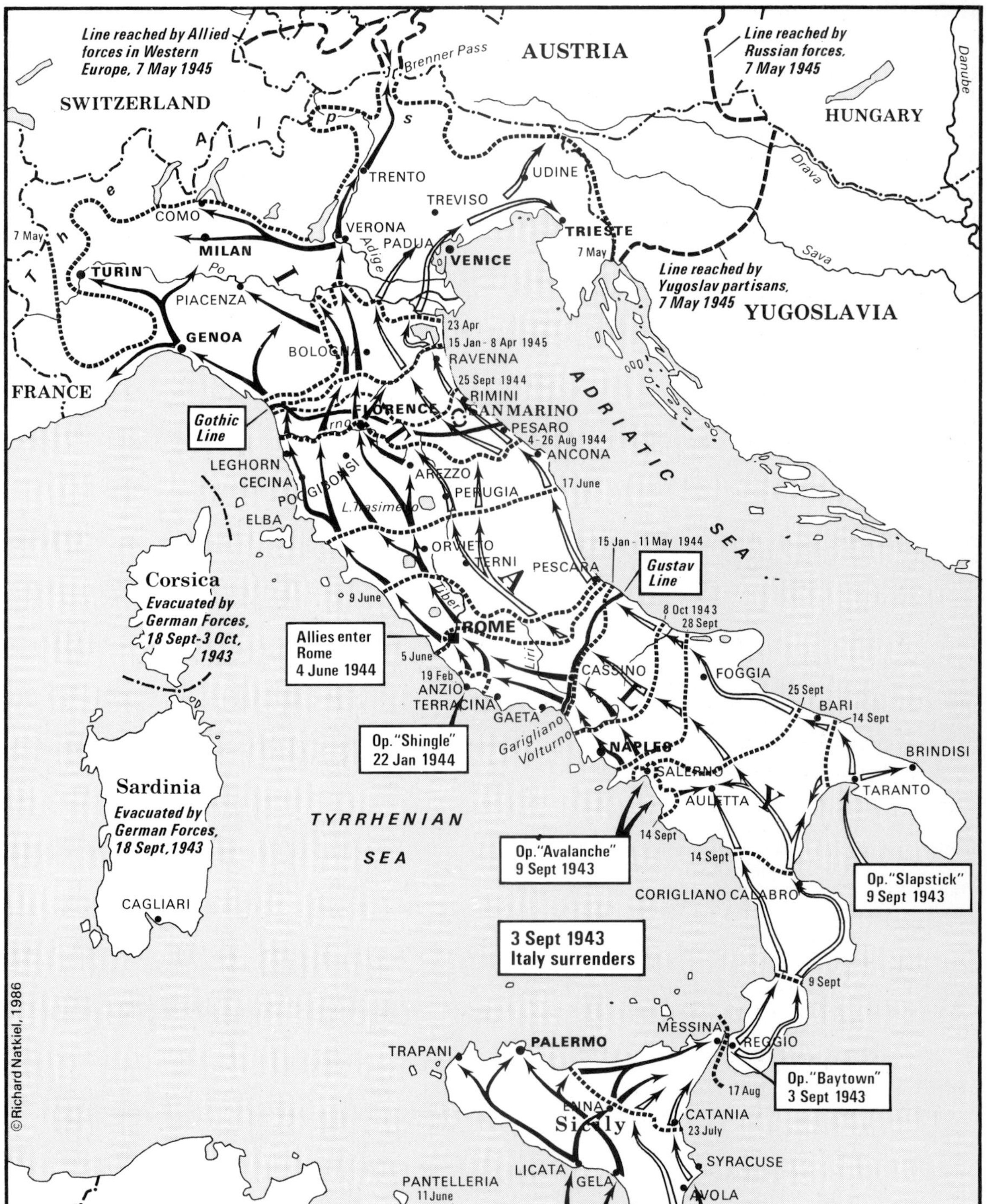

Right: A general map of the Italian campaign.

paring the main American attempt to push inland. German artillery in the mountains will prove to be a major obstacle. To the south Montgomery's advance up the toe of Italy is slowed by demolitions and bad roads.

World War II: Italian Surrender As the Italian fleet is en route to Malta to surrender to the Allies, German glider bombs sink one ship and damage several others; but the bulk of the fleet will reach Malta. There is some fighting in Rome between Italian and German troops, and the government is forced to leave the city, allowing the Germans to take over.

10 SEPTEMBER 1943

World War II: Corsica and Sardinia Germans begin to evacuate their garrison from the Italian island of Sardinia. Some will go on to Corsica, a French island, but starting on 14 September the French will rise against them. By 4 October Free French forces will liberate Corsica.

11 SEPTEMBER 1943

World War II: Operation Avalanche For the second day in a row American and British corps advance with initial success at Salerno but are then driven back by the Germans, who are quickly bringing in reinforcements. There are heavy enemy attacks on Allied transports. Elsewhere, the British take Brindisi without opposition.

World War II: New Guinea A major pocket of enemy resistance falls as the Japanese garrison at Salamaua pulls out and the Australians move in. To the north Allied forces are closing in on the enemy at Lae.

12 SEPTEMBER 1943

World War II: Italy In a daring operation German parachutists rescue Mussolini from his arrest in the Abruzzi Mountains. From Germany the Italian dictator will proclaim his resumption of authority, but few will heed him.

13 SEPTEMBER 1943

World War II: Operation Avalanche Trying to drive a wedge between the American and British beachheads at Salerno, German Panzer divisions attack, driving US forces from Persano and breaching the Allied line in several places. However, naval gunfire contains the Nazi advance and in the next days prevents any significant enemy gains, though the Allied position at Salerno remains shaky.

15 SEPTEMBER 1943

World War II: Italy There is something of a lull at Salerno as the Germans regroup. They now have available the equivalent of about four divisions, including some 100 tanks. The Allies have seven divisions and twice as much armor and can now make practical plans to expand the beachhead. To the south Montgomery's advance gradually quickens its pace. After a failed German attack tomorrow Nazi General Kesselring will concede Salerno and order his forces back to the Volturno River.

16 SEPTEMBER 1943

World War II: New Guinea The Australians take the important eastern coast town of Lae, though most of the Japanese garrison escapes to the north.

17-18 SEPTEMBER 1943

World War II: Central Pacific Land-based B-24 Liberator bombers attack Tarawa on the 17th. The next day aircraft from four carriers follow suit.

18-19 SEPTEMBER 1943

World War II: Italy Following a German pullout, the Allies occupy the island of Sardinia.

20-21 SEPTEMBER 1943

World War II: Solomons On these two days Americans find the enemy has been evacuated from Sagekarasa and Arundel Islands.

21 SEPTEMBER 1943

World War II: Italy The Allies are on the move into the continent, the Germans falling back everywhere except in the vital passes leading to Naples. Today General Clark's Fifth Army wheels to the left toward Naples as Montgomery's Eighth Army moves to the east side of the country.

23 SEPTEMBER 1943

World War II: Italy The British X Corps begins attacks to clear the passes toward Naples. The terrain and tenacious German defense delay progress, but the attacks press on.

25 SEPTEMBER 1943

World War II: Solomons The Japanese begin to evacuate Kolombangara; the garrison there has been isolated by American capture of the other islands in the New Georgia group.
World War II: Russia The Soviets take Smolensk and Roslavl, perhaps their most important successes since the victory at Kursk. From here to the south the Germans are retreating behind the Dnieper River, where Hitler has ordered them to make a stand. However, the Soviets will break through at several points on the Dnieper in the first week of October.

27 SEPTEMBER-1 OCTOBER 1943

World War II: Italy: The Fall of Naples The people of Naples rise against the Germans and fight for three days, suffering heavy losses. On 1 October General Clark's US Fifth Army takes the city. Before evacuating, the Germans damage many cultural institutions and burn thousands of books to punish the Italians for their 'betrayal.' The Allied advance will immediately push on to the north. Hitler orders General Kesselring to hold a line south of Rome during the coming months.

6-9 OCTOBER 1943

World War II: Solomons Americans land unopposed at Vila, on Kolombangara, on the 6th, completing the occupation by the 9th.

12 OCTOBER 1943

World War II: New Britain In a surprise attack preparing for a major invasion of New Britain Island, Operation Cartwheel, 349 planes of the American Fifth Air Force drop 350 tons of bombs on the Japanese naval base at Rabaul. Many of the defending aircraft are shot down, and several enemy ships are damaged in the harbor.

12-13 OCTOBER 1943

World War II: Italy The US Fifth Army assaults German lines along the Volturno River, north of Naples, in the beginning of the hard-fought battles on the way to Rome. The German defense on the river is energetic, and the Allied advance is also hindered by swollen waters and roadless hills. Given the wet weather, the Allied advance must depend on three or four major roads until the ground hardens in the spring. On the 13th Italy, now led by Marshal Badoglio, declares war on Germany, but the country will remain under Allied military control until the end of the war.

14 OCTOBER 1943

World War II: Air War A force of 291 Flying Fortresses from the Eighth Air Force bombs the German ball-bearing works at Schweinfurt. Though the raid does considerable damage, 60 planes go down, and 140 are damaged. With this, and the downing of 88 aircraft during the last week, the Eighth has taken insupportable losses. Accordingly, the USAAF abandons long-range, unescorted daylight attacks for the time being.

15 OCTOBER 1943

World War II: Italy Canadian troops take Vinchiaturo. The battle line in the Fifth Army's sector has now moved north of the Volturno. German resistance there is still strong, but the Nazis are preparing to fall back to two intermediate defensive lines – the Barbara and Reinhard Lines. This pullback will begin on the 16th, with Allied forces pursuing.

The F6F Hellcat, most important US carrier fighter of the war, first saw action on 31 August 1943, just 18 months after the prototype first flew.

19-30 OCTOBER 1943

World War II: Diplomacy In Moscow representatives of the USSR, Great Britain, the US and China discuss issues of mutual interest. They sign a four-power agreement on postwar treatment of the Axis powers and on the creation of an international organization to work for peace.

28 OCTOBER-3 NOVEMBER 1943

World War II: Solomons A Marine parachute battalion lands by sea on Choiseul in a diversion preparing a major attack on Bougainville. After a series of sharp actions the Marines are withdrawn.

30 OCTOBER 1943

World War II: Italy On the west coast the Fifth Army takes Mondragone, having penetrated the Germans' Barbara Line there. Inland other units of the army continue their advance over hilly terrain and tenacious enemy defenses.

NOVEMBER-DECEMBER 1943

World War II: Battle of the Atlantic In the last two months of the year 78 Allied North Atlantic convoys make their passage without loss. Seventeen U-Boats are sunk, along with 12 of 17 U-Boat tankers.

1 NOVEMBER 1943

World War II: Solomons Beginning another gruelling Pacific campaign US forces land on the large island of Bougainville. They are opposed by some 60,000 land and navy forces under General Hyakutake. By the end of today 14,000 men have landed despite some opposition. A Japanese fleet leaves Rabaul under Admiral Omori to attack the American task force.

2 NOVEMBER 1943

World War II: Solomons Just after midnight Admiral Merrill's Task Force 39 finds Omori's squadron on radar; the Japanese are steaming toward Bougainville. A confused night action ensues in which the Americans fight by radar, sinking a cruiser and a destroyer and damaging most of the other Japanese ships. The Americans lose a destroyer. On Bougainville the Americans, having wiped out the local garrison, extend their beachhead over the next days.
World War II: New Britain The Japanese base at Rabaul is attacked by about 160 land-based aircraft from the Fifth Air Force; some 20 planes on each side are lost. On the 5th carrier-based American planes will attack a Japanese naval squadron off Rabaul.
World War II: Command General Carl Spaatz takes command of all US Air Forces in the Mediterranean.

5 NOVEMBER 1943

World War II: Italy The American Fifth Army begins major attacks against the Reinhard Line. The tenacious German defense, which is aided by mountainous terrain and bad weather, will bring the Allied advance to a halt for a time.

6 NOVEMBER 1943

World War II: Russia Soviet troops recapture Kiev, their third-largest city. Stalin makes a celebratory broadcast to the Russian people.

9 NOVEMBER 1943

World War II: Solomons American Marines, advancing inland against enemy resistance on Bougainville, run into the main body of a Japanese regiment in the jungle, and a fierce battle develops; the Japanese will pull back tomorrow. Meanwhile, there is a second wave of American landings.

11 NOVEMBER 1943

World War II: New Britain In further preparations for a ground invasion Admirals Sherman and Montgomery lead two carrier task forces to attack the Japanese base at Rabaul. The 185 attacking American pilots down 70 enemy aircraft, while losing only two, and strike enemy ships as well.

15 NOVEMBER 1943

World War II: Italy Field Marshal Harold Alexander calls off the Fifth Army's attacks on the German Reinhard Line. Allied casualties have been heavy and to little avail; the armies will pause to mop up and regroup.

18 NOVEMBER 1943

World War II: Air War RAF Bomber Command begins the 'Battle of Berlin,' which will include 9100 sorties against the German capital, as well as others on various targets. The campaign will end on 24 March 1944.

20 NOVEMBER 1943

World War II: Invasion of Tarawa After massive preparatory bombing and shelling 18,600 Marines under General J.C. Smith land on Tarawa Atoll in the Gilberts, to the northeast of the now Allied-dominated Solomons. Supporting the landing is a task force of battleships and carriers under Admiral Hill. The Japanese garrison comprises 4800 men under Admiral Shibasaki. The Marines run into a storm of fire from surviving enemy bunkers that kill or wound 1500 men of the first 5000 to land, and reserves are delayed by the living and dead Marines lying on the fringes of the beach. A separate landing on Makin Atoll today is more successful.

22 NOVEMBER 1943

World War II: Invasion of Tarawa After two days of terrible fighting the Marines have consolidated their position on Tarawa, though the Japanese continue to fight fiercely for every inch of ground and to mount suicidal counterattacks. The Americans also advance on Makin, land on Abimama and secure Butaritari.

22-25 NOVEMBER 1943

World War II: Allied Planning Roosevelt and Churchill meet in Cairo with Chiang Kai-shek, the Chinese Nationalist leader. They agree that Japan must accept such terms as restoration of all Chinese territory, independence for Korea and surrender of the Pacific islands it has siezed since 1941.

23 NOVEMBER 1943

World War II: Fall of Tarawa By noon the battle on Tarawa is over. American losses have been 1000 killed and 2000 wounded in the process of annihilat-

Some of the Overlord planners. L to r: Bradley, Ramsay, Tedder, Eisenhower, Montgomery, Leigh-Mallory and Bedell-Smith.

ing the enemy garrison. As they will on later campaigns, the Japanese fight to the death; the only prisoners are 17 wounded soldiers and some Korean laborers. In proportion to the forces engaged it has been the most costly military operation in US history. The invasion, however, has proved a successful trial of the techniques of amphibious warfare. The Americans also complete the capture of Makin.
World War II: German Planning Hitler views a test of the new German jet airplane, the Messerschmitt Me 262, which will become operational in June 1944.

28 NOVEMBER 1943

World War II: Italy The British Eighth Army breaks through German lines in an offensive across the Sangro River.

28 NOVEMBER-1 DECEMBER 1943

World War II: Allied Planning Churchill, Roosevelt, and Stalin and their staffs meet for the first time at Teheran, Iran. They agree on the timing of the invasion of northern France and on plans for a supporting invasion of southern France. Stalin promises to join the war against Japan when Germany is defeated.

30 NOVEMBER 1943

World War II: Command General Alexander Vandegrift, who was outstanding during the Marine operations in Guadalcanal, is named commandant of the US Marine Corps as of 1 January.

World War II: Italy The British offensive is making good progress, now having cleared the first ridge beyond the Sangro River. The American Fifth Army begins diversionary attacks on the lower reaches of the Garigliano River.

1 DECEMBER 1943

World War II: Air War A new variant of the American Mustang fighter, the P-51B, fitted with a British Merlin engine, is used operationally for the first time over Belgium. This aircraft and its subsequent variants will transform the Allied strategic-bombing campaign by its unprecedented combination of range and performance as an escort fighter.

2 DECEMBER 1943

World War II: Italy British units and the newly-arrived US II Corps (General Keyes) begin the main Fifth Army attack on the German line in the Liri Valley. Other American units push forward to the right, and the Eighth Army advances in the east. Tomorrow Allied forces will be at Monte Camino and Monte Maggiore.

4 DECEMBER 1943

World War II: Marshall Islands To soften it for a coming invasion, US carriers and cruisers attack Kwajalein, sinking six Japanese transports and damaging two cruisers. American flyers down 55 enemy aircraft while losing five of their own.

7 DECEMBER 1943

World War II: Italy With the peaks south of the Mignano Gap now in Allied hands after bitter fighting, the second phase of the Fifth Army's attack begins in the mountains of central Italy. Operating on a broader front, the US II and VI Corps move against strong German positions on Monte Sammucro and San Pietro, while the British Eighth Army attacks Orsogna. Besides the problems of terrain, weather and enemy resistance, the Italian Campaign is now hampered by a drain of manpower to England, where vast forces are being gathered for Operation Overlord – the invasion of Normandy and Western Europe.

Amphibious DUKWs rush in under German fire to bring supplies to the Anzio beachhead. Sound in concept, the Anzio operation was bungled in execution.

11 DECEMBER 1943

World War II: Italy Fighting in the Fifth Army's sector has continued now for several days with no decisive gains for either side; Allied momentum is being worn down by a hard-slogging and demoralizing campaign. The British, however, have pushed across the Moro River in strength.

15 DECEMBER 1943

World War II: New Britain Now that the Australians have taken the important Japanese New Guinea supply base at Lae, New Guinea, General MacArthur has ordered a campaign against Rabaul; lying at the eastern tip of New Britain, it is the main enemy naval base in the southwest Pacific area. In the first major island invasion of Operation Cartwheel a cavalry regiment lands from LST's at Arawe off New Britain in a diversion for the main landings set for the 26th.

17 DECEMBER 1943

World War II: Italy The Allied drive gains a little momentum in the mountains: today the Germans begin to withdraw some troops from the key point of San Pietro and from other positions to the north. Monte Sammucro is now in Allied hands. Tomorrow the Fifth Army will take Monte Lungo despite violent German counterattacks. The British are on the move to the east against heavy resistance.

24-29 DECEMBER 1943

World War II: Allied Command In a series of announcements in London and Washington the leaders are announced for Operation Overlord, the coming Allied invasion of Europe: General Dwight D. Eisenhower will be supreme Allied commander for the invasion, with Air Marshal Arthur Tedder as his deputy. Admiral Bertram Ramsay and Air Marshal Trafford Leigh-Mallory will lead the naval and air forces, and General Bernard Montgomery will lead the British armies. General Henry Wilson becomes supreme commander for the Mediterranean, with General Jacob Devers as his deputy. General Harold Alexander commands in Italy. General Ira Eaker commands the Mediterranean Air Forces, and General Oliver Leese takes over the British Eighth Army. General Carl Spaatz is appointed to command all US Strategic Bomber Forces against Germany, and General James Doolittle will lead the Eighth Air Force. General George C. Marshall remains the American chief of staff.

24 DECEMBER 1943

World War II: Air War The US Eighth Air Force makes a major strike against German launching sites being built for the V-1 flying bomb in the Pas de Calais area.

26 DECEMBER 1943

World War II: North Atlantic The German battleship *Scharnhorst* tries to attack an Allied convoy in the North Atlantic but is surprised and sunk by the British battleship *Duke of York*.
World War II: New Britain After the usual preliminary bombardment the 1st Marine Division opens the Operation Cartwheel campaign on Rabaul, making landings near Cape Gloucester. While Japanese attacks sink a destroyer in the task force, the landings are otherwise without incident. In the next days the beachhead will be extended toward an enemy airfield. This will be the pattern of many Pacific island invasions to come.

JANUARY-MARCH 1944

World War II: Battle of the Atlantic German U-Boats are losing the battle with Allied shipping. Although they sink 54 allied ships during these months, they lose 60 boats. On 22 March Admiral Doenitz will order U-Boats to disperse from their 'Wolf Packs' and operate independently.

4-5 JANUARY 1944

World War II: Italy The final phase of the Allied winter offensive begins. Units of the Fifth Army launch attacks on a ten-mile front toward the south end of the German Gustav Line between Naples and Rome.

10 JANUARY 1944

World War II: National President Roosevelt submits a $70 billion budget, most of it for the war effort.

14 JANUARY 1944

World War II: New Britain American forces have not been able to expand their perimeter significantly from the Cape Gloucester area, though Japanese attacks have not scored positive success either.

15 JANUARY 1944

World War II: Italy As of today, the Fifth Army has closed up to the Gustav Line all along its front. American troops capture Monte Trocchio, the last important bastion before the defenses of the Rapido Valley and the formidable German position at Cassino, which is the linchpin of the Gustav Line. Despite the heavy fighting of the past weeks, the Fifth must continue to attack in order to draw off German reserves, that to support a coming Allied amphibious landing at the coastal city of Anzio – Operation Shingle.

16 JANUARY 1944

World War II: Allied Command General Eisenhower arrives in London to take up his duties as Supreme Commander, Allied Expeditionary Force, and to lead what will become known as 'the crusade in Europe' to free the Continent from the German conquest. Eisenhower brings immense skills in logistics to the myriad problems of organizing Operation Overlord, with its millions of troops and mountains of matériel.

18 JANUARY 1944

World War II: Italy By daybreak British units of the Fifth Army have cracked German positions on the Garigliano River; they then push forward from the north bank. German General Kesselring agrees to move reserves from Anzio to meet this attack – which is just what the Allies wanted.

22 JANUARY 1944

World War II: Italy: Operation Shingle Allied forces make an amphibious landing at Anzio and Nettuno, about 30 miles south of Rome, in an attempt to outflank the Gustav Line across central Italy and to capture Rome. The Germans are caught off guard – only 13 of the 36,000 Allied troops landing on the first day are killed, and by tomorrow some 50,000 will be ashore. Reacting quickly, however, German commander Kesselring calls in reserves from far afield.

23 JANUARY 1944

World War II: Italy The Allies consolidate their beachhead at Anzio and push forward slowly, due more to the cautiousness of American General John P. Lucas than to enemy resistance. Before long Kesselring will have ten divisions in place to oppose the Allies' four divisions – Operation Shingle is ill-fated in its attempt to capture Rome quickly. Elsewhere in Italy today the Fifth Army is repulsed in an attempt to force the Rapido River, one of several fruitless attacks on the Gustav Line over the next days.

27 JANUARY 1944

World War II: Russia The Red Army finally lifts the siege of Leningrad, which has been in effect since September 1941. Several hundred thousand civilians of the city have died of starvation and disease.

30 JANUARY 1944

World War II: Italy At the south end of the Gustav Line the British break through and capture Monte Natale. Opposite the key point of Monte Cassino, US forces hold a line on the west bank of the Rapido. At Anzio, Allied attacks take heavy punishment; a Ranger battalion leading the American assault loses all but six men in killed or captured. These attacks at Anzio continue with heavy losses and no worthwhile gains for the next three days.

31 JANUARY 1944

World War II: Marshalls Under the overall command of Admiral Raymond A. Spruance, with General Holland Smith commanding the various landing forces, the major American operation on the Marshall Islands gets underway with landings on Kwajalein Atoll and nearby islands. Commanding Task Force 58 at sea is Admiral Marc A. Mitscher. As usual, Japanese defenses on the beaches are an intricate system of barricades, concrete pillboxes, gun emplacements and underground shelters. The landings are bitterly contested, especially on Namur, and the enemy mounts counterattacks during the night. But by 2 February the US will have established a major base on Majuro. Task force carriers also mount attacks on Eniwetok and Maleolap. By now the US command has settled firmly on the strategy of 'island hopping' – seizing key islands from which to mount attacks on further targets while leaving smaller enemy-held islands to wither on the vine.

2 FEBRUARY 1944

World War II: Marshalls The American occupation of the islands of Roi and Namur is complete. The Japanese have lost virtually every man of the 3700 defenders; American casualties number 740 killed and wounded. The battle for Kwajalein continues.

World War II: Italy The Germans have halted the Allied drive from Anzio; tomorrow night a major German counterattack will begin. At the main battle front before Cassino the Allied offensive is stalling.

The ruins of the sixth-century Benedictine abbey in Monte Cassino, bombed by the Allies because they mistakenly thought it a German command post.

4 FEBRUARY 1944

World War II: Marshalls All organized Japanese resistance in the Kwajalein Atoll has been subdued. Most of Admiral Akiyama's 8700-strong garrison are dead; only 265 have been captured, most of them Korean laborers or wounded. Altogether, the Americans have landed 41,000 men, of whom 370 have been killed and 1500 wounded. The grim process of mopping up small enemy pockets will continue over the next days.

10 FEBRUARY 1944

World War II: New Guinea Australian forces advancing from Sio link up with Americans near Saidor. The occupation of the Huon Peninsula is virtually complete.

11 FEBRUARY 1944

World War II: Italy German counterattacks are making headway at Anzio. Around Cassino an American division makes a final unsuccessful attempt to move forward the last few hundred yards to the Cassino monastery, the symbol of the Allies' frustration in this bitter campaign.

12 FEBRUARY 1944

World War II: Bismarcks Marines on New Britain take Gorissi, just east of Cape Gloucester. The Allies land on Rooke Island in the Bismarck Sea.

15 FEBRUARY 1944

World War II: Italy: Bombing of Monte Cassino The medieval monastery at the crest of Monte Cassino is bombed at the request of the New Zealand Corps, and the historic buildings are completely wrecked. It has been claimed that the Germans are using the monastery as a command post; in fact, the Germans move in only after the bombing, finding the ruins provide excellent cover.

16 FEBRUARY 1944

World War II: Italy Supported by the Luftwaffe, the Germans begin a major attack on the Anzio beachhead, driving the Allied forces back. By the 18th Kesselring will decide that the enemy beachhead cannot be wiped out, but clearly it can be contained. Meanwhile, over the next days another series of futile attacks will be made at Cassino by New Zealand and Indian troops.

17 FEBRUARY 1944

World War II: Marshalls The first US landings on Eniwetok Atoll are carried out against the Japanese garrison of some 3400 men.

17-18 FEBRUARY 1944

World War II: Carolines Ships from the task forces of Admirals Mitscher and Spruance mount a heavy attack on the Japanese base at Truk and on nearby enemy warships. The Japanese lose several ships and 250 planes, the Americans less than 30 planes, with one US carrier damaged.

18 FEBRUARY 1944

World War II: Marshalls With land-based artillery support, as well as naval and air support, American forces land on Engebi, driving off Japanese counterattacks.

20-27 FEBRUARY 1944

World War II: Air War In what is known as 'Big Week' the US Strategic Air Force conducts a series of massive air raids on the centers of the German aircraft industry at Brunswick, Leipzig, Regensburg and other cities. There are heavy Allied losses in bombers and fighters, but the raids seriously harm the Luftwaffe.

21 FEBRUARY 1944

World War II: Japan Prime Minister General Tojo becomes chief of the Army General Staff in place of Field Marshal Sugiyama. Navy Minister Shimada takes on an additional office, replacing Admiral Nagano as chief of staff.

23 FEBRUARY 1944

World War II: Marshalls The fighting for Parry comes to an end, and with it the battle for the whole Eniwetok Atoll. US losses are 300 dead and 750 wounded; the Japanese garrison has fought practically to the last man – there are 66 prisoners out of a force of 3400.

World War II: Italy General Truscott takes over command of the VI Corps at Anzio, replacing General Lucas. Ironically, that battle has now settled down to the sort of careful position warfare that is Lucas's style. Allied forces will turn back another German offensive on the 28th.

29 FEBRUARY 1944

World War II: Admiralty Islands A thousand men of the 5th Cavalry Regiment land at Hyane Harbor on Los Negros. General MacArthur and the Seventh Fleet's Admiral Kinkaid are present offshore; they decide to convert the landings from the planned reconnaissance-in-force to a full-scale occupation.

3 MARCH 1944

World War II: Italy There is another flurry of activity at Anzio, where the American 3rd Division holds back an attack near Ponte Rocco. After this failure the Germans will go on the defensive.

World War II: Admiralty Islands The Japanese mount a strong night attack on Los Negros. The newly-reinforced Americans inflict heavy losses, dissipating much of the Japanese strength on the island.

6-8 MARCH 1944

World War II: Air War Escorted by some 800 fighter planes, 660 US bombers make the first American daylight raid on Berlin; a second attack is mounted on the 8th with 580 bombers. US losses in both raids amount to some 10 percent, but these and regular ensuing raids will gradually weaken German morale, if not industrial capacity.

8 MARCH 1944

World War II: Solomons The Japanese begin attacks on the American position on Bougainville, shelling airfields and infiltrating American lines. US forces will gain the upper hand on the 12th after heavy fighting and then mount successful counterattacks to recapture lost territory.

US *Essex*-class carriers at Ulithi atoll. By 1945 there would be more *Essex*'s than all the rest of the world's fleet carriers combined.

World War II: Burma The Japanese offensive *U-Go* begins, the objective being to destroy British forces around Imphal and Kohima, India, and then to push on through passes to Dimapur, cutting off the Chinese and American forces in the north. By the end of the month the British will have fallen back to Imphal, there to be surrounded by the Japanese.

12 MARCH 1944

World War II: Admiralty Islands A small American force lands on Hauwei Island. Despite strong enemy resistance, the landing force will overrun the island tomorrow and begin preparing an upcoming operation on Manus. The latter will find success within the week.

15-23 MARCH 1944

World War II: Italy After a lengthy stalemate at Cassino, the key point to breaking through the German Gustav Line, the Allies launch a major bombing raid and tank assault. Losses are so high that the attack is called off on the 23rd, not to be resumed until May. The Allies are now thoroughly stalled in Italy.

24 MARCH 1944

World War II: Solomons The last significant Japanese effort on Bougainville comes to an end. There will be small skirmishes in the coming months, but the enemy on the island is worn out after taking some 8000 casualties in the last two weeks; American losses have been 300.

25 MARCH 1944

World War II: Admiralty Islands Organized enemy resistance ends on Los Negros, and a final US attack on Manus crushes most of the remaining enemy forces.

A USAAF B-29 Superfortress on a Chinese airfield. The B-29 was specially designed to have the range to reach Japan's home islands from distant bases.

29 MARCH 1944

World War II: Relief The US Congress approves a joint resolution authorizing up to $1.35 billion for the United Nations Relief and Rehabilitation Agency. This is the start of what will become a massive postwar effort to aid the millions of people whose lives were disrupted by the war.

30 MARCH-1 APRIL 1944

World War II: Carolines Admiral Spruance leads a detachment of Task Force 58 in attacks on Palau Island. The Japanese have dispersed their fleet but still suffer damage to a warship and lose much supply shipping.

30 MARCH 1944

World War II: Air War The RAF raids Nuremberg, losing 96 planes from an attacking force of 795 – the worst losses for the RAF during the war.

2 APRIL 1944

World War II: Eastern Europe The first Russian troops cross into Rumania.

8 APRIL 1944

World War II: Burma Having surrounded the British at Imphal, India, the Japanese now encircle British forces at Kohima. The defenders will be supplied by air.

8-10 APRIL 1944

World War II: Russia The Russians take Odessa, a primary port on the Black Sea, and the Germans begin to fall back in the Crimea.

17 APRIL 1944

World War II: China The Japanese mount offensives on Chennault's B-29 bases in Hounan. The newest and largest US bomber, the long-range B-29 has been designed to conduct raids on the Japanese home islands, but it lacks bases sufficiently close to Japan.

18 APRIL 1944

World War II: Operation Overlord: Approach The British Government bans all coded radio and telegraph transmission from London and elsewhere in the British Isles. Diplomatic bags are censored, and most diplomats forbidden to leave the country. These and other measures are designed to tighten security around the mounting preparations for the most grandiose and daring amphibious operation in all of military history, Operation Overlord, the D-Day invasion of Normandy.

22 APRIL 1944

World War II: New Guinea Now that the Allies have secured much territory to the east, US operations begin against the Japanese in the Hollandia area of Netherlands New Guinea. The landing force of 84,000 men is under the overall command of General Robert Eichelberger, hard-fighting field commander of the Buna campaign. The Japanese defenders, numbering some 11,000, are caught off guard by the landings and in the first few days put up little resistance to the American advance.

28 APRIL 1944

World War II: Washington Secretary of the Navy Frank Knox dies; he has played a large part in the revival of the US fleet since Pearl Harbor. Admiral James V. Forrestal will be named to the position on 10 May and will pursue his duties with great imagination and vigor.

29-30 APRIL 1944

World War II: Carolines On these days Admiral Mitscher's Task Force 58 sends heavy air strikes against the Japanese base at Truk, destroying nearly all its planes, against little loss for Allied pilots. Next day, Admiral Oldendorf leads nine cruisers and eight destroyers to shell targets in the Sawatan Islands, southeast of Truk.

MAY 1944

World War II: Operation Overlord: Approach The principal efforts of the Allied air forces based in Britain turn to preparations for the Normandy landings: the RAF flies 28,500 sorties on small targets in France – stores, dumps, rail and training centers – while American heavy bombers strike rail centers, oil productions areas, communications and manufacturing centers.

3 MAY 1944

World War II: Japan Admiral Toyoda is named commander in chief of the Japanese Combined Fleets after the death in an air crash of Admiral Koga.

9 MAY 1944

World War II: Russia Sevastopol falls to the Red Army.

9-13 MAY 1944

New Guinea There is constant skirmishing, with occasional fullscale fights, around the US beachheads at Hollandia, but the Japanese are ill-supplied and weak and achieve little.

11-18 MAY 1944

World War II: Italy: The Fall of Cassino The reorganized Allies – British, Americans, Canadians, French, New Zealanders, Poles and Indians – launch a new offensive on German positions in the bombshattered town and monastery of Cassino. Despite the usual strong enemy resistance, the Allies break through this major bastion of the Gustav Line and drive to the north. Meanwhile, French units advance rapidly in the east. The stalemate in Italy is broken; by 1 June the Allies will be ready to make the final drive to Rome.

US General Joseph Stillwell (second from right) confers with one of his Chinese division commanders during the Burma campaign in May 1944.

17 MAY 1944

World War II: Burma An American commando group called Merrill's Marauders (commanded by General Frank D. Merrill) helps Chinese forces capture Myitkyina airfield. This operation is in support of an advance from India by Chinese divisions under crusty US General Joseph Stilwell. 'Vinegar Joe' is commander of all Chinese forces; as such, he is much resented by Nationalist Chinese leader Chiang Kai-shek, who gives him little help. Though the Japanese are still in control of Burma, Stilwell and his air commander, Chennault, have established Allied supremacy in the air, and his ground forces are gearing up to take the offensive.
World War II: New Guinea US forces land on Insumarai Island and on the nearby mainland at Arare.

18 MAY 1944

World War II: German Command Berlin announces that Field Marshal Gerd von Rundstedt is to be Commander in Chief West, with Rommel and Blaskowitz his subordinates. Rommel will be quick to quarrel over strategy with Rundstedt.
World War II: Admiralty Islands The US Sixth Army announces that the campaign to take these islands is finished. The Americans have lost 1400 dead and wounded; the Japanese 3820 dead and 75 prisoners.

20 MAY 1944

World War II: Air War Polish Resistance fighters secure a test version of a German V2 ballistic missile that lands outside Warsaw. They dismantle the rocket and ship the parts to London, seven weeks before the first V2 lands. Germany is currently preparing to launch V1 robot flying bombs against England.

23 MAY 1944

World War II: Italy Having bogged down at Anzio since their landing on January 22, Allied forces there launch a major offensive to break out. By the end of the day German lines are penetrated. From Anzio these Allied units will drive northward toward Rome.

24 MAY 1944

World War II: Burma Stilwell's advancing Chinese troops are halted by strong Japanese counterattacks south of Myitkyina.

27 MAY 1944

World War II: New Guinea US forces land on Biak Island, finding little initial resistance from the Japanese garrison of 11,000 men – which, for a change, is nearly equal to the Allied strength. Tomorrow the Americans will be hit by a fierce counterattack, but the beachhead will hold. There is a similar situation at Arare.
World War II: Operation Overlord: Approach The loading of the gigantic Allied assault force begins.

1 JUNE 1944

World War II: Italy The US II and VI Corps begin a drive toward Rome, attacking through the Alban Hills and toward Albano and Valmonte on either side. Since the German Caesar Line has now been breached by these advances, Kesselring orders a fighting withdrawal north, declaring Rome an open city and thus conceding it to the Allies.
World War II: Operation Overlord: Approach The BBC sends a code message giving a general warning to the French Resistance that invasion in imminent. The Germans understand the rough significance of this message (a poem by Verlaine) and alert some of their units. However, Hitler has been deceived by a massive Allied hoax to convince him that the main invasion is to come directly across the English Channel to the Pas de Calais area. Thus, believing the Normandy assault is a diversion, Hitler makes no special preparations to defend Normandy.

4 JUNE 1944

World War II: Overlord: Approach The convoys for the invasion are at sea, but because of bad weather expected on 5 June they turn back to wait. After consulting his meteorological staff, late in the evening Eisenhower makes the momentous decision to go ahead with the invasion on 6 June, when a break in the weather is expected. If there is no break, the greatest invasion in history may be a disaster. Eisenhower is led to this decision because the necessary low tide occurs only about three days a fortnight. If he does not go ahead by the 7th he must wait until July, jeopardizing the security and morale of the invasion as well as giving the enemy time to strengthen defenses. On the German side, the bad weather has put the leaders off their guard; Rommel is in Germany for his wife's birthday, and some junior officers are away in Brittany.

5 JUNE 1944

World War II: Italy: Entry into Rome Though advance units of the US 88th Division entered Rome yesterday, today Allied forces make their triumphal march into the city and push on beyond in pursuit of the retreating Germans. As usual, the German retreat is accompanied by skillful rearguard actions and demolitions.
World War II: New Guinea On Biak, American units are advancing successfully against pockets of suicidal Japanese resistance.
World War II: Operation Overlord: Approach A second message that the invasion is imminent is sent to the French Resistance. Again the Germans hear the message, but they do not alert the Seventh Army in Normandy. As the landing ships near the coast on rough seas, airborne troops are sent on their way from airfields in southern England.
World War II: Burma At Kohima an Allied flanking attack forces the encircling Japanese off the Aradur spur and into retreat. Now the road to Imphal must be cleared.

6 JUNE 1944

World War II: Operation Overlord: Plans and Preparations The plan is to land units of four army corps and three airborne divisions on the beaches of Normandy between Caen and Valognes. Normandy has been selected for a number of reasons – topography, its relative closeness to England and the fact that it is a less obvious invasion point and thus more lightly defended than the Pas de Calais. Operation Overlord is the largest invasion in the world's history; it is intended to bring decisive victory in Europe. Eisenhower commands 45 divisions; there are nearly three million American, British and Canadian troops, along with 5000 large ships, 4000 landing craft and more than 11,000 aircraft, as well as two elaborate prefabricated harbors called *Mulberries*. (Made from old ships, huge blocks of concrete and steel and metal roadway, they will be sunk off the beaches and become ports for unloading troops.) The landing areas are separated into five codenamed beaches. West to east they are: General Omar Bradley's American VII Corps (General Collins) will land on *Utah* beach and his V Corps (General Gerow) on *Omaha*; British forces will land on *Gold* and *Sword*, with Canadians between on *Juno*. Overall commander of ground forces is Field Marshal Sir Bernard Montgomery. Thousands of preparatory air attacks on targets in France have been carefully orchestrated to avoid giving away the real location of the landings. These raids have been successful, but air strikes after the invasion will be still more so, delaying German reinforcements in reaching Normandy.
World War II: Operation Overlord: German Dispositions In France, Belgium and Holland the Germans have 60 divisions, including 11 armored, though many of the divisions are not highly mobile and many are understrength. The supreme commander is Field Marshal Gerd von Runstedt; commanding in the Normandy area is Field Marshal Erwin Rommel. (By now, however, Hitler is so intimately involved in directing the details of German operations as to hamstring the chain of command – and he still expects the main invasion to come at Pas de Calais.) The Allied landings will at first largely be opposed by units of the German Seventh Army. Shortages of materials have made the German beach

Scottish regimental pipers parade in Rome in June 1944 to celebrate the liberation of the first Axis capital to fall to the Allies in the war.

defenses considerably weaker than they are supposed to be, and reserves are not readily obtainable. Behind the defenses of Normandy lies the German Atlantic Wall, its fortifications stretching from Norway to Spain.

An American LCT plows across the Channel toward Normandy on the fateful morning of 6 June 1944.

World War II: Operation Overlord: Airborne Landings Two US airborne divisions begin to drop shortly after midnight of D-Day inland from the western-flank beach *Utah*. One division has the task of taking the exits on the various causeways through the area; the other, dropped further inland, is to clear territory around the Merderet River. Inexperienced pilots disperse these paratroops, but this has the fortunate effect of confusing the Germans, and one enemy commander is killed, adding to the confusion. In a multitude of small gallant and successful American actions, the capture of St. Mère Eglise stands out. On the left (eastern) flank, a British airborne group seizes crossings on the Orne and the Caen Canal, storms a battery, blows up bridges and ties up part of a Panzer division during the landings.

World War II: Operation Overlord: The Landings The first wave of infantry and armored troops are dispatched from thousands of landing craft and wade ashore on a 50-mile front at 6:30 in the morning, with Allied aircraft blanketing the overcast skies and striking German positions (the Luftwaffe in the area is so weak that it downs only one Allied plane). Action on the five beaches varies greatly in intensity. At *Utah* General Collins' US VII Corps has trouble with choppy seas, but gets ashore with little resistance; the troops advancing inland are held up mostly by marshy ground. By the end of the day 23,250 men have gone ashore at *Utah*, with less than 200 killed. The situation is far different at *Omaha*. Despite a heavy preceding bombardment from air and naval forces, General Gerow's US V Corps has immense difficulty: the terrain favors the well-entrenched defenders, rough seas swamp amphibious tanks and wash up some landing craft sideways onto the beach and air support bombs fall too far inland, while rocket craft are aiming short, threatening Allied soldiers. As soon as the barrage lifts, blistering German fire begins. The American infantrymen lie in the surf or take cover behind beach obstacles and tanks and suffer galling casualties. As the tide comes in, and with it subsequent waves of troops, a slow advance begins, with individual leaders inspiring forward momentum. This, combined with a renewed bombardment by destroyers against enemy strongpoints, is the story for the rest of the day. By nightfall there are 34,250 battered Americans ashore at *Omaha*, but none more than a mile from the beach. More than 1000 are dead and many more wounded, but this landing has broken the main thrust of enemy resistance. Elsewhere the story is better. At *Gold*, despite heavy enemy fire, General Bucknall's XXX Corps quickly clears the beaches, and the advance inland is fairly rapid – though the designated objective of Bayeux and the road to Caen are not reached. Altogether 25,000 British are landed, with about 500 killed. At *Juno* 21,400 Canadians make good progress toward Breteville and Caen, their amphibious tanks silencing German strongpoints. At *Sword* General Crocker's British I Corps has cleared the beach exits before ten o'clock after heavy fighting. Commando units hurry inland to aid the paratroops along the Orne, but regular infantry are slowed by German resistance. By late afternoon Biéville is reached, where the troops fight off an enemy Panzer division. At nightfall the British have 28,850 men ashore on *Sword*. Overall, the first day of Operation Overlord has been a great success for the Allies. They have almost 150,000 men ashore, and their aircraft are preventing the Germans from building up superior forces in Normandy. Casualties, while extensive, have in fact been lighter than expected.

By the evening of D-Day the Normandy beaches were littered with beached landing craft and smashed or drowned equipment, but some 150,000 troops were on shore. By 12 June the number would be 326,000.

7 JUNE 1944

World War II: Operation Overlord Although the Allies have not reached the objectives set for the first day of Operation Overlord, they are everywhere solidly established along the Normandy coast. The priorities are to link up the four beachheads (*Gold* and *Juno* are already joined) and to expand inland. Today there is some progress toward these goals. Meanwhile, the British around Caen are holding up German reinforcements, which gives the Americans at *Omaha* especially a welcome respite to consolidate and expand.
World War II: New Guinea American forces on Biak capture an airfield. There is fighting elsewhere on the island, with small groups of Japanese resisting fiercely, and this fighting will go on for some time.

8 JUNE 1944

World War II: Operation Overlord The second wave of Allied troops is now largely ashore. A division of the VII Corps begins an advance toward Cherbourg, and there is heavy fighting near Azeville, which will fall tomorrow. Units of the V Corps take Isigny but cannot yet link with the *Utah* force. The British establish a vital link between *Gold* and the American *Omaha*. The next day will see slow but steady progress; *Utah* and *Omaha* will link up on the 10th.

9 JUNE 1944

World War II: Italy The Allies are advancing steadily to the north. Today US forces take Tarquinia, Viterbo and Vetrella, while the British advance toward Terni and Orvieto. Allied forces are reorganized as American units are pulled out of line for an invasion of southern France.

11 JUNE 1944

World War II: Marianas Admiral Mitscher's Task Force 58 sends fighter strikes against Saipan, Tinian and other islands in the group, shooting down 36 Japanese planes. Another task group sinks several enemy ships. Admiral Spruance is in overall command of the Marianas campaign from the cruiser *Indianapolis*.

12 JUNE 1944

World War II: Operation Overlord The US 4th Division is involved in a series of actions against German strongpoints at Montebourg, Crisbecq and near Azeville. The Germans will only hold at Montebourg. Other units of the VII Corps are fighting their way across the Cotentin Peninsula and southwest from Carentan. V Corps is helping in these attacks as well as advancing toward St Lô; in this sector Caumont is taken and the Forêt de Cerisy and the Bayeux road reached. The third wave of troops is now largely ashore. At this stage there are 326,000 men, 104,000 tons of supplies and 54,000 vehicles ashore for the Allied armies in France.

12-13 JUNE 1944

World War II: Marianas Three groups of US carriers continue attacks on Tinian and Saipan, while another concentrates on Guam. In response to these assaults Japanese Commander in Chief Admiral Toyoda sends fleets from Tawitawi and Batjan. These fleets are considerably outnumbered by the Americans; Toyoda plans on land-based aircraft support from the Marianas and elsewhere, but he has not been informed by local commanders that Japanese land bases are severely damaged by the American carrier strikes.

A nervous Navy officer scans the skies as Allied brass land in Normandy. Behind him, from the left, Generals Marshall, Arnold and Eisenhower.

13 JUNE 1944

World War II: Air War Germany's first pilotless, jet-propelled V1 flying bombs are launched for England. Of the ten fired, four cross the Channel successfully, and one lands in London, killing six civilians. Londoners will dub the weapon the 'Buzz Bomb,' from is characteristic sound.

14 JUNE 1944

World War II: Operation Overlord A third US Corps, XIX, becomes operational between the V and VII Corps sectors. General de Gaulle visits the beachhead and takes measures to prepare for the restoration of French civil government in recaptured territory.

14-17 JUNE 1944

World War II: Battle of the Philippine Sea: Approach The main US carrier forces which have been operating against the Marianas spend most of the period replenishing. Two groups led by Admiral Clark do, however, attack Iwo Jima, Chichi Jima and Haha Jima. By the 17th all are on their way to a rendezvous west of the Marianas, with Japanese fleets closing to intercept.

15 JUNE 1944

World War II: Air War US B-29 Superfortresses from China bomb Kyushu, the first such air raid on a Japanese main island.
World War II: Marianas: Invasion of Saipan While the heavy surface ships of Task Force 52 keep shelling, the main phase of the Saipan landings gets under way under the name Operation Forager. Altogether, there are 67,000 Marines in the land force; Japanese defenders number some 30,000. After three hours of air and naval bombardment the attacks go in north and south of Afetna Point, finding fierce enemy resistance, but the Marines get well ashore during the day and at night repulse counterattacks.

17 JUNE 1944

World War II: Operation Overlord Rommel, Rundstedt and Hitler meet at Soissons. Both generals want to order withdrawals to better positions. Flying into one of his rages, Hitler accuses the army of cowardice and overrules them; he insists that V1 attacks will force Britain out of the war. (Increasingly, Hitler will place his hope on the advent of some 'miracle weapon.') In the fighting, a division of the US VII Corps reaches the west coast of the Cotentin Peninsula near Barneville. The German divisions cut off to the north are refused permission to attempt a breakout.
World War II: Italy A French division lands on Elba; they will complete occupation of the island on 19 June.

18 JUNE 1944

World War II: Marianas: Saipan The advance of the 4th Marine Division reaches the west side of Saipan at Magicienne Bay, cutting the Japanese forces in two. Offshore, Japanese air strikes sink three American ships.
World War II: Battle of the Philippine Sea One of the most decisive air-naval engagements of the war begins when US forces make their rendezvous west of the Marianas. Scout planes from the approaching Japanese fleet spot the American ships. The Japanese plan to launch an air strike early tomorrow and refuel and rearm on Guam, not realizing that the Guam airfield has been too badly damaged by American attacks to be of much use.

19 JUNE 1944

World War II: Battle of the Philippine Sea Early in the morning Japanese search planes find Task Force 58, while their own fleet remains undetected. The Japanese have some 550 land- and carrier-based planes, to the Americans' 950 carrier-based aircraft. The Japanese carriers launch 372 planes in four waves, which the Americans quickly find on radar and send up planes to meet. The US fighters intercept some 50 miles out; in the ensuing battle most of the enemy planes fall to American airborne and AA fire, and few reach their targets – the only damage is one bomb hit on the battleship *South Dakota*. The Japanese lose 240 aircraft, the Americans only 29. Fifty more enemy planes are destroyed on the way to Guam and on the ground there. The list of Japanese misfortunes is completed when the valuable carriers *Taiho* and *Shokaku* are sunk by US submarines. The American victory has been so relatively easy that US flyers and gunners call the day 'The Great Marianas Turkey Shoot.'
World War II: Operation Overlord Various American units complete the clearance of Montebourg and Valognes. For three days there will be gales in the channel which damage both Mulberry harbors, the one at *Omaha* irreparably.

20 JUNE 1944

World War II: Battle of the Philippine Sea The Japanese carriers do not realize the extent of their aircraft losses and withdraw to refuel. Admiral Mitscher sails in pursuit and in the afternoon sends 216 planes to attack. They meet only 35 defending fighters and break through to sink the carrier *Hiyo* and damage two others. In the action 20 American planes are lost and a further 72 crash in attempting to land on their carriers at night. (A feature of US operations is the care taken of the pilots – only 16 flyers and 33 aircrew are not picked up today. By contrast the

The first wave of landing craft heads for Omaha Beach on 6 June. More than 1000 US soldiers would die there by the day's end.

Above: General Charles de Gaulle, leader of the Free French forces in World War II. After years of bearing the humiliation of the defeat of 1940 his hour of triumph would come on 26 August 1944 when newly-liberated Paris gave him a hero's welcome.

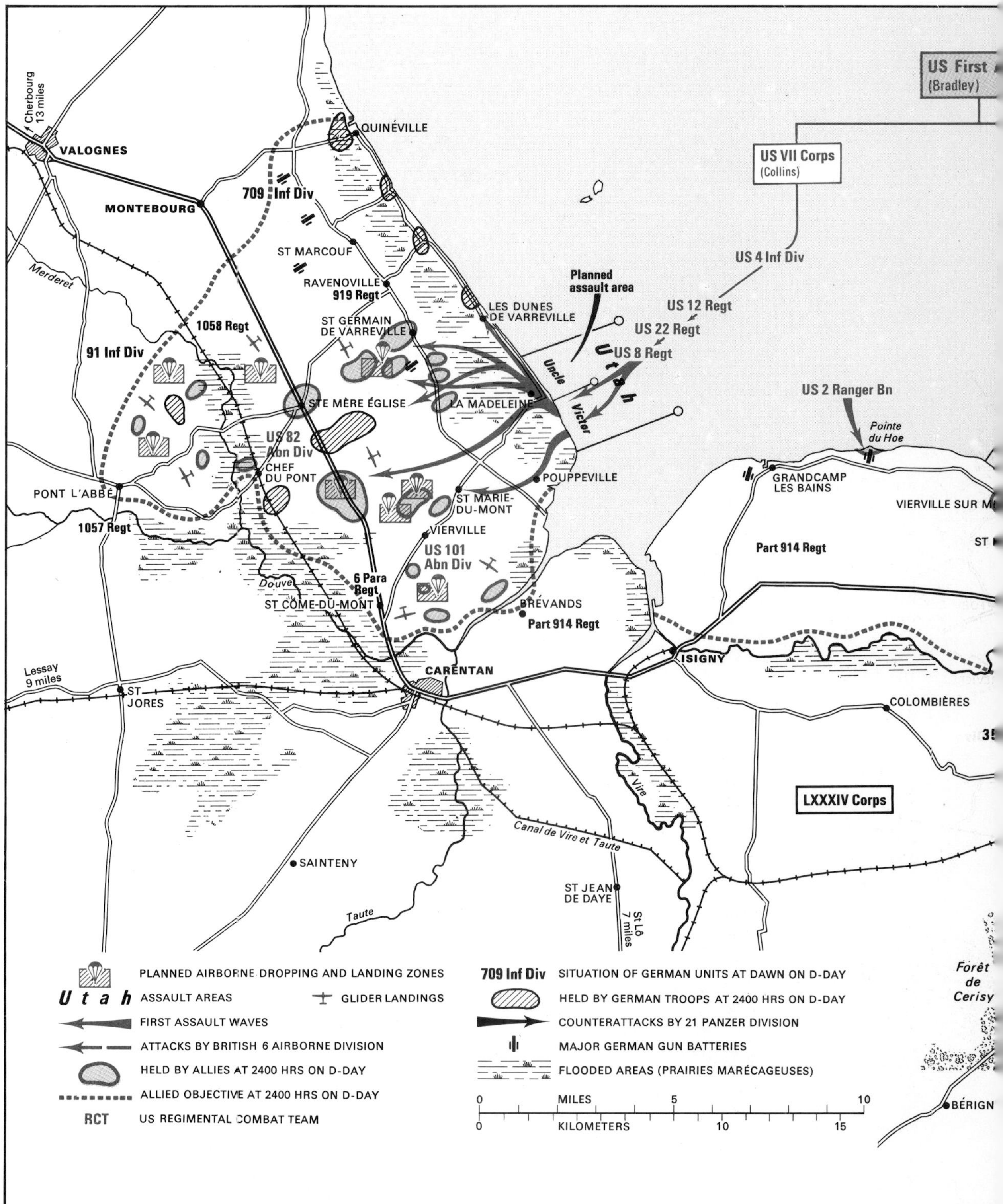

Right: A map of the Overlord landings.

Japanese have saved almost none of their pilots.) In the first time the Japanese have committed their carriers to battle since early 1943 they have lost 395 planes and nearly that many trained pilots, as well as three carriers. During the night the enemy retreats and Mitscher does not follow.

22 JUNE 1944

World War II: National President Roosevelt signs the Servicemen's Readjustment Act, providing financial aid to veterans for education, housing and other needs. This act will soon become widely known – and beloved – as the GI Bill.
World War II: Operation Overlord The final battle for Cherbourg begins with a two-hour air raid in which the Allies drop over 1000 tons of bombs. Despite this preparation, the three attacking divisions of the US VII Corps still meet strong resistance.
World War II: New Guinea Operations against the Japanese persist on Biak; today American troops believe they have cleared the west, but during the night there is renewed enemy activity. On the mainland there is fighting near Aitape and Sarmi.
World War II: Burma The Japanese begin to retreat from the Kohima-Imphal area; they are taking ever heavier losses, both in combat and as a result of food shortages. Allied troops, even when surrounded, have been adequately supplied by air.

24 JUNE 1944

World War II: Marianas: Saipan US forces have completed clearing the southern part of Saipan, but for days there has been fierce fighting on Mount Tapotchau; tomorrow, Marines will fight their way to the top.
World War II: Bonin Islands Enemy bases on Iwo Jima and Chichi Jima are attacked by American carrier aircraft; the Japanese lose 66 planes.

25 JUNE 1944

World War II: Italy In the steady advance of the Allies up the Italian boot the US 36th Division takes Piombino on the western coast. (Directly after, this division will be taken out of line to prepare for planned landings in the south of France, codenamed Operation Anvil.) Inland there are fairly successful British and French attacks against the German Albert Line west of Lake Trasimeno.

27 JUNE 1944

World War II: Operation Overlord After hard fighting against determined German defenders the Americans complete the capture of Cherbourg, the first major French port to come under Allied control. It will be some time before the port can be made operational because of booby traps and demolitions; once functional, however, it will prove valuable.

28 JUNE 1944

World War II: New Guinea On Biak, US forces have nearly completed the agonizing process of clearing the western caves of enemy. Japanese strength on the island has now largely been dissipated, and the main task for the Americans is mopping up.

30 JUNE 1944

World War II: Operation Overlord The last German forces in the Cotentin Peninsula either surrender to the Americans or are wiped out. Major British and American units are still battling on the approaches to Caen and St. Lô, respectively. Since D-Day the Allies have landed 630,000 men, 600,000 ton of supplies and 177,000 vehicles in Normandy; casualties to date have been 62,000.

1-22 JULY 1944

International Delegates from 44 nations meet at a resort hotel in New Hampshire, Bretton Woods, for an economic and financial conference. They agree to set up an International Monetary Fund and an International Bank for Reconstruction and Development. Many of their decisions will govern international finance for the next quarter-century.

2 JULY 1944

World War II: New Guinea An American-Australian force lands on Numfoor Island; in the next days will come the now-familiar and ghastly process of expanding the beachhead against suicidal enemy resistance.

3 JULY 1944

World War II: Operation Overlord US forces begin a major drive south from Normandy's Cotentin Peninsula, aiming to reach a line from Coutances to St. Lô. This will become known as the 'Battle of the Hedgerows' because Germans are in a maze of narrow lanes with high hedges – ideal terrain to defend, as the American soldiers will soon discover.
World War II: Italy French troops capture Siena; to their right the British advance toward Arezzo and on the left the US forces reach Rosignano on the Tyrhennian coast.

6 JULY 1944

International General Charles de Gaulle visits Washington for talks about the postwar status of his administration and aid for Free French forces.
World War II: German Command Berlin announces that Field Marshal Hans Gunther von Kluge has replaced Field Marshal Gerd von Rundstedt as Commander in Chief West.
World War II: Marianas: Saipan The Americans push forward toward the north end of the island. The senior Japanese commanders, Admiral Nagumo and General Saito, both commit suicide while their remaining subordinates plan a final fanatical attack. (Many civilians join in the defense, since Saipan is Japanese home territory, and the population is primarily Japanese rather than Melanesian.)

7 JULY 1944

World War II: Marianas: Saipan Practically the whole of the Japanese garrison, now reduced to about 3000 men, and with civilian supporters alongside often wielding knives, mount a wild attack on the American line south of Makunsha Village. They succeed in coming to close quarters, but by about midday they are being driven off with terrible losses. The Japanese believe that suicide in support of the Emperor is the most honorable of deaths. It is in these days that some American soldiers will observe a large segment of the civilian population – men, women and children – deliberately walking into the sea.

9 JULY 1944

World War II: Operation Overlord Caen finally falls to a major British and Canadian attack.
World War II: Marianas: Saipan US forces overcome the last organized resistance in Saipan. The Japanese have suffered an estimated 27,000 military and civilian casualties and only 1780 have been taken prisoner. American forces have suffered 3400 dead and 13,000 wounded.

13 JULY 1944

World War II: Russia After several days of vicious street fighting, the Lithuanian city of Vilnius falls to the Russians.

17 JULY 1944

World War II: Western Front While returning to his headquarters Field Marshal Rommel is severely wounded in his car by an Allied air attack. Kluge assumes Rommel's duties in France, as well as his own as commander in chief.

18 JULY 1944

World War II: Operation Overlord St. Lô, a crucial road junction linking Normandy and Brittany, effectively falls to US forces after a long and difficult approach.
World War II: Italy Part of the US IV Corps begins to attack Leghorn on the west coast, while other units take Pontedera on the River Arno. On the east coast Polish troops take Ancona; tomorrow's capture of Leghorn and that of Ancona will ease Allied supply problems.

World War II: Japan Yesterday a new navy minister, Admiral Nomura, replaced Admiral Shimada; today General Tojo resigns as prime minister and chief of staff, to be replaced in the latter post by General Umezu. These and other changes are manifestations of growing sentiment for peace by some Japanese statesmen; however, concerned about an unfavorable peace, all wish to maintain the appearance of a strong front.

20 JULY 1944

World War II: Germany A bomb explodes near Hitler in his headquarters in East Prussia, but he escapes serious injury. A group of officers and politicians has plotted to assassinate the dictator and seize power. Before the day is over several leaders of the plot are identified and executed; other active or alleged conspirators will follow them in death – some by torture, on Hitler's orders. For Hitler himself, the effect of the plot is to contribute to his growing instability – he has largely lost his military acumen and seems well on the way to losing his sanity.

21 JULY 1944

National Meeting in Chicago, the Democrats nominate Franklin Delano Roosevelt for an unprecedented fourth term as president. Senator Harry S Truman of Missouri will become his running mate.
World War II: Marianas Another major push in this Japanese home territory begins when troops of General Geiger's III Amphibious Corps land on Guam to moderate resistance. In the course of the campaign 54,900 American troops will be landed to operate against the 19,000 Japanese defenders.

23 JULY 1944

World War II: Russia The Red Army captures Pskov – the last major town of the prewar Soviet Union in German hands.
World War II: Marianas The Marines are trying to link up their two beachheads on Guam; today one division extends the northern beachhead to Point Adelup. Units from the southern landing cut off the main enemy airfield on the island.

24 JULY 1944

World War II: Marianas General Schmidt's V Amphibious Corps lands 15,600 men on Tinian Island; the approximately 6200 defenders cannot prevent the Americans from establishing a solid beachhead. Napalm is used in the engagements for the first time in the Pacific.

25 JULY 1944

World War II: Operation Overlord The St. Lô 'breakout,' called Operation Cobra, begins when General Omar N. Bradley's First Army launches a coordinated offensive to cut off the German forces in Brittany and sweep across France. More than 3000 planes operate today, including 1500 heavy bombers. Some of the latter aim short and cause many casualties, including killing General Lesley J. McNair, commander of the US Army Ground Forces. Nonetheless, the VII and VIII Corps make good initial progress. Meanwhile, the British and Canadians are still operating around Caen.

26 JULY 1944

World War II: Strategy Roosevelt meets with General MacArthur and Admiral Nimitz in Honolulu. MacArthur argues for an attack on the Philippines, but the navy commander suggests that they be bypassed and that the next major target should be Formosa. This disagreement will become heated.

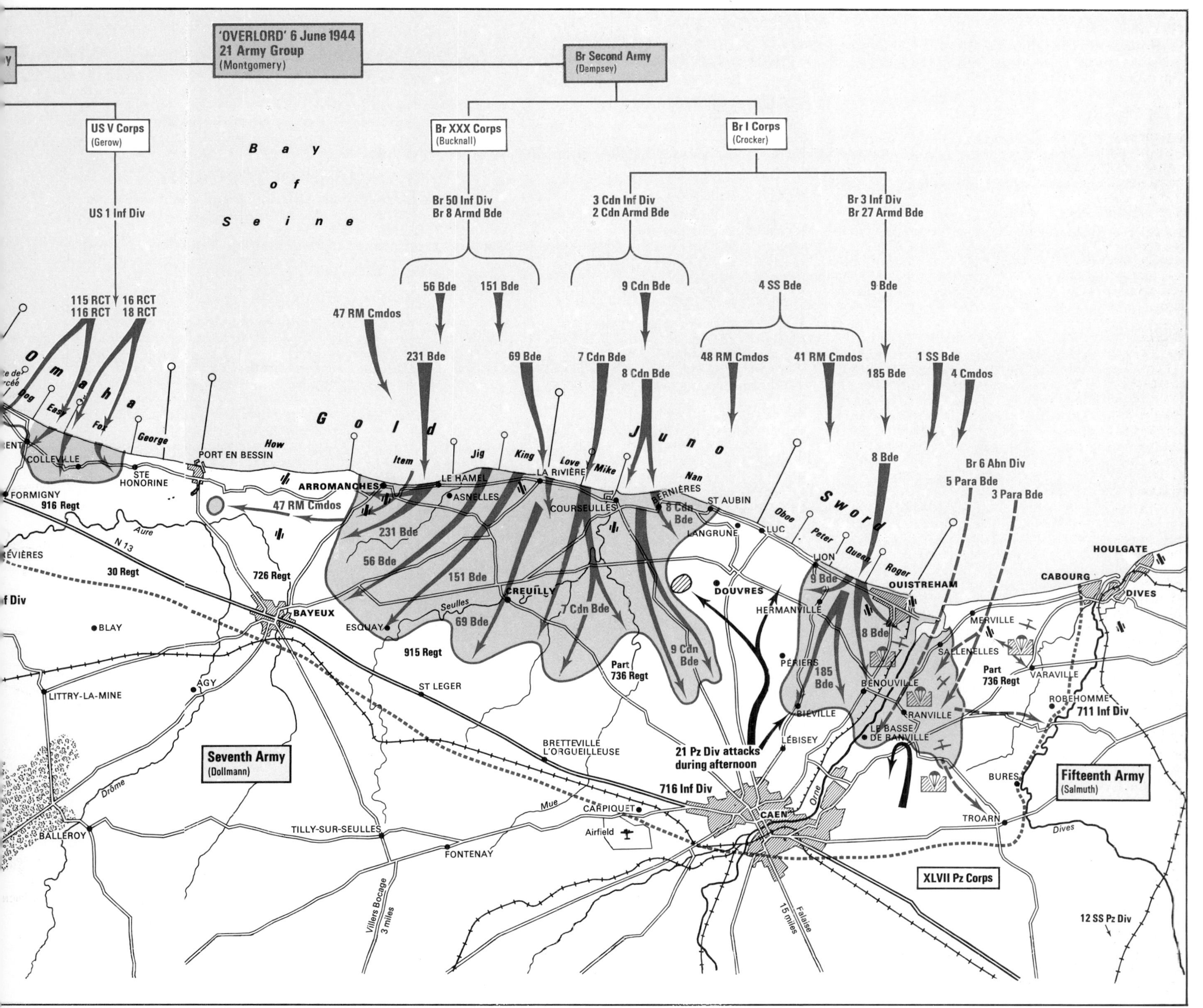

Patton confers with Eisenhower. The promise that Patton had shown in Tunisia and Sicily was more than fulfilled in his brilliant French campaign.

28 JULY 1944
World War II: Operation Overlord A US armored division enters Coutances, the first objective of Operation Cobra. The advance is making steady progress against intense enemy resistance.

29 JULY 1944
World War II: New Guinea On Biak the Americans complete the destruction of a Japanese pocket around Ibdi. The island is finally essentially won; there will be no more organized fighting.

30 JULY 1944
World War II: Marianas The main town on Tinian, also named Tinian, is taken by US forces. On Guam, American forces have now largely cleared the southern half of the island.
World War II: New Guinea US forces land on the Vogelkop Peninsula.

AUGUST 1944
World War II: Air War Among the usual massive bombing operations on European targets this month – many against V-weapon sites – are 'shuttle' raids by the Eighth Air Force in which planes fly to Russia and then to Italy, attacking on each leg. In Japan, there are B-29 Superfortress raids on Nagasaki and Yawata in Japan, in addition to the usual attacks on targets in New Guinea and the Marianas.

1 AUGUST 1944
World War II: Northern France The objectives of Operation Overlord have been won. The invasion has been secured, and the Allies prepare to mount their great offensive in Western Europe. Today General George S. Patton's Third Army becomes operational; it will find historic success in coming operations. US forces are now organized as 12 Army Group (Bradley), First Army (Hodges) and Third Army. The British Second Army and the First Canadian Army form 21 Army Group under Montgomery, who, as well, retains overall direction of Allied ground forces. Eisenhower continues as supreme commander. Patton's main initial task with the Third Army is to overrun Brittany. The First Army will advance on Mortain, and the British and Canadians will continue to attack between Caumont and Caen.
World War II: Marianas On Tinian the last organized resistance comes to an end. As usual, the Japanese garrison has been completely wiped out; there are over 6000 enemy dead and 250 prisoners while the Americans have lost 390 killed and 1800 wounded.

1 AUGUST-2 OCTOBER 1944
World War II: Poland Patriots of the Home Army begin operations inside Warsaw. The rising is timed so that when the Russians arrive in Warsaw, which is expected soon, they will find an established Polish Government. But the Russians halt; they insist that this is dictated by logistical problems, but others accuse Stalin of wanting to give the Germans time to wipe out anti-communist forces in Poland. In any case, that is what happens, despite Allied airlifts (in which the Russians refuse to cooperate). By 2 October 200,000 Poles have reportedly been killed, and central Warsaw is in ruins.

3 AUGUST 1944
World War II: Burma Mytkyina is finally taken by a Chinese and American attack after the bulk of the Japanese garrison has slipped away.

4 AUGUST 1944
World War II: Italy As South African units enter Florence, the Allied forces in Italy pause to regroup for a major offensive against the German Gothic Line.

5 AUGUST 1944
World War II: Northern France Patton's Third Army is making superb progress: in Brittany Vannes is liberated, while other units attack near St. Malo and reach the outskirts of Brest. The VII Corps reaches Mayenne and Laval.

7 AUGUST 1944
World War II: Northern France The Germans begin a major counterattack just east of Mortain; the blow falls between the VII and XIV Corps. Mortain is retaken by the enemy, but Allied air strikes help to prevent more serious loss.

10 AUGUST 1944
World War II: Northern France Operation Cobra is still making a remarkable advance: British troops take Vimont, south of Caen; the three corps of the Third Army are fighting vigorously, having taken St. Malo, Dinard, Nantes and Le Mans. Around Mortain the Germans have to pull back slightly due to American pressure.
World War II: Marianas The Marines wipe out the last serious opposition in the north of Guam. There are various small groups of Japanese holding out in jungle hideouts (one survivor will show up in 1972). The Americans have taken 7000 casualties, including 1300 dead; there are less than 100 Japanese prisoners out of a garrison of at least 10,000.

12 AUGUST 1944
World War II: Northern France The first PLUTO (Pipe Line Under the Ocean) is in operation carrying fuel from the Isle of Wight to Cherbourg.

15 AUGUST 1944
World War II: Northern France The British enter Tinchebray from the north. Other British and Canadian units are attacking strongly along a line from there to east of Falaise. From south of Tinchebray to Argentan, US forces are attacking northward. Trapped German units begin a desperate retreat to the east. Field Marshal Kluge is forced to take cover from Allied air attacks for most of the day; his long absence from HQ increases Hitler's suspicions that Kluge is disloyal.
World War II: Southern France The Allies launch a new front against the Germans, invading southern France at beachheads between Cannes and Toulon. This is Operation Dragoon, changed from the original codename Anvil due to compromised security. The landing forces are from General Alexander Patch's US Seventh Army and General Jean de Lattre de Tassigny's II French Corps. French commando units also land from the sea in the first wave, and thousands of paratroops drop inland near Le Mury. German units in the area are helpless to stop the Allied drive up the Rhone Valley.

17 AUGUST 1944
World War II: German Command Hitler dismisses Field Marshal Kluge, appointing Field Marshal Walther Model as Commander in Chief West. Kluge will commit suicide tomorrow rather than face a treason trial.
World War II: New Guinea American holdings near Aitape are extended; on Numfoor the last significant Japanese force is brought to battle and largely destroyed.

18 AUGUST 1944
World War II: Northern France The Falaise-Argentan gap is nearly closed by the junction of Polish and American troops at Chabois; the last enemy troops will slip through the gap on the 20th. Meanwhile, advance units of the Third Army reach Versailles on the outskirts of Paris.

19 AUGUST 1944
World War II: Northern France Eisenhower had originally planned to bypass Paris, feeling that trying to clear the Germans out might hold up the Allied advance. But today the French Resistance changes all bets by setting off an uprising in the city. German commander Chollitz, contrary to Hitler's orders to fight until Paris is 'a field of ruins,' comes to terms with the Resistance leaders, preparing the way for an unobstructed Allied entry into Paris. Tomorrow, the Germans will arrest Marshal Henri Philippe Pétain, sometime hero of the Battle of Verdun in World War I and now the leader of their puppet Vichy government, for refusing to go to an area secure from the Allies.

20 AUGUST 1944
World War II: New Guinea The fighting on Biak comes to an end after 4700 Japanese have died; American casualties are 1550.
World War II: Eastern Front The Red Army begins an offensive into Rumania; that country will surrender on the 23rd.

21 AUGUST-7 OCTOBER 1944
International At Dumbarton Oaks, an estate in Washington, DC, representatives from the US, Britain, the USSR and China meet to discuss the postwar formation of an international organization for promoting peaceful solutions to international problems.

21 AUGUST 1944
World War II: Northern France All the Allied armies begin a rapid advance to the northeast in pursuit of the broken and retreating German forces. Although at this stage the invasion of France is behind schedule, the advance in the next few weeks will make up the time. Patton's Third Army now has bridgeheads over the Seine thirty miles west of Paris; on the right flank the advance reaches Sens.
World War II: Southern France Aix-en-Provence is taken by units of the US VI Corps.

24 AUGUST 1944
World War II: Southern France The Allied advance takes Cannes, Grenoble and Arles.

25 AUGUST 1944
World War II: Liberation of Paris General Philippe Leclerc's 4th Armored Division enters Paris; tomorrow, cheering crowds of Parisians will watch American and French forces, with General Charles de Gaulle among them, parade down the Champs Elysées. In the countryside the Allies are still moving steadily northeast.
World War II: Italy The British-Polish-Canadian Eighth Army begins a new offensive over the River Metauro on the German Gothic Line. The enemy is taken by surprise and begins to withdraw.

28 AUGUST 1944
World War II: Northern France US First Army units cross the Marne at Meaux, and Patton's Third Army is moving toward Reims.
World War II: Southern France The last German forces in Toulon and Marseilles surrender, effectively ceding southern France. The Allies have close to 190,000 men ashore now for Operation Dragoon, and American units are pushing toward Lyon.

29 AUGUST 1944
World War II: War Crimes The Russians and the Polish communists jointly announce that they have discovered evidence that the Germans have murdered some 1.5 million people in the former Majdanek concentration camp. This is the first of many such appalling revelations.

Massed columns of American infantrymen march down the Champs-Elysées in the most spectacular of the parades celebrating the liberation of Paris.

30 AUGUST 1944

France The provisional Government of General de Gaulle is established in Paris.

SEPTEMBER 1944

World War II: Atomic Research Work at the Los Alamos, New Mexico, atomic bomb development site has now proceeded so far that a special bomber unit is established and begins training. Some of the scientists involved are beginning to have doubts about the morality of continuing their work, especially since the war seems nearly won, but work continues.
World War II: Allied Strategy There is an increasingly acrimonious debate among the Allied generals as to how best to exploit the German collapse. Eisenhower and others believe in a broad-front advance, with Allied armies moving in concert and sharing supplies and support. Montgomery and his circle support a 'wedge-thrust' plan to cross Belgium, encircle the industrial Ruhr Valley and cross the Rhine. Eisenhower will determinedly insist on a broad front. Part of the debate is a simple power struggle between the imperious Montgomery and the conciliatory-but-tough Eisenhower. The debate will go on for months – and for decades after the war.

1 SEPTEMBER 1944

World War II: Northern France The Canadians liberate Dieppe, British forces take Arras north of the Somme and the US First Army approaches St. Quentin and Cambrai. On the right flank the Third Army takes Verdun and Commercy, but also comes to a temporary halt due to gasoline shortage: the rapid Allied advance is creating immense supply problems.
World War II: Southern France Narbonne and St. Agrève fall to French forces.
World War II: Italy The Eighth Army continues its attacks on the Gothic Line in the Adriatic sector.
World War II: Eastern Front The Russian advance reaches the Danube on the Bulgarian frontier.
World War II: Greece German forces begin withdrawing from the mainland and adjacent islands.

2 SEPTEMBER 1944

World War II: Finland Prime Minister Hackzell announces that Finland is breaking diplomatic relations with Germany and demands that all German troops be withdrawn. Finland and the USSR will sign an armistice on the 10th.
World War II: Italy San Giovanni is taken and the eastern end of the Gothic Line has been overrun.

3 SEPTEMBER 1944

World War II: Western Front The British enter Brussels, Belgium, also taking Tournai and Abbeville; tomorrow they will enter Antwerp. The Third Army begins crossing the Moselle as the First Army takes Mons. Lyons falls to French forces.

5 SEPTEMBER 1944

World War II: Western Front As US forces take Namur and Charleroi, Hitler brings Field Marshal Rundstedt back to command the overwhelmed Nazi armies in the west.

8 SEPTEMBER 1944

World War II: Air War The first German V2 rocket strikes England. Much faster and more powerful than the V1 bombs, the V2's will take a heavy toll, psychological and physical, on British civilians in the closing months of the war, but it will fail to be the 'miracle weapon' that Hitler hopes will bring England to her knees.

Belgian crowds cheer as units of the British Guards Armored Division roll into Brussels on 3 September 1944. Antwerp would fall the next day.

10 SEPTEMBER 1944

World War II: Western Front Troops from the US First Army enter Luxembourg, and the Canadians are attacking near Zeebrugge in northwest Belgium. To placate Field Marshall Montgomery amidst their quarrels about strategy, General Eisenhower agrees to Montgomery's proposal for an airborne operation to take the bridges over a series of canals and rivers in Holland. Under the codename Operation Market Garden, this is designed to speed the advance across the Rhine into Germany. It is based on the erroneous assumption that the enemy has only light forces in the target areas and will not be able to prevent the advance of ground forces to link up with the paratroops.

11-16 SEPTEMBER 1944

World War II: Allied Planning At a second Quebec Conference (known as the Octagon Conference) Roosevelt and Churchill discuss strategies for final defeat of the Germans and Japanese, as well as their status in the postwar world.

11 SEPTEMBER 1944

World War II: Western Front Operation Dragoon forces moving up from the south of France take Dijon and make their first linkup with Overlord units.

12 SEPTEMBER 1944

World War II: Western Front The 12,000-strong German garrison at Le Havre surrenders to the British. Units of the US First Army are gathering on the German border between Aachen and Trier, threatening the German West Wall.

13 SEPTEMBER 1944

World War II: Rumania An armistice between Rumania and the Allies is signed; the terms, dictated by the Russians, include reparations and cession of territory.

14 SEPTEMBER 1944

World War II: Italy With the capture of Zollara the Eighth Army has cleared the Gemmano Ridge of enemy and is able to push forward to the Marano River.

15 SEPTEMBER 1944

World War II: France The justice commissioner orders the arrest of Marshal Pétain and his Vichy Cabinet for their collaboration with the Germans.
World War II: Moluccan Islands American forces land unopposed on Morotai; General MacArthur watches from offshore. By October there will be over 30,000 men on the island.
World War II: Palau Islands Marine landings on the coast of Peleliu meet moderate resistance on the beaches, but fighting inland is fierce; the Japanese have a formidable defense system in a complex of caves.
World War II: Western Front The US First Army breaches the German West Wall, taking Maastricht and Eisden; meanwhile, the Third Army takes Nancy and Epinal. The former Operation Dragoon forces moving up from the south of France come under General Eisenhower's command.
World War II: Italy The Eighth Army creates a bridgehead over the Marano River.

US troops gather around their commander, General Douglas MacArthur, on the invasion beach of the Philippine island of Leyte, 20 August 1944.

17 SEPTEMBER 1944

World War II: Operation Market Garden The ill-fated Operation Market Garden commences. Its plan, primarily Montgomery's, calls for three airborne divisions to seize a series of bridges and canal lines in Holland, allowing the main Allied forces to hasten their advance into Germany. The operation is predicated on German weakness in the area, but the real enemy strength, particularly near Arnhem, is greater than Montgomery realizes. Two of the units will achieve their objectives – the US 82nd Airborne is dropped and takes bridges over the canals north of Eindhoven, and the 101st Airborne secures bridges at Grave and Nijmegen. The farthest bridge is over the lower Rhine at Arnhem, and the British 1st Airborne Division is dropped outside town to mount that attack. In fighting there today, a battalion reaches one end of the bridge but then is cut off from the remainder of the division, which is soon also fighting for its life. The deciding factor will be whether the British XXX Corps can advance fast enough overland to aid the paratroops.

World War II: Palau Islands Americans land on Angaur to operate against a 1600-man Japanese garrison. Tomorrow there will be an advance inland there, but on Peleliu the Marines will find themselves under heavy attack, and the fighting on Angaur will heat up soon.

18 SEPTEMBER 1944

World War II: Operation Market Garden The British XXX Corps links up with the US 101st Airborne at Eindhoven and Veghel; to the north, the two other Market Garden divisions are fighting hard.

19 SEPTEMBER 1944

World War II: Operation Market Garden In the morning the XXX Corps links up with the 82nd Airborne at Grave, and together the troops attempt to move toward Nijmegen. At Arnhem the main body still cannot reach the battalion which holds the north end of the bridge. Elsewhere, German resistance comes to an end in Brittany

20 SEPTEMBER 1944

World War II: Operation Market Garden The infantry and paratroops, now moving overland, take Nijmegen and the vital bridge over the Waal before the Germans can destroy it. At Arnhem the British paratroops are driven away from the bridge in desperate fighting. Tomorrow they will make a stand west of town.

21-24 SEPTEMBER 1944

World War II: Philippines Twelve carriers from Admiral Mitscher's Task Force 38 attack targets on Luzon, especially near Manila. In operations since 31 August, TF 38 has destroyed at least 1000 Japanese aircraft and sunk 150 ships of all types. American losses have been 72 planes, 18 of them in accidents.

22 SEPTEMBER 1944

World War II: Palau Islands A new Marine division is brought in to replace some of the units which have taken heavy losses in attacks on Peleliu's Mount Umurbrogol. Tomorrow, Ulithi Atoll, just north of the Palaus, will be occupied, to become a major naval base by the end of the war.

25 SEPTEMBER 1944

World War II: Operation Market Garden While the British paratroops near Arnhem are being worn down by severe fighting and shortages of food and ammunition, the XXX Corps has been able to move only a few miles east of Eindhoven. It is finally decided to evacuate as many of the surviving Arnhem fighters as possible across the Rhine. During the night 2400 of the 10,000 who landed get away; about 1100 have been killed and 6400 taken prisoner. Though the lower bridges were taken as planned, the operation against the bridge at Arnhem has been an unqualified disaster – later memorialized as 'A Bridge Too Far.' Tomorrow the Allies will begin consolidating their positions in Belgium and Holland.

World War II: Italy The US Fifth Army has completed its penetration of the German Gothic Line. The Allied campaign in Italy has made excellent progress, despite having been demoted to the status of a diversion for operations in France, but there have been some 50,000 casualties in the process. The great offensive will now largely pause for some weeks on a line running east-west across Italy from north of Rimini to north of Florence and Pisa.

2 OCTOBER 1944

World War II: Western Front The US First Army begins a new offensive against the Siegfried Line in Germany between Aachen and Geilenkirchen. On the 3rd breakthroughs will begin, but fighting in that area and around Metz will be especially bitter: the Germans are now struggling for their own soil.

9-20 OCTOBER 1944

World War II: Diplomacy Churchill and Anthony Eden visit Moscow for talks with the Russians on the political future of eastern Europe. Stalin insists that Poland, Bulgaria and Rumania are to remain in the Soviet 'sphere of influence'; Greece can come under British sway; Hungary and Yugoslavia are to come under both nations' influence. The British (and later Americans) will make the fateful decision to go along with Stalin because of the immediate need of continuing Russian help in the war.

10 OCTOBER 1944

World War II: Ryukyu Islands The main American carrier force, Mitcher's Task Force 38 (part of Admiral Halsey's Third Fleet), begins a series of operations with attacks on Onami-O-shima, Okinawa and Sakashima; all are effective against Japanese planes and shipping.

12-14 OCTOBER 1944

World War II: Formosa Task Force 38 sends over 2000 fighter sorties against Formosa; most of the Japanese planes challenging this attack are intercepted and destroyed.

A general map of the Battle of Leyte Gulf, by far the largest naval battle ever fought.

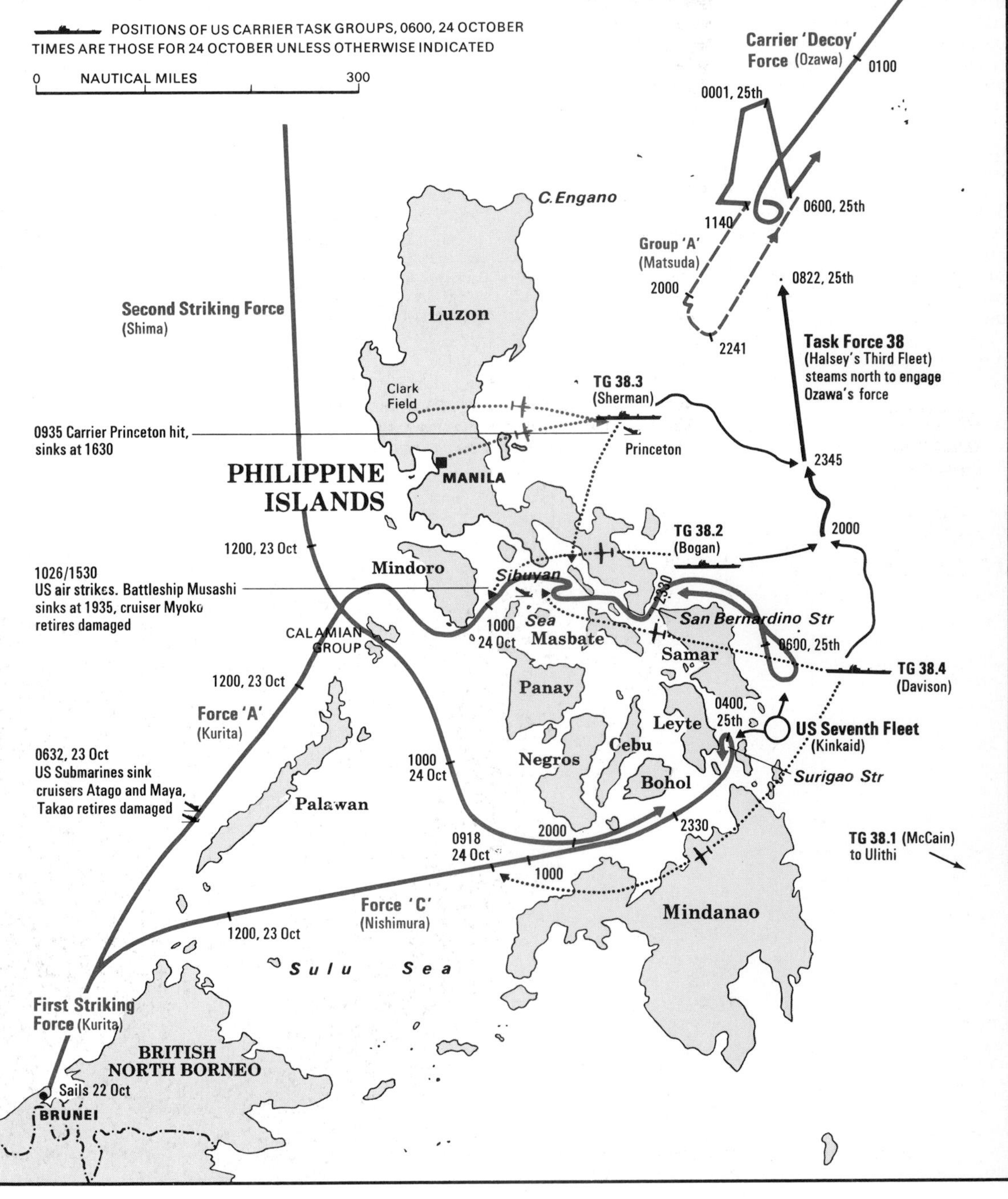

13 OCTOBER 1944

World War II: Western Front US troops have fought their way into Aachen, where a bitter street-by-street struggle begins.

14 OCTOBER 1944

World War II: German Command Suspected of complicity in the July plot against Hitler, Field Marshal Erwin Rommel is given the choice of a public trial or suicide; Rommel kills himself.
World War II: Palau Islands New Marine units take over at Peleliu, where fighting is still severe.

16-19 OCTOBER 1944

World War II: Invasion of Leyte Preliminary air attacks and fleet movements for a US landing on Leyte take place. Japanese forces lose heavily in these operations.

20 OCTOBER 1944

World War II: Invasion of Leyte US forces invade Leyte Island in the Philippines; General MacArthur comes ashore and broadcasts to the people, thus fulfilling his promise of March 1942: 'I shall return.' There is little fighting on the beaches, as Japanese defenders retire to inland positions to await reinforcements. By nightfall 132,000 Americans are ashore, but there are some 270,000 Japanese ground troops in the Philippines. The Japanese decide to commit the bulk of their navy in a last-ditch effort to stop this invasion.
World War II: Eastern Front A combined Russian and Yugoslav Partisan attack completes the liberation of Belgrade, Yugoslavia.

21 OCTOBER 1944

World War II: Western Front After weeks of severe fighting in the area German Forces in Aachen surrender; much of the city is in ruins.
World War II: Palau Islands Japanese resistance on Angaur ends; they have lost 1300 dead and 45 prisoners, the Americans 265 dead and 1335 wounded. The larger islands are left with their Japanese garrisons isolated and impotent.

22 OCTOBER 1944

World War II: Battle of Leyte Gulf As US land forces make progress on Leyte, units of the Japanese fleet converge on the area to commence the largest naval battle in history. The plan is complex. Admiral Ozawa's lightly-armed carriers will move down from Japan as a decoy to lure away Halsey's Third Fleet to the north. The surface ships of Admiral Shima's strong Second Fleet will make converging attacks – the 1st Attack Force under Admiral Kurita through the San Bernardino Strait in the north, and the C Force under Admiral Nishimura through the Surigao Strait in the south. Presuming success in destroying American warships in the Gulf, Shima's 2nd Attack Force is to follow and operate against supply shipping and then join with the other forces to attack the beachheads. The Japanese are considerably outnumbered, hence the importance of drawing off Halsey's Third Fleet, which has all the main carriers, and leaving isolated the surface units of Admiral Thomas C. Kincaid's Seventh Fleet.

23 OCTOBER 1944

World War II: Battle of Leyte Gulf Kurita's 1st Attack Force is sighted by two US submarines, which attack and sink two heavy cruisers. Receiving the report, the groups of Task Force 38 east of the Philippines prepare for battle.

24 OCTOBER 1944

World War II: Battle of Leyte Gulf Kurita's 1st Attack Force is found by scout planes and attacked throughout the day by US carrier aircraft, which sink the giant battleship *Musashi* and inflict other damage. Kurita suddenly turns his force back, convincing Halsey that he is withdrawing for good, but in the evening Kurita again reverses course. Meanwhile, Halsey has learned of Ozawa's decoy force and turns north to engage – just as the Japanese had hoped. Ground forces on Leyte continue to advance.

25-26 OCTOBER 1944

World War II: Battle of Leyte Gulf Nishimura's and then Shima's forces try to push through the Surigao Strait; American PT Boats and destroyers sink several enemy ships, and Admiral Jesse B. Oldendorf's old battleships (some survivors of Pearl Harbor) sink six more trying to break through. In the action the Japanese lose two battleships. The surviving Japanese forces then withdraw from the Surigao Strait. Sailing south along the Samar Coast, Kurita's 1st Attack Force engages Kinkaid's Seventh Fleet to great effect, sinking three ships and damaging others. But then Kurita, fearful of American planes, makes the fateful decision to withdraw. Had he sailed on, he might have caused havoc in the American transport fleet. While Kurita is withdrawing there are Japanese *Kamikaze* (suicide plane) attacks which sink four American escort carriers and damage others. These are the first significant premeditated enemy suicide-plane strikes. While these actions are being fought Halsey is leading the Third Fleet north in pursuit of Ozawa, who has thus fulfilled his decoy mission. Halsey mounts air strikes, but then hears news from the other battles and turns part of his fleet south; he thereby loses his chance to destroy Ozawa, and his ships reach the San Bernardino Strait too late to engage Kurita. On the 26th American air attacks sink more enemy ships. Overall, the Battle of Leyte Gulf has been a shattering defeat for Japan, which has lost three battleships, its entire complement of four carriers, ten cruisers and nine destroyers. US forces have lost three small carriers, two destroyers and a destroyer escort. In the future, operations of the Japanese Fleet will be even more circumscribed; their only hope now is in *Kamikaze* suicide attacks, which have been very successful so far and in the coming weeks of regular naval skirmishes will find further success.

The Battle of Leyte Gulf: The crew of the sinking Japanese carrier *Zuikaku*, veteran of Pearl Harbor, cheer their Naval Ensign for the last time.

OCTOBER 1944

World War II: China General Joseph Stilwell, chief of US forces in China and effectively the American ambassador to China, is recalled to Washington. A blunt but realistic soldier, Stilwell has been openly critical of Chiang Kai-chek and his Nationalist supporters; Stilwell has also antagonized some American authorities by calling for more cooperation with the communist Chinese in the war against Japan. Stilwell is replaced as military commander by Major General Albert C. Wedemeyer, while Major General Patrick J. Hurley is appointed as US ambassador. Both these men will also see some need for cooperation between the Nationalists and the Communists in China's war against the Japanese, but both will also make no secret of their preference for the Nationalists.

7 NOVEMBER 1944

National Franklin D. Roosevelt wins an unprecedented fourth term as president, beating Republican Thomas E. Dewey with some 53 percent of the vote.

8 NOVEMBER 1944

World War II: Western Front The last German resistance on Walcheren is overcome, and the remainder of the garrison surrenders. Patton's Third Army begins an offensive around Metz in northeastern France, the eventual objective being the Saar River just over the German border.

15 NOVEMBER 1944

World War II: Western Front South of Metz the Third Army cuts the rail line to Saarebourg, and from there to north of St. Dié ground is gained all along the front.
World War II: Mapia Island US troops occupy this small island north of New Guinea, easily overcoming a small Japanese garrison. The forces at sea include both American and British ships under Admiral Lord Ashbourne.

19 NOVEMBER 1944

World War II: Western Front The Allies are advancing all along the front. The British make ground near Venlo, and the Ninth Army occupies Geilenkirchen. To the south the Third Army completes the isolation of Metz (the city will fall on the 22nd). Still further south the French reach the outskirts of Belfort, while other units have penetrated to the Swiss border north of Basle.

21 NOVEMBER 1944

World War II: Leyte The US march from the north coast is meeting strong resistance in the Ormoc Valley. Other units push up from the south.

23 NOVEMBER 1944

World War II: Western Front At the north end of the front the Germans pull back deeper into Holland; by contrast, other German forces begin a series of sharp attacks against the US Ninth Army west of the Roer. French troops of the US Seventh Army reach Strasbourg. Tomorrow the Third Army will make crossings over the Saar about 25 miles north of Saarbrücken – Patton is now knocking at the German West Wall.

24 NOVEMBER 1944

World War II: Air War American B-29's make their first raid on Tokyo from bases in the Marianas. Such attacks will escalate in the coming months.

28 NOVEMBER 1944

World War II: Western Front The first Allied convoy reaches Antwerp. The opening of the port means the end of major Allied fuel and supply shortages.

10 DECEMBER 1944

World War II: Leyte After heavy fighting US troops take Ormoc, the main Japanese base on Leyte. The bulk of the enemy forces have now pulled away to the northwest. On the 15th US forces will land on the island of Mindoro, meeting almost no resistance.

15 DECEMBER 1944

World War II: Command Congress establishes the rank of General of the Army, which will become known as 'Five-star General.' Receiving the new insignia are George Marshall, Dwight D. Eisenhower, Douglas MacArthur and USAAF commander Henry 'Hap' Arnold.

16 DECEMBER 1944

World War II: Battle of the Bulge Out of the blue comes Hitler's last, convulsive drive to throw back the Allies from the western borders of Germany. Under the codename *Watch on the Rhine* 38 German divisions under Field Marshal Walther Model strike west into the lightly defended American positions in the Ardennes forest of France. Hitler's objective is to drive through to Antwerp, splitting the Allied forces in two. Due to complete surprise, in the first days the Germans carve a great bulge in the Allied front – thus the name of the battle.

19 DECEMBER 1944

World War II: Battle of the Bulge General Eisenhower assigns Montgomery to head operations to the north of the expanding German salient, and Bradley to the south. The German drive has gained much ground, but US forces are impeding them in small pockets of resistance, especially at vital road junctions and bridges. If the Germans are to press the offensive they must do so quickly before the bad weather clears enough to allow Allied forces to move up and Allied aircraft to intervene.

22 DECEMBER 1944

World War II: Battle of the Bulge The advancing Germans have surrounded General Anthony C. McAuliffe's 101st Airborne Division at Bastogne in the southern Ardennes. Presented with an enemy demand for surrender, McAuliffe makes his immortal reply in a single word: 'Nuts.' Meanwhile, the weather is clearing, and the German generals are beginning to realize that the objective of reaching Antwerp is impossible. Nonetheless, the German attack goes on, though impeded by the resistance in Bastogne.

24 DECEMBER 1944

World War II: Battle of the Bulge On this Christmas Eve the German offensive runs afoul of American units on the Meuse River outside Dinant. There the US 2nd Armored Division annihilates the German spearhead. Meanwhile, Patton's Third Army has turned to strike the southern shoulder of the salient, and beleaguered Bastogne is being supplied by air. It is the beginning of the end for Hitler's last great drive.

26 DECEMBER 1944

World War II: Battle of the Bulge One of Patton's armored divisions breaks through to relieve Bastogne after McAuliffe's determined holdout. The Allied counteroffensive is taking shape.

31 DECEMBER 1944

World War II: Leyte There are heavy Japanese assaults in northwest Leyte, but American forces turn them back. Elsewhere on the island resistance is all but ended. In the fighting for Leyte Japanese casualties have been around 70,000, almost all killed. American losses have been 15,500 dead and wounded.

Surrounded US troops in Bastogne in the Battle of the Bulge refused to surrender. Here supply trucks enter the city after its relief.

1 JANUARY 1945

World War II: Air War Some 800 German planes make a surprise attack on Allied airfields in Belgium and Holland. Though the strike destroys or damages 260 planes, the attackers lose 200, critically depleting the waning remaining strength of the Luftwaffe.

2 JANUARY 1945

World War II: Battle of the Bulge In the Ardennes, Third Army troops take several towns. Hitler refuses to allow retreats. In Alsace the Seventh Army is being pushed back by the Germans.

2-8 JANUARY 1945

World War II: Philippines A large American convoy leaves Leyte for the invasion of Luzon. The ships are much harassed by Japanese midget submarines, small surface ships and Kamikazes. The cruiser *Boise*, with General MacArthur aboard, narrowly escapes a torpedo attack. The night of 7-8 January sees the last surface engagement of the Luzon campaign, with a Japanese destroyer sunk.

3 JANUARY 1945

World War II: Battle of the Bulge In the Ardennes the fighting continues. Now US forces are squeezing the bulge in a pincers, the Third Army from the south and the First Army from the north.

9 JANUARY 1945

World War II: Invasion of Luzon Operation Mike 1, the massive US landings on Luzon at Lingayen Gulf, is begun. General Yamashita's 260,000 Japanese ground troops on the island will not intervene in the first two days, but invading ships and troops come under heavy air attack. The inevitable severe ground fighting will begin on the 11th. At sea Kamikaze attacks will be a continuing problem.

11 JANUARY 1945

World War II: Battle of the Bulge Units of the Third Army and the British XXX Corps join up near St. Hubert as the German salient in the Ardennes is further reduced. To the south the Seventh Army is beginning to stand up against enemy attacks around Bitche.

12 JANUARY 1945

World War II: Eastern Front A major Soviet offensive begins all along the front from the Baltic to the Carpathians; underequipped German forces will soon fall back.

19 JANUARY 1945

World War II: Luzon US ground attacks on Luzon have been pressing forward, today concentrating to the south of the beachhead in the direction of Manila.

20 JANUARY 1945

National Roosevelt is inaugurated for his fourth term as president, with new Vice-President Harry Truman being sworn in as well. In his speech the president promises to continue work for Allied victory and for the establishment of peace and security in the postwar world.

World War II: Hungary The Hungarian Provisional Government concludes an armistice with the Allies and agrees to pay reparations and to join the war against its former ally Germany.

World War II: Burma Converging Allied attacks from Burma and China have essentially reopened the vital Burma Road, now called the Stilwell Road, climaxing efforts that began in 1943 (General Stilwell himself was relieved in October 1944, having lost the power struggle with Chiang Kai-shek). On 4 February the first truck convoys will arrive over the road into China; now supplies will not have to be flown in over the 'Hump' of the Himalayas.

21-22 JANUARY 1945

World War II: Formosa and Ryukyus There are ongoing operations in this area by Admiral Mitscher's Task Force 38. Over 1150 sorties are flown over Formosa on the 21st. Meanwhile, Japanese strikes damage three American carriers. On the 22nd Okinawa is the main target. Since 30 December the carriers have sunk 300,000 tons of enemy shipping and shot down 615 Japanese planes, while losing 201 planes and 167 pilots.

23 JANUARY 1945

World War II: Battle of the Bulge St. Vith falls to American tank units. German forces are falling back throughout the Ardennes salient, meanwhile losing heavily to Allied air attacks.

27 JANUARY 1945

World War II: Battle of the Bulge Troops from Patton's Third Army cross the Our River and take Oberhausen. The Battle of the Bulge is now effectively at an end, the German gains retaken and the Allies once again at the West Wall. Though the offensive, the greatest pitched battle of the war on the Western Front, has delayed the Allied advance some six weeks, the Germans have suffered over 100,000 casualties and lost much matériel. American casualties have been around 76,000.

31 JANUARY 1945

World War II: Eastern Front Russian troops reach the Oder River, less than 50 miles from Berlin, where they will halt to mop up and regroup.

World War II: Luzon The US advance on Manila is making steady progress as waves of new Allied troops are landed on Luzon.

3 FEBRUARY 1945

World War II: Western Front French and American units complete the capture of Colmar. As other Allied armies keep up the pressure on the Germans all along the front, the US First Army is beginning operations to seize dams on the Roer River. Tomorrow the Allies will announce that all enemy forces have been expelled from Belgium.

4 FEBRUARY 1945

World War II: Luzon On Luzon advance units of the 1st Cavalry Division reach the outskirts of Manila from the north, while the 11th Airborne approaches from the south. In the city 20,000 Japanese troops are prepared to fight to the end.

4-11 FEBRUARY 1945

World War II: Yalta Conference At Yalta, in the Crimea, Roosevelt and Churchill (having spent a few days conferring on Malta) join Stalin to discuss the final phase of the war. Anxious to gain Soviet help against Japan, Roosevelt and Churchill promise territorial concessions in the Sakhalin and Kurile Islands. The three leaders also carve up the map of Europe, agreeing on the postwar borders of such Eastern European countries as Poland, in return for which Stalin makes empty promises of fair elections. Roosevelt, severely weakened by what will prove to be his last illness, is willing to trust Stalin far more than is

Churchill, Roosevelt and Stalin meet in Yalta in February 1945. The agreements reached here would profoundly affect the postwar settlement.

Churchill, and Roosevelt's approach prevails. Finally, all agree to call a meeting of the United Nations in San Francisco on 25 April to establish a permanent international organization.

8-9 FEBRUARY 1945

World War II: Western Front Canadian forces begin an operation to clear the territory between the Maas and Rhine Rivers; advance units of the Third Army have moved beyond the Our River. On the 9th British and Canadian troops reach the critical divide of the Rhine River at Millingen.
World War II: Luzon Fighting rages inside and outside Manila against fanatical Japanese resistance.

13 FEBRUARY 1945

World War II: Luzon US troops have now closed the neck of the Bataan Peninsula on southern Luzon and are advancing down to clear out enemy forces.
World War II: Eastern Front After a battle lasting almost two months the last of the 100,000 Germans in Budapest surrender to the Red Army.

13-15 FEBRUARY 1945

World War II: Air War A series of RAF and US firebomb raids devastates Dresden, Germany, leaving 70,000 dead in the fire storm (many of those killed are refugees from the Eastern Front). The raid seems vindictive rather than strategic, since Dresden is not an important military target but rather an important cultural center.

16 FEBRUARY 1945

World War II: Luzon Two battalions, one seaborne and one airborne, land on the fortress island of Corregidor in Manila Bay. A bitter struggle develops among the tunnels and gun emplacements of the island; US troops are quickly reinforced.

18 FEBRUARY 1945

World War II: Western Front As the Allies close in on the Rhine the US Third Army breaks the Siegfried Line north of Echternach.

19 FEBRUARY 1945

World War II: Invasion of Iwo Jima After months of preparatory shelling and air strikes 30,000 Marines land on Iwo Jima, halfway between Guam and Japan (750 miles away). General Kuribayashi commands a garrison of about 21,000 Japanese, who have prepared elaborate concrete fortifications and underground defenses. The topography of the island is dominated by 600-foot high Mount Suribachi on the southern tip. The defenders mount savage resistance, but this fails to prevent the Marines from consolidating their beachhead and fighting across to the other side of the island before the end of today. Part of metropolitan Japan, Iwo Jima lies within fighter range of Tokyo and thus is of immense potential use to the Allies.

21 FEBRUARY 1945

World War II: Luzon American forces complete the capture of the Bataan Peninsula on Luzon. Fighting on Corregidor continues.

23 FEBRUARY 1945

World War II: Western Front The US First and Ninth Armies begin operations across the Roer River, heading for the Rhine.
World War II: Iwo Jima Most of Mount Suribachi is taken by American forces during the day, and the US flag is hoisted on the summit. A photograph of this event will become a symbol of American triumph in the Far East during the war. To the north of the beachhead the painful US advance continues against fanatical Japanese opposition.

26 FEBRUARY 1945

World War II: Luzon Fighting on Corregidor ends. US forces find more than 5000 Japanese dead on the tiny island; there are 19 prisoners. American casualties are around 1000.

3 MARCH 1945

World War II: Iwo Jima The area of the island which has come to be known as 'The Mincer' is finally cleared by the Marines after a vicious struggle. The Americans now hold three airfields on the island.
World War II: Luzon Japanese resistance in Manila comes to an end after a bitter month-long fight by MacArthur's troops. The 20,000 defenders have been wiped out and the city devastated.

7 MARCH 1945

World War II: Western Front: Crossing of the Rhine A major watershed in the invasion of Germany is reached when the advance of the US 9th Armored Division (First Army) reaches the Rhine opposite Remagen and finds the Ludendorff Bridge there still standing. Troops are immediately rushed across the river, and brilliant staff improvisation sends more units hurrying to join them. (Hitler sacks Field Marshal Rundstedt for the mistake of leaving the bridge intact.) Other units of the First Army complete the capture of Cologne.

9-10 MARCH 1945

World War II: Air War Over Tokyo 279 Superfortresses rain 1650 tons of incendiary bombs in a strike specifically designed to destroy the wood and paper homes of Japanese civilians. As many as 120,000 people die in the horrific fire storm, making this the most devastating air attack of the war – even more so than the later atomic attacks on Hiroshima and Nagasaki. These attacks will continue on Japanese cities.

10 MARCH 1945

World War II: Philippines American infantry forces land on Mindanao. Meanwhile, fighting continues

In one of the war's most famous pictures US Marines raise the flag on Iwo Jima's Mount Suribachi.

The Allied advance into Germany was facilitated by the discovery of a Rhine bridge at Remagen that the Germans had failed to destroy.

on Luzon and Japanese resistance ends on the island of Palawan.

15 MARCH 1945

World War II: Western Front In Operation Undertone the American Third and Seventh Armies begin an offensive to clear the triangle between the rivers Saar, Moselle and Rhine. This operation will wind up successfully on 25 March. On the 17th the German bridge at Remagen collapses under the strain of heavy use and German bomb attacks, but engineers have built other bridges, and Allied troops continue pouring over the Rhine.

16 MARCH 1945

World War II: Philippines A US division lands on Basilan Island. Here, as on other small islands in the area, the pattern will be to subdue the Japanese in the first few days, then to withdraw, leaving the mopping up to Filipino guerrillas.

18-21 MARCH 1945

World War II: Japan The carriers of Mitscher's Task Force 58 carry out a series of attacks on the Japanese home islands. Kamikaze planes attack in reply and are most effective, damaging six carriers; the 832 killed on the *Franklin* make this the heaviest casualty list of any US ship in the war.

20 MARCH 1945

World War II: Burma The 19th Indian Division of the British Commonwealth forces completes the capture of Mandalay.

20-25 MARCH 1945

World War II: Western Front On the 20th General Patch's Seventh Army takes Saarbrücken and Zweibrücken to the east. Meanwhile, Patton's Third Army is moving up fast; on the 22nd Patton will drive across the Rhine near Nierstein as other units of his army complete mopping up west of the Rhine. On the 23rd British units will cross the Rhine south of Wesel, to be followed soon by other Allied crossings. At Remagen the First Army has expanded the bridgehead some 30 miles wide and 19 miles deep. By the 25th the Germans have abandoned resistance west of the Rhine and are in full retreat to the east. Hitler has ordered a total scorched-earth policy on all fronts, but some subordinates try to prevent this being carried out. By now the German army is drafting teenagers for the final defense.

23-31 MARCH 1945

World War II: Ryukyu Islands US naval forces mount massive air and naval strikes on the Ryukyu Islands in preparation for landings on Okinawa. The Japanese reply with deadly Kamikaze attacks.

26 MARCH 1945

World War II: Iwo Jima The few hundred Japanese troops remaining on the island mount a final suicide attack; they are wiped out by Marine units which are finishing off the last enemy pockets. Just over 200 of the Japanese garrison of 20,700 remain alive as prisoners. American casualties have been almost 6000 dead and 17,200 wounded, plus 90 seamen killed. Admiral Nimitz observes, 'uncommon valor was a common virtue' in capturing Iwo Jima. The percentage of US casualties has been one of the worst in US history, equalled only by Pickett's Charge at Gettysburg.

27 MARCH 1945

World War II: Air War The last German V2 rocket strikes near London. The 1115 rocket hits have killed over 2700 British civilians, while others have killed thousands in Antwerp, Brussels, and Liège.
World War II: Philippines Cebu City is taken by the US landing force. On this and the other islands the Japanese are beginning to withdraw to inland strongholds where mopping up will usually be the task of Filipino guerrillas.

28 MARCH 1945

World War II: Western Front Marburg is taken by the US III Corps, which has made a rapid advance from the Remagen bridgehead. Meanwhile, General Eisenhower sends a message to Stalin informing him that the Allies intend to advance across southern Germany and Austria rather than head straight for Berlin. The British object strongly both to the warning and the strategy, arguing in favor of reaching Berlin before the Soviets. With many implications for postwar Berlin and Europe, the American strategy prevails.

1 APRIL 1945

World War II: Invasion of Okinawa Supported by the largest naval operation yet in the Pacific, US forces invade Okinawa, the largest of the Ryukyu Islands just south of Japan. There are some 450,000 Army and Marine Corps personnel under General Simon B. Buckner, Jr. in the invading force. The 130,000 Japanese troops on the island are largely in caves to the south of the landings and thus mount no resistance in the first few days, but the fighting will thereafter be severe.
World War II: Western Front The US First and Ninth Armies link up at Lippstadt, cutting off 325,000 German troops in the Ruhr.
World War II: Philippines While a regiment lands unopposed in southeast Luzon, US forces southeast of Manila are making steady but extremely difficult progress.

5 APRIL 1945

World War II: Command It is announced that General MacArthur will take control of all army forces in the Pacific and Admiral Nimitz all naval forces, in preparation for the invasion of Japan.
World War II: Japan The government resigns, to be replaced by a new cabinet under Admiral Suzuki. The new leaders agree that no reasonable offer of peace should be turned down. Meanwhile, word arrives from the Russians that they will not renew their 1941 nonaggression pact.

6-9 APRIL 1945

World War II: Battle of the South China Sea On 6 April the giant Japanese battleship *Yamato* leaves the Inland Sea accompanied by other ships on a mission

Japan's *Yamato*, like her sister ship *Musashi*, was the largest (over 70,000 tons), most heavily armed (nine 18 in guns) battleship ever built.

to Okinawa. The *Yamato* has only enough fuel to reach Okinawa; the plan is to beach the ship off Okinawa and from that position to shell US forces in the area. The flotilla is sighted and reported by US submarines. Also on the 6th there are severe Kamikaze attacks on Allied shipping around Okinawa; two carriers are hit, along with 25 other ships. On 7 April a swarm of 380 American planes attack the *Yamato* which takes ten torpedo and five heavy bomb hits before going down. On the 8th and 9th the enemy attacks taper off after further strikes on American warships, but despite considerable damage inflicted, the Japanese operation has been futile and suicidal.

8 APRIL 1945

World War II: Burma British Commonwealth forces have now captured Mandalay and Meiktila and are ready for a rapid advance to finish a long, frustrating campaign in Burma.
World War II: Eastern Front In Austria, Soviet and German troops are battling fiercely in Vienna.
World War II: Okinawa The American advance has now cut off the neck of the Motobu Peninsula, and Marine units begin to clear the area of enemy forces.

9 APRIL 1945

World War II: Italy The British Eighth Army begins a major spring offensive toward Ferrara and Bologna; the US Fifth Army will join the operation on the 14th, and all forces will drive forward steadily.

11 APRIL 1945

World War II: Western Front Having pushed past the famous Krupp munition works at Essen, the US Ninth Army reaches the Elbe River south of Magdeburg, there to establish a bridgehead on the east bank. Also today, Weimar falls to the US Third Army; meanwhile, the British advance in the north.

11-14 APRIL 1945

World War II: Okinawa The Japanese mount furious Kamikaze attacks on Task Force 58, scoring hits on the battleship *Missouri* and the carrier *Enterprise* on the 11th and a number of other ships over the next three days. Nonetheless, American operations against Okinawa and Japanese air bases continue.

12 APRIL 1945

Death of Roosevelt While vacationing at Warm Springs, Georgia, President Roosevelt suffers a massive cerebral hemorrhage and dies. Vice-President Harry S Truman is sworn in as president, assuming the monumental tasks of replacing a major world leader in completing the most devastating war in history. Among the subjects on which Truman receives his first briefings will be the atomic-weapons project.

13 APRIL 1945

World War II: Western Front The full horror of German atrocities begins to appear to the West with the liberation of the Belsen and Buchenwald concentration camps by Allied forces. In this week many towns, including Brunswick, Baden-Baden, Bamberg and Jena, fall to the Allies. Today the US Ninth Army seizes a second bridgehead over the Elbe, and Vienna surrenders to the Russians (by now the two fronts have almost merged).
World War II: Luzon In Manila Bay, US forces land at Fort Drum and begin to pour 5000 gallons of fuel oil into the concrete fortifications, with their unknown number of Japanese defenders. The oil is then set afire and burns for five days. On 16 April Fort Frank will be seized, completing the capture of Manila Bay.

16 APRIL 1945

World War II: Eastern Front Deciding Eisenhower's 28 March message was a ruse to cover an American sprint to Berlin, Stalin orders Soviet forces to mount a major offensive against the city. The Germans are far outnumbered and can do little but delay the advance.

18 APRIL 1945

World War II: Western Front As the US Seventh Army assaults Nuremberg (it will fall on the 20th), the last German forces in the Ruhr pocket surrender. German commander Model commits suicide. Also today, Patton's troops cross the Czechoslovakian border after a whirlwind advance.

21 APRIL 1945

World War II: Italy Polish troops capture Bologna; the main forces of the US Fifth Army have now fought their way into the Lombardy Plain and are advancing quickly into the Po Valley, where the Germans will prove powerless against the Allied advance.

22-27 APRIL 1945

World War II: Diplomatic Gestapo head Heinrich Himmler sends a secret message to the British and Americans stating that Germany will surrender to them but not to the Soviets. The Allies reject this offer on the 27th and repeat their demands for unconditional surrender. On the 23rd Luftwaffe commander Hermann Goering sends a telegram to Hitler offering to take over leadership if Hitler is unable to continue. The enraged Führer orders Goering's arrest.

25 APRIL 1945

International: The UN Conference Representatives of 50 nations begin a meeting in San Francisco to draw up a document establishing the United Nations Organization, a focal point for the hopes of a war-weary civilization. The UN Charter will be signed on 23 June.
World War II: Western Front: Meeting on the Elbe The Red Army completes its encirclement of Berlin as Russian and American patrols make a historic first meeting on the Elbe River near Torgau. Elsewhere, the Third Army crosses the Danube and attacks Regensburg; tomorrow Bremen will fall to the British.

28 APRIL 1945

World War II: Death of Mussolini As US forces occupy Genoa and other cities, Mussolini and his mistress are caught and shot by Italian partisans; today the bodies are hung upside down in the main square of Milan.
World War II: Battle of Berlin The Russian siege of Berlin continues; the Soviets have now penetrated to within a mile of the bunker where Hitler and his staff have taken refuge: the final noose is tightening around the now-impotent figure who proclaimed the Thousand-Year Reich.
World War II: Western Front The US Seventh Army takes Augsburg in an advance south toward Austria. In the north the British Second Army is advancing from the Elbe River to the Baltic Sea.
World War II: Okinawa US forces are fighting on the Shuri Line, employing tanks, flame throwers and artillery in attempts to destroy strong Japanese defenses.

29 APRIL 1945

World War II: Victory in Italy The surrender of the German forces in Italy is signed at Caserta in the south. In the rapid Allied advance to the north Venice is liberated.
World War II: Holocaust Third Army troops liberate the concentration camp at Dachau, a few miles outside Munich; there they find 30,000 starved and devastated survivors, many of whom will die despite the best Allied efforts. Tomorrow the Seventh Army will occupy Munich.

30 APRIL 1945

World War II: Suicide of Hitler Having prepared his Political Testament, married his mistress, Eva Braun, and appointed Admiral Doenitz as his successor, Adolf Hitler shoots himself in his Berlin bunker; Braun poisons herself at his side. As Hitler had instructed, their bodies are doused with gasoline and burned outside the bunker. Meanwhile, the Soviets reach the Reichstag from the north, and fighting rages in the streets of Berlin. American troops have been ordered to stay in positions along the Elbe and Milde Rivers, leaving Berlin to the Russians.
World War II: Okinawa Japanese counterattacks and infiltration attempts around the Shuri Line are suppressed; there is particularly fierce fighting in the Maeda and Kochi Ridge positions.

US First Army soldiers reach out to greet their Soviet counterparts at the historic meeting on the wrecked Elbe River bridge at Torgau in April 1945.

MAY 1945

World War II: Air War American bombers drop 24,000 tons of bombs on Japan, the targets including Nagoya, Tokyo and Oshima. Many Allied aircraft are involved in food drops into Holland.

1 MAY 1945

World War II: Collapse of Germany New Führer Doenitz broadcasts rather pathetically, 'It is my duty to save the German people from destruction by the Bolshevists.' Propaganda minister Goebbels and his wife commit suicide after poisoning their six children. Top Hitler aid Martin Bormann flees the bunker, probably to die nearby (though later rumors will place him in South America). Soviet troops will complete the capture of Berlin on 2 May. The US Seventh Army drives south into Austria, while the British advance north, reaching the Baltic tomorrow.

3 MAY 1945

World War II: Collapse of Germany Soviet forces have now reached the Elbe west of Berlin and have made contact there with the US First and Ninth Armies and, to the north, with the British Second Army. The only major German forces still fighting Soviet armies are those isolated in Latvia and those in Austria and Czechoslovakia, the latter two under pressure from Allied forces on both Eastern and Western fronts, as well as from Italy.
World War II: Burma The vital city of Rangoon is recaptured by the 26th Indian Division without resistance from the Japanese.

3-29 MAY 1945

World War II: Okinawa A fierce Japanese counter-offensive strikes from the south on 2-4 May, but the attacks do not break the American front. At sea the Japanese mount a series of Kamikaze raids on American and British warships in the area; the 560 suicide planes severely damage several Allied carriers and battleships, sink destroyers, and hit many other smaller ships.

4 MAY 1945

World War II: Collapse of Germany Doenitz sends envoys to Montgomery's headquarters at Luneburg Heath and they agree on the surrender of German forces in Holland, Denmark and north Germany, effective 5 May.

5 MAY 1945

World War II: Collapse of Germany Soviet units seize the German rocket development center at Peenemünde. Nazi scientists captured there, though

The gutted Reichstag, symbol of the devastation visited on Berlin by Allied air raids and, even more, by the Red Army's conquest of the city.

responsible for the deaths of thousands of Allied civilians, will become the foundation of both the Russian and American missile and space programs.

5-6 MAY 1945

World War II: Collapse of Germany On these days the German Army Group G surrenders to the US 6th Army Group in Bavaria, and the US Third Army takes Pilsen in their drive through Czechoslovakia. Patton is ordered, much to his disgust, to halt his Third Army advance there and allow the Soviets to occupy the rest of the country, as previously decided. In Prague, meanwhile, Czech resistance elements are engaged in a fierce battle with German SS units.

7 MAY 1945

World War II: German Surrender In the small red schoolhouse that houses Eisenhower's headquarters in Reims, France, General Alfred Jodl signs an unconditional German surrender. General Walter B. Smith, Eisenhower's chief of staff, signs for the Allies; British, French, Soviet and American representatives are present. Hostilities are to end at 12:01 AM on 8 May. Meanwhile, at sea off the Firth of Forth two Allied merchant ships are the last victims of German U-Boats.

8 MAY 1945

World War II: VE Day The British and Americans celebrate VE (Victory in Europe) Day. Truman, Churchill and King George VI make special broadcasts as millions of civilians on both continents dance in the streets. German forces surrender in Prague and Latvia.

9 MAY 1945

World War II: Europe As the German surrender is ratified in Berlin, the last German soldiers holding out in Prussia and Pomerania surrender, among them Goering and Kesselring.

15 MAY 1945

World War II: Okinawa In weeks of operations on the island the pattern has become one of heavy fighting, slow US advances and costly, only partly successful, Japanese counterattacks. There are particularly fierce battles on Sugar Loaf and Conical Hills; the Japanese Shuri Line will finally break near the end of the month.

23 MAY 1945

Britain After the Labour Party leaves the coalition government, Churchill resigns and forms a caretaker government; elections will be held in July.
War Criminals Gestapo chief Heinrich Himmler has been captured by the British, but he commits suicide.

JUNE 1945

World War II: Air War B-29 Superfortress bombers fly 6500 missions over Japan, striking numerous targets. By now the heart of Tokyo is nearly destroyed. The Fourteenth Air Force raids targets in China, joined by planes based in the Philippines and on Okinawa.

1-13 JUNE 1945

World War II: Okinawa The US Task Force 38 completes nearly three months of operations off Okinawa. During these days it sustains much damage from Kamikaze attacks, and on 5 June a typhoon causes more damage. Meanwhile, on the island the Japanese defenders of the Shuri Line have retired to the Oruku Peninsula, where they mount still more resistance to the Marines. By the 13th, however, it will become apparent that the last stages of opposition have been reached when Japanese soldiers begin committing suicide.

5 JUNE 1945

International The Big Four (US, Great Britain, France, USSR) make arrangements to divide Berlin, as well as for the occupation of Germany under the Allied Control Commission.

18 JUNE 1945

World War II: Okinawa General Buckner, commander of US forces on the island, is killed by Japanese artillery fire when on a visit to the front. General Joseph Stilwell takes over command.

22 JUNE 1945

World War II: Okinawa Fighting on Okinawa comes to an end after a truly horrible campaign. US forces have lost 12,500 dead and 35,500 wounded. The Navy has had 36 ships sunk and 368 damaged. In the air the Americans have lost 763 planes. Given their concept of noble death for the homeland, the Japanese tolls are far worse: 120,000 military and 42,000 civilian dead, an estimated 7830 planes downed and, among other vessels sunk, the battleship *Yamato*, one of the two largest ships ever built (the other being the *Musashi*, sunk last year). For the first time, however, there are significant numbers of Japanese prisoners – 10,755. It will be some consolation that the struggle for Okinawa will prove to be the last major land battle of the war.

28 JUNE 1945

World War II: Luzon General MacArthur announces that operations on Luzon are over after five months and 19 days. Over 12,000 Americans have been killed. Isolated enemy pockets remain to be mopped up.

29 JUNE 1945

World War II: Planning Plans for an invasion of Japan are approved by President Truman. They provide for landings in Kyushi on 1 November (Operation Olympic) and on Honshu near Tokyo on 1 March, 1946. It is expected that this final campaign will be far bloodier than those on Iwo Jima and Okinawa.

11 JULY 1945

International The Inter-Allied Council for Berlin holds its first meeting. The Soviets agree to turn over administration of allocated sectors to the British and Americans, who themselves allocate parts of their sectors to France.

16 JULY 1945

World War II: Atomic Research After years of secret research American atomic scientists see the results of their efforts on the Manhattan Project: the first atomic bomb test is mounted successfully at Alamogordo, New Mexico. The explosion of the approximately 15-kiloton weapon is visible and audible up to 180 miles away.

17 JULY-2 AUGUST 1945

World War II: Potsdam Conference At Potsdam, near Berlin, Churchill, Truman and Stalin meet to clarify and implement agreements reached at Yalta and other conferences vis-a-vis Germany and the former occupied countries of Europe. The British delegation leaves between 25-28 July because of the election results; on their return Clement Attlee is the new Prime Minister and representative. On the 24th Truman will inform Stalin of a major new weapon but does not identify it as atomic (Stalin probably knows all about it through his spies). On the 26th the Allies authorize a broadcast to Japan of what is known as the Potsdam Declaration – a demand for unconditional surrender, qualified only by the assurance that there is no intention of reducing Japan to poverty in the postwar world; it says nothing of the disposition of Emperor Hirohito. Japan will not accept the Declaration.

29-30 JULY 1945

World War II: Pacific The US cruiser *Indianapolis*, returning to the US after delivering an atomic bomb to the Marianas air base, is sunk by a Japanese submarine. The loss is not discovered for three days, and many of the 316 survivors are not found for several days more.

Marines hurdle a stone wall in the bitter struggle for Okinawa. In the nearly three-month campaign some 12,500 US servicemen lost their lives.

The remains of the Hiroshima Fire Department, 4000 feet from ground zero when the first atomic bomb was dropped on the city by the B-29 Superfortress *Enola Gay* on 6 August 1945.

6 AUGUST 1945

World War II: Bombing of Hiroshima The first atomic bomb used in war is dropped on Hiroshima, Japan from a B-29 called the *Enola Gay*, named after pilot Paul Tibbets' mother. A uranium fission type, the bomb yields the equivalent of 20,000 tons of TNT. Sixty percent of the city is destroyed in the blast and the firestorm that follows; some 80,000 Japanese civilians are killed, other thousands horribly burnt or given radiation poisoning; cancer from radiation exposure will kill uncounted victims over the next 40 years. Though the March bombing raids on Tokyo were worse in the immediate effect, the blast at Hiroshima commences a new, bomb-haunted era of the world's history.

8 AUGUST 1945

World War II: USSR Enters the Pacific War The Soviet Union declares war on Japan and minutes later launches a massive invasion of Manchuria with one and a half million men on three fronts; Japanese defense lines are soon smashed.

World War II: Bombing of Nagasaki The USAAF drops its second (and last) atomic bomb on Nagasaki, killing 40,000 Japanese. President Truman makes a broadcast threatening Japan with total destruction by atomic bombs; the Japanese Supreme War Council decides late in the night that they will accept defeat if the monarchy is to be maintained – a proviso that is soon abandoned.

14 AUGUST 1945

World War II: Surrender of Japan At a government meeting Emperor Hirohito ends the wrangling of his leaders by ordering the war to end. He records a radio message to the Japanese people saying that they must 'Bear the unbearable.' Despite an effort by dissident officers to steal the recording, it is transmitted to the Allies, who announce that Japan accepts unconditional surrender.

China Communists are now to be cut off from any active role in postwar China.

15 AUGUST 1945

World War II: VJ Day As the Allies deliriously celebrate today as VJ Day, Hirohito's broadcast goes out to the Japanese people.

17 AUGUST 1945

International The Allies divide Korea at the 38th parallel, with US troops to move into the southern portion and Soviet troops into the north. These are presumed to be temporary occupations.

29 AUGUST 1945

Japan General MacArthur is named Supreme Commander of Allied Powers in Japan; he will supervise the postwar reconstruction of the country.

AUGUST-DECEMBER 1945

China With the collapse of Japan, China is now set to become the stage for one of the great 'power plays' in history. The two principal antagonists are the Kuomintang, or Nationalists, led by Chiang Kai-shek, and the Communists, led by Mao Tse-tung. Behind them lie the yet-to-emerge superpowers, the USA and the USSR. The conflict begins as a race between the Nationalists and Communists to liberate as much of China from the Japanese occupation forces as possible. The US has about 60,000 military personnel (in all branches) in China as the war ends, and almost immediately begins to use its air and naval forces to transport some 450,000 Nationalist troops from Chiang's bases in central and southern China to major cities in the north and east. Not unnaturally, the Chinese Communists will increasingly turn to the Russians for aid (even though at this time Mao is well disposed toward the USA, and Stalin has indicated support for Chiang's Nationalist government). The Russians, having invaded Manchuria on 9 August, are now proceeding to loot its factories and physical facilities. Meanwhile, in the parts of China liberated by the Nationalists, some 350,000 Japanese troops are not only not being imprisoned but are being allowed to keep their weapons and are openly used by the Nationalists and their American sponsors as guards, workcrews and general support troops against the Communists.

AUGUST 1945-FEBRUARY 1946

Vietnam Because of his relations with the OSS during WW II and because he regards the United States as the friend of all struggling peoples, Ho Chi Minh writes at least eight letters during these months to President Truman and the US State Department asking for US aid in gaining Vietnam's independence from France. There is no record of US officials ever answering these appeals. The US Government at this time is in a quandary, not wanting to support French colonialism but not wanting to turn Vietnam over to a communist administration.

2 SEPTEMBER 1945

World War II: Japanese Surrender Ceremonies The Japanese surrender is signed on the USS *Missouri* in Tokyo Bay. Foreign Minister Shigemitsu leads the Japanese delegation. General Douglas MacArthur accepts the surrender on behalf of the Allies. In a memorable remark at the end of the ceremonies MacArthur says, 'These proceedings are now closed.' The 'proceedings' to which he seems to allude were nothing if not impressive. Of the estimated 55,000,000 people killed in World War II – among them some 20,000,000 Russians dead and 6,000,000 Jews murdered by the Nazis – 405,399 American soldiers lost their lives.

Vietnam In Hanoi, with American OSS officers at his side, Ho Chi Minh proclaims the Independent Democratic Republic of Vietnam. Ho even quotes from the American Declaration of Independence, and he has high hopes of gaining support from the US in maintaining an independent state of Vietnam.

8 SEPTEMBER 1945

Korea The first American troops, commanded by Lt. General John R. Hodge, begin to arrive in Korea to accept the surrender of the Japanese below the 38th parallel. Short of men and weary from the war, the US military government assigns some Japanese administrators to the new government because they were the most experienced. This antagonizes many Koreans.

12 SEPTEMBER 1945

Vietnam British troops arrive in Saigon to accept surrender of the Japanese. Most Vietnamese expect the Allies to support their independence. While the US does in principle favor a provisional international trusteeship for Vietnam, after Roosevelt's death the US signs a credit agreement with France for supply of vehicles and relief equipment to French authorities in Indochina. This is seen as US endorsement of the French reconquest.

26 SEPTEMBER 1945

Vietnam In Saigon, Lieutenant Colonel A. Peter Dewey, head of the American OSS mission in Vietnam, is driving a jeep when he is shot by Vietminh troops (who evidently think he is French). Dewey thus becomes the first of some 56,000 Americans who will eventually die in hostilities in Vietnam.

OCTOBER 1945

China As it has become apparent that the Nationalist Chinese need all the help they can get in their race with the Communists, the US sends in some 53,000 Marines, assigned to occupy Peking, Tientsin and nearby railroads, coal mines and other facilities, thus freeing Nationalist troops to fight elsewhere. This action will only temporarily bolster Chiang's fight but will make him feel that he can count on the US to support him to the end.

United Nations On 24 October the United Nations Charter comes into force; there are 29 signatories at this stage.

NOVEMBER 1945

China A major debate is now engulfing the US government and the political scene in general over just what the US role in China has been and should

General Marshall with Chinese leaders during his fruitless mission to end the civil war. L to r: Chou En-lai, Marshall, Chu Teh, Cheng Kai-min, Mao.

be. A well-organized group generally known as the 'China Lobby,' tends to blame the State Department and various 'communist sympathizers' with having brought about the present crisis and wants to commit more US support to the Nationalists. But many Americans with no ideological or other commitment to China are questioning why US troops remain in China; there are reports filtering back of incidents that are putting US personnel at risk of being injured or killed. The debate over 'who lost China' will rage for many years.

20 NOVEMBER 1945

War Crimes The trial of 21 major German war leaders begins at Nuremberg, Germany (and will continue until October 1946). This is the first such trial under international law and will be criticized by some on grounds that the crimes in question had not hitherto been defined by law. The Nuremberg trials will give a full and public account of the atrocities of the Nazi regime.

23 NOVEMBER 1945

China General Albert Wedemeyer, commander of the US armed forces in China, cables the Army chief of staff in Washington that if the US is to be effective in supporting the unification of China and Manchuria he will need still more US troops than the 110,000 already present. Although no more troops will be sent, the orginal plan of withdrawing all American forces from China by the end of 1945 is now abandoned. Once again, Chiang Kai-shek will read this as signalling that with such US support he need not cooperate or compromise with the Communists.

28 NOVEMBER 1945

China President Truman, trying to stem the controversy over China, appoints General George C. Marshall, just retired as US Army chief of staff, as his special representative to that country (with the personal rank of ambassador but not as the official ambassador). Marshall's mission is to bring the Nationalists and the Communists together in some sort of coalition to rule China, and thus avoid the civil war that is shaping up.

20 DECEMBER 1945

China General Marshall arrives in China to commence what will turn out to be a thoroughly frustrating year trying to get the Nationalists and Communists to compromise and cooperate. Although Marshall will obtain a few temporary results, the situation essentially moves along its own course. The Communists remain convinced that time is on their side and that Chiang Kai-shek is unable to make any substantial reforms.

JANUARY-JUNE 1946

China US forces in China continue to provide air and sea transportation to move the Nationalist troops around China, as well as providing equipment and training; the Americans even assign large units to various Chinese cities. At times the US soldiers find themselves confronting Russian and Communist Chinese forces, but the Americans generally withdraw rather than engage in overt hostilities. In an incident at Tangku the Communists try to seize a US Marine Corps ammunition depot but are driven off after a two-hour firefight.

China President Chiang Kai-shek announces a truce between his Nationalist government and Mao Tsetung's Communists, the truce expedited by US envoy General George Marshall. But the Chinese civil war will resume hostilities on 14 April.

5 MARCH 1946

International In a speech at Westminster College in Fulton, Missouri, former British Prime Minister Winston Churchill calls for closer Anglo-American military cooperation in resisting Russian expansionism, and says, 'From Stettin on the Baltic to Trieste on the Adriatic an iron curtain has descended across the Continent . . . Police governments are pervading from Moscow.' His speech popularizes the term 'iron curtain,' but American leaders are not yet fully responsive to the Soviet threat. Resisting alliances, for some time America will look to the UN to provide international security.

JULY 1946

China In some of the most serious confrontations yet, seven US Marines are kidnapped east of Peking and held by the Communist Chinese for several days before being released. Then at the end of the month the Communists ambush a US Marine motor convoy carrying UNRRA supplies between Tientsin and Peking; three Americans are killed and 12 wounded.

1 JULY 1946

Atomic Testing The US begins underwater atomic tests at Bikini in the Marshall Islands. Part of the ensuing fallout will be the introduction in Paris of the Bikini bathing suit, claimed to have the 'ultimate impact' of the bomb test.

30 SEPTEMBER 1946

War Crimes The Nuremberg international tribunal announces the verdicts in its trial of accused Nazi war criminals. Of the 22 defendants, only three are acquitted; the rest receive sentences ranging from ten years' imprisonment to death. Before he can be hanged Hermann Goering will commit suicide.

1 OCTOBER 1946

Korean War: Approach Under-Secretary of State Dean Acheson states unequivocally that the United States intends to remain in Korea until that country is united and free. Under a wartime agreement proposed by the US, and intended to be temporary, the Korean peninsula has been divided at the 38th parallel, the northern half occupied by the Soviets and the southern half by the US. But the Russians have firmly settled in, gradually cutting off communications between north and south Korea, extending communist control over the occupied territory and fortifying the 38th parallel. Despite Acheson's proclamation, however, Washington does not yet view Korea as essential to Western security.

23 NOVEMBER 1946

Vietnam Beginning their long and ultimately futile effort to hold on to colonial Indochina, French forces bomb Haiphong, killing some 6000 Vietnamese.

19 DECEMBER 1946

Vietnam: The Indochina War In Hanoi the Democratic Republic of Vietnam launches its first attack against the French. Following months of steadily deteriorating relations, the attack has the support of most Vietnamese and begins what comes to be known as the Indochina War.

JANUARY 1947

Greece The makings of a full-fledged civil war are now apparent in Greece as the former guerrillas of both persuasions – communist and non-communist – begin to train their guns on one another in an effort to see who will take over postwar Greece. The British government under Churchill had planned to maintain its support for the Greek government, but due to Britain's own economic and financial problems it now admits that it can no longer assume the burden in Greece. The British government approaches the US, which agrees to take over the role as main supporter of the Greek government in its growing struggle with the communists.

Harry S Truman was the only US president to hold office during two major American foreign wars.

8 JANUARY 1947

China General George Marshall flies from China practically at the same moment that President Truman announces that Marshall is to become the new Secretary of State. One of the reasons Marshall leaves so abruptly is that he is disgusted with the situation in China and with the actions of both sides. China is now undergoing a full-scale civil war. Although the Nationalists control almost all the major cities, the Communists control the countryside and thus most of the food supplies and raw materials. The Nationalists have by now imposed a National Assembly and a constitution, but these are facades for a corrupt government and a bankrupt economy. Marshall's departing statement makes it clear that he regards both the Nationalists and Communists as responsible for the strife that now splits the country.

FEBRUARY 1947

China The bulk of the 100,000 or so American military personnel in China begin to be withdrawn.

12 MARCH 1947

The Truman Doctrine Before a joint session of Congress the president proposes a new foreign policy to 'support free peoples who are resisting subjugation by armed minorities or by outside pressure.' Aimed at containing communist expansion, the policy is immediately dubbed the Truman Doctrine. Its first effort will be to give $400 million in emergency aid to anti-communist governments in Greece and Turkey.

19 MARCH 1947

China In the Chinese civil war Chiang's Nationalists capture the Communist capital of Yenan. Mao's forces will rally for a series of victories that result in Communist control of Manchuria by the end of the year.

31 MAY 1947

Hungary In the first challenge to the Truman Doctrine, Russian-backed communists seize control of Hungary.

5 JUNE 1947

The Marshall Plan At a Harvard commencement address Secretary of State George Marshall proposes a massive plan of aid to war-torn Europe, the enemy being 'hunger, poverty, desperation and chaos,' the goal being 'the revival of a working economy in the world so as to permit the emergence of political and social conditions in which free institutions can exist.' Formally called the European Recovery Program but known as the Marshall Plan, the program will over the next years distribute some $12 billion in American aid to 17 countries; despite steady Russian attempts to sabotage it, the program will be an historic success in its twin aims of helping revive the European economy and blocking the spread of Soviet-style communism in Western Europe.

As Berlin children watch, a C-54, part of the US airlift during the 1948 Soviet blockade of the city, prepares to land at Tempelhof Airport.

26 JULY 1947

National Reorganizing the nation's military, the National Security Act designates a National Military Establishment of all services, to be administered by a cabinet-level secretary of defense. Under the secretary are three Joint Chiefs of Staff representing the Army, Navy and Air Force. Later the Marine commandant and a chairman are added to the joint chiefs, and in 1949 the whole will be renamed the Department of Defense. On 17 September Navy Secretary James V. Forrestal will become the first secretary of defense.

17 SEPTEMBER 1947

Korean War: Approach The US refers the issue of Korean independence to the United Nations, which passes a resolution calling for free elections in that country.

NOVEMBER 1947

Greece Since the US has assumed responsibility for supporting the Greek government in its struggle against the communist forces the US has voted some $200 million in aid to Greece. By 1953 the US will have given Greece almost $2 billion in military and economic aid. But during this month, a new step is taken with the formation of a joint Greek-American general staff – effectively, US military personnel will begin to have an increasingly active role in planning the strategy and tactics of the Greek civil war that will continue for another two years. In February 1948 General James Van Fleet will arrive in Greece to assume command of the Joint US Military Advisory and Planning Group (JUSMAPG).

23 JANUARY 1948

Korean War: Approach The Soviet government notifies the United Nations Temporary Commission on Korea that the Commission will not be allowed into North Korea to supervise UN-mandated elections.

25 FEBRUARY 1948

Czechoslovakia Soviet-supported communists seize control of the country.

1 APRIL 1948

The Berlin Blockade The Soviet military government in Berlin begins a land blockade of Allied sectors of the city by refusing passage to US and British supply trains. During the next two months the Russians will effectively isolate Berlin from all contacts with the West.

1 MAY 1948

North Korea Soviet-supported communists proclaim a People's Republic in Pyongyang, with jurisdiction over all Korea.

25 JUNE 1948

The Berlin Airlift To bypass the Russian land blockade from their sector surrounding the city American C-47 'Gooney Birds' begin to arrive in West Berlin with supplies. Over the next year US and British aircraft will fly a steady stream of 2.3 million tons of food and coal into the city.

Berliners take inventory of US aid delivered under the Marshall Plan, a program meant to help Europe rebuild and to halt the spread of communism.

15 AUGUST 1948

Korean War: Approach The Republic of Korea (ROK) is proclaimed, with Syngman Rhee installed as president in the new capital of Seoul. Though this ends the American occupation, the US leaves advisors to train South Korean military forces and in December will agree to provide economic assistance. In fact, this outcome is exactly what the American Joint Chiefs of Staff have planned: the US is now resigned to a divided Korea and has little desire to become involved in fighting communists in a strategically unimportant country. The intention is to make the new South Korean regime capable of resisting any communist aggression.

1 SEPTEMBER 1948

China Mao's forces have made enough gains to proclaim a North China People's Republic.

9 SEPTEMBER 1948

Korean War: Approach The Korean People's Democratic Republic is established under the presidency of communist leader Kim Il Sung. His government in the north, which claims authority over all Korea, is modeled on the USSR's and commands most of the industrial capacity of the peninsula.

NOVEMBER 1948

China Mukden, the principal city in Manchuria, falls to the Communists despite a last-minute effort by US air transports to reinforce the Nationalist troops there. Chiang's US military adviser, General David Barr, advises Washington that it is 'the beginning of the end.' During the night of 16-17 November, the last 800 members of the US Military Advisory Group are flown out of Chiang's capital, Nanking, and elsewhere the last US military personnel are being withdrawn.

2 NOVEMBER 1948

National The presidential elections result in a surprise victory for incumbent Harry S Truman, who defeats Governor Thomas E. Dewey by 2.2 million popular votes and 114 electoral votes.

23 DECEMBER 1948

War Crimes Convicted as war criminals, ex-Premier Tojo and six other war leaders are hanged in Tokyo after the US Supreme Court rejects their appeal. The next day General MacArthur closes out Japan's major war-crimes cases by releasing all others accused.

12 JANUARY 1949

Korean War: Approach Dean Acheson, soon to be Marshall's successor as Secretary of State, reaffirms the United Nations' responsibility to provide military security to Pacific area nations. He does not include Korea within the US defense perimeter; Korea is expected to defend itself, backed by a vague 'commitment of the entire civilized world.' Current American military doctrine has drastically reduced conventional forces, expecting US superiority in air power and atomic weapons to provide security and leaving international disputes to the UN.

Marshall's successor as secretary of state was the tough and brilliant Dean Acheson.

15-21 JANUARY 1949

China Communist forces score a major victory by occupying Tientsin; on 21 January they will take Peiping, and Chiang Kai-shek will resign. America has had thousands of noncombatant military forces in China since 1946 and has spent billions of dollars over the years in trying to prop up the inept Chiang's Koumintang (KMT) forces. Now the guerrilla tactics of Mao Tse-tung's Chinese Communist Party (CCP) are on the verge of conquering the entire gigantic country. Fearing too much direct military involvement might precipitate war with Russia, Washington will pull all American troops out of China in February. Mao will then turn to Stalin for help, and the two great Communist countries will enter into an uneasy alliance. On 25 March, Mao will set up the capital of Communist China in Peiping, now renamed Peking.

4 APRIL 1949

International Twelve nations sign the North Atlantic Treaty, a defense agreement that lays the foundation of the North Atlantic Treaty Organization (NATO). Under the pact the US, Canada, Britain, France and eight other Western European nations agree that 'an armed attack against one or more of them in Europe and North America shall be considered an attack against them all.

8 APRIL 1949

Germany It is decided to merge the US occupation zone in Germany with those of France and Britain, contingent on the establishment of a German civilian administration; occupation troops will remain for security reasons. The Federal Republic of Germany will be established on 21 May.

12 MAY 1949

Berlin Blockade The Soviet Union lifts its Berlin blockade, again allowing truck and train traffic to pass through East Germany to West Berlin. The airlift into Berlin will continue until 30 September in order to build up stockpiles of supplies against another emergency. During the blockade there have been as many as 900 flights a day; in the process, only 70 American and British lives have been lost. The newly-created US Air Force has shown its ability to mobilize in a crisis, and its leaders have honed their skills at logistics to a fine edge.

29 JUNE 1949

Korean War: Approach The US removes the last of its troops from South Korea, leaving behind a group of around 500 military advisors. ROK president Syngman Rhee is decidedly unhappy about the withdrawal, especially since America has supplied his largely untrained army with few fighting planes and tanks. (Washington fears the truculent Rhee might use them to invade North Korea). By this time Russia has pulled most of its troops out of the North but has supplied the North Korean army much modern weaponry.

2 SEPTEMBER 1949

Korean War: Approach The United Nations Commission on Korea reports that it is unable to settle differences between the Republic of Korea in the south and the Democratic People's Republic in the north, and that civil war is possible.

23 SEPTEMBER 1949

Atomic testing President Truman makes the sobering announcement that Russia has just tested an atomic device and thus has nuclear capabilities. American military doctrine, predicated on an atomic-weapons monopoly, has now become moot; meanwhile, inspired by Mao's success, anti-Western uprisings are flaring all over Asia.

1 OCTOBER 1949

China In Peking, the Communist People's Republic of China is proclaimed, with Mao Tse-tung as chairman. The USSR recognizes the regime immediately, followed soon by Britain and others. The US refuses recognition.

14 JANUARY 1950

Vietnam Despairing of any reconciliation with France, Ho Chi Minh declares that the only true legal government is his Democratic Republic of Vietnam. The Soviet Union and China extend recognition, and China will start supplying modern weapons to the Vietminh.

31 JANUARY 1950

National President Truman announces that he has instructed the Atomic Energy Commission to produce a hydrogen bomb – a superweapon far more destructive than those dropped on Japan.

15 FEBRUARY 1950

Moscow Russia and China sign a 30-year friendship and mutual defense pact.

8 APRIL 1950

Cold War Over the Baltic Sea a Soviet fighter shoots down an unarmed US Navy patrol plane, ostensibly for violating Soviet air space over Latvia. The bodies of the ten crew members are never found. Similar incidents will occur throughout the years ahead, ending variously in negotiations, apologies, charges or countercharges.

8 MAY 1950

Vietnam In response to the Communist victory in China, Secretary of State Dean Acheson announces that the US will provide economic and military aid to French-controlled Vietnam. This marks a fateful step toward US involvement in that country.

25 JUNE 1950

Korean War: Invasion of South Korea In a massive surprise attack two columns of North Korean communist troops with Soviet-made weapons and tanks surge across the 38th parallel in an invasion of South Korea. DPRK Premier Kim Il Sung has built an army of some 135,000, many of them Soviet-trained. Kim also has assurances of material support from Stalin, who feels that a swift conquest will forestall American intervention, and encouragement from Mao Tse-tung. America has prepared the way by repeated official statements that Korea is not strategically significant. US intelligence, meanwhile, has failed to discern the communist military buildup on the border over the past weeks. Syngman Rhee's ROK forces are some 100,000 lightly-armed and green troops; they are able to mount little resistance to the communist's drive toward the capital of Seoul.

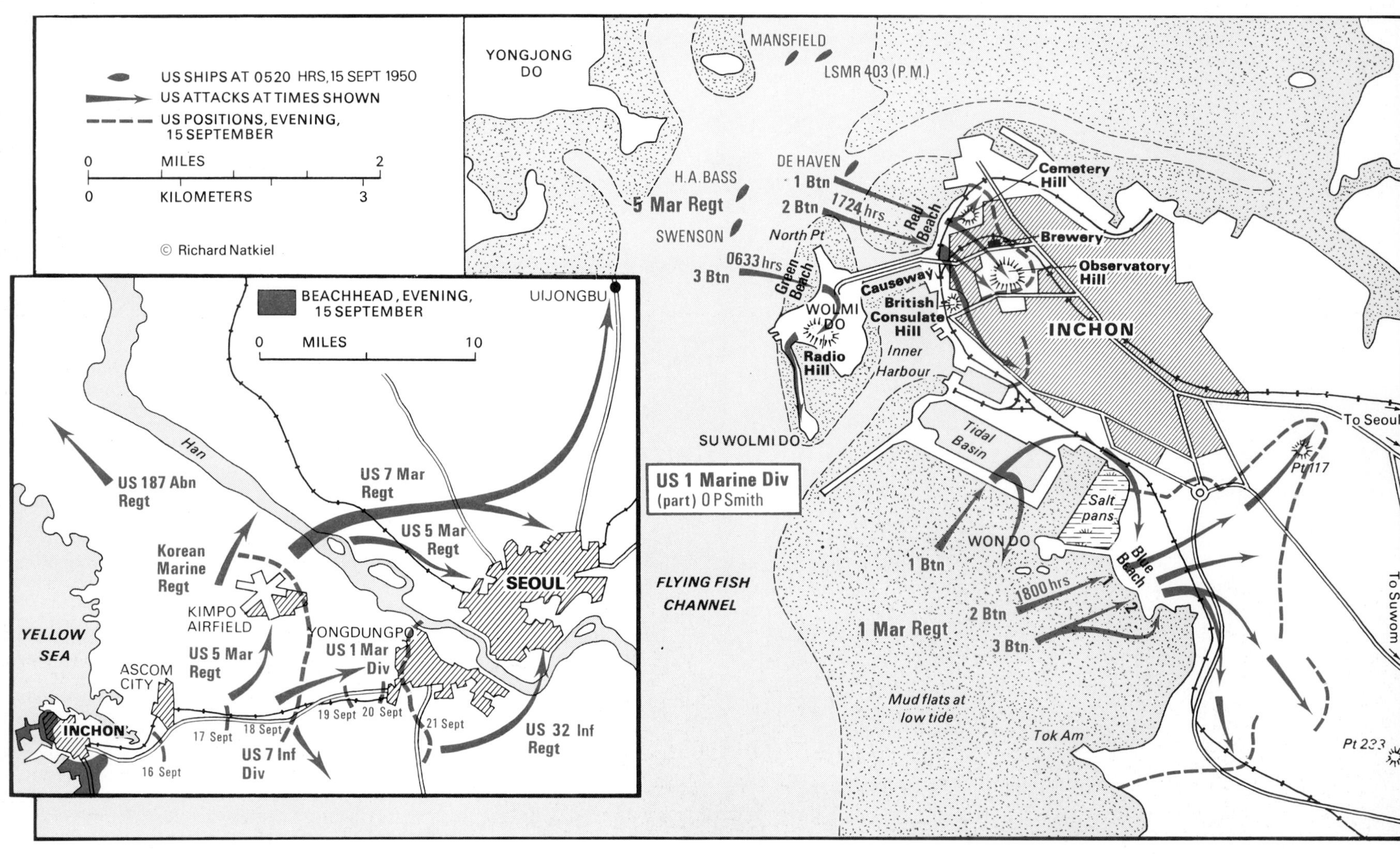

A map of General MacArthur's masterly landing at Inchon which transformed the Korean War in 1950.

President Truman hears the news at his home in Independence, Missouri, and hastens back to Washington to confer with advisors.

26 JUNE 1950

Korean War: Washington Concluding that the communist invasion of Korea is Soviet-instigated, Truman decides that the US cannot stand aside if it is to maintain credibility in containing the Russians. The Americans, however, are unprepared for this kind of war. The prospect of a limited conventional war with a communist satellite nation on the continent of Asia has never been seriously addressed by American military planners. Truman's first moves are to mobilize US forces and to ask the UN for aid and sanctions. Acting in emergency session, and with the Soviet representative absent, the UN Security Council orders North Korea to cease its aggression. Meanwhile, Truman directs the US Navy and Air Force to support ROK forces in Korea.

27 JUNE 1950

Korean War: UN When North Korea ignores the UN demand to pull back, the Security Council adopts a US resolution calling for members to help South Korea 'repel the armed attack.' Eventually 20 governments will contribute troops or other aid to the war, making it officially a UN action, but most of the fighting will be done by the US. Today Truman appoints General Douglas MacArthur as commander in chief of UN forces; also today, elements of the US Far East Air Forces first engage communists on the East Coast of South Korea. Meanwhile, Seoul is nearly surrounded by enemy and the South Korean government and most ROK troops are in flight.

Vietnam President Truman announces he is accelerating a program of military aid for Vietnam that he began in April. Funneled through Paris, the aid includes a military mission and advisors. Having indirectly been supporting the buildup of an anti-communist Vietnamese Army since 1946 the US, by November 1952, will be carrying more than half the cost of the Indochina War.

28 JUNE 1950

Korean War The capital of South Korea falls to the North Koreans.

29 JUNE 1950

Korean War: South Korea General MacArthur and his staff fly to Suwon, 20 miles south of Seoul, to assess the situation; he reports to Washington that ROK troops seem 'incapable of gaining the initiative,' and that the enemy will overrun the peninsula unless the US provides immediate and massive aid. At this point the nearest American infantry regiment is in Hawaii, 4000 miles away.

30 JUNE 1950

Korean War: Washington President Truman sends US infantry forces to South Korea and authorizes them to conduct missions above the 38th parallel. He also extends the draft for another year and orders the Navy to blockade the Korean coast.

JULY 1950

Korean War: US Forces MacArthur flies in a makeshift unit of 500 inexperienced American troops from Japan and names them Task Force Smith, after their commander, Colonel C.B. Smith. Equipped largely with outdated WW II equipment, these men are sent northward to Osan, where they clash with North Korean infantry and tanks before pulling back. The US Seventh Fleet successfully evacuates American civilians from Korea. Total US Army strength at the beginning of the war is only some 600,000 men. The Air Force is outfitted with leftover WW II fighters and bombers; the newer jet fighters are currently based in Japan, out of range of Korean targets. During the month National Guard and reserve troops will be called up; a total of eight Army and one Marine divisions will be committed to the fighting in Korea. These troops will in the first weeks of the war face nightmarish fighting in heavy rain and mud and rice paddies against a determined and numerically superior enemy. It will be some time before US tactics change from the style of the last war and adapt to the rainy weather and mountainous terrain of Korea or to the guerrilla tactics of the enemy, who are adept at infiltrating UN lines in small units. US troops are unused to fighting sustained defensive actions against a large enemy force; early battles will often end with panicky and disastrous retreats. Finally, the Americans will learn to withdraw in good order and, when on the offensive, to build forward airstrips rapidly and bring in troops by air. By 5 Septem-

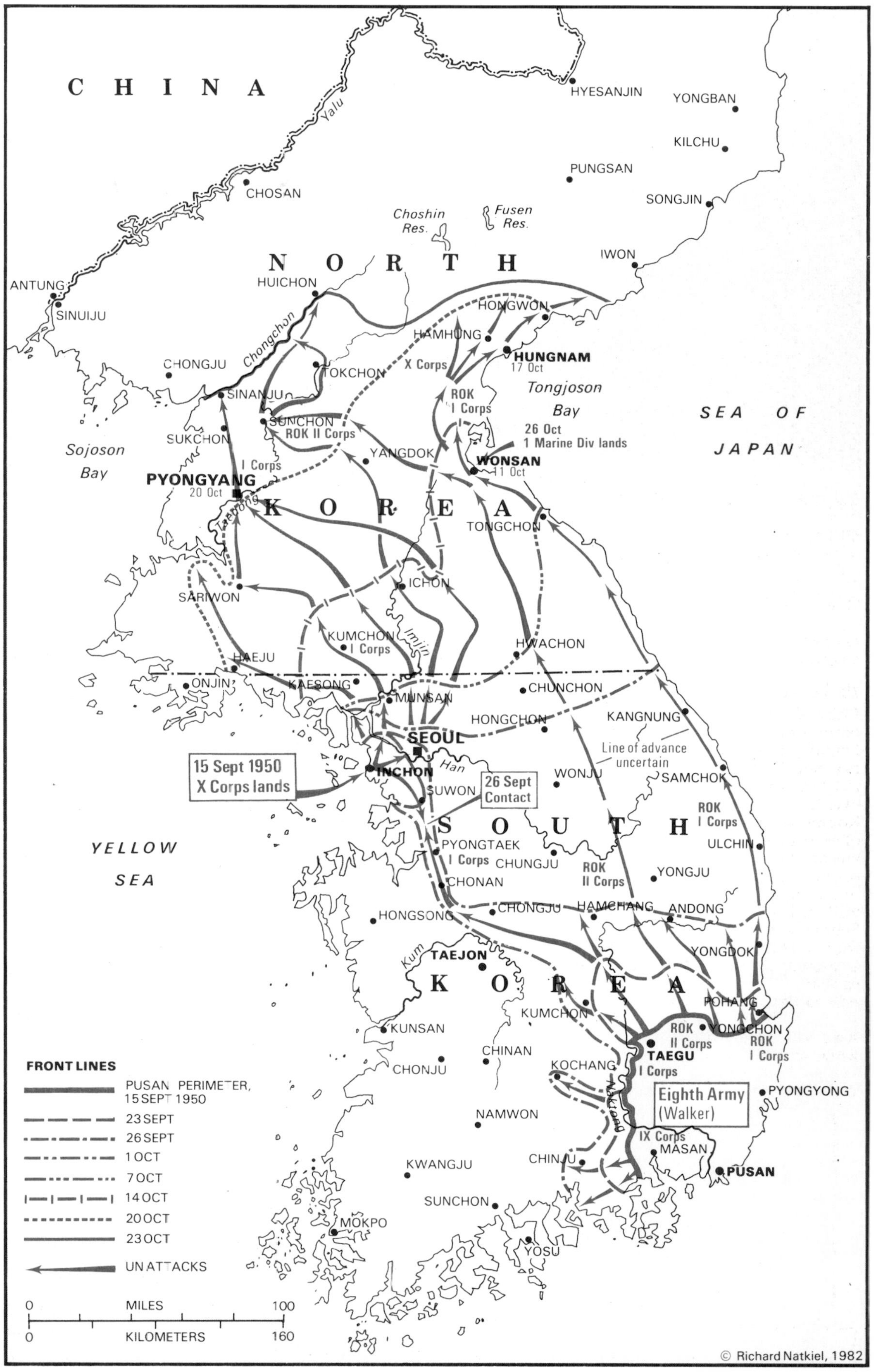

Right: A general map of the Korean War in 1950.

Below: Marines storm over the sea wall at Inchon on ladders fixed to the bow of their landing craft. The enemy was caught completely by surprise.

Marine infantry advance after having knocked out an enemy bunker during the UN counteroffensive that followed the Chinese intervention.

ber, North Korean forces have virtually overrun all Korea, driving the UN and ROK forces into a small perimeter at the southeastern tip of the peninsula that hugs the port of Pusan. However, there General Walton Walker is able to stabilize the 'Pusan perimeter.'

20 JULY 1950

Korean War: National President Truman asks Congress to pass a $10 billion rearmament program and proposes a partial mobilization of US resources.

3 AUGUST 1950

Vietnam A US Military Assistance Advisory Group (MAAG) of 35 men arrives in Vietnam to teach anti-communist troops receiving US weapons how to use them.

5 AUGUST-15 SEPTEMBER 1950

Korean War: Battle of the Pusan Beachhead North Korean forces mount a series of uncoordinated probing attacks along the UN-held Pusan perimeter, but this offensive is not able to crack the perimeter. The US Seventh Fleet contributes much to the defense, pouring shells into enemy positions and blockading the sea routes. Navy and Marine planes, joined in mid-August by Australian fliers, hold off the North Korean Air Force.

Korean War: Inchon Landing: Planning General McArthur plans a bold counteroffensive in 'Operation Chromite.' He proposes to launch a massive amphibious operation from the Yellow Sea onto the west coast of Korea – at Inchon, 20 miles west of Seoul. The goal is to cut off the enemy south of the 38th parallel and then to push on to the northern boundary of Korea at the Yalu River, while UN forces in the Pusan perimeter break out to mop up in the south. The Joint Chiefs of Staff twice reject this plan, reasoning that UN troops are poorly trained and equipped for such an operation, that it is typhoon season, that the landings would have to be made precisely at high tide or the troops would be disastrously marooned on mile-wide mud flats and that the area is protected by enemy shore batteries. MacArthur argues that those very factors will make a landing at Inchon likeliest to achieve surprise. And, indeed, the North Koreans have concluded that Inchon is safe; thus they ignore the buildup of American naval forces in the area when MacArthur's improbable plan is finally approved by the Joint Chiefs. On 1 September, Navy Lieutenant Eugene Clark lands near Inchon; over the next two weeks, working at night and hiding during the day, he meticulously maps for MacArthur all enemy defenses in the harbor. The intrepid Clark will greet the landings by turning on a lighthouse beacon to guide the soldiers.

15 SEPTEMBER 1950

Korean War: Inchon Landing At 6:33 in the morning, under the overall command of General Edward Almond, the US 5th Marines spearhead the assault, landing at Green Beach on the island of Wolmi, which guards the harbor of Inchon. While some units scale the seawall on ladders, others smash holes into the wall with LST's and blast it with dynamite. The defenders are taken completely by surprise; the island is won in 45 minutes, and artillery, tanks and more infantry follow the Marines. Just to the south, at 8:00, the 1st Marine regiment disembarks on to Red and Blue Beaches. By nightfall the beachhead is secure, and Inchon is threatened from the west and south. The second phase of the war has begun.

17-27 SEPTEMBER 1950

Korean War: Inchon The UN forces press eastward, surrounding Seoul in a pincers. Meanwhile, at the Pusan perimeter on the southeastern coast, General Walker's 8th Army has been delayed by North Korean counterattacks from its scheduled breakout. Accordingly, MacArthur plans a second landing from the Yellow Sea 100 miles south of Inchon; this will prove unnecessary when communist forces, realizing they are about to be cut off, begin withdrawing to the north on 23 September. Walker's forces are then able to break out on the 27th.

26 SEPTEMBER 1950

Korean War: Seoul MacArthur's United Nations forces complete the recapture of the South Korean capital of Seoul after days of bitter house-to-house fighting. It has been an extraordinary victory for General MacArthur and will be called by many the greatest strategic envelopment in history. It will certainly not have the effect of making the proud general feel any more humble.

29 SEPTEMBER 1950

Korean War: North Korean Retreat With enemy forces in full retreat and over 125,000 captured, US and South Korean troops reach the 38th parallel. General MacArthur's call for surrender of the North Korean Army is ignored. In turn, UN military leaders will ignore a series of Chinese threats to intervene.

9 OCTOBER 1950

Korean War: Invasion of North Korea Authorized by the UN General Assembly, General MacArthur orders the crossing of the 38th parallel and the invasion of North Korea. Washington has gained this authorization by assuring the UN that 'no major Soviet or Chinese Communist forces' have entered North Korea and that there is no threat of such. Washington regards the Chinese threats as a bluff, though it has forbidden UN aircraft to fly missions north of the Yalu River into Manchuria.

14 OCTOBER 1950

Korean War: US Strategy President Truman and General MacArthur meet on Wake Island in the Pacific to plan strategy above the 38th parallel. The general assures the president that even if China were to enter the war they would not commit more than 60,000 troops, and Truman is satisfied. As they talk some 300,000 Chinese Communist 'volunteers' are massing along the Yalu River.

20 OCTOBER 1950

Korean War: Invasion of North Korea After a two-day fight General Walker's 8th Army captures Pyongyang, the capital of North Korea, and continues northward toward the Yalu.

26 OCTOBER 1950

Korean War: Wonsan Making an inexplicable strategic error, MacArthur has ordered, despite the opposition of subordinates, that the X Corps be re-embarked at Inchon and sailed around the peninsula to make an amphibious landing today at Wonsan on the east coast. In the first place, it would have been easier for the troops to move there overland; secondly, ROK troops have already taken Wonsan on the 11th.

Korean War: Invasion of North Korea A ROK division reaches the Yalu River; there they stumble on a body of Chinese Communist troops massing for attack. The Chinese virtually annihilate the ROK division. At the same time, elements of another ROK division find strong Chinese resistance at Sudong. Such scattered encounters with Chinese forces continue over the next few days, but American leaders refuse to believe there is a real threat from Manchuria.

1 NOVEMBER 1950

Korean War: Limited Chinese Intervention People's Republic of China (PRC) troops suddenly materialize east of Unsan and overwhelm the 6th ROK infantry.

Marines bring in two North Korean prisoners. Both are regular army soldiers who had changed into civilian clothes in hopes of avoiding capture.

Marines watch as a Corsair hits an enemy position on their route of advance. Techniques of close air support greatly improved during the war.

Soon the American 8th Cavalry find themselves under attack by the PRC in their chilling style: a mortar and rocket barrage, then masses of horn- and whistle-blowing Chinese troops attacking in waves. After a night of this the Cavalry regiment is shattered. The Chinese troops withdraw, and the UN forces continue their advance north.

8 NOVEMBER 1950

Korean War: Air War The first all-jet dogfight in history occurs between US F-80 Shooting Stars and Soviet-built MiG-15s. One MiG is shot down.

20 NOVEMBER 1950

Korean War: Invasion of North Korea Several US units reach the Yalu River, on the border of Manchuria. MacArthur's forces have now retaken virtually the whole of Korea.

24 NOVEMBER 1950

Korean War: Invasion of North Korea General MacArthur flies to North Korea to supervise personally the final drive to the Yalu, which is intended to wrap up the war and is known as the 'Get the Boys Home By Christmas' offensive. MacArthur plans to send General Almond's X Corps on the right wing and General Walker's 8th Army on the left, to envelop the enemy on the northern edge of the country. (Walker's army includes American, ROK, British, and Turkish troops). Altogether, MacArthur commands some 200,000 men.

25 NOVEMBER-5 DECEMBER 1950

Korean War: Full-Scale Chinese Intervention After extensive preparations and many warnings that have been ignored by the American command, PRC troops fall on to the right flank of the 8th army in central North Korea, the beginning of an all-out offensive by some 200,000 Chinese. The initial attack virtually annihilates the ROK II Corps and devastates the US 2nd Army Division. Fighting rages throughout the night, wave after wave of attacks striking US positions. UN forces begin pulling back. One of the most gruelling marches begins at the Chosin Reservoir, where General Oliver Smith's 1st Marine Division is surrounded by enemy and is sapped by temperatures so cold that carbines cannot be used. Smith's Marines fight their way to Hagaru, at the south end of the reservoir, where they receive airdrops of food and supplies amidst further vicious enemy attacks. At Koto-ri, Marine units will be attacked from the west and east, battling seven different PRC divisions over a period of two weeks. The first phase of the UN forces' withdrawal is completed on 5 December with the abandonment of Pyongyang, the North Korean capital.

19 DECEMBER 1950

NATO The North Atlantic Council names Dwight D. Eisenhower supreme commander of Western European defense forces.

Korean War: Washington As UN troops retreat before the Chinese and North Korean forces back across the 38th parallel, President Truman has declared a state of national emergency, the ultimate source of the perceived threat being Russia.

23 DECEMBER 1950

Korean War: Allied Retreat In a scene reminiscent of Dunkirk in WW II, a fleet of 109 vessels is moving the exhausted X Corps and its equipment from the UN perimeter at Hungnam after their fighting retreat through mountain passes in the dead of a bitter winter. The ships will evacuate 91,000 Korean civilian refugees, 105,000 UN troops, over 17,000 vehicles and 375,000 tons of supplies. By 25 December the X corps will be back in the Pusan perimeter, where the UN forces had first been driven. Despite massive UN infantry operations and widespread air strikes, the communists have driven their enemy right back where they came from. Meanwhile, the 8th Army is amidst a three-week, 300-mile retreat to the 38th parallel. (In a reorganization, the X Corps will now become part of the strategic reserve of the 8th Army). The Red forces have gotten good MiG-15 airplanes and pilots from Russia, but the UN will retain complete control of the sea.

Korean War: Command In Korea today General Walton Walker, commander of the 8th Army, is killed in a jeep accident. MacArthur brings in General Matthew Ridgway both to replace Walker and to take on overall command of ground forces in the war. MacArthur assumes command of UN operations on ground, sea and air.

Vietnam The US signs a Mutual Defense Assistance Agreement with France, Vietnam, Cambodia and Laos (the French Associated States). Congressman John F. Kennedy asserts America has allied itself with a desperate French attempt to hang on to the last of its empire. By 1954, American military aid to Vietnam will top $2 billion.

29 DECEMBER 1950

Korean War: Strategy Debate Broaching, and not for the first time, the issue that will become his Waterloo, General McArthur states that the Korean conflict has become an 'entirely new war' and that the situation must be met with attacks into Communist China itself, against what he calls the 'privileged sanctuaries' of the PRC north of the Yalu River, their bridges and road and supply lines. Going farther, MacArthur presses for a blockade of China and an invasion of the country by Chiang Kai-shek's 'free Chinese' army from Formosa. MacArthur's extravagant proposal will not and cannot be implemented. Washington, and especially Britain, are convinced that it might bring Russia into hostilities and touch off a global atomic war. Moreover, it might galvanize anti-Western sentiment in Vietnam, Malaya, the Philippines and elsewhere in Asia. Finally, America is determined that the war must, at least in appearance, continue to be a UN rather than a US war, an international effort to put down communist aggression. This is not solely a clash of military and political agendas: Eisenhower is against attacking China, and JCS Chairman Omar Bradley will later tell Congress that MacArthur proposed 'the wrong war, at the wrong place and at the wrong time, and with the wrong enemy.' On 6 December President Truman attempted to muzzle his brilliant but outspoken general, ordering MacArthur to make no public statements on either military or political matters without approval. Today the JCS directs MacArthur to continue fighting in Korea but reiterates that there will be no operations elsewhere and no 'unleashing' of Chiang. The objective is to restore the prewar status quo in Korea.

1-4 JANUARY 1951

Korean War: Chinese Invasion of South Korea In their second major offensive 400,000 Chinese and 100,000 North Korean troops break through the 8th Army lines along the 38th parallel. On the 4th the Communists will recapture Seoul. This time Ridgway will manage a relatively orderly withdrawal of UN forces, despite the obstruction of thousands of civilians and ROK soldiers fleeing the city. Ridgway will set up a new defensive perimeter about 50 miles south of the 38th parallel; he now has about 365,000 ground troops under his command.

25 JANUARY 1951

Korean War: Allied Counteroffensive General Ridgway, having stabilized his lines south of the 38th parallel, orders the 8th Army to begin moving north.

Above: Seated behind MacArthur is General Matthew Ridgway, the commander primarily responsible for containing the Chinese offensive in 1951.

Right: A full-page newspaper headline reports the dismissal of MacArthur for insubordination.

11 FEBRUARY 1951

Korean War: Allied Counteroffensive Communist counterattacks stop the new UN northward drive at Chipyong and Wonju in central Korea. There a unit of the 2nd Division, with the aid of a French battalion, will fight a total of five communist divisions for a week until Cavalry tanks arrive to drive the enemy away, leaving 2000 Chinese dead. To the west UN forces successfully advance to the Han River near Seoul.

7 MARCH 1951

Korean War: Allied Counteroffensive In the second stage of his offensive, which will be named 'Operation Ripper,' General Ridgway's objectives are to retake the port of Inchon and the Kimpo airfield west of Seoul, to occupy Seoul itself, along with other key points on the 38th parallel, to capture a large enemy supply base near Seoul and generally to inflict as many casualties on the enemy as possible. The last objective will not be gained, but the others will.

14 MARCH 1951

Korean War: Allied Counteroffensive The capital of South Korea once again changes hands, recaptured by UN troops.

21 MARCH 1951

Korean War: Washington Defense Secretary George Marshall announces that the United States armed forces stand at 2.9 million, twice what they were prior to the Korean conflict. As of today US casualties in the war have been 33,237 dead, 103,376 wounded and 410 missing.

24 MARCH 1951

Korean War: Strategy Debate Despite President Truman's muzzle order, and having learned that the president is preparing a peace initiative, General MacArthur releases to the press what he calls a fresh plan to end the war. In fact it is a rehearsal of what MacArthur has said before: he threatens Red China with a devastating attack if it does not get out of Korea. In the ensuing confusion Truman is forced to hold back his peace plan. He also begins seriously to contemplate one of the most politically and militarily delicate steps of his presidency: cashiering MacArthur.

31 MARCH 1951

Korean War: Allied Counteroffensive Ridgway's 8th Army has pushed beyond the 38th parallel and is preparing the next move, which will be to assault the 'Iron Triangle,' an area formed by lines linking Chorwon, Kumwha and Pyongyang at (the apex).

5 APRIL 1951

Cold War: National After a controversial trial in which they have been found guilty of giving top-secret information on nuclear weapons to Russia, Julius Rosenberg and his wife Ethel are sentenced to death.

Korean War: Strategy Debate In a letter to House Minority Leader Joseph Martin, General MacArthur tosses on the last straw; he reiterates his demand for an invasion of China, stating that in Korea 'we fight Europe's war with arms while the diplomats there still fight it with words,' and ends with his familiar slogan, 'There is no substitute for victory.'

11 APRIL 1951

Korean War: Dismissal of MacArthur Having conferred with and gained the support of Generals Bradley and Marshall and other advisors, President Truman in a hastily-drafted and curt letter relieves General Douglas MacArthur of his command. Taking over operations in Korea will be General Matthew Ridgway, who has in fact already turned the war around. Public rage over MacArthur's dismissal will be spectacular: flags will be flown at half mast, Senators will threaten impeachment proceedings and Red-baiter Joseph McCarthy will call Truman 'a s.o.b. who decided to remove MacArthur when drunk.' A Gallup poll will find the public 69 percent to 29 percent against the president. History, however, will see Truman's removal of a popular war hero as one of the most courageous and farsighted acts of his presidency.

19 APRIL 1951

Korean War: Dismissal of MacArthur General MacArthur makes an emotional address to a joint session of Congress, again calling for naval and air strikes against China. Regarding his future, he quotes the old army song, 'Old soldiers never die, they just fade

FINAL ★★★

DAILY NEWS

Copr. 1951 by News Syndicate Co. Inc. NEW YORK'S PICTURE NEWSPAPER Trade Mark Reg. U. S. Pat. Off.

3¢

Vol. 32. No. 249 New York 17, Wednesday, April 11, 1951★ 88 Main+12 Brooklyn+8 Queens Pages 3 Cents

EXTRA

TRUMAN FIRES M'ARTHUR

Gives Ridgway Command Of U. S. Forces in Far East

Special to The News.

Washington, D. C., Wednesday, April 11.—President Truman early today relieved Gen. MacArthur of his command in the Far East and appointed Gen. Matthew B. Ridgway as his successor.

Truman said at 1 A. M. in a news conference unprecedented since World War II:

"With deep regret I have concluded that General of the Army Douglas MacArthur is unable to give his wholehearted support to the policies of the United States Government and the United Nations in matters pertaining to his official duties.

"In view of these specific responsibilities imposed upon me by the Constitution of the United States and the United Nations, I have decided that I must make a change in the command of the Far East.

"Full and vigorous debate on matters of national policy is a vital element in the Constitutional system of our democracy.

"It is fundamental, however, that military commanders must be governed by the public directives issued to them in the matter provided by our laws and Constitution.

"In time of crisis, this consideration is particularly compelling."

For the days' events leading up to the ouster of Gen. MacArthur, turn to page 2.

away.' MacArthur has been one of the great generals of his time and a magnificent peacetime leader of postwar Japanese recovery, but he has of late been insubordinate and seemingly blind to the larger implications of his public utterances. He has denounced politicians who 'invariably in the past have propagandized a policy of defeatism and appeasement in the Pacific,' and these include his current bosses. He will later, in private, declare that a theater commander should have *carte blanche* to act as he pleases. Great as he is, MacArthur's insistance on policymaking has been deemed intolerable in a society governed by elected leaders.

22-30 APRIL 1951

Korean War: Communist Spring Offensive Communist forces begin a spring offensive with a night attack on an ROK division near the center of the UN perimeter. The ROK troops flee under the assault of horn-blowing and grenade-hurling enemy, but American General James Van Fleet quickly plugs the gap. A few days later the Reds cut a highway into Seoul and attempt to retake the city; Van Fleet's defensive lines keep the enemy at bay. During the last week of the month UN fliers average nearly 100 missions a day against the Reds. The US F-86 Sabre jet fighter has replaced the older F-80 and has established a clear superiority over the MiG. UN fliers will average 13 MiG kills for every US jet lost, though UN losses to Red anti-aircraft fire remain worrisome. Having failed to cross the Han River into Seoul, the first phase of the new communist offensive grinds to a halt at the end of April after having cost some 70,000 Red casualties, compared to 7000 for UN forces.

27 APRIL-7 MAY 1951

NATO The USA and Denmark sign an agreement on 27 April allowing America to use bases on Greenland for the duration of the North Atlantic Treaty. On 7 May the first contingent of 200 US troops lands on Iceland, also as part of NATO's agreements.

10 MAY 1951

Korean War: Communist Spring Offensive Learning of an impending new communist offensive General Van Fleet orders 500 miles of barbed wire plus mines and booby traps placed in front of his lines.

15 MAY 1951

Korean War: Communist Spring Offensive During the night 30 Chinese and North Korean divisions strike the US X Corps and ROK III Corps in the center of the UN perimeter. Tomorrow, in fierce fighting, the Reds will break through the ROK lines, but American forces will shift to close the gap.

20 MAY 1951

Korean War: Offensive and Counteroffensive The second communist spring offensive ends. There have been some 900 American casualties and an estimated 35,000 losses for the communists. The enemy's primary gain has been to shift one American division five miles south. Today General Van Fleet launches a counteroffensive that by the end of the month will take UN forces to Kansong, above the 38th parallel on the east coast, to Munsan on the west and to the Hwachon Reservoir in the center.

24 MAY 1951

NATO An advance force of 5000 men of the US Army's 4th Division embarks from New York, the first American troops specifically committed to NATO. They will be followed within weeks by the 2nd Armored Division and by units of the US Air Force, the first of millions of US military personnel who will serve in NATO forces abroad.

11 JUNE 1951

Korean War: UN Counteroffensive UN troops have taken the base of the Iron Triangle – the towns of Chorwon and Kumhwa – and are advancing towards the apex at Pyongyang; but Red resistance will stiffen to hold the latter.

19 JUNE 1951

Korean War: National Congress extends the military draft to July 1955 and lengthens the period of service to two full years; the draft age is now 18½.

25 JUNE 1951

Korean War: Peace Proposals Soviet United Nations delegate Jacob Malik calls for negotiations between the sides in Korea. The People's Republic of China approves the idea.

27 JUNE 1951

Korean War: Strategy Debate A Senate committee which has been investigating the firing of General MacArthur issues a statement that US objectives remain unchanged. After what has emerged in the committee hearings much of the furor over the firing has died down, and Truman's action is receiving increasing public and official approval.

Soldiers of the US Army's 25th Infantry Division seek cover behind a jumble of rocks as a barrage of North Korean mortar shells creeps towards them.

30 JUNE 1951

Korean War: Peace Proposals General Ridgway makes a radio broadcast offering to negotiate with the communists.

8 JULY 1951

Korean War: Peace Talks Begin Formal truce talks begin at Kaesang, on the 38th parallel. Vice-Admiral Turner Joy heads the UN delegation, and General Nam Il of North Korea the communist delegation. Among the first decisions made is that there will be no cease-fire during negotiations. Thus, during the talks, both sides will use the time to attempt to improve their military positions. Most of the 'negotiating' will be a matter of hurling accusations and propaganda back and forth across the table. Through the summer and indeed for the next two years of sullen and snail-paced peace talks, the military situation will remain virtually stalemated. But it will nevertheless be bloody, Americans fighting and dying for minor strategic objectives with names such as Hill 1179, Heartbreak Ridge and the Punch Bowl. The air war will also continue, USAF units operating mainly in the west, and Navy carrier-based units in the east.

23 JULY 1951

NATO Near Paris the new NATO headquarters are opened by Supreme Commander General Dwight D. Eisenhower, who says the occasion underlines NATO's intention 'to preserve peace and not to wage war, and lift from the hearts of men the fear of cell blocks and slave camps.'

22 AUGUST 1951

Korean War: Peace Talks After no real progress, the peace talks are broken off by the communists; they charge that UN aircraft have bombed the site of the conference.

7 SEPTEMBER 1951

Vietnam The US signs an agreement with Saigon for direct aid to South Vietnam; no longer will aid be funneled through France. American civilian government employees join the military already there.

15-20 SEPTEMBER 1951

NATO Meeting in Ottawa, Canada, the NATO council agrees to invite Turkey and Greece to become members, which they will do in February 1952.

24 SEPTEMBER 1951

Vietnam America is now committed to aiding the French in their fight against Ho Chi Minh's Viet Minh; today a French carrier arrives in Indochina with American-supplied fighters and light bombers.

18 OCTOBER 1951

Cold War In one of a continuing series of Cold War border incidents, the East German People's Police seize the village of Steinstuecken, just inside the US sector of West Berlin. (The East Germans claim this was 'historically' a part of their Soviet zone.) The three-mile square suburb and its 194 inhabitants are returned to US control after the American general threatens reprisals.

10 NOVEMBER 1951

Middle East Defense Command Britain, France, Turkey and the US announce plans for a Middle East defense command against outside aggression, with a statement of principles to the Arab nations and Israel asserting that the command will not interfere with regional politics but will advise Middle East states. South Africa and Australia will soon join the command.

12 NOVEMBER 1951

Korean War: Peace Talks Peace talks resume at Panmunjon, near Kaesong. The communists agreed to a renewal of talks in early October, after General Van Fleet had mounted a successful offensive to drive back enemy forces from the Seoul-Chorwon rail line, the Hwachon Reservoir and part of the Iron Triangle.

23 NOVEMBER 1951

Korean War: Peace Talks At Panmunjon the sides agree to a cease-fire along a demarcation line that is to be considered permanent if a full armistice agreement is not reached by the end of 1951. The line runs from just below Panmunjon in the west, goes up to below Pyonggang in central Korea and continues to below Kosong on the east coast. The cease-fire will not last, however; as negotiations continue through 1952 the conflict will settle into a stalemated trench warfare reminiscent of WW I, punctuated by minor raids and skirmishes that produce a steady stream of casualties.

27 DECEMBER 1951

Korean War: Peace Talks The trial armistice ends with no extension proposed. The main unresolved issues are airport construction in North Korea and, more serious, the matter of prisoner exchange.

JANUARY 1952

Egypt Egypt has been trying to get Britain to withdraw from the Suez Canal, which has already been closed to Israeli shipping since 19 May 1950. Now, in their frustration, thousands of Egyptians sack and burn companies owned by or operated for Britons and Americans in the main Egyptian cities.

8 JANUARY 1952

International President Truman and Britain's once-again Prime Minister Winston Churchill wind up a conference in Washington with a statement that the US agrees not to launch an atomic attack on Communist Europe without the consent of Britain. In February, Britain will become the third country to have the atomic bomb.

20 FEBRUARY 1952

NATO At a meeting of the NATO council in Lisbon delegates decide to create a European army of 50 divisions provided by member nations for the defense of Western Europe. (That troop strength will never be achieved.) US Secretary of State Dean Acheson reiterates that NATO is a defensive alliance.

4 MARCH 1952

Korean War: Propaganda The communists, as they have before, accuse the UN forces of dropping cholera-infected insects in North Korea. These germ warfare charges, which are entirely fabricated, are supported by 'confessions' from brain-washed or tortured UN fliers in Red captivity, and will be widely believed in the Communist world.

Korean War: Peace Talks The talks have achieved agreement on all substantial issues but one – the repatriation of Red prisoners. The UN has some 170,000 such prisoners, of which nearly a third have declared that they do not want to go home. The UN insists that each prisoner be given a choice of whether or not to repatriate. The Reds insist that all prisoners must be returned. Negotiations deadlock.

28 APRIL 1952

NATO General Matthew Ridgway is named supreme commander of Allied forces in Europe, replacing General Eisenhower, who has resigned to run for the Republican presidential nomination.

MAY-JUNE 1952

Cold War As a result of the signing on 26 May of a 'peace contract' between the West German government and the US, Britain and France (and more basically, of the setting up of a European Defense Community), the USSR and the communist leaders of East Germany protest that this contract is illegal. Hundreds of communist sympathizers invade the US sector of Berlin and fight with police. The East Germans announce that no travel to or from West Berlin or West Germany will be allowed after 30 May. By the end of June, the East Germans are building a 500-mile-long barbed wire fence along the 'no man's land' between East and West Germany.

4 NOVEMBER 1952

National Eisenhower, running as a Republican, wins the presidency, garnering 442 electoral votes to 89 for Democrat Adlai E. Stevenson. Besides being a war hero, Eisenhower has gained votes by declaring he will go to Korea, implying he will seek to end the war.

5 DECEMBER 1952

Korean War Eisenhower visits Korea in an attempt to find a way to break the stalemate in truce talks. Reviewing the front lines with his experienced military perceptions, he concludes that there is no easy solution for the conflict.

2 FEBRUARY 1953

China In a major US Far East policy change President Eisenhower announces that the US 7th Fleet will no longer block a Nationalist attack from Taiwan (Formosa) against the Chinese mainland.

In his 1952 presidential campaign Eisenhower had promised to go to Korea to end the fighting there. He did so in December as president-elect, but what effect his visit had on negotiations is moot.

A French Army Sikorski S-55 lets down to evacuate wounded from their besieged Indochinese base at Dien Bien Phu in March 1954.

5 MARCH 1953

USSR Premier Josef Stalin dies in Moscow; Georgi M. Malenkov will be the new premier. The death of Stalin will lead to a modest thaw in East-West relations and will perhaps contribute to the coming settlement in Korea.

26 MARCH 1953

Vietnam In talks with French Premier Mayer, President Eisenhower makes a commitment of aid to France in the latter's war in Indochina. The president will provide $60 million to France in May, and by 1954 America will be financing three-quarters of France's war against the Viet Minh.

28 MARCH 1953

Korean War: Peace Talks In a move that breaks the deadlock communist representatives agree to accept a UN offer to exchange sick and wounded POWs. However, communist leaders soon decide to try and achieve a big military victory before concluding negotiations.

10 JUNE 1953

Korean War: Communist Offensive The last confrontation of the Korean War occurs: nearly a million Chinese and North Korean troops make a push against the 800,000 UN troops in the Iron Triangle and Punch Bowl areas. By mid-July the inconclusive fighting will have claimed 70,000 Red casualties.

19 JULY 1953

Korean War: Peace Talks At Panmunjon a final armistice agreement is reached and a *de facto* boundary is worked out along the existing battle lines. It will become known as the Demilitarized Zone (DMZ).

27 JULY 1953

End of the Korean War UN and North Korean officials sign a truce ending the war after three years of fighting. Dead in the war are 116,000 UN troops, 54,000 of them American; 1,500,000 North Koreans and Chinese have been killed or wounded. The pact provides for a cease-fire and a DMZ separating North and South Korea around the 38th parallel. Following a mutual aid pact with South Korea, US forces will remain there, and US military and economic aid will continue over the decades of continual tension and frequent border incidents. (No formal peace treaty has been concluded to this time: the situation remains an armed truce.) The pact is a makeshift but is beneficial to both sides. America has succeeded in its minimum goal of restoring the prewar status quo, both China and the US have succeeded in keeping the war from spreading to their own or European soil and the superpowers have not unleashed their atomic arsenals. In the war there has been considerable technical progress, such as increased use of jets and helicopters, and social progress, such as the integration of whites and blacks in the US army. But the war has also profoundly deepened Cold War tensions and has had the effect of greatly increasing US military preparedness, which had ebbed after the end of World War II. Finally, the experience has introduced Americans to a concept new in their history: war in which total victory is not the goal.

SEPTEMBER 1953

NATO NATO forces throughout West Germany, southeastern Europe, and the North Atlantic – involving hundreds of thousands of personnel in all branches – conduct the largest peacetime maneuvers ever staged as a demonstration of their readiness against any attacks from the USSR and its allies.

30 SEPTEMBER 1953

Vietnam Eisenhower approves $385 million over the $400 million already budgeted for military aid to Vietnam. By April 1954 aid to Indochina has reached $1.13 billion out of a total foreign aid budget of nearly $4 billion.

18 FEBRUARY 1954

Vietnam At a Big Four meeting in Berlin the US, Britain, France and Russia discuss the issues arising from a deteriorating military situation in Indochina, where the French have been fighting Ho Chi Minh's Communist Vietminh since 1946. Currently the US is financing three-quarters of the Indochinese War.

13 MARCH 1954

Vietnam: Battle of Dienbienphu Some 40,000 Vietminh troops under General Vo Nguyen Giap attack the French garrison at Dienbienphu. Chinese-supplied heavy artillery rings the 15,000 French troops that General Henri Navarre has placed behind enemy lines to defend Laos from Vietminh incursions and to turn the course of the long war toward a French victory. But after the Vietminh have shelled their airstrip for five days, it is clear the French are doomed, since all their supplies must come in by air.

7 APRIL 1954

Washington At a news conference discussing the importance of defending Dienbienphu, Eisenhower observes, 'You have a row of dominoes set up, and you knock over the first one, and what will happen to the last one is . . . that it will go over very quickly. So you have the beginning of a disintegration that will have the most profound influences.' This is the first public statement of the 'domino theory' that will contribute much to pulling America into war in Southeast Asia.

26 APRIL 1954

International The Far Eastern Conference begins in Geneva, Switzerland. The siege at Dienbienphu continues to humiliate the French and to bolster Ho Chi Minh's Democratic Republic of Vietnam.

7 MAY 1954

Vietnam: The Fall of Dienbienphu The French garrison at Dienbienphu surrenders to the Vietminh; after losing over 35,000 killed and 48,000 wounded. The French are ready to end a long war that has been financially and militarily disastrous. With the Western powers in disarray, and Britain in particular firmly against Western intervention, the momentum and initiative in Geneva fall to the Vietminh and the East. Negotiations will go on into July.

1 JUNE 1954

Vietnam War: Approach Colonel Edward G. Lansdale, USAF, arrives in Saigon as chief of the Saigon Military Mission. Denoted an 'Assistant Air Attache,' he is in fact a CIA man assigned to run covert paramilitary operations against the Communist Vietnamese.

20-21 JULY 1954

International: The Geneva Accords The Big Four countries and the Vietminh reach agreements ending the Indochina War. Among the stipulations: hostilities will cease in Vietnam, Cambodia and Laos; Vietnam will 'temporarily' be divided at the 17th parallel, the South under Ngo Dinh Diem in Saigon, the North under Ho Chi Minh in Hanoi, pending reunification through nationwide elections in 1956; the two sections will be separated by a demilitarized zone. Though there is general agreement on the terms, the main document is never officially signed by the participating governments. There are many problems with the Geneva Accords. Ho has agreed to them under pressure from the Soviets, and especially from Chinese delegate Chou En-lai; the Vietminh will therefore feel their revolution has been betrayed to some extent by the Chinese – their ancient enemies and presently uneasy allies under the Communist banner. For South Vietnam the selection of Diem as Premier will prove unfortunate; Diem is an ardent nationalist, but also an autocratic leader who favors the elite Catholic minority and who has little popular support. In August the US National Security Council will call the Geneva settlement a 'disaster' that 'completed a major forward stride of communism which may lead to the loss of Southeast Asia.' At this point, the American Military Assistance Advisory Group (MAAG) has 342 men.

AUGUST 1954

Vietnam As a result of the terms of the Geneva Accords a stream of almost one million refugees begins flowing from North to South Vietnam, many with American assistance. The majority of the refugees are Catholics; others include factions opposed to the Vietminh. They will furnish Prime Minister Diem with a fiercely anti-communist constituency in the South.

8 SEPTEMBER 1954

SEATO The US joins other countries in signing a collective defense treaty for the Pacific. The Southeast Asia Treaty Organization (SEATO) will be composed of Australia, Britain, New Zealand, Pakistan, the Philippines, Thailand and the US. Secretary of State Dulles makes American involvement in SEATO contingent on 'communist aggression.'

OCTOBER 1954

Vietnam War: Approach The Vietnamese Marine Corps is formally organized with US Marine Colonel Victor J. Croizat as its senior US advisor.

24 OCTOBER 1954

Vietnam War: Approach President Eisenhower sends a letter to Diem stating that US aid to Diem's government is contingent upon assurances of the 'standards of performance [Diem] would be able to maintain in the event such aid were supplied.' Later, President Johnson will cite this letter as the starting point of US commitment to South Vietnam. Diem agrees to the 'needed reforms' stipulated as a precondition for receiving aid, but few of these reforms will ever be pursued.

NOVEMBER 1954

Vietnam War: Approach On the basis of Diem's promise of reforms Eisenhower announces on the 3rd that he is sending General J. Lawton Collins to Vietnam to 'coordinate the operation of all US agencies in that country.' Arriving in Saigon on the 17th, Collins affirms $100 million in US aid to South Vietnam and announces that 'The American mission will soon take charge of instructing the Vietnamese Army.'

DECEMBER 1954

North Vietnam Hanoi concludes its first aid agreement with China, providing for the delivery of transportation, communications and water-works supplies.

3 FEBRUARY 1955

South Vietnam After months of prodding by US advisors Diem introduces the first of a series of agrarian reform measures. But these fall far short of true reforms; although one million peasant tenants receive some relief, an equal number receive no land at all. At length Diem's land reform program will take back what the peasants have been given by the Vietminh and return it to the landlords: by 1960, 75 percent of the land will be owned by 15 percent of the people, creating much peasant unrest to be exploited by the communists.

28 MARCH 1955

South Vietnam After provocations by Diem fighting breaks out between troops loyal to Diem and the Binh Huyen and Hoa Hao sects, who blockade the city. In the next weeks Saigon will become a battlefield.

27 APRIL 1955

Washington After meeting with General Collins, Secretary of State John Foster Dulles reluctantly agrees to replace Diem and cables the embassy in Saigon to find an alternative. However, CIA Colonel Lansdale, who helped Diem during the last coup attempt, once more rallies to Diem and presses the US to support the Prime Minister.

28 APRIL 1955

South Vietnam With Lansdale's encouragement Diem mounts a successful counterattack against the sects. Washington then orders the American Embassy to burn Dulles's order of the previous day. By the end of May, Diem will have prevailed in Saigon, but most of the over 2000 Binh Xuyen, Cao Dai and Hoa Hao sect fighters who withdraw into the Mekong Delta will later reemerge to fight Diem as Vietcong.

14 MAY 1955

Warsaw Pact The USSR, Albania, Bulgaria, Czechoslovakia, Hungary, Poland, Rumania and East Germany sign the Warsaw Pact, a treaty of mutual defense similar but opposed to NATO.

6 JUNE 1955

North Vietnam Foreign minister Pham Van Dong states that Hanoi is prepared to open consultations with South Vietnam in preparation for holding nationwide elections in July 1956, as per the Geneva Accords.

6 JULY 1955

South Vietnam Diem declares that since the Geneva Accords were never officially signed, South Vietnam is not bound by them. Although he does not reject the 'principle of elections,' any proposals from the Vietminh are out of the question 'if proof is not given us that they put the higher interest of the national community above those of Communism.' During the next two weeks China and the Soviet Union will announce some $300 million in aid to North Vietnam.

23 OCTOBER 1955

South Vietnam A referendum deposes Vietnam's nominal head of state, Bao Dai, once the French puppet Emperor, and replaces him with Diem.

26 OCTOBER 1955

South Vietnam Diem proclaims the Republic of South Vietnam with himself as its first president, prime minister, defense minister and supreme commander of the armed forces. The new regime is recognized immediately by the US and several allies.

As a result of the Geneva Accords the Vietminh leader Ho Chi Minh became ruler of North Vietnam. The US considered this settlement a 'disaster.'

When the 1954 Geneva Accords 'temporarily' divided Vietnam into North and South, the controversial Ngo Dinh Diem became premier of South Vietnam.

21 NOVEMBER 1955

METO US representatives attend the opening session of members of the Baghdad Pact – a mutual defense treaty including Turkey, Pakistan, Iran, Iraq and Great Britain. Although the American representatives do not yet sign the treaty, they observe and sit on committees. This defense chain along Russia's Asian frontier links up with NATO and SEATO. However, pro-Russian Egypt refuses to join what will finally be called the Middle East Treaty Organization (METO).

13 DECEMBER 1955

North Vietnam Agrarian reform begins to be pursued with a vengeance in North Vietnam, tribunals of the poor and landless trying landlords in a rural reign of terror that will claim over 15,000 victims. This campaign will be repudiated by Hanoi in July 1956, to be replaced by 'A Campaign for the Rectification of Errors.' Ho Chi Minh, now named party chairman, will remark of the attempts at rectification that 'one cannot awaken the dead.'

MAY 1956

Vietnam War: Approach In violation of the Geneva Accords the United States sends 350 additional military men designated Temporary Equipment Recovery Team (TERM) to Saigon under the pretext of helping redistribute equipment abandoned by the French; they will stay on as part of MAAG.

26 JULY 1956

Suez Crisis Egyptian President Gamal Abdel Nasser nationalizes the Suez Canal after the West, in view of Nasser's pro-Soviet posture, withdraws an offer of financial support for a proposed Aswan Dam.

31 OCTOBER – 5 NOVEMBER 1956

Suez Crisis President Eisenhower opposes force in settling the crisis surrounding Israeli occupation of the Sinai Peninsula (called the '100-hours War') in the wake of the Suez issue. On 5 November the US achieves a ceasefire in the Sinai, and a United Nations force is sent to prevent further clashes between Egypt and Israel. The Suez Canal will reopen to maritime traffic on 7 March 1957.

6 NOVEMBER 1956

National The Eisenhower-Nixon ticket wins over Stevenson by a landslide.

2 DECEMBER 1956

Cuba With an invading force Fidel Castro lands on Cuban soil to begin a guerrilla campaign against President Fulgencio Batista.

5 JANUARY 1957

Eisenhower Doctrine President Eisenhower asks Congress for the right to use economic aid and, when necessary, military force to resist communist aggression in the Middle East. Becoming known as the Eisenhower Doctrine, this policy will be approved by Congress on 7 March.

The largest US troop deployment between the Korean and Vietnam wars, the by-invitation intervention in Lebanon in 1958, proved a diplomatic success.

5-19 MAY 1957

South Vietnam The scattered resistance to Diem begins to pull together: some 6000 hard-core guerrillas will begin, under the direction of Hanoi, a program of harassment, sabotage, and terror to destabilize the Diem government. By the end of the year over 400 minor South Vietnamese officials will be assassinated by what comes to be called the Vietcong – from the word for communist, *Cong-san*.

3 JUNE 1957

International The US joins the Baghdad Pact (METO) and reaffirms its determination to aid the member nations – Turkey, Iraq, Iran, Pakistan and Britain – in countering communist aggression.

24 JUNE 1957

Vietnam War: Approach The US Army's 1st Special Forces Group is activated in Okinawa and begins to train members of the ARVN, who will become the nucleus of the Vietnamese Special Forces.

22 OCTOBER 1957

Vietnam War: Approach Communist insurgency in South Vietnam begins in earnest, Hanoi organizing 37 armed companies in the Mekong Delta. Today the first US casualties occur when 13 Americans are wounded in three terrorist bombings of MAAG and US Information Service installations in Saigon.

14 MAY 1958

Lebanese Crisis The US Navy's 6th Fleet doubles its strength in the Mediterranean. Arms are airlifted into Beirut to safeguard Lebanese independence and US citizens from the threats of the USSR and the newly-formed United Arab Republic. The Nasser-headed UAR, a union of Egypt, Yemen and Syria, is supported by many Moslems in a Lebanon divided between Christians and Moslems.

15 JULY 1958

Deployment in Lebanon President Eisenhower announces that he has ordered US Marines into Lebanon at the request of Lebanese President Camille Chamoun, who fears that the country will be unable to survive the agitation of Moslem rebels allegedly supported by the UAR and the USSR. In 'Operation Bluebat,' Marines secure a beachhead at Beirut and move into the city, meeting no resistance from Lebanese troops as other US forces arrive by air. By the 20th there will be some 14,000 American military personnel in the city. These forces will be withdrawn by 15 October 1958, having met with only sporadic sniper fire that kills one soldier. On the American side, this Lebanese intervention will be described by the Pentagon as 'not war, but like war,' and by the anti-Chamoun faction as an 'American bridgehead to secure Lebanon from a Syrian invasion that never was.' In any case, during the occupation Chamoun loses office to General Fuad Shebab. With this, the largest American troop deployment between the Korean and Vietnam Wars, the US honors its commitments in the Middle East and also gains international respect by not interfering with domestic politics in Lebanon.

DECEMBER 1958

Vietnam War: Approach The CIA comes into possession of a directive from Hanoi to its headquarters for the Central Highlands stating that the communist heirarchy has decided to 'open a new stage of the struggle' and move into overt insurgency against the government in South Vietnam.

7 JANUARY 1959

Cuba Rebels have overthrown the dictator Batista, and the US recognizes Fidel Castro's new government.

4 APRIL 1959

Vietnam War: Approach Speaking at Gettysburg College in Pennsylvania, President Eisenhower affirms 'the inescapable conclusion that our own national interests demand' support of a non-communist regime in South Vietnam.

MAY 1959

North Vietnam Hanoi's leaders formally take control of the insurgency in the South. The tempo of the war speeds up as more southern cadre members infiltrate back into the South along an improved Ho Chi Minh Trail. Stretching down through Laos near the western border of Vietnam, this trail will be the lifeline of the communist war effort. Though for years it will be attacked by land and air, it will never be shut down for long.

8 JULY 1959

Vietnam War: Approach Major Dale R. Buis and Master Sergeant Chester M. Ovnand become the first Americans killed in Vietnam hostilities when guerrillas strike a MAAG compound in Bienhoa, 20 miles northeast of Saigon.

AUGUST 1959

South Vietnam The Vietcong campaign of assassination of local officials in the South picks up – between 1959 and 1961 the number killed rises from 1200 to 4000 per year. Diem reacts by appointing more military men to administrative posts, indirectly aiding the strategy of the insurgents by neglecting the social and economic needs of local populations. At the end of the month the Diem government will be returned to office by an election in which only supporters of the government are allowed to vote; even the non-Communist opposition is excluded, and some of its leaders are prosecuted.

7-9 OCTOBER 1959

CENTO In Washington the Council of Ministers of the Baghdad Pact (METO) meet under its new name, Central Treaty Organization (CENTO), signifying location between the NATO and SEATO regions.

17 JANUARY 1960

South Vietnam A popular uprising begins in Ben Tre Province, about 100 miles from Saigon in the Mekong Delta. Villagers armed with mattocks, swords and other hand weapons join slightly better-armed dissidents to storm civil guard posts and overthrow village administrations. Largely a reaction to oppressive measures employed by the Diem regime, the Hanoi-directed peasants organize a defense and survive a counterattack. For the first time, a popular armed uprising wins victory on a provincial scale.

4 FEBRUARY 1960

Cuba Castro signs a commercial pact with the USSR, which also expresses willingness to sell Cuba military planes. On 18 February, Eisenhower will order seizure of any military supplies en route to Cuba.

5 FEBRUARY 1960

Vietnam War: Approach The South Vietnamese government requests that the US double MAAG strength from 342 to 685. This request will be approved in April.

5-11 MAY 1960

U-2 Incident An American U-2, a high-altitude reconnaissance plane, piloted by Francis Gary Powers, is shot down over the Soviet Union. Premier Nikita Khrushchev refuses to participate in a planned Paris summit conference scheduled for May unless President Eisenhower apologizes for such spy flights over the USSR. The conference does not take place. Powers will be convicted of espionage in Moscow in August and sentenced to a ten-year term, but he will be freed in February 1962 in exchange for a Soviet spy.

8 NOVEMBER 1960

National John F. Kennedy is chosen the nation's 35th president, the first Catholic and the youngest man (43) ever elected. He defeats Republican Richard M. Nixon by a margin of little more than 100,000 popular votes. His vice-president is Lyndon B. Johnson.

11-12 NOVEMBER 1960

South Vietnam Military units under the direction of Colonel Nguyen Van Thi and Colonel Vuong Van Dong surround Diem in the presidential palace in an effort to force reforms. Diem stalls until loyal troops arrive. From this time on many in the military, including Diem's former allies, plot coups against him.

20 DECEMBER 1960

South Vietnam: Formation of the NLF Hanoi announces formation of the National Front for the Liberation of the South – more commonly known as the National Liberation Front or NLF – at a congress held in the South. The NLF is a broad communist-controlled coalition of over a dozen political parties and religious groups. The Saigon regime will call the NLF the 'Vietcong,' for Vietnamese Communists, and this label comes to be applied generally to supporters of the insurgency in the South. By the end of the year some 4500 former South Vietnamese in the North have infiltrated back to the South. US forces in Vietnam now number 900.

3 JANUARY 1961

International The US severs diplomatic relations with Castro's Cuba.

19 JANUARY 1961

Washington Outgoing President Eisenhower cautions incoming President Kennedy that unstable Laos is the 'key to the entire area of Southeast Asia' and might even require military intervention. Kennedy will increase US presence in the area by sending a carrier task force to the Gulf of Siam.

One of many Cold War crises occurred when US spy-plane pilot Francis Gary Powers was downed in the USSR in 1960. Here he appears in a Soviet court.

Some of Fidel Castro's Cuban troops cluster about a light antiaircraft gun after their 1961 victory over CIA-sponsored invaders at the Bay of Pigs.

23 MARCH 1961

Vietnam War: Approach One of the first American aircraft casualties in Indochina, an SC-47 intelligence-gathering plane en route from Vientiane in Laos to Saigon, is shot down over the Plain of Jars while checking radio frequencies used by Russian planes delivering arms to the Pathet Lao.

17-20 APRIL 1961

Cuba: The Bay of Pigs Invasion An anti-Castro Cuban exile force of 1453 men, organized, equipped and trained by the CIA, lands at Cuba's Bay of Pigs. This ill-planned and ill-executed invasion, organized during the Eisenhower administration but approved by Kennedy, is easily crushed by Castro's forces, who capture 1179 invaders and kill the rest. The debacle is a serious blow to American prestige, strengthens the Castro regime and will embolden the Russians to send missiles to Cuba. On 24 April a shaken Kennedy will take full responsibility for the US part in the invasion.

26-29 APRIL 1961

Vietnam War: Approach President Kennedy meets with the National Security Council to decide whether to send troops into communist-threatened Laos. It is also recommended to expand South Vietnam's forces to prevent an invasion of South Vietnam from Laos. Debate within the administration over the extent of US involvement in Southeast Asia will become heated in the next months, the actions reflecting the indecisiveness of that debate.

11 MAY 1961

Vietnam War: Approach Kennedy approves sending 400 Special Forces troops and 100 other US military advisors to South Vietnam, on the same day ordering clandestine warfare against North Vietnam, to be conducted by South Vietnamese agents directed and trained by the US. Kennedy's orders also call for infiltration of ARVN forces into Laos to strike communist bases and supply lines.

3-4 JUNE 1961

International President Kennedy and Soviet Premier Khrushchev confer in Vienna. No substantive agreement is reached on such issues as nuclear testing, disarmament and Germany. The leaders do, however, agree on a neutral Laos, though Kennedy rejects neutrality for Vietnam, believing that South Vietnam is the best place to make US power credible.

JULY 1961

Vietnam War: Approach General Lansdale submits a report on the 'First Observation Group,' the clandestine warfare unit ordered by Kennedy in May. About to expand to 805 men, the group's focus will shift from the Vietcong to North Vietnam. On 2 July Hanoi captures at least three members of Lansdale's command when their plane goes down. Meanwhile, the Army of the Republic of Vietnam (ARVN) has been fighting pitched battles with the communists. On 16 July, in what is described as the bloodiest battle since Dienbienphu, 169 guerrillas are killed by ARVN forces in the Plain of Jars marsh, 80 miles west of Saigon. During August there will be 41 engagements between government troops and insurgents in the South.

12-13 AUGUST 1961

Berlin Wall The Communist East German regime closes the border between East and West Berlin, erecting a concrete-block wall along most of their border with West Berlin.

21 SEPTEMBER 1961

Vietnam War: Approach The US Army's 5th Special Forces Group, 1st Special Forces, is activated; later they will be in charge of all Special Forces operations in Vietnam and will be known as the Green Berets.

11 OCTOBER 1961

Vietnam War: Approach As both the National Security Council and the Joint Chiefs of Staff urge commitment of troops to Vietnam, Kennedy decides to send General Maxwell Taylor to study the situation. In November, Taylor will also call for a 'massive joint effort' with the South Vietnamese against the Vietcong. Kennedy will hold back from commitment of major forces, but in November he will order that military aircraft be sent to Vietnam and that US advisors be increased from 1000 to 16,000 over two years.

NOVEMBER 1961

Vietnam War: Approach US Special Forces medical specialists are deployed to provide assistance to the *montagnard* tribes around Pleiku. Out of this will develop the Civilian Irregular Defense Group (CIDG), a program of organized paramilitary forces among the ethnic and religious minorities of South Vietnam and the chief concern of the US Special Forces during the war.

11 DECEMBER 1961

Vietnam War: Approach Two US Army helicopter companies, the first direct military support for South Vietnam, arrive in Saigon. The 33 twin-rotor Vertol H-21C Shawnees are accompanied by 400 US troops to fly and maintain them. They will be used for airlifting ARVN troops into combat.

16 DECEMBER 1961

Vietnam War: Approach Operation 'Farm Gate' aircraft are authorized to fly combat missions, provided a Vietnamese crew member is aboard. The first mission will be flown by T-38's on 13 January 1962. Because the 1954 Geneva Agreements prohibit bringing bombers into Indochina, US B-26 and SC-47 bombers will be redesignated 'reconnaissance bombers.'

31 DECEMBER 1961

Vietnam War: Approach According to MAAG, US military forces in South Vietnam have reached 3200; total insurgent forces are estimated at 26,700. Fourteen Americans have been killed or wounded in com-

An aerial view of a montagnard resettlement area in Vietnam. The US trained the montagnards to be fierce opponents of the Viet Cong.

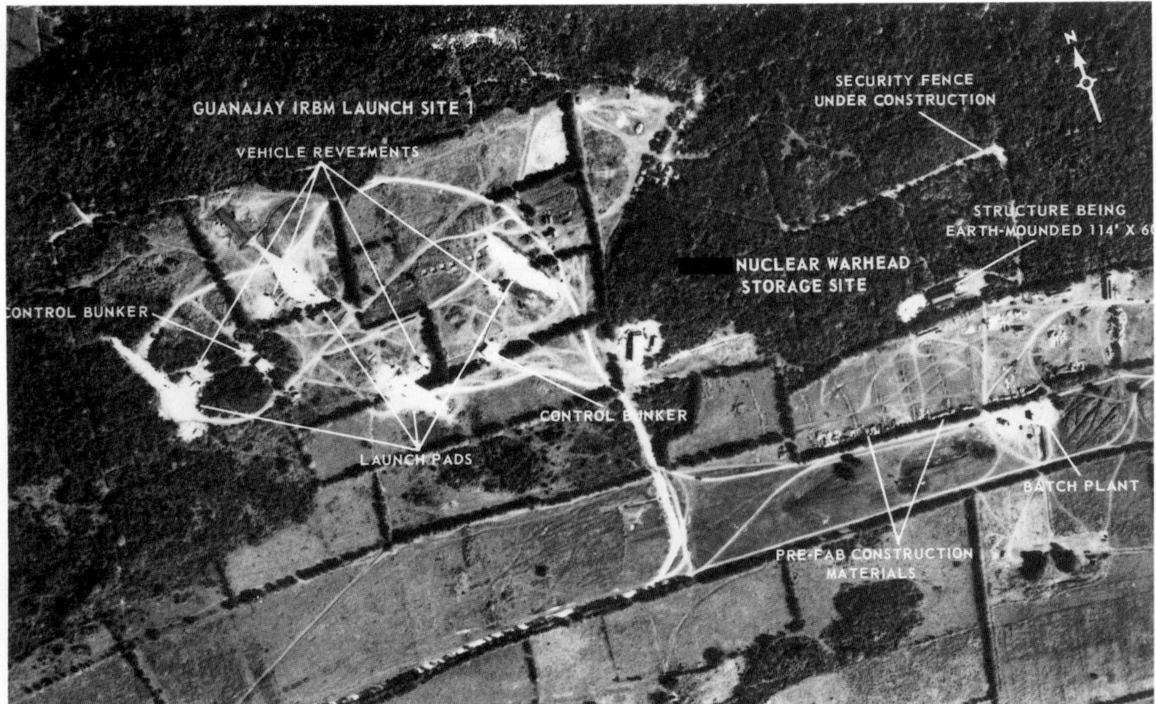

The USSR's attempt to build missile sites in Cuba provoked the most serious crisis of the Cold War. Here, a 1962 US aerial photo of such a site.

bat. Two Army helicopter units are flying combat missions. 'Jungle Jim' air commandos are instructing the South Vietnamese Air Force. US Navy Mine Division 73 is sailing from Danang along the coastline. US aircraft from Thailand and Seventh Fleet carriers are flying surveillance and reconnaissance missions over Vietnam. And six C-123 aircraft equipped for defoliant operations are ready to enter the South. In all $65 million of US military equipment and $136 million in economic aid have been delivered to South Vietnam in 1961.

12 JANUARY 1962

Vietnam War: Approach In Operation Ranch Hand, US planes begin a program that will dump some 19 million gallons of defoliating herbicides, largely Agent Orange, over 10-20 percent of Vietnam and parts of Laos in 1962-1971. Designed to expose roads and trails used by Vietcong forces in the thick jungle, the operation will have little success. It will, however, expose thousands of soldiers and civilians of both sides to dioxin, which is suspected of causing cancer and birth defects.

8 FEBRUARY 1962

Vietnam War: Approach The Military Assistance Command, Vietnam (MACV), headed by General Paul D. Harkins, is installed in Saigon as the US reorganizes its military command in South Vietnam. Henceforth the conduct of the war will be directed by MACV, which supervises MAAG.

27 FEBRUARY 1962

South Vietnam Two South Vietnamese pilots flying US planes bomb and strafe the presidential palace, primarily out of frustration at Diem's failure to prosecute the war effectively. Diem and family miraculously escape injury, but Diem hereafter will retreat deeper into himself, delegating more authority to his brother Nhu, who is rarely seen in public.

22 MARCH 1962

South Vietnam Operation Sunrise, South Vietnam's first long-range counteroffensive against the Vietcong, is launched in Binh Duong province, 35 miles north of Saigon. Central to the operation is the idea of 'strategic hamlets.' This program to forcibly relocate peasants into armed stockades, theoretically depriving the Vietcong of their support, proves ill-conceived, expensive and ineffective.

15 APRIL 1962

Vietnam War: Approach The first US Marine air units sent to Vietnam, 15 combat helicopters of the 362nd Marine Medium Helicopter Squadron, arrive at their base near Soc Trang. They will form a task unit dubbed 'Shoofly,' carrying ARVN supplies and troops.

17 MAY 1962

Thailand Three thousand US Marines begin landing at Bangkok, Thailand, in response to troop movements near the Thai border by the Soviet-supported Laotian Pathet Lao army. This US show of force, ordered by President Kennedy at the request of the Thai government, will be out of Thailand by the beginning of August, after a declaration of Laotian neutrality signed in Geneva in July.

22-28 OCTOBER 1962

The Cuban Missile Crisis A Soviet buildup of nuclear missiles in Cuba is revealed to the American people by President Kennedy, who, after consulting with his advisors and deciding against an invasion of Cuba, orders a naval and air blockade on further shipment of military equipment to the island nation. Following a confrontation that takes the world as close as it has ever come to nuclear war, Kennedy and Khrushchev agree on 28 October on a formula to end the crisis that saves face for both. On 2 November Kennedy reports that Soviet missile bases in Cuba are being dismantled. Among the fruits of this crisis are a determination to prevent similar incidents in the future; thus a telephone hotline will be installed between Moscow and Washington, and in July 1963 the two nations will sign a Nuclear Test Ban Treaty.

31 DECEMBER 1962

South Vietnam By the year's end Saigon claims that 4077 strategic hamlets have been completed, now housing 39 percent of the South Vietnamese, but these figures are probably exaggerated. Regular ARVN troops number 200,000. Approximately 11,000 US advisory and support personnel are now in Vietnam; 109 Americans have been killed or wounded this year. US aviation units have flown over 50,000 sorties, about half of them combat support missions. Chinese-armed communist guerrilla forces in South Vietnam are estimated at 25,000, with active Vietcong sympathizers numbered at 150,000. The Vietcong are now killing or kidnapping 1000 local officials per month.

26 FEBRUARY 1963

Vietnam War: Approach US helicopters are ordered to shoot first at enemy soldiers while escorting ARVN troops.

8 MAY 1963

South Vietnam: Buddhist Uprising Twenty thousand Buddhists in Hué, celebrating the traditional birthday of Buddha, are fired upon by order of a Catholic official. Nine persons are killed, including seven children and one woman. Diem blames the incident on the Vietcong and refuses Buddhist demands that the officials responsible be punished, though three are later dismissed. In Vietnam, Buddhists form at least 70 percent of the population and Catholics less than 10 percent, but the government and army are Catholic-dominated. Buddhist protests will hereafter crystallize the growing resentment of Diem's regime. Tri Quang, a politically sophisticated monk, stirs up the people against Diem and warns the US that it must make him reform.

11 JUNE 1963

South Vietnam Buddhist monk Quang Duc publicly burns himself in a plea for Diem to show 'charity and compassion' to all religions. Diem remains stubborn despite repeated US requests, and his committee of inquiry backs his cover story that Vietcong are responsible for the Hué incident. More Buddhist monks will immolate themselves during the next weeks. Madame Nhu, wife of Diem's brother and self-styled First Lady of Vietnam, will call the immolations 'barbecues' and offer to supply matches.

27 JUNE 1963

South Vietnam President Kennedy appoints Henry Cabot Lodge, his former Republican political opponent, to succeed Nolting as ambassador to Vietnam. In Washington the Kennedy administration begins seriously considering a coup against Diem. Next month General Tran Van Don will inform CIA operative Lucien Conein that certain officers are planning such a coup.

20-22 AUGUST 1963

South Vietnam Diem accepts the proposal of Tran Van Don and other generals that he declare martial law in order to prosecute the war more effectively. The generals' real purpose is to consolidate control for a coup. Diem, scheming also, accepts in order to implicate the army in a planned crackdown on the Buddhists. On the 21st troops loyal to Diem and Nhu – but disguised as regular soldiers – attack Buddhist temples and sanctuaries in several cities, destroying property and beating, jailing and murdering hundreds of monks, nuns, students and ordinary citizens. Demonstrations against the regime break out, but at first Diem's ruse works, and the army is blamed for the attacks on Buddhists. On the 22nd Diem's foreign minister and the American ambassador resign in protest. Ambassador Lodge reports to Washington that Nhu is behind the attacks against the Buddhists and that the plotting generals are hoping for US support. Washington will withhold such support but will issue a demand that Diem get rid of Nhu. This puts the generals on notice that if Nhu stays the US will probably support their coup.

26 AUGUST 1963

South Vietnam Meeting with Lodge for the first time, Diem refuses to drop Nhu or to discuss reforms. Lodge now presses the Kennedy administration, still bitterly divided over Vietnam policy, to support the dissident generals.

22 OCTOBER 1963

South Vietnam The situation in South Vietnam has now approached chaos. MACV commander General Paul Harkins informs plotter General Don that he knows of the coup and considers it a mistake. In response, the following day Don tells CIA operative Lucien Conein, who has actively promoted the coup, that he has postponed the takeover; Conein assures Don that Harkins speaks only for himself.

29 OCTOBER 1963

Washington Now leaning toward Harkins' and Taylor's opposition to the coup, Kennedy cables Lodge to ask the generals to postpone the attempt. Lodge never delivers the message.

1-2 NOVEMBER 1963

South Vietnam: The Fall of Diem Dissidents organized by key generals of the South Vietnamese Army lay siege to the presidential palace, which is captured by the morning of the 2nd. Unable to summon any support, Diem and Nhu flee. Early on the 2nd Diem begins negotiating with the generals, who have assured Lodge that Diem's life will be spared. Diem finally agrees to surrender, and a US armored personnel carrier picks up him and Nhu. En route, Diem and Nhu are murdered on orders of General Minh. Hearing the news in Washington, President Kennedy is visibly horrified. But in Saigon, Ambassador Lodge welcomes the insurgent generals to his office to congratulate them.

4 NOVEMBER 1963

South Vietnam The US recognizes the new provisional government of South Vietnam, which is controlled by the Revolutionary Military Committee headed by General Duong Van Minh. The new government announces, 'the best weapon to fight communism is democracy and liberty.'

22 NOVEMBER 1963

National: Assassination of Kennedy Kennedy is fatally wounded by communist-sympathizer Lee Harvey Oswald as the president rides in a motorcade through Dallas. Vice-President Lyndon B. Johnson is sworn in as president soon afterward. Johnson takes office having scarcely been briefed by Kennedy on important details of the situation in Vietnam; his advisors will continue to add to the confusion.

DECEMBER 1963

North Vietnam Ho Chi Minh and senior staff assess accomplishments and plan for the future. Acting on a report that the Vietcong are poorly organized and prepared, the Hanoi leadership decides to start sending regular North Vietnamese troops into the South via the Ho Chi Minh Trail.

31 DECEMBER 1963

Vietnam War: Approach A total of 489 Americans have been killed or wounded in Vietnam since January, well over four times the previous year's total. There are at least 16,500 American servicemen in South Vietnam, which has received $500 million in US aid this year.

2 JANUARY 1964

Vietnam War: Approach President Johnson receives a military report outlining an elaborate series of clandestine operations against North Vietnam. Known as Oplan 34A, it will go into effect on 1 February and consists of three main elements. The first involves a mixture of operations including spy flights over the North, kidnapping of North Vietnamese for intelligence gathering, parachuting of sabotage and psychological-warfare teams into the North, commando raids to strike roads and bridges and the like: these will be controlled from Saigon by the MACV chief, though most of the participants are to be South Vietnamese or Asian mercenaries. The second element of Oplan 34A involves bombing raids against communist forces in Laos, to be done with American planes bearing Laotian Air Force markings. The third prong consists of USN destroyer patrols in the Gulf of Tonkin, both as a show of force and to collect intelligence; these patrols are code-named DeSoto Mission.

30 JANUARY 1964

South Vietnam The military junta that killed Diem and has ruled since is toppled from power in a bloodless coup led by Major General Nguyen Khanh, who proclaims himself chief of state and pledges victory over the Communists. Three more changes of government will ensue during this year, the US futilely trying to bolster each one, but none will have broad internal support or any real competence to govern or to fight.

16 FEBRUARY 1964

Vietnam War: Approach American deaths in fighting and from terrorist raids have become common in South Vietnam. Today a bomb explodes at a movie theater in the American community, killing three Americans and wounding 50. Meanwhile, the ARVN is fighting the Vietcong daily, but to little effect.

1 MARCH 1964

Vietnam War: Approach Deputy Secretary of Defense for International Security Affairs William Bundy sends President Johnson recommendations for extending the war against North Vietnam – including blockading Haiphong harbor and bombing North Vietnamese railways. Bundy points out that such actions will require some form of legislative endorsement short of a declaration of war; he recommends that the president obtain such a resolution from Congress.

23 MARCH 1964

Cambodia Talks between Cambodia and South Vietnam over border violations collapse. Cambodian leader Prince Sihanouk calls for a Geneva conference to insure Cambodian neutrality; he has denied that Cambodia provides sanctuaries for Vietcong.

9-15 APRIL 1964

South Vietnam: Ground War The war is escalating steadily. On 9-12 April, major fighting in the Mekong Delta sees 50 Army of the Republic of Vietnam (ARVN) losses, while four Americans are killed. In a five-day Kien Long battle from 11-15 April, the heaviest fighting to date, ARVN forces retake a position but lose 70 South Vietnamese guardsmen and 55 ARVN dead, while some 175 Vietcong are killed.

17-23 APRIL 1964

Laos In a crisis that will have far-reaching consequences for the US role in Southeast Asia, Laotian leader Souvanna Phouma, failing in an attempt to unite warring factions toward demilitarizing and neutralizing Laos, threatens to resign. Finally Souvanna gains control of a US-supported coalition government, but the communist Pathet Lao reject the coalition and go on the offensive.

25 APRIL 1964

Command President Johnson announces that General William Westmoreland will replace General Harkins as head of the US MACV as of 20 June.

14 JUNE 1964

Laos Despite the protests of Souvanna Phouma and US denials, Americans have participated in air strikes against the Pathet Lao in Laos. Today the US military allows its own pilots operating out of Thailand to hit 'targets of opportunity' in Laos.

23 JUNE 1964

Washington President Johnson announces that Henry Cabot Lodge has resigned as ambassador to South Vietnam and that General Maxwell Taylor will be his replacement.

A funeral cortege escorts the casket of President John F. Kennedy, slain in Dallas on 22 November 1963, down Pennsylvania Avenue in Washington.

JULY 1964

Vietnam War: Approach Both sides are now engaged in a barely-secret war in violation of the 1954 Geneva Accords. The Ho Chi Minh trail is being turned into a major route to carry supplies and North Vietnamese regular troops infiltrating into South Vietnam. At the same time, modern Soviet and Chinese machinery is expanding North Vietnam's warmaking capacity by building roads and bridges and support facilities – antiaircraft defenses, underground barracks, workshops, warehouses, depots and hospitals. On the other side, the clandestine activities under Oplan 34A are well underway, and US military advisers are operating with the Laotian army on the ground, supported by US air strikes.

30-31 JULY 1964

Vietnam War: Approach Around midnight six South Vietnamese PT boats fire on two islands in the Tonkin Gulf, Hon Me and Hon Ngu. While monitoring

In April 1964 President Johnson named General William Westmoreland to head the rapidly growing US Military Assistance Command, Vietnam (MACV).

The M-21 Shawnee was the first of many helicopter types to serve in Vietnam. The use of helicopters revolutionized the conduct of the war.

radio transmissions in the Gulf the USS *Maddox*, a DeSoto Mission ship, will report sighting patrol boats but will be told that these are the friendly PT boats.

2 AUGUST 1964

Vietnam War: Approach Captain John Herrick of the *Maddox*, finding himself under fire by three North Vietnamese patrol boats, fires back. The enemy torpedoes do not connect. The *Maddox* sinks one enemy, and called-in US jets cripple the others. Hearing the news, Johnson is cautious, but US military command puts land and sea forces in the area on alert and orders ships into the Gulf. American ships will stand by as South Vietnamese PT boats mount further attacks along the coast on 2-4 August.

4 AUGUST 1964

Vietnam War: Gulf of Tonkin Incident About eight o'clock in the evening the *Maddox* intercepts North Vietnamese radio messages that give Captain Herrick the impression that their patrol boats are planning an attack. Herrick quickly calls in air support, but neither he nor the pilots can find the enemy. Then, at about ten o'clock, a radar officer reports enemy torpedoes coming in, and Herrick orders evasive maneuvers and return fire. After two hours of firing into the night US officers report sinking two or three North Vietnamese ships. In fact, no one really knows what happened, or even if enemy were actually in the area: Herrick will report to Admiral U.S. Grant Sharp that the radar and sonar information was ambiguous. When word of the Tonkin 'engagement' arrives in Washington, Johnson is cautious at first but, after National Security Council prodding, orders retaliatory air strikes. After receiving word from Admiral Sharp that he is satisfied the Tonkin attack was genuine the president meets with Congressional leaders to inform them of the second unprovoked attack (the first being that of 2 August), of the imminent reprisal strikes and of his intention to ask for a Congressional resolution. By 2320 hours Defense Secretary Robert McNamara is informed that US bombers are flying to their targets; at 2336 hours Johnson appears on national television to announce that the reprisal strikes are underway because of the unprovoked attack on US ships. The president assures the world that, 'We still seek no wider war.' In fact, today's events put into operation months of military planning that commences America's longest and most bitter war.

5 AUGUST 1964

Vietnam War: Gulf of Tonkin Incident US planes from the carriers *Ticonderoga* and *Constellation* fly 64 sorties along the Gulf of Tonkin, destroying or damaging North Vietnamese PT boats, an oil storage depot and anti-aircraft installations. Two US planes are damaged, and two are shot down; one of the downed pilots, Lieutenant Everett Alvarez Jr, becomes the first of 600 US airmen captured by the Communists during the war.

Vietnam War: Tonkin Gulf Resolution Aides to the president present to Congress the resolution drafted earlier by William Bundy; it would give the president authority to 'take all necessary measures to repel any armed attack against the forces of the United States and to prevent further aggression . . . including the use of armed force, to assist any member or protocol state of the Southeast Asia Collective Defense Treaty.' In short, carte blanche.

7 AUGUST 1964

Vietnam War: Tonkin Gulf Resolution The Senate approves the Resolution by a vote of 82-2, the House by 416-0. The two dissenting Senators are Wayne Morse and Ernest Gruening, who have received hints that the *Maddox* was engaging in covert actions against North Vietnam. Predictably, the USSR and China have condemned the American actions and pledged support for North Vietnam. Supporting the US so far are Britain, Laos and the Inter-American Naval conference. After an August tour of Western Europe by Henry Cabot Lodge to drum up support, most of the governments will pledge non-military technical aid to South Vietnam, but none will ever provide military support. Meanwhile, debate in the UN is heated but inconclusive.

16-25 AUGUST 1964

South Vietnam The Military Revolutionary Council elects Nguyen Khanh president of Vietnam on the 16th, but opposition to his government soon flares, led by Buddhists and students; by the last weeks of the month, Saigon is engulfed in virtual anarchy, and violence is spreading to other cities. On the 25th Khanh will withdraw the new constitution that gives him power, but this apparent resignation will not stem the violence.

26-29 AUGUST 1964

South Vietnam A provisionary triumvirate of Generals Khanh, Duong Van Minh and Tran Thien Khiem is appointed to lead for two months until elections can be held, Khanh meanwhile holding the title of prime minister. This cosmetic change does nothing to stem the violent unrest spreading across the country. The US, worried about the image of a puppet government, does its best to support the new situation. In September, Khanh will try to buy off the Buddhists and will dissolve the triumvirate.

13-14 SEPTEMBER 1964

South Vietnam Dissident generals fail in a coup attempt against Khanh after Air Vice Marshal Nguyen Cao Ky threatens to bomb the insurgents' headquarters. This crisis encourages the National Liberation Front (NLF), the political arm of the Vietcong, to order a step-up in operations.

30 SEPTEMBER 1964

Vietnam War: Protest The first major demonstration by students and faculty opposed to the US role in the Vietnam War takes place at the University of California at Berkeley. However, polls show that a majority of Americans support the President's actions.

OCTOBER 1964

Vietnam War: Covert War Both sides are now blatantly escalating their clandestine operations. Tactical units of the North Vietnamese Army (NVA) are beginning a steady influx into the South over the Ho Chi Minh Trail, while the US continues to support the various groups operating under Oplan 34A.

14 OCTOBER 1964

Vietnam War: Laos The US authorizes its Yankee Team jets to fly cover missions with Laotian Air Force planes that are bombing communist routes and strongholds in Laos. Meanwhile, ARVN troops are operating inside the border; Prince Souvanna Phouma is not informed of this so that he can honestly deny the incursions and keep up – as he will do successfully throughout the war – the image of Laotian neutrality.

20-28 OCTOBER 1964

Cambodia Cambodian leader Prince Norodom Sihanouk has been vigorously demanding respect for his country's neutrality, while the US and South Vietnam have repeatedly charged that the Vietcong are using Cambodian territory to move troops and supplies. During this week a series of military incursions across the border by both sides, which produce a number of deaths, bring relations among Cambodia, South Vietnam and the US to their lowest point yet, but all three back away from a complete break.

24-29 OCTOBER 1964

South Vietnam Phan Khac Suu, a civilian, is appointed figurehead chief of state in order to break some of the military dominance of the government. Khanh resigns as premier on the 26th, to be succeeded by Tran Van Huong.

South Vietnamese troops (ARVN) herd captured Viet Cong onto a US-piloted UH-1 helicopter.

1 NOVEMBER 1964

Vietnam War: Raid on Bienhoa Vietcong raiders infiltrate the US air base at Bienhoa, 12 miles north of Saigon, and launch a surprise mortar attack. Before the Vietcong flee with no known losses they kill five US troops and two Vietnamese and wound about 76. They destroy six B-57's and damage 20 other aircraft. President Johnson's advisors suggest a strong response, but, being virtually on the eve of the election, Johnson only orders replacing the planes.

3 NOVEMBER 1964

National Lyndon Johnson is re-elected president by a landslide over Republican Senator Barry Goldwater, in part because many believe that Johnson is less likely to escalate the US involvement in Vietnam.

18 NOVEMBER 1964

Vietnam War: Ground War In the largest airborne strike of the war to date 116 US and South Vietnamese helicopters fly some 1100 ARVN troops into Bing Dyong and Tayninh Provinces to take what is described as a major Vietcong stronghold; but the operation only makes light contact with the enemy. The operation shows the new nature of this war, when helicopters can airlift troops and supplies quickly into any area; this will make possible a mobility unprecedented in warfare.

1 & 3 DECEMBER 1964

Vietnam War: Planning In two meetings at the White House, President Johnson and top-ranking advisers agree somewhat ambivalently to a two-phase bombing plan first suggested by Ambassador to South Vietnam Maxwell Taylor. Phase I is to involve US air strikes against communist infiltration routes and facilities in the Laotian panhandle; phase II, which will be kept secret for some time, will extend the air strikes to a widening selection of targets in North Vietnam.

4 DECEMBER 1964

Vietnam War: Ground War The Vietcong move into Phuoc Ty Province, southeast of Saigon, and commence a series of offensive operations that will culminate in a major defeat of ARVN forces at Binh Gia, 40 miles from Saigon.

7-11 DECEMBER 1964

Vietnam War: South Vietnam After conferences with Premier Huong and other South Vietnamese leaders Ambassador Taylor announces additional US aid to build up ARVN forces by another 100,000 men.

14 DECEMBER 1964

Vietnam War: Operation Barrel Roll Phase I of the bombing plan approved by President Johnson on 1 December begins with US planes attacking 'targets of opportunity' in northern Laos. These raids will be kept secret.

19-20 DECEMBER 1964

South Vietnam General Khanh, Air Commodore Ky and others stage yet another bloodless coup and take over the government to re-install military rule. Summoning some of the leaders to the US Embassy, Ambassador Taylor scolds them like schoolchildren: 'We Americans [are] tired of coups . . . Now you have made a real mess.' Inevitably, Taylor's ensuing attempts to persuade Khanh and the others to restore civilian government will be met by defiance.

31 DECEMBER 1964

Vietnam War: State of the War Although none of the combatants has formally declared war, it is undeniable that a fullscale war is now being waged in Vietnam and the adjacent territories of Laos and Cambodia. The US has about 23,000 military personnel in the South, all still designated as 'advisors'. South Vietnam has some 265,000 in its regular ARVN forces but also supports paramilitary and militia forces of some 290,000. South Korea, Australia and New Zealand have contributed advisors, and Thailand and the Philippines are ready to do so. It is estimated that some 34,000 communist troops are fighting fulltime in the South under the NLF banner; they have largely been trained in the North and have infiltrated the South via the Ho Chi Minh Trail, which is being greatly expanded. The communists can count on another 80,000 part-time activists, who, with a combination of terrorism and 'political education,' are gaining power over many of the South Vietnamese people. Official US figures for the year show 140 dead in combat, 1138 wounded and 11 missing. South Vietnamese estimates show some 7000 killed, 16,700 wounded and 500 missing. US estimates of enemy killed are 17,000, with some 4200 captured.

2 JANUARY 1965

Vietnam War: Battle of Binh Gia The six-day battle that has been fought in and around the village of Binh Gia ends with a clear defeat of South Vietnamese forces. Nearly 300 ARVN troops are dead, and some 300 are wounded. Five Americans have been killed and three are missing – the highest US casualties in battle to date. Most sobering, though, is the fact that the South Vietnamese, despite the advantage of tanks, artillery and helicopters, could not withstand the more flexible tactics of the Vietcong.

8 JANUARY 1965

Vietnam War On a typical day of fighting an ARVN company is ambushed by Vietcong, and one US officer is killed; an American soldier is wounded in a skirmish at Tanbu; US and South Vietnamese planes drop bombs and napalm over Phuoc Tuy Province to destroy a Vietcong regiment; and the ARVN claims to have killed 53 guerrillas in a fight at Quangnam and to have routed attackers in the area of Hué.

9 JANUARY 1965

South Vietnam After weeks of negotiations, continuing violent demonstrations around the country, and US pressure, Vietnamese civil and military leaders reach a compromise that agrees to restore the civilian government, with Tran Van Huong remaining as premier, and proposes a new constitution.

27-28 JANUARY 1965

South Vietnam The Armed Forces Council ousts Premier Huong and his civilian government in a bloodless coup; General Nguyen Khanh is empowered to establish a stable government.

FEBRUARY 1965

Vietnam War: Operation Open Arms The South Vietnamese government's plan to win over defectors from the Vietcong is now underway and will report some success in ensuing months, though it will not come close to disrupting the NLF 'shadow government' that now controls much South Vietnamese territory.

7 FEBRUARY 1965

Vietnam War: Attack at Pleiku Vietcong attack the US helicopter base at Camp Halloway and simultaneously blow up the barracks of US military advisors near Pleiku, in the Central Highlands; the Vietcong also destroy part of a fuel depot in Phuyan Province. Eight Americans are killed, 126 wounded and a number of aircraft destroyed or damaged. McGeorge Bundy, in Saigon, telephones the president to urge immediate retaliatory air raids against North Vietnam. President Johnson convenes his top advisors and says he is ordering retalitory air raids; all present except Senator Mike Mansfield and Vice-President Humphrey concur.

Vietnam War: Operation Flaming Dart In the retaliatory raids, called Operation Flaming Dart, 49 US Navy jets – A-4 Skyhawks and F-8 Crusaders – from the Seventh Fleet drop bombs and rockets on enemy barracks and staging areas at Donhoi, 40 miles north of the 17th parallel in North Vietnam. Among other results, these and ensuing raids on the 8th and 11th will convince the Russians to supply the North with surface-to-air missiles.

Behind a cluster of Hawk antiaircraft missiles the US ambassador to South Vietnam, Maxwell Taylor, confers with Air Force officers at Danang airbase.

10 FEBRUARY 1965

Vietnam War Vietcong guerrillas blow up the US barracks at Quinhon, 75 miles east of Pleiku on the central coast; 23 US personnel are killed.

13 FEBRUARY 1965

Vietnam War: Operation Rolling Thunder President Johnson decides to undertake the sustained bombing of North Vietnam that he and his advisers have discussed for a year. Called Operation Rolling Thunder, it will continue, with occasional suspensions, until 31 October 1968.

16-17 FEBRUARY 1965

South Vietnam The Armed Forces Council appoints Dr. Phan Huy Quat as premier and reappoints Phan Khac Suu as chief of state.

22-26 FEBRUARY 1965

Vietnam War: US Military General Westmoreland cables Washington to ask for two battalions of US Marines to protect the US base at Danang. Despite the objections of Ambassador Taylor, the JCS support the request, and on the 26th Washington agrees. Thus comes the fateful step of overt American troop commitment in the fighting. In early March, Taylor pressures the South Vietnamese government into 'inviting' the Marines; General Nguyen Van Thieu, chief of the Armed Forces Council, will ask that the entry of the Marines be 'inconspicuous.'

2 MARCH 1965

Vietnam War: Operation Rolling Thunder Over 100 USAF jet bombers strike an ammunition depot at Xombang, 10 miles inside North Vietnam, while 60 South Vietnam Air Force planes bomb the Quangkhe naval base, 65 miles north of the 17th parallel. These raids are intended to force the communists to the bargaining table, but Hanoi will refuse to negotiate until US forces withdraw.

3 MARCH 1965

Vietnam War: Air War USAF jets strike targets along the Ho Chi Minh Trail in Laos. Now that such raids are no longer secret the US State Department announces that they are authorized by powers given to the president by the Tonkin Gulf Resolution.

8 MARCH 1965

Vietnam War: First US Marine Landing Two battalions of US Marines, 3500 men, land on Red Beach Two, north of Danang. Wearing full battle gear and

President Lyndon B. Johnson, Kennedy's successor, inherited the Vietnam War, escalated it and in the end became its political victim.

carrying M-16's, the Marines are met by sightseers, ARVN officers and Vietnamese girls with leis. Landings of men, tanks and artillery will continue until 12 March. The troops are assigned to protect the large American air base at Danang.

24 MARCH 1965

Vietnam War: Protest The first so-called 'teach-in' is conducted at the University of Michigan; some 200 faculty hold special seminars while regular classes are cancelled. This form of protest eventually spreads to many colleges and universities.

30 MARCH 1965

Vietnam War: Terrorism A bomb explodes in a car parked in front of the US embassy in Saigon, virtually destroying the building. Nineteen Vietnamese, two Americans and a Filipino are killed, and 183 others are injured. Congress will appropriate funds to reconstruct the embassy.

APRIL 1965

Vietnam War: Naval Trying to stop the supplies that stream down the coast from the North, the US Seventh Fleet establishes a blockade under the name Operation Market Time. Its main assignment is to monitor the movement of junks, of which some 1000 per day ply the coastline; however, it will prove virtually impossible to locate all the clandestine craft carrying supplies to the Vietcong.

3-5 APRIL 1965

Vietnam War: Operation Rolling Thunder US and South Vietnamese planes make a series of raids on bridges and roads in North Vietnam. Four Russian-built MiG fighters attack the US planes in the first reported combat by the North Vietnamese Air Force. These raids are also the farthest north in the ongoing Rolling Thunder operations, and the first explicitly aimed at non-military targets. Six US planes are shot down in these raids.

6 APRIL 1965

Vietnam War: US Government McGeorge Bundy drafts and signs National Security Action Memorandum 328 on behalf of President Johnson. This pivotal document constitutes 'marching orders' authorizing US personnel to take the offensive to secure 'enclaves' and to support ARVN operations.

7 APRIL 1965

Vietnam War: US Government In a major policy speech at Johns Hopkins University, President Johnson says that the US is ready to engage in 'unconditional discussions' to settle the war – though in fact he mentions several conditions. He also calls for a vast economic plan for Southeast Asia.

8 APRIL 1965

Vietnam War: North Vietnam Before the National Assembly, Premier Pham Van Dong sets forth four conditions that the North Vietnamese require for negotiations: independence for all Vietnamese, non-intervention by foreign powers, political settlement of all issues and reunification of the country.

10-14 APRIL 1965

Vietnam War: US Military The 5000 US Marines already stationed around Danang are reinforced by another battalion, some of which are sent to Phu Bai, south of Hue. Marine tactical aircraft – Phantom II jets – also arrive. On the 14th the JCS order an airborne brigade to Bienhoa-Vungtau.

15-16 APRIL 1965

Vietnam War: Air War Among extensive air missions today, US and South Vietnamese planes fly the largest strike of the war, dropping 1000 tons of bombs on a Vietcong stronghold in Tayninh Province.

19-20 APRIL 1965

Vietnam War: Planning In Honolulu, McNamara, JCS Chairman Earle Wheeler and other high-ranking military and civilian leaders meet with General Westmoreland and Ambassador Taylor. The conferees agree to double US military forces, from the present level of 40,200 to 82,000, and to bring the commitment of Australia and South Korea up to some 7250 men.

26 APRIL 1965

Vietnam War: Operation Rolling Thunder Secretary McNamara reports that although virtually around-the-clock air raids against North Vietnam have 'slowed down the movement of men and materiel . . . infiltration of both arms and personnel into South Vietnam' has increased.

28-29 APRIL 1965

Dominican Republic President Johnson sends 405 Marines and airborne units to the Dominican Republic, now in the throes of a military power struggle, to protect US citizens in the Caribbean nation and 'to see that no communist government is established.' Fighting will continue despite a 5 May truce, by which date the US has 12,439 soldiers and 6924 Marines in the strife-torn nation. At the end of May, OAS troops will replace US forces.

MAY 1965

VietnamWar: US Military The Marines in Vietnam, now designated the III Marine Amphibious Force (MAF), are settling into three enclaves: Danang, Phu Bai and Chu Lai. Various disputes among American commanders include the matter of the Marines' defensive 'enclave' strategy, as opposed to the offensive 'search-and-destroy' approach that Westmoreland prefers. For the next two years the Marines will pursue a pacification strategy in the three provinces of I Corps, their area of responsibility. They will expend considerable energy in civic action and village welfare work, but this will ultimately bear little fruit.

3-12 MAY 1965

Vietnam War: US Military About 3500 men of the 173rd Airborne Brigade are brought into Vietnam, the first US Army combat units assigned there. The brigade includes the war's first US artillery unit.

7 MAY 1965

Vietnam War: US Military Some 6000 Marines begin building a jet air base at Chu Lai, about 55 miles south of Danang.

16 MAY 1965

Vietnam War: US Military In one of several such mishaps, an accidental explosion of a bomb on the ground at Bienhoa air base triggers other explosions that leave 27 US servicemen dead and some 95 injured; over 40 planes, including ten B-57's, are destroyed.

19 MAY 1965

Vietnam War: Operation Rolling Thunder After a bombing halt that does not produce the desired peace overtures from Hanoi, US bombers begin Phase II of Operation Rolling Thunder. Targets north of 20 degrees latitude are authorized, but pilots are not to enter a 30-mile buffer zone along the Chinese border, or to operate within 30 miles of Hanoi or 10 miles of Haiphong.

27 MAY 1965

Vietnam War: Naval Augmenting the vital role now being played by US aircraft carriers, whose planes participate in many raids in both South and North, US warships today begin to fire on Vietcong targets in the central area of South Vietnam.

28 MAY-1 JUNE 1965

Vietnam War: Ground War In Quangngai Province, Vietcong forces ambush a battalion of ARVN troops; reinforcements are called for, but a US Marine battalion fails to arrive in time, and ARVN reinforcements are also ambushed. Only three US advisers and

US A-1E Skyraiders sortie to attack a Viet Cong position. The Air Force's hope that airpower would prove effective against counterinsurgency was ultimately doomed to disappointment.

Above: Marines land at Danang, one of the main 'enclaves' the US sought to defend so as to free the ARVN for offensive operations.

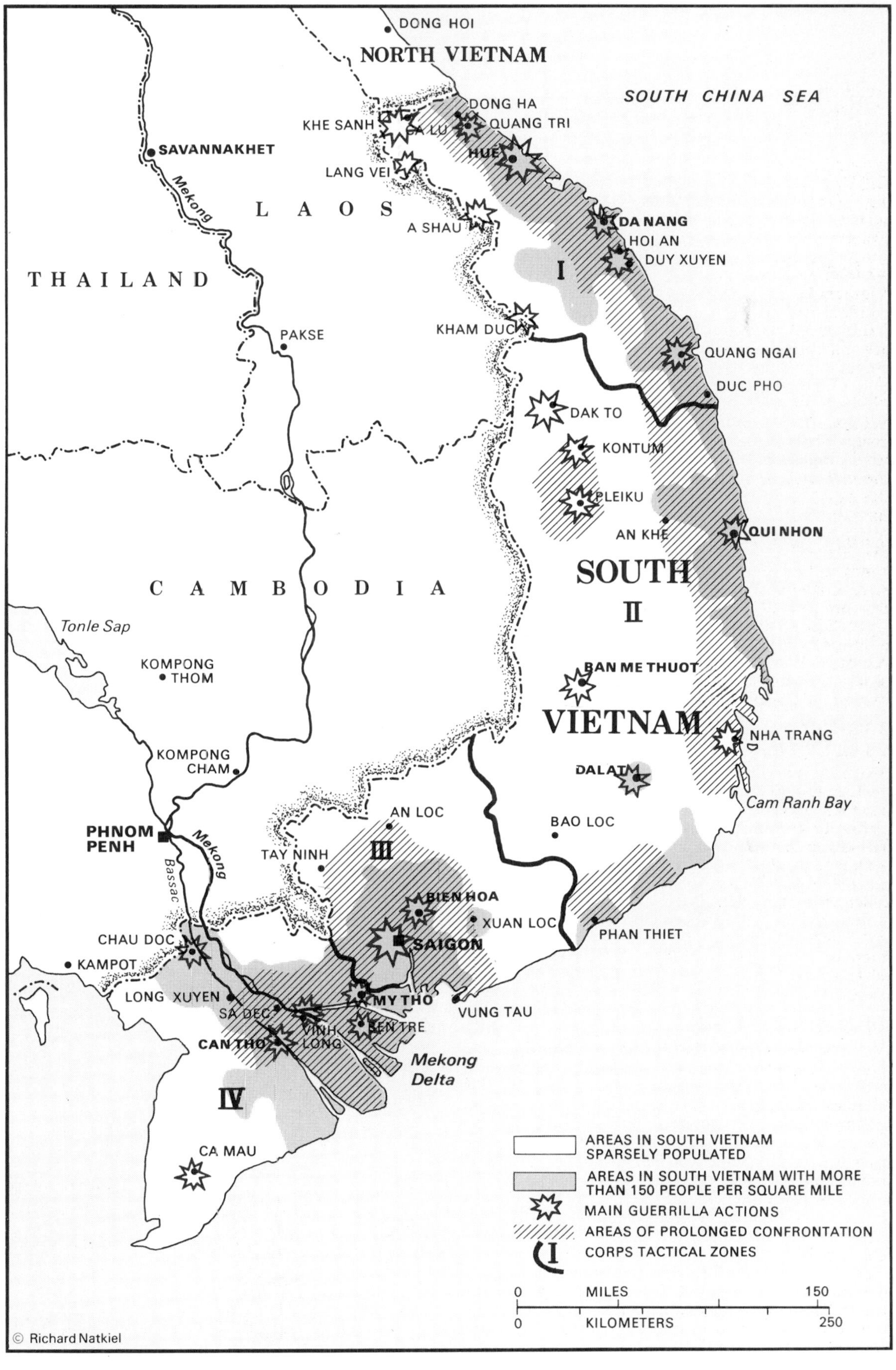

Right: A general map of the Vietnam War.

about 60 ARVN troops manage to get away; losses are 392, though Vietcong losses are reported at several hundred.

JUNE 1965

Vietnam War: US Military US forces in Vietnam are still directed to operate under the 'enclave strategy.' The Marines are at Danang, Phu Bai and Chu Lai, and the Army at Vungtau. US forces are expected to defend these coastal areas, leaving ARVN troops to operate in the rest of the country. US forces in Vietnam are now around 42,200; deployment of another 21,000 will be announced on 26 June.

4 JUNE 1965

Vietnam War: Command Major General Lewis Walt takes command of the III Marine Amphibious Force and the 3rd Division from Major General William Collins.

8-9 JUNE 1965

Vietnam War: US Policy The State Department issues a press release stating that 'American forces would be available for combat support together with Vietnamese forces when and if necessary.' In other words, Americans may now take a direct combat role, and public outcry about this is quick to arise within the growing American anti-war movement. Attorney General Nicholas Katzenbach will assure Johnson that the Tonkin Gulf Resolution empowers the president to commit large-scale forces without Congressional approval.

10-13 JUNE 1965

Vietnam War: Ground War Some 1500 Vietcong attack the district capital of Dongxoai, northeast of Saigon, and overrun the town's military headquarters and an adjoining militia compound. US helicopters fly in ARVN reinforcements, but the enemy renews the attack and soon isolates and cuts down the ARVN troops. Heavy US air strikes eventually help to drive off the Vietcong, but not before the ARVN has lost some 800-900 troops and the US has lost seven killed, 12 missing and 15 wounded.

12-19 JUNE 1965

South Vietnam Mounting Roman Catholic opposition to Premier Quat's government leads him to resign. On the 19th, Air Vice-Marshal Nguyen Cao Ky assumes the premiership of the ninth government within the last 20 months. Promising to rule with an iron hand, he starts by demanding full mobilization.

17 JUNE 1965

Vietnam War: Operation Arc Light For the first time, 27 B-52 Stratofortresses fly from Guam to bomb a Vietcong concentration in Binh Duong Province. Such flights, under the aegis of the Strategic Air Command, are known as Operation Arc Light; some military leaders question the worth of such raids, and this one fails to suppress enemy activity.

26 JUNE 1965

Vietnam War: US Policy General Westmoreland is given formal authority to commit US forces to battle when he decides they are necessary 'to strengthen

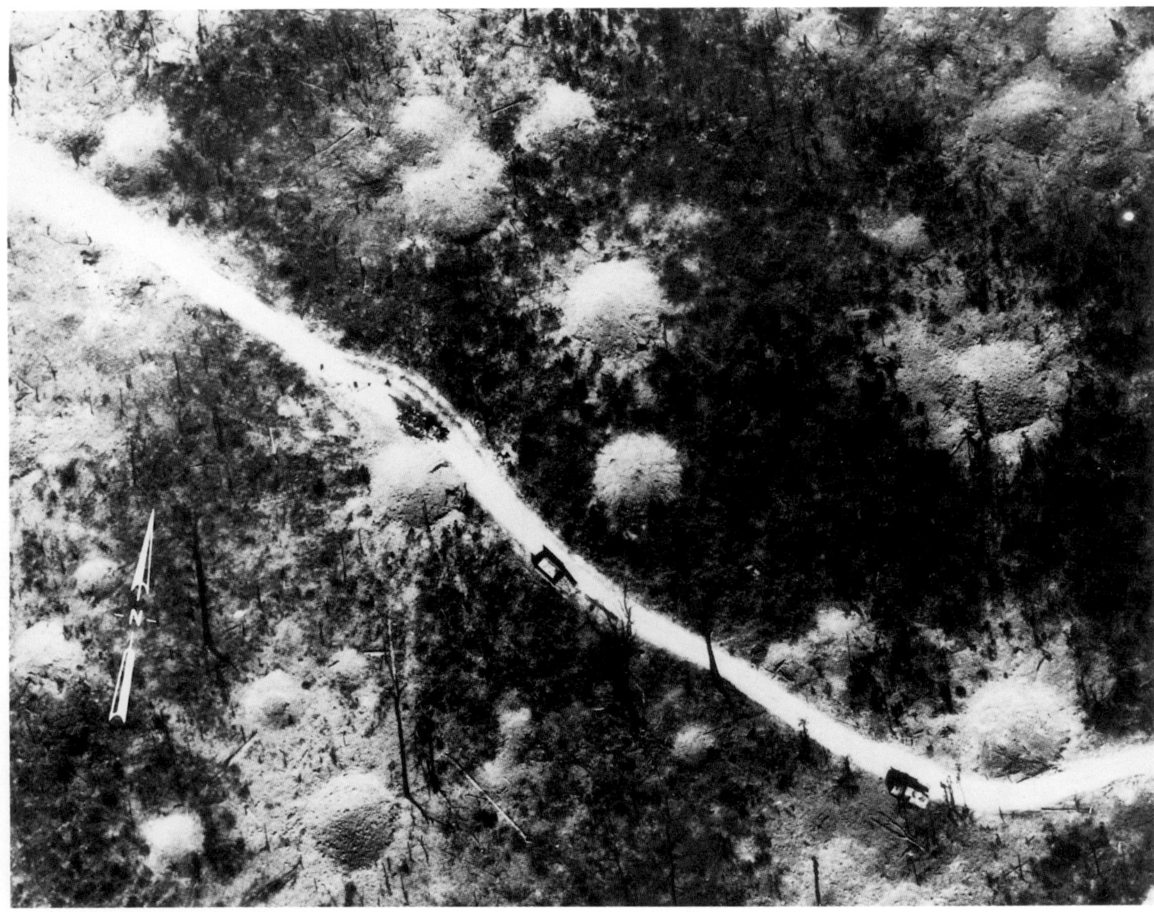

One damaged and two intact North Vietnamese trucks on the Ho Chi Minh Trail, North Vietnam's primary supply route to the south throughout the war.

the relative position of the GVN [Government of Vietnam] forces.'

28-30 JUNE 1965

Vietnam War: Ground War In the first major offensive by US forces, 3000 troops of the 173rd Airborne Brigade, in conjunction with 800 Australian soldiers and a Vietnamese airborne unit, is aimed at a jungle area known as War Zone D, 20 miles northeast of Saigon. The operation is called off after three days when it fails to make major contact with the enemy; one American is killed, and nine Americans and four Australians are wounded.

JULY 1965

Vietnam War: US Military There are now some 51,000 US servicemen in Vietnam, and General Westmoreland has requested another 125,000. Bombing sorties over North Vietnam have increased from 3600 in April to 4800 in June.

11 JULY 1965

Vietnam War: US Policy Secretary of State Dean Rusk states that the 'idea of sanctuary is dead,' – that is, that the US will attack any part of North Vietnam it chooses to.

24 JULY 1965

Vietnam War: Operation Rolling Thunder Four US F-4C Phantom jets escorting a formation of bombers over Kangchi, 55 miles northwest of Hanoi, are fired at for the first time by Soviet SAM-2 anti-aircraft missiles from an unknown launching site.

26 JULY 1965

Vietnam War: US Policy President Johnson announces he will increase US strength in Vietnam to 125,000 men. To support the buildup, draft quotas increase from 17,000 to 35,000; on 4 August the president will ask Congress for an additional $1.7 billion to support the war.

18-21 AUGUST 1965

VietnamWar: Operation Starlite In Operation Starlite about 5500 of General Lewis Walt's Marines destroy a Vietcong stronghold near Vantuong, 16 miles south of the air base at Chu Lai. The Marines not only battle on the ground but in tunnels and caves that the enemy use as hideouts; US planes and warships support the fighting. The Marines lose 45 and claim to have killed 688 Vietcong. This engagement is the first all-US battle of the war and the first involving tanks. It is also the first regimental-size battle for US forces since the Korean War.

3 SEPTEMBER 1965

Vietnam War: Operation Rolling Thunder US and South Vietnamese planes fly a record 532 missions over North Vietnam in one day, including a joint launch from three offshore carriers.

17-19 SEPTEMBER 1965

Vietnam War: Air War In three incidents US planes strike so close to the DMZ that at least 60 South Vietnamese civilians are reported killed or wounded. While Westmoreland orders special cautions to avoid civilian casualties, he also calls for redrawing the borders of the 'free strike' zone.

10-14 OCTOBER 1965

Vietnam War: Ground War In its first operation since arriving last month the US 1st Air Cavalry Division joins South Vietnamese marines in a major drive against some 2000 enemy near Ankhe in the Central Highlands. Though unable to trap the NVA division, they do reopen the Pleiku-Ankhe highway and destroy an enemy hospital.

15-16 OCTOBER 1965

Vietnam War: Protest At a rally David Miller becomes the first anti-war protester to burn his draft card, which the government has recently decreed a crime; Miller is arrested by FBI agents. On the 16th protest marches against the war in some 40 US cities will be echoed by demonstrations in London, Rome and other European capitals. Japan will announce that it refuses, even if formally requested, to send troops to Vietnam.

19-27 OCTOBER 1965

Vietnam War: Pleime Assault Enemy forces launch a heavy assault against the US Special Forces camp at Pleime in the Central Highlands. During a week of savage fighting defenders, including *montagnards*, Green Berets and South Vietnamese, repel repeated Vietcong attacks, aided by ARVN reinforcements and numerous air strikes.

23 OCTOBER-20 NOVEMBER 1965

Vietnam War: Battle of the Ia Drang Valley In an extension of the clash at the Pleime camp ARVN and US 1st Air Cavalry Division units seek to destroy enemy forces operating in Pleiku Province. The operation concludes with a week of bitter fighting when retreating NVA troops try to protect an important staging area and supply base in the Ia Drang Valley. It is the bloodiest battle of the war to date. In one engagement 500 NVA ambush a battalion, wiping out most of a company. US casualties number about 300. Estimated Vietcong and North Vietnamese casualties are 1800. The battle ends with the communists withdrawing under pursuit into Cambodia.

30 OCTOBER 1965

Vietnam War: Counter-Protest In New York 25,000 persons march in support of US policy in Vietnam. Most Americans and government leaders still support the war, but doubts and anti-war activity are growing.

Vietnam War: Ground War US Marines repel a 'human wave' assault 10 miles from Danang, killing 56 Vietcong. A search of the dead uncovers a sketch of Marine positions on the body of a 13-year-old boy who had sold drinks to the Americans the previous day.

2 NOVEMBER 1965

Vietnam War: Protest To express his opposition to the war Norman Morrison, a 32-year-old Quaker, immolates himself in front of the Pentagon. Another Quaker and a Catholic will do likewise in coming months.

5 DECEMBER 1965

Vietnam War: North Vietnam A Peking pact is signed between China and North Vietnam whereby China is to provide large amounts of materiel for the war. In February the USSR will sign a similar pact. Soviet defensive SAM (surface-to-air-missile) sites have been in place around Hanoi since April, and have made a number of kills of allied planes.

8-19 DECEMBER 1965

Vietnam War: Ground War A joint ARVN-USMC operation to clear Vietcong from the Que Son Valley begins when enemy units destroy two ARVN battalions before they can be reinforced. In subsequent fighting, however, allied troops, supported by B-52 strikes, overcome stiff resistance and accomplish the objective.

15 DECEMBER 1965

Vietnam War: Operation Rolling Thunder In the first attack on a major industrial target in the North, US planes drop 12 tons of bombs on a vital power plant near Haiphong, the nation's chief port.

31 DECEMBER 1965

Vietnam War: State of the War Some 180,000 US military personnel are now in South Vietnam; General Westmoreland has requested another 250,000 for the

Soldiers of the 7th Marine Division move along the dikes of a South Vietnamese rice paddy in the course of a 1965 Search-and-Destroy mission.

coming year and expects to get them. US forces are now reporting significant casualties: some 1350 killed, 5300 wounded and 150 missing or captured during 1965. South Vietnam reports 11,100 killed, 22,600 wounded and 7400 missing among the military; and increasing numbers of South Vietnamese civilians are casualties of the war. South Vietnam claims to have killed 34,585 communist troops and to have captured 5746. Operation Rolling Thunder has flown 55,000 sorties and dropped 33,000 tons of bombs; 171 US aircraft have been lost. There is no indication, however, that these air raids are having a significant effect on North Vietnam, either in its military operations or on its willingness to negotiate. It is estimated that some 36,000 North Vietnamese Army (NVA) troops have now infiltrated the South, mostly via the Ho Chi Minh Trail, which has been vastly improved despite steady US air strikes. The kind of ground fighting that is developing is unlike anything seen in warfare before: there are no front lines, but rather the war is mostly fought by relatively small helicopter-borne operations into communist-controlled areas, supported by air strikes. Tanks and conventional large troop movements have rarely proven effective. Once allied troops move out of an area, the enemy often moves right back in.

8-14 JANUARY 1966

Vietnam War: Ground War General Westmoreland's 'search-and-destroy' strategy has now replaced the former 'enclave' strategy. In these days a massive search-and-destroy operation by US forces, supported by Australian and New Zealand troops, converges on the Vietcong's Iron Triangle stronghold northwest of Saigon. Although they fail to make contact with any large enemy units the allies do uncover and destroy a huge Vietcong tunnel network before pulling out.

24 JANUARY-6 MARCH 1966

Vietnam War: Ground War in the largest search-and-destroy operation to date – Operation Masher/ White Wing/ Thang Phong II – US air cavalry, ARVN and Korean forces sweep through Binh Dinh Province. In late January these forces link up with Double Eagle, a USMC operation. Altogether, reported enemy casualties number 2389.

31 JANUARY 1966

Vietnam War: US Policy President Johnson announces on television that a 37-day bombing pause is being ended since it has produced no sign of negotiation from Hanoi. The communists have used the time to good advantage by accelerating their buildup of supplies and troops in the South. In the last months America has made wide-ranging peace overtures, but these and ensuing ones, some through the UN, have been rebuffed. Clearly, Hanoi feels it is winning the war and therefore will not agree to the US demand to withdraw from the South.

9-11 MARCH 1966

Vietnam War: Ground War Communist troops wipe out the US Special Forces camp at A Shau near the Cambodian border after two days of savage fighting. Total disaster is averted when allied helicopters lift out 12 of 17 Green Berets and 172 of the 400 ARVN.

10 MARCH-15 APRIL 1966

South Vietnam Dismissal of Buddhist General Thi triggers widespread, often violent, anti-government and anti-American demonstrations by Buddhists. On 14 April the Ky government will temporarily end the unrest by promising to dissolve the ruling military junta and hold elections for a Constituent Assembly.

1 APRIL 1966

Vietnam War: Terrorism In one of many such terrorist events Vietcong commandos set off explosives at a Saigon hotel housing US troops, killing three Americans and four South Vietnamese. As intended, this demonstrates that allied troops are not safe anywhere in the country.

1 MAY 1966

Vietnam War: Cambodia US artillery shells targets in Cambodia after US troops operating on the South Vietnam side of the Caibac River come under fire from the Cambodian shore. This is the first time the US has intentionally fired on Cambodian soil and will increase ongoing and bitter Cambodian protests about violations of its neutrality. There is no doubt, however, that Vietcong and NVA are active within the Cambodian border.

5 MAY 1966

Vietnam War: Washington The national Vietnam debate continues as Senate Foreign Relations Committee Chairman William Fulbright declares the US is 'succumbing to the arrogance of power' by confusing 'its power with virtue and its major responsibilities with a universal mission.' Johnson will be quick to rebuff this blow to his war policy from a respected figure within his own party.

Danang interceptor pilots race to man their F-102s against possible enemy air attack in 1966. The NVA in fact had no air-ground attack capability.

29 JUNE 1966

Vietnam War: First Bombing of Hanoi and Haiphong Pursuing a suggestion of presidential advisor and leading hawk Walt Rostow, US bombers attack fuel-storage installations near Hanoi and Haiphong, destroying an estimated 50 percent of the North's fuel supply. These are the first raids in the immediate vicinity of the two cities and constitute a major escalation of the air war. Congressional reaction to these raids will range from applause to denunciation. Historians will debate the raids' military and political consequences for many years to come.

15 JULY-3 AUGUST 1966

Vietnam War: Operation Hastings A force of more than 8500 US Marines and 2500 ARVN troops launch a massive drive called Operation Hastings in Quangtri Province, below the Demilitarized Zone. The target is a communist force of 8000-10,000 who are attempting to take control of Quangtri Province. After losing 824 men, North Vietnamese troops pull out of the area.

30 JULY-5 AUGUST 1966

Vietnam War: Air War For the first time, US B-52's intentionally bomb targets in the DMZ – a communist camp and supply area north of the Benhai River. Inevitably, such raids cause extensive civilian casualties.

3 AUGUST-18 SEPTEMBER 1966

Vietnam War: Operation Prairie US Marines begin a sweep just south of the DMZ against three battalions of NVA. Two companies of Marines encounter a large enemy force three miles south of Zone 2; outnumbered, the Americans are unable to break out until 18 September. Enemy casualties are estimated at 1099.

11 SEPTEMBER 1966

South Vietnam Voters elect a Constituent Assembly that is to draft a new constitution and pave the way for restoration of civilian government in 1967. The Vietcong unsuccessfully try to disrupt the election by terrorist attacks.

15 OCTOBER-26 NOVEMBER 1966

Vietnam War: Operation Attleboro Though most of the war is being fought in daily, small and deadly operations in the countryside – a guerrilla war to match the communist style –, General Westmoreland prefers to mount large-scale conventional operations. In these weeks a heavy concentration of US troops moves into Tayninh Province near the Cambodian border, around 50 miles north of Saigon, and sweeps the area in search of Vietcong. On 3 November they fight one of the war's biggest battles, involving the US First and 25th Infantry Divisions, the 196th Light Infantry Brigade, the 173rd Airborne Brigade and at least two ARVN battalions. Engagements continue through 12 November. At the height of the fighting 20,000 allied troops, a record number, are committed against the Vietcong and NVA concentration; 1100 of the latter die in the engagements.

24-26 OCTOBER 1966

Vietnam War: Manila Conference President Johnson meets with leaders of the six other nations involved in the war – Australia, New Zealand, the Philippines, Thailand, South Korea and South Vietnam. The allies pledge political self-determination and overall cooperation. On the military front they pledge to withdraw troops six months after North Vietnam ceases its aggression. On 26 October Johnson pays a visit to the US base at Camranh Bay, where he decorates wounded soldiers.

25 OCTOBER-23 NOVEMBER 1966

Vietnam War: Naval The US Navy increases attacks against North Vietnamese coastal shipping and shore installations in the Donghoi area. By 23 November more than 230 Communist vessels are reported sunk. The US has also developed a 'riverine' force of floating barracks, patrol boats, landing craft and helicopters that operate in the waterways of the Mekong Delta.

7 NOVEMBER 1966

Vietnam War: Protest Attempting to speak at Harvard University, Secretary McNamara is assailed by Students for a Democratic Society (SDS) and others, who shout him down and finally lie down in front of his car. McNamara is finally escorted from the campus by police. On 15 November, Brown students will storm the stage where JCS Chief Earle Wheeler is speaking.

4 DECEMBER 1966

Vietnam War: Attack on Tansonnhut A Vietcong unit penetrates the 13-mile defense perimeter around Saigon's Tansonnhut Airport and shells the field for hours. US and South Vietnamese security guards finally drive off the attackers, killing 18 but also taking casualties. The guerrillas return at night and resume the attack before again being repulsed.

13-14 DECEMBER 1966

Vietnam War: Operation Rolling Thunder US planes bomb a railroad yard six miles north of Hanoi and a truck depot two miles to the south. North Vietnam and her allies immediately condemn the raid as striking civilians; the American response will claim the targets were military and all bombs perfectly accurate. On the 26th, after a report by *New York Times* editor Harrison Salisbury describing destruction in North Vietnam, the US Defense Department will concede that civilians in the North have been bombed accidentally.

31 DECEMBER 1966

Vietnam War: State of the War During 1966 the US has increased its forces in Vietnam to 280,000, with another 60,000 aboard ships operating off the coast. By the end of the year South Vietnamese forces number about 750,000, South Korean 46,000, Australian 550, Thai 180, New Zealand 150 and Philippine 1000. Estimates of communist strength are around 275,000, including 45,000 North Vietnamese regulars. Infiltration of personnel and supplies from the North continues unabated, despite massive bombing raids on the Ho Chi Minh Trail. Operation Rolling Thunder is now in overdrive. The year's total number of individual flights was 148,000, total bomb tonnage 128,000, number of aircraft lost 318 and operational costs of the air war over a billion dollars. The CIA estimates North Vietnamese casualties from bombing raids at 24,000, some 80 percent of them civilian. The Department of Defense reports that 5008 US servicemen have been killed and 30,093 wounded this year, for a total of 6664 Americans killed and 37,738 wounded since January 1961. South Vietnamese combat fatalities totaled 19,110 during 1966. The South Vietnamese claim to have killed 61,631 Vietcong this year. The North Vietnamese claim to have killed 240,000 allied troops, including 100,000 Americans.

2 JANUARY 1967

Vietnam War: Operation Rolling Thunder In what is described as the biggest air battle of the war US Air Force F-4 Phantom jets down seven communist MiG-21s. The Phantoms were flying cover for US planes attacking surface-to-air missile (SAM) sites in the Red River Delta.

8-26 JANUARY 1967

Vietnam War: Operation Cedar Falls About 16,000 US and 14,000 South Vietnamese troops mount an operation to disrupt insurgent activities near Saigon. This offensive, the largest of the war to date and one involving tanks and bulldozers, has as its primary targets the Thanhdien Forest Preserve and the Iron Triangle, a 60-mile-square area of jungle believed to contain VC base camps and supply dumps. US infantrymen destroy a massive tunnel complex in the Triangle, apparently a headquarters for guerrilla raids and terrorist attacks on Saigon. The tunnels also contain a half-million pages of documents detailing communist operations and command structure – this find is the greatest intelligence breakthrough of the war. Bensuc a village regarded as hostile, is leveled after its 3800 inhabitants are resettled. The operation ends with 711 of the enemy reported killed and 488 captured. The Vietcong will immediately reoccupy the territory.

Right: A camouflaged commando of a crack US Navy SEAL team stalks the enemy in Vietnam.

Below: SEALs (an acronym for Sea, Land and Air) were used primarily in riverine operations.

2 FEBRUARY 1967

Vietnam War: Ground War In a large-scale offensive called Operation Gadsden, around 7000 US troops sweep through War Zone C near the Cambodian border to discourage enemy troop movement. As allied offensive operations large and small increase, other US and ARVN forces pursue the 'pacification' program in the villages and hamlets, isolating and relocating the inhabitants in an attempt – mostly futile – to break up the Vietcong influence and infrastructure.

11 FEBRUARY 1967

Vietnam War: Ground War After a cease-fire during the Tet lunar new year the US and South Vietnam launch 16 separate operations. One of them, Operation Lam Son 67, involves several battalions of the First Infantry Division in clearing guerrillas from villages in an area 13 miles south of Saigon.

22 FEBRUARY 1967

Vietnam War: Operation Junction City Operation Junction City, an effort to smash the Vietcong's War Zone C stronghold near the Cambodian border, begins with over 25,000 US and ARVN troops – the war's largest offensive so far. The first day's operation is supported by 575 US plane sorties, a record for a single day.

2 MARCH 1967

Vietnam War: Air War In one of many such incidents the friendly village of Languei south of the DMZ is accidentally hit by American bombs, killing at least 83 civilians and wounding 176.

10 MARCH-1 APRIL 1967

Vietnam War: Operation Junction City Communist forces mount a series of attacks in strength on the US Operation Junction City in War Zone C. During a fierce enemy attack on the 19th US defenders fire 2500 artillery rounds at the Vietcong. Then, on the 21st, the enemy mounts an unprecedented daylight attack with human wave tactics on Firebase Gold. As the VC come to hand-grenade range the Americans call in armor and infantry reinforcements with 200 machine guns; the communists try unsuccessfully to climb on to the armored vehicles. The enemy finally withdraw leaving 600 dead. In the final battle on 31 March – 1 April, US troops kill 591 Vietcong, while suffering 10 fatalities and 64 wounded. In April the enemy will fade away into the jungle, and Westmoreland will declare a victory.

Opposite top: A map of the air war in Vietnam.

Opposite: Trucks and M-113 armored personnel carriers of the US 11th Armored Cavalry Regiment assemble for the 1967 assault on the Viet Cong in War Zone C called Operation Junction City.

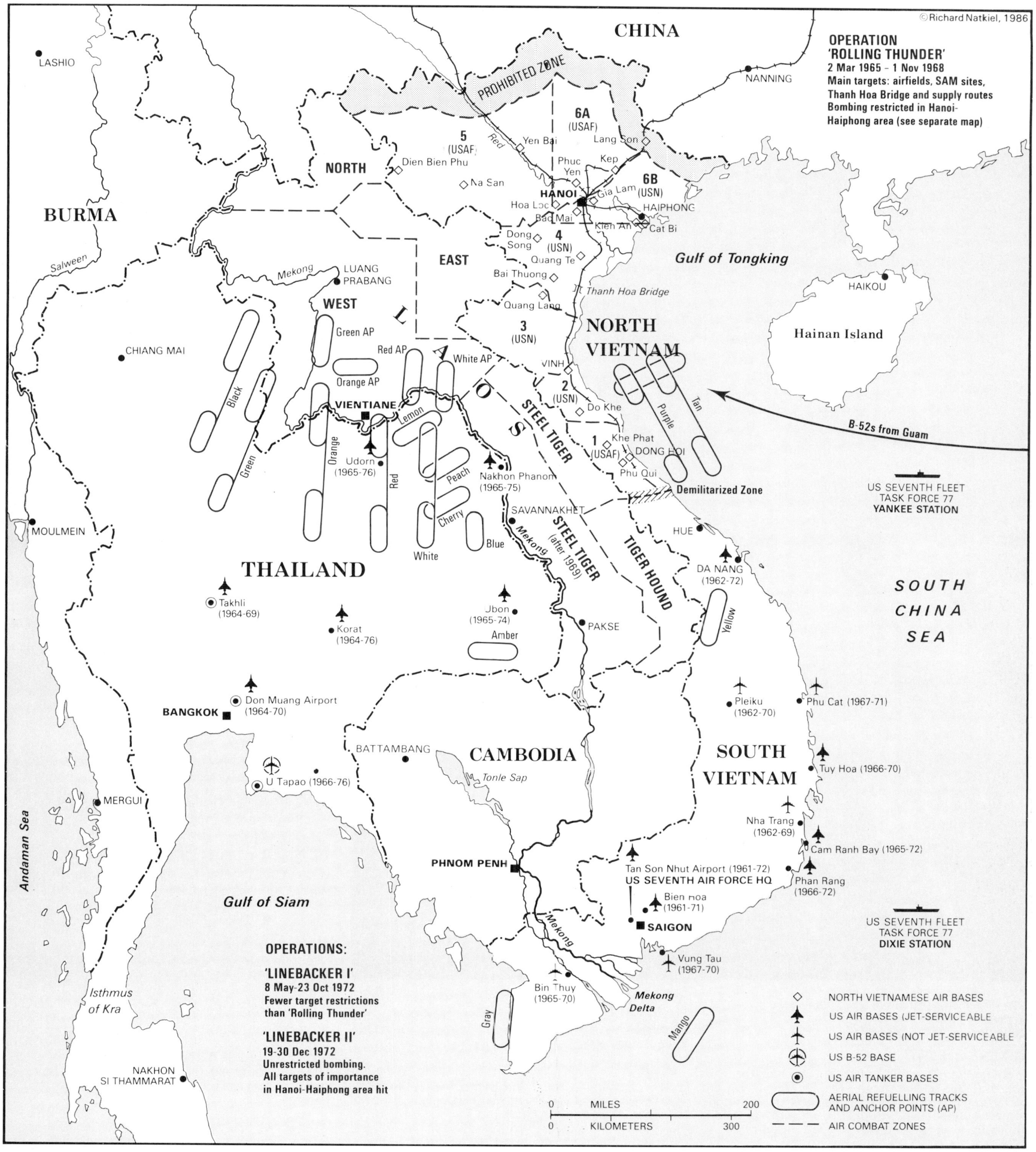
©Richard Natkiel, 1986
OPERATION 'ROLLING THUNDER'
2 Mar 1965 - 1 Nov 1968
Main targets: airfields, SAM sites, Thanh Hoa Bridge and supply routes
Bombing restricted in Hanoi-Haiphong area (see separate map)
CHINA
PROHIBITED ZONE
BURMA
THAILAND
LAOS
NORTH VIETNAM
SOUTH VIETNAM
CAMBODIA
Hainan Island
Gulf of Tongking
SOUTH CHINA SEA
Gulf of Siam
Andaman Sea
Isthmus of Kra
B-52s from Guam
US SEVENTH FLEET TASK FORCE 77 YANKEE STATION
US SEVENTH FLEET TASK FORCE 77 DIXIE STATION
Demilitarized Zone
STEEL TIGER
STEEL TIGER (after 1969)
TIGER HOUND
NORTH
EAST
WEST
5 (USAF)
6A (USAF)
6B (USN)
4 (USN)
3 (USN)
2 (USN)
1 (USAF)
Tan Son Nhut Airport (1961-72)
US SEVENTH AIR FORCE HQ
OPERATIONS:
'LINEBACKER I'
8 May-23 Oct 1972
Fewer target restrictions than 'Rolling Thunder'
'LINEBACKER II'
19-30 Dec 1972
Unrestricted bombing.
All targets of importance in Hanoi-Haiphong area hit
NORTH VIETNAMESE AIR BASES
US AIR BASES (JET-SERVICEABLE
US AIR BASES (NOT JET-SERVICEABLE
US B-52 BASE
US AIR TANKER BASES
AERIAL REFUELLING TRACKS AND ANCHOR POINTS (AP)
AIR COMBAT ZONES
0 MILES 200
0 KILOMETERS 300

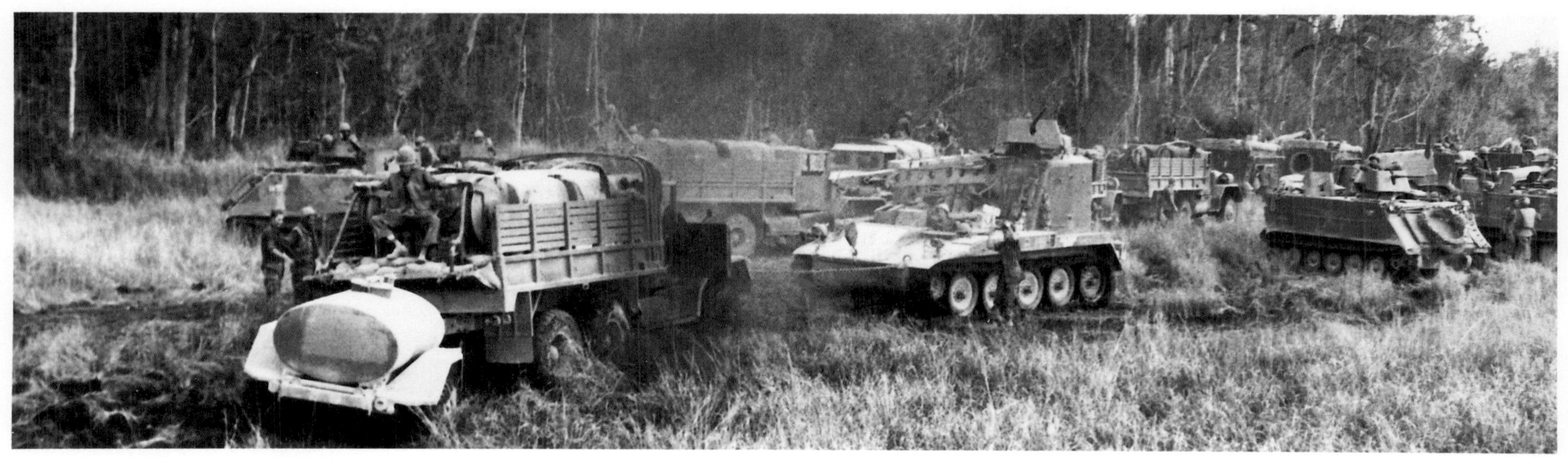

US artillerymen load 155mm shells onto trucks in preparation for Operation Junction City, one of the largest battles before the Tet Offensive.

21 MARCH 1967

Vietnam War: Peace Overtures It is disclosed that Ho Chi Minh has turned down President Johnson's bid for direct peace talks. Ho reiterates a demand that the bombing stop and US troops be withdrawn unconditionally from the South before talks take place.

25 MARCH 1967

Vietnam War: Protest In Chicago, Reverend Martin Luther King leads a large anti-war march and declares the Vietnam War is 'a blasphemy against all that America stands for.' King will receive much criticism for his new anti-war activities, many saying he should stick to civil rights, but he will labor to create a link between the growing peace movement and the civil rights movement.

6 APRIL 1967

Vietnam War: Ground War About 2500 VC and North Vietnamese troops carry out four closely-coordinated attacks on the city of Quangtri. Some 125 ARVN troops and four US Marines are killed.

15 APRIL 1967

Vietnam War: Protest Parades to protest US policy in Vietnam are held by over 100,000 people in New York and some 20,000 in San Francisco. Among those speaking are Martin Luther King and Dr. Benjamin Spock; 200 youths burn draft cards in Central Park.

20 APRIL 1967

Vietnam War: Operation Rolling Thunder For the first time the US bombs inside Haiphong, attacking two power plants with 86 carrier-based planes.

24 APRIL-5 MAY 1967

Vietnam War: Ground War In a fierce 12-day battle US Marines defeat NVA troops on three hills near the airstrip at Khe Sanh in Quangtin Province. US forces lose 160 killed and 746 wounded – half the combat strength of two Marine battalions.

25-28 APRIL 1967

Vietnam War: Congress Objection to the war is heating up both outside and inside government. On the 25th major Senate speeches attacking administration policies in Vietnam are delivered by Democratic Senators George McGovern, Robert Kennedy, Frank Church and Ernest Gruening. Republican Senator Charles Percy has recently called for peace talks with Vietcong participation.

2 MAY 1967

Vietnam War: International Protest Called by British philosopher Bertrand Russell, members of an 'International Tribunal on War Crimes' convenes in Stockholm. The tribunal will charge the US with crimes of aggression including 'widespread, systematic and deliberate' bombing of civilians.

15-23 MAY 1967

Vietnam War: Ground War US Marine positions between Dongha and Conthien, just south of the DMZ, are pounded by NVA artillery; over 100 Americans are killed or wounded in heavy fighting. On 18 May 5500 US and South Vietnamese troops invade the DMZ to smash a Communist buildup in the area; the North Vietnamese call this violation of the DMZ a 'brazen provocation' and a violation of the Geneva Accords.

19 MAY 1967

Vietnam War: Washington Sentiment within the administration for cutting back the war is growing; today Secretary of Defense McNamara sends a memo to the president that mashals the arguments against widening the ground war and sharpens the case for curtailing the air war. He recommends deployment of only 30,000 more troops for General Westmoreland, whose troop requests have escalated steadily. On 31 May the JCS will issue a sharp rebuttal to McNamara's memo. During the summer the administration will decide on a troop increase, but it will be considerably less than Westmoreland has asked for.

22 JUNE 1967

Vietnam War: Ground War A 130-man US airborne company is hit by a North Vietnamese ambush near Dakto, 28 miles northeast of Saigon; 80 Americans are killed and 34 wounded.

JULY 1967

Vietnam War: Ground War On 2 July, US Marines are ambushed by 500 NVA troops near Conthien, south of the DMZ. Reinforcements are brought in by both sides as the fighting heats up, and Marine casualties finally total 96 killed and 211 wounded. Over the next two weeks other Marines in the Conthien area are heavily attacked, with losses of 159 dead. Enemy dead are put at 1301. Meanwhile, still other US positions are hit by severe enemy mortar, rocket and artillery fire on 4-6 July.

16 JULY-31 OCTOBER 1967

Vietnam War: Operation Kingfisher A three-month US offensive in northern South Vietnam ends after the loss of 340 Marines dead and 3086 wounded. Enemy losses are unknown but are presumed high.

23 JULY 1967

Vietnam War: Ground War In a five-hour battle US infantry virtually wipes out an NVA company near Ducco in the Central Highlands.

29 JULY 1967

Vietnam War: Naval 134 crewmen are killed aboard the US carrier *Forrestal* in the Gulf of Tonkin as fire sweeps across the deck, ignited by a punctured Skyhawk fuel tank. This is the worst naval accident in a war zone since WW II.

30 JULY 1967

Vietnam War: National A Gallup poll reports that 52 percent of Americans disapprove of Johnson's handling of the war; 41 percent think the US should not have gone in at all; 56 percent believe the US is losing the war or making no progress.

11-21 AUGUST 1967

Vietnam War: Operation Rolling Thunder President Johnson and his advisors have largely been controlling the air war from the White House, and Johnson has recently stepped up the attacks, despite the objections of McNamara and others. In these days the president directs extensive bombing on North Vietnamese targets near Hanoi and Haiphong, many near the Chinese border. On the 11th two Navy jets stray off course into China; on the 21st China will claim to have shot down two US jets within its border.

3 SEPTEMBER 1967

South Vietnam In elections under a new constitution Nguyen Van Thieu, already serving an appointed role as chief of state, is elected president of South Vietnam, with Nguyen Cao Ky as vice-president. They defeat ten other candidates, some of whom will charge the election was rigged. The Constituent Assembly will eventually endorse the elections.

13-16 SEPTEMBER 1967

Vietnam War: Ground War In Operation Coronado 5, one of a series of offensives in the Mekong Delta, US infantry and ARVN forces battle the Vietcong 47 miles southwest of Saigon.

14-15 SEPTEMBER 1967

Vietnam War: Peace Proposals Hints of peace talks have accelerated in the past months. Two separate news reports indicate that Hanoi is interested in talks; the condition is the ceasing of US bombing attacks in the North. American officials will reply that it is the bombing that will force the North to negotiate. Debate about the political effect of bombing will recur often, most notably in December 1972.

A Viet Cong base camp is hit by US UH-1 "Huey" helicopters. Vietnam saw the first use of helicopters as ground attack aircraft.

28 SEPTEMBER 1967

Vietnam War: Operation Rolling Thunder Navy pilots from the *Coral Sea* knock down part of the last intact major road and rail bridge into Haiphong. Four other bridges have been destroyed since 11 September. On 2 October, American officials will report that the recent step-up of bombing has slowed, but by no means stopped, the supply of military equipment into Hanoi.

4 OCTOBER 1967

Vietnam War: Ground War The US reports that a month-long communist siege of the Marine base at Conthien has been broken. An estimated 3000 NVA troops have been killed or wounded in the daily artillery exchange that began on 1 September.

5-14 OCTOBER 1967

Vietnam War: Operation Rolling Thunder A North Vietnamese education minister charges that a US air raid on a school killed 33 children and wounded 28. On the 14th an Australian correspondent will report a US attack levelling a hospital complex and quote the Haiphong mayor as saying a third of the city's residential areas have been destroyed in the recent US raids.

13-14 OCTOBER 1967

Vietnam War: Ground War US positions around Conthien again come under heavy North Vietnamese shelling. On the 14th communist attempts to penetrate the positions will be thrown back in fierce hand-to-hand fighting.

21-23 OCTOBER 1967

Vietnam War: Protest Two days of anti-war demonstrations take place in Washington, involving some 50,000 people and including a vigil at the Pentagon in which 647 are arrested for trying to break in. This protest is paralleled by demonstrations across Western Europe and in Japan.

24-25 OCTOBER 1967

Vietnam War: Operation Rolling Thunder The huge Phucyen airfield, 18 miles from Hanoi, is struck for the first time. It is believed to be the largest MiG base in the North. Severe US air attacks continue on Hanoi and Haiphong.

3-22 NOVEMBER 1967

Vietnam War: Battle of Dakto One of the bloodiest and most sustained battles of the war is fought between US and NVA troops in the Central Highlands around Dakto, near the Cambodian border, the site of a large US military complex. Around 5000 American troops face some 6000 communists. The climax of the fighting comes in a savage battle on 19-22 November for Hill 875, where the 173rd Brigade loses 158 men – 30 to misdirected friendly air fire – in driving the North Vietnamese from their defense line. In the 19 days of action communist fatalities are estimated at 1455, while 285 US soldiers are killed, 985 wounded and 18 missing.

25 NOVEMBER 1967

Vietnam War: Washington After months of growing private disillusionment with the air war that he had originally promoted, Robert S. McNamara in an emotional farewell resigns as secretary of defense to become president of the World Bank. He will be replaced by Clark Clifford, who will follow McNamara on the path of disillusion.

21 DECEMBER 1967

Vietnam War: Peace Proposals After meeting today in Canberra, Presidents Johnson and Thieu will issue a communique stating that Thieu is ready 'to discuss relevant matters with any individual now associated with the NLF' but not to recognize the communist political organization in the South as an independent government.

26-27 DECEMBER 1967

Vietnam War: Cambodia In the ongoing exchange of Cambodian protests about violations of its territory and US charges that the communists are operating there, Prince Sihanouk warns that if US troops should be ordered to invade Cambodia in search of VC and NVA his government will retaliate by asking China and Russia for military aid.

31 DECEMBER 1967

Vietnam War: State of the War By the end of the year the US contingent in Vietnam is over half a million; ARVN regulars total some 200,000. It is estimated that communist forces now number about 250,000, with at least that many in irregular and political units. Since February the allies have dropped over a million and a half tons of bombs, while losing 328 US planes. Additionally, since 1961 more than 500 helicopters have been downed in combat, and 1000 other aircraft have been lost in accidents. In the fiscal year ending in June the war cost the US $21 billion. As many young people avoid the draft, the Marines are finding it hard to find qualified soldiers and officers. US casualties during the year are 9353 dead – more than the total of all previously killed in the war – and 99,742 wounded. (Rapid helicopter evacuation of wounded has, however,saved a higher percentage than in any previous war.) The South Vietnamese armed forces report 11,135 killed. The allies claim to have killed around 90,400 enemy soldiers and some 25,000 enemy civilians, but by now it is generally known that estimates are greatly inflated.

20 JANUARY-14 APRIL 1968

Vietnam War: Siege of Khe Sanh One of the greatest and most critical campaigns of the war begins at Khe Sanh, 14 miles below the DMZ and six miles from the Laotian border. Seized and activated by the US Marines last year, it is used as a staging area for forward patrols. The battle begins on 20 January with a brisk firefight between Marines and NVA entrenched between two hills northwest of the base. Next day, enemy forces overrun the village of Khe Sanh and long-range artillery opens fire on the US base itself, hitting its main ammunition dump and starting a blaze that slowly detonates 1500 tons of explosives. As the incessant barrage keeps the Marines pinned down in trenches and bunkers, General Robert Cushman calls for massive artillery and air strikes to dislodge the enemy. These strikes will drop some 5000 tons of bombs daily, exploding the equivalent of five Hiroshima-sized atomic bombs in the area. Commanding the enemy attack is North Vietnamese General Vo Nguyen Giap, who earned his reputation when he beat the French at Dienbienphu, and who has led the NVA ever since. Giap has planned a complex campaign to devastate the US and South Vietnamese forces; the attack at Khe Sanh is the prelude to that offensive, which will break out during the Tet (lunar new year) holiday. Using an approach similar to the one that defeated the French, Giap hopes to make Khe Sanh another Dienbienphu. The peak of the siege at Khe Sanh comes on 23 February when 1300 artillery rounds hit the Marine positions. The relief of Khe Sanh, called Operation Pegasus, begins in early April when Air Cavalry and ARVN fight their way toward the base from the east and south, while Marines push westward to reopen Route 9. The siege is finally lifted on 6 April when the cavalrymen link up with the 9th Marines south of the Khe Sanh airstrip. In a final and bloody clash on Easter Sunday three Marine companies and an NVA division struggle for control of Hill 471 overlooking Route 9; the enemy is finally driven away.

Marines at Khe Sanh watch smoke from a fuel dump hit by NVA mortars. The January 1968 attack on the base was a prelude to the Tet Offensive.

23 JANUARY 1968

North Korea A USN intelligence vessel, the *Pueblo*, is seized along with 83 crew by North Korean patrol boats in the Sea of Japan.

30 JANUARY-10 FEBRUARY 1968

VietnamWar: Tet Offensive Thousands of VC guerrillas have infiltrated Saigon and other major cities, dressed as civilians and carrying hidden weapons. At dawn on the first day of the usual Tet truce these soldiers, supported by incoming VC and NVA forces, launch Giap's offensive, the largest and best-coordinated communist operation of the war. The 84,000 attackers drive into the center of South Vietnam's seven largest cities and strike 30 provincial capitals, ranging from the Delta to the DMZ. Among the cities taken during the first days are Hué, Dalat, Kontum and Quantri. At the same time, enemy forces shell numerous allied airfields and bases. In Saigon a 19-man Vietcong suicide squad seizes the US Embassy and holds a section of it for six hours until they are all killed by an assault force of US paratroops. Nearly 1000 VC are believed to have infiltrated Saigon; it requires a week of intense fighting through the streets, and some 79 separate engagements by some 11,000 allied troops, to dislodge them. Yet by 10 February the Tet Offensive is largely crushed, though it takes almost a month of savage house-to-house fighting to regain the former Imperial capital of Hué from 5000 infiltrators and 7000 enemy reinforcements (who during the month execute some 3000 civilians). In Pleiku the battle rages for five days, in Phan Thiet for eight. At Lang Vei, southwest of Khe Sanh, NVA troops overrun a Green Beret camp, killing ten Americans and 225 South Vietnamese and Montagnard irregulars before the rest make their escape. Casualties in the overall fighting are severe on both sides. In the first 14 days the VC and NVA lose some 32,000 killed; allied dead are numbered at 1000 for the US and 2000 for the ARVN. On 2 February, President Johnson announces that the enemy have suffered complete military defeat, an appraisal General Westmoreland echoes four days later in a statement declaring that allied forces have killed more enemy troops in the past week than the US has lost in the entire war. Johnson and Westmoreland are correct: General Giap's offensive has been a horribly costly failure. Not only are communist troops defeated in every engagement, but the popular support that the communists had expected to find has not appeared, and the ARVN has fought well. Nonetheless, in the end the Tet offensive will be a psychological and political disaster for the US. Watching the fighting on TV, American citizens, unused to seeing the horrors of war so graphically portrayed, will be disheartened by the communists' organization, fighting power and ability to penetrate any part of the country – as symbolized by the bloody shambles of the US embassy in Saigon. Thus, paradoxically, a communist military defeat is transformed into a political victory.

20 FEBRUARY 1968

Vietnam War: Washington The Senate Foreign Relations Committee opens hearings to investigate American policy in Vietnam. Early sessions focusing on the Gulf of Tonkin Incident will raise the issue of a 'credibility gap' concerning the administration's version of the incident.

23 FEBRUARY 1968

Vietnam War: Planning JCS Chairman Earle Wheeler and General Westmoreland confer in South Vietnam in the wake of the Tet offensive. Wheeler suggests the administration might make the long-delayed decision to call up the reserves and then allow broadening of the war into Laos and Cambodia. Westmoreland estimates that this new effort will require another 206,000 troops. When Wheeler presents his report in Washington on the 28th – making it clear that the Vietcong have, contrary to previous American estimations, gained greatly in strength during the years of major American commitment – Johnson will defer a decision on the 206,000 troops and ask new Defense Secretary Clark Clifford to review US policy.

4 MARCH 1968

Vietnam War: Washington In a memo to the president Defense Secretary Clark Clifford and his advisory group suggest sending 22,000 troops and waiting for developments before sending more. In fact, Clifford is turning against the war and will form a secret alliance within the administration to change Johnson's mind about US commitment. Clifford has come to this conclusion after finding that military leaders can offer him no prospects for a forseeable end to the fighting and no long-range goal other than wearing the enemy down by attrition.

16 MARCH 1968

Vietnam War: Massacre at My Lai In what will become the most notorious atrocity committed by US troops in Vietnam, American soldiers sweep through the South Vietnamese hamlet of My Lai, gunning down at least 300 unarmed civilian men, women and children. The massacre is revealed to the world in November 1969. In March 1971 Army Lieutenant William Calley will be found guilty of the murders by a court-martial and sentenced to hard labor for life (but will be released in a few years).

31 MARCH 1968

Vietnam War: US Government In a televised speech to the nation – one written by the Clifford group to replace an early sabre-rattling draft – Johnson is conciliatory, saying that in hopes of peace he has ordered a halt to most air and naval bombardments of North Vietnam. He will also send another 13,500 troops – far less than Westmoreland has requested. In closing Johnson stuns the world with the announcement, 'I shall not seek, and I will not accept, the nomination of my party for another term as your president.' Now Johnson himself has become another casualty of the Vietnam War.

3 APRIL 1968

Vietnam War: Peace Proposals Hanoi announces its readiness to negotiate with the US on ending the war; Johnson replies that 'we will establish contact with representatives of North Vietnam.'

8 APRIL-31 MAY 1968

Vietnam War: Ground War The largest allied operation to date, involving 42 US and 37 Vietnamese battalions, is launched against Communists within the Capital Military District; reported enemy casualties are 7645. On 11 April, Defense Secretary Clifford announces that some reservists will be called up and that the American troop ceiling in Vietnam has been raised to 549,500.

Army Lieutenant William L. Calley marches to the court martial that will sentence him to prison for life for guilt in the March 1968 My Lai massacre.

22 APRIL 1968

Vietnam War: US Policy Clifford says that the South Vietnamese have 'acquired the capacity to begin to insure their own security [and] they are going to take over more and more of the fighting.' This is the first public statement of a policy that will later be called 'Vietnamization.'

3 MAY 1968

Vietnam War: Peace Talks The US and North Vietnam agree to begin formal negotiations in Paris on 10 May. Xuan Thuy will head the North Vietnamese delegation, Averell Harriman the American. Each side restates its negotiating position: the North insists on the four-point plan enunciated by Ho Chi Minh some years ago; the US calls for an end to communist infiltration of the South and neighboring countries.

5-13 MAY 1968

Vietnam War: Second Communist Offensive To try and reverse their losses during the Tet offensive and to influence the coming negotiations in Paris, the communists begin their second large-scale offensive

US Navymen jump ashore from a river patrol boat to attack a Viet Cong stronghold in the Mekong Delta during the aftermath of the Tet Offensive.

Members of the joint US-South Vietnamese Coastal Group inspect a fishing sampan for possible enemy supplies or personnel.

of the year by shelling 119 cities, towns and military barracks. Heavy action continues for a week. The principal target is Saigon, where, following a major ground assault, the fighting quickly spreads around the city. The battle climaxes on 12 May when US jets pound a final Vietcong stronghold around the Y bridge, preparing for a US infantry assault. An estimated 5270 North Vietnamese are killed in this offensive, compared to 154 Americans and 326 South Vietnamese. It is another severe communist military defeat, but it goes almost unnoticed by discouraged US civilians at home.

11 MAY 1968

Vietnam War: Peace Talks In Paris American and North Vietnamese negotiators agree that both South Vietnam and the NLF will be excluded from the peace talks. The South Vietnamese government will protest its being omitted. The talks immediately deadlock over US demands for troop withdrawals and Communist demands for a bombing halt.

25 MAY-4 JUNE 1968

Vietnam War: Ground War The Vietcong launch their third major assault of the year on Saigon. In Cholon allied forces use helicopters, fighterbombers and tanks to dislodge Vietcong infiltrators.

1 JUNE 1968

South Vietnam Recent government directives on pacification indicate that since the Tet offensive the program's focus has shifted from school-building, health care and other social initiatives to an emphasis on training self-defense teams and bolstering hamlet security. Since the Vietcong 'shadow government' in the countryside has been weakened by losses sustained as a result of the Tet Offensive, these efforts will bear some fruit in the next year.

10 JUNE 1968

Vietnam War: Command In another hint of changing US policy, General William Westmoreland has been reassigned from commanding in Vietnam to become chairman of the Joint Chiefs of Staff. At a Saigon news conference on the day he is to turn over command to General Creighton Abrams, Westmoreland defends his attrition policy and denies that the military situation is stalemated.

19 JUNE 1968

South Vietnam President Thieu signs a general mobilization bill subjecting to induction all men between 18 and 43.

27 JUNE 1968

Vietnam War: Ground War US command in Saigon confirms that American forces have begun to evacuate the military base at Khe Sanh in favor of a more 'mobile posture.' This and other such voluntary pullbacks from hard-won positions will be much criticized by those who feel that they show inconsistency in US strategic thinking. The evacuation of Khe Sanh does, at the least, seem to imply a re-evaluation of the earlier US policy of trying to maintain defensive 'enclaves' in the field.

1 JULY 1968

Vietnam War: Air War US B-52 bombers resume raids north of the DMZ.

3 JULY 1968

Vietnam War: Casualties US command in Saigon releases figures showing that more Americans were killed during the first six months of 1968 than in all of 1967.

5-8 AUGUST 1968

Vietnam War: National In his speech in Miami accepting the Republican presidential nomination Richard Nixon pledges to 'bring an honorable end to the war in Vietnam.' He will later announce he has 'a secret plan to end the war.'

18-27 AUGUST 1968

Vietnam War: Ground War In the heaviest fighting in three months communist forces mount 19 separate attacks on allied positions throughout South Vietnam. The struggle for Tay Ninh begins after 600 VC infiltrate the provincial capital and attack government offices and installations. US reinforcements are rushed to the scene and after a day of house-to-house fighting expel the attackers. The last significant enemy offensive against the US begins on 24 August near Tam Ky City; this is repulsed on the 27th, and thereafter the communists will be reluctant to battle with US forces. Since the January Tet offensive General Giap has sacrificed an estimated 60,000 casualties without any tangible military gains. Much recrimination will follow in North Vietnamese command circles: the North has underestimated American fighting power and has overestimated communist sympathies in the South.

26-29 AUGUST 1968

Vietnam War: Protest In Chicago, as Vice-President Hubert Humphrey receives the presidential nomination over anti-war candidate Eugene McCarthy, police and troops battle outside the convention hall with over 10,000 rioting anti-war demonstrators. During the first half of the year there have been 221 major demonstrations against the war on 101 college campuses.

11-16 SEPTEMBER 1968

Vietnam War: Ground War In another assault on Tay Ninh 1500 communist troops enter the city after mortar and rocket attacks. The next day, 2000 ARVN reinforce the local garrison and after four days of heavy fighting drive the enemy from the city.

31 OCTOBER 1968

Vietnam War: End of Operation Rolling Thunder In a move intended to break the stalemated Paris peace talks – in which both sides have softened their positions – President Johnson announces an end to US bombing of North Vietnam, thus winding up the Rolling Thunder raids that began in 1965. (Major air strikes will continue in the South and on the Ho Chi Minh Trail in Laos.) The president further discloses that Hanoi has agreed to allow South Vietnamese participation in the peace talks, while the US has agreed to an NLF role – though this stops short of recognition of the NLF. Domestically, the president's speech draws widespread acclaim; reaction in Saigon is subdued.

1 NOVEMBER 1968

Vietnam War: Phoenix Program It is announced that among US efforts to bolster pacification will be the new Phoenix Program, a hamlet security initiative relying on centralized intelligence gathering aimed at destroying the Vietcong infrastructure in the South. It will become one of the most controversial operations undertaken by the US in Vietnam, critics charging that it involves extensive use of torture and assassination. In any event, some 20,000 suspected Vietcong cadres and sympathizers will die during Phoenix, which the communists will later admit was a serious blow to their operations.

6 NOVEMBER 1968

National In one of the nation's closest presidential elections, Richard M. Nixon wins over Hubert H. Humphrey by less than a million votes. The new vice-president is Spiro T. Agnew.

15-26 NOVEMBER 1968

Vietnam War: Ground War US reconnaissance reports that NVA troops and supply movements north of the DMZ have quadrupled since the bombing halt. On the 26th US and ARVN forces enter the buffer zone for the first time since the halt and drive the enemy back from advanced positions.

12 DECEMBER 1968

Vietnam War: Peace Talks After steady pressure from the US, South Vietnam has agreed to join the Paris peace talks with the North and the NLF. But the talks deadlock again, the issues now including the seating arrangement and what it implies about the importance of the four participants.

31 DECEMBER 1968

Vietnam War: State of the War While some US officials still claim that the allies are making progress against the communists, few others really believe that the war is going to be decided on the battlefield: after Tet the US is clearly losing heart, and the fighting abilities of the ARVN are debatable, though apparently improving. In 1968, 14,314 Americans have died in Vietnam, along with 20,482 ARVN and 978 other allied soldiers. Estimates of Vietcong and NVA deaths are as high as 100,000 for the year. Little wonder that as President Johnson ends the year with only a few weeks left in his long political career, he is reported to be 'haunted' by the war.

4 JANUARY 1969

Vietnam War: Diplomatic President-elect Nixon announces that he will ask Ellsworth Bunker to continue as ambassador to South Vietnam. Tomorrow Nixon will name Henry Cabot Lodge to succeed W.

Averell Harriman as chief negotiator at the still-deadlocked Paris peace talks.

5 JANUARY 1969

Vietnam War: Riverine War The US Navy announces it has established the final link of interlocking river patrols along a 150-mile stretch of the Cambodian-South Vietnamese border. The patrols involve over 100 vessels in an effort to stop the flow of communist men and supplies from Cambodia into the South.

16 JANUARY 1969

Vietnam War: Peace Talks An agreement is reached in Paris for opening expanded talks. Representatives of the US, South Vietnam, North Vietnam and the National Liberation Front will sit at a circular table without nameplates or other markings. This ambiguous compromise allows the US and the South to speak of only two sides, while allowing the communists to speak of four. The sessions will still make little progress.

In the course of an international trip President Richard Nixon made a surprise 5½-hour visit to Vietnam on 30 July 1969. Here he talks with soldiers at Di An, a US Army base about ten miles northeast of Saigon.

18 JANUARY 1969

Vietnam War: US Policy President Thieu confirms that he has requested the withdrawal of some US troops from South Vietnam in 1969. Though the outgoing Johnson has requested over $25 billion to fight the war this year, that figure represents a $3 billion reduction from last year – the first such reduction of the war and an indication of American de-escalation.

22 FEBRUARY-MARCH 1969

Vietnam War: Ground War As the usual Tet ceasefire ends, communists fire mortar and rocket rounds into Saigon for the first time since October. On the 23rd the Communists begin what comes to be called the 'post-Tet' offensive on Saigon and 115 other targets. On 6 March, American military command will report over 453 Americans dead in the first week of fighting and 2593 wounded; it will estimate communist casualties at 6752, with civilian casualties in the hundreds. As usual, the fighting will result in the communists taking no major military objectives but causing many casualties – and winning a psychological victory in the minds of the American people at home by reasserting their strength and ubiquity. In the second week of fighting 336 US soldiers die, 1694 are wounded and 259 ARVN are killed. From 9-15 March, 351 Americans will be killed.

18 MARCH 1969

Vietnam War: Secret Bombing of Cambodia President Nixon orders US B-52's to attack suspected communist positions in Cambodia for the first time in the war. The mission, formally designated Operation Breakfast but finally known as the 'Menu' bombings, will involve a total of 3630 flights and some 110,000 tons of bombs dropped over Cambodia through April 1970. This bombing of Cambodia and all subsequent 'Menu' bombings will be kept secret from the American public and the US Congress. Among other things, the bombings will have a destabalizing effect on the Cambodian government.

3 APRIL 1969

Vietnam War: US Policy New Secretary of Defense Melvin Laird says the US is moving to 'Vietnamize' the war as rapidly as possible. America has already begun to turn over major military supplies to the South Vietnamese.
Vietnam War: Casualties US combat deaths for the week of 23-29 March raise the toll to 33,641 Americans killed in eight years of war – 12 more than fell during the Korean War. The communist offensive continues.

24-25 APRIL 1969

Vietnam War: Air War In two days of the heaviest bombing raids of the war, almost 100 B-52's drop nearly 3000 tons of bombs on a northwest border area.

9 MAY 1969

Vietnam War: US Government *New York Times* correspondent William Beecher publishes an article describing the secret US bombing raids in Cambodia. Immediately, presidential National Security Advisor Henry Kissinger asks the FBI to find the leak that led to Beecher's article. During the next two years Alexander Haig, a key Kissinger assistant, will transmit the names of National Security Council staff members and reporters who are to have their phones tapped by the FBI.

10-20 MAY 1969

Vietnam War: Battle of Hamburger Hill US and ARVN forces battle North Vietnamese troops for Hill 937, one mile east of the Laotian border. The battle is part of an allied sweep of the Ashua valley called Operation Apache Snow; its purpose is to cut off enemy there and stop infiltration from Laos. US paratroops, pushing northeast, find communist forces entrenched on Hill 937 and fierce fighting breaks out. The enemy withstands air strikes, artillery barrages and ten infantry assaults before 1400 allied troops fight their way to the summit. There are 597 NVA reported killed; US casualties are put at 56 killed and 420 wounded. Due to the intense fighting, Hill 937 is dubbed 'Hamburger Hill.' Commanders will order the hill abandoned on 28 May.

8 JUNE 1969

Vietnam War: US Withdrawal Begins At a Midway Island meeting between President Nixon and South Vietnamese President Thieu, Nixon announces that 25,000 US troops will be withdrawn before the end of August. The two leaders underscore the point that American forces will be replaced by South Vietnamese troops. The announcement produces gloom in Saigon and approval in the US.

10 JUNE 1969

South Vietnam The NLF announces the establishment of a Provisional Revolutionary Government (PRG) to rule South Vietnam. It is no different in substance from the NLF but is a clearer challenge to the Thieu government for political control of the South.

13 JUNE 1969

Vietnam: Air War Today Laotian premier Souvanna Phouma acknowledges publicly for the first time that US planes regularly carry out bombing raids in Laos. American B-52 missions over the Ho Chi Minh Trail there rise to 5567 in 1969; the planes, no longer permitted to bomb North Vietnam, are increasingly diverted to Laos and, in secret, to Cambodia.

8 JULY 1969

Vietnam War: US Withdrawal The American withdrawal begins as 814 men return to the US. In April, US forces in Vietnam had peaked at 543,000.

25 JULY 1969

US Policy: Nixon Doctrine At a news briefing in Guam, President Nixon discusses the future role of the US in Asia and the Pacific after the Vietnam War is over. Quickly dubbed the 'Nixon Doctrine,' these remarks are interpreted to mean that while the US will have primary responsibility for the defense of allies against nuclear attack, the non-communist Asian nations must bear their own burden of defense against conventional attack and their own responsibility for internal security.

3-9 AUGUST 1969

Vietnam War: Ground War In the lowest weekly US death toll since 12 August 1967, 96 Americans are reported killed.

4 AUGUST 1969

Vietnam War: Peace Talks Henry Kissinger and NLF negotiator Xuan Thuy hold the first of their secret meetings in Paris. Their only agreement is to keep open the new secret channel of communication.

17-26 AUGUST 1969

Vietnam War: Ground War US troops report killing at least 650 NVA in a fierce battle in the Queson Valley, 30 miles south of Danang. More than 60 Americans are reported dead in the fighting.

3 SEPTEMBER 1969

North Vietnam: Death of Ho Chi Minh Having led the Vietnamese Communist struggle against the French and the US since 1946, Ho Chi Minh dies in Hanoi at the age of 79. He will be succeeded by a collective leadership including Le Duan, Truong Chin, General Vo Nguyen Giap and Premier Pham Van Dong.

16 SEPTEMBER 1969

Vietnam War: US Withdrawal President Nixon announces a second round of US troop withdrawals of around 35,000 men. Such announcements – with accompanying lowering of draft calls – will accelerate in coming months as Vietnamization takes hold.

15 OCTOBER 1969

Vietnam War: Protest Hundreds of thousands of Americans participate in Moratorium Day events across the nation. In November, more than 250,000 will gather in Washington for the largest anti-war demonstration to date; the activities will be punctuated with tear-gas and arrests. Major protests are also mounted in England and Europe.

20 NOVEMBER 1969

Vietnam War: Peace Talks Henry Cabot Lodge resigns as head of the American delegation in Paris; he will be replaced by Philip Habib.

31 DECEMBER 1969

Vietnam War: State of the War It is clear that the new administration is making changes. Nixon is withdrawing US forces from their June peak of 543,000; they are now down to some 479,000, the lowest number in two years. American forces are also being withdrawn from Thailand, and the Australians and Philippines are beginning to withdraw. The communists also seem to be cutting back; they are now at an estimated 240,000, down from 290,000 in 1968. However, the war is far from over for Americans: US combat deaths in 1969 come to 9414, against 14,592 in 1968; to date, some 40,000 Americans have lost their lives in the fighting, 260,000 have been wounded and some 1400 listed as missing or captured. At least 6000 South Vietnamese civilians have been killed by terrorists this year.

17-18 JANUARY 1970

Vietnam War: Air War B-52 raids are mounted against North Vietnamese and Pathet Lao forces in northern Laos. The Nixon administration will attempt to cover up this extension of raids further north, but they will soon be revealed, producing strident Congressional and public criticism.

30 JANUARY 1970

Vietnam War: Air War After a 28 January incident in which a US reconnaissance plane was downed by a missile inside North Vietnam and American planes returned to attack the missile base, the US admits at the Paris peace talks that it sends planes daily over the North with fighter escorts, but denies that this violates last year's understanding about the bombing halt.

18 FEBRUARY 1970

Vietnam War: Protest The jury in the tumultuous trial of the 'Chicago Seven' (one of the original eight is to be tried separately) finds the defendants not guilty of conspiring to incite a riot in connection with the violence that took place in Chicago during the 1968 Democratic Convention. Five of the men are found guilty on a lesser charge of crossing state lines to incite a riot.

21 FEBRUARY 1970

Vietnam War: Peace Talks Presidential assistant Henry Kissinger and Le Duc Tho, a ranking member of the Hanoi Politburo, hold the first of three largely fruitless secret meetings in Paris.

18-20 MARCH 1970

Cambodia After much internal uproar over continuing communist activities in Cambodia, General Lon Nol, premier and defense minister, overthrows Prince Norodom Sihanouk in a bloodless coup. As Sihanouk flees to the communists for help, Lon Nol will head a troubled anti-communist administration. On the 20th Lon will ask for US and South Vietnamese aid in operating against Vietnamese communists within Cambodia.

27-28 MARCH 1970

Vietnam War: Invasion of Cambodia South Vietnamese troops, supported by artillery and air strikes, launch their first major operation into Cambodia.

28 APRIL 1970

Vietnam War: Invasion of Cambodia President Nixon authorizes commitment of US combat troops, in cooperation with ARVN units, against communist troop sanctuaries in Cambodia. Three National Security Council staff members and key aides to Kissinger resign in protest over the invasion. In announcing the operation on television on 30 April, Nixon will say that the intention is not to occupy Cambodian territory, since the border areas are 'completely occupied and controlled by North Vietnamese forces,' and adds, 'if . . . the world's most powerful nation . . . acts like a pitiful, helpless giant, the forces of totalitarianism . . . will threaten free nations and free institutions throughout the world.'

1 MAY 1970

Vietnam War: Invasion of Cambodia An offensive into Cambodia's Fishhook area is launched by a combined force of 8000 US and 2000 ARVN soldiers.

1-2 MAY 1970

Vietnam War: Air War Heavy bombing raids are carried out against targets in North Vietnam.

4 MAY 1970

Vietnam War: Killings at Kent State Campus reaction to the Cambodian invasion results in a confrontation between students and National Guard at Kent State University in Ohio. Four students die after guardsmen fire into the demonstrators. The tragedy will trigger other protests that shut down many American campuses and involve a wide range of citizens in anti-war activities for the first time.
Vietnam War: Cambodian Invasion About 20 miles north of the Fishhook area US troops reach a large communist base known as The City. Tomorrow, Nixon will make a 'firm commitment' to withdraw

Anti-war protesters gather on the Capitol steps in Washington on the evening of 14 October 1969. This was a prelude to a nationwide 'Vietnam Moratorium Day' that was held on the 15th.

US helicopters swarm about a landing zone where they are delivering supplies to support the South Vietnamese incursion into Laos in early 1971.

US troops from Cambodia in 3-7 weeks and not to penetrate farther than 21 miles without Congressional approval.

20 MAY 1970

Vietnam War: Invasion of Cambodia Supported by US air power and advisers, ARVN soldiers open a new front in Cambodia, 125 miles north of Saigon, bringing the number of South Vietnamese troops in the country to 40,000.

24 JUNE 1970

Vietnam War: US Government Reflecting frustration with the course of the war and their lack of control over it, the Senate votes 81-10 to repeal the Tonkin Gulf Resolution, which has given the president power to pursue the undeclared war.

29-30 JUNE 1970

Vietnam War: Invasion of Cambodia US combat troops end two months of operations in Cambodia and return to South Vietnam. A reported 354 Americans have been killed and 1689 wounded in the operation; ARVN casualties are 866 killed and 3724 wounded. South Vietnamese troops will remain in Cambodia into the summer, supported by US bombing, and will make occasional raids across the border well into 1971.

5 NOVEMBER 1970

Vietnam War: Ground War Releasing the lowest weekly death toll in five years, US command reports 24 Americans dead in combat in Indochina for the week of 25-31 October. It is also the fifth consecutive week that the US death toll has been below 50.

21 NOVEMBER 1970

Vietnam War: Ground War A combined Air Force and Army team of 50 Americans, led by Colonel 'Bull' Simon, lands by helicopter at the Sontay prison camp near Hanoi in an attempt to free American POW's supposed to be there. In support, US planes attack communist strongholds around the camp. The force finds no US prisoners, but kills 25 guards before escaping safely.

Vietnam War: Air War An hour after the Sontay raid US warplanes carry out their heaviest and most sustained bombing of North Vietnam since November 1968. Some 200 fighter-bombers and 50 support planes strike a wide variety of military targets. Defense Secretary Laird will claim that the strikes were all below the 19th parallel and in response to attacks on US reconnaissance planes.

31 DECEMBER 1970

Vietnam War: State of the War By year's end US forces in Vietnam are down to about 280,000. As both sides avoid large-unit confrontations, the 4204 dead US soldiers are largely victims of booby-traps, mortar attacks and sniper fire rather than battle. The progress of Vietnamization is shown by the 20,914 ARVN killed. An estimated 25,000 South Vietnamese civilians have been killed and another 6000 executed by the Vietcong for serving in the Saigon government. The invasion of Cambodia underlines how widespread and interrelated are the ongoing hostilities throughout Indochina. In Paris the peace talks are still stalemated.

3 JANUARY 1971

VietnamWar: Air War South Vietnam, Laos and Cambodia see intensive bombing raids by a large force of US B-52's and some 300 fighter-bombers. They are operating against communist supply and infiltration routes – and supporting Pathet Lao and Khmer Rouge (communist Cambodian) troops – along the Ho Chi Minh Trail.

22-24 JANUARY 1971

Vietnam War: Cambodia Communist commandos shell central Pnompenh, the capital, for the first time, while also penetrating the airport and destroying much of its military fleet. US air operations are greatly stepped up; later in the week Cambodian government forces clash with communists in several battles near Pnompenh.

8 FEBRUARY-6 APRIL 1971

Vietnam War: Operation Lam Son 719 The South Vietnamese army, aided by heavy US air support, launches Operation Lam Son 719 against the Ho Chi Minh Trail in Laos. In exceptionally heavy fighting the drive makes headway for a week, but then bogs down before stiffening enemy resistance. The ARVN will pull out of Laos in late March with up to 3800 killed and 5200 wounded; American losses include 450 dead and 104 helicopters downed. (Congress has banned US ground troops in Laos and Cambodia, but not air operations.) Both sides claim victory; in any case, traffic on the Ho Chi Minh Trail is soon back to normal.

18-23 APRIL 1971

Vietnam War: Air War US jets carry out the 30th raid since 1 January against missile sites and antiaircraft positions inside North Vietnam; it is the heaviest six-day period of raids since the November 1968 bombing halt.

3-5 MAY 1971

Vietnam War: Protest Militant anti-war demonstrations in Washington – with extensive participation by the Vietnam Veterans Against the War – end with 12,614 protestors arrested. Most of those arrested will be released within a day. At the same time, somewhat smaller demonstrations supporting the war are mounted this year by conservative, religious and labor groups.

13 JUNE-30 DECEMBER 1971

Vietnam War: Pentagon Papers The *New York Times* publishes portions (leaked mainly by Daniel Ellsberg, a disenchanted former Defense Department employee) of a 47-volume Pentagon analysis of how the US commitment in Indochina grew over a period of three decades. Their publication, with revelations of governmental coverups, bad judgment and general lack of direction about the war, creates a nationwide furor, with Congressional and diplomatic reverberations as all branches of government debate what constitutes 'classified' material and how much should be made public. Administration attempts to get an injunction against further publication will be turned down by the Supreme Court on 30 June.

1 JULY 1971

Vietnam War: US Withdrawal In the single largest troop pullout since phased withdrawal began in 1969, 6100 US soldiers from the Central Highlands depart, beginning a wind-down of the American combat role in that region. The majority of the some 236,000 US troops remaining in Vietnam are in the bitterly-contested northernmost provinces of the South. By the end of the month all US Marine combat units will be gone, leaving only Marine advisors and embassy guards. On the 9th the US will complete the DMZ turnover to the ARVN.

15 JULY 1971

US Government President Nixon discloses that he will visit Peking in 1972. The news, a prelude to long-delayed American recognition of Communist China, stuns the world – not least the North Vietnamese, who see the visit as courting their prime ally.

26 SEPTEMBER-9 OCTOBER 1971

Vietnam War: Cambodia These days show how the war is now being fought, as the much-improved Army of the Republic of Vietnam (ARVN) has taken over most of the fighting. The war has intensified along the Cambodian-South Vietnamese border, the ARVN, with US help, fighting off communist attacks. The allies begin a counteroffensive on the

A Navy RA-3 photo reconnaissance plane is set to take off from the *Coral Sea* to try to assess air strike damage in North Vietnam in 1972.

29th to reopen Route 22 between Tayninh and Krek. The 20,000 ARVN in Cambodia are reinforced, and the US command moves 1500 of its troops, with armored vehicles, to the front just inside South Vietnam. American B-52 bombers batter North Vietnamese positions inside Cambodia. During the offensive Saigon forces are able to lift two communist sieges of ARVN bases.

8 OCTOBER 1971

Vietnam War: Ground War After 399 days US Operation Jefferson Glenn in Thua Thien Province ends with a reported 2026 enemy casualties. This is the last major operation involving US ground forces.

19 NOVEMBER 1971

Vietnam War: Cambodia Relentless North Vietnamese and Vietcong pressure on the capital city of Pnompenh leads to a Cambodian call for more South Vietnamese military assistance. The ARVN will arrive in strength, with heavy US air support and – despite a Congressional ban – with US military advisors.

26 DECEMBER 1971

Vietnam War: Air War In the sharpest escalation of the war since the end of saturation bombing in November 1968 US fighter-bombers strike North Vietnamese airfields, missile sites and other targets for five straight days. Pentagon figures show that US planes, as many as 250 on a mission, have attacked northern targets over 100 times in 1971, a figure comparable to all US air activity in the previous 26 months. This step-up of the air war spurs new protests in the US.

31 DECEMBER 1971

VietnamWar: State of the War The gradual US withdrawal from the Indochina conflict is reflected in reduced casualty figures: the number of Americans killed in action drops to 1386 from the previous year's total of 4204. South Vietnam has lost some 21,500 soldiers, while the estimated – and probably inflated – communist dead total 97,000. US troops levels are now down to 159,000 and falling rapidly.

1 JANUARY 1972

Vietnam War: Air War In an attempt to disrupt an anticipated new communist Tet offensive US jets in January make nearly a third as many 'protective reaction' strikes in North Vietnam as in all of 1971.

13 JANUARY 1972

Vietnam War: US Withdrawal Nixon announces that withdrawals of 70,000 US troops in the next three months will reduce US strength in South Vietnam to 69,000. US combat deaths are now down to less than ten per week.

21 FEBRUARY 1972

International President Nixon begins his momentous visit to China, which he describes as a 'journey for peace.' The visit will conclude with pledges of normalization of relations. China continues to supply North Vietnam with arms and materiel, but relations between the two states are beginning to erode.

30 MARCH 1972

Vietnam War: Communist Spring Offensive Behind a wedge of Soviet-made tanks some 120,000 North Vietnamese cross the DMZ in the heaviest offensive since the sieges of Conthien and Khe Sanh in 1968. Hanoi believes that, with only 95,000 US troops now in the South and negotiations still shaky, this is the time for a major push. After initial losses over the next five weeks, including all of Quang Tri Province, ARVN and US resistance will stiffen. On 6 April, US planes will begin a course of retaliatory bombing that will climax on 16 April with strikes on fuel and supply facilities near Hanoi and Haiphong (the first raids in those areas in more than three years and the first ever with the massive B-52 bombers) and with the mining of major harbors in Haiphong and elsewhere. The public announcement on 8 May of the harbor minings will lead to anti-war demonstrations in the US, denunciations from the Communist Bloc and lukewarm support from European allies.

22 MAY 1972

Summit Meeting In the first peacetime visit to the Soviet Union by an American president, Nixon begins a week of talks with Russian leaders in Moscow. The summit will culminate in a landmark arms pact designed to balance missile forces and halt the nuclear arms race, as well as a trade agreement and a plan for a joint Soviet-US space mission in 1975.

JUNE 1972

Vietnam War: Air War Under President Nixon the number of USAF fighter-bombers and aircraft carriers in Southeast Asia has tripled, and the B-52 force is being quadrupled.

3 JUNE 1972

Vietnam War: War Crimes A secret Army analysis of the My Lai massacre concludes that the entire command structure of the American division suppressed information on the massacre. Further accusations of US atrocities will be made by American journalists in the next months.

20 JUNE 1972

Vietnam War: Command Nixon appoints General Creighton W. Abrams, commander of US forces in Vietnam, to be US Army chief of staff.

11 AUGUST 1972

Vietnam War: US Withdrawal The last US ground combat unit in Vietnam, the 3rd Battalion, 21st Infantry, is deactivated, leaving less than 44,600 US servicemen in the country – excluding Seventh Fleet sailors and military airmen. Heavy US air strikes continue in the North.

15 SEPTEMBER 1972

VietnamWar: Ground War In Saigon's most significant victory since the beginning of the communist spring offensive ARVN troops recapture the city of Quang Tri after four days of fierce combat. However, the rest of Quang Tri Province and much of the Central Highlands are still under communist control, and the North Vietnamese offensive continues.

3 OCTOBER 1972

Vietnam War: Air War The Department of Defense reports that over 800,000 tons of 'air ammunition' have been used over Indochina so far this year, compared with 763,160 for all of 1971. During the war to date the US has dropped on Indochina more than three times the tonnage of all Allied bombing in WW II.

26 OCTOBER 1972

Vietnam War: Peace Talks Returning from South Vietnam, Henry Kissinger says that peace is 'within reach in a matter of weeks or less.' The announcement, following mutual softening in negotiating positions and a preliminary draft of a cease-fire (which Thieu resists bitterly), comes just two weeks before the American presidental elections and thus strengthens Nixon's already strong position. But the agreement will soon break down, and negotiations will resume.

7 NOVEMBER 1972

National Richard Nixon is re-elected president over George McGovern, carrying all states but Massachusetts, with 97 percent of the electoral votes, in the lowest turnout since 1948. The Democrats widen their majority in Congress. Nixon pledges to secure 'peace with honor in Vietnam.'
Vietnam War: Air War US B-52's set a record for concentrated bombing of a single province – Quangtri – in a single day.

16 DECEMBER 1972

Vietnam War: Peace Talks Kissinger breaks silence on the ongoing secret talks and announces that they have failed to achieve what Nixon regards as a 'just and fair agreement to end the war.' The deadlock centers on the nature of an international supervisory team and on US insistence on Saigon's sovereignty over South Vietnam. Kissinger charges that Hanoi is to blame for the failure to reach an agreement.

18 DECEMBER 1972

Vietnam War: Christmas Bombing After the latest negotiating deadlock the Nixon administration announces the resumption of bombing and mining of North Vietnam, saying that full-scale raids will continue until 'such time as a settlement is arrived at.' US aircraft, beginning the most concentrated air offensive of the war (known as Linebacker II), will in 11 days drop 40,000 tons of bombs, mostly over the densely populated area between Hanoi and Haiphong. Hanoi will call the raids barbaric and insane.

31 DECEMBER 1972

Vietnam War: Christmas Bombing The most intense US bombing operation of the Vietnam War ends in light of a scheduled resumption of secret peace talks. During the bombing the North Vietnamese launched their entire stock of over 1200 Soviet surface-to-air missiles, downing 15 giant B-52's and 11 other US aircraft; 93 American flyers are dead, missing or captured. The raids have stimulated anti-war sentiment around the world, but they appear to have brought the North Vietnamese back to the bargaining table.

8-23 JANUARY 1973

Vietnam War: Peace Talks Kissinger and Le Duc Tho resume peace talks in Paris. A preliminary agreement is reached on 9 January, and a joint announcement issued on 18 January says that the two will meet again on 23 January to complete the agreement. As a result, on the 15th Nixon suspends hostilities against North Vietnam – but not in the South, where the war intensifies as both sides try to gain territory before a cease-fire. On the 23rd, after an agreement is initialed, a cease-fire is scheduled to go into effect at 0800 hours 28 January, Saigon time. Truces are also planned in Laos and Cambodia.

27 JANUARY 1973

Vietnam War: South Vietnam As of today Saigon controls about 75 percent of South Vietnam's territory and 85 percent of its population. The Army of the Republic of South Vietnam is well-equipped with US weapons and will continue to receive US aid after the ostensible cease-fire; the South Vietnamese Air Force is now the fourth largest in the world. The CIA estimates North Vietnamese presence in the South at 145,000 men.
Vietnam War: National Defense Secretary Melvin Laird announces the end of the military draft in America.
Vietnam War: Casualties The last US serviceman to die in combat in Vietnam, Lieutenant Colonel William B. Nolde, is killed by an artillery shell at Anloc. US involvement in the war, which began 20 years ago under the Truman administration, has claimed 56,379 American lives, nearly a million esti-

The culmination of years of negotiation, both open and secret, came in Paris on 27 January 1973 with the signing of the 'Agreement Ending the War.'

mated communist dead and several million Vietnamese civilians presumed dead. The official cost of the war will be set by the US at $139 billion; only WW II cost more.

Vietnam War: Paris Peace Accords 'An Agreement Ending the War and Restoring Peace in Vietnam' is signed in Paris by the US, North Vietnam, South Vietnam and the National Liberation Front (Vietcong). Among its stipulations: a cease-fire throughout Vietnam; withdrawal of all US troops and advisors (now totalling about 23,700) and dismantling of all US bases within 60 days; release of all US and other POW's within 60 days; continuance in place of North Vietnamese troops in the South; withdrawal of all foreign troops from Laos and Cambodia; the DMZ as provisional dividing line pending eventual peaceful reunification of the country; an international control commission to supervise the agreement; continuance of the Thieu government in the South pending elections; respect for the South Vietnamese people's 'right to self-determination'; no military movement across the DMZ. Few of these provisions will be honored: both sides will continue military build-up and hostilities, America will continue bombing Cambodia into August and in a little over two years the North will invade and conquer the South.

7 FEBRUARY 1973

National: Watergate Investigation The Senate establishes a Select Committee on Presidential Campaign Activities to investigate the Watergate conspiracy; hearings will begin in May. Over the next months unfolding revelations about Watergate and other criminal efforts, and a subsequent high-level attempt to cover them up, will weaken the Nixon administration bit by bit as legal prosecutions and forced resignations climb the ladder toward the White House and the president.

12-27 FEBRUARY 1973

POWs The return of US POWs begins with North Vietnam's release of 142 men in Hanoi. The release program will continue, though the question of whether all POWs and MIAs have been accounted for by the North will persist until the present.

MARCH 1973

North Vietnam Spurred by recent ARVN gains and the absence of American bombs, Hanoi launches a logistical program to prepare for a major offensive.

29 MARCH 1973

South Vietnam The last US troops depart, leaving only a Defense Attaché office and a few Marine guards at the American Embassy in Saigon. Some 8500 US civilians stay on.

POWs Hanoi releases the last 67 of its acknowledged POWs, bringing the total number relased to 587.

16 JUNE 1973

International Soviet leader Leonid Brezhnev begins talks with President Nixon. The two will agree to avoid confrontations that might precipitate a nuclear war and will prepare for negotiation of a strategic arms limitation treaty.

16 JULY 1973

National The Senate Armed Forces Committee begins hearings on US secret bombing raids into Cambodia during 1969 and 1970. The fact that the Senate was given false reports about the bombings will merge with the developing Watergate investigation to destroy the Nixon presidency.

10 OCTOBER 1973

National Vice President Spiro Agnew resigns after pleading 'no contest' to a charge of tax evasion stemming from illegal payments by contractors who sought favors while Agnew was governor of Maryland. Nixon will nominate House minority leader Gerald R. Ford to succeed Agnew, and Congress will approve.

7 NOVEMBER 1973

National Congress passes the War Powers Act over the president's veto. The bill is an attempt to restrain the executive's power to commit US troops into foreign countries for indefinite periods without Congressional approval.

27 JANUARY 1974

Vietnam Since the January 1973 truce and supposed cease-fire 13,788 South Vietnamese soldiers, 2159 South Vietnamese civilians and 45,057 Communist soldiers have died in the ongoing fighting.

27-30 JULY 1974

National After six months of investigation by the Senate Watergate Committee, the House Judiciary Committee votes three articles of impeachment against President Nixon, charging obstruction of justice, abuse of power and contempt of Congress.

9 AUGUST 1974

National President Nixon resigns, and Vice-President Gerald R. Ford is sworn in as the nation's first unelected president. On 8 September President Ford will issue Nixon an unconditional pardon, arousing criticism that will later contribute to Ford's losing the presidency.

11 AUGUST 1974

South Vietnam Congress settles on $700 million in military aid to South Vietnam (the 1973 figure was $2.8 billion, the 1975 figure will be $300 million). In December, South Vietnam will report that 80,000 of its soldiers have been killed in the year's fighting.

24 MARCH 1975

Vietnam: Ho Chi Minh Campaign Having captured Phuoc Long Province in January and Banmethout in March, and with the ARVN withdrawing in disorder from the Central Highlands, Hanoi's Ho Chi Minh Campaign begins; it is intended to conquer the South before the rains begin in May.

1 APRIL 1975

Vietnam: Ho Chi Minh Campaign The communist offensive continues to make giant strides, pushing the ARVN back in waves. More than half of South Vietnam's territory is now controlled by the North Vietnamese. During the first week of April, communist forces push into Long An Province, just south of Saigon. Thousands of refugees are in flight from the offensive. In America, the government and the people are doing their best to ignore the final collapse of all America fought for in Vietnam.

16 APRIL 1975

Cambodian Holocaust Under insurgent military pressure from all sides the Lon Nol government surrenders to the Khmer Rouge, ending the five-year war. A new constitution in December will establish a People's Assembly headed by Pol Pot, whose regime will pursue one of the most inhuman campaigns of murder in history. Its victims over the next three years will number an almost unbelievable two to four million Cambodians.

29-30 APRIL 1975

Vietnam: Fall of Saigon The Saigon government surrenders to the victorious communists. Option IV, the largest helicopter evacuation on record, begins removing the last Americans from Saigon, among them US Ambassador Graham Martin. In 19 hours 81 helicopters carry more than 1000 Americans and almost 6000 Vietnamese to offshore carriers. Thousands of 'boat people' will flee South Vietnam as the communists consolidate their hold; many of the fugitives will eventually be picked up by US ships off the coast.

14 MAY 1975

International: *Mayaguez* Incident President Ford orders a ground, air and sea operation to recover the US cargo vessel *Mayaguez*, seized by the Cambodian Khmer Rouge two days ago in the Gulf of Siam; the communists accused the ship of spying. Both the

As North Vietnamese troops near the city in 1975 frantic Saigonese scramble onto a bus bound for the relative safety of the US embassy.

Mayaguez and its crew are recovered, but in the process 38 American Marines are killed and 49 are wounded.

16 MAY 1975

Refugees Congress votes $405 million to aid South Vietnamese refugees, of whom 130,000 will resettle in the US.

28 MAY 1976

International The US and the Soviet Union sign a five-year agreement limiting underground nuclear explosions and providing for on-site inspection.

2 JULY 1976

Vietnam After almost 20 years of continuous warfare North and South Vietnam are officially reunited into one nation, with Hanoi as its capital. North Vietnamese prime minister Pham Van Dong becomes prime minister in the new Northern-dominated government. Saigon will later be renamed Ho Chi Minh City.

2 NOVEMBER 1976

National Jimmy Carter defeats Gerald Ford to become the nation's 39th president, taking 297 electoral votes to the incumbent's 241.

3 MAY 1977

US/Vietnam The two countries begin talks in Paris toward normalizing relations. Although both sides will express satisfaction over the discussions, the US still refuses to provide financial assistance. Vietnam will be admitted to the UN in September with no US objections.

21 SEPTEMBER 1977

International The USA, USSR and 13 other nations sign a nuclear nonproliferation pact aimed at limiting the spread of atomic weapons.

17 SEPTEMBER 1978

International Private talks, mediated by President Carter, between Egyptian President Anwar Sadat and Israeli Prime Minister Menachem Begin end today at Camp David, Maryland. Concluding a diplomatic triumph for Carter, the two sign the 'Camp David Accords,' establishing a timetable for peace negotiations that will lead to a peace treaty in March 1979.

27 NOVEMBER 1978

Refugees The US decides to raise the ceiling on 'boat people' to 47,000 allowed to settle in the US; these people are among the hundreds of thousands fleeing persecution in Laos, Cambodia and Vietnam.

16 JANUARY 1979

Iran Ending 37 years of rule, the last few under an increasing escalation of unrest and governmental repression, Shah Mohammed Reza Pahlavi leaves Iran. The new ruler will be Ayatollah Khomeini, who will institute a strict Islamic regime with a violently anti-American cast (the US has been a major supporter of the Shah).

18 JUNE 1979

International President Carter and Soviet President Leonid Brezhnev sign the SALT II agreement in Vienna; the treaty, limiting long-range nuclear missiles and bombers, will never be ratified by Congress, but both sides will comply with it into the Reagan administration.

4 NOVEMBER 1979

Iran Hostage Crisis Around 500 Iranian students seize the US embassy in Teheran, taking about 90 hostages including 65 Americans. The militants vow to hold the hostages until the Shah, who is receiving medical treatment in the US, is returned to Iran to stand trial. In response, President Carter will order deportation of Iranian students in America, suspend Iranian oil imports and freeze Iranian assets in the US. By the end of the month the students will release female, black and non-American hostages, but the rest will remain captive until 1981, putting a fatal strain on American public support of Carter.

12 DECEMBER 1979

International NATO members, except France and Greece, agree to install 572 American medium-range nuclear missiles in Europe by 1983. These missiles will be the first in Europe capable of hitting targets within the Soviet Union.

24 JANUARY 1980

International In a major policy shift, President Carter announces that his administration is willing to sell weapons to Communist China. This decision is part of the administration's response to a Soviet armed intervention in December to support their puppet government in Afghanistan. Soviet forces will be unable to subdue Afghan guerrilla resistance over the next years.

24 APRIL 1980

Iran Hostage Crisis After several months of diplomatic maneuvers to gain the release of the hostages President Carter calls off a secret military rescue mission that has become a debacle: three of eight helicopters involved in the mission break down, and in attempting to escape after the abort, another helicopter collides with a transport plane, killing eight Americans. This ill-fated rescue attempt leads Secretary of State Cyrus Vance (who opposed the scheme) to resign.

4 NOVEMBER 1980

National Ronald Reagan resoundingly defeats Jimmy Carter for president, winning 489 electoral votes to 49 for Carter. The victory reflects public dissatisfaction with Carter's inability to make progress against inflation, to bring the Iran hostages home or to halt the Russian invasion of Afghanistan.

20 JANUARY 1981

Iran Hostage Crisis As Ronald Reagan is sworn in as president the 52 remaining American hostages are released after 444 days of captivity. In exchange for the hostages the US has agreed to some Iranian demands, including unfreezing most Iranian assets in America.

2 MARCH 1981

El Salvador With a brutal civil war raging in El Salvador between leftist guerrillas and government troops supporting President José Napoleon Duarte, the Reagan administration announces it will send 20 more advisors and $25 million in military equipment to help the Duarte junta.

2 OCTOBER 1981

Military Procurement President Reagan presents a five-point program to strengthen America's military defense system and calling for building 100 B-1 bombers and 100 MX missiles. In general, Reagan will significantly escalate the military budget while slashing away at nonmilitary spending. Reagan's goal is to build up both US nuclear capacity and also its conventional forces.

19 MARCH 1982

Central America The Reagan administration increases the number of US military advisors in El Salvador to 100 and sends a contingent of Green Berets to Honduras to train soldiers patrolling that country's border with El Salvador. The administration has also begun turning its attention to Nicara-

Hundreds of thousands of South Vietnamese fled the country after the North's victory. Here, refugee boats seen from a US ship in the South China Sea.

Families greet the last 52 hostages returning from 444 days of captivity in Iran on 20 January 1981, the same day Ronald Reagan is inaugurated.

gua, where leftist Sandanista revolutionaries ousted dictator Anastsio Somoza in 1979; the US accuses the Sandanistas of trying to help Cuba export revolution to other Central American countries.

6 JUNE 1982

Lebanon The Israeli army invades southern Lebanon, claiming it must drive out Palestinians who have shelled Israel from this area. The country is already devastated by a civil war between Moslem and Christian factions.

19-30 AUGUST 1982

Lebanon Israel agrees to a plan calling for a multinational peacekeeping force of troops from the US, France, and Italy to move into Beirut as the Israelis and their Syrian and Palestinian enemies mutually withdraw (this withdrawal will be indefinitely delayed). US Marines land on the 25th, to be withdrawn temporarily in September.

17-18 SEPTEMBER 1982

Lebanon Christian Phalangist militiamen are allowed by the Israeli Army to enter Palestinian refugee camps in West Beirut, where the Christians massacre 800 men, women and children. In the wake of this atrocity US, French and Italian troops will immediately return to Beirut to try and keep peace.

13 NOVEMBER 1982

Vietnam War Memorial The Vietnam War Memorial is dedicated in Washington, DC. Designed by Yale student Maya Ying Li, it consists of two sunken black granite walls simply inscribed with the names of all Americans killed in the war. The monument receives much initial criticism because it carries no inscription characterizing the war and no heroic statuary; but over the years it will become a focus for the nation's conscience, perhaps the most telling and moving war memorial of all.

14 FEBRUARY 1983

Central America Around 1600 US and 4000 Honduran troops engage in war games near the border of Nicaragua, which has increasingly been the target of Reagan sabre-rattling. In March the ruling Nicaraguan Sandanistas will charge that 2000 American-backed rebels have invaded from Honduras.

23 MARCH 1983

Strategic Defense Initiative President Reagan calls for development of a new anti-missile system deployed in space to be developed over the next years, involving a vast coordination of as-yet undeveloped technologies, including nuclear-powered lasers and particle beams. The system is called the Strategic Defense Initiative but comes popularly to be called 'Star Wars.' A major shift in US military doctrine from nuclear retaliation to destroying enemy missiles in flight, the program will receive both massive funding in the next years and massive criticism from those who claim it is destabilizing or unworkable. The USSR denounces SDI as an offensive system intended to carry warfare into space, but plainly the Soviets are worried about the technological advantages the program might give the US.

18 APRIL 1983

Lebanon The US embassy in Beirut is almost demolished by a car-bomb that kills over 50 people; it is believed that this action is sponsored by radical Iranian Moslems. In August escalating attacks by Druse Moslem militia will kill four US Marines and four French soldiers of the peacekeeping force.

25 MAY 1983

El Salvador Navy commander Albert Schaufelberger is killed by leftist guerrillas in El Salvador.

12-19 OCTOBER 1983

Grenada Maurice Bishop, leftist Prime Minister of the tiny Caribbean island nation, is arrested by a more radical group led by General Hudson Austin; a week later Bishop and 16 supporters are killed by the insurgents. The US has been concerned about Cuban support of the Grenadan leftists and about Cuban military advisors in Grenada. Moreover, the deteriorating conditions after the coup threaten some 700 Americans, most of them medical students, on the island.

23 OCTOBER 1983

Lebanon A truck filled with explosives, driven by a suicidal Moslem, crashes into the US Marine barracks in Beirut; in the ensuing explosion 237 Marines are killed and 80 wounded. A coordinated bombing of French military quarters claims 58 dead. The Islamic Holy War, a pro-Iranian Shiite Moslem group, is apparently responsible. President Reagan and military leaders will receive much criticism for inadequate precautions and for sending the Marines to police the civil war in Lebanon in the first place.

25 OCTOBER 1983

Invasion of Grenada Early in the morning 1900 US Marines and Army Rangers and 300 Caribbean troops invade Grenada, meeting much more resistance than had been expected from Grenadan leftists and some 600 Cuban military advisors. Most of the resistance is put down on the first day, but around 400 Grenadans and Cubans hole up and resist with mortar and sniper fire for several days. By 28 October some 6000 US Marines, Rangers and paratroops are on the island; mopping up goes on for nearly three weeks, by which time 18 US troops have been killed and 116 wounded. Enemy dead are put at 25 Cubans and 45 Grenadans; the remaining Cubans and Communist-Bloc diplomats are expelled. Extensive caches of ammunition and weapons for the Cuban troops are discovered around the island. For their part, most of the islanders seem to welcome the invasion, but world opinion is largely critical, with a wide-margin UN General Assembly resolution 'deeply deploring' the invasion and British Prime Minister Margaret Thatcher expressing 'very considerable doubts.' The last US military forces will depart in mid-December, leaving 300 noncombat troops on the island.

7 FEBRUARY 1984

Lebanon In effect conceding defeat of the US peacekeeping force in Lebanon after the bombing of the Marine barracks in Beirut, President Reagan orders the Marines to withdraw from the country.

APRIL 1984

Nicaragua It is revealed that the US has mined harbors in Nicaragua; this being a violation of international law, conservative Senator Barry Goldwater observes 'I don't see how we are going to explain it.' After Congressional and worldwide condemnation of the mining, the administration announces that it has been halted.

MAY 1984

Middle East As part of the hostilities in the long-running war between Iraq and Iran, both countries attack neutral shipping in the Persian Gulf; the countries attacked decline a US offer of air protection for the ships, but Saudi Arabia accepts American anti-aircraft missiles.

6 NOVEMBER 1984

National Ronald Reagan is returned to the Oval Office by a landslide, carrying 49 states. The Republicans retain control of the Senate; the Democrats control the House.

24 APRIl 1985

Nicaragua Despite mighty efforts by the administration, the House kills a resolution giving aid to the anti-Sandanista Contra rebels in Nicaragua. However, Sandanista leader Daniel Ortega quickly alienates the US Congress from his government by visiting Russia on 28 April to discuss assistance; in June, Congress will approve $27 million in nonmilitary aid for the Contras.

OCTOBER 1985

***Achille Lauro* Incident** Yet another terrorist incident unfolds in the Middle East when four Palestinians seize the Italian cruise ship *Achille Lauro* near Port Said, Egypt, on the 7th. On the 9th the hijackers surrender after killing American tourist Leon Klinghoffer and throwing his body overboard. Egypt releases the terrorists to the anti-Israeli Palestine Liberation Organization, placing them on an airliner to Tunis on the 10th. President Reagan orders Navy F-14 fighters to intercept the airliner; they successfully force the plane to land in Italy, where the hijackers are arrested and charged with murder and kidnapping.

Above: The presidency of Ronald Reagan saw a rise in military spending, a new assertiveness in US foreign policy and the most impressive gains in international arms control yet made.

Right: A crippled veteran gazes thoughtfully at the Vietnam War Memorial in Washington, DC.

15 APRIL 1986

Attack on Libya Having gained 'irrefutable' proof of Libyan involvement in a 5 April terrorist bombing of a discotheque in West Berlin that killed two and injured 200, President Reagan orders a US bombing attack on the Tripoli area, among the targets being the headquarters of militantly anti-American Libyan leader Muammar al-Quaddafi. The 32 planes also strike the airport, a suspected terrorist training site, and military barracks, losing one F-111 and two crew dead to anti-aircraft fire. Though Quaddafi is uninjured, little will be heard of him for months after the raid.

25 JUNE 1986

Nicaragua Following a similar Senate vote, the House approves giving $100 million in military aid to the Nicaraguan Contras.

5 OCTOBER 1986

Nicaragua A major scandal over covert activities within the Reagan administration begins to unfold when a plane is shot down by the Sandanistas in Nicaragua. Dead in the crash are two Americans, but surviving American Eugene Hasenfus will reveal during his trial in Nicaragua that the CIA was involved in these flights over the past year to supply the Contras – despite a preceding Congressional ban on aid to the anti-communist rebels. Hasenfus will be convicted at the trial, but then released to the US. Polls show that most Americans are against aid to the Contras, and the rebels have been charged with drug-smuggling and terrorism.

11-12 OCTOBER 1986

Iceland Summit At a summit meeting between President Reagan and Soviet President Mikhail Gorbachev in Reykjavik, Iceland, the Soviet leader surprises the Americans with a wide-ranging proposal for arms reductions, all of it predicated on US abandoning of 'Star Wars' research. When Reagan refuses to compromise the summit breaks up with no substantial agreements; but in the aftermath the meeting proves to be a decisive advance in ongoing US/Russian arms-reduction talks and will lead to far more fruitful summit meetings in the future.

3-6 NOVEMBER 1986

Iran-Contra Affair First in a Beirut magazine, then in American papers, the story breaks that America has sold military arms to arch-enemy Iran in exchange for the release of three American hostages held by Moslem extremists. The next weeks will see a gradual unravelling of the affair, with much government denial and obfuscation. During this time it will be discovered that some of the money from the arms sales was earmarked for the Contras in Nicaragua, despite a Congressional ban on such aid.

5 MAY 1987

The Iran-Contra Affair A Joint Congressional Committee opens public hearings on the Iran-Contra affair. Weeks of testimony by figures involved (including former national security advisors Robert McFarlane and Admiral John Poindexter and national security staff member Colonel Oliver North) will reveal a secret apparatus within the White House that conducted foreign policy initiatives – including selling arms to Iran to influence terrorists and supplying the Contras – without the knowledge of the public and even, apparently, of President Reagan. One of the principals in the affair, former CIA director William Casey, has recently died, taking with him a good many details of this fabric of covert operations.

17 MAY 1987

Persian Gulf For some time US Navy ships have been escorting US merchantmen in the Persian Gulf to protect them from air or sea attack by either of the participants in the long-standing Iran-Iraq war. Today an Iraqi warplane makes a mistaken attack on the frigate USS *Stark*. A sea-skimming Exocet missile hits the *Stark*, tearing a hole in her side and killing 37 crewmen, but the ship survives. Iraq apologizes immediately, but the incident raises troubling questions about the Navy's proper role in the Gulf and about what 'rules of engagement' US warships should follow in the future when exposed to possible attack.

22 JULY 1987

Persian Gulf Kuwaiti tankers begin sailing in the Persian Gulf under American flags and with American naval protection, part of President Reagan's controversial program to protect neutral shipping from the depredations of Iraq and Iran.

22-31 JULY 1987

International Soviet leader Mikhail Gorbachev, in an interview published on 22 July, says the USSR would like to eliminate intermediate nuclear forces throughout the world. On 23 July, at the Geneva arms-control talks, the Soviets formally offer to stop basing nuclear warheads anywhere in their territory if the US would reciprocate. On 31 July the Soviets present a draft treaty on reducing long-range nuclear weapons, but they make it conditional on America's curbing its Strategic Defense Initiative ('Star Wars').

28 AUGUST-3 SEPTEMBER 1987

Persian Gulf Iran and Iraq step up the 'tanker war' in the Persian Gulf, and 20 ships of both sides are hit during these six days.

21 SEPTEMBER 1987

Persian Gulf A US Navy helicopter gunship fires on and hits an Iranian ship laying mines in the Persian Gulf. Three Iranian sailors are killed and 26 are taken prisoner; the latter are turned over to the Iranians.

8 OCTOBER 1987

Persian Gulf US Navy helicopter gunships sink three Iranian patrol boats in the Persian Gulf after one fired on the helicopters that were patrolling the passage of oil tankers.

15 OCTOBER 1987

Persian Gulf Off Kuwait the tanker *Sungari,* flying the Liberian flag but American owned, is struck by an Iranian missile.

General Manuel Noriega, Panamanian strongman and convicted drug lord, successfully resisted all US efforts to dislodge him until December 1989.

A Nicaraguan anti-Sandinista Contra guerrilla. The Reagan administration's support of the Contras was one of the president's most controversial policies.

16 OCTOBER 1987

Persian Gulf The Kuwaiti tanker *Sea Isle City*, flying the US flag, is struck by an Iranian missile; 18 seamen are injured.

19 OCTOBER 1987

Persian Gulf In retaliation for Iranian attacks on tankers the US first warns Iranians to abandon an offshore oil rig used as a base for gunboats and then four US destroyers fire on the rig and destroy it.

8 DECEMBER 1987

International: INF Treaty Soviet leader Mikhail Gorbachev, in Washington for the long-promised summit meeting, signs the first treaty (known as the Intermediate-Range Nuclear Forces – or INF – Treaty) calling for the dismantling of Soviet and American nuclear weapons: the Soviets will dismantle 859 intermediate- and short-range missiles (300-3400 miles) and the US will dismantle 1752. The treaty calls for each country to station inspection teams in the other to see that the provisions are carried out. The US Senate will ratify this treaty on 27 May 1988.

17 FEBRUARY 1988

Lebanon US Marine Lt. Colonel William Higgins, on temporary assignment to the UN peacekeeping force, is kidnapped near the city of Tyre. His abductors charge that Higgins is working for the CIA. He becomes the 20th foreigner held hostage in Lebanon.

26 FEBRUARY 1988

Panama The US conflict with Panamanian strongman General Manuel Noriega has been heating up since US federal grand juries have indicted him on charges of aiding international drug traffickers. With US encouragement, Panama's President Eric Arturo Delvalle has tried to fire Noriega, but today the pro-Noriega National Assembly ousts Delvalle, and he goes into hiding in fear for his life.

2 MARCH 1988

Panama The US State Department advises US banks to disburse no more money to Noriega and the present Panamanian government. Strikes will spread throughout Panama, and the US government will put its payments to the Panama Canal Commission in escrow, but Noriega will survive.

17 MARCH 1988

Central America Over 3000 US combat soldiers are landed at an air base in Honduras after that country claims that Nicaraguan troops have crossed its border in pursuit of Contra forces. The Contras are never engaged, and the US troops are withdrawn starting 28 March.

23 MARCH 1988

Nicaragua After three days of talks Nicaraguan Defense Minister Humberto Ortega and Contra leader Adolfo Calero sign an agreement for a 60-day ceasefire and for continuation of negotiations. The refusal of the US Congress to appropriate more military aid has forced the Contras to this, but the Congress, on 30-31 March, will approve $47.9 million in humanitarian aid.

5-7 APRIL 1988

Panama The US sends 1300 Marines to support security duties at US bases in Panama. On 8 April 800 other Marines will arrive for a previously scheduled jungle training course.

14 APRIL 1988

Persian Gulf A US Navy frigate hits an underwater mine in the Persian Gulf; ten sailors are injured.

The wreckage of the residence of Libyan leader Muammar al-Quaddafi in the aftermath of the US air strike on Tripoli on 15 April 1986.

18-19 APRIL 1988

Persian Gulf In a series of engagements between US Navy and Iranian vessels and airplanes several Iranian boats are sunk, and one US helicopter is lost, with its two crewmen.

3 JULY 1988

Persian Gulf In the Persian Gulf the crew of the guided missile cruiser USS *Vincennes,* mistaking an approaching airplane for an Iranian military aircraft, fires off SM-2MR missiles that down an Iranian airliner, killing all 290 passengers and crew. President Reagan calls it a tragic but understandable accident because the ship had been involved only shortly before this in a skirmish with Iranian boats.

28 JULY 1988

US-Vietnam Officials of these countries reach an agreement to conduct a survey to resolve questions about US military personnel still carried as Missing in Action during the Vietnam War.

10 AUGUST 1988

National President Reagan signs a measure calling for the creation of a $1.25 billion trust fund to compensate Japanese-Americans who were forced to relocate during World War II.

12 OCTOBER 1988

National The US Congress passes a bill calling for the closing of many obsolete military facilities. If carried through, this would mean the end of some of the best-known military bases in the US.

8 NOVEMBER 1988

National The Republican ticket of George Bush and J. Danforth Quayle defeats the Democratic ticket of Michael Dukakis and Lloyd Bentsen, Jr., by a margin of 54 percent to 46 percent of the popular vote and 426 to 112 of the electoral college votes.

7 DECEMBER 1988

USSR Soviet President Mikhail Gorbachev announces a plan to reduce overall Soviet armed forces by 500,000 men and to reduce Soviet conventional arms in European Russia and Eastern Europe by 10,000 tanks, 8500 artillery pieces and 800 aircraft. Although the move is unilateral, it will put pressure on the new Bush administration to reciprocate and will intensify the growing debate in NATO about the alliance's proper military posture. Even with the proposed Soviet cuts, the Warsaw Pact will still enjoy a 3:2 quantitative conventional superiority over NATO.

21 DECEMBER 1988

Libya-USA President Reagan, in an interview with ABC News, says that the US is 'discussing' with its allies the possibility of taking some military action against a new chemical plant in Libya that the US charges is designed to make chemical warfare weapons. Libya denies this, but most US allies are convinced that the plant at least has the potential to make such weapons.

4 JANUARY 1989

Libya-USA Two US Navy F-14 fighter planes, on a training exercise in international waters off Libya, shoot down two Libyan MiG-23 fighters that they claim were pursuing them and were armed. Libya claims its planes were unarmed, though aerial photographs indicate the contrary. The US denies that the incident has any connection with the controversy over the Libyan chemical weapons plant.

11 JANUARY 1989

International At a conference of 149 nations in Paris delegates agree to 'solemnly affirm their commitment not to use chemical weapons and condemn such use.' This represents a compromise between those who want nations such as the USA and the USSR to destroy their stockpiles of weapons and those who want to force less developed nations to promise not to make any chemical weapons of their own.

31 JANUARY 1989

Iran-Contra Affair The trial of former Marine Lt. Colonel Oliver North opens in federal district court in Washington, D.C. As the first of those implicated to stand trial, North has fought to have the entire case against him dismissed on the grounds that he cannot get a fair trial without breaching national security. Although the charges are reduced to 12 felony counts relating to his personal actions, implicit questions will inevitably be raised about the policies of the Reagan administration. On 4 May North will be found guilty on three of the counts.

19 APRIL 1989

US Navy During firing practice in a training exercise off Puerto Rico there is an explosion in the second gun turret on the battleship USS *Iowa,* and 47 seamen are killed or burnt to death almost instantly. The exact cause, whether a human or mechanical failure, remains in doubt, but it is an especially bitter loss because the *Iowa* fought through World War II and the Korean War without suffering any casualties among its crew.

7 MAY 1989

Panama National elections take place amid massive intimidation and vote fraud by Noriega henchmen. Despite this, it soon becomes clear that the anti-Noriega candidates have won an overwhelming victory. Noriega responds by declaring his own candidates the winners and by having thugs beat up two of the leading opposition candidates in the streets of Panama City. Outraged, President Bush calls on Noriega to resign and sends an additional 2000 US troops to Panama to protect US interests there.

30 MAY 1989

NATO A simmering debate in NATO is, at least for the moment, put to rest when President Bush persuades other NATO leaders to accept the US view that negotiations with the Soviets on conventional arms reductions should precede discussions on reducing short-range nuclear forces (SNF). The earlier insistance by some NATO members, led by West Germany, that SNF talks begin immediately is indicative of growing divergences of opinion within the alliance.

20 DECEMBER 1989

Panama US Army and Marine forces invade Panama. The intention is to oust strongman Manuel Noriega and bring him to the United States, where he is wanted on drug charges, as well as to install in his stead the government of Guillermo Endara, who won the national election in May. There is sporadic resistance by Noriega henchmen in Panama City, but by Christmas the country has been pacified, with US battle deaths amounting to less than 30. Noriega himself eludes capture and is given sanctuary in the Panama City offices of the Papal Nuncio, from which the Vatican will refuse to release him into US or Panamanian custody.

Vice President George Bush (with wife Barbara) in New Orleans to receive the Republican nomination for the presidency. Bush won the election by an overwhelming 426 electoral votes.

Index

Page numbers in *italics* refer to illustrations

Acknowledgments

The publisher would like to thank the following people who helped in the preparation of this book: David Eldred, who designed it; John Kirk, who edited the text; Rita Longabucco, who did the picture research; and Elizabeth McCarthy, who prepared the index.

Picture Credits

The Bettmann Archive: 10(both), 11(top), 13(bottom), 14(both), 16(top), 22(top), 24(top), 30(top), 32(bottom), 34(top left, bottom), 35(top), 39, 40(bottom right), 41, 42(top), 49(top left), 102(top), 113(bottom), 114(bottom), 116(both), 119(bottom), 120(bottom), 121(top).
Brompton Photo Library: 104(top), 117(top), 118(bottom), 125(both), 137(bottom), 139(bottom), 140(top), 152(both), 163(top).
Anne S. K. Brown Military Collection, Brown University: 20(bottom), 28(top), 50(top), 61(top), 63(top right), 66, 71(bottom), 76(top), 78(left), 80(both), 83(both), 98(bottom).
Bundesarchiv: 114(top right), 129(bottom), 131(left).
Chicago Historical Society: 57(bottom), 62(top), 72(top), 75.
Dwight D. Eisenhower Library: 160(bottom).
Illinois State Historical Library: 49(bottom), 60(top).
Imperial War Museum: 117(bottom), 128(top both), 130(both), 132(top), 135, 136(bottom), 143(bottom).
LBJ Library: 168(top).
JFK Library: 165(top).
Library of Congress: 8(both), 9, 12(top), 13(top), 15(both), 22(bottom), 23(bottom), 26(both), 29, 30(bottom), 31, 33(both), 36(both), 42(bottom), 44(both), 49(top right), 52(both), 53(both), 54(both), 55(top), 56, 58(both), 60(bottom), 61(bottom), 62(bottom), 63(top left, bottom), 64, 65(top both), 67(both), 68(top), 70(bottom), 71(top), 72(bottom), 74(top, bottom right), 76(bottom left), 77, 78(right), 79(both), 81, 82(top), 85(bottom), 86(bottom), 87(bottom), 88(both), 89(top), 90(bottom), 92(top), 93, 96(top), 97(both), 100, 101(bottom), 103(bottom), 106(top), 114(top left).
Museum of the City of New York: 47.
Museum of the Confederacy: 70(top).
National Archives: 18, 48(top right), 59, 68(bottom), 76(bottom right), 86(top), 94(all three), 98(top), 103(top), 105(top), 110(both), 111(top), 112(top), 113(top), 122(both), 126(bottom), 133, 134(bottom), 136(top), 148(bottom).
National Gallery of Art: 25(bottom).
National Maritime Museum: 16(bottom), 19(bottom).
Richard Natkiel: 21, 25(top), 40(top, bottom left), 45(right), 51, 55(bottom), 75(bottom left), 92(bottom left), 110(bottom), 120(top both), 124(top, center), 128(bottom), 132(bottom), 140-141(bottom), 144(bottom), 154(bottom), 155(top), 169(bottom), 173(top).
Courtesy of The New York Historical Society: 48(top left, bottom).
New York Public Library, Picture Collection: 46(top), 73.
New York Public Library, Prints Division: 24(bottom), 28(bottom).
Reuters/Bettmann Newsphotos: 186(all three).
H. Armstrong Roberts: 89(bottom).
FDR Naval Collection, FDR Library: 43(bottom), 46(bottom).
Smithsonian Institution National Anthropological Archives: 91, 92(bottom right).
South Dakota State Historical Society: 95.
State Historical Society of Wisconsin: 20(top).
Sutro Library: 12(bottom), 90(top).
Title Guarantee Company: 11(bottom).
UPI/Bettmann Newsphotos: 115, 118(top), 121(bottom), 138(both), 147(both), 149, 154(top), 161(both), 162(bottom), 166(top), 167, 168(bottom), 176(top), 178, 179, 180, 181, 182(both), 185(bottom), 187.
U.S. Department of Defense (all branches): 19(top), 23(top), 27, 34(top right), 35(bottom), 37, 38(top), 43(top), 45(bottom left), 50(bottom), 65(bottom), 69, 82(bottom), 84, 85(top), 87(top), 96(bottom), 99, 101(top), 102(bottom), 104(bottom), 105(bottom), 106(bottom), 107(both), 108(both), 109, 112(bottom), 119(top), 124(bottom), 126(top), 127, 129(top), 131(right), 134(top), 137(top), 139(top), 142, 143(top), 144(top), 145, 146, 148(top), 150(both), 151, 155(bottom), 156(both), 157, 158(top), 159, 163(bottom), 164, 166(bottom), 169(top), 170(both), 171, 172(both), 173(bottom), 174, 175(both), 176(bottom), 177, 183, 184.
U.S. State Department Photo: 153(top).
Virginia State Library: 57(top).
The White House, Jack Kightlinger: 185(top).
WW: 153(bottom), 160(top), 162(top), 165(bottom).